AUTISM SPECTRUM DISORDERS

FOUNDATIONS, CHARACTERISTICS, AND EFFECTIVE STRATEGIES

E. Amanda Boutot

Texas State University

Brenda Smith Myles

Chief of Programs
Autism Society of America

Boston   Columbus   Indianapolis   New York   San Francisco   Upper Saddle River
Amsterdam   Cape Town   Dubai   London   Madrid   Milan   Munich   Paris   Montreal   Toronto
Delhi   Mexico City   Sao Paulo   Sydney   Hong Kong   Seoul   Singapore   Taipei   Tokyo

Vice President and Editor in Chief: Jeffery W. Johnston
Executive Editor: Ann Castel Davis
Editorial Assistant: Penny Burleson
Vice President, Director of Marketing: Quinn Perkson
Marketing Coordinator: Brian Mounts
Senior Managing Editor: Pamela D. Bennett
Project Manager: Wanda Rockwell
Creative Director: Jayne Conte
Cover Designer: Suzanne Duda
Cover Art: Magumi Takamura/Jupiterimages/Getty Images, Inc.
Full-Service Project Management: Jogender Taneja/Aptara®, Inc.
Printer/Binder: R.R. Donnelley & Sons Company
Text Font: Garamond

Credits and acknowledgments borrowed from other sources and reproduced, with permission, in this textbook appear on the appropriate page within text.

Every effort has been made to provide accurate and current Internet information in this book. However, the Internet and information posted on it are constantly changing, so it is inevitable that some of the Internet addresses listed in this textbook will change.

Library of Congress Cataloging-in-Publication Data
Boutot, E. Amanda
    Autism spectrum disorders : foundations, characteristics, and effective
strategies / E. Amanda Boutot, Brenda Smith Myles.
        p. cm.
    ISBN-13: 978-0-205-54575-9
    ISBN-10: 0-205-54575-0
    1. Autistic children—Education—United States.   2. Autistic youth—
Education—United States.   3. Inclusive education—United States.
I. Myles, Brenda Smith.   II. Title.
    LC4718.B68 2011
    371.94—dc22

                                              2009041555

10 9 8 7 6 5
Prentice Hall
is an imprint of

www.pearsonhighered.com

ISBN 10:   0-205-54575-0
ISBN 13: 978-0-205-54575-9

BRIEF CONTENTS

CONTENTS

PREFACE

This book is an introductory text on Autism Spectrum Disorders (ASD). Given the increasing prevalence of children and youth with ASD in public schools and the extraordinary number of opinions and options for educating these students, this book will be valuable for pre-service teachers and in-service teachers seeking a deeper understanding of autism as well as a clear explanation of intervention strategies. This book will be useful for special and general education courses covering the autism spectrum, as well as other courses dealing with the spectrum such as psychology, school psychology, speech pathology, occupational therapy, and child development.

Our goal in developing this text was to provide a comprehensive, up-to-date, research-based introduction to and overview of Autism Spectrum Disorders (ASD) for future educators. Our primary aim was to bring together, in one textbook, all of the things instructors need to present a broad, yet in-depth, overview of ASD, rather than having to pull pieces from multiple sources. We developed this book to provide necessary background information so that students studying the autism spectrum would (a) understand the disorder, including its many manifestations and associated characteristics; (b) understand and appreciate the issues faced by the families of children on the autism spectrum so that students could more empathetically work with them; and (c) have sufficient information on the myriad instructional strategies from which students with autism may benefit, and based on this knowledge, be able to make an appropriate decision as to which strategy may benefit a particular student and why. Most importantly, we wanted to provide sufficient information in the major areas related to educating students with autism so that future teachers would not have to fall back on what is found in the media, on the Internet, or through their own sometimes limited experiences. One of the most important concepts a student in an introduction to ASD course can understand is that no two individuals with ASD are alike, and there is no quick fix or "one size fits all" for working with this population. Our hope is that this message is clear. We wanted to create a source so that future teachers can be informed consumers within the field of Autism Spectrum Disorders.

We recognize that with any introductory text the information presented is not exhaustive, and leaves many unanswered questions. This book was never intended to be a methods text or a cookbook for teachers of children with autism; indeed, in some areas we have only scratched the surface. However, if Introduction to Autism were the only course on ASD that a future teacher or other professional were to take, if structured according to the organization of this text, we believe it would provide a sufficient foundation and enough tools to be successful with this population. Our hope is that readers will refer to the many resources provided herein to advance their own study of the research-based practices used to work with students with ASD in schools.

ORGANIZATION OF THE TEXT

Instructors will find that we have tried to include the major issues and questions faced by teachers and future teachers of students on the autism spectrum. We called upon the expertise of multiple individuals from a variety of disciplines (e.g., Occupational Therapy, Psychology, Special Education, Speech-Language Pathology) to aid in writing chapters that are factual and up-to-date. We organized the book around the way that we teach introductory autism courses, and instructors of introduction to ASD courses will hopefully find the progression of information as useful for their courses as we do for ours. We begin with a comprehensive overview of ASD in Chapter 1, including neurological underpinnings of the disorder. We feel this information provides a necessary framework for how ASD may affect an individual, as well as an understanding of the many varied manifestations ASD may take. For future teachers, information on how to develop a program for students with ASD is critical, including how to assess to determine what to teach, developing IEP objectives, and creating systems for on-going progress evaluation; this information is provided in detail in Chapter 2. What to teach is followed by how to teach, including how to make decisions on the instructional strategies one should choose for individual students. We provide a framework and structure for making programming and instructional decisions through Chapter 3, the Evidence-Based Practices chapter; it includes a model for determining which strategies may be most appropriate for particular students based on that child's individual strengths and needs. We are especially proud of Chapter 4, which deals with working with families of children on the spectrum, because this is a frequently cited concern among teachers and future teachers alike. By including this chapter early in the book (and early in a course) we hope to provide a basis for understanding of family issues that will foster consideration of the family in each of the key areas discussed through the rest of the text. Setting up a classroom for student success and specific details on various skill instruction (e.g., behavior, communication, social) follows; however, there is no way to provide in-depth "how to" information in an introductory course. The overview provided in the remaining chapters should deliver sufficient detail for future teachers to support appropriate decision making, including in which areas to receive additional, more advanced training. Toward the end of our course, we focus on transition to adulthood and adult service needs of individuals with ASD. The final chapter of the text is on transition and adulthood and provides the reader with a broad context for the future of the students with whom they will work; it presents an overview of transition services as well as research on best practices for adolescents and adults on the autism spectrum. Overall, the text provides a comprehensive review of the major concepts encountered in the field today, with particular emphasis on connecting these concepts to the real world of teaching.

FEATURES OF THE TEXT

Each chapter begins with learning objectives, which serve as an advanced organizer to guide the reader through the more salient concepts that will be presented. At the end of each chapter are study questions, derived directly from the learning objectives, to promote self-reflection of the reader. Throughout each chapter we provide real-life scenarios, anecdotes, and case studies to support the concepts presented. In addition, in each chapter we provide synopses of current or classic research (Research Boxes), which further support these concepts. Information related to diversity is included in each chapter through Diversity Boxes, and the Trends and Issues Boxes provide current information on important topics in the field. Each chapter has a list of key terms to guide study; a list of Internet resources is also available in most chapters for those wishing to take their studies beyond this text.

ACKNOWLEDGMENTS

I would like to thank the individuals who helped in the development of this book. I am incredibly grateful to the support of the Pearson editing and publishing team: Ann Davis, Penny Burleson, and Sheryl Langner. If an award for patience is available, I would like to nominate these three women, who never once made me feel like the novice that I clearly was! I wish to also thank those who contributed their time and expertise to the individual chapters: Ruth Aspy, Gena Barnhill, Scott Bellini, Jenny Clark Brack, Christina Carnahan, Tricia Cassel, Yu-Chi Chou, Charles Dukes, Jennifer S. Durocher, Ketty Patino Gonzales, Barry G. Grossman, HyoJung Lee, Melissa L. Olive, Jonathan Tarbox, Kai-Chien Tien, Jennifer Loncola Walberg, and Elizabeth West. I am especially grateful to

Dr. Charles Dukes, my friend and colleague, who provided additional insight and lent his "ear" whenever I called; he is a true professional. I wish to also personally thank Ms. Claire Seymour, whose dedication to the completion of this project went above and beyond the call of duty.

This text would not have been possible without the wise and valuable comments and suggestions of those who served as reviewers: Kevin J. Callahan, University of North Texas; Thomas McLaughlin, Gonzaga University; Shanon Taylor, University of Nevada—Reno; Jane R. Wegner, University of Kansas; and Thomas Williams, Virginia Tech. Thank you so much for your time and energy.

Finally, I wish to extend a very special thank you to Dr. Brenda Smith Myles, one of the greatest ASD advocates I know, who assisted in conceptualizing this project from the beginning and was instrumental in helping to pull together all of the talented contributors. Dr. Myles provided me with guidance and encouragement throughout the entire process and her editorial comments and suggestions were invaluable. I am honored to have shared this editorship with her.

EAB
Austin, Texas

1

Overview of Autism Spectrum Disorders

Ketty Gonzalez, Ph.D.
Tricia Cassel, Ph.D.
Psychologists in Private Practice
E. Amanda Boutot, Ph.D. BCBA
Texas State University

CHAPTER OBJECTIVES

After reading this chapter, learners should be able to:

1. Describe the characteristics of Autism Spectrum Disorders.
2. Explain how Autism Spectrum Disorders are identified and diagnosed.
3. Identify the differences among the Autism Spectrum Disorders.
4. Discuss causal theories associated with autism.
5. Describe the neurological impact of autism.

 CASE STUDY Examples

Case of Robert

Robert was only 7 years old and his parents had no idea how they would be able to manage getting him through the next 11 years of school. While Robert had always been a bit temperamental and knew what he wanted, his parents never had any significant difficulties parenting him until he began preschool at age 3.

From the time he entered preschool, Robert was ostracized by his peers because of his lack of social graces and high activity level. In fact, Robert was labeled as "hyperactive" from the moment he set foot in school. He would not sit down during Circle Time, refused to share his toys, and would frequently hide under a table. Robert's mother took him to his pediatrician, who felt that Robert was a little overactive but that he would "grow out of it." Unfortunately, things continued to go badly in school. Robert always seemed upset about something and occasionally bit or physically fought with his peers. Time-outs had no effect, and he was kicked out of two preschools. Robert was labeled a "bad seed." Robert's parents did not understand why Robert would behave this way at school, while at home he could spend hours with his trains. They started to believe that the teachers were right and that they were doing something wrong.

Unfortunately, kindergarten was not any better, and his teacher suggested that Robert may have **Attention–Deficit/Hyperactivity Disorder (ADHD)**. A school psychologist confirmed this suspicion. Then, in addition to his aggressive behavior, Robert began to lag behind his classmates in penmanship and coloring. He was also terrible at sports and always the last child picked for a team. Robert started getting stomachaches every morning before school.

By the time Robert entered first grade he hated school and wondered why he did not have any friends. His parents started to consider homeschooling him. At home, his parents were sometimes puzzled by Robert. His facial expressions did not always match his mood and sometimes he would have explosive meltdowns, making his parents feel as if he were a time bomb ready to explode at any moment. His parents also began noticing that Robert did not understand jokes and had difficulty following movie plots. They began to worry that perhaps he was not very intelligent. In addition to diagnosing Robert with ADHD, doctors also suggested that he may have early onset bipolar disorder, which could explain Robert's explosive behavior. Something called Oppositional Defiant Disorder (ODD) was also mentioned.

In the summer between first and second grade, Robert attended a summer camp, and one of the counselors suggested to his parents that an assessment test for Asperger Syndrome should be given to Robert. His parents took him to a university-based clinic, where they were immediately told that while Robert certainly exhibited many symptoms consistent with ADHD, a significant number of his problems were not explained by ADHD. After a thorough assessment, Robert was diagnosed with Asperger Syndrome. Recommendations included treating the co-occurring ADHD symptoms through a combination of medication and behavioral techniques, didactic sessions for his parents, specific behavioral recommendations, school accommodations, plus therapies for specific deficits. Robert's parents were worried, but relieved, with the diagnosis. At this time, Robert is getting ready to start middle school. Although things are not perfect and he continues to struggle, he has made much progress socially and has one good friend who was described as somewhat odd himself. However, the match between the two of them has done wonders for Robert's self-esteem and he enjoys going to school again.

Case of Jacob

Jacob's parents first became concerned about his development when he was around 18 months old, when they realized he was not talking, or even babbling, like other children his age. As Jacob got a little older, he showed limited interest in playing with his toys and tended to line them up or examine them while waving them in front of his face. He occasionally babbled, but this babbling did not seem to be an attempt to communicate. In fact, Jacob rarely communicated with his family unless he wanted something. Even when something was important to him, he rarely made eye contact with his mother or smiled at her. Jacob frequently flapped his arms, spun around in circles, or tensed his body when he was upset or excited. Jacob's parents had him evaluated when he was almost 3 years old. Results of the evaluation indicated that Jacob had severe deficits in the three areas associated with autism. Jacob is now 5 and continues to flap his arms and rock back and forth. He does not have friends, nor does he have any interest in other children. Although he can be loving with his family, it is always on his terms. Jacob is able to say several words, but mainly uses pictures to communicate with his family. He is obsessed with Thomas the Tank Engine™ and carries a train with him wherever he goes.

Case of Tim

Before the children were settled, Tim showed a Harry Potter card to one of his classmates, who quickly grabbed it, started taunting him, and would not give the card back. Although Tim was 6 inches taller and 40 pounds heavier than his tormentor, he made only half-hearted attempts to grab it back, but the other boy was quicker. Tim looked very lost and did not appear to know how to proceed. The clinician who was observing Tim in school finally could not control herself and felt compelled to intervene by standing close to the tormentor and demanding the return of the card in a menacing tone. The class was large, with 38 students, and the teacher was busy settling the children down and did not realize what was happening. The clinician is hopeful that the little tormentor learned his lesson.

Case of Josh

During his assessment, Josh was playing with his older brothers and appeared to enjoy the train set. However, when they gave him a train that unexpectedly made a noise Josh threw it down, kicked it, and left. Later in the play, one of Josh's brothers leaned on a toy that made noise and Josh got upset, covered his ears, and kicked the toy bins. Each of Josh's brothers made attempts to deactivate the toy and apologized to Josh, assuring him they would not play with other noise-making toys. Throughout the entire assessment, Josh's family was careful to avoid anything that might make noise and upset him.

Case of Jorge

When seen in the office, Jorge continuously hit his face with a pencil when he was not engaged in testing. He had a history of unusual behaviors. For example, he would hit himself almost continuously with long, hard objects (e.g., pencils, tongue depressors) when he was anxious or depressed. At home he would continuously run from one wall to another and touch them. He had engaged in self-mutilating behaviors, such as peeling the skin of his fingertips until they bled.

Case of Jack

Jack frequently looked at the clock and told the examiner what time it was or what time it almost was (e.g., "It's almost 10 o'clock."). Jack knew that he was leaving at 11:45 and attempted to stop in the middle of a task when the clock reached 11:45. When he was asked to continue, he looked slightly concerned, paused, and continued working. When the clock was removed for the afternoon session, Jack repeatedly asked for it and wondered if it was broken. He asked the examiner to fix it and put it back on the wall. Jack frequently glanced toward the spot on the wall where the clock used to be. On the second day of testing, a different room was selected—one without a clock. Jack immediately said that the room was "different" and asked where the clock was in the room. He frequently asked the examiner what time it was and became noticeably upset when she did not tell him.

Case of Matthew

Each day, Matthew got on the bus immediately after school. Unfortunately, one day his bus left without him. Matthew, an 11-year-old boy with a gifted IQ, was paralyzed by the fact that he had missed the bus. He sat down on the school parking lot and cried until his panicked mother showed up at the school 2 hours later. Matthew was unable to think of an alternative solution to his problem, even though he could see the school office from where he had been sitting.

Case of Natalie

Natalie was 4 when she was first seen by a diagnostician. Her mother had made the appointment because Natalie constantly claimed that she was King Arthur. The examiner observed Natalie at preschool. During free play on the playground Natalie played by herself with the sand. She constantly talked to herself and acted as if she was in a fantasy world of knights and horses. For example, she climbed the play equipment and started shouting orders to the "laborers." When she started playing by herself in a playhouse, the examiner joined her. She allowed the examiner to participate in her play, as long as the examiner followed her script. The theme of the play was castles, dragons, and rescuing princesses in distress. Natalie knew the names of many of the knights from King Arthur's Court and played this way for approximately 15 minutes. During this period she exhibited enthusiasm and good eye contact. When asked about her play, she indicated that she knew it was fantasy.

Case of Andrew

Andrew immediately and spontaneously said hello to the examiner when he saw her for the first time and happily accompanied her to the office. His affect was consistently elevated, whether he was working, playing, or talking. He constantly and exuberantly laughed aloud when he found anything amusing, which happened every 5 minutes or so. Eye contact was within normal limits. Although in school he was out of control and, as a result, had been kicked out of three different elementary schools, in the one-to-one testing situation with an adult, he demonstrated none of the behaviors he exhibited in school. In fact, Andrew was a great pleasure to test.

Case of David

David failed his freshman year at an Ivy League school. Past diagnoses had included Attention-Deficit/Hyperactivity Disorder (ADHD), Oppositional Defiant Disorder (ODD), depression as a child, and Tourette's Syndrome and Obsessive-Compulsive Disorder (OCD) in college. His IQ was 145 and he had obtained combined SAT scores of 1470. During college, David was unable to get to his classes on time or plan and turn in his assignments, so he failed academically. David's room was messy, as he did not pick up after himself, did not do laundry, and had poor hygiene. His parents rated him on the Vineland Adaptive Behavior Scales II as having the adaptive behavior of a 9-year-old child.

Case of Benny

Benny was 9 years old and hated to write. No matter how much he tried, his handwriting was always messy and poorly spaced. In addition, it took him a much longer time to write than his peers. Because of his problem writing, Benny had to invest so much time remembering and executing letters that he would forget what he was supposed to write and would try to keep his writing as short as possible. Unfortunately, he was now in fourth grade, and his teacher expected her class to write essays. The first day of school the teacher asked the class to write a four-paragraph essay about their summer vacation. Benny stared at his paper, put his head down, and began to cry.

INTRODUCTION

One in 150 individuals in the United States is diagnosed with an **Autism Spectrum Disorder (ASD)**, resulting in a new diagnosis every 20 minutes, according to the Centers for Disease Control (2008). This represents a substantial increase in overall **prevalence** over the last two decades. In 1990, for example, that figure was 5 to 10 in 10,000. In fact, autism is the fastest growing childhood disorder and is more common than childhood cancer, cystic fibrosis, and multiple sclerosis combined (Autism Society of America, 2008). Teachers in public schools today will almost certainly encounter a student with an ASD, and for those entering the field of special education, the chances are probably greater that you will win the lottery than not have a student with ASD during the course of your career. Autism is a relatively young disorder, having only been recognized in the early 1940s. Therefore, what we know and understand about ASD is still in its infancy; there is still much unknown and misunderstood about this exceptionality. The purpose of this chapter is to provide the reader with a basic overview to help guide understanding of the complexities of ASD. This text is written for teachers who are both new to the field and for those who have taught children with autism for years. It is our intention that the information provided herein will aid you in providing the most successful learning experience possible for your students with ASD. The field of ASD is ever changing; what we understand today is far different from what we know of yesterday and this will likely not be the same as that of tomorrow. Teachers are encouraged to remain current on the research, trends, and issues related to educating students with ASD, because information continually shifts and changes. The more teachers understand the students they teach, the better able they are to teach them.

AUTISM SPECTRUM DISORDERS

There are five **Pervasive Developmental Disorders (PDDs)** listed in the *Diagnostic and Statistical Manual of Mental Disorders*, Fourth Edition, Text Revision (***DSM-IV-TR***; American Psychiatric Association [APA], 2000), the publication that psychiatrists and psychologists use to diagnose psychiatric disorders, psychological problems, and learning difficulties, among others. The *DSM-IV-TR* lists explicit criteria for each PDD, some of which are presented in Figure 1.1. In general, PDD involves deficits in language and communication, unusual interests and behaviors, and the "heart" of ASD: difficulties engaging in appropriate social interactions.

1. Autism
   a. Extreme difficulties and delays in the area of language and social functioning. Children may also have repetitive behaviors such as rocking back and forth or flicking light switches.
   b. There are both high- and low-functioning children with autism.
2. Asperger Disorder
   a. Children experience extreme social difficulties without a language delay.
   b. There are many similarities to children with **high-functioning autism**.
3. Rett's Disorder
   a. A genetic condition in which girls develop normally until they are approximately 5 years old.
   b. They frequently have extreme behavior and social problems and develop severe mental retardation.
   c. The disorder is characterized by wringing hand movements.
4. Childhood Disintegrative Disorder
   a. Children develop normally until between the ages of 2 and 4 and then show drastic declines in social, cognitive, and language functioning.
5. PDD-NOS
   a. This category is a "catchall" for children not fitting neatly into other categories but who still have severe difficulties in at least one area (i.e., the child has difficulties only in language and does not meet criteria for an ASD in social interaction or behaviors and interests).

FIGURE 1.1   What Are the PDDs in the *DSM*?

Our discussion will focus on the three disorders that make up the autism spectrum: **Autistic Disorder** (commonly known as autism), **Asperger Disorder** (also known as Asperger Syndrome or AS), and Pervasive Developmental Disorder—Not Otherwise Specified (known as PDD-NOS). These three disorders are also known as Autism Spectrum Disorders, or ASD.

Briefly, according to *DSM-IV-TR*, the primary difference between children with autism and children with AS is that (a) children with autism show a delay in language (i.e., they do not use single words by age 2 and communicative phrases by age 3) that is not shown in children with AS; and (b) children with AS show no cognitive delays. In essence, if a child has such a delay in functional language (defined for practical purposes as the ability to have enough language to get needs and wants met), she cannot be given a diagnosis of AS. In addition, a child with AS cannot have a cognitive delay or a delay in **adaptive behavior** (which is mastery of personal demands that are expected of someone at a particular chronological age). If a child meets some but not all of the criteria for autism or AS, then that child is diagnosed with PDD-NOS. Figure 1.2 delineates the *DSM-IV-TR* criteria.

Clinical experience and research reveal that some of the diagnostic criteria in the *DSM-IV-TR* are not consistent with current research. For example, children with AS almost invariably have delays in their adaptive behavior (Lee & Park, 2007), and some may have early language delays (Miller & Ozonoff, 2000).

Classic Autism

When a layperson thinks about a child with autism, he probably visualizes the child as having what clinicians may call *classic autism*. Classic autism was first described in 1943 (Kanner, 1943), but was not included in the *DSM-III* until 1980. To date, the definition in the *DSM* has been revised three times. Children with classic autism may be nonverbal. Alternatively, they may have significant language difficulties, so that their language may consist primarily of echolalia (immediate repetitions

1. Deficits in Reciprocal Social Interaction	
Difficulty using nonverbal behaviors to regulate social interaction	Trouble looking others in the eye
	Little use of gestures while speaking
	Few or unusual facial expressions
	Trouble knowing how close to stand to others
	Unusual intonation or voice quality
Failure to develop age-appropriate peer relationships	Few or no friends
	Relationships only with those much older or younger than the child or with family members
	Relationships based primarily on special interests
	Trouble interacting in groups and following cooperative rules of games
Little sharing of pleasure, achievements, or interests with others	Enjoys favorite activities alone (e.g., television shows, toys) without trying to involve other people
	Does not try to call others' attention to activities, interests, or accomplishments
	Little interest in or reaction to praise
Lack of social or emotional reciprocity	Does not respond to others; "appears deaf"
	Not aware of others; "oblivious" to their existence
	Strongly prefers solitary activities
	Does not notice when others are hurt or upset; does not offer comfort
2. Deficits in Communication	
Delay in or total lack of development of language	No use of words to communicate by age 2
	No simple phrases (e.g., "More milk") by age 3
	After speech develops, immature grammar or repeated errors
Difficulty holding conversations	Has trouble knowing how to start, keep going, and/or end a conversation
	Little back-and-forth; may talk on and on in a monologue
	Fails to respond to the comments of others; responds only to direct questions
	Difficulty talking about topics not of special interest
Unusual or repetitive language	Repeating what others say to them (echolalia)
	Repeating from videos, books, or commercials at inappropriate times or out of context
	Using words or phrases that the child has made up or that only have special meaning to him/her
	Overly formal, pedantic style of speaking (sounds like "a little professor")
Play that is not appropriate for developmental level	Little acting-out scenarios with toys
	Rarely pretends an object is something else (e.g., a banana is a telephone)
	Prefers to use toys in a concrete manner (e.g., building with blocks, arranging dollhouse furniture) rather than pretending with them
	When young, little interest in social games like peekaboo, ring-around-the-rosie, and the like

FIGURE 1.2 *DSM-IV-TR* Symptoms Examples

3. Restricted, Repetitive Behaviors, Interests, or Activities	
Interests that are narrow in focus, overly intense, and/or unusual	Very strong focus on particular topics to the exclusion of other topics
	Difficulty "letting go" of special topics or activities
	Interference with other activities (e.g., delays eating or toileting due to focus on activity)
	Interest in topics that are unusual for age (sprinkler systems, movie ratings, astrophysics, radio station call letters)
	Excellent memory for details of special interests
Unreasonable insistence on sameness and following familiar routines	Wants to perform certain activities in an exact order (e.g., close car doors in specific order)
	Easily upset by minor changes in routine (e.g., taking a different route home from school)
	Need for advanced warning of any changes
	Becomes highly anxious and upset if routines or rituals not followed
	Lining up objects
Repetitive motor mannerisms	Flapping hands when excited or upset
	Flicking fingers in front of eyes
	Odd hand postures or other hand movements
	Spinning or rocking for long periods of time
	Walking and/or running on tiptoe
Preoccupation with parts of objects	Uses objects in usual ways (e.g., flicks doll's eyes, repeatedly opens and closes doors on toy car), rather than as intended
	Interest in sensory qualities of objects (e.g., likes to sniff objects or look at them closely)
	Likes objects that move (e.g., running water, spinning wheels)
	Attachment to unusual objects (e.g., strings)

FIGURE 1.2 *DSM-IV-TR* Symptoms Examples (*continued*)

Note: To obtain a diagnosis of Autistic Disorder, the child has to display

    Six symptoms: At least two from Area 1, one from Area 2, and one from Area 3.
    Delays in at least one of the following three areas (starting before age 3):
        social interaction
        language as used in social communication
        symbolic/imaginative play

To obtain a diagnosis of Asperger Disorder, the child has to display

Three symptoms: At least two from Area 1 and one from Area 3.
No significant delay in functional language
No significant delay in cognitive development
No significant delay in:
    self-help skills
    adaptive behavior
    curiosity about the environment
No schizophrenia or another PDD

To obtain a diagnosis of Pervasive Developmental Disorder Not Otherwise Specified(PDD-NOS), the child has to have a severe and pervasive impairment in any or all of the three areas. However, the child does not display the needed number of symptoms, as outlined above, or the symptoms started after age 3, or the exclusionary criteria are not met (e.g., there is a significant delay in cognitive development, but the child would otherwise meet criteria for Asperger's Disorder).

Thomas the Tank Engine	Planets/Outer space
Yu-Gi-Oh!™ and Pokémon	Disney
Animals (especially for girls)	Weather
Reptiles (including dinosaurs) and sea life (love those sharks)	Numbers and letters
Bugs	Books

FIGURE 1.3   Common Interests We Have Encountered

of what they hear) or delayed echolalia (repetitions of what they have heard from others prior to three conversational turns)—very commonly, from television. Approximately 25% of these children may show normal language development when very young, but then regress and lose their skills (Volkmar & Klin, 2005). Children with classic autism are commonly not interested in other children, and those who are may not express this desire in a typical way. These individuals also experience behaviors commonly identified in the third group of symptoms. That is, they may rock back and forth, flap their hands, and show special interests in unusual objects or topics (see Figure 1.3). However, these behaviors may not manifest until the child is approximately 3 years of age (APA, 2000). This means that, if a child is formally evaluated at age 2, he may not meet full criteria for Autistic Disorder.

Many children with classic autism also have below-average intelligence, with some estimates suggesting that approximately 75% of children with autism have a cognitive disability (Edelson, 2006). Children with classic autism are sometimes classified based on their intelligence quotients (IQ): those with higher IQs (i.e., standard scores above 70) may be referred to as having high-functioning autism (HFA), and those with IQs below 70 (the cut-off for mental retardation) are classified as low functioning.

It is well established that children with autism are more likely to be male than female. Estimates range from 1.3 to as many as 16 boys for every girl diagnosed, although most recent trends suggest a ratio of 4 boys for every girl diagnosed (Thompson, Caruso, & Ellerbeck, 2003; Volkmar, Paul, Klin, & Cohen, 2005). Some research suggests that girls affected with classic autism are more likely to be severely impaired (Brown, 2004; Roberts, 2003), so the ratio of boys to girls is even higher in high-functioning children with autism and those with AS.

Clinically, children with autism often display a flat affect or a limited or depressed range of facial expressions. At other times, however, they may display an overly exaggerated affect. A common mistake among professionals is thinking that because a child seems attached to his parents he cannot have autism. In fact, many children with autism are very attached to their parents (Rutgers, VanJzendoorn, & Bakermans-Kranenburg, 2007).

Asperger Disorder

AS was first identified by Hans Asperger, an Austrian pediatrician, in 1944. Dr. Asperger described a group of boys who had difficulty engaging in social interaction and noted that many of these boys' family members evidenced similar difficulties. AS was not introduced in the United States until 1991, when Dr. Asperger's original paper was translated into English (Frith, 1991).

The primary *DSM-IV-TR* criterion that differentiates AS from autism is that children with autism have a "functional" language delay while those with AS do not. However, research has failed to conclusively show that AS and HFA are, in fact, different disorders (Macintosh & Dissanayake, 2004;

Ozonoff, South, & Miller, 2000; Tryon, Mayes, Rhodes, & Waldo, 2006; Verte, Geurts, Roeyers, Oosterlaan, & Sergeant, 2006). For the purpose of this text, however, we will continue to discuss HFA and AS as two distinct disorders, although characteristics may be similar.

Although prevalence is not known, it is estimated that less than 5% of children have AS (Baird et al., 2000; Chakrabarti & Fombonne, 2001; Ozonoff & Rogers, 2003; Sponheim & Skjeldal, 1998). It is fairly well established that approximately four out of five children diagnosed with AS are boys, although there are some estimates placing this ratio at 8:1 males over females (Chakrabarti & Fombonne, 2001).

Children with autism in schools are frequently identified according to the Individuals with Disabilities Education Act (IDEA) criteria. These criteria were written broadly to also include children with AS and those with PDD-NOS. Thus, students who have a medical diagnosis of AS and PDD-NOS may be identified by a school team as having autism. Not all, however, are served under IDEA; some have an individualized 504 Plan and receive modifications and accommodations under Section 504 of the Rehabilitation Act. Table 1.1 provides an overview of the differences between IDEA and 504. For more information about 504, please see the resources section at the end of this chapter. Table 1.2 provides an example of a 504 Plan for a child with AS in a public school.

TABLE 1.1   Comparison of 504 and IDEA

504 vs. IDEA	
504	**IDEA**
Antidiscrimination law	Funding law
Prevents discrimination in institutions receiving federal funds	Provides services in all public schools
No specific eligibility requirements	Specific eligibility requirements (13 disability categories)
Covers children who are at risk for disabilities	Covers only children at risk for disabilities from 0 through age 8 as determined by states
Disability must limit one or more major life activities	Disability must adversely affect educational performance
Provides for comparable education to those without disabilities	Provides for an education that provides some meaningful benefit
Requires reasonable accommodations	Requires modifications and accommodations that permit achievement of some educational benefit
No parental notice required	Parental notice required for assessments, meetings, changes of placement
No meeting required for services or changes of placements	Team meetings required for services and changes of placement
504 plans have no specific requirements	IEPs have specific requirements
Manifestation meeting required for expulsion	Manifestation meeting required for expulsion
Expelled children do not continue to receive services	Expelled children must continue to receive services
No transition services required	Transition services required by age 16

TABLE 1.2   Sample 504 Plan for a Student with Asperger Syndrome

Student: Joaquin
Grade: 5

Need Area	Specific Modifications and Accommodations	Person/s Responsible
Attention	• Seating away from distractions • Option to take tests in quiet location (e.g., Resource Room)	General education teacher
Organization	• Opportunity to e-mail himself assignments, etc., daily rather than using an academic planner • Set of textbooks at home for homework use • Personal schedule located on his desk; checklist format so that he can check off tasks when complete • Color-coded notebooks and spirals for different classes; color-coded textbook covers • Extra pencils and other supplies in each classroom and at home • A checklist for "Getting Started" on assignments, which is posted in the corner of his desks at school (both classrooms) and his work space at home (e.g., 1-Write heading; 2-Read directions out loud; etc.)	General education teacher Parents
Sensory & Motor	• Personal space, "Office" (e.g., study carrel) in a corner of the classroom for use when he is feeling overwhelmed by noise in the classroom • Opportunity to type assignments rather than write • Yellow notebook paper to cut glare from florescent lights • Orange "Break" cards: three per day to place on his desk to signal his need for a walk or to go to the motor lab and jump for 5–10 minutes • Opportunities built into his daily schedule to take a walk (e.g., deliveries to other classrooms or the office) and to get sensory input (e.g., carrying the heavy playground equipment basket to recess, pushing the LCD projector cart, etc.)	General education teacher Occupational therapist consult Behavior specialist consult
Behavioral/ Social	• Social script cards indicating appropriate responses to various issues (e.g., what to do if someone makes fun of you, what to say when you do not understand an assignment, etc.) • Social skills training once weekly (Friday Lunch Bunch) • Token system for appropriate behavior, completed assignments, on-task behavior, etc. • Self-management for on-task behavior • Frequent breaks and frequent reinforcement	General education teacher Special education teacher consult Counselor Behavior specialist consult
Other	• Calculator to check math problems • Extra time on tests • Directions provided visually	General education teacher

DIAGNOSING AUTISM SPECTRUM DISORDERS

The diagnosis of AS and related disorders has received a lot of attention from parents, professionals, and researchers in the past few years. Diagnosing a child with classic autism has been made much easier with empirically based instruments that have been developed in the past few years. However,

Autism: A developmental disability significantly affecting verbal and nonverbal communication and social interaction, generally evident before age 3, that adversely affects a child's educational performance. Other characteristics often associated with autism are engagement in repetitive activities and stereotyped movements, resistance to environmental change or change in daily routines, and unusual responses to sensory experiences. The term does not apply if a child's educational performance is adversely affected primarily because the child has a serious emotional disturbance as defined below. From http://www.ericdigests.org/1999-4/ideas.htm, retrieved March 11, 2008.

FIGURE 1.4   IDEA Definition of Autism

diagnosing a child or adult with HFA or AS, despite age, is part science and part art. Research, however, shows that the diagnosis of ASD made by a clinician is relatively stable (Chawarska, Klin, Paul, & Volkmar, 2007; Turner, Stone, Pozdol, & Coonrod, 2006).

When diagnosing ASD, the clinician (a psychologist, psychiatrist, or physician) will meet with the parent(s) and the child. Various tools may be used to help make a formal diagnosis, yet no single assessment measure is considered "the" one for diagnosis. Further, in public schools, the definition of autism is sufficiently broad as to encompass AS as well and may not include any specific assessment measure, although schools routinely use some formal measurement tool when determining eligibility of special education (see Figure 1.4). Descriptions of some of the measures used by clinicians as well as school psychologists follow.

The Autism Diagnostic Interview–Revised (ADI-R; Lord, Rutter, & Le Couteur, 1994) is a comprehensive interview conducted with the parent or caregiver of the individual being assessed. It is designed to assess the extent of autistic symptoms in individuals with a mental age of 2 and above. The 85-page interview booklet with 93 items takes approximately 1½ to 2½ hours to administer and score. Questions in the ADI-R are in the following sections: background information, introductory questions, early development, loss of language or other skills, language and communicative functioning, social development and play, favorite activities and toys, interests and behaviors, and general behaviors. Despite its length, it is still only one piece of the diagnostic puzzle and should never be used as the sole diagnostic tool. It is frequently used for research and is an important clinical tool, but can be cumbersome and time-consuming.

The Autism Diagnostic Observation Schedule–Generic (ADOS-G) is a semi-structured assessment designed to assess the three areas of impairment associated with autism (Lord, Rutter, DiLavore, & Risi, 1999). It takes approximately 30 to 45 minutes to administer. The ADOS-G consists of four modules, based on the cognitive and language levels of the individual being assessed. For instance, Module 1 is for young children or children with no language, while Module 4 is administered to adults who speak in full sentences. Modules 1 and 2 are largely play based and assess constructs such as joint attention (defined as the process of sharing one's experience of observing an object or event, by following gaze or pointing gestures), reciprocal play, social interest, and eye contact. Modules 3 and 4 assess imaginary play, but are largely interview based, particularly Module 4. Interview questions focus on social stressors, descriptors of emotions, adaptive behavior, and daily life events. Both modules provide an opportunity for the assessment of language and conversational skills, appropriate eye contact, and imagination. All modules of the ADOS-G allow for an assessment of repetitive and stereotyped interests and behaviors, although these do not form part of the diagnostic algorithm (i.e., the way we quantify the findings to decide whether the individual meets criteria for an ASD).

The Social Communication Questionnaire (SCQ; Berument, Rutter, Lord, Pickles, & Bailey, 1999) is a 40-item questionnaire that contains the algorithm items from the ADI-R in a yes/no format.

Designed to screen for ASD, there are two forms of the SCQ: the Lifetime and Current versions. The Current form investigates the child's behavior over the past 3 months. The Lifetime form assesses ASD symptoms across the lifetime of an individual, with a particular focus on the time when a child was between 4 and 5 years of age.

The Social Responsiveness Scale (SRS; Constantino, 2003) is a 65-item rating scale that measures the severity of autism spectrum symptoms, including social impairments, social awareness, social information processing, capacity for reciprocal social communication, social anxiety/avoidance, and autistic preoccupations and traits as they occur in natural social settings. It is completed by a parent or teacher in 15 to 20 minutes.

Also available to assess autism symptoms are several screening instruments, including the Modified–Checklist for Autism in Toddlers (M-CHAT; Robins, Fein, Barton, & Green, 2001), Asperger Syndrome Diagnostic Scale (ASDS; Myles, Bock, & Simpson, 2000), and the Childhood Autism Rating Scale (CARS; Schopler, Reichler, & Renner, 1980). However, some of these instruments have limited standardization and may not be appropriate for children across a variety of age and ethnic groups. Thus, while you can get an impression of the child's symptoms by using one or more of these scales, clinical experience and knowledge are an integral part of the diagnostic process. For instance, you may need to do something more unconventional, such as taking an adult to lunch to see how she reacts to social situations. For children, observing a child at school lets one know how the child interacts with his peers during recess, versus one-on-one in an adult's office. Such observations are critical, particularly when working with children who are considered higher functioning.

In addition to obtaining a valid estimate of a child's level of autism symptoms, a clinician or the school team should obtain a reliable estimate of the child's functioning in other areas, including adaptive behavior and cognitive functioning. Adaptive functioning refers to a child's ability to care for himself. For instance, young children should be able to tell a parent if they are hurt or do not feel well. Teenagers should be capable of fixing simple snacks and meals for themselves and independently addressing personal hygiene needs. Unfortunately, research and clinical experience show that even children with AS who have high IQs show delays in adaptive functioning (Barnhill et al., 2000; Lee & Park, 2007; Myles et al., 2007). There are many questionnaires designed to assess a child's adaptive functioning. Two of the most popular are the Adaptive Behavior Assessment System (ABAS-II; Harrison & Oakland, 2003) and the Vineland Adaptive Behavior Scale (VABS-II; Sparrow, Bella, & Cicchetti, 2005). Both measures have parent/caretaker and teacher forms.

In addition to adaptive behavior, it is also important to gain a valid estimate of a child's cognitive abilities. The most commonly used instruments to test children's cognitive abilities are the different Wechsler scales (e.g., the Wechsler Preschool and Primary Scale of Intelligence–III [WPPSI-III; Wechsler, 2002] and the Wechsler Intelligence Scale for Children–Fourth Edition [WISC-IV; Wechsler, 2004]). Other scales, such as the Mullen Scales of Early Learning (Mullen, 1995), the Stanford Binet–Fifth Edition (Roid, 2004), and the Kaufman Assessment Battery for Children–Second Edition (Kaufman & Kaufman, 1983), can also be used with young children and/or children with limited verbal abilities.

Comorbid and Differential Diagnosis in ASD

Comorbid diagnoses are two or more diagnoses that co-occur. We have already discussed the **comorbidity** between autism and mental retardation and have also described learning difficulties associated with AS. However, other disorders are also likely to co-occur in children in the autism spectrum (Zafeiriou et al., 2007). It is important to understand that a child with an ASD may have another disorder, but that this does not preclude a diagnosis of an ASD.

DEPRESSION As children with AS mature, they frequently want friends. However, not surprisingly, this can be a very difficult task to accomplish, and they may begin to realize that they are different from the other children in their class. As children repeatedly fail at social interactions and are ridiculed by their peers, they become increasingly at risk for depression (Klin, McPartland, & Volkmar, 2005).

ANXIETY Individuals with AS live in a world that frequently appears overstimulating and unpredictable (Klin et al., 2005). In essence, they do not understand the rules of the world in which they live. It is then no wonder that anxiety disorders co-occur with AS. Generalized Anxiety Disorder (GAD), a condition characterized by a persistent state of worrying, is one of the most common comorbidities associated with AS (Ghaziuddin, 2002). Symptoms of anxiety tend to increase during times of stress. Given the highly stressful world in which these individuals live, the relationship is obvious.

BOX 1.1   Research Notes Box

Children with early onset psychotic disorders or bipolar disorder can also frequently appear to have autism. In fact, some children with chromosome deletion disorders can appear to have autism, a psychotic disorder, or both (Vorstman et al., 2006). Children with ASD generally have more psychiatric disturbances (e.g., depression or bipolar disorder) than children without ASD (Bradley & Bolton, 2006). Bradley and Bolton (2006), in a study of children with ASD and peers, found that 3 of the 41 children with autism had a comorbid bipolar episode while none of the comparison children had such a diagnosis.

OBSESSIVE COMPULSIVE DISORDER Obsessive Compulsive Disorder (OCD) is another anxiety disorder. Individuals with OCD are plagued with obsessions and/or compulsions that they find difficult to control. The restricted and repetitive interests of children with ASD, as well as their atypical motor mannerisms, have the flavor of and may actually meet criteria for an additional diagnosis of OCD (Ghaziuddin, 2002). Distinguishing between ASD symptoms of a restricted pattern of interests that do not reach the intensity of OCD is difficult. This process is called **differential diagnosis**.

ATTENTION DEFICIT DISORDERS Attention problems, such as those associated with ADHD, can sometimes look like AS, particularly in severe cases (Myles et al., 2007).

NONVERBAL LEARNING DISABILITIES Children with a nonverbal learning disability (NLD) have social difficulties similar to children with AS (Minshew, Sweeney, Bauman, & Webb, 2005). NLD characteristics include average or high IQ; good rote memory; strong vocabulary; concrete and literal thinking and language interpretation; poor **social skills**; difficulty processing nonverbal communication, including body language and facial expressions; difficulty adjusting to changes in routines; motor awkwardness; and an apparent lack of "common sense" (Tanguay, 1998). There is a great deal of overlap between NLD and AS: studies at the Yale Child Study Center have found that 80% of persons with AS also met diagnostic criteria for NLD, although those with NLD met the AS diagnostic criteria much less frequently (Dinklage, 2005). The primary difference between the two diagnoses appears to be that while AS is diagnosed on behavioral observations, identifying NLD requires a focus on academic difficulties (particularly in math and spelling) incongruent with intellect (Dinklage, 2005).

Introduction to Autism Spectrum Disorder Diagnosis across the Lifespan

There are several "red flags" that serve as potential indicators of an ASD diagnosis. These are common areas of concern as well as behaviors that tend to cluster based on the age of the child (Figure 1.5).

1. Frequent meltdowns
2. Emotional lability
3. Symptoms of ADHD (e.g., teachers complain the child is unable to sit still or will not sit during "Circle Time")
4. Overly perfectionistic
5. Sensory issues (such as dislikes being touched or bathed)
6. Unusual fears
7. Discrepancy between behavior at home and at school (the child the school complains about is not the child at home!)

Red Flags for Diagnosis Asperger Syndrome at Any Age
1. Three or more previous referrals and diagnoses
2. Charming with adults (including at the assessor's office), but fails at interactions with same-aged peers
3. Child has difficulty discussing emotional states and showing insight into others' emotional states
4. Affective expressions may appear overly restricted or heightened
5. Shows few gestures and has difficulty reading nonverbal cues of others

FIGURE 1.5   Red Flags for Diagnosis of Asperger Syndrome in Preschool Children

ASD are often not recognized as such in young children with HFA or AS; so many such children are referred for diagnosis only when they enter school. In fact, the average age for a diagnosis of a child with AS is between 7 and 11 years old (Howlin & Asgharian, 1999; Mandell, Novak, & Zubritsky, 2005).

POSSIBLE CAUSES OF AUTISM SPECTRUM DISORDERS

Historical Context

As recent as the 1980s, practitioners believed that the cause of autism was what was termed *Refrigerator Mothers.* Specifically, Bruno Bettleheim (1967), a professional in the 1960s, believed that autism was caused by the child's parents (the mother in particular) not providing love or attention and was, in fact, cold to the child—hence the term *refrigerator.* Ivar Lovaas, well-known behavioral interventionist, also held this belief. The common practice of the day was to remove the child from his parents and place the parents in psychotherapy. Today, thanks to the work of individuals such as psychologist Bernard Rimland (1964), a father of a child with autism, we understand that autism is not caused by parents.

Role of Environment

The exact cause of ASD is unknown. Some believe that the environment plays a role in the development of autism. Environmental contributors may include pre-, peri-, and postnatal factors (such as second and third trimester uterine bleeding, Rh incompatibility, high bilirubin levels at birth, and oxygen supplementation at birth), as well as the recently publicized Measles, Mumps, and Rubella (MMR) vaccines. Further, some suggest that food allergies or deficiencies in certain vitamins and minerals may be a contributing factor in the development of ASD (cf., Croen, Grether, Yoshida, Odouli, & Van de Water, 2005).

Genetics

Researchers, practitioners, and parents are all invested in investigating possible causes of ASD. Research clearly indicates that ASD have a genetic component (cf., Bolton, Macdonald, Pickles, & Rios, 1994; Constantino et al., 2006; Constantino & Todd, 2003; Landa & Garrett Mayer, 2006; Pickles et al., 2000; Rutter, 2000; Veenstra, Vanderweele, & Cook, 2003; Watson et al., 2007; Zwaigenbaum et al., 2005). Although the extent of this relationship has not yet been determined, and no single gene has been identified as a cause in every case, "approximately 5% of individuals with autism have an identified chromosomal abnormality" (Whitman, 2004, p. 120). Faulty genes have been found on the long arm (q) of chromosomes 2, 3, 6, 7, 13, and 15 and on the short arm (p) of chromosomes 1, 11, 13, 16, and 19 (Whitman, 2004, p. 121). According to Whitman, 2004, the "most commonly reported anomaly in research studies is the duplication of a section of the long arm of chromosome 15" (p. 120). Various autistic characteristics are associated with varying locations of genetic differences. For example, the 7q region impacts the development of the frontal, parietal, and temporal lobes, all of which are associated with significant functioning in autism, and speech delays are linked with an area on chromosome 2 (Whitman, 2004).

The role of genetics in autism has been clearly established. Research indicates that siblings of a child with autism also have a risk of related difficulties. More than 10% of siblings of children with autism show deficits associated with an ASD diagnosis, such as abnormalities in eye contact, imitation, social smiling, and disengagement of visual interest (Landa & Garrett Mayer, 2006; Zwaigenbaum et al., 2005). Deficits in language and cognitive abilities have also been noted in ASD siblings before the age of 5 (Watson et al., 2007). This is much higher than the risk for the general population. Other research indicates that if one identical twin has autism, the chance for the other twin to have autism is 60%, but that the risk for the twin to be somewhere on the autism spectrum is 90%. However, if autism was caused purely by heritability, we would expect the concordance rates of identical twins to be closer to 100% (Ozonoff & Rogers, 2003; Rutter, 2000).

Other psychiatric disorders, such as depression or anxiety, are found at higher than average levels in family members of those with an ASD. Researchers have even proposed that a broad autism phenotype exists within families (Goin-Kochel, Abbacchi, & Constantino, 2007). This refers to a set of autistic-like subclinical symptoms in members of the families of children on the autism spectrum. Symptoms range from slow or impaired language development to shyness (Ozonoff & Rogers, 2003). As researchers continue to investigate the genetic underpinnings of autism, we will begin to learn more about the broad autism phenotype.

CHARACTERISTICS OF AUTISM SPECTRUM DISORDERS

Language Deficits

AUTISM   Although many children with autism may not speak, as noted previously, they may display echolalia. Echolalia was once thought to be nonfunctional; however, it is now recognized that echolalia may in fact be the child's way of speaking (cf., Quill, 1995). For example, I knew a 5-year-old with autism whose speech consisted almost exclusively of echolalia in particular, delayed echolalia that included songs and quotes from television. His teacher noted increased singing during story time after recess. The school team asked if I could assist in decreasing this distracting behavior. When I came to observe, I noted that Keith sang only commercial themes, and that they were all for food. Given that story time was just before lunch, I wondered if he might be hungry. We asked his mother to send a snack that he could eat just before story time to see if this might be the issue. Once he began eating a snack to tide him over for lunch, the singing stopped. Although Keith did not have the functional speech to tell us he was hungry, his echoed singing provided the clue necessary to get his need met. Teachers are, therefore, encouraged to become "investigators" when students with autism are engaging in echolalia and/or challenging behaviors.

When someone has limited or no speech, she will use other methods to communicate wants and needs. Carly, a child with autism who was completely without speech, used symbols as an alternative/augmentative communication (see Chapter 12, Assistive Technology) system. One day she wanted a drink of water, but the teacher's back was turned. Carly touched a card symbolizing water that was on a table rather than bringing it to her teacher. Because the teacher could not see Carly, she did not realize that Carly was asking for a drink. When the teacher did not respond to Carly's initiation, Carly approached her teacher and bit her, effectively saying, "Pay attention to me, I want some water!" Carly's story clearly indicates that all behaviors have a communicative function and teachers should first consider what a child might be trying to tell them when a behavior occurs.

Other children with autism will have speech, although it may be delayed and/or limited. For these children, speech may consist of a single word utterance or approximations of words to communicate entire thoughts. Still others may have seemingly adequate speech, but have difficulties with forms of language similar to those with AS (see section below). It is important to note that language deficits in children with autism are not static; a child may have no speech, but that does not imply that he will never develop speech. With appropriate instruction, including augmentative and alternative communication systems (AACs), children with autism can develop speech.

ASPERGER SYNDROME   As per the *DSM-IV-TR*, language milestones for children with AS are at the same level as those of typically developing children. However, children with AS still show important language *differences* that need to be addressed. While their *functional* language (i.e., grammar, sentence structure, pronunciation, vocabulary) may be adequate, their language *pragmatics* are almost invariably deficient. "Pragmatics" refers to the rules and social components associated with language. For instance, there are certain routines that people typically use when first meeting another person (e.g., saying "Nice to meet you," shaking hands). A child with AS may not necessarily understand these social norms and may, for example, immediately ask someone she met how old she is or how much she weighs. In school, a student with AS may want to talk incessantly about his special interest and will not understand why peers are not fascinated listening to him speak about decks on cruise ships. So, while this child's ability to *produce* language may not have been delayed, his ability to use language *adaptively* may indeed be severely delayed. It is important to remember that the needs of children with AS vary greatly; their pragmatic deficits may range from subtle to significant Likewise language challenges may appear different based on the structure of the learning environment and social demands.

Children with AS may also have difficulty understanding the semantics or the meaning of language. For example, in a clinical examination of a child, a psychologist introduced a set of dolls by saying that they would play with "my family." The child looked very confused, wondering how the examiner's family could be a set of dolls. The subtleties of language and sarcasm are lost on many children with AS. They frequently do not understand sarcasm or subtle jokes and may be quite literal thinkers. For instance, a student with AS may be the only child in the classroom who does not understand a joke. However, some parents work extremely hard to socialize their child, and the child may be able to use these learned skills in combination with strong cognitive skills to understand, and even tell, jokes. For example, one child we know was chosen master of ceremonies for a school pep rally and, because of direct instruction, was able to make jokes and spontaneous, funny remarks about classmates and teachers. Do not assume that a child does not have AS because she is funny and can use sarcasm.

Some children with AS may also use language in unusual ways, such as using inappropriately formal words. They may also describe things in somewhat odd or indirect ways (Attwood, 1998;

Bashe & Kirby, 2001), such as calling a person by the color of her shirt rather than by her name. For example, one child we know used to call his school "1214," which was the number in front of the school's main building.

USING LANGUAGE IN ODD WAYS

Adrian, a boy with AS, once stood outside his parents' bathroom door, where they mistakenly thought they could hide while having an argument. When he knocked on the door and his parents came out, he calmly remarked that, "this does not seem to be a festive moment between the two of you."

Children with AS frequently have difficulty in conversations and following up on statements made by others (Attwood, 1998). For instance, if somebody said, "My parents are not from this area," a typical child may follow up and ask where her parents live, while a child with AS may ignore this statement completely and talk about something else without acknowledging this remark. Conversations with a child with AS do not generally "flow" as they do with neurotypical children. There may be frequent, long, and awkward pauses wherein one party will be uncomfortable, while the child with AS will be oblivious that he should be feeling awkward. For those children with particularly intense interests, others may notice that the conversation invariably ends up on this topic. Similarly, a discussion with an individual with AS may sound more like a lecture rather than a conversation (Bashe & Kirby, 2001). While this may be uncomfortable for the conversation partner, the child with AS will be comfortable talking about a topic for which he has a "script." Children with AS have a sketchy understanding of social norms, which makes it likely that they will make inappropriate remarks or not notice odd turns of conversations. Even if they do notice an awkward turn, they may lack the resources they need to repair the conversation.

Individuals with AS have challenges related to understanding nonverbal communication, including gestures, facial expression, and proximity, which some experts estimate accounts for as much as 70% to 90% of communication. In addition to difficulties with nonverbal aspects of communication, children with AS may also have difficulty processing language in highly distractible environments (Twachtman-Cullen & Twachtman-Reilly, 2007).

THE LITERAL INTERPRETATION OF LANGUAGE

The examiner told Susie that she had a friend who was a dentist who had given her several boxes of free toothpaste. The examiner told Susie, "I have so much toothpaste I don't have anywhere to sit." Susie looked at her and seriously said, "Maybe you should buy another chair."

Children with AS may also have overly formal or pedantic language (Frith, 1991; Twachtman-Cullen & Twachtman-Reilly, 2007). For example, they may always begin their questions with "I would like to inquire about. . . ." They may also speak with an unusual rate, volume, or pitch, or may speak in an extremely loud or monotone voice (Gillberg, Gillberg, Rastam, & Wentz, 2001).

Children with AS may use functional echolalia. While unique, this language generally has an adaptive purpose. For instance, a child who has difficulty processing information or remembering a question may repeat this question to themselves before giving an answer. For instance, when one child was asked "Is this like your boat?" he repeated "Is this like my boat?" several times, seemingly to help himself remember the question as he thought about his answer.

Many young children vocalize their thoughts as they play or interact with another person. While this is developmentally appropriate for young children, by the time a child goes to school this type of behavior is no longer acceptable. Children with AS, however, may continue this self-verbalization into their teen years (Attwood, 1998). This behavior can interfere with the ability to attend and learn in the classroom, as a child with AS may be too busy rehearsing what to say to attend. Children or adults with AS may also rehearse via whisper what they are going to say in a conversation to themselves before speaking, which greatly disrupts the normal flow of conversation.

Social Differences

AUTISM   From birth, human beings are social creatures; infants as young as a few hours old have been noted to look toward speakers and to attempt to imitate facial expressions. It should come as no surprise, then, that one of the earliest symptoms of autism noted by parents are differences in social behaviors. The word "autism" comes from the Greek "aut" meaning *self.* Kanner, in his early description of what was then called "Kanner's Syndrome" described the children as "unto themselves" and, thus, described their behaviors as "autistic." Although the stereotyped child with autism is thought to prefer to be alone and left in his own world, many children with autism express love and affection for familiar people, including parents and teachers. As noted previously, it is a myth to think that children with autism do not love or experience emotions. The differences we see in children with autism frequently have to do with the *way* in which they experience emotions or interact.

Theory of Mind   The ability to understand that others have thoughts, perspectives, and opinions other than our own is known as *theory of mind* or mind blindness, and there is substantial research supporting this as a deficit area for persons on the autism spectrum (Baron-Cohen, 1995; Kerr & Durkin, 2004). Many people with ASD have difficulty taking the perspective of another into consideration during conversation, may believe that others have the same thoughts and opinions as they do, and may fail to understand why someone would make a particular choice or do something because they themselves would not do so. This can contribute to significant difficulty in social situations (Hill, 2004).

Kevin, an 8-year-old with autism, would continually attempt to talk with his teacher about events from a movie his teacher had never seen. He would become angry when his teacher would ask a question, insisting that she already knew the answer. Despite her best efforts to explain to Kevin that she had never seen the movie, Kevin continued to talk to his teacher as if she had, and continued to become angry when she "acted dumb" or asked "dumb" questions, because in Kevin's mind, everyone had the same information that he had.

Joint Attention   As noted previously, children with autism, contrary to previously held beliefs, can form meaningful relationships with caregivers and others in their environment. They can engage in attachment behaviors, make eye contact, show affection, and even engage in routine social play. Behaviorally, lack of joint attention is observed in a lack of pointing behaviors in youngsters with autism, such as to show someone something of interest. Further, persons with limited joint attention may not follow the point or gaze of another person or engage in gaze shift from point of reference to person and back again. Joint attention abilities are seen as crucial to communication—particularly nonverbal social communication—and critical for socialization (cf., Mundy, Fox, & Card, 2003; Mundy & Vaughn, 2001–2002). In fact, Mundy and Crowson (1997) suggested challenges in joint attention can discriminate children with autism from their peers. In addition to being a key feature of autism, joint attention may also be a critical skill for instruction.

Play   Although the *DSM-IV-TR* lists "lack of imaginative play" as a language deficit, we will discuss it here as a social deficit. Play development follows a somewhat predictable pattern. Beginning at birth, typically developing children seem almost "hardwired" to play (Boutot & Guenther, in press; Wolfberg & Schuler, 2006). However, children with autism do not follow the typical patterns of play development, preferring to play alone, with unusual objects, or seemingly not at all (Wolfberg, 2004).

Marty was 2 years old when he began therapy to learn play and language skills. As he entered the therapy room each day, he approached a yellow school bus, one of his favorite toys. However, instead of rolling the bus, or putting the accompanying toy characters in the bus, Marty would repeatedly open and close the doors, becoming extremely distressed when this activity was interrupted. Further, when offered a toy train whose doors did not open, Marty would turn it over and spin the wheels. Marty was eventually taught to play appropriately with these toys, but his initial response to them was to engage in *self-stimulatory behaviors,* by opening and closing doors and spinning wheels. Such unusual behaviors not only prevent a child like Marty from learning how to play appropriately with typical toys, but also may limit their interaction with other children. Typically developing children will begin to play alongside others in parallel play by age 2 and to cooperatively engage in play with another child by age 3 (Boutot & Guenther, in press). Children with autism, however, given their other social, language, and stereotypical play differences, often continue in solitary or parallel play well beyond what is age typical. This lack of typical play may further result in limited opportunities for development in other areas, including social, language, motor, and cognition—areas that are enhanced naturally through play for neurotypical children (Boutot & Guenther, in press; Wolfberg, 2003). Many parents of children with autism report that failure of their child with autism to "play like the other kids" was one of the first things they noticed. Play differences are so important in early identification of autism that they are appearing in early autism screening measures (i.e., M-CHAT; see above section).

Imitation   Typically developing children learn many important behaviors, including social skills, through imitation of others. They are able to attend to and imitate behaviors that they see as important or key to a particular goal. For example, a child who observes a sibling being given a lollipop to keep him quiet in church may determine that in order to get a lollipop, he too must cry. It is well documented in the literature that children with autism have difficulty with imitation skills, so much so that researchers (cf., Mundy & Crowson 1997; Stone, Coonrod, Pozdol, & Turner, 2003) have identified lack of imitation as a reliable early indicator of autism. In order to imitate, one must first be able to attend, which is a common difficulty for persons with autism. Difficulties with attending appear to be related to several factors, including distractibility, weak central coherence (see cognition section that follows), and a general lack of interest in the social behaviors of others. For this reason, early intervention programs for children with autism often focus on imitation as a key, or pivotal, skill (Koegel, Harrower, & Koegel, 1999). As with all characteristics, they vary from person to person.

ASPERGER SYNDROME   In addition to the social deficits defined by the *DSM-IV-TR* and listed above, children with AS have more subtle social deficits (cf., Baron-Cohen, 1995; Carter, Meckes, Pritchard, Swensen, Wittman, & Velde, 2004). For example, children and adolescents with AS may have an inaccurate concept of personal space and may stand too close or too far away from another person. Similarly, children with AS may have difficulty walking next to or with another person. Children with AS also show differences in eye contact. For some, their eye contact may be fleeting or extremely brief, while others may have unusually long or intense periods of eye contact. In addition, research suggests that children on the autism spectrum focus their gaze more toward a speaker's mouth than at their eyes as compared to typically developing children (cf., Klin, Jones, Schultz, Volkmar, & Cohen, 2002).

Some children with AS may appear uninterested in others and may be described as self-centered (cf., Wheelwright et al., 2006). In reality, they lack the skills to initiate and maintain interactions with others. Social attempts are also impacted by the rigid behavior of individuals with AS, which makes it difficult for them to play cooperatively with other children. They may want to "run the show" and tell the other children what to do (the old adage "my way or the highway"). Thus, some children with AS may gravitate toward younger or older peers and/or adults, as they are more accommodating to their needs. However, even in these situations individuals with AS have challenges as they may want to tell other adults or their teacher what to do or how to solve a particular problem. One child we know became extremely upset when her teacher rearranged the computers in the classroom because the teachers did not use the optimal arrangement. The girl with AS emphatically scolded the teacher for selecting an inefficient configuration.

Given that children with AS may be extremely rigid, it makes sense that they are also rule-governed (cf., Crooke, Hendrix, & Rachman, 2007; Tsatsanis, Foley, & Donehower, 2004). This inflexibility often impedes functioning. For instance, one child refused to hang his pajamas on the hanger his mother bought for his door because the packaging noted that it was for towels. A child with AS may turn into the class policeman, notifying the teacher of the slightest infraction, oblivious of the social repercussions.

Emotional Expressions and Affect   Children with AS may have a restricted range of facial expressions or display limited affect. For example, a parent once made the comment about her 11-year-old son that only once in his entire life had she been able to tell he was happy. Other parents may assert that their child with AS is more negative than other children. These children may whine or cry more than others and tend to see the glass as half empty rather than half full (Barnhill, 2001). Parents and professionals may tend to think of children with AS as always showing reduced or flattened emotional expressions. However, this is not always the case, and some children appear to be consistently happy. They may also have usual and intensely positive affective expressions. Caution is needed in the interpretation of facial expressions as they may not match emotional state.

In addition to differences in emotional expressions, children with AS frequently have difficulty describing internal emotional states (Losh & Capps, 2006). While they are able to tell others something that makes them happy or sad, they have an extremely difficult time explaining these feelings. In addition, they have difficulty attributing how their actions may make others feel (Barnhill, 2001).

It is important for parents and professionals to remember that many children with AS experience grave social challenges at school, and they may have more success at home when interacting with adults, with younger or older children, or are left to do as they please.

Sensory Concerns

AUTISM   Almost all children with autism have some differences in **sensory** input (Baranek, 2002; Myles et al., 2004). Although we have separated them for purposes of this textbook, it is important to note that sensory issues for children with autism and those with AS have some similarities (Myles et al., 2003). Sensory issues for persons with ASD are either hypersensitivity (over) or hyposensitivity (under) (see Chapter 11). Children who have an oversensitivity to light, for example, may become agitated in a room in which there are florescent bulbs. A child who experiences an undersensitivity to tactile stimulation, for example, may prefer heavy pressure or brushing with a firm-bristled brush to stimulate his sense of touch. While current diagnostic criteria do not include sensory processing abnormalities, teachers should be aware that sensory issues may exist for their students with autism and should plan to support them as needed (see Chapter 11 for more information). However, it is also important to note that while sensory differences are common, they are not the same for all persons with autism, and some may experience no differences.

ASPERGER SYNDROME   Research shows that the majority of individuals with AS have sensory issues (Henry & Myles, 2007; Myles et al., 2004) and these challenges may become more evident when the child is overly tired or stressed (Myles et al., 2004; Pfeiffer, Kinnealey, Reed, & Herzberg, 2005).

In fact, a study that compared the sensory profile of students with AS to neurotypical peers found that in 22 out of 23 sensory comparisons, those with AS had marked sensory impairments as compared to peers (Dunn et al., 2002). Sensitivity can occur in virtually any sensory modality, but the most common sensitivities are in the auditory, tactile, and multisensory areas (Myles, Cook, Miller, Rinner, & Robbins 2000).

Three types of auditory stimuli have been described by adults with AS. One category refers to sudden or unexpected noises—as simple as an air conditioner turning on or a pen top clicking. The second category is high-pitched noises, such as those coming from the motors of small kitchen appliances. The final category includes complex or multiple sounds occurring at once. Thus, the "buzz" of people talking at a social gathering may be extremely overwhelming for somebody with AS. Sound sensitivities make the world a difficult place to live in. Imagine attempting to go to the supermarket if you have difficulty integrating multiple sources of sensory information. There are multiple noises, such as the cash registers, people walking, people talking to each other, and announcements over the loud speaker. Most typically developing individuals are able to tune this out and attend to only the most important stimuli (i.e., getting the food you want and paying for it). However, this is a virtually impossible task for somebody with auditory sensitivity, and it is a very difficult concept for others to understand (Myles & Adreon, 2001; Dunn et al., 2002).

Parents frequently report that their child with auditory sensitivity covers up her ears when confronted with an aversive sound. In fact, it is estimated that more than 85% of children with auditory sensitivity exhibit this type of behavior (Myles & Adreon, 2001). Children may also go to great lengths to avoid unpleasant stimuli, such as avoiding birthday parties.

Tactile sensitivity is also quite common in children and adults with AS. This refers to an extreme sensitivity to touch or to the way things feel. Some children may resist being picked up, held, or hugged by their parents because the pressure of touch is uncomfortable. Many parents report that bath time is a struggle because of sensory issues. For instance, one parent had an extremely difficult time washing (and later brushing) her child's hair because her scalp was extremely sensitive. Another parent indicated that her child's toes were extremely sensitive, making it difficult to wash his feet. Children with tactile sensitivity may also be unable to tolerate certain types of clothing or fabrics, so it is common to find that many require that the tags be cut out of shirts. One 10-year-old child with AS was knowledgeable about the thread count of sheets and could sleep only on the highest quality sheets. Similarly, children with tactile sensitivity tend to prefer certain clothes and will wear only them, which results in their parents buying the same shirts or pants in varying sizes to accommodate their child as he grows.

Related to tactile sensory processing, one of the most concerning areas for parents may be a child's decreased sensitivity to pain.

Other children with AS may be seemingly unaware of the weather and wear warm clothes during the summer or lightweight clothing during the winter. Others may not be able to stand the heat of a summer day and will refuse to go outside at all.

Some children are sensitive to the taste and textures of food. For instance, some children may prefer only bland food or be unable to tolerate any mixing of foods on their plates. Other children may be able to eat only food with certain textures. For instance, some children will only eat crunchy foods, while others will only eat soft foods.

Approximately one half of children and adults with AS experience sensitivity to visual stimuli (Myles et al., 2000). For example, some children and adults report being extremely uncomfortable with certain types of lighting. Others indicate that they see colors differently, and some have even become artists known for their unusual work with color (Attwood, 1998). See Figure 1.6 for examples of sensory integration difficulties.

Tactile

Tags in cloths

Dislike being touched or hugged

Difficulties during bathing or hair brushing

Knowledgeable about things like thread count

Cannot eat certain foods

**Some children require a great deal of tactile stimulation (might hit themselves)

Auditory

 Cover up or put fingers in ears (e.g., many children do not like noises from fireworks or the vacuum cleaner)

 Constantly tells others to "stop yelling"

Smell

 Notices and complains when parents switch cleaning products

 Frequent smelling of fingers, food, or toys

Visual

 Wears sunglasses indoors or when the sun is not shining

 Intense, unusual preferences for certain colors

FIGURE 1.6   Some Examples of Sensory Integration Difficulties

Repetitive Behaviors and Restricted Interests

In this section we will overview some of the **repetitive behaviors** (sometimes called "self-stimulatory behaviors," such as rocking or hand flapping) and restricted interests often associated with autism and AS. As previously noted, ASD manifests in individuals in vastly different ways, and no two individuals may share the exact same characteristics. The same is true for repetitive behaviors and restricted interests. Further there are varying degrees of such behaviors, and these too differ from person to person.

AUTISM   Until 1988, many Americans had not heard the term *autism*. In 1988 Dustin Hoffman won an Oscar for his portrayal of an adult with autism in the movie "Rainman." In the movie, Hoffman's character Ray displayed many repetitive, also known as self-stimulatory, behaviors and ritualistic behaviors, common to persons with autism. For example, Ray had to eat a particular food on a particular night and had to purchase his underwear from one particular store. In addition, he would robotically repeat his needs over and over again, becoming increasingly agitated if they were not met. Ray also rocked back and forth on his heels, particularly when anxious or in a novel situation. This portrayal of an individual with autism was for many people the first glimpse of autism.

 Stereotypical Mannerisms   Hand flapping, finger flicking, rocking, spinning objects or self: these are all examples of stereotypical mannerisms or behaviors that may be common for people with autism. There is some evidence to suggest that these behaviors serve to calm persons with autism when their anxiety level increases—the behaviors serving as the routine they lack and crave (see next section). While the antecedent and purpose may be unclear, what is clear is that all persons with autism, by its definition, will have some stereotypic behaviors at some time, and they may increase or decrease in frequency and/or intensity based on age and situation. It is also possible that persons with low-functioning autism have more intense and more obvious forms of stereotyped behaviors compared with those with HFA or AS.

Insistence on Sameness   According to the *DSM-IV-TR*, resistance to change and insistence on sameness are qualifying characteristics of autism. Tommy, an 18-year-old with autism is nonverbal and also has a cognitive disability. He insists that each family member sit in a specific chair at the table. When they do not, he becomes aggressive in his attempts to physically move them to their "correct" location. The need for sameness can often be seen when a routine is violated or when objects are rearranged. At this time, teachers and parents may observe challenging behaviors, increased self-stimulatory behaviors, and/or attempts to escape the environment. Routines are often not obvious to families and school staff and quite often make themselves known when one is disrupted. Although nonverbal with very poor adaptive behavior skills, Hu had a keen eye for detail. One day upon entering the classroom, he bolted from the teacher and ran to "fix" a chair that was out of place. Before Hu could begin his day, he needed the chair to be in its "correct" position, which was inches from where it was when he entered the room. While sometimes inhibitory, the need for sameness can also be viewed as a strength of persons with autism. Teachers and parents can work to create meaningful routines and a predictable environment for a child with autism to enhance independence. Chapter 6 provides additional information on environmental arrangement.

Self-Injurious Behaviors and Aggression   Although uncommon, some individuals with autism, particularly those with classic autism and who are nonverbal, may engage in self-injurious behaviors (SIBs (Murphy, Hall, Oliver, & Kissi-Debra, 1999). SIBs are often thought to be related to either sensory processing or communicative issues (cf., Fectau, Mottron, Berthiaume, & Burack, 2003). Even so, SIBs should be addressed immediately (see Chapter 7 for information on how to address SIBs for persons with autism). Head banging, eye poking, skin picking, head hitting, and lip biting are examples of SIBs.

Some individuals with classic autism exhibit aggressive behavior toward others. Aggression toward others should be considered within the context of communication (see the example of Hu in the previous section); in other words, the individual with autism is attempting to communicate, and aggression is his way of doing so. For example, people with autism may engage in aggressive behaviors when a routine has changed, when they are anxious, or when they perceive a threat. Autism is, if nothing else, enigmatic and heterogeneous.

Savant Skills   Specialized or splinter skills are sometimes evident in individuals with autism. These are also known as savant skills. In the movie "Rainman," Ray had the ability to count cards in the movie, a seemingly impossible skill given his limitations in many other areas, such as self-help and communication. Jonah, an adult with classic autism, has an ability to calculate days of the week; that is, when given any date, he can quickly indicate the day of the week on which it did or will fall. It is estimated that only 1% of people with classic autism have a splinter skill or are savant (Hermelin, 2001).

ASPERGER SYNDROME   Children with AS may show a pattern of unusual behaviors or restricted interests. In fact, in a Web-based survey, 100% of parent respondents indicated that their child had at least one interest that was unusual in its intensity of scope (Bashe & Kirby, 2001). While most children have interests, children with AS may take their interests to extreme levels. These interests are typically unusually intense or of unusual content (Winter-Messiers, 2007). They may remain consistent over time, or they may change. In addition to changing over time, these interests may manifest differently in people of various ages, as they are frequently age appropriate, such as Thomas the Tank Engine™ at age 3 or Pokémon™ at age 7 (Winter-Messiers et al., 2007). Young children can develop intense interests in pretending to be animals or people. Children with such interests may be avid learners of their chosen topic and talk about it incessantly (Frith, 1991). However, others may learn to control themselves in order to be more socially appropriate.

Children with AS may rely greatly on routines and may have compulsions or rituals. These rituals may become more complex over time, such as lining up 12 animals before bed instead of the original 3 (Attwood, 1998).

Children with AS may show a similar pattern of behavior in their play by which they repeatedly play in the same way. This type of repetitive play, also called perseveration, is common in children with autism and in children with AS (cf., Hill, 2004). For example, one parent commented that her child would organize shapes all day long if allowed. Another child played with his figurines by repetitively crashing them against each other.

Rigid Behavior   Children with AS are not able to adjust to change as easily as typically developing children. This may translate into difficulty with transitions or difficulty with flexible thinking and problem solving (cf., Iovannone, Dunlap, Huber, & Kincaid, 2003). For example, if a child with AS becomes convinced that a problem has to be solved in a certain way, it could be very difficult to teach him otherwise. Maria, a 12-year-old with AS, became upset in math class when the teacher said there were two ways to solve a problem. When the teacher demonstrated both methods, Maria became very upset and insisted that one method had to be inaccurate.

This rigidity, combined with the social deficits inherent in AS, clearly makes it difficult for these children to play appropriately with peers. Parents frequently report that their child *has* to play their way and that they are unwilling to give in to their peers. For instance, many typical children take their playmates' wishes into consideration when determining what game to play. This is not the case with children with AS, who may like to direct the game and each person's part. When challenged by other children, they may become extremely angry or upset.

Imagination   Some children with AS show a limited ability to create an imaginary world and are content with their restricted areas of interests. However, there is a subgroup of these children who love pretend play and particularly enjoy drama. These children tend to play by themselves (at times playing each of the characters involved) rather than inviting others into their group. For some children, imaginary friends are their only companions (Attwood, 2007).

Older children and teenagers with AS may create or appear to live in imaginary worlds. It has been hypothesized that this allows children to escape from a social world that they do not understand and where, despite trying, they are not fully accepted (Attwood, 2007). This imaginary world may coincide with special interests. For instance, a child interested in dinosaurs may pretend to live among them or write scripts about dinosaurs. Other children may appear to "live" in a television show that they have written.

Motor Deficits

AUTISM   Motor problems are not uncommon in children with autism, although they are not part of the defining set of characteristics. Common problems may include dyspraxia, which is essentially difficulty with motor planning and may manifest itself in both fine/gross motor planning as well as oral motor planning related to speech. Dyspraxia can make learning new tasks difficult, despite otherwise good motor ability (Whitman, 2004). Other issues common to children with autism relative to motor abilities include difficulty with motor skills requiring balance (potentially due to disturbances in the vestibular sensory system), awkward movements, and toe walking. In addition, developmentally, delayed motor milestones are commonly reported by parents, including slow to sit up, slow to crawl, and slow to walk. Fine motor issues, such as difficulty cutting with scissors and poor penmanship, are also commonly noted by teachers and parents and frequently addressed through occupational therapy. As always, it is important to note that motor difficulties are not a defining feature of autism and are not seen in every individual.

ASPERGER SYNDROME   Research suggests that children with AS have difficulties with fine and gross motor coordination (Ghaziuddin & Butler, 1998). Children with gross motor deficits are often identified as awkward or clumsy. Physical education classes are typically difficult for children with AS, as they do not excel at sports requiring coordinated physical activity. For example, they frequently have extreme difficulty catching a ball or balancing on one foot. When one combines their social deficits with their lack of athletic ability, it is not surprising that these children are typically the last ones picked for a team or are left out entirely.

Within the area of fine motor skills, their graphomotor (motor abilities needed to write) functioning is frequently impaired (Myles et al., 2003), which makes their handwriting labored and illegible. It is thus not surprising that many report disliking writing (Church, Alisanki, & Amanullah, 2000).

Similarly, their manual dexterity is frequently poor, and using both hands together may frequently be a challenge. Seemingly simple things, such as tying shoes, can be a great challenge for a child with AS. These children may also struggle to learn to ride a bicycle or to roller-skate (Attwood, 1998).

Cognition

Research supports several areas of cognition that are impacted by autism, including memory, metacognition, executive functioning, central coherence, and abstract thought (for review, see Whitman, 2004). Because the nature of cognitive issues for individuals with autism are similar to those with AS, we will present them together in this section.

MEMORY   Children with autism as well as AS may have better memories for rote information and may recall facts better when presented visually rather than auditorially (cf., Williams, Goldstein, & Minshew, 2006). Complex information and information that lacks meaning for them may also be difficult for students with autism to recall. Memory is further hampered when the volume of information is too great or when it requires semantic understanding that the child lacks (cf., Garcia-Villamisar & Della Sala. 2002).

METACOGNITION   *Metacognition* refers to one's ability to understand not only how one thinks or learns, but also to understanding one's limitations and strengths relative to knowing. For persons on the autism spectrum, there is some research to support a relative lack of self-awareness that would preclude metacognition. This limitation can be seen in the inability of some individuals with ASD to generalize newly acquired skills across environments without direct instruction. Related to generalization of skills, Whitman (2004) wrote: "A person has to know what skills they possess, what skills are required in new situations they encounter, and whether they possess the skills necessary to perform in new situations" (p. 68). Therefore, lack of metacognitive understanding may limit one's ability to transfer knowledge from one situation to another.

EXECUTIVE FUNCTIONING   Executive functioning includes the ability to (a) organize and plan, (b) use working memory, (c) inhibit and control impulses, (d) manage time and priorities, and (e) use new strategies based on situational and historical context (Baron-Cohen, 1995). Behaviorally, executive functioning deficits may be seen through inflexibility, lack of spontaneity, slow reaction time, apparently random actions or impulsivity, or distractibility—particularly in a new situation (Hill, 2004). Executive functioning also plays a role in pretend play, which is known to be deficient in many children with autism (Wolfberg, 2004).

CENTRAL COHERENCE   It has been suggested that individuals with autism have a weak central coherence. That is, they have the ability to focus on detail but do not perceive the essence or entirety of a situation (Frith & Happe, 1994). Behaviorally this can be seen in a student who attends to irrelevant features of materials or the environment to the exclusion of more salient features. Consider Luke, a 14-year-old with classic autism. Luke's therapists had been teaching him to identify common nouns, including "bird," for some time. Once they believed he recognized a particular item as a bird, they would test his knowledge by placing "bird" in an array of several items he had previously learned, and asking him to identify the bird. Although they had been sure of his understanding of the concept of *bird,* upon presentation with three items that included a flower, Luke continually chose "flower" instead of "bird" when asked. Upon reflection, staff realized that both the bird and the flower were red. Luke had selected the bird each time, not on its salient bird-like qualities, but on the basis of an irrelevant stimulus—its color.

Teachers and parents will frequently choose to use line drawings rather than photographs of items for individual schedules or communication systems because of this tendency to focus in on irrelevant content. For example, Keith's teachers used photographs for his schedule system. Each picture was of an actual place or activity that Keith would encounter in his day. The picture of the speech therapist had her placed in front of a bulletin board. After a few months of school, during which time Keith had displayed great ability to use his schedule, he suddenly became noncompliant when it was time for speech therapy. Staff later realized that the therapist had changed her bulletin board; it was not the same as in the picture. Keith did not want to go into her room because he believed it to be a novel situation; he had focused on an irrelevant stimulus—the background—rather than the speech therapist.

ABSTRACT THOUGHT   As previously mentioned, some individuals on the autism spectrum may have difficulty with humor, metaphorical language, or idioms. These difficulties can be explained by a deficiency of abstract thought. More specifically, people with ASD are concrete, literal thinkers, and have difficulty understanding and processing abstract concepts or ideas (cf., Minshew, Myere, & Goldstein, 2002). Temple Grandin, an adult with HFA, has written about how it feels to have autism. Specifically, Dr. Grandin talks about how she processes information "in pictures" (see her book, *Thinking in Pictures: And Other Reports from My Life with Autism;* Grandin, 1995) and that abstract concepts do not lend themselves to these photographic images. For example, try to "picture" the concept of a *dog.* You may imagine your own dog, a dog you know, or some dogs you've seen. Now picture the concept of *love*; what images do you see? Whatever they are, they are likely much less specific to the concept than when you thought of *dog.* People with autism, then, may have specific difficulties with "picturing" abstract concepts, particularly those with which they have not had personal experience.

Summary

"If you've seen one student with autism . . . you've seen one student with autism." One of the most important concepts to remember is that ASD are heterogeneous, impacting each individual differently. A mistake commonly made by teachers of children with autism is that, based on experience with a handful of children, they "know" autism. While they may share a great many characteristics, no two individuals with ASD are alike, and the differences may profoundly impact how they learn and process information. This chapter covered the diagnosis and characteristics of autism, along with causal theories and historical perspectives. This information is intended to aid teachers in better understanding the individual students with whom they work and to provide a broad base of information. It is not intended to cover the entirety of possibilities relative to the characteristics of autism and its presentation within specific individuals. Teachers are encouraged to learn all they can about autism in general, and their students in particular, in order to be most effective in their instruction.

Chapter Review Questions

1. What are the characteristics of ASD? (Objective 1)
2. What are the main diagnostic criteria for ASD? (Objective 2)
3. What are the similarities and differences between the three main PDDs? (Objective 3)
4. What causes autism? (Objective 4)
5. How are each of the characteristics of autism associated with particular neurological impairment? (Objective 5)

Key Terms

Adaptive behavior *6*
ADI-R *12*
ADOS-G *12*
Asperger Disorder *6*
Attention–Deficit/Hyperactivity Disorder (ADHD) *2*

Autistic Disorder *6*
Autism Spectrum Disorder (ASD) *5*
Comorbidity *13*
Differential diagnosis *14*
DSM-IV-TR *5*

High functioning autism *6*
Pervasive Developmental Disorders (PDDs) *5*
Prevalence *5*
Repetitive behaviors *23*
Social skills *14*

Internet Resources

Diagnosing Autism: One Family's Journey:
http://childnett.tv/videos/services?page=1
National Institute of Mental Health:
http://www.nimh.nih.gov/publicat/autism.cfm
Descriptions of ADOS and ADI:
http://www.umaccweb.com/diagnostic_tools/index.html

Nonverbal Learning Disabilities:
http://www.NLDline.com and
http://www.NLDontheweb.org
Autism Speaks:
http://www.autismspeaks.org/
Autism Diagnostic Observation Schedule:
http://www.google.com/search?hl=en&q=Autism+Diagnostic+Observation+Schedule

References

American Psychiatric Association. (1994). *Diagnostic and statistical manual of mental disorders* (4th ed.). Washington, DC: Author.

American Psychiatric Association. (2000). *Diagnostic and statistical manual of mental disorders* (4th ed., text revision). Washington, DC: Author.

Attwood, T. (1998). *Asperger's syndrome: A guide for parents and professionals.* Philadelphia: Jessica Kingsley.

Attwood, T. (2007). *The complete guide to Asperger's Syndrome.* London: Jessica Kingsley.

Autism Society of America. (2008). From http://www.autism-society.org, retrieved March 17, 2008.

Baird, G., Charman, T., Baron-Cohen, S., Cox, A., Swettenham, J., Wheelwright, S., et al. (2000). A screening instrument for autism at 18 months of age: A 6-year follow-up study. *Journal of the American Academy of Child and Adolescent Psychiatry, 39,* 694–702.

Baranek, G. (2002). Efficacy of sensory and motor interventions for children with autism. *Journal of Autism and Developmental Disorders, 32,* 397–422.

Barnhill, G. P. (2001). Social attribution and expression in adolescents with Asperger Syndrome. *Focus on Autism and Other Developmental Disabilities, 16,* 46–53.

Barnhill, G. P., Hagiwara, T., Myles, B. S., Simpson, R. L., Brick, M. L., & Griswold, D. E. (2000). Parent, teacher, and self-report of problem and adaptive behaviors in children and adolescents with Asperger Syndrome. *Diagnostique, 25*(2), 147–167.

Baron-Cohen, S. (1995). *Mind blindness: An essay on autism and theory of mind.* Cambridge, MA: MIT Press.

Bashe, P. R., & Kirby, B. L. (2001). *The OASIS guide to Asperger Syndrome: Advice, support, insights, and inspiration.* New York: Crown.

Berument, S. K., Rutter, M., Lord, C., Pickles, A., & Bailey, A. (1999). Autism Screening Questionnaire: Diagnostic validity. *British Journal of Psychiatry, 175,* 444–451.

Bettleheim, B. (1967). *The empty fortress.* Toronto, CA: Collier-Macmillan.

Bolton, P., Macdonald, H., Pickles, A., & Rios, P. (1994). A case-control family history study of autism. *Journal of Child Psychology and Psychiatry, 35,* 877–900.

Boutot, E. A., & Guenther, T. (in press). *Play-based applied behavior analysis: Teaching young children with autism to and through play.* Shawnee Mission, KS: Autism Asperger Publishing Company.

Bradley, E., & Bolton, P. (2006). Episodic psychiatric disorders in teenagers with learning disabilities with and without autism. *British Journal of Psychiatry, 189,* 361–366.

Brown, R. T. (Ed.). (2004). *Handbook of pediatric psychology in school settings* (27th ed.). Mahwah, NJ: Lawrence Erlbaum Associates.

Carter, C., Meckes, L., Pritchard, L., Swensen, S., Wittman, P. P., & Velde, B. (2004). The friendship club: An after-school program for children with Asperger Syndrome. *Family and Community Health, 27,* 143–150.

Centers for Disease Control and Prevention. Autism Information Center. From http://www.cdc.gov/ncbddd/autism/, retrieved March 18, 2008.

Chakrabarti, S., & Fombonne, E. (2001). Pervasive developmental disorders in preschool children. *Journal of the American Medical Association, 285,* 3093–3099.

Chawarska, K., Klin, A., Paul, R., & Volkmar, F. (2007). Autism Spectrum Disorder in the second year: Stability and change in syndrome expression. *Journal of Child Psychology and Psychiatry, 48,* 128–138.

Church, C., Alisanki, S., & Amanullah, S. (2000). The social, behavioral, and academic experiences of children with Asperger syndrome. *Focus on Autism and Other Developmental Disabilities, 15,* 12–20.

Constantino, J. N. (2003). *Social responsiveness scale (SRS).* Los Angeles: Western Psychological Services.

Constantino, J. N., Lajonchere, C., Lutz, M., Gray, T., Abbacchi, A., McKenna, K., et al. (2006). Autistic social impairment in the siblings of children with pervasive developmental disorders. *The American Journal of Psychiatry, 163,* 294–296.

Constantino, J., & Todd, R. D. (2003). Autistic traits in the general population: A twin study. *Archives of General Psychiatry, 60,* 5824–5530.

Croen, L. A., Grether, J. K., Yoshida, C. K., Odouli, R., & Van de Water, J. (2005). Maternal autoimmune diseases, asthma and allergies, and childhood autism spectrum disorders: A case control study. *Archives of Pediatrics and Adolescent Medicine, 159,* 151–157.

Crooke, P. J., Hendrix, E., & Rachman, J. Y. (2007). Brief report: Measuring the effectiveness of teaching social thinking to children with Asperger Syndrome and high-functioning autism. *Journal of Autism and Developmental Disorders, 38,* 581–591.

Dinklage, D. (2005). *Asperger disorder and nonverbal learning disabilities: How are these two disorders related to each other?* From http://www.addforums.com/forums/archive/index.php/t-22779.html, retrieved March 20, 2008.

Dunn, W., Myles, B. S., & Orr, S. (2002). Sensory processing issues associated with Asperger Syndrome: A preliminary investigation. *The American Journal of Occupational Therapy, 56*(1), 97–102.

Edelson, M. G. (2006). Are the majority of children with autism mentally retarded? A systematic evaluation of the data. *Focus on Autism and Other Developmental Disabilities, 21,* 66–83.

Fecteau, S., Mottron, L., Berthiaume, C., & Burack, J. A. (2003). Developmental change of autistic symptoms. *Autism, 7,* 255–268.

Frith, U. (1991). Asperger and his syndrome. In U. Frith (Ed.), *Autism and Asperger Syndrome* (pp. 1–36). New York: Cambridge University Press.

Frith, U., & Happe, F. (1994). Autism: Beyond "theory of mind." *Cognition, 50,* 115–132.

Garcia-Villamisar, D., & Della Sala, S. (2002). Dual-task performance in adults with autism. *Cognitive Neuropsychoogy, 7,* 63–74.

Ghaziuddin, M. (2002). Asperger Syndrome: Associated psychiatric and medical conditions. *Focus on Autism and Other Developmental Disabilities, 17,* 138–144.

Ghaziuddin, M., & Butler, E. (1998). Clumsiness in autism and Asperger Syndrome: A further report. *Journal of Intellectual Ability Research, 42,* 45–48.

Gillberg, C., Gillberg, C., Rastam, M., & Wentz, E. (2001). The Asperger Syndrome (and high-functioning autism) Diagnostic Interview (ASDI): A preliminary study of a new structured clinical interview. *Autism, 5,* 57–66.

Goin-Kochel, R., Abbacchi, A., & Constantino, J. H. (2007). Lack of evidence for increased genetic loading for autism among families of affected females. *Autism, 11,* 279–286.

Grandin, T. (1995). *Thinking in pictures: And other reports from my life with autism.* New York: Doubleday.

Harrison, P., & Oakland, T. (2003). *Adaptive behavior assessment system* (2nd ed.). San Antonio, TX: Pearson.

Henry, S. A., & Myles, B. S. (2007). *The Comprehensive Autism Planning Systems (CAPS) for individuals with Asperger Syndrome, autism and related disabilities: Integrating best practices throughout the student's day.* Shawnee Mission, KS: Autism Asperger Publishing Company.

Hermelin, B. (2001). *Bright splinters of the mind.* London: Jessica Kingsley.

Hill, E. L. (2004). Executive function in autism. *TRENDS in Cognitive Science, 8,* 26–33.

Howlin, P., & Asgharian, A. (1999). The diagnosis of autism and Asperger Syndrome: Findings from a survey of 770 families. *Developmental Medicine and Child Neurology, 41,* 834–839.

Iovannone, R., Dunlap, G., Huber, H., & Kincaid, D. (2003). Effective educational practices for students with autism spectrum disorders. *Focus on Autism and Other Developmental Disabilities, 18,* 150–165.

Kanner, L. (1943). Autistic disturbances of affective contact. *Nervous Child, 2,* 217–250.

Kaufman, A. S., & Kaufman, N. L. (1983). *Kaufman assessment battery for children.* San Antonio, TX: Pearson.

Kerr, S., & Durkin, K. (2004). Understanding of thought bubbles as mental representations in children with autism: Implications for theory of mind. *Journal of Autism and Developmental Disorders, 34,* 637–648.

Klin, A., Jones, W., Schultz, W., Volkmar, F., & Cohen, D. (2002). Defining and quantifying the social phenotype in autism. *American Journal of Psychiatry, 159,* 895–908.

Klin, A., McPartland, J., & Volkmar, F. (2005). Asperger syndrome. In F. Volkmar, R. Paul, A. Klin, & D. Cohen (Eds.), *Handbook of autism and pervasive developmental disorders* (3rd ed., pp. 88–125). Hoboken, NJ: John Wiley & Sons.

Klin, A., Schultz, R., & Cohen, D. (2000). Theory of mind in action: Developmental perspectives on social neuroscience (pp. 357–388). In S. Baron-Cohen, H. Tager-Flusberg, & D. Cohen (Eds.), *Understanding other minds: Perspectives from developmental neuroscience* (2nd ed.). Oxford: Oxford University Press.

Koegel, L. K., Harrower, J., & Koegel, R. L. (1999). Support for children with developmental disabilities participating in full-inclusion classrooms through self-management. *Journal of Positive Behavior Interventions, 1,* 26–34.

Landa, R., & Garrett Mayer, E. (2006). Development in infants with autism spectrum disorders: A prospective study. *Journal of Child Psychology and Psychiatry, 47,* 629–638.

Lee, H. J., & Park, H. R. (2007). An integrated literature review on the adaptive behavior of individuals with Asperger syndrome. *Remedial and Special Education, 28,* 132–139.

Lord, C., Rutter, M., DiLavore, P., & Risi, S. (1999). *Autism Diagnostic Observation Schedule (ADOS) manual.* Los Angeles: Western Psychological Services.

Lord, C., Rutter, M., & Le Couteur, A. (1994). Autism Diagnostic Interview—Revised: A revised version of a diagnostic interview for caregivers of individuals with possible pervasive developmental disorders. *Journal of Autism and Developmental Disorders, 24,* 659–685.

Losh, M., & Capps, L. (2006). Understanding of emotional experience in autism: Insights from the personal accounts of high-functioning children with autism. *Developmental Psychology, 42,* 809–818.

Macintosh, K. E., & Dissanayake, C. (2004). Annotation: The similarities and differences between autistic disorder and Asperger's Disorder: A review of the empirical evidence. *Journal of Child Psychology and Psychiatry, 45*, 421–434.

Mandell, D. S., Novak, M. M., & Zubritsky, C. D. (2005). Factors associated with the age of diagnosis among children with autism spectrum disorders. *Journal of the American Academy of Child and Adolescent Psychiatry, 45,* 657.

Miller, J. N., & Ozonoff, S. (2000). The external validity of Asperger Disorder: Lack of evidence from the domain of neuropsychology. *Journal of Abnormal Psychology, 109*, 227–238.

Minshew, N. J., Meyer, J., & Goldstein, G. (2002). Abstract reasoning in autism: A dissociation between concept formation and concept identification. *Neuropsychologyy, 16*, 327–334.

Minshew, N. J., Sweeney, J. A., Bauman, M. L., & Webb, S. J. (2005). Neurologic aspects of autism. In F. R. Volkmar, R. Paul, A. Klin, & D. Cohen (Eds.), *Handbook of autism and pervasive developmental disorders* (3rd ed., pp. 473–514). New York: Wiley.

Mullen, E. M. (1995). *Mullen scales of early learning.* San Antonio, TX: Pearson.

Mundy, P., & Crowson, M. (1997). Joint attention and early social communication: Implications for research on intervention with autism, *Journal of Autism and Developmental Disorders 27*, 653–676.

Mundy, P., Fox, N., & Card, J. (2003). EEG coherence, joint attention and language development in the second year. *Developmental Science, 6*(1), 48–54.

Mundy, P., & Vaughn, A. (2001–2002). Joint attention and its role in the diagnostic assessment of children with autism. *Assessment for Effective Intervention, 27,* 57–60.

Murphy, G., Hall, S., Oliver, C. M. & Kissi-Debra R. (1999). Identification of early self-injurious behavior in young children with intellectual disability. *Journal of Intellectual Disabilities Research* 43, 149–163.

Myles, B. S., & Adreon, D. (2001). *Asperger syndrome and adolescence: Practical solutions for school success.* Shawnee Mission, KS: Autism Asperger Publishing Company.

Myles, B. S., Bock, S. J., & Simpson, R. L. (2000). *Asperger Syndrome diagnostic scale.* Austin, TX: Pro-Ed.

Myles, B. S., Cook, K. T., Miller, N. E., Rinner, L., & Robbins, L. (2000). *Asperger Syndrome and sensory issues: Practical solutions for making sense of the world.* Shawnee Mission, KS: Autism Asperger Publishing Company.

Myles, B. S., Hagiwara, T., Dunn, W., Rinner, L., Reese, M., Huggins, A., et. al. (2004). Sensory issues in children with Asperger syndrome and autism. *Education and Training in Developmental Disabilities, 39*(4), 283–290.

Myles, B. S., Huggins, A., Rome-Lake, M., Hagiwara, T., Barnhill, G. P., & Griswold, D. E. (2003). Written language profile of children and youth with Asperger Syndrome. *Education and Training in Developmental Disabilities, 38*, 362–370.

Myles, B. S., Lee, H. J., Smith, S., Tien, K., Chou, Y., Swanson, T. C. & Hudson, J. (2007). A large-scale study of the characteristics of Asperger Syndrome. *Education and Training in Developmental Disabilities, 42*, 448–459.

Myles, B. S., & Southwick, J. (2005). *Asperger Syndrome and difficult moments: Practical solutions for tantrums, rage, and meltdowns.* Shawnee Mission, KS: Autism Asperger Publishing Company.

Ozonoff, S., & Rogers, S. J. (2003). From Kanner to the millennium: Scientific advances that have shaped clinical practice. In S. Ozonoff, S. J. Rogers, & R. L. Hendren (Eds.), *autism spectrum disorders: A research review for practitioners* (pp. 3–33). Washington, DC: American Psychiatric Publishing.

Ozonoff, S., South, M., & Miller, J. N. (2000). *DSM-IV*-defined Asperger Syndrome: Cognitive, behavioral and early history differentiation from high-functioning autism. *Autism, 4*, 29-46.

Pfeiffer, B., Kinnealey, M., Reed, C., & Herzberg, G. (2005). Sensory modulation and adolescents with Asperger's Disorder. *The American Journal of Occupational Therapy, 59*, 335–345.

Pickles, A., Starr, E., Kazak, S., Bolton, P., Papanikolaou, K., Bailey, A., et al. (2000). Variable expression of the autism broader phenotype: Findings from extended pedigrees. *Journal of Child Psychology and Psychiatry, 41*, 491–502.

Quill, K. A. (1995). *Teaching children with autism: Strategies to enhance communication and socialization.* New York: Delmar Publishers.

Rimland, B. (1964). *Infantile autism: The syndrome and its implications for a neural theory of behavior.* Upper Saddle River, NJ: Prentice Hall.

Roberts, M. C. (Ed.). (2003). *Handbook of pediatric psychology* (3rd ed.). New York: Guilford.

Robins, D. L., Fein, D., Barton, M. L., & Green, J. A. (2001). The Modified Checklist for Autism in Toddlers: An initial study investigating the early detection of autism and pervasive developmental disorders. *Journal of Autism and Developmental Disorders, 31,* 131–144.

Roid, G. J. (2004). *Standford-Binet intelligence scales.* Rolling Meadows, IL: Riverside.

Rutgers, J., VanJzendoorn, M. J., & Bakermans-Kranenburg, M. H. (2007). Autism and attachment. *Autism, 11,* 187–200.

Rutter, M. (2000). Genetic studies of autism: From the 1970s into the millennium. *Journal of Abnormal Child Psychology, 28*(1), 3–14.

Schopler, E., Reichler, R. J., & Renner, B. R. (1980). *The childhood autism rating scale.* Los Angeles: Western Psychological Services.

Sparrow, S. S., Balla, D. A., & Cicchetti, D. V. (2005). *Vineland Adaptive Behavior Scales: Interview edition survey form manual* (2nd ed.). Circle Pines, MN: American Guidance Service.

Sponheim, E., & Skjeldal, O. (1998). Autism and related disorders: Epidemiological findings in a Norwegian study using ICD-10 diagnostic criteria. *Journal of Autism and Developmental Disorders, 28,* 217–227.

Stone, W., Coonrod, E. E., Pozdol, S. L., & Turner, L. M. (2003). The parent interview for autism—clinical version (PIA-CV). *Autism, 7,* 9–30.

Tanguay, P. B. (1998). *Nonverbal learning disorders: What to look for.* From http://www.nldontheweb.org/tanguay_3.htm, retrieved March 20, 2008.

Thompson, T., Caruso, M., & Ellerbeck, K. (2003). Sex matters in autism and other developmental disabilities. *Journal of Learning Disabilities, 7,* 345–362.

Tryon, P. A., Mayes, S. D., Rhodes, R. L., & Waldo, M. (2006). Can Asperger's Disorder be differentiated from autism using *DSM-IV* criteria? *Focus on Autism and Other Developmental Disabilities, 21,* 2–6.

Tsatsanis, C., Foley, C., & Donehower, C. (2004). Contemporary outcome research and programming guidelines for Asperger Syndrome and high-functioning autism. *Topics in Language Disorders, 24,* 249–259.

Turner, L. M., Stone, W. L., Pozdol, S. L., & Coonrod, E. E. (2006). Follow-up of children with autism spectrum disorders from age 2 to age 9. *Autism, 10,* 243–265.

Twachtman-Cullen, D., & Twachtman-Reilly, J. (2007). Communication and language issues in less able school-age children with autism. In R. L. Gabriels & D. E. Hill (Eds.), *Growing up with autism: Working with school-age children and adolescents* (pp. 73–94). New York: Guilford.

Veenstra Vanderweele, J., & Cook, E. H. J. (2003). Genetics of childhood disorders: XLVI. Autism, Part 5: Genetics of autism. *Journal of the American Academy of Child and Adolescent Psychiatry, 42*(1), 116–118.

Verte, S., Geurts, H. M., Roeyers, H., Oosterlaan, J., & Sergeant, J. A. (2006). Executive functioning in children with an Autism Spectrum Disorder: Can we differentiate within the spectrum? *Journal of Autism and Developmental Disorders, 36,* 351–372.

Volkmar, F., & Klin, A. (2005). Issues in the classification of autism and related conditions. In F. Volkmar, R. Paul, A. Klin, & D. Cohen (Eds.), *Handbook of autism and pervasive developmental disorders* (3rd ed., pp. 5–41). Hoboken, NJ: John Wiley & Sons.

Volkmar, F. R., Paul, R., Klin, A., & Cohen, D. (Eds.). (2005). *Handbook of autism and pervasive developmental disorders: Volume. 1: Diagnosis, development, neurobiology, and behavior* (3rd ed.). Hoboken, NJ: John Wiley and Sons.

Vorstman, J. A. S., Morcus, M. E. J., Duijff, S. N., Klaassen, P. W. J., Heineman-de Boer, J. A., Beemer, F. A.; et al. (2006). The 22q11.2 deletion in children: High rate of autistic disorders and early onset of psychotic symptoms. *Journal of the American Academy of Child and Adolescent Psychiatry, 45,* 1104–1113.

Watson, L., Baranek, G. T., Crais, E., Reznick, S., Dykstra, J., & Perryman, T. (2007). The first year inventory: Retrospective parent responses to a questionnaire designed to identify one-year-olds at risk for autism. *Journal of Autism and Developmental Disorders, 37,* 49–61.

Wechsler, D. (2002). *Wechsler preschool and primary scale of intelligence–III.* San Antonio, TX: Harcourt Assessment.

Wechsler, D. (2004). *Wechsler adult intelligence scale–IV.* San Antonio, TX: Harcourt Assessment.

Wheelwright, S., Baron-Cohen, S., Goldfeld, N., Delaney, J., Fine, D., Smith, R., Weil, L., & Wakabayashi, A. (2006). Predicting autism spectrum quotient (AQ) from the systemizing quotient-revised (SQ-R) and empathy quotient (EQ). *Brain Research, 1079,* 47–56.

Whitman, T. L. (2004). *The development of autism: A self-regulatory perspective.* London: Jessica Kingsley.

Williams, D., Goldstein, G., & Minshew, N. (2006). The profile of memory function in children with autism. *Neuropsychology, 20,* 21–29.

Winter-Messiers, M. A., (2007). From tarantulas to toilet brushes: Understanding the special interest areas of children and adolescents with Asperger Syndrome. *Remedial and Special Education, 28,* 140–152.

Winter-Messiers, M. A., Herr, C. M., Wood, C. E., Brooks, A. P., Gates, M. A. M., Houston, T. L., & Tingstad, K. I. (2007). How far can Brian ride the 4448 Express? A strength-based model of Asperger Syndrome based on special interest areas. *Focus on Autism and Other Developmental Disabilities, 27,* 67–79.

Wolfberg, P. J. (2003). *Peer play and the autism spectrum: The art of guiding children's socialization and imagination.* Shawnee Mission, KS: Autism Asperger Publishing Company.

Wolfberg, P. J. (2004). Guiding children on the autism spectrum in peer play: Translating theory and research into meaningful practice. *The Journal of Developmental and Learning Disorders, 8,* 7–25.

Wolfberg, P. J., & Schuler, A. L. (2006). Promoting social reciprocity and symbolic representation in children with ASD: Designing quality peer play interventions. In T. Charman & W. Stone (Eds.), *Early social communication in autism spectrum disorders* (pp. 180–218). New York: Guilford.

Zafeiriou, D., Ververi, A., & Vargiami, E. (2007). Childhood autism and associated comorbidities. *Brain & Development, 29,* 257–272.

Zwaigenbaum, L., Bryson, S., Rogers, T., Roberts, W., Brian, J., & Szatmari, P. (2005). Behavioral manifestations of autism in the first year of life. *International Journal of Developmental Neuroscience, 23,* 143–152.

2

Assessment for the Purpose of Instructional Planning for Students with Autism Spectrum Disorders

Jennifer Stella Durocher
University of Miami

CHAPTER OBJECTIVES

After reading this chapter, learners should be able to

1. Describe components of a core battery for the assessment of students with ASD.

2. List two standardized tests that can be used to assess each domain included in the core battery and discuss their pros and cons.

3. Explain the difference between formal and informal assessment measures and the utility of each approach in instructional planning for students with ASD.

4. Describe common characteristics of individuals with ASD and how they may affect (a) the child's ability to engage in the evaluation process and (b) the selection of evaluation procedures.

5. Discuss the pros and cons of "breaking standardization" during assessment.

6. Describe the type of information that can be obtained through observations of the child during test administration.

7. Summarize the National Research Council's recommendations for educating children with ASD, including the "characteristics of effective interventions" and the "six kinds of interventions that should have priority."

8. List several assessment instruments and curricula that can be used to assist in identifying developmentally appropriate goals and objectives for students with ASD.

CASE STUDY Examples

Case of Nicole

Nicole is 4 years and 1 month old. She was evaluated to determine an appropriate diagnosis for her and to consider potential program options for her. Currently, Nicole has a formal diagnosis of language disorder by her neurologist, but the possibility of an Autism Spectrum Disorder has been raised. According to parent report, Nicole experienced a regression in her language skills between the ages of 2 and 3 years, particularly with respect to the desire to speak. Nicole's mother reported that Nicole will often avoid eye contact and does not show an interest in approaching other children to play, although she does respond positively to peers' approaches. Nicole also is delayed in the areas of pretend play and use of gestures and often has difficulty answering simple questions. In addition, Nicole has overly intense areas of interest (such as numbers, letters, and words) and will form "attachments" to objects which she may insist on carrying with her (e.g., an Easter basket with letters on it).

Evaluation of Nicole consisted of parent interview and administration of an autism diagnostic measure (the ADOS) and a developmental battery (the Mullen Scales of Early Learning) to Nicole. On the ADOS, Nicole met cut-offs for autism in the areas of Qualitative Impairments in Reciprocal Social Interaction (score = 11; cutoff = 7) and Communication (score = 6; cutoff = 4), resulting in a total score of 17, which also exceeded the cutoff for autism (cutoff = 12).

Nicole's performance on the Mullen indicated that, overall, she is performing within the Very Low range of intellectual functioning (SS = 54, 1st percentile). Her skills were relatively evenly delayed across the areas of fine motor development (8th percentile, Age-Equivalent = 42 months), expressive language (1st percentile, Age-Equivalent = 29 months), receptive language (1st percentile, Age-Equivalent = 23 months) and nonverbal problem solving (1st percentile, Age-Equivalent = 31 months).

What can we make of these results? Aside from answering the diagnostic question, there's probably not much else we can take from these findings, other than the fact that Nicole would likely meet criteria for a diagnosis of autism and that her cognitive skills are delayed. A much more useful approach for instructional planning would be to analyze the specific types of tasks that Nicole was able to complete successfully and compare them to those that were answered incorrectly. We could also obtain additional information that would be useful for instructional planning by reviewing the descriptions of her social, communication, and play behaviors on the ADOS. This information would help us describe her present levels of performance and identify priority educational needs (PENS).

On the fine motor domain of the scale, Nicole was able to string beads, stack 12 blocks vertically, imitate a 4-block train, cut a 1-inch strip of paper, reproduce a number of drawings with a crayon (circle, diagonals, square, and line), and draw in a path while staying inside the lines. She had difficulty when asked to screw and unscrew a nut and bolt, cut a 2-inch paper strip, fold paper according to a model, and could not copy letters or words. She was also observed to have difficulty writing her name, although it was not part of the assessment battery. With respect to Nicole's visual reception (i.e., nonverbal problem solving) skills, she was able to sort objects by category (spoons vs. blocks), match shapes and pictures, match by size and color (simultaneously), and recall pictures and object placements after a delay. She was inconsistent in her ability to match letters and discriminate spatial positions in drawings and was unable to demonstrate number awareness ("give me six blocks"). However, letters and words were observed to be a high interest area for Nicole. While she had difficulty with the matching task on this test, observations indicate that she can name all the capital letters of the alphabet and can read some words. Thus, her score on this subtest may not accurately depict her skill level in this area.

In the area of receptive language, Nicole recognized body parts and colors, comprehended basic questions, and followed two-step related commands. However, she was much more inconsistent in her ability to point to pictures of named items (e.g., shoe, doll) and action words (e.g., eating, sleeping) and was unable to correctly identify positional concepts (e.g., in, behind, under, beside), follow two-step unrelated commands, or identify objects according to their function. Expressively, Nicole was able to repeat two-number sequences (e.g., 3–4, label pictures of common objects. She consistently used two-word phrases and inconsistently spoke in three- to four-word sentences but did not spontaneously use pronouns. She could count to 3, but had difficulty when asked to count to 12.

Based on the above description of the tasks that Nicole was able to perform during a commonly used standardized developmental assessment, it is clear that the addition of this information will also allow us to create a much more meaningful description of her present level of performance than we would have been able to by reviewing her scores alone. In addition, we were also able to outline four priority educational needs to address in an Individualized Education Program (IEP) for Nicole.

Case of Bobby

Bobby is a 16-year-old high school student who was diagnosed with autism when he was 2 years old. At the present time, Bobby's parents are most concerned about his increasingly challenging behavior and wish to obtain updated information regarding his overall abilities, insight into the function of his challenging behavior, and strategies for intervention. Overall, the goal of the evaluation was to assist the family with behavioral and educational planning for Bobby. Bobby was administered several tasks in order to estimate his nonverbal cognitive abilities, which were found to be in the mildly impaired range (WISC-IV Perceptual Reasoning Index = 55; DAS Nonverbal Composite = 60). Adaptive behavior functioning (ABAS-II General Adaptive Composite = 48) was also in the impaired range.

Behavioral observations included as part of the evaluation contributed a great deal of information about Bobby's functioning and suggest areas to target for intervention. In general, Bobby appeared to prefer to engage in isolated activities, such as drawing, listening to music on his CD player, and watching videos. On occasion, Bobby would participate in short interactions where he would allow the examiners to comment on his activities and sometimes answered questions about what he was doing. In addition, Bobby's behavior was observed to vary dramatically across situational contexts (i.e., unstructured, child-directed vs. structured, clinician-directed). Bobby was generally resistant when presented with structured activities, such as formal testing. He willingly reviewed a schedule of the day's activities; however, he frequently and emphatically indicated displeasure about one or more of the activities (e.g., "No stories!"). It became apparent that Bobby was easily overwhelmed by the amount and perceived difficulty of the tasks. For example, he would look at a list of words on a reading/decoding task and exclaim, "It's too much!" At such times, Bobby would refuse to begin the task. Attempts to minimize the amount of stimuli presented (e.g., covering lines and revealing them a row at a time), were usually successful in assisting

Bobby in initiating the task. However, Bobby would often stop in the middle of the task, stating "That's enough!" "No more work!" or "It's too hard!" He could sometimes be persuaded to continue with the promise of a break; however, at other times, the task had to be discontinued at that point (which he was often able to resume after a break). Typically, Bobby indicated his frustration with the task (e.g., "It's too hard!"), while also expressing frustration toward the examiner (e.g., "Go away!" "Don't come in again!" and "I'm not your friend!"). Despite Bobby's apparent frustration, he would frequently continue with the task if the examiner ignored his disruptive behavior and redirected him to the task at hand by stating calmly that it was time to work and reviewing the day's schedule. An additional strategy that was sometimes successful was having the examiner respond by stating that Bobby was hurting the examiner's feelings and/or making the examiner sad. This tended to evoke an empathic response from Bobby (e.g., "What happened?"), and he would then begin working cooperatively for a short time.

Observations suggest that Bobby tends to become angry and/or frustrated when test questions began to exceed his ability level or when he perceives the tasks to be too "large" or difficult (even if they are within his ability level). In response to this "flood" of anxiety, Bobby attempts to escape or avoid the activity through whining or refusing (e.g., "It's too many," "Go away," etc.). When these strategies are ineffective, Bobby's behavior escalates and he begins to yell and/or "threaten." While it was clear that the tasks were truly distressing for him, there also appeared to be a learned component to these behaviors. It is likely that these behaviors have been effective in allowing Bobby to escape from task demands and may have even influenced the type of demands that others place upon him. Further contributing to Bobby's behavioral challenges are his language impairments. Bobby was not able to use his language to ask for assistance with difficult tasks, negotiate with others around the amount and type of work to be done, or use more socially desirable language to request that tasks discontinued, especially when in an anxious or agitated mood state.

These observations illustrate the usefulness of a "process-oriented" approach to assessment. Instead of focusing primarily on cognitive and academic skills, the clinicians were able to contribute significantly to instructional planning by highlighting behavioral challenges and communicative difficulties that are critical areas to address in programming for Bobby. Further, the examiners focused on evaluating strategies for managing Bobby's behavior during the assessment process (by using visual supports and altering the presentation format) which will allow educators to implement appropriate supports in the classroom during instructional activities.

INTRODUCTION

Assessment is a necessary step in the overall program planning for students with Autism Spectrum Disorders (ASD). However, students with ASD are likely to present unique challenges and issues during formal evaluation, which may impact the success of the evaluation process and the utility of the assessment data (Klin, Saulnier, Tsatsanis & Volkmar, 2005). Since instructional programming is based on information regarding a student's present levels of performance and identification of priority educational needs (PENS), accurate and useful assessment data are critical to programming success (see Table 2.1)

This chapter will provide a summary of the symptoms and characteristics of ASD that will impact the assessment process and describe the components of a core "best practices" assessment of

TABLE 2.1   Present Levels of Performance, PENS, and Potential Skills for Intervention

Present Levels of Performance	Priority Educational Needs	Potential Target Skills
Can sort objects by category; match shapes, colors, and pictures; identify uppercase letters; and read a few words	Cognitive Skills	• Identify lowercase letters • Match letters and words • Sight word recognition • 1:1 correspondence
Can follow simple one- and two-step commands, and receptively identify body parts and colors	Receptive Language	• Follow two-step unrelated commands (hang up your backpack and go sit down) • Receptive vocabulary: nouns, verbs, object functions and prepositions
Speaks in short (two- to three-word) phrases and can label pictures of objects	Expressive Language	• Expand length of utterances to three- to four-word sentences • Use pronouns in spoken language • Expressive vocabulary for verbs (action words) • Counting to 20
Can copy shapes and cut 1-inch strips of paper	Fine Motor Skills	• Cut 2- and 3-inch paper strips • Cut shapes • Write her name and uppercase letters

individuals with ASD. Formal and informal assessment procedures and instruments for the evaluation of ASD will be described. Finally, this chapter will close with a description of recommendations for necessary areas of intervention and curricula.

SYMPTOM PRESENTATION IN ASD

Autism Spectrum Disorders are included under a class of disorders referred to as Pervasive Developmental Disorders (PDDs) within *the Diagnostic and Statistical Manual of Mental Disorders*–Fourth Edition–TR (*DSM–IV–TR;* APA, 2000). The *DSM–IV–TR* lists five specific PDDs: Autistic Disorder, Asperger's Disorder, Pervasive Developmental Disorder–Not Otherwise Specified (PDD-NOS), Rett Disorder, and Childhood Disintegrative Disorder. These disorders are diagnosed based on a set of criteria provided in the *DSM–IV* and include impairments in three general domains of functioning:

• Delayed and atypical development in social reciprocity and relatedness
• Delayed and atypical development of language, communication, and play skills
• The presence of repetitive and restricted patterns of behaviors, interests, and activities

In addition, individuals with ASD may also exhibit associated disturbances in areas such as cognition and information processing, attention, executive functioning, and sensory processing. These core ASD deficits and associated impairments will ultimately have a direct effect on the assessment process.

Social Impairments

Due to deficits in the social domain, clinicians will often find that it is more difficult to establish **rapport**, or a comfortable cooperative relationship, with the student during the evaluation process. Students with ASD may not respond to the usual methods of establishing rapport, including the use of informal conversation and the use of social praise to motivate the child to cooperate with the testing procedures. In addition, children with ASD (particularly younger children) may be unfamiliar with basic social behaviors that will impact the evaluation process and the child's performance, such as sitting quietly at a table, taking turns, or returning test materials after an item is completed. Finally, impairments in the use and understanding of nonverbal communication (such as eye contact and gesture use) may lead the child to miss important components of task instructions and/or respond in line with test specifications (such as pointing to the correct answer).

Language/Communication Impairments

Language and communication deficits also present major challenges to conducting an effective evaluation. The majority of children with ASD have receptive language difficulties. This is true even for "higher-functioning" individuals with ASD who have cognitive and expressive language abilities that are within the expected range for their age (Filipek et al., 1999). These difficulties may impact the ability of the child to adequately understand orally presented instructions, which will certainly impact task performance. For some children, there is also a great deal of scatter in their receptive language skills, with understanding of more difficult words and concepts in the face of unfamiliarity with easier vocabulary. This discrepancy often results in inconsistent responding patterns that may be interpreted as noncompliance by the examiner. Such receptive language problems, and attempts by the examiner to "gain compliance," increase the likelihood of behavioral problems during the evaluation, which stem from language expectations which are too high for the child's abilities.

Further, even for those individuals with adequate receptive language skills, deficits in pragmatics (use of language in a social context) may still be apparent. Such difficulties may include a tendency to be overly literal and concrete in interpreting instructions and problems with interpreting nonverbal behaviors and turn-taking skills. The effect of these pragmatic language difficulties on the evaluation process, however, may be more difficult to initially notice. As an example, a student who was asked to produce a written essay on an academic achievement test repeatedly refused to begin the task, stating that he didn't "know how to." At this point, it would be common for the examiner to move on to the next item and/or task with the assumption that the student lacked the necessary skills to correctly respond to the test item. Upon follow-up questioning by the examiner, it became apparent that the student did, in fact, have experience writing essays. However, he knew how to write an essay only in French. Apparently, the student had written essays only in French class and was unable to spontaneously apply that experience to the current testing situation. The student readily began the task when the examiner indicated to "write the essay just like you would in French, but use English instead."

Finally, expressive language difficulties also affect task performance in the testing environment. Many cognitive assessment measures assess verbal as well as nonverbal problem-solving skills. For students who are nonverbal or minimally verbal, requirements of verbal subtests will likely be beyond their language abilities. Students with better language abilities are likely to be able to respond to such tasks, but may still encounter problems. Difficulties may include word-finding problems and difficulty formulating and generating answers and/or the use of unusual or idiosyncratic language which may impact the examiner's understanding of their responses.

Presence of Restricted, Repetitive, and Stereotyped Interests, Behaviors, and Activities

The behavioral challenges inherent to ASD also create unique problems during the testing session. Students with ASD often exhibit strong interest in idiosyncratic objects and events that will affect manipulation of the testing materials (such as flapping materials, rubbing surfaces, and/or visual inspection of items). Thus, it may be quite difficult to obtain cooperation from the child in using materials as intended, retrieving materials from the child to demonstrate the task, and/or removing the materials in order to present the next task. In addition, students may be overly reliant on routines and often have extreme reactions to changes. Interrupting or redirecting the child in such instances may trigger a variety of behavioral responses that can interrupt assessment procedures.

BOX 2.1   Diversity Notes

A commonly accepted premise today is that autism "knows no racial, ethnic, or social boundaries" according to the Autism Society of America. Unfortunately, the accuracy of this premise is called into question as researchers (and clinicians alike) have tended to pay little attention to racial and/or cultural differences in autism. Dyches and colleagues present a provocative paper raising a number of questions for further examination in the field. Specific questions for consideration included:

- Are there differences in the prevalence of autism across race/ethnicity?
- Are there factors that may influence children from different races/cultures who are identified as having an ASD (including cultural differences in how symptoms are viewed and defined, stigmatization of disability status, potential bias from clinicians in diagnosis, etc.)?
- Are there differences in family adaptation to the autism diagnosis?

Dyches and colleagues suggest that the relative paucity of research into the specific challenges faced by families from diverse backgrounds should be a concern to the professionals who work with these families. Because of the paucity of research in this area, what we know about the characteristics of best practice in assessment and intervention for ASDs may not apply to individuals and families of different cultural, racial, and/or ethnic backgrounds.

Source: Information from Dyches, T. T., Wilder, L. K., Sudweeks, R. R., Obiakor, R. E., & Algozzine, B. (2004). Multicultural issues in autism. *Journal of Autism and Developmental Disorders, 34,* 211–222.

THE SPECTRUM NATURE OF ASD

Another important consideration for assessment is the spectrum nature of ASD. Autism is referred to as a "spectrum" condition, meaning that the symptoms of ASD fall along a spectrum, or continuum. As the word "spectrum" implies, ASD affects each individual differently and to varying degrees. Figure 2.1 presents the characteristics of ASD that may impact the assessment process. Symptoms can occur in any combination and can range from the very mild to the severe. In addition, individuals may differ significantly in their overall language and cognitive abilities. In the area of language development, children may range from completely nonverbal to highly verbose. Further, individuals also vary along a continuum with respect to cognitive functioning, from the mental retardation/intellectual disability range to the gifted range. However, there is some evidence that there may be changes in the number of individuals who fall within the intellectually disabled range.

- Difficulty establishing rapport with examiner
- Lack of motivation to please examiner
- Limited flexibility and/or overly reliant on nonfunctional routines or rituals
- Difficulty understanding and following instructions and generating verbal responses due to language deficits
- Unique learning profiles
  - Stimulus overselectivity (such as attending to irrelevant stimuli, difficulty switching between tasks, and a desire to use materials in unique or unusual ways)
  - Attending to materials, and persisting in completing tasks
  - Inconsistent responding across items on a task
  - Inability to demonstrate skills that child can do at home (generalization problems)
- Interfering and challenging behaviors

FIGURE 2.1   Characteristics of Students with ASD That Affect the Evaluation Process

While the prevalence of comorbid mental retardation/intellectual disability in ASD was estimated to be approximately 70% to 75% of individuals during the previous decade (Filipek, et al., 1999; National Research Council, NRC, 2001), more recent prevalence studies now report rates of comorbid intellectual disability of just under 50% (Yeargin-Allsopp, Rice, Karapurkar, Doernberg, Boyle, & Murphy, 2003).

Thus, the spectrum nature of ASD results in a great degree of heterogeneity across children which is likely to affect the process of conducting the evaluation; there will be no "one size fits all" approach to testing strategies and instrument selection, requiring a great deal of knowledge and flexibility on the part of the examiner.

Learning Challenges Associated with ASD

Students with ASD often exhibit uneven learning profiles marked by "scatter" in skill development. Such students may function at or above age level in some areas, but well below age level in others. This pattern also results in a scattered profile of results on formal testing measures, as well as inconsistent performance within individual subtests that will affect not only test results but instructional programming as well.

Coupled with inconsistent skill acquisition, students with ASD also exhibit inconsistencies in responding, even for skills that have been mastered. Such difficulties are frequently referred to as problems with **generalization**. Despite having acquired given skills, individuals with ASD often have difficulties "showing what they know" in the evaluation setting and fail to demonstrate skills that they can successfully perform in the home and/or at school. Generalization difficulties also can manifest as an inability to demonstrate a skill under different conditions than those in which the skill was learned (e.g., with different materials and/or verbal instructions). Deficits in skill **maintenance** are also characteristic of children with ASD; children may "lose" skills if they are not consistently practiced and/or used in the child's daily life. Again, these difficulties have implications for the testing setting, as parents often proclaim that the child possesses skills that were not exhibited during the evaluation session. This is often an accurate statement; however, difficulties with generalization and maintenance of skills have direct relation to instructional programming. Skills that have been "mastered" but cannot be demonstrated across people, settings, and materials should take first priority as instructional goals and objectives.

Challenges may also be displayed in areas associated with the core deficits of ASD. For example, there may be significant problems with orienting to the examiner and task materials and distractibility. Further, attention and persistence may vary significantly across tasks with reduced motivation for non-preferred activities. Individuals may also be hypersensitive to sounds and visual stimuli in the environment, display self-stimulatory behaviors, and become preoccupied by oral exploration of items. Difficulties with tasks requiring sequential steps or that have multiple stimuli and **stimulus overselectivity** may also be observed. Overselectivity refers to the tendency of individuals with ASD to focus on a restricted range of available environmental cues, such as focusing on one feature of an object while ignoring other equally important features. For example, a student may respond to extraneous and/or irrelevant details (such as the model of the car in a picture) and fail to pay attention to the more salient and important aspects of stimuli on which the task depends (such as object identification, color identification, and/or object function). Overselectivity will have a significant impact on behavior during both assessment and instructional tasks.

THE ASSESSMENT PROCESS

Assessment is more than the administration and interpretation of test results. In contrast to "testing," assessment is much broader, being conceptualized as a systematic process for gathering information (or data) for use in making diagnostic, legal, and/or educationally relevant decisions. Data collected during the assessment process generally falls within two main types of procedures: formal and informal.

Formal Assessment Approaches

Simply put, formal assessments are the conventional methods of testing that the majority of people are familiar with, such as tests like the SAT and their other aptitude measures. Formal assessments are generally used to compare a student's performance in some domain with that of his or her peers. Norm-referenced tests are the most commonly used formal assessment procedure; such tests have specific standards that outline the basis of comparison and administration guidelines, resulting in them also being referred to as **standardized tests**.

The standard of comparison for **norm-referenced tests** is a representative "student body" comprising individuals of the same age, grade-level, gender and/or disability category; comparing one student's performance to others in a similar category or categories. The development of norm-based standardized tests requires that a representative population of students (the standardization sample) is assessed in order to derive the norms to be used for comparison. While this is a process that is more complex than described herein, it involves ensuring that a large enough number of students are assessed across age and grade levels, racial and ethnic categories, socioeconomic status, and geographical region, among others. Based on this information, data is mathematically computed and summarized through statistical procedures in order to generate a range of standardized scores upon which comparisons can be made.

Standardized scores are converted from raw scores and are then used to interpret the student's performance; scores are then reported as scaled scores, standard scores, stanines, percentiles, and/or age-equivalents. Standard scores are the most commonly reported type of score, in which the mean (or average) and the standard deviation (a measure of variation) have been assigned preset values, typically with a mean of 100 and the standard deviation at 15. Percentiles allow performance to be compared to other students by ranking performance within a range of 1 to 99, with the 50th percentile indicating the median (or middle) score. A percentile rank reflects the percentage of students who scored as well as or lower than the student being tested. As an example, a percentile score of 82 indicates that the student's performance exceeded that of 82 percent of the comparison group.

In addition, the standardization procedures for norm-referenced tests also apply to administration of test items, with strict guidelines for implementation. Since these tests are used as comparisons between students, they must be administered under similar circumstances in each instance of test taking. This is a major advantage of standardized tests; because they are so specific with respect to their implementation, they are quite easy to administer. All the materials are provided and are held constant across administrations, both over time and across child, allowing for every administration to be conducted in same manner, thereby increasing reliability of results.

However, this approach is not without its disadvantages. Such measures often do not provide an adequate amount of information in order to fully assess the student's level of achievement with respect to what has and has not been learned, or to reach conclusions regarding whether the student meets the standards set for specific grade levels and/or content areas. Thus, this information is only moderately helpful in describing **present levels of performance** during the IEP process (described in more detail later in the chapter).

Also included under formal assessment procedures are **criterion-referenced tests** (which are discussed under informal measures as well). In contrast to norm-based assessments, criterion-referenced tests measure a child's performance and compare it to a specific, typically curricular, standard instead of to other students' performance. Criterion-referenced tests occur when individuals are measured against defined (and objective) criteria and are often, but not always, used to establish a person's competence (whether he or she can do something). Essentially, criterion-referenced tests are able to track or measure a student's mastery of specific skills. The main basis of comparison is between students' performance and a specified level of mastery or achievement. Placement tests and state "accountability tests" (such as the Florida Comprehensive Assessment Test or FCAT) are examples of criterion-referenced competency tests that are commercially available and have standardized administration procedures.

Informal Assessment Approaches

Informal assessments are centered on content and individual performance, rather than on comparisons to other students. As such, these approaches do not necessarily require a defined reference group, but rather compare the child's performance to expected skills and abilities as set forth by developmental standards and/or the curriculum. Most informal assessment tools and measures are not standardized and therefore do not provide information about psychometric properties of the assessment (such as reliability and validity). Nonetheless, this approach does have some advantages over standardized tests. Standardized measures generally assess a larger breadth of skills than informal measures; however the skills included in the assessment may be selective rather than comprehensive and there may be relatively few items for each individual skill area. Informal measures tend to focus on subskills within a curriculum or developmental area in much greater depth (representing a smaller range of skills) and much more thoroughly. Therefore, informal measures are often preferred for goal setting and in determining appropriate instructional strategies.

Types and Goals of Informal Assessments

Informal assessments are sometimes referred to as performance-based measures whose main goal is to inform instruction. Since informal assessments make up such a broad range of procedures, there are a number of different types of assessments that fall under this category.

Criterion-referenced assessments are often considered to be an informal assessment procedure as well. In criterion-referenced assessments, specific criterion serve as the standard for what every student is expected to know, and scores are set to allow comparisons to these benchmarks. Thus, an individual's skill mastery is measured and performance is compared to curricular standards, rather than to a normative group. Criterion-referenced assessments tell us how well students are performing with respect to specific goals or standards, rather than just indicating how their performance compares to a norm group of local or national students. Therefore, in criterion-referenced assessments, it is possible that none (or all) of the examinees will reach a particular goal or performance standard. This approach allows for determination of individual needs and abilities which aid in the selection of areas to target in intervention, allowing instructional goals and approaches to be specifically tailored to a child.

Many informal assessments are **curriculum-based**. As discussed earlier, the standard of comparison for such measures is the curriculum and students are evaluated as to whether or not they have mastered the skills specified in the curriculum. Thus, these measures directly assess "school skills," which easily translate to instructionally relevant goals and objectives. **Curriculum-based measurement (CBM)** is a type of curriculum-based assessment strategy that differs primarily with respect to the types of skills selected for assessment and the frequency with which assessment takes place. Brief probes (behavior/data sampling) are collected to sample critical target behaviors and are administered frequently; data are then graphed and the results are analyzed. This process of graphing student performance allows for the identification of whether or not adequate progress is being made and/or when changes need to be made to improve the rate of skill acquisition.

Some other informal assessment procedures include inventories and quizzes, work-sample analysis, task analysis, and portfolio assessment. In **work sample analysis**, samples of the student's work are observed to study responses (both correct and incorrect) in order to shed light on areas of successful performance and those areas in which the student still needs assistance. Errors are often examined in more detail in order to identify error patterns that may suggest where the learning process has broken down for the student. **Task analysis** approaches involve the study of task demands, in which complex tasks are broken into teachable subcomponents or steps. Because of this feature, task analysis is considered to be an instructional technique as much as it is an assessment strategy. The major goal of this strategy is to allow for a direct relation to specifying the instructional sequence for a specific task. A further informal strategy is **portfolio assessment**. A portfolio assessment involves collecting work products that demonstrate improvement over time in the objectives and goals that have been set for the student. This approach is the most common type of alternative assessment used in classrooms today. It is important to keep in mind that the products selected for inclusion in the portfolio should be consistent with the instructional goals for the student.

Final informal assessment approaches consist of dynamic assessment and diagnostic teaching procedures. Dynamic assessment can be conceptualized as a "learning potential" assessment that differs from traditional testing in terms of the nature of the examiner–student relationship and the type and content of feedback offered. In addition, while formal assessment (and other informal assessment approaches) tend to emphasize the *product* of student learning (i.e., the student's level of performance), in a dynamic assessment, the examiner is interested in both the product and the *process* of student learning. During **dynamic assessment**, the examiner not only gives performance-contingent feedback on the student's correct and incorrect responses, but also offers instruction in response to student failure aimed at enhancing the student's achievement. Diagnostic teaching involves very similar concepts and approaches. In this approach, the focus is on interpreting the student's interactions with the learning environment and involves taking observational notes regarding the way in which the student approaches a task, handles frustration, self-corrects errors, and engages in problem-solving strategies (Carlson et al., 1998). Another way in which diagnostic teaching can be conducted is to present the same task to the student, while systematically altering task requirements, such as presentation or response modes and observing their effects on student performance. In essence, both approaches involve the systematic manipulation of the testing and/or instructional conditions to determine the most appropriate strategy for teaching a particular skill to a given student; performance is assessed under standard instructional conditions, aspects of the task or teaching approach are modified, and performance is assessed again under these modified conditions and compared with previous performance. These strategies offer a clear advantage for instructional programming in that they provide necessary insight that will allow educators to alter how they teach according to the type of conditions under which the student is most likely to be successful.

SPECIAL ASSESSMENT GUIDELINES FOR STUDENTS WITH ASD

A thorough and comprehensive assessment, including both formal and informal assessment procedures, is crucial to understanding and appropriately assisting individuals with ASD. Specifically, assessment of individuals with ASD should provide information as to how the individual's development compares to other children his or her age and the specific symptoms, strengths, and challenges exhibited by the child. Further, changes in the individual's development over time should be documented, including skills mastered, rate of skill acquisition, and the maintenance and generalization of mastered skills. Finally, there should be a clearly articulated plan at the outset for linking assessment results to intervention planning and program monitoring. The above-mentioned assessment goals are best accomplished by utilizing a process-oriented approach.

A **process-oriented assessment** is based on idea that the assessment process itself represents a feedback mechanism or a circular process, whereby some portion of the system's output is returned (or fed back) to the input system. An overview of a process-oriented assessment for students with ASD is presented in Figure 2.2.

The aim of a process-oriented assessment is to measure the student's learning and performance over time, allowing data to continually guide goal setting and programming. As such, this approach is particularly well suited for data collection and evaluation that will be ongoing in nature. A major assumption of this approach is that instruction is most effective when it is based on (a) identification of objectives that match student strengths, weakness, and learning styles; (b) instruction that matches clearly defined and measurable objectives; (c) continual assessment of the student's performance relative to objectives; and (d) adjustments to goal selection, instructional programming, and teaching strategies based on feedback on student performance.

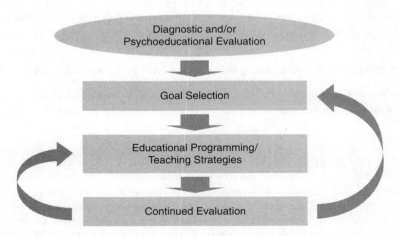

FIGURE 2.2   Process-Oriented Assessment Approach for Students with ASD

Further, best practice assessment guidelines for individuals with ASD have been published, emphasizing four general themes (Klin, Saulnier, Tsatsanis, & Volkmar, 2005; Ozonoff, Goodlin-Jones, & Solomon, 2005). First, assessment must utilize a developmental perspective. Using a developmental framework provides a benchmark for understanding the severity or quality of delays or deviance. Delays in one developmental area can significantly impact the acquisition of later developmental milestones. In addition, whenever possible, assessments of ASD should be multidisciplinary, including a range of professionals with specific perspectives and areas of expertise (such as psychologists, speech and language pathologists, psychiatrists, neurologists and other medical specialists, educational specialists, and/or social workers).

Further, information should be collected from multiple sources, across multiple contexts/settings, and utilizing multiple strategies. Sources include interactions with the individuasl with ASD; their parents, teachers, therapists, and service providers; and their siblings and/or peers. Settings for assessment include not only the evaluation room, but home, school, and/or community settings as well. There are many important reasons to collect assessment data across multiple settings. First, symptoms of ASD are often dependent on characteristics of the environment (e.g., situation-specific). Therefore, the child may demonstrate more adaptive and functional skills within a one-to-one testing situation, but have much more difficulty in less structured settings, such as with peers on a playground or in a distracting classroom situation. In contrast, due to difficulties with adapting to changes in routines and environments, along with generalization difficulties, structured one-to-one evaluation sessions may fail to capture the full range of skills that the individual possesses. Therefore, the child may look much more competent in a known environment (such as the classroom) than in an evaluation room without familiar, well-practiced routines and materials. Assessment must also utilize a wide range of strategies and assessment procedures, including observations, administration of formal standardized and informal curriculum-based assessments, and completion of ratings scales and inventories by individuals familiar with the child's day-to-day functioning, such as parents and teachers.

Finally, and perhaps most importantly, decisions regarding assessment methods and approaches to be used need to be individualized based on the child's age, developmental level, specific diagnosis, and areas of need. Necessary components include a review of available records, including anecdotal reports, work samples, behavioral charting systems, report cards, previous diagnostic evaluations, and **Individualized Education Programs (IEPs)**. Additional information can be obtained through parental interviews regarding the child's developmental, educational, and medical histories, as well as by conducting observations across multiple settings.

Types and Goals of Formal Assessment of Individuals with ASD

Formal assessments generally involve both **diagnostic** as well as **psychoeducational** components. Guidelines for goals within each type of assessment, specific to individuals with ASD, are offered.

BOX 2.2   Research Notes # 1

With the increased interest in early identification and the belief that early intervention for ASD will lead to more optimal outcomes, researchers have begun to focus on studying the long-term outcomes of young children with ASD who have participated in specialized early intervention services. Turner and colleagues followed 26 children (22 male, 4 female) who received clinical diagnoses of either autism ($n = 18$) or PDD-NOS ($n = 8$) under the age of 3 and evaluated them 5–7 years after their initial evaluations.

Results indicated considerable improvement in cognitive scores for a large number of children in the sample, compared with initial cognitive scores at age 3. At age 3, 84% of the children had cognitive scores below the threshold for intellectual disability (less than 70), which decreased to only 28% of children by follow-up (mean age = 7.9 years). In addition, at follow-up, 72% of children obtained scores in the borderline to average ranges in comparison to only 16% at age 3. Further, and most encouragingly, 56% of the children were scoring in the average range or above at follow-up.

Results from this study are important because they suggest that cognitive scores may change dramatically between the ages of 2 and 9 for students with ASD. Cognitive scores increased for most children, with 68% of scores rising at least 15 points. Findings indicated that, on average, cognitive scores at outcome increased 23 points, and nine children increased more than 30 points. Higher initial cognitive scores appeared to be more stable than lower scores, as all four children who attained cognitive scores above 70 at age 2 obtained average scores at age 9. Results further revealed that there were some initial characteristics of children that were associated with better outcomes at follow-up. Children with better outcomes tended to have a younger age of diagnosis, higher initial development quotient and language scores, and received more hours of speech and language therapy services.

Source: Information from Turner, L. M., Stone, W. L., Pozdol, S. L., & Coonrod, E. E. (2006). Follow-up of children with autism spectrum disorders from age 2 to age 9. *Autism, 10,* 243–265.

DIAGNOSTIC ASSESSMENT   Diagnostic assessment for ASD is typically the first formal assessment process that a family will undergo. The overall goal of such an assessment is to obtain an initial diagnosis, through consideration of other disorders with similar presenting problems and symptoms. Through the diagnostic evaluation, clinicians seek to determine whether the child's behavioral difficulties are consistent with a diagnosis with the autism spectrum, or rather, can be better explained by another disorder such as an intellectual disability/mental retardation or a language disorder. The process of receiving a diagnosis or label is important for a number of reasons. Most importantly, accurate diagnosis facilitates the selection of additional assessment components, as well as identification of appropriate intervention approaches. Further, symptom presentation is often related to other domains of interest, including cognitive abilities, joint attention, language, and social development. Early diagnosis also has far-reaching implications for prognosis and family adjustment. Early identification allows for early entry into intervention as well as assisting families in understanding their child's difficulties. Diagnosis is the first step in providing families with the tools they will need to advocate for services for their child and become active participants in their child's intervention.

Documentation of diagnostic status is often necessary for access to services or funding mechanisms. Accurate classification is important from an educational standpoint in that it is used to determine eligibility for school-based special educational placement and related services. State and federally funding social service and health care agencies also rely on diagnostic reports in order to document eligibility for services.

Finally, diagnostic evaluations offer a basis from which to prescribe or plan interventions, by specifying child characteristics across core and associated impairment areas in ASD, such as specific deficits and skills in the areas of social, communication, and play skills as well as restricted, repetitive, and stereotyped behaviors and sensory processing disturbances that may interfere with instruction. Such information, collected during the initial evaluations stage, can also be important in documenting progress and evaluating intervention efforts. In this regard, it is equally important that intervention consider goals for outcomes that reflect areas that are relevant to symptom presentation.

PSYCHOEDUCATIONAL EVALUATION   Psychoeducational evaluation should also be incorporated into the initial assessment stages, as the emphasis of this approach is to gather information across multiple domains of functioning that can be used to guide educational programming. The major goal of a psychoeducational evaluation is to obtain a better understanding of the student's strengths and weaknesses in order to provide a baseline of skills from which to plan intervention (Klin, et al., 2005). Ultimately, this information will be used to create an individualized education program (IEP) that takes into account developmental level, strengths and needs, likes and dislikes, behavioral difficulties, effective teaching strategies, and motivational systems. Information relevant for program evaluation can be provided through the psychoeducational process and can be complemented with consistent application of informal assessment strategies during instruction. Such informal procedures allow for documentation of progress toward goals over time through continued evaluation of a child's characteristics (learning readiness, academic strengths and weaknesses) with frequent comparisons between current and previous functioning.

A "Best Practices" Assessment Battery for ASD

Best practices in the assessment of ASD specify that an adequate assessment must lead to an appropriate intervention plan (Perry, Condillac, & Freeman 2002). Therefore, it will be important to use guidelines for priority areas for intervention in ASD as a basis for the evaluation, in order to ensure that all important areas are assessed. According to recommendations put for by the National Research Council (NRC, 2001), areas that should be prioritized in intervention programs for students with ASD include language and communication development, social and play skills, fine and gross motor development, development of cognitive and functional academic skills, and skills needed for success in a regular classroom, including flexibility, organization, and engagement in the learning process. An overview of Best Practices in the assessment of individuals with ASD is presented in Figure 2.3.

- Maintain a developmental approach.
  - Using a developmental framework provides a benchmark for understanding the quality and/or severity of areas of delay and/or deviance.
- Assessment of ASD should be multidisciplinary.
  - Whenever possible, professionals from multiple disciplines should be part of the evaluation process, including psychology, psychiatry, speech and language, occupational therapy, and other medical disciplines (audiology, neurology, pediatrics).
- Assessment should include information from multiple sources and settings.
  - Symptoms of ASD are often dependent on the characteristics of the environment and performance is often dependent on these environmental task demands.
- Assessment methods should be individualized based on age, developmental level, and diagnosis; and areas of need and should include, at a minimum:
  - A review of records
  - A family interview regarding developmental and medical history
  - Natural and structured observations in multiple settings
  - Standardized and informal tools

FIGURE 2.3 Guidelines for a Best Practices Assessment of Autism Spectrum Disorders

Sources: Information adapted from Klin, A., Saulnier, C., Tsatsanis, K., & Volkmar, F. R. (2005). Clinical evaluation in autism spectrum disorders: Psychological assessment within a transdiciplinary framework. In F.R. Volkmar, R. Paul, A. Klin & D. Cohen (Eds.), *Handbook of Autism and Pervasive Developmental Disorders, 3rd ed., Vol II* (pp. 863–881). Hoboken, NJ: John Wiley & Sons; and Ozonoff et al. (2005). Evidence-based assessment of autism spectrum disorders in children and adolescents. *Journal of Clinical Child and Adolescent Psychiatry, 34,* 523–540.

COMPONENTS OF A CORE ASSESSMENT BATTERY

Klin et al. (2005) offer that "developmentally based assessment of cognitive, social communicative and adaptive skills provides the essential bases on which decisions on diagnosis, eligibility for services, and program planning have to be made" (p. 772). Elements of a core assessment battery include those domains that are both necessary and sufficient for an evaluation of a suspected ASD, and are typically included as part of the diagnostic evaluation. These core domains include developmental and/or intellectual assessment of cognitive abilities, speech and language skills, and adaptive behavior functioning. Figure 2.4 provides a recommended evidence-based assessment battery for students with ASD.

Cognitive/Intellectual Assessment

Cognitive/intellectual assessment is necessary for the evaluation of individuals suspected of meeting criteria for ASD and for differentiating between individuals with ASD and those with a primary diagnosis of mental retardation/intellectual disability. Thus, intellectual assessment allows for the differential diagnosis of conditions that may affect language and cognitive development, including ASD, general developmental delay, intellectual disability, and language disorders. Cognitive assessment is also necessary because many diagnostic assessment measures for ASD require that behaviors

---

Core Assessment Battery—Necessary assessment domains for diagnosis and eligibility determination, as well as preliminary planning of priority instructional needs.

- Assessment of *specific symptoms of autism* using a variety of autism diagnostic measures, combined with parent interview
- Assessment of *intellectual functioning* to allow clinicians to frame the interpretation of other evaluation results
- Assessment of *language,* including receptive, expressive, and pragmatic language abilities
- *Adaptive behavior* assessment in order to rule out co-occurring intellectual disability/mental retardation as well as setting appropriate goals in treatment planning. This domain should include self-help, recreational/leisure and community-based skills

Additional Assessment Domains—Additional assessment domains that will provide information about additional priority educational needs to guide IEP development

- *Neuropsychological assessments* including attention and executive functioning, memory, and processing
- *Developmental, pre-academic and academic functioning* in order to identify patterns of strengths and weaknesses in the student's individual learning profile
- *Prevocational and vocational skills* for students approaching transition-age to plan for post-school activities and outcomes
- *Emotional functioning* to assess comorbid anxiety and depression that may need to be targeted
- *Motor skills and sensory processing* to set appropriate instructional objectives, supports, and accommodations
- *Reinforcement assessment* in order to determine effective learning and behavioral supports
- *School, family, and community contexts* because the goal of assessment should be to understand how ASD affects individuals in the course of daily life

FIGURE 2.4   A Recommended Evidence-Based Assessment Battery for Students with ASD

Source: Information from Ozonoff et al. (2005) and Klin et al. (2005)

be interpreted against the child's developmental level; without a measure of intellectual ability, it is often very difficult to ascertain whether a given behavior is appropriate for the child's level of development and skills. Further, intellectual ability is one of the best predictors of long-term prognosis for individuals with ASD, and therefore can be used to provide family members with preliminary information regarding the child's expected developmental trajectory.

The inclusion of standardized intelligence tests is especially important given prevailing misconceptions (or "myths") regarding the measurement of cognitive abilities in individuals with ASD. Such "myths" include the idea that measurement of IQ is irrelevant for individuals with autism; many erroneously believe that because of motivational difficulties, individuals with ASD are often "untestable" on standardized tests and therefore, it is not possible to accurately measure their cognitive abilities. This assumption results in the viewpoints that it is not possible to know the true intellectual capabilities of someone with ASD and/or that all individuals with ASD are actually quite intelligent, but do not demonstrate the skills they have due to problems with motivation and attention.

BOX 2.3   Research Notes # 2

"Despite the general agreement that cognitive ability is a critical component of treatment research in addition to the clinical need for IQ information, there is no consensus about the most appropriate test instrument(s) to measure cognitive functioning in this population" (Delmolino, 2006, p. 959). So, a study was conducted to assess the usefulness of the PEP-R as a measure of general cognitive development in young children with autism. Participants consisted of 27 children with autism or PDD-NOS (23 boys and 4 girls) with a mean age of 44 months (3.8 years) at the time of testing.

In order to answer this question, Delmolino administered the PEP-R along with a standardized intelligence test (the Stanford-Binet Intelligence Scales—Fourth Edition) and compared the scores. Findings of the current study indicate that the PEP-R is an instrument that is correlated significantly with estimates of cognitive functioning obtained with the SB-FE. Correlations between the DQ scores obtained on the PEP-R and the Composite IQ score on the SB-FE were .73, indicating a high degree of consistency in scores across the 2 measures.

Further, Delmonico offered that the PEP-R has "some potential advantages for testing this population including flexibility, range of appealing materials, lack of timed items, and separation of language items from general assessment items that are not dependent on language and its utility for educational programming" (p. 962). These findings suggest that developmental assessment instruments, such as the PEP-R, can be useful tools to use when estimating cognitive functioning of children with autism, in addition to serving a role in educational programming.

Source: Information from Delmolino, L. M. (2006). Brief report: Use of DQ for estimating cognitive ability in young children with autism. *Journal of Autism and Developmental Disorders, 36,* 959–963.

Speech and Language Assessment

Speech and language assessment is the second critical area to include in a core assessment battery for the diagnosis of ASD. As with intellectual ability, understanding of the child's language abilities, particularly when compared against their cognitive abilities, is important for the differential diagnosis process (specifying the most appropriate diagnosis). Further, language abilities are also important indicators of prognosis. Research suggests that individuals with the best prognosis for outcome are those who, by the age 5, have developed the spontaneous and communicative use of language and the ability to speak in phrases.

Assessment of Adaptive Behavior

Assessment of adaptive behavior serves as the final core assessment battery component, as it is also important for the differential diagnosis of ASD from intellectual disability/mental retardation (ID/MR). Adaptive behavior refers to "real life" skills that are necessary for people to live independently and to function safely and appropriately in daily life, including skills such as self-care, socialization, communication, safety, food preparation, ability to follow community rules, money management, shopping, and cleaning. By definition, individuals with ID/MR must exhibit deficits in adaptive behavior in addition to impaired intellectual functioning (APA; *DSM-IV-TR*). In addition to differential diagnosis, ASD can co-occur (or be comorbid) with ID/MR. Adaptive behavior assessment is critical to diagnosing the presence of both conditions, if appropriate. Further, adaptive behavior is important to include in diagnostic evaluations because such measures give a more comprehensive picture of the students' various capabilities and weaknesses than measures of IQ alone. Functional skills that should be the focus in instructional programs can also be revealed through this approach.

COGNITIVE ASSESSMENT

Developmental and Intelligence Tests

According to the practice parameters for the screening and diagnosis of ASD, "knowing the child's cognitive status is important in determining his overall level of functioning. This is, in turn, important when trying to establish a discrepancy between the child's level of social function and the overall cognitive and adaptive function, a key criterion in the diagnosis of autism" (Filipek et al, 1999, p. 462). As mentioned previously, intellectual functioning is generally considered as a predictor of outcome; however, it should be recognized that the predictive validity of such scores is not necessarily high. Research has indicated that there may be relatively low stability in IQ scores for children with ASD, with a significant proportion of children exhibiting changes in cognitive functioning over time (Sigman & Ruskin, 1999; Turner et al., 2006). Scores are relatively less stable, and reliable, the younger the child is at the time of administration of the intelligence test. For a list of commonly used measures of intelligence for students with ASD, refer to Table 2.2.

Recommendations for test selection include choosing measures that (a) are appropriate for both the child's chronological age and estimated mental age; (b) provide a full range (in the lower direction) of raw to standard scores conversions for the child's chronological age; (c) sample both verbal and nonverbal intellectual skills; and (d) measure and score verbal and nonverbal skills separately from one another.

In addition to the above specifications, it is often useful for tests to also have visually interesting materials and allow for subtests to be administered in flexible, rather than fixed, sequence. Some assessment instruments may be more useful than others in maintaining a child's interest, tapping into strengths as well as weaknesses, gathering information about learning style, and generating meaningful (e.g., valid and reliable) test scores. With respect to the latter, it is critical to consider both floor and ceiling effects when selecting measures. The majority of assessment tests organize test items in a sequential manner, with easier/earlier occurring skills preceding more difficult ones. However, due to the uneven developmental profile observed in many children with ASD, this approach may not accurately reflect the full range of skills the child possesses. For example, due to language difficulties, a child may reach the **ceiling** (the item in which administration of a subtest ceases due to a series of incorrect responses) on a certain test item, but be able to pass visual-spatial and memory tasks at a higher level.

Therefore, it is recommended that the following aspects of instruments be evaluated when attempting to select an appropriate measure for a particular child: the range of easy to difficult items, the number of items at each difficulty level, the normative age range and raw to standard score conversion charts, whether the test provides "out of level" norms, the manner in which test items are

TABLE 2.2 Recommended Measures for the Assessment of Intellectual Assessment for Individuals with ASD

Measure	Test	Publisher & Date	Type	Scores	Skills Measured	Age Range
Developmental Assessment	*BRIGANCE (IED-II)*	Curriculum Associates, 2005	Standardized/ Norm-referenced; Criterion-referenced	Quotients; Percentiles; Age-equivalents	• Motor • Language • Academic/Cognitive • Daily Living • Social-emotional	Birth to 7 years
	Battelle Developmental Inventory-2 (BDI-2)	Riverside, 2004	Standardized/ Norm-referenced	Standard and Scaled scores; Percentiles; Age-equivalents	• Communication • Adaptive • Personal-Social • Motor • Cognitive	Birth to 7.11 years
	PEP-III	WPS, 2005	Standardized/ Norm-referenced	Developmental Quotient (DQ); Composite scores; Age-equivalents	• Fine motor • Gross motor • Visual reception	6 months to 7 years
	Mullen	Pearson, 1995	Standardized/ Norm-referenced	Early Learning Composite (DQ); Domain T-scores; Percentiles; Age-equivalents	• Communication Composite • Motor Composite • Maladaptive Behavior Composite • Expressive Language	Birth to 68 months
Intellectual/ Cognitive Assessment	*K-ABC-II*	Pearson, 2004	Standardized	IQ and Subtest Standard and Scaled scores; Percentiles; Age-equivalents	• Mental Processing (Full Scale IQ) • Nonverbal IQ • Simultaneous Processing • Sequential Processing • Planning • Learning	3.0 years to 18.0 years

Test	Publisher, Year	Type	Scores	Domains	Age Range
SB–5	Riverside, 2003	Standardized	IQ and Subtest Standard and Scaled scores; Percentiles	• Full Scale IQ • Verbal IQ • Nonverbal IQ • Fluid Reasoning • Knowledge • Quantitative Reasoning • Visual-Spatial Processing • Working Memory	2.0 years to 85 years
WPPSI–III	PsychCorp, 2002	Standardized	IQ and Subtest Standard and Scaled scores; Percentiles	• Full Scale IQ • Verbal IQ • Performance IQ	2.6 years to 7.3 years
WISC–IV	PsychCorp, 2003	Standardized	IQ and Subtest Standard and Scaled scores; Percentiles	• Full Scale IQ & Index Scores: • Verbal Comprehension • Perceptual Reasoning • Processing Speed • Working Memory	6.0 years to 16.11 years
Leiter–R	Stoelting, 1997	Standardized	Standard and Scaled scores for domains; Percentiles	Nonverbal IQ assesses matching, concept formation, and reasoning	2 years to 20.11 years

Source: Information from Klin et al., (2005) and Ozonoff et al., (2005)

presented to the child (verbally, visually, with demonstration or modeling etc.) and/or the presence of "practice" or "teaching" items. Further, to obtain the most useful results, it is also recommended that clinicians choose measures that minimize language demands and/or assess nonverbal problem solving independently from verbal skills, have a "backup" instrument readily accessible to allow for switching tests depending on the child's ability level and/or interests, and consider administering subtests from different instruments to get a more thorough picture of ability level.

With these suggestions in mind, appropriate and widely used developmental tests, including those for younger, and/or less verbal individuals with ASD, are listed in Table 2.4 and described in detail below. Because educators are less likely to administer and interpret the results of intelligence (IQ) tests, only brief details regarding the most commonly used tests are provided.

Developmental Assessments

Developmental assessments are similar to intelligence tests, but are typically intended for infants through early school-age students. Like IQ tests, developmental assessment measures are usually norm-referenced standardized assessments. However, because they are intended for a younger age group, the types of skills measured are often different from those included on IQ tests. The types of skills assessed on developmental measures relate easily to the domains frequently targeted in preschool and early elementary school, such as fine motor skills, vocabulary, preacademic concepts (color and shape identification, matching, sorting, classification/categorization) and academic skills (counting, one-to-one correspondence, number and letter identification, sight word identification, etc.). Thus, these batteries are especially well-suited for use by educators and school psychologists alike.

On developmental measures, the child's current abilities are compared to the expected scope and sequence of skill acquisition in typically developing students, and a developmental quotient (DQ) norm-based score is derived. This DQ provides an estimate of cognitive functioning; however, "the concept of IQ is avoided in young children because of the close interdependence of cognitive functioning with other domains of development" (Klin et al., 2005, p. 790). Nonetheless, developmental quotient scores and IQ scores are **correlated** with one another (Delmolino, 2006).

ADDITIONAL COMPONENTS OF AN ASSESSMENT BATTERY FOR ASD

In addition to the core assessment components, evaluation of students with ASD may benefit from inclusion of other measures and domains that can serve to enhance understanding of the student's strengths and difficulties, as well as approach to problem-solving and learning style. Inclusion of these measures is consistent with a process-oriented assessment approach that is focused on understanding how the child learns, rather than what the child has learned.

A major assessment area in this approach includes **information processing**, which can include some or all of the following areas:

- *Auditory/Phonological Processing*, including auditory memory, letter-sound correspondence, phonemic discrimination and segmentation, and the synthesis of sounds into words. These abilities underlie fundamental reading processes and can indicate when the student may have difficulty with the attainment of literacy skills.
- *Visual Processing and Visual-Motor Integration*, including visual discrimination, spatial awareness, eye-hand coordination, and ability to translate visual perception into motor functioning (which involves motor control, accuracy, and coordination as well as psychomotor speed). These abilities typically underlie successful performance in academic areas such as mathematics and writing.

- *Memory and Learning* processes are critical for adequate functioning in school and daily life. Memory refers to the encoding, storage, and retrieval of information. The types of memory systems that appear to be most important, and which may be the focus of assessment, include short-term memory, working memory, and long-term memory and retrieval. Such assessment tasks generally repeat the same information and/or stimuli over a number of times to assess the efficiency and accuracy of storage and retrieval of new information. These tests can provide insight into the manner in which the individual is likely to learn best and the ease with which they are likely to learn new tasks. A process-oriented approach to learning and memory tasks is critical as it will reveal important information about the strategies that the individual is using to complete the task; dynamic assessment approaches may be especially useful in highlighting additional strategies that may improve performance and thus enhance efficiency of learning.
- *Attention and Executive Functions* include the areas of sustained and selective attention, initiation and inhibition, planning and organization, problem solving, self-monitoring, and cognitive flexibility. Research has consistently indicated that individuals with ASD often have a pattern of executive functioning impairments including selective focus on irrelevant details, initiation and planning difficulties, and the ability to be flexible in problem-solving strategies and behavior. Since attention and executive functioning are critical to school (and workplace) success, they should be a focus of both assessment and intervention efforts.

Research with individuals with ASD has consistently demonstrated specific information-processing profiles, including relatively good performance on tasks that rely on rote, mechanical, or perceptual processes, and impaired performance on tasks requiring higher-order conceptual processes, reasoning, interpretation, integration, or abstraction (Minshew & Goldstein, 1998 as cited in Ozonoff et al., 2005).

In addition, other areas that may impact behavior and instructional planning include sensory processing (including under- and oversensitivities to specific stimuli including sounds, lighting, touch, temperature, etc.), emotional and behavioral functioning (including interfering or challenging behaviors and emotional issues such as anxiety and/or depression), preference assessments (including information about what the child will "work" to obtain). These should be included in the assessment process when relevant.

Assessment Strategies for Individuals with ASD

Due to learning challenges outlined earlier in the chapter, children with ASD may present particular challenges during assessment that may make generating meaningful estimates of performance on standardized tests difficult. Such children are often colloquially referred to as "untestable." However, Ozonoff and colleagues believe that "untestability" primarily reflects a lack of availability of appropriate tests and/or clinician experience; "when experienced clinicians evaluate children with autism, few should be untestable" (Ozonoff et al., 2005, p. 529).

While the focus of the chapter thus far has been primarily on standardized assessment procedures and instruments, it is important to keep in mind the overarching purpose of assessment—namely, to provide information that will be useful for program planning. Therefore, while standardized, norm-based scores are important for documenting eligibility for special education services and revealing areas of educational priority, scores do not "tell the whole picture." In fact, for some children, the obtained "scores will hardly convey the most important information to the special educators whose mission is to address the child's needs while capitalizing on their strengths" (Klin et al., 2005, p. 791). Therefore, no child is truly "untestable." Even if scores generated are not considered to be a valid reflection of the child's overall skills, useful information can still be obtained. The likelihood of the latter is significantly increased when the assessment process includes effective use of behavioral observations and the provision of **adaptations** to evaluation procedures.

Clinicians have an ethical obligation to make such adaptations when working with special populations, both in instruction as well as in assessment. Adaptations will inform instructional planning by providing the most accurate possible estimate of the child's abilities in the constructs of interest, by minimizing the impact of test-taker attributes. In addition, the inclusion of adaptations to test procedures during the assessment process provides some ecological (or "face") validity to parents that the child was given every opportunity to demonstrate the skill in question. Further, all of the strategies provided below are applicable for use during instructional tasks. Adaptations provided during assessment (whether formal or informal) and their subsequent effect on the student's performance directly relate to the process of developing an IEP. Adaptations allow for "testing the limits" and provide more valid information regarding what the student knows, providing a more accurate picture of the child's present level of performance. In addition, by trying out different strategies, educators are armed with more complete knowledge regarding potential accommodations to include in the IEP.

ADAPTATIONS FOR TESTING DIFFICULT TO TEST CHILDREN   Suggestions for testing difficult to test children include (a) selecting appropriate measures; (b) presenting detailed descriptions of behavioral observations during the assessment procedures; (c) utilizing environmental supports and reinforcement strategies; and (d) altering or making **modifications** to standardization procedures.

Behavioral observations during testing often provide critical information regarding preferred types of tasks, task persistence and frustration level, attention to details, instructions and materials, attention span across preferred and non-preferred tasks, length of time the child will attend and work before becoming disengaged, and approach to problem solving (i.e., trial and error, deliberation, etc.). In addition, useful information can be obtained regarding strategies that increase cooperation and performance.

Environmental supports and reinforcement strategies improve cooperation and performance during the testing situation by making adjustments to the testing environment, in order to increase the child's attention and success on tasks. Such approaches inform instruction by systematically assessing the level and type of environmental structure needed for task completion and social engagement. The first step in this process involves creating a comfortable testing environment by conducting the evaluation in a child-friendly environment with familiar adults present and/or in familiar locations (e.g., the classroom rather than the clinician's office). Testing can be completed with the child standing near the table, seated on a familiar person's lap (for younger children), and/or on the floor if needed. It is also helpful, if space allows, to create clearly identified "work" and "play/break" areas.

Visual strategies are also an effective addition to the testing session and may include a "first-then" or "work-play" visual schedule, the use of work systems (e.g., "finished basket") to demonstrate task completion, and visual, token, or word schedules to communicate the number and type of tasks to be completed. Visual cues for requests (e.g., a "break" card, reinforcer choice boards, and/or token or penny boards) can also help less verbal students to signal the need for a break and to increase motivation for task completion.

With respect to reinforcement, there are three main goals for the use of reinforcers during testing: (a) to improve task compliance and effort by increasing motivation, (b) to assist in the identification of functional reinforcers for the child that can be incorporated into his or her instructional program, and (c) to assess for preferred stimuli, any self-stimulatory behaviors, preoccupations, and circumscribed interests. Some strategies and guidelines for using reinforcers during testing include asking the child's parent and/or teacher about preferred and non-preferred stimuli and having them bring preferred snacks and favorite toys or materials to the testing session, trying out a full range of different reinforcers to assess their value, varying reinforcers throughout the session to prevent satiation, assessing the schedule of reinforcement that results in optimal performance, evaluating the child's response to social praise as a reinforcer, using planned ignoring for minor disruptive behavior, and considering using escape from tasks or "work" as a reinforcer.

In contrast to the above mentioned adaptations, breaking standardization during testing is typically done through making modifications to the test procedures.

BOX 2.4   Trends and Issues # 2

When, Why, and How to Break Standardization Procedures

Perry and colleagues (2002) provide some thoughts and guidelines related to the issue of "breaking standardization," along with a number of useful testing strategies. According to the authors, making adaptations when required for persons from special populations is ethically responsible practice in order to reduce the effect of characteristics of the test-taker that are not relevant to the construct being tested and/or the primary focus of the assessment. Such adaptations may include presentation or response formatting changes, modifications to timing or the testing environment, using portions of tests, or using substitution tests.

It is important to keep in mind that such adaptations and modifications will invalidate the scores obtained. However, this problem can be minimized by first administering the tests under standardized conditions and then making modifications in order to "test the limits" and provide qualitative information regarding the student's performance. In such a case, scores would be reported based on the standardized administration. In addition, behavioral observations would then be provided regarding (a) what modifications were made and (b) how these adaptations influenced performance. Some possible modifications are offered:

1. Be flexible in the order of presentation of subtests and subtest items:
   • Administer subscales in a different order to maximize cooperation.
   • Begin with a task that you know the child likes (puzzles).
   • Intersperse easy and more difficult items (behavioral momentum).
   • Present tasks so that stressful language items are balanced by more enjoyable visual motor tasks.
   • Start at the beginning of a particular subscale (easiest item) rather than the age-suggested start point.
   • Repeat tasks the person enjoyed following some frustrating task, prior to a break.
2. Change the manner in which instructions are given:
   • Use a multiple-choice or fill-in-the-blank format rather than an open-ended style.
   • Paraphrase instructions and/or simplify language to match the child's language level.
   • Use phrases that are more familiar to the child (e.g., "match" vs. "find me another one just like this").
   • Use generic verbal prompts. For example, for a picture vocabulary task, we may ask: "What is this? This is a _____."
   • Use visual supports to aid in the comprehension of instructions.
3. Modify the response and presentation formats:
   • Allow untimed responses.
   • Allow different modes of responding, including nonverbal (pointing, gestures), etc.
   • Administer task with different materials, which may be more familiar, motivating, or interesting.
   • Administer items in naturalistic settings and/or on another day.
   • Use dynamic assessment/diagnostic teaching approaches (teach the task).

Source: Information from Perry, Condillac, & Freeman (2002). Best practices and practical strategies in the assessment and diagnosis of autism. *Journal on Developmental Disabilities, 9,* 61–75.

Such strategies significantly alter the task demands and/or the construct being measured. However, this approach can be useful in gathering information about optimal levels of performance and useful instructional approaches for the child and relies on the informal assessment procedures referred to as diagnostic teaching and dynamic assessment. Areas of "emerging" skills and evaluation of specific instructional strategies and approaches can be highlighted that will prove useful in guiding instructional programming and IEP development.

Linking Assessment to Intervention

Once the data is collected and the evaluation is completed, the assessment results must be linked to instructional programming. The NRC (2001) guidelines for necessary components of interventions for ASD provide a good starting place for creating an instructional plan for a student with ASD (see Box 2.5). The NRC (2001) recommendations for preschool children with ASD specified that children be enrolled in early intervention programs as soon as an ASD is seriously considered. In addition, active engagement in intensive instructional programming (a minimum of a full school day, at least 5 days a week – 25 hours a week) for the full year was considered essential. Further, the

BOX 2.5   Trends and Issues # 1

Guidelines for Selecting Appropriate Educational Objectives for Children with ASD

Appropriate objectives should be observable, measurable behaviors that can be reasonably accomplished within a 1-year time frame. In addition, these objectives should have a direct impact on enhancing the child's ability to participate fully in education, the community, and family life. The following areas should be targeted for development:

- *Social skills* that will enhance participation in family, school, and community activities. Suggestions for target areas include imitation skills, responding to and initiating interactions with peers and adults, and parallel and interactive play skills with peers and siblings.
- *Language and nonverbal communication skills* including expressive (verbal) language, receptive language, and use of eye contact and gestures to communicate with others.
- *Development of a functional and symbolic communication system* that should emphasize identifying a system that allows children to communicate their wants and needs, and to make choices that affect them, to the greatest extent possible.
- *Fine and gross motor skills* that will assist in achieving age-appropriate functional activities.
- *Cognitive skills* including the development of basic concepts, life skills, symbolic play, and academics. Goals for cognitive development should be carried out in the context in which the skills are expected to be used and functional academic skills should be taught when appropriate.
- *Behavioral goals* that are focused on skill development (communication skills, self-regulation skills, etc.) to replace more challenging and/or problematic behaviors. Behavioral strategies should be positive and proactive, incorporate information about the contexts in which the behaviors occur, and include a range of behavioral techniques that have empirical support.
- *Independent organizational and self-help skills* that underlie successful participation in the home, school, and broader community (independent task completion, asking for assistance, following directions and instructions, etc.).

Source: Information from: National Research Council (2001). Conclusions and Recommendations. *Educating Children with Autism.* Washington DC: National Academy Press.

educational environment should allow for repeated teaching of instructional goals around short intervals with one-to-one and small group instruction. The importance of specifying mechanisms for ongoing evaluation of the program and the child's progress, with adjustments made accordingly, was also stressed.

DEVELOPMENT OF THE INDIVIDUALIZED EDUCATION PROGRAM (IEP)

The assessment process leads directly to the development of an IEP for the student. The IEP is a written document that describes the special education and related services to be provided in order to meet the specific needs of a child with a disability, and is comprised of six required parts:

1. *Description of the child's present level of performance, or functioning:* The first step in developing an IEP involves a description of the child as he or she is at the present time. This section of the IEP highlights the child's current academic and behavioral skills, interests, and learning style, and discusses the implications of the child's disability on academic and non-academic (e.g., social, communication) achievement. From this description, the IEP team develops a list of areas of instructional priority, often referred to as priority educational needs (PENS). Since instructional programming is based on information regarding a student's present levels of performance, learning style, and preferences, and identification of PENS, the assessment process and its resulting data are critical to successful instructional planning.

2. *Annual goals and objectives:* **Goals** and **objectives** are based upon the information described above, namely descriptions of the child's present level of performance and identification of priority educational needs. Goals and objectives are descriptions of the skills that the child will attain within a specified period of time. Goals are typically written to reflect annual expectations for progress, whereas objectives typically reflect short-term steps (often quarterly) toward the attainment of the annual goal. Goals and objectives should take into account the above referenced NRC (2001) recommendations for programming for students with ASD, and target each identified area of priority educational need.

3. *Related services:* The IEP also describes services that will be provided in order to supplement the educational services provided in the classroom. Related services are those services that are necessary in order to effectively implement the IEP and designed to ensure that the child is able to benefit from special education in the least restrictive environment. Examples of possible related services include counseling; occupational, physical, and/or speech and language therapies; parent training; and assistive technology.

4. *Educational placement:* Placement refers to the educational setting in which the IEP will be implemented and is chosen based on the setting in which the goals and objectives will be appropriately met. If the classroom setting is not a general education classroom, the IEP must specify the amount of time (if any) that the child will participate in the general education classroom and include a statement ensuring that the least restrictive environment was considered.

5. *Time and duration of services:* This step in the IEP process specifies starting and ending dates for goals, objectives, and related services. In addition, the frequency of any related service is also specified. For example, the IEP might specify that speech and language therapy will be delivered twice a week for 30 minutes each session for the duration of the IEP. Because special education law (IDEA) requires annual review of services provided in the IEP, long-term duration for services should be projected no further than 1 year.

6. *Evaluation of the IEP:* The final step in IEP development is specifying how student progress toward short-term objectives and annual goals will be measured or evaluated. Following a

process-oriented assessment approach will ensure that this step is not overlooked. In addition, well-written goals and objectives (described below) automatically build in an evaluation process by allowing for growth and development to be tracked.

Creating Annual Goals and Objectives

Annual goals and objectives will be based upon comprehensive assessment data (both formal and informal) and should incorporate the NRC (2001) recommendations referenced in this chapter. Given the challenges associated with ASD, annual goals should address, at minimum, the following areas: social functioning; nonverbal communication skills; receptive, expressive and pragmatic language; fine and/or gross motor skills; academic skills; and behavioral, organizational, and/or self-help skills.

Annual goals should (a) clearly state what the student is expected to accomplish in a 1-year time frame, (b) be worded as a positive statement (what the student *will* accomplish, versus what the student will no longer do), and (c) be worded to be clearly observable and measurable. Well-written IEP goals and objectives tend to follow a specific formula consisting of five questions, which when used, will result in a statement that is objective, observable, and measurable.

1. Who will demonstrate what behavior or skill?
2. How will this skill be demonstrated? What will the skill look like as it is demonstrated and/or at what level will the skill be demonstrated?
3. Where or under what condition will the skill be demonstrated?
4. How frequently will the skill be demonstrated (What are the criteria for mastery)?
5. By when will the skill be demonstrated?

Examples of some poorly written goals (and their improvements) are provided in Table 2.3. Further examples are available in the following texts: *Creating a Win-Win IEP for Students with*

TABLE 2.3   Writing Goals and Objectives

Poorly Written Goal	Well-Written Goal
John will improve his communication skills with peers and adults in the classroom.	John will independently respond to single-answer questions by pointing to (or picking up) a picture card on four out of five opportunities during circle and snack activities.
Susan will stop calling out in class.	Susan will independently raise her hand and wait for teacher acknowledgement before speaking during independent and group work on three out of five opportunities.
When it is time for Michael to sort the silverware, he will put the silverware as accurately as possible.	Michael will independently sort 10 forks, 10 knives, and 10 spoons into the correct sections of a silverware tray, with 90% accuracy for 3 consecutive days.
Mark will increase letter recognition.	When presented with three alphabet cards, Mark will point to named letter on four of five trials over three consecutive sessions per letter. And/Or: Given a field of five alphabet cards and their corresponding matches, Mark will independently match letters to sample on 9 out of 10 trials over three consecutive sessions.
Jacob will improve his listening skills.	Jacob will follow two-step directions when presented by the teacher during group instruction with no more than one verbal prompt on four out of five opportunities.

Autism (Fouse, 1999), *Negotiating the Special Education Maze* (Anderson, Chitwood, Hayden, & Takemoto, 2008) and *Writing Measurable IEP Goals and Objectives* (Bateman & Herr, 2006).

Designing an appropriate instructional program requires more than just accurate assessment data, but it cannot be done in its absence. In addition to linking assessment data to the creation of goals and objectives within the student's IEP (see Box 2.6), adequate instructional planning also must include a plan for actually teaching the specified skills. In this respect, educators may benefit from the use of curricula developed specifically for students with ASD to guide their instructional approaches. A list of and commercially available curricula and resources that can assist in identifying appropriate instructional targets and in writing clear, objective, measurable goals and objects is provided in Table 2.4.

BOX 2.6   Trends and Issues # 3

A Checklist for Linking Assessment Results to Instructional Planning

The following guidelines are suggested for ensuring that assessment results are utilized in the most useful way possible in designing an appropriate instructional program. Key steps in the instructional planning process are listed, along with links between the assessment process and creation of an individualized education program (IEP) for students with ASD.

❑ Was the assessment multidisciplinary? Was it conducted by personnel with background experience and skills in the areas listed below?
  ❑ Child development
  ❑ Autism Spectrum Disorders
  ❑ Behavior
  ❑ Communication
  ❑ Experience with the specific child across a variety of settings and situations
❑ Are the following areas documented in the assessment report?
  ❑ Determination and statement of eligibility
  ❑ The child's developmental level(s)
  ❑ Implications of eligibility and developmental levels for behavior
  ❑ Assessment of ALL areas related to the suspected disability (see below)
❑ Are all the required components of the IEP documented, including the following?
  ❑ Present level of performance (based on a variety of assessment findings)
  ❑ Measurement of existing objectives and progress toward mastery
  ❑ New goals and objectives written for *all areas related to assessment*
  ❑ Description of how new objectives will be measured to determine progress
  ❑ Discussion of placement related to the LRE requirement
  ❑ Description of services and settings, including the frequency and duration of service
  ❑ Long-term goals of the parents
❑ Do the outlined goals, objectives, and services address all areas of need?
  ❑ Implications of Autism Spectrum Disorders on behavior and development
  ❑ Language and communication
  ❑ Social development
  ❑ Behavior
  ❑ Cognitive development
  ❑ Gross and fine motor skills
  ❑ Family participation
  ❑ Transition from school to work

❑ Does the program description provide for coordination, collaboration, ongoing training, and supervision of all service providers and parents?

❑ Does the data collection described in the child's or student's plan provide for the documentation of necessary information? Does the documentation establish timelines and identify criteria for making decisions?

❑ Data collection should allow for documentation of whether objectives have been met, history of student progress toward goals, provision of services, and curricula used.

❑ Timelines for initiation of service, periodic assessment and data collection, and dates for reevaluation should be specified.

❑ Decision-making criteria should be specified in order to allow for evaluation of program effectiveness.

❑ Were dates set for further program evaluation and planning?

Source: Information from Collaborative Work Group on Autistic Spectrum Disorders (July 1997). *Best Practices for Designing and Delivering Effective Programs for Individuals with Autistic Spectrum Disorders.* California Department of Education: Sacramento, CA.

TABLE 2.4 Commercially Available Curricula and Assessment Instruments that Provide Curricular Input

Curriculum/ Assessment Instrument	Description	Skills Addressed
Psychoeducational Profile: Third Edition (PEP-3)—Assessment Instrument Schopler, Lansin, Reichler, & Lee (2005)	• The assessment approach of this instrument maps easily onto instructional planning efforts • Graphically charts uneven and idiosyncratic development as well as emerging skills • Also includes a Caregiver Report that estimates the child's developmental level compared with typical children. The report consists of three subtests: Problem Behaviors, Personal Self-Care, and Adaptive Behavior	• Cognitive Verbal/Preverbal • Expressive Language • Receptive Language • Fine Motor • Gross Motor • Visual-motor Imitation • Affective Expression • Social Reciprocity • Characteristic Motor Behaviors • Characteristic Verbal Behaviors
TEACCH Transition Assessment Profile (TTAP) Second Edition Mesibov, Thomas, Chapman, & Schopler (2007)	• Revision of the *Adolescent and Adult Psychoeducational Profile (AAPEP)* • Assessment instrument developed for adolescent and older children with Autism Spectrum Disorders • Three different environmental contexts assessed • Allows for direct relation to instructional planning that satisfies Individuals with Disabilities Education Act (IDEA) transition planning requirements	• Vocational Skills • Vocational Behavior • Independent Functioning • Leisure Skills • Functional Communication • Interpersonal Behavior

TABLE 2.4   (Continued)

Curriculum/ Assessment Instrument	Description	Skills Addressed

BRIGANCE
(IED–II) Criterion-
Referenced
Skill Areas
Brigance (2004)
	• In addition to being a standardized norm-based assessment instrument, the Brigance (IED-II) is also a criterion-referenced measure
	• Directly relates to instructional areas to be targeted in programs for young children
	• Provides developmental sections with comprehensive skills sequences
	• Also allows for program evaluation
		• Preambulatory Motor Skills
		• Gross-motor Skills and Behaviors
		• Fine-motor Skills and Behaviors
		• Self-help Skills
		• Speech and Language Skills
		• General Knowledge and Comprehension
		• Social-emotional Development
		• Early academic skills sections:
		  • Readiness
		  • Basic Reading Skills
		  • Manuscript Writing
		  • Basic Math

Individual Goal Selection *Curriculum (IGS)* Romanczyk, Lockshin, & Matey (1994)	• A curriculum that is based on principles of Applied behavior analysis • Skills are analyzed in relation to the target or goal behaviors, which are broken down to their essential elements • Allows for identification of skills to target in the child's intervention program that are tailored to the child's difficulties	• Maladaptive Behavior • Attentive Skills • Speech • Receptive Language • Expressive Language • Concept Formation • Gross Motor Skills • Self-Help and Daily Living Skills • Social Skills • Reading • Fine Motor Skills • Written Communication • Arithmetic • Cultural Skills • General Information • School-related Skills • Life Relevant Skills • Leisure Skills • Emotional and Self-control
The Assessment of Basic *Language and Learning* *Skills–Revised (ABLLS–R)* Partington (2008)	• An assessment, curriculum guide, and program monitoring device • Based on the principles of Applied behavior analysis • Provides criterion-referenced information regarding current skills and deficits in 25 areas, along with a curriculum that can serve as the basis for the selection of educational objectives	• Cooperation and Reinforcer Effectiveness • Visual Performance • Receptive Language • Motor Imitation • Vocal Imitation • Requests • Labeling • Intraverbals • Spontaneous Vocalizations • Syntax and Grammar • Play and Leisure

(continued)

TABLE 2.4   (Continued)

Curriculum/ Assessment Instrument	Description	Skills Addressed
	• Information obtained from the completed assessment can be used to develop an effective Individualized Education Program (IEP)	• Social Interaction • Group Instruction • Classroom Routines • Generalized Responding • Reading, Math, Writing, Spelling • Eating • Dressing , Grooming, Toileting • Gross Motor Skills • Fine Motor Skills
A Work in Progress: Behavior Management Strategies and a Curriculum for Intensive Behavioral Treatment of Autism Leaf & McEachin (1999)	• A curriculum based on principles of Applied behavior analysis • Instructional programs fit roughly into four categories • Also provides suggestions for toilet training, eating, play and social skills, sleep problems, and dealing with disruptive and self-stimulatory behaviors	• Imitation: verbal and motor • Language and Communicative Concepts: labeling, pronouns, yes/no, following instructions, prepositions, plurals, attributes, asking questions, conversation • Cognitive: same and different, first and last, before and after, quantities • Academic and Pre-academics: reading, writing, stories, sequencing, recall
Behavioral Intervention for Young Children with Autism Maurice, Green, & Luce (1996)	• A curriculum based on principles of Applied behavior analysis	• Attending • Imitation • Receptive Language • Expressive Language • Abstract Language • Pre-academics • Academics • School Readiness • Self-help • Socialization

Summary

Instructional planning for students with ASD requires knowledge and experience and a range of approaches and strategies. Programming is only as useful as the foundation on which it is based; assessment provides that solid foundation. The ultimate goal of assessment is to obtain data that can be used to devise an appropriate intervention plan. There are many approaches for assessment of individuals with ASD from diagnostic to psychoeducational evaluations, and including formal and informal measures. The range of available assessment tools and strategies is wide, allowing clinicians the flexibility to select a battery of measures that is individualized to the assessment questions and student's characteristics. In addition to assessment scores, the use of modifications during testing greatly increases the chance of success in formal testing situations and provides insight in to the student's learning process and preferences. These strategies can provide a comprehensive picture of the student that will ensure the greatest success in developing the most appropriate instructional plan possible.

Chapter Review Questions

1. Explain why intellectual performance, speech and language, and adaptive behavior are all considered core assessment domains for the evaluation of ASD. Why are norm-referenced tests preferred for these assessments? (Objective 1)

2. Discuss three ways in which the characteristics of individuals with ASD may affect the evaluation process and selection of evaluation procedures. (Objective 2)

3. Describe several ways that standardized test administration procedures can be modified for students with ASD. Why might you use such procedures? How would you interpret the results? (Objective 3)

4. What does research suggest about the stability of evaluation results over time for individuals with ASD? What factors are related to outcome and how do these correspond to what is viewed as best practices for assessment and intervention? (Objectives 4 and 5)

5. Discuss the way that behavioral observations during test administration can assist in the development of appropriate goals, objectives, and accommodations for a student. (Objective 6)

6. The National Research Council discusses their general recommendations for educating children with ASD. List the six interventions that were mentioned as priority instructional areas and a target goal in that area for a student with whom you've worked. (Objective 7)

7. Discuss the NRC recommendations with respect to the "characteristics of effective interventions." (Objective 7)

Key Terms

Adaptations *56*
Assessment *42*
Ceiling *51*
Correlated *54*
Criterion-referenced assessments *43*
Criterion-referenced tests *43*
Curriculum-based *44*
Curriculum-based measurement *44*
Developmental assessments *54*
Diagnostic assessment *47*

Dynamic assessment *44*
Generalization *41*
Goals *59*
Individualized Education Program (IEP) *46*
Informal assessments *43*
Information processing *54*
Maintenance *41*
Modifications *56*
Norm-referenced tests *42*
Objectives *59*

Portfolio assessment *44*
Present levels of performance *43*
Process-oriented assessment *45*
Psychoeducational Evaluation *47*
Rapport *39*
Standardized tests *42*
Stimulus overselectivity *42*
Task analysis *44*
Work sample analysis *44*

Internet Resources

http://www.autismsocietyofwa.org/files/bestpracticesguide.pdf
A PDF file entitled: "Best Practices for Designing and Delivering Effective Programs for Individuals with Autistic Spectrum Disorders." This is a guide sponsored by the California Departments of Education and Developmental Services that outlines recommendations of a collaborative work group for the assessment and treatment of students with ASD.

The guide provides information on assessment domains and measures, as well as curricula and instructional approaches.

http://smhp.psych.ucla.edu/qf/autism.htm
An online clearinghouse of links to websites containing information on the topic "Educating Children with Autism." Links are organized by subtopics, which include "Guides to Autism

Disorders," "Education and Management (Teaching Strategies)," "Implementation and Legislation," and "Support/Network Resources" among others.
http://www.polyxo.com
Polyxo.com—Teaching Children with Autism is a resource for parents, professionals, or anyone interested in teaching children with autism or other related developmental disorders. Contains curriculum resources and data collection forms.

References

American Psychiatric Association (2001). *Diagnostic and Statistical Manual of Mental Disorders— Fourth Edition, Text Revision (DSM-IV-TR).* Washington DC: Author.

Anderson, W., Chitwood, S., Hayden, D., & Takemoto, C. (2008). *Negotiating the special education maze: A guide for parents and teachers* (4th ed.). Bethesda, MD: Woodbine House.

Bateman, B. D., & Herr, C. M. (2006). *Writing measurable IEP goals and objectives.* Verona, WI: Attainment Company, Inc.

Brigance, A. H. (2004). *BRIGANCE Inventory of Early Development–II (IED–II).* North Billerica, MA: Curriculum Associates, Inc.

California Department of Developmental Services. (2003). *autism spectrum disorders–Changes in the California caseload. An update: 1999–2003.* Sacramento, CA: California Health and Human Services Agency.

Collaborative Work Group on Autistic Spectrum Disorders (July 1997). *Best practices for designing and delivering effective programs for individuals with autistic spectrum disorders.* Sacramento, CA: California Department of Education.

Delmolino, L. M. (2006). Brief report: Use of DQ for estimating cognitive ability in young children with autism. *Journal of Autism and Developmental Disorders, 36,* 959–963.

Dyches, T. T., Wilder, L. K., Sudweeks, R. R., Obiakor, R. E., & Algozzine, B. (2004). Multicultural issues in autism. *Journal of Autism and Developmental Disorders, 34,* 211–222.

Filipek, P. A., Accardo, P. J., Baranek, G. T., Cook, E. H. Jr., Dawson, G., Gordon, B., Gravel, J. S., Johnson, C. P., et al. (1999). The screening and diagnosis of autistic spectrum disorders. *Journal of Autism and Developmental Disorders, 29,* 437–482.

Fouse, B. (1999). *Creating a win-win IEP for students with autism: A how-to manual for parents and educators.* Arlington, TX: Future Horizons.

Klin, A., Saulnier, C., Tsatsanis, K., & Volkmar, F. R. (2005). Clinical evaluation in autism spectrum disorders: Psychological assessment within a transdiciplinary framework. In F. R. Volkmar, R. Paul, A. Klin, & Cohen D. (Eds.), *Handbook of autism and pervasive developmental disorders* (3rd ed., Vol II, pp. 863–881.). Hoboken, NJ: John Wiley & Sons.

Leaf, R., & McEachin, J. (1999). *A work in progress: Behavior management strategies and a curriculum for intensive behavioral treatment of autism.* Los Angeles, CA: DRL Books.

Maurice, C., Green, G., & Luce, S. C. (1996). *Behavioral intervention for young children with autism.* Austin, TX: PRO-ED.

Mesibov, G., Thomas, J. B., Chapman, S. M., & Schopler, E. (2007). *TEACCH Transition Assessment Profile (TTAP)* (2nd ed.). Austin TX: PRO-ED.

National Research Council, Committee on Educational Interventions for Children with Autism (2001). *Educating children with autism* (C. Lord & J. P. McGee (Eds.). Washington, DC: National Academies Press.

Ozonoff, S., Goodlin-Jones, B. L., & Solomon, M. (2005). Evidence-based assessment of autism spectrum disorders in children and adolescents. *Journal of Clinical Child and Adolescent Psychiatry, 34,* 523–540.

Partington, J. W. (2006). *The assessment of basic language and learning skills-Revised (ABLLS–R).* Pleasant Hill: CA: Behavior Analysts, Inc.

Perry, A., Condillac, R. A., & Freeman, N. L. (2002). Best practices and practical strategies in the assessment and diagnosis of autism. *Journal on Developmental Disabilities, 9,* 61–75.

Rohde, T. E., & Thompson, L. (2007). Predicting academic achievement with cognitive ability, *Intelligence, 35*, 83–92.

Romanczyk, R. B., Lockshin, S., & Matey, L. (1995). *Individual goal selection curriculum (IGS).* Appalachian, NY: CBTA.

Schopler, E., Lansing, M. D., Reichler, R. J., & Marcus, L. M. (2003). *Psychoeducational Profile: Third Edition (PEP–3).* Los Angeles, CA: Western Psychological Services.

Sigman, M., & Ruskin, E. (1999). *Change and continuity in the social competence of children with Autism, Down syndrome, and developmental delays.* Monograph of the Society for Research in Child Development. London, England: Blackwell.

Turner, L. M., Stone, W. L., Pozdol, S. L., & Coonrod, E. E. (2006). Follow-up of children with autism spectrum disorders from age 2 to age 9. *Autism, 10,* 243–265.

Yeargin-Allsopp, M., Rice, C., Karapurkar, T., Doernberg, N., Boyle, C., & Murphy C. (2003). Prevalence of autism in a US metropolitan area. *JAMA, 289,* 49–55.

3

Evidence-Based Practices for Educating Students with Autism Spectrum Disorders

E. Amanda Boutot, Ph.D. BCBA
Texas State University

Charles Dukes, Ph.D. BCBA
Florida Atlantic University

CHAPTER OBJECTIVES

After reading this chapter, learners should be able to:

1. Compare and contrast evidence-based practices for students with Autism Spectrum Disorders.

2. Identify the components of effective instruction for students with Autism Spectrum Disorders.

3. List and describe three theoretical perspectives underlying intervention for students with Autism Spectrum Disorders.

4. Describe the rationale behind a Multi-theoretical Approach to the education of students with Autism Spectrum Disorders.

5. Identify ways of determining effective treatment for students with Autism Spectrum Disorders.

INTRODUCTION

As you have learned in the previous chapter, autism is a perplexing developmental disorder characterized by severe social, communicative, and cognitive deficits (Kasari, 2002). The onslaught of children being diagnosed with autism has created a challenge for educators and therapists: how to best serve children and youth with autism and their families. Parents are often faced with the daunting task of choosing the "right treatment option." Teachers are often caught between the service delivery system embraced by parents and the services the school actually provides. It is not uncommon for parents and educators to disagree about the manner in which services should be delivered. There has been great controversy surrounding the treatment of children and youth with autism (Maurice, Green, and Luce, 1996). The controversy surrounding treatments for students with autism can make service delivery for students with autism a difficult and complex venture (Freeman, 1997). There is a great need for a better understanding of what constitutes *evidence-based practice* in the era of autism. Whereas other disciplines may have historical or theoretical bases for generally accepted appropriate practices, autism is a relatively new field, fraught with myth and fad treatments, making it difficult to distinguish between that which is a truly viable treatment option and that which is not.

BOX 3.1   Trends and Issues Notes #2

Parents of children with autism at some point received a diagnosis for their children and for many, this time served as a major turning point in their lives. Diagnosis is only the beginning of an extended process to understand the symptoms associated with the condition and efforts to procure the most effective and efficient services to improve skills. There are a number of studies indicating that the stress and anxiety associated with parenting a child with autism may exceed that of parenting a child with other conditions (e.g., Down's Syndrome) (see Siklos & Kearns, 2006). This body of work has spawned a focus on social supports for parents. Social supports has been defined as "information leading the person to believe that she is cared for and loved, valued and esteemed, and is important in a network of mutual obligation and communication" (Cobb, 1976). Examples of social support may include involvement of extended family or friends in the care of the child or respite care available on a consistent basis. While it is difficult to quantify the impact of such supports, it is much easier to qualify the impact of these supports. Parents who have more supports report less stress and anxiety. This may be especially important for families who have a child who engages in high frequency problem behavior. This area of inquiry will be increasingly important as the population of children with autism begins to age and families seek assistance for their children after they are no longer eligible for school-based services.

For further reading, refer to the partial list of works below:

Lounds, J., Seltzer, M., Greenberg, J. S., & Shattuck, P. T. (2007). Transition and change in adolescents and young adults with autism: Longitudinal effects on maternal well-being. *American Journal on Mental Retardation, 112*(6), 401–417.

Siklos, S., & Kerns, K. A. (2006). Assessing the need for social support in parents of children with autism and Down syndrome. *Journal of Autism and Developmental Disorders 36*(7), 921–933.

EVIDENCE-BASED PRACTICES: DEFINITION AND RATIONALE

The Individuals with Disabilities Education Act (IDEA, 2004) requires that public schools use evidence-based practices, sometimes referred to as scientifically based practices, when working with students with disabilities, just as the No Child Left Behind Act (NCLB, see Box 3.2) does for typically developing children. Although current literature supports many methodologies as "Promising practices," few would be considered "scientific" (Simpson, 2005). Evidence-based practice is defined by Simpson (2005) as "interventions and treatments . . . that have undergone a substantial amount of rigorous research." In other words, research resulting in "evidence that repeatedly and consistently proves that children and youth with Autism Spectrum Disorders (ASD) display a significant increase in skill acquisition as a consequence of the intervention" (p. 10). Although multiple treatment

BOX 3.2 Trends and Issues Notes #1

Children and adolescents generally receive the greatest proportion of their treatment through school-based educational programs. The reauthorization of the Elementary and Secondary Education Act of 2001(commonly referred to as No Child left Behind) and the Individuals with Disabilities Education Improvement Act of 2004 have introduced both educators and parents to the term *evidence-based practices*. The purpose of introducing evidence-based practices emanates from the need for educators to identify treatments that have been clearly defined and tested and that yield clear results about the effectiveness of the treatments. The legislative requirement for evidence has spawned two major responses from researchers in special education. First, standards have been set so that treatments can be categorized based on the extent of support available for its effectiveness. (See Umbarger, 2007, for a brief introduction to standards.) For example, applied behavior analysis (ABA) has extensive support from different empirical investigations with different populations across time. In contrast, the use of Vitamin B_{12} lacks the same amount of empirical support and would not be rated as high as those interventions utilizing the principles of ABA. Second, several researchers have conducted extensive reviews of the extant literature to bring together definitive statements about those treatments that have the greatest amount of support and can be classified as evidence-based. These meta-analytic studies literally research the research so that it is possible to indicate those treatments that meet the specifications set forth in the legislation. Science does not remain at a standstill, and more evidence is always invited and even demanded to ensure that any new evidence can be juxtaposed to the current evidence and if necessary, our knowledge must be adjusted to match the new evidence. It will not be an easy task to collect and disseminate information in relation to evidence-based practices, but many in the field recognize the vital nature of this task and will work toward increasing the use of evidence-based practices.

For further reading, refer to the following list of works:

Horner, R. H., Carr, E. G., Strain, P. S., Todd, A. W., & Reed, H. K. (2002). Problem behavior interventions for young children with autism: A research synthesis. *Journal of Autism and Developmental Disorders, 32*(5), 423–446.

Levy, S., Kim, A., & Olive, M. L. (2006). Interventions for young children with autism: A synthesis of the literature. *Focus on Autism and Other Developmental Disabilities, 21*(1), 55–62.

Umbarger, G. T. (2007). State of the evidence regarding complementary and alternative treatments for Autism Spectrum Disorders. *Education and Training in Developmental Disabilities, 42*(4), 437–447.

options are available to parents and professionals, the sometimes slow pace of the scientific process makes it difficult to discern that which is considered truly scientific practice. In essence, there is a time lag between the development of treatments and the validation of the treatment.

Many disciplines define **evidence-based practices** as treatments or approaches that have been found effective through replicated research. Specifically, questions are posed, followed by the creation of a hypothesis, which is then tested. If a particular hypothesis is tested on several different occasions with different participants (in this case students with autism) and the results are favorable, then a tentative decision is made that the particular treatment in question has an evidence base. "Ultimately, such research should be able to demonstrate that there is a causal relationship between an educational intervention and immediate or long-term changes that occur in development, behavior, social relationships, and/or normative life circumstances" (National Research Council, 2001, p. 193). Testing a hypothesis is carried out by using a particular research design. Generally, research designs can be categorized into two broad categories: single-subject designs (also known as within-subject or single-case designs) and group designs (also known as between-subject or experimental designs). Experimental designs may include matched-subject designs, control group designs, and so forth, and rely on appropriate reliability measures.

A great deal of research in the area of autism is conducted through single-subject design methodologies and case studies. There are two major reasons for the paucity of experimental or group designs to answer questions. First, although the number of children diagnosed with autism is steadily increasing, autism is considered a low-incidence disability, making it difficult to secure a large enough sample of subjects for most group designs. Second, due to the heterogeneity of the population, it is challenging to match subjects according to specific characteristics. For example, in a number of studies investigating the effects of schooling on children's intelligence, many children are matched using a construct called *socioeconomic status* or *SES*. This construct is often measured by asking mothers to identify their highest level of education. In the case of students with autism, researchers are often interested in the manifestation of symptoms (e.g., behavioral or communication patterns). It may be difficult or even impossible to identify children with the same behavioral or communication profiles, which would enable a researcher to match children for a particular study. This difficulty does not completely eliminate the possibility of using group designs, but it does mean that a number of researchers ask questions that can be more easily answered using different experimental methods. The use of single-subject designs and case studies is considered by those in the field of autism as appropriate given the challenges of experimental designs (Odom, et al., 2004). However, using single-subject designs can present challenges in identifying evidence-based practices for treatment and instruction for individuals with autism and leaves the door open for practices that are less appropriate or that work for fewer individuals.

Simpson and colleagues attempted to categorize treatment options for students with autism by ranking each as either "scientifically based," "promising," "limited supporting information," or "not recommended" (2005). We have defined *scientifically based* above. Promising practices are those that "have (a) been widely used for several years without any or with few adverse outcomes, and/or (b) undergone research that suggests that children and youth with ASD respond favorably and display skill acquisition as a consequence of the intervention" (Simpson, 2005, p. 11). Practices with limited supporting evidence are those that have undergone limited study, are not "widely utilized," or "reflect a wide range of results (poor to favorable)" (p. 11). Interventions were deemed not recommended when they had "undergone a substantial amount of rigorous research and the evidence proves that the intervention or treatment does not increase skill acquisition or favorable results" and/or have resulted in detrimental outcomes for students with autism (p. 11). We summarize Simpson's categorization of common educational interventions or strategies in Table 3.1.

To help us better understand what we mean by evidence-based practice, Green (2008) suggests that "popularity should not be mistaken for proof; enthusiasm is no substitute for evidence; it just does not stand to reason that all interventions are comparably effective" (p. 6). Although many interventions, programs, approaches, and strategies are promoted through the media and Internet, at conferences, and in books, not all would be considered evidence based. According to Dr. Green, *evidence-based* means that the proposed intervention has been scientifically validated through direct, controlled analyses (Green, 2008). Further, such studies should involve "careful selection and assessment of participants" as well as "objective, accurate, and reliable measurement" of the effects of the intervention under study. Finally, she suggests that interventions should be replicated by multiple investigators, "not just on a person or group, especially if they are the principal developers/promoters of the intervention" (p. 8), and that all studies be published in peer-reviewed scientific journals (Green 2008). While it is clear that evidence-based practice may be best, practitioners and families may wonder, what harm is there in using a strategy or approach with limited support? According to Dr. Green, interventions supported primarily by "opinions, speculations, personal accounts, and

TABLE 3.1   Overview of Simpson's Categorization of Practices for Students with ASD

Scientifically Based Practices	Promising Practices	Limited Supporting Evidence Practices	Practices Not Recommended
• Applied behavior analysis (ABA) • Discrete trial teaching (DTT) • Pivotal response training (PRT) • Learning Experiences: An Alternative Program for Preschoolers and Parents (LEAP)	• Play-oriented strategies • Assistive technology • Augmentative alternative communication (AAC) • Incidental teaching • Joint action routines (JARS) • Picture exchange communication system (PECS) • Structured teaching (TEACCH)	• Gentle teaching • Option method (Son-Rise) • Floor time • Pet/Animal therapy • Relationship development intervention (RDI) • Fast ForWord • Van Dijk approach • Cartooning • Cognitive scripts • Power cards • Auditory integration training (AIT) • Art therapy • Music therapy	• Holding therapy • Facilitated communication

Source: From Simpson, R. L. (2005). *Autism Spectrum Disorders: Interventions and treatments for children and youth.* Thousand Oaks, CA: Corwin Press.

uncontrolled or poorly controlled studies "have many risks, including, "wasted money, time, and energy; exploitation of vulnerable people; physical and emotional injuries; lost opportunities to make real advances; (and) reinforcement and perpetuation of practices that impede progress" (p. 7). Therefore, the best way to reduce these risks, according to Green, is to use evidence-based practices, or in some cases, those that are considered promising.

As can be seen, evidence-based practices are sometimes difficult to define, and some practices that may be useful for a particular student, although "promising," do not meet the criteria. An alternative way to identify best practices is to consider the theoretical construct from which treatments and instructional strategies are derived. In the field of autism, there are three such theories: behavioral, developmental, and perceptual-cognitive (Scheuermann & Webber, 2002). Each theory has served as the foundation for the development of specific instructional strategies that can be used effectively with individuals with autism. It is important here to make reference to the progression of science and how scientists understand the development and use of theories much differently than the general public. In the general public, it is not uncommon for theories to be likened to opinions or statements that do not have substantive proof. Theories play a much different role in the practice of science. Specifically, theories are used to guide the manner in which scientists ask questions, develop hypotheses, and design experiments. The key for scientists is to formulate theories that serve as an explanation or more specifically, serve predictive purposes. In other words, for scientists, theories provide a guide to approach a particular problem. Theory helps scientists formulate thoughts about what they should find (when conducting an experiment or implementing an intervention) and define the parameters for analyzing a particular problem. A simple yet powerful example comes from one of the most rigorous natural sciences: physics. In actuality, gravity was at one time a theory. Predictions were made based on the theory of gravity which was a hypothesized understanding of how gravity might work. Based on these speculations, experiments were designed and carried out.

This same kind of logic operates when discussing theories in social sciences as well. For example, **applied behavior analysis** is based on the **behavioral theory**. Generally, this theory asserts that a great deal of behavior can be explained by analyzing the interactions between humans and their environments, making it possible to predict much of human behavior. Thus, the predictive value of a particular theory is absolutely essential to both scientists and practitioners, as theories guide one's thinking and help clarify what one may expect to find under certain conditions. Whitman (2004) suggests that "theories are not either wrong or right, but rather are more or less useful. Theories that allow more precise and accurate predictions to be made and/or lead to the design of effective interventions are more useful and for that reason are characterized as having greater validity" (p. 101). Further, "theory formulation in the area of autism is particularly difficult because of the number and heterogeneous nature of the symptoms" (p. 102). Whereas evidence-based practices should guide our thinking about autism intervention, theoretical understandings are necessary in order to make decisions about those potentially beneficial practices for which evidence is as yet only promising. There are many professionals who may hold an almost slavish adherence to a particular theory, and we do not advocate this position. Instead, we believe that those responsible for assisting students with autism should understand and thoroughly examine the theoretical underpinnings of many approaches to better understand the thinking behind the approach, which will enable them to identify effective treatments. One of the purposes of this chapter is to serve as an introduction to future chapters on specific instructional and treatment methodologies by describing the theoretical underpinnings and the research backing each. Further, the authors posit a model of treatment and instruction that utilizes a Multi-theoretical Approach, combining all three theoretical orientations to provide the most effective practices for individual students. Finally, the authors make a case for the need for increased research in the area of evidence-based practices in autism, specifically related to the Multi-theoretical Approach.

THEORETICAL BASES FOR AUTISM INTERVENTION

Behavioral Theory

In the behavioral theory, autism is a syndrome of behavioral deficits and excesses that have a biological basis but are nonetheless amenable to change through carefully orchestrated, constructive interactions with the physical and social environment (Green, 2001). Proponents of the behavioral theory posit that students without disabilities learn directly from interactions with others in school, home, and/or community. While interacting in these environments on a daily basis, it is highly probable that students without disabilities will learn communication, social, and behavioral skills. In contrast, children with autism need highly structured learning opportunities to learn the skills necessary to interact with others. Behavioral theory is grounded in the science of applied behavior analysis (ABA). ABA is a scientific approach used to examine human behavior. The science relies on careful observation, measurement, and recording to bring about socially significant behavioral change (Schreibman & Winter, 2003). Behavioral theory calls for the arrangement of the learning environment, use of prompting and shaping techniques, and attention to immediate reinforcing feedback (Quill, 1995). In addition to the teaching of communication, social, and behavioral skills, behavioral theorists also concern themselves with reducing inappropriate behavior. Managing or reducing inappropriate behavior begins with a process designed to help parents and professionals to understand the purpose or function of the behavior. Then, a replacement or alternative behavior is identified and taught to children, "replacing" the inappropriate behavior (Jordon, 2001). There are several well-researched approaches to the treatment of autism based on behavioral theory, including **discrete trial training (DTT)**, **pivotal response training (PRT)**, and incidental teaching. In the following section, we discuss DTT. In later sections Multi-theoretical Approaches and developmental approach respectively we will discuss PRT and incidental teaching.

BOX 3.3 Research Notes

It is widely accepted that children with autism should receive early intervention often if there is to be improvement in behavioral, communication, and social skills. The debates about the nature of treatment can easily fill entire volumes. The fundamental issue at hand is the type, frequency, and intensity of treatment. Of the early intervention educational programming available, which program offers the best possibilities for skill improvement? This question will be answered differently by adherents of various educational programs. In 2007, Reed and colleagues attempted to answer some questions about the effectiveness of educational programming by conducting a study in which three different programs were compared. The researchers compared the effectiveness of applied behavior analysis (ABA), special nursery school placements, and portage (a home-based program used in the United Kingdom focusing on increasing attentional responses including joint attention). The controversies surrounding treatment options can be traced to the seminal study conducted by Lovaas (1987), in which his results seemingly indicated that children with autism can "recover" from the major symptoms of autism. The results of this study have been questioned on a number of different levels, but Reed and colleagues sought to conduct their investigation to question three major aspects of the original Lovaas study. First, the study by Reed, et al., was conducted in a community setting (e.g., preschool and home) as opposed to a clinic setting used by Lovaas. This allowed comparison of programs that are implemented in real-world contexts. Second, in the Reed study, the same measures were used at both pre- and posttest, while the Lovaas study utilized two different IQ tests for comparison of behavior before and after treatment (which, as noted by Reed, et al., is a threat to internal validity). The third issue that Reed and colleagues attempted to address through their study was the level of functioning of the participants in the study. As noted by Reed, et al., "the sample chosen for the study reported by Lovass (1987) were verbal, relatively high-functioning participants, who may have performed equally well with any intervention" (p. 419). The results of the Reed study indicate that there was no significant difference between ratings of autism symptom severity as measured by the Gillman Autism Rating Scale (GARS) between any of the three programs, though the ABA program produced the most significant gain on both intellectual and educational functioning. In terms of adaptive behavior or one's ability to meet the social requirements of one's community appropriate for one's age, the special nursery program produced the greatest improvements. Although these results should be interpreted with caution, as the sample sizes were small (12–19 children) and the participants were not randomly assigned, the study adds to the current knowledge base about early intervention programming and its possibilities.

Source: Reed, P., Osbourne, L. A., & Corness, M. (2007). The real-world effectiveness of early teaching interventions for children with autism spectrum disorder. *Exceptional Children, 73*(4), 417–433.

Discrete Trial Training Interventions

One of the most extensively studied approaches derived from ABA is a procedure called discrete trial training or discrete trial teaching (DTT; Smith, 2001). In DTT, skills are taught through discrete teaching trials that consist of a trainer-provided antecedent (an instruction and/or stimulus), a behaviorally defined response from the child, and a consequence that rewards a correct response or marks an incorrect response (Mastergeorge, Rogers, Corbett, & Solomon, 2003), known as the three-term contingency. The three-term contingency refers to the antecedent, the behavioral response, and the consequence; together they make up a discrete trial. It is critical to "target" specific skills and teach these skills to students with autism. In the absence of directed, structured, and frequent learning opportunities, students with autism will not acquire the skills necessary to engage in appropriate interactions in several different environments. DTT has been shown to help students with autism develop skills in naming and requesting objects, asking questions, initiating and maintaining conversation, describing items, and making social greetings (Lovaas, 2002). The wide-scale success of DTT has brought both praise and debate about the merits of the technique. In spite of the many documented success stories, there is concern that the lessons learned within the contrived learning environments do not generalize across more typical environments (e.g., home and community). Although the controversy rages on, many families and professionals have found great success.

Developmental Theory

Developmental theorists in the field of autism contend that the resulting neurological differences from autism lead to delays in language, cognitive, social, and motor development for the child (Scheuermann & Webber, 2002). Thus, working from this model of intervention, it would be wise for the educator to teach the child developmentally appropriate skills, beginning with what the child has not mastered and working toward age-appropriate and functional skills. **Developmentally appropriate practices (DAP))** are a well-recognized collection of practices used for young children both with and without disabilities. Thus, many early interventionists and early childhood special education teachers may be most familiar with these approaches. However, for students with disabilities, the developmental perspective has received relatively little attention in the past. The developmental perspective prescribes teaching methods that are more naturalistic in focus, including incidental and milieu (teaching in the natural environment) instructional strategies.

Incidental teaching involves "teaching a child a particular skill in the context of its use" (Pierce & Schreibman, 1997, p. 208). Incidental teaching strategies are also rooted within the field of ABA and thus, may be thought of as both behavioral and developmental in nature. Behaviorally, incidental teaching involves sabotaging the environment to set up learning opportunities in order to remediate deficit skills, most often related to language (Zagar & Shamow, 2005). With ABA incidental strategies are used to generalize skills taught through discrete trial training to a more natural learning environment, allowing them to be maintained by more natural consequences (Zagar & Shamow, 2005). For both the behavioral and developmental theories, incidental teaching involves giving the child more child control of the learning situation than the teacher, as well as teaching "in the context of everyday situations and naturally occurring stimuli" (Zagar & Shamow, p. 308). Incidental teaching involves several components: using novel materials, having teachers join the activities with the children, offering choices, using incidental strategies (e.g., placing a preferred item out of reach, requiring the child to make a communicative request for it), "using comments and questions to facilitate the child's interest and/or play-related talk," generating elaboration of child's talk, and inviting interaction with peers (Kohler, Anthony, Steighner, & Hoyson, 2001, p. 95). In this way, incidental teaching strategies take advantage of teachable moments and set up the environment so that those moments are highly likely to happen.

One way to differentiate incidental teaching from discrete trial teaching is to consider the following examples, both of which involve taking a walk around the block with a child with autism. In the first example, the adult may point to objects and ask the child "What is it?" or ask the child to point to items named and provide praise when the child is correct and corrective feedback when the child is incorrect. This is an example of DTT because the adult is leading and making specific instructional demands on the child, using the three-term contingency ("What is it?" serves as the antecedent, the child's point is the behavior, and praise is the consequence). In the second example, the adult waits until the child shows an interest in a particular object through looking, naming, or pointing toward it. The adult may then repeat the child's utterance, make a statement of her own, or inquire about the child's interest; praise may be non-contingent or may be delivered when the child shows an interest in something, but is not based on accuracy of a response. This second example is of incidental teaching because the adult is allowing the child to take the lead and basing any instruction on the child's motivation and interest; there is no three-term contingency used in this example.

Several models have emerged from the developmental approach. The Denver Model at the University of Colorado Health Science Center; the Developmental Intervention Model at the George Washington University School of Medicine; the Douglas Developmental Center at Rutgers University; Learning Experiences, an Alternative Program for Preschoolers and their Parents (LEAP) at the University of Colorado School of Education; the Walden Early Childhood Programs at the Emory University School of Medicine; and the Developmental Individual-Difference Relationship-Based Model. Several researchers have investigated the utility of the developmental approach. Milieu procedures have been linked with increasing opportunities for children to use language (Camarata & Nelson, 1992; Hart & Risley, 1968; Halle, Marshall, & Spradlin, 1979; Warren, McQuarter, & Rogers-Warren, 1984).

Child choice is one aspect of the developmental model that has received attention in research. Utilizing child choice in instruction has led to increased noun acquisition, increased use of grammatical structures, increases in verbal initiations and verbal responses, increases in communication of wants and needs, increased meal-time requests in home and community settings, and to generalization of appropriate verbal skills to new settings (Camarata & Nelson, 1992; Cavallaro & Bambara, 1982; Halle, Marshall, & Spradlin, 1979; Koegel, Schreibman, Good, Cerniglia, Murphy, & Koegel, 1989; Warren, McQuarter, & Rogers-Warren, 1984; Yoder, Karser, Alpert, & Fischer, 1993). In addition, the use of direct and natural consequences has been shown to lead to more rapid acquisition of target behaviors, increases in expressive single words and word approximations, and increases in syntax use (Charlop, Schreibman, & Thibodeau, 1985; Koegel, O'Dell, & Koegel, 1987; Koegel & Williams, 1980). These studies demonstrate that the use of the developmental approach can improve many skills for students with autism. The developmental approach has also been found to increase cognitive levels; increase communication through gestures, signs and words; enhance social and emotional growth; increase shared attention and regulation; increase engagement; increase affective reciprocity (i.e., social-emotional response to another's emotional expression); increase problem solving; improve symbolic and creative use of ideas; improve logical and abstract use of ideas and thinking; improve social skills, compliance, toileting, self-help skills, and pre-academic skills; and improve physical development (Greenspan & Wiedner, 1999; Harris et al., 2000; Rogers et al., 2000; Strain & Cordisco, 1994; Strain & Hoyson, 2000). Further, the developmental approach has been found effective in improving functional verbal language, responsiveness to adults, tolerance and participation with typical peers, independence in daily living, and emotional thinking (Greenspan & Wiedner, 2001; McGee et al., 2000).

Developmental theory posits that through naturalistic settings, materials, interactions, and consequences (specifically natural reinforcement), students with autism learn functional skills and improve generalization of already learned skills. This theory is particularly practical for skills such as two-way and functional communication, play, and social skills because these are skills typically learned in the natural environment. Further, students with autism often have difficulty generalizing skills from one setting, presentation stimulus, or person, to another. The developmental theory's reliance on instruction in the natural environment can aid in generalization of skills. The developmental theory alone, however, may not be appropriate for some skills that require more direct instruction.

Perceptual-Cognitive Theory

The **perceptual-cognitive theory** originates from the belief that students with autism have sensory, perceptual, and thinking differences resulting from brain malfunction. The theory suggests that these children are overly stimulated by the external senses and have difficulty processing sensory information (Scheuermann & Webber, 2002). Given these difficulties, the perceptual-cognitive theory places a priority on teaching in very structured and routinized environments, working toward independence of thought and behavior. Further, cognitive processing problems create the need for teachers to present information in specific ways, such as providing instructions one step at a time, and limiting extraneous verbalizations. Following are some common strategies for working with students with autism, guided by the perceptual-cognitive theory.

VISUAL CUES AND ENVIRONMENTAL SUPPORTS   The perceptual-cognitive approach relies heavily on visual cues and supports, such as providing picture or three-dimensional schedule systems depicting the child's activities for the day. The approach teaches children top-down or left-right orientation through visual cues and supports. The approach further provides visual cues for common tasks such as washing hands or playing with toys. These visual cues involve picture symbols for each component of the task, posted in sequential order. The goal of visual cues such as these is to fade the necessity for adult prompting, providing the child with the opportunity to practice skills independently using only the visual cue as a support. Another example of visual cues and supports is the use of color. A learning environment may have colored baskets for different categories of instructional materials. For example, yellow baskets may be used for building blocks, and blue baskets may be used for art supplies. The purpose of color cueing is to aid children as they learn categorization skills as well as to help them begin to recognize expectations for different activities without an adult prompt. For instance, if the yellow basket is on the floor, the child will come to expect to build blocks, whereas if the blue basket is out, he or she will come to expect to sit at the table for an art activity. In this way, independence is fostered.

ROUTINES   Students with autism often have difficulty with changes in routine and with transitions from one activity to the next. The perceptual-cognitive approach addresses these challenges through the establishment of routines and other cueing practices. As much as possible, teachers should set a routine that does not change from day to day or week to week except in emergencies. This provides a sense of structure and safety to the child's world by making expectations clear and providing predictability. Cues can be added to ease transitions. For example, the use of a kitchen timer to signal the end of one activity, if used consistently, will help to prevent common resistance to changes in activities. It is also important to prepare the child in advance for changes in routine. The use of the visual schedule system provides the visual support for this preparation.

ATTENTION AND IMITATION   A final key component to the perceptual-cognitive theoretical approach is teaching students with autism to attend and imitate. Because of their perceptual and cognitive difficulties, paying attention and imitating can be challenging areas for students with autism. To address these challenges, teachers should incorporate attending skills and imitation (both verbal and nonverbal) into the lesson plan.

The goal of the perceptual-cognitive approach is to provide children with autism with the necessary supports to overcome the perceptual and cognitive processing challenges while promoting independence and self-reliance. Whereas these supports are necessary for intervention early on, the goal of fading the supports as the child gets older and more independent is critical.

Research into the efficacy of the perceptual-cognitive approach has noted its utility for children with autism by several researchers. The most well-known program utilizing the perceptual-cognitive approach is the Treatment and Education of Autistic and related Communication-handicapped Children

(TEACCH) model. This model was developed at the University of North Carolina at Chapel Hill. Research suggests that the TEACCH model increases independence, self-management, and task completion (Marcus, Schopler, & Lord, 2001; Schopler, Lansing, & Waters, 1983). Another model program utilizing the perceptual-cognitive approach is the Princeton Child Development Institute, which uses graduated guidance to increase imitation and completion (MacDuff, Krantz, & McClannahan, 1993). Environmental supports have been found to increase a child's understanding of his or her world, acceptance of change, and independence (Bryan & Gast, 2000; Quill, 1997; Simpson & Myles, 1993), as well as increasing adaptability and flexibility during times of transition (Orelove, 1982). Visually cued instruction is a key component of the TEACCH program and inherent in the perceptual-cognitive approach. The use of visual cues has been linked with increases in social-communicative behaviors such as joint attention, prelinguistic communicative gestures, and receptive language (Quill, 1996; Quill & Grant, 1996). Further, increases in independence, less dependence on adults, less confusion and resistance to changes, improved understanding of activities and expectations (MacDuff, Krantz, & McClannahan, 1993), and improved generalization and maintenance of daily living skills have been noted with the use of visual cues (Pierce & Schriebman, 1994). Another aspect of the visual cue is the Social Story (Gray & Garand, 1993), which is often used with high-functioning students with autism to improve social, communication, and behavior skills. Numerous studies are under way or have been published indicating that this type of visual support is effective for this population (Bernard-Ripoll, 2007; Crozier & Tincani, 2007; Gray & Garand, 1993; Okada, Ohtake, & Yanagihara, 2008; Reynhout & Carter, 2007; Scottane, 2008). Similar to the visual cues mentioned above are the use of graphic symbols and graphic phrase and sentence strips to improve language. Use of these types of visual supports improved labeling, commenting on actions, asking "wh" (e.g., what, where, and why) questions, spontaneous commenting, and functional communication with peers (Hunt, Alwell, & Goetz, 1985; Kistner, Robbins, & Haskett, 1988; Quill, 1992; Vicker, 1991; Wolfberg & Schuler, 1993).

Combination Approaches

NATURALISTIC BEHAVIORAL INTERVENTIONS   PRT is a play-based, naturalistic intervention for students with autism targeting "pivotal" behaviors that impact many areas of functioning (Schreibman & Winter, 2003). The naturalistic behavioral interventions, while still grounded in ABA, grew out of a call for different teaching techniques that began with child-initiated communication and sessions conducted "without a table and chair." The approach requires professionals and parents to "follow the child" through a session and allow the child to learn communication through natural opportunities (e.g., requesting a cup of juice from the table). Mastergeorge and colleagues (2003) identified a number of key differences between DTT and naturalistic approaches like PRT: (a) child initiation of communication rather than adult directiveness, (b) use of intrinsic rather than extrinsic reinforcement, and (c) instruction in the natural context rather than at a table using drill and practice. The strength of behavioral approaches is well documented. However, students require other approaches to initiate the use of skills they have acquired, transfer those skills to new settings, and reduce their reliance on cues from the teacher (Smith, 2001).

THE STAR PROGRAM   Strategies for Teaching based on Autism Research (STAR, Arick, Loos, Falco, & Krug, 2004) is described by the authors as a "comprehensive behavioral program for students with autism . . . [which] uses applied behavioral analysis methodology to provide an instructional base for teaching" (p. 1). The STAR program may be thought of as a Multi-theoretical Approach to autism treatment, as discussed in the next section, because of its use of a combination of three instructional strategies, each of which entails aspects of the differing theoretical constructs previously described. The instructional strategies used in the STAR Program include DTT (behavioral theory), PRT (combined behavioral and developmental theories), and the use of functional routines instruction (perceptual-cognitive theory). The authors conducted a study of 67 children with autism ages 2–6 (at baseline) using the STAR program (Arick et al., 2003). After staff received comprehensive training and several baseline assessments were conducted with each of the children, the children participate in home- or school-based STAR programs. At the beginning of the program, children were given a pretest. At the end of 16 months, the children were given a posttest. Results were analyzed based on the pretest and posttest. At the posttest, significant gains were found in socialization and language. Specifically, over the 16-month period, 36% of the participants showed gains of 16 months or more; the average gain for all children was 10 months (Arick et al., 2003). Further, significant decreases in autistic behavior and social characteristics associated with autism were noted. Another study by Young (2006) found similar results, specifically that children taught via the STAR program made an average of 1 month's gain in expressive verbal language for each month of intervention. Both studies reported that there appeared to be no correlation between a participant's chronological age and these language gains; ". . . children were just as likely to make gains at any chronological age" (Arick et al., 2003, p. 81). These studies suggest that using a combination approach that targets specific, individual areas of child need can lead to improvements in targeted skills.

MULTI-THEORETICAL APPROACH

Although each of the three primary theoretical approaches has merit and efficacy for many children, no one approach can be said to work for *every* child with autism (Scheuermann, Webber, Boutot, & Goodwin, 2003). The heterogeneity of students with autism necessitates that educators provide instruction utilizing a variety of approaches, based on the individual needs of each student. Teachers who must choose one program over another are placed in the difficult situation of perhaps ignoring a technique that may have merit. Box 3.3 provides research-based support for the notion that various skills can be improved through various techniques. Even the most successful treatment can offer only substantial improvement in about 60–70% of the children to which they are applied (Schreibman & Winter, 2003). Unless teachers have been trained in other approaches, they cannot make appropriate instructional decisions for their students if one approach fails. Having training in a variety of approaches allows teachers to make decisions based on individual student needs, rather than on the one or two approaches with which they are familiar. We advocate a Multi-theoretical Approach. A **Multi-theoretical Approach** borrows from each theoretical perspective, and based on careful assessment, combines to create the most effective instructional package for the individual student. The well-documented research into the treatment of autism has yielded valuable information about effective and ineffective interventions. Several features shared by most efficacious treatments, regardless of model, philosophy, or type, have been identified: they begin early, are intensive, are individualized and developmentally appropriate, and are family centered, involving parents at every level (Ozonoff & Rogers, 2003). The multi-theoretical perspective maintains that neurological differences resulting from autism leave children with deficits in processing, leading to learning and developmental challenges that cannot be overcome through one perspective alone. A Multi-theoretical Approach, heavily influenced by the principles of ABA may maximize a child's chances for success by focusing on his or her individual needs. Professionals who practice only one approach are limiting their effectiveness. Table 3.2 provides an overview of the various theoretical perspectives and their respective interventions according to Simpson's levels of supporting evidence.

Keys to the use of a Multi-theoretical Approach include individualized assessment, family and child-centered programming decisions, and ongoing data collection and program evaluation using ABA methodologies (i.e., maintenance and generalization). Determining which strategies to use from each theoretical perspective should be decided based on a comprehensive and individualized assessment using multiple assessment procedures. Below are several considerations when working from a multi-theoretical perspective. Figure 3.1 provides some questions to consider when designing

TABLE 3.2   Theoretical Approaches and Supporting Evidence

	Level of Supporting Evidence			
Theory	**Scientifically-Based Practices**	**Promising Practices**	**Limited Supporting Evidence Practices**	**Practices Not Recommended**
Behavioral Theory	• Applied behavior analysis (ABA) • Discrete trial Training (DTT) • Pivotal response training (PRT)			
Perceptual-Cognitive Theory		• Augmentative alternative communication (AAC) • Picture exchange communication system (PECS) • Structured teaching (TEACCH)	• Social Stories™ • Cartooning • Cognitive scripts • Power cards	• Facilitated communication
Developmental Theory		• Incidental teaching • Joint action routines (JARS) • Play-oriented strategies	• Gentle teaching • Option method (Son-Rise) • Floor time • Relationship development Intervention (RDI)	

1. Does the student, or do some of the skills to be taught, require direct instruction, with skills broken down into small units and/or free of competing stimuli?
2. Does the student learn better visually?
3. Does the student seem to "need" order and consistency?
4. Does the student need help generalizing skills to the natural environment?
5. Does the student appear unmotivated to learn with natural reinforcement?

Other questions to consider:
6. What treatment or intervention strategies and programs have been used in the past?
7. How successful were previous strategies and programs at teaching new skills?
8. How successful were previous strategies and programs at teaching functional skills?
9. How successful were previous strategies and programs at helping the student generalize skills?
10. How successful were previous strategies and programs at maintaining a skill over time?
11. Is there one approach or strategy that seems to work best for this student?
12. Is there one approach or strategy that seems to be least effective for this student?

FIGURE 3.1   Questions to Consider for Choosing a Multi-Theoretical Approach

a Multi-theoretical Approach. Note that there are no "No" responses that lead to alternative approaches. Teachers are encouraged to consider appropriate components from all approaches based on the child's strengths and the family's needs.

CHILD AND FAMILY-CENTERED DECISION MAKING

It is important to note that by advocating the "Multi-theoretical" Approach, we are not endorsing what some critics call "eclectic" approaches. *Eclectic* implies a randomness in selection of strategies, based on variables such as availability of the treatment or training, or someone's personal or professional bias. In using a Multi-theoretical Approach, teachers take a much more systematic approach to determining which strategies may be most effective for a given child, based on that child's needs and strengths, not on some arbitrary variable. The decision regarding the skills to be taught, and the best method through which to teach them, should be based on a valid and up-to-date assessment as well as on the wants and needs of the individual child and family. Each child has abilities, strengths and skill deficits that may be more successfully enhanced or remedied in response to one methodology than another. Box 3.4 and 3.5 discuss the role of families in decision making as well as cultural influences that should be considered when working with families. Child and family-centered decision making should always seek to promote the goals of the Multi-theoretical Approach as the overarching objectives of any programming.

> ## BOX 3.4   Diversity Notes #1
>
> The vast diversity in the United Sates is readily apparent with no more than a cursory look at the changing demographics of schools, clinics, and the like. This trend has far-reaching implications for the diagnosis and service delivery to families from diverse backgrounds. In 2007, Welterlin and LaRue reviewed a large sample of the current knowledge available on serving the needs of immigrant families who have a child with a disability, most notably autism. In spite of the paucity of information, this work yielded notable information regarding the way families interpret disability and some recommendations for service delivery to families. In regard to interpretation of disability, it is known that families from diverse backgrounds may interpret both symptoms and behavior differently than families from the majority culture. For example, it is not uncommon for Native Americans to view an individual with a disability as possessing special insight into our world. Second, the well-accepted Western notion of intervention, specifically for the purposes of ameliorating the effects of disability, may be a foreign concept to immigrant families. Some families may view themselves as holding primary responsibility for any intervention, whereas others may feel as if interventions intended to change behavior are simply misguided. The implications of this review are twofold. First, practitioners should be aware of the families' interpretation of disability and their current strengths that may contribute to the success of a treatment plan. This information will assist both families and practitioners to ensure that treatment plans are acceptable to all. Second, practitioners should incorporate strategies into any treatment plan that respect and promote the knowledge of families. This recognition of perspective should also facilitate the development of effective treatment planning.
>
> *Source:* Information from Welterlin, A., & LaRue, R. H. (2007). Serving the needs of immigrant families of children with autism. *Disability and Society, 22*(7), 747–760.

BOX 3.5   Diversity Notes #2

Families of children with autism are often faced with a number of different challenges in caring for their children. Often, these difficulties are not confined to diagnosis, but persist well after. As parents attempt to negotiate different social service agencies, schools, and medical facilities, there is often a need for parental support. There are a number of different sources of family support, but a common source of support is found in a support group. Currently, there is little information available about families who join support groups or why they join them. Mandell and Salzer (2007) conducted a study to investigate these questions. The researchers distributed their survey through community-based service agencies. A total of 1,018 respondents answered questions about themselves and provided reasons why they chose to attend a support group. Information from the study was split into different categories for analysis. Specifically, respondents were divided into those who reported attending a support group at least once and those who reported never attending. The most interesting findings are based on those reporting attending a support group at least once. Two thirds of the sample reported attending a support group at least once. Of this sample, an overwhelming majority was white, earned incomes over $40,000 a year, lived in a suburban area, had a college degree, were married or living with a partner, and were referred to the support group by a trained clinician. Perhaps most significantly, African American families were much less likely to participate in support groups. The authors offer some interpretation for this finding. It may be that some groups take comfort in talking about their concerns, or some groups may have more time and resources to seek out different support mechanisms. The availability of information about families from diverse backgrounds is so spare that it is difficult to draw any broad conclusions, but this work is a worthy beginning.

Source: Information from Mandell, D. S., & Salzer, M. S. (2007). Who joins support groups among parents of children with autism? *Autism, 11*(2), 111–122.

Data-Driven Instruction

One cannot know the effectiveness of any instructional approach, no matter how well-documented in the research, unless data is collected and analyzed regarding its use within the framework of an individualized instructional program. Thus, the use of ABA techniques for data collection, analysis, and documentation is advocated in the Multi-theoretical Approach. Ongoing formative as well as summative evaluation must be conducted and changes in programming made to ensure maximum success of each student.

Systematic Generalization

Once skills have been mastered, they should be systematically revisited to ensure they are maintained across time. Further, **systematic generalization** of skills must be planned in advance to ensure that such generalization of skills will occur.

The ultimate goal of intervention from a multi-theoretical perspective is threefold. First, interventions should lead to the child's maximum and age-appropriate participation in the natural environment and with typical peers. Second, intervention should be age appropriate and functional for the child. Third, intervention should support the child and his or her family in maximizing the child's potential both now and in the future; as such, generalization of skills and independence are paramount.

Implications for Practice

The treatment of autism is currently a challenge for teachers and families alike. The selection and implementation of an intervention may "look" different for each child in need of services. For this reason, it is necessary to conduct research in several areas to gain insight into the utility and effectiveness of the Multi-theoretical Approach. It is possible that some of this information will come directly from many of the education programs designed to deliver services to students with autism. Thus, we suggest several questions that may help to guide critical reflection as well as ignite research so that both professionals and families can gain a better understanding of the Multi-theoretical Approach. First, we pose a question for critical reflection: What are the current intervention packages teachers and parents use and how are these packages chosen? (The reasons behind making such choices will be of special interest.) It is possible that some highly skilled practitioners have already "discovered" the brilliance of a Multi-theoretical Approach. More research is necessary to understand the decision-making process about these combination approaches to assist those who may be attempting to understand various intervention packages. The final two questions are intended to ignite research, but have implications for classroom practices. How do intervention packages differ for children of varying ages? (Many families choose entirely different interventions after children reach the age of 6.) There is not only a need to understand the decision-making process educational professionals (i.e., teachers) use to choose and implement interventions, but it is also critical to understand how and why families may embrace or perhaps completely reject a particular intervention. Communication and cooperation between school and home is essential. Thus, it is important to understand how and why both professionals and families make decisions about interventions. Our final question deals directly with the outcomes of interventions: How effective are treatment packages and in what combination? It is important for teachers and families to thoroughly understand how intervention packages can be put together for the most efficient and effective results. The severity and impact of autism on families requires that teachers and families choose the most appropriate treatment package for students with autism. Effective treatment for children with autism is possible and has been demonstrated in a number of different settings under a host of conditions. Yet, questions remain about how such programming can be identified and implemented on a wide scale. It is possible that a number of families and professionals have a narrow focus about treatment and do not appreciate the strength of a Multi-theoretical Approach. We believe that information is emerging and will continue to grow, demonstrating that a Multi-theoretical Approach may contribute to the literature on evidence-based strategies for use with children and youth with autism.

SELECTING AN INSTRUCTIONAL APPROACH

We have provided an overview of what it means for an intervention approach to be evidence based as well as theoretically sound. However, how does a team (including a child's teacher and family) use this knowledge to make appropriate decisions? To begin to examine how one makes programming decisions for students with ASD, let us first consider the goals of such programming. Specifically, what is the purpose of the education we seek to provide? The ultimate goal of any educational program is to provide the student with the skills necessary to be maximally independently functioning within his or her natural environment. In order to achieve this goal, we suggest consideration of four principles of educating students with ASD.

Principles of Educating Students with ASD

Westling and Fox (2004) provide us with a philosophy for educating students with significant disabilities, including autism. According to this philosophy, students with ASD should:

- Receive an education that is qualitatively equal to that received by students without disabilities or those with other disabilities
- Receive an IEP that represents their unique individual needs

- Spend time with others, especially those without disabilities (e.g., not in isolation)
- Receive early intervention services as soon as possible
- Receive training until they are ready for adulthood
- Receive an education that "maximizes their learning, growth, and development" (p. 31)
- Receive an education that is not unnecessarily intrusive or different from the education of others
- Receive an education that promotes independence and self-sufficiency

According to this philosophy, then, the goal is to provide students with ASD with educational opportunities to participate actively and successfully in the mainstream of society by promoting the principles of self-determination, independence, normalization, and functionality.

PRINCIPLE OF SELF-DETERMINATION   Individuals are said to be self-determined if they can (a) make choices, (b) make decisions about their actions, (c) set goals for themselves, (d) recognize their own abilities (strengths and needs), and (e) advocate for themselves. People with disabilities have long had a history of potential learned helplessness, particularly those with more significant disabilities (Scheuermann & Webber, 2002). Learned helplessness occurs in individuals when they become conditioned to allowing others to make decisions and do things for them. Consider the case of Jonathan, a 17-year-old with autism and intellectual disabilities. Jonathan had learned to do a great many things for himself at school, and his parents were surprised to learn at his transition meeting that he was able to make his own snacks, do laundry, and tie his shoes. His mother stated that she had been tying his shoes every day since he first began to walk, and it never occurred to her to allow Jonathan to do it himself. She stated that she had attempted to teach him when he was in elementary school, but it took him so long to get them tied in the morning that they were often late getting out of the house. This represents an example of learned helplessness. Jonathan was capable, but allowed his mother to tie his shoes because she always had and she would. If we are to prevent learned helplessness in people with autism, we must give them ample opportunities to perform skills on their own, as well as teach them how to do so. Further, as teachers, it is incumbent that we ensure that families and other caregivers are aware of the individual's abilities and are willing to give them more independence, even if it means that it takes longer to get out of the house in the morning.

Although independence is key to **self-determination**, one can receive support and still be self-determined. It is necessary for people with autism to have a voice and choices in order to achieve self-determination. People with autism must be given opportunities to enjoy a myriad of experiences, just as typically developing children do, if they are to be aware enough of their options to make informed choices as they grow older. Consider April, a 15-year-old with autism. Her family met with the school team to discuss community-based instruction opportunities that might provide April with work experience the following school year. When asked what she wanted to do, April was unable to come up with a response, even with prompting by family and teachers. Her family admitted that they rarely went anywhere on weekends except to the homes of relatives or to church. April had not had enough experiences to be aware of jobs she might enjoy. The teaching staff spent the next school year providing April with as many different community experiences as they could. At the end of that year, she was able to tell them that she wanted to work at the community pool because she had learned to swim and loved to be near the water. If provided opportunities, children with autism, like all children, will have a broader base from which to make personal decisions. Further, they will have a better awareness and understanding of their own abilities and limitations, which also aid in decision making. However, choices about one's career are not the only choices we make as individuals. Many students with autism have difficulty making decisions as simple as where to sit at lunch or what shirt to wear because they are accustomed to someone making those decisions for them. Teachers and families should start early teaching children with autism to make their own choices by providing multiple opportunities throughout the day for them to make choices. For example, when Gigi was 3 years old, her family gave her two choices for as many things as they could think of throughout the day: the pink dress or the purple one, the red bowl or the yellow one, hold Mommy's hand or Daddy's, and so on. When she was older, Gigi was able to make her own choices and speak for herself, rather than wait for someone to do it for her. Teaching young children to make their own choices and have their own voice teaches early self-determination.

PRINCIPLE OF INDEPENDENCE   A primary goal of education for students with autism is to maximize their independence in all activities and across all settings. Independence is achieved when one uses only those supports that are absolutely necessary for functioning. Although teachers and parents frequently must use some level of prompting when teaching new skills, prompts and cues must be faded to promote independence. Further, independence cannot be achieved until individuals have opportunities to do things for themselves in the natural setting (e.g., the real world) and are provided training in doing so. Therefore, goals and objectives for students with autism should include statements of how skills are to be generalized to the natural setting, as well as prompt-fading techniques that will be used to promote maximum independence.

PRINCIPLE OF NORMALIZATION   **Normalization** occurs when the activities, materials, and settings in which a person engages are the same as those in which persons without disabilities of the same age, gender, and culture are engaged (Nirje, 1969; see Perske, 2004, for an updated review). In short, normalization helps individuals with autism "fit in" with those without disabilities. Fitting in cannot occur if the person with autism is not provided opportunities to participate in the activities and environments in which others without disabilities are participating. In other words, the first step is opportunity. Second, teachers and families need to ensure that once in the environment, the child with autism has the skills necessary to engage in the same or similar activities as others. Finally, we know that persons with autism often have difficulties, including social skill deficits, language deficits, or stereotypical behaviors, that may set them apart from typically developing peers, especially in a "typical" activity or setting. Therefore, teachers and families must ensure that these differences do not pose a barrier to successful fitting in for the person with autism. Consider Austin, a 10-year-old with high-functioning autism. His family wanted him to play soccer and signed him up to play on one of the local teams. His parents decided that since Austin could speak well enough, they would not tell the coaches and players about his autism; they felt it might negatively impact their impression of him and prevent him from making friends. After several practices, during which Austin could physically do everything that the other players could do, his parents felt that their decision was a good one. However, at the first game, Austin was very excited and began engaging in more of his self-stimulatory behaviors than he had at practices. He flapped his hands wildly in front of his face and made a loud "eeeeeee" sound whenever someone came near him on the field. When on the sidelines, he sat on his heels and rocked, only flapping when the players came near where he was sitting. His parents noticed that the coaches and some of the boys (both on their team and the other team) began to look at him warily, and some boys were even imitating Austin's hand flapping and laughing. His parents began to question their decision not to inform his coaches and teammates, which in hindsight may have made them more tolerant of Austin's differences. As this scenario illustrates, simply being in the same location does not guarantee fitting in. Although the Inclusion Movement has helped to make students without disabilities more tolerant of those with autism (Boutot & Bryant, 2005), misunderstandings can occur when the behavior of children with autism is very different from what is expected, or when they lack the appropriate skills to fit in and participate in an activity. Therefore, along with providing opportunities, successful participation should be incorporated into programming for individuals with autism in order to promote the principle of normalization.

PRINCIPLE OF FUNCTIONALITY   A skill is said to be functional when someone has to do the skill for the child if the child cannot do it himself (Brown, Nietupski, & Hamre-Nietupski, 1976). In other words, a skill is considered functional only if it is something the child actually needs to be able to do in his everyday life in the natural environment. Functional skills can also be thought of as those skills that are meaningful to the child, necessary for current or future independence, and/or when they promote opportunities to fit in with age and cultural groups. For example, skills that can assist in meeting the principle of normalization may be considered functional. Consider the case of Chloe, who is a 7-year-old with low-functioning autism. Her occupational therapist wants her to work on her pincer grip (used to pinch and pick up items). Chloe's teacher created a game wherein Chloe uses her pincer grasp to put clothespins on and take them off of a coffee can over and over. In Chloe's natural environment (home and school) clothespins are never in use (except for this activity). One could argue that while this activity does aid with improving her pincer grasp, the act of taking off clothespins and putting them on a coffee can is one she will rarely (if ever) use in the real world. A better idea might have been to provide her with "chip clips" to take off and put back on her favorite bag of chips (thereby including a natural motivation for the task), or picking up raisins (a favorite food) using the pincer grasp. In other words, the teacher should think of materials and activities for this skill that will better meet the principle of **functionality**.

Determining Appropriate Strategies for Individual Students

Refer again to Table 3.2 on page 80. Table 3.2 provides the scientific support level for a variety of commonly known instructional strategies for students with autism according to theory. As can be seen in this table, if teachers followed only one theoretical approach (developmental for example), they would be limiting the amount of evidence-based practices they provided (in this case, none). Further, if teachers relied solely on those approaches found by Simpson (2005) to be scientifically based (e.g., ABA), they would not address the perceptual-cognitive theory, the strategies of which may also hold some benefit for a given child. As discussed earlier, we support a Multi-theoretical Approach, which uses a combination of strategies based on the needs of the individual child. Although research supports ABA as the evidence-based strategy for working with students with autism (as will be discussed in more detail in Chapter 6), determination of the exact combination of strategies from the differing perspectives must be made on an individual basis. It would be unethical for us to prescribe a combination for each and every student with autism, because each has his or her own unique needs, which may be addressed in a number of different ways. However, we can provide guidelines for determining which combination might be most appropriate for an individual student. Table 3.3 lists the characteristics of children with autism that lend themselves to each theoretical orientation. From this table, teachers can identify those characteristics that appear most similar to those of particular students with whom they work and make a case for specific interventions based on these characteristics. Further, we have included those strengths of individuals with autism that may make the effectiveness of a particular theoretical approach more effective. Note that there are few specific strengths designated for the behavioral theory. Behavioral theory is useful for students of varying levels of ability and disability, and, particularly with ABA, no prerequisite skills are necessarily required for it to be effective. While the skills noted as strengths in the other two categories are not prerequisites per se, if one finds that a particular approach is not working well, it may be wise to re-examine the student's abilities to determine the degree to which lack of certain skills—attending skills, for example may be preventing improvement. Applied behavior analysis techniques within the behavioral theory are often used to teach such early, or prerequisite, skills to students. It is important to continually monitor any program of intervention closely to determine the degree to which it is successful for an individual child.

TABLE 3.3   Core Deficits of Autism Spectrum Disorders and Strengths of Students with ASD

	Behavioral Theory	Perceptual-Cognitive Theory	Developmental Theory
Core Deficit Areas that may be Improved by Each Perspective	• Slow in processing • Distractible • Difficulty with memory • Weak central coherence • Easily confused by inconsistent stimuli • Executive functioning difficulties • Difficulty attending • Difficulty imitating	• Sensory over-selectivity • Sensory underselectivity • Auditory processing difficulties • Use of self-stimulating behaviors (motor or vocal) as a means of calming self in stressful or new situations	• Slow to generalize acquired skills • Dependent on prompts/cues • Resistant to changes in expected instructional routine • Able to attend • Able to imitate
Strengths of Students with Autism who may Benefit from Each Perspective		• Visual learners • Rule-oriented • Appear to use Self-Stimulating Behaviors as Calming Strategy for Stressful or New Situations	• Able to attend to adults • Able to differentiate demands • Able to follow commands • Able to imitate

Summary

From the fist moment a family receives a confirmation that a child does indeed have autism, thoughts about treatment begin. The path from diagnosis to treatment can be riddled with challenges and uncertainties, but there are efforts to facilitate an easier process for families when making choices about treatment. The communities of professionals who serve children with autism have and continue to be highly concerned about making the best possible treatment available to all families. In fact, recent federal legislation has also addressed this issue (e.g., NCLB and IDEIA). Clearly, there are efforts on a number of fronts to identify and disseminate information about effective treatments. In this chapter, we have discussed a number of the issues surrounding the identification and dissemination of effective treatment. First, even referring to a treatment as evidence-based is a task within itself. The criteria for evidence are not always easily accessible because the progression of science takes time. Nevertheless, there are clearly treatment options that have a great deal of support behind them and should be considered when making treatment decisions. Second, the issue of dissemination can also be a challenge. How exactly does information get disseminated to ensure that families and practitioners not only access the information, but also truly understand its application? Finally, making treatment decisions is one of the most significant challenges a family can face. Of the treatments available, which one should be chosen? This question is by no means simple, as there are a number of implications from any one choice that is made regarding treatment. In spite of these challenges, there is clearly a light at the end of the tunnel. The professional community has and will continue to identify effective treatments for children with autism. In addition, families are becoming ever more engaged in treatment for their children and are making sound decisions about treatment and in turn helping other families make the same sound decisions. Although there is a need for further investigation to identify evidence-based treatments, we have a store of knowledge that is readily available for our use, and the prospects seem to be bright for the future.

Chapter Review Questions

1. Compare and contrast evidence-based practices. List evidence-based practices for educating students with autism. (Objective 1)
2. What are the components of effective instruction for students with Autism Spectrum Disorders? (Objective 2)
3. List and describe three theoretical perspectives underlying intervention for individuals with Autism Spectrum Disorders. (Objective 3)
4. What is the rationale behind a Multi-theoretical Approach to the education of students with Autism Spectrum Disorders? (Objective 4)
5. What are ways of determining effective treatment for individual students with Autism Spectrum Disorders? (Objective 5)

Key Terms

Applied behavior analysis   73
Behavioral theory   73
Developmentally appropriate practices (DAP)   75
Developmental theory   76

Discrete trial training (DTT)   74
Evidence-based practices   70
Functionality   86
Multi-theoretical Approach   79
Normalization   85

Perceptual-cognitive theory   77
Pivotal response training (PRT)   74
Self-determination   84
Systematic generalization   82

Internet Resources

Cambridge Center for Behavioral Studies: *http://www.behavior.org/autism/*
Center for Evidence-based Practices: *http://www.evidencebasedpractices.org/*
Division TEACCH: *http://www.teacch.com/welcome.html*

National Association for the Education of Young Children: *http://www.naeyc.org/*
National Autism Center: *http://www.nationalautismcenter.org/*

References

Arick, J. R., Loos, L., Falco, R., & Krug, D. A. (2004). *The STAR program: Strategies for teaching based on autism research (Program Manual)*. Austin, TX: Pro-Ed, Inc.

Arick, J. R., Young, H. E., Falco, R. A., Loos, L. M., Krug, D. A., Gense, M. H., et al. (2003). Designing an outcome study to monitor the progress of students with Autism Spectrum Disorders. *Focus on Autism and Other Developmental Disabilities, 18*(2), 75–87.

Bernad-Ripoll, S. (2007). Using a self-as-model video combined with social stories to help a child with Asperger Syndrome understand emotions. *Focus on Autism and Other Developmental Disabilities, 22*(2), 100–106.

Boutot, E. A., & Bryant, D.P. (2005). Social status and social network affiliation of children with Autism Spectrum Disorders in inclusive settings. *Education and Training in Developmental Disabilities, 40*(1), 14–23.

Brown, L., Nietupski, J., & Hamre-Nietupski, S. (1976). Criterion of ultimate functioning. In M. A. Thomas (Ed.), *Hey, don't forget about me! Education's investment in the severely, profoundly, and multiply handicapped* (pp. 2–15). Reston, VA: Council for Exceptional Children.

Bryan, L. C., & Gast, D. L. (2000). Teaching on-task and on-schedule behaviors to high-functioning children with autism via picture activity schedules. *Journal of Autism and Developmental Disorders, 30,* 553–567.

Camarata, S. M., & Nelson, K. E. (1992). Treatment efficiency as a function of target selection in the remediation of child language disorders. *Clinical Linguistics and Phonetics, 6,* 167–178.

Cavallaro, C. C., & Bambara, L. M. (1982). Two strategies for teaching language during free play. *Journal of the Association for Persons with Severe Handicaps, 7,* 80–91.

Charlop, M. H., Schreibman, L., & Thibodeau, M. G. (1985). Increasing spontaneous verbal responding in autistic children using a time delay procedure. *Journal of Applied Behavior Analysis, 18,* 155–166.

Crozier, S., & Tincani, M. (2007). Effects of social stories on prosocial behavior of preschool children with Autism Spectrum Ddisorders. *Journal of Autism and Developmental Disorders, 37*(9), 1803–1814.

Freeman, B. J. (1997). Guidelines for evaluating intervention programs for children with autism. *Journal of Autism and Developmental Disorders, 27,* 641–651.

Gray, C. A., & Garand, J. D. (1993). Social stories: Improving responses of students with autism with accurate social information. *Focus on Autistic Behavior, 8*(1), 1–10.

Green, G. (2001). Behavior analytic instruction for learners with autism: Advances in stimulus control technology. *Focus on Autism and Other Developmental Disabilities, 16,* 72–85.

Green, G. (2008). *Evidence-based practice: Improvement or illusion?* Paper presented at the Association for Behavior Analysis International Autism Conference, Atlanta, GA.

Greenspan, S. I., & Wieder, S. (1999). A functional developmental approach to Autism Spectrum Disorders. *The Journal for the Association for Persons with Severe Handicaps, 24,* 147–161.

Greenspan, S. I., & Wieder, S. (2001). *Floor time techniques and the DIR model: For children and families with special needs.* Bethesda, MD: Interdisciplinary Council on Developmental and Learning Disorders.

Halle, J. W., Marshall, A. M., & Spradlin, J. E. (1979). Time delay: A technique to increase language use and facilitate generalization in retarded children. *Journal of Applied Behavior Analysis, 12,* 431–439.

Harris, S. L., Handleman, J. S., Arnold, M. S., & Gordon, R. F. (2000). The Douglas Developmental Disabilities Center: Two models of service delivery. In S. L. Harris & J. S. Handleman (eds.), *Preschool education programs for children with autism* (2nd ed., pp. 233–260). Austin, TX: Pro-Ed.

Hart, B. M., & Risley, T. R. (1968). Establishing use of descriptive adjectives in spontaneous speech of disadvantaged preschool children. *Journal of Applied Behavior Analysis, 14,* 389–409.

Horner, R. H., Carr, E. G., Strain, P. S., Todd, A. W., & Reed, H. K. (2002). Problem behavior interventions for young children with autism: A research synthesis. *Journal of Autism and Developmental Disorders, 32*(5), 423–446.

Hunt, P., Alwell, M., & Goetz, L. (1985). *Teaching conversational skills to individuals with severe disabilities with a communication book adaptation: Instructional handbook.* San Francisco: San Francisco State University.

Jordon, R. (2001). *Autism with severe learning difficulties.* London: Human Horizons Series.

Kasari, C. (2002). Assessing change in early intervention programs for children with autism. *Journal of Autism and Developmental Disorders, 32,* 447–461.

Kistner J., Robbins, F., & Haskett, M. (1988). Assessment and skill remediation of hyperlexic children. *Journal of Autism and Developmental Disorders, 18,* 191–205.

Koegel, R. L., O'Dell, M. C., & Koegel, L. K. (1987). A natural language paradigm for teaching nonverbal autistic children. *Journal of Autism and Developmental Disabilities, 17,* 187–199.

Koegel, R. L., Schreibman, L., Good, A., Cerniglia, L., Murphy, C., & Koegel, L. K. (1989*). How to teach pivotal behaviors to children with autism: A training manual.* Santa Barbara, CA: University of California.

Koegel, R. L., & Williams, J. A. (1980). Direct vs. indirect response-reinforcer relationships in teaching autistic children. *Journal of Abnormal Child Psychology, 8,* 537–547.

Kohler, F. W., Anthony, L. J., Steighner, S. A., & Hoyson, M. (2001). Teaching social interaction skills in the integrated preschool: An examination of naturalistic tactics. *Topics in Early Childhood Special Education, 21*, 93–103, 113.

Levy, S., Kim, A., & Olive, M. L. (2006). Interventions for young children with autism: A synthesis of the literature. *Focus on Autism and Other Developmental Disabilities, 21*(1), 55–62.

Lounds, J., Seltzer, M., Greenberg, J. S., & Shattuck, P. T. (2007). Transition and change in adolescents and young adults with autism: Longitudinal effects on maternal well-being. *American Journal on Mental Retardation, 112*(6), 401–417.

Lovaas, O. I. (2002). *Teaching individuals with developmental delays: Basic intervention techniques.* Austin, TX: Pro-Ed.

Lovaas, O. I. (1987). Behavioral treatment and normal educational and intellectual functioning in young autistic children. *Journal of Consulting and Clinical Psychology, 55*(1), 3–9.

MacDuff, G. S., Krantz, P. J., & McClannahan, L. E. (1993). Teaching children with autism to use photographic activity schedules: Maintenance and generalization of complex response chains. *Journal of Applied Behavior Analysis, 26*, 89–97.

Mandell, D. S., & Salzer, M. S. (2007). Who joins support groups among parents of children with autism? *Autism, 11*(2), 111–122.

Marcus, L., Schopler, E., & Lord, C. (2001). TEACCH services for preschool children. In S. L. Harris & J. S. Handleman (Eds.), *Preschool education programs for children with autism* (2nd ed., pp. 215–232). Austin, TX: Pro-Ed.

Mastergeorge, A. M., Rogers, S., Corbett, B. A., & Solomon, M. (2003). Nonmedical interventions for Autism Spectrum Disorders. In S. Ozonoff & S. Rogers (Eds.), *Autism Spectrum Disorders: A research review for practitioners* (pp. 133–160). Washington, DC: American Psychiatric Publishing.

Maurice, C., Green, G., & Luce, S. C. (1996). *Behavioral intervention for young children with autism.* Austin, TX: Pro-Ed.

McGee, G. G., Morrier, M. J., & Daly, T. (2000). The Walden early childhood programs. In S. L. Harris & J. S. Handleman (Eds.), *Preschool education programs for children with autism,* (2nd ed., pp. 157–190). Austin, TX: Pro-Ed.

National Research Council (2001). *Educating children with autism.* Washington, DC: National Academy Press.

Nirje, B. (1969). The normalization principle and its human management implications. In R. Kugel & W. Wolfensberger (Eds.), *Changing patterns in residential services for the mentally retarded* (pp. 181–195). Washington, DC: President's Committee on Mental Retardation.

Odom, S. L., Brown, W. H., Frey, T., Karasu, N., Smith-Canter, L. L., & Strain, P. S. (2003). Evidence-based practices for young children with autism: Contributions for single-subject design research. *Focus on Autism and Other Developmental Disabilities, 18*, 166–181.

Okada, S., Ohtake, Y., & Yanagihara, M. (2008). Effects of perspective sentences in social stories(tm) on improving the adaptive behaviors of students with Autism Spectrum Disorders and related disabilities. *Education and Training in Developmental Disabilities, 43*(1), 46–60.

Orelove, F. P. (1982). Developing daily schedules for classrooms of severely handicapped students. *Education and Treatment of Children, 5*, 59–68.

Ozonoff, S., & Rogers, S. (2003). From Kanner to the millennium: Scientific advances that have shaped clinical practice. In S. Ozonoff & S. Rogers (Eds.), *Autism Spectrum Disorders: A research review for practitioners* (pp. 3–36). Washington, DC: American Psychiatric Publishing.

Perske, R. (2004). Nirje's eight planks. *Mental Retardation, 42*, 147–150.

Pierce, K., & Schreibman, L. (1994). Teaching daily living skills to children with autism in unsupervised settings through pictorial self-management. *Journal of Applied Behavior Analysis, 27*, 471–482.

Pierce, K., & Schreibman, L. (1997). Increasing complex social behaviors in children with autism: Effects of peer-implemented pivotal response training. *Journal of Applied Behavior Analysis, 28*, 285–295.

Quill, K. A. (1992). Using pictographic symbols in the communication training of echolalic children with autism. Unpublished manuscript.

Quill, K. A. (1995). Enhancing children's social-communication in verbal children. In K. A. Quill (Ed.), *Teaching children with autism:*

Strategies to enhance communication and socialization. (pp. 163–184). New York: Delmar.

Quill, K. A. (1996). *Helping a child with PPD: Guidelines for families.* Wareham, MA: Autism Institute.

Quill, K. A. (1997). Instructional considerations for young children with autism: The rationale for visually cued instruction. *Journal of Autism and Developmental Disorders, 27,* 697.

Quill, K. A., & Grant, N. (1996, July). *Visually cued instruction: Strategies to enhance communication and socialization.* Proceedings of the Autism Society of America National Conference, Milwaukee, WI.

Reed, P., Osbourne, L. A., & Corness, M. (2007). The real-world effectiveness of early teaching interventions for children with Autism Spectrum Disorder. *Exceptional Children, 73*(4), 417–433.

Reynhout, G., & Carter, M. (2007). Social story™ efficacy with a child with autism spectrum disorder and moderate intellectual disability. *Focus on Autism and Other Developmental Disabilities, 22*(3), 173–182.

Rogers, S. J., Hall, T., Osaki, D., Reaven, J., & Herbison, J. (2000). The Denver model: A comprehensive, integrated educational approach to young children with autism and their families. In S. L. Harris & J. S. Handleman (Eds.), *Preschool education programs for children with autism* (2nd ed., pp. 95–133). Austin, TX: Pro-Ed.

Scattone, D. (2008). Enhancing the conversation skills of a boy with Asperger's Disorder through social stories™ and video modeling. *Journal of Autism and Developmental Disorders, 38*(2), 395–400.

Scheuermann, B., Webber, J., Boutot, E. A., & Goodwin, M. (2003). Problems with personnel preparation in Autism Spectrum Disorders. *Focus on Autism and Other Developmental Disabilities, 1,* 197–206.

Scheuermann, B., & Webber, J. (2002). *Autism: Teaching does make a difference.* Belmont, CA: Wadsworth.

Schopler, E., Lansing, M., & Waters, L. (1983). *Individualized assessment and treatment for autistic and developmentally disabled children: Vol. 3. Teaching activities for autistic children.* Austin, TX: Pro-Ed.

Schreibman, L., & Winter, J. (2003). Behavioral intervention therapies. *The Exceptional Parent, 33*(11), 64–71.

Siklos, S., & Kerns, K. A. (2006). Assessing the need for social support in parents of children with autism and Down Syndrome. *Journal of Autism and Developmental Disorders, 36*(7), 921–933.

Simpson, R. L. (2005). *Autism Spectrum Disorders: Interventions and treatments for children and youth.* Thousand Oaks, CA: Corwin Press.

Simpson, R. L., & Myles B. S. (1993). Successful integration of children and youth with autism in mainstreamed settings. *Focus on Autistic Behavior, 7,* 1–12.

Smith, T. (2001). Discrete trial training in the treatment of autism. *Focus on Autism and Other Developmental Disabilities, 16,* 86–92.

Strain, P. S., & Cordisco, L. (1994). LEAP Preschool. In S. L. Harris & J. S. Handleman (Eds.), *Preschool education programs for children with autism* (2nd ed., pp. 225–244). Austin, TX: Pro-Ed.

Strain, P. S., & Hoyson, M. (2000). On the need for longitudinal, intensive social skill intervention: LEAP follow-up outcomes for children with autism as a case-in-point. *Topics in Early childhood Special Education, 20,* 116–122.

Umbarger, G. T. (2007). State of the evidence regarding complementary and alternative treatments for Autism Spectrum Disorders. *Education and Training in Developmental Disabilities, 42*(4), 437–447.

Vicker, B. (1991, July). *The minimally verbal individual with autism and the role of augmentative communication.* Paper presented at the Autism Society of America Conference, Indianapolis, IN.

Warren, S. F., McQuarter, R. J., & Rogers-Warren, A. K. (1984). The effects of teacher mands and models on the speech of unresponsive language-delayed children. *Journal of Speech and Hearing Research, 49,* 43–52.

Welterlin, A., & LaRue, R. H. (2007). Serving the needs of immigrant families of children with autism. *Disability and Society, 22*(7), 747–760.

Westling, D. L. & Fox, L. (2004). *Teaching students with severe disabilities* (3rd ed). Upper Saddle River, NJ: Merrill/Pearson Education.

Whitman, T. L. (2004). *The development of autism: A self-regulatory perspective.* London: Jessica Kingsley Publishers.

Wolfberg, P. J., & Schuler, A. L. (1993). Integrated play groups: A model for promoting the social and cognitive dimensions of play in children with autism. *Journal of Autism and Developmental Disorders, 23*, 467–489.

Yoder, P. J., Kaiser, A. P., Alpert, C., & Fischer, R. (1993). Following the child's lead when teaching nouns to preschoolers with mental retardation. *Journal of Speech and Hearing Research, 36*, 158–167.

Young, H. E. (2006). An examination of the variables that affect the outcomes of children with Autism Spectrum Disorders. *Dissertation Abstracts International, 68*(3), (ProQuest No. AAT 3255176).

Zager, D., & Shamow, N. (2005). Teaching students with Autism Spectrum Disorders. In D. Zager (Ed.), *Autism Spectrum Disorders: Identification, education, and treatment* (3rd ed.). Mahwah, NJ: Laurence Erlbaum Associates.

4

Working with Families of Children with Autism

E. Amanda Boutot, Ph.D. BCBA
Texas State University

Jennifer L. Walberg, Ph.D.
DePaul University

CHAPTER OBJECTIVES

After reading this chapter, learners should be able to:

1. Discuss the impact of autism on all members of a family.
2. Describe selection of interventions in home-based services.
3. Discuss the changing effects of ASD through the lifespan.
4. Discuss transition issues and their impact on the family.
5. Describe ways to support family members with a child with an ASD.

 CASE STUDY Case Study Examples

Case of Will

Soon after Shannon and Matt were married, they discovered they were expecting their first child. They were elated. They notified their families, registered with the baby store, and cleared out the spare room of their house. Their own parents were thrilled; this would be the first grandchild on either side. Shannon's pregnancy progressed without much concern; she was only 32 so did not need to have an amniocentesis, although she did opt for a blood test to be sure that the baby was otherwise healthy. It was. At her 20-week appointment, the doctor did an ultrasound and informed the parents that they were having a boy. They were ecstatic. They painted the room blue, Matt's parents sent a crib and other baby furniture, and Shannon's mom began knitting a blanket to welcome home the baby; they began thinking of names. After much debate, they decided on William Sullivan, to honor each of their grandfathers. When she was 34 weeks along, the couple's best friends Susan and Steven threw a baby shower at their favorite restaurant and invited all of their friends and family. Despite the burden of being 8 months pregnant, Shannon was overjoyed, and looking more and more forward to meeting baby "Will." Finally, at 39½ weeks, as she was preparing for bed one night Shannon's water broke. She and Matt hurried to the hospital, calling family and friends on the way: "HE'S ALMOST HERE!" A little more than 12 hours later, Shannon gave birth to a 7-lb., 6 oz. baby boy with a healthy APGAR score and a loud cry. The new parents were exhausted, but overjoyed; Will was perfect.

The days and weeks that followed were a blur for the couple. Shannon was breastfeeding, but Will had trouble latching on. He finally learned to suck correctly, but still he slept in fits and starts, and seemed to have trouble finding a comfortable spot. Whenever Shannon tried to pick him up to console him, it seemed only to trouble him more; he seemed to quiet down only when in her arms when he was eating. Shannon was exhausted and Matt could do little to help her. Will would scream when anyone other than his mother held him. At his 2-week visit to the pediatrician, the doctor told the couple that this was perfectly normal and suggested that they give Will some breast milk in a bottle so that Matt could feed him, too. They tried this, but Will seemed to prefer to be fed lying down in his crib, which resulted in him spitting up most of what he drank. The couple was beginning to get frustrated. The pediatrician then suggested that perhaps Will needed a different type of milk, and suggested a formula for "fussy" babies. Matt immediately went out and bought four large containers, thinking that this surely would be the cure for Will's constant crying. However, even with the new formula, Will cried and cried when he wasn't eating or sleeping. Shannon read everything she could find on the Internet about fussy, colicky babies and tried every home remedy she found. Despite all their best efforts, Will continued to be a very fussy baby.

The first 6 months with Will were difficult on the couple, who were still newlyweds. Matt's parents took over for them one Saturday night so that the couple could take a much needed overnight "vacation" to their favorite bed-and-breakfast. This would be the last trip they would take as a couple for the next 4 years.

As Will approached his first birthday, Shannon, who was staying home with him, began to worry about how he was developing. She and Will belonged to a Mother's Morning Out program at the neighborhood recreation center, and she had developed a friendship with some of the other moms. One day she noticed that many of the other children were interacting with their mothers, trying to speak, and engaging in more social forms of play than Will. She asked Jamie, one of the other moms, how long her son Mac had been doing those things. She did not like Jamie's response: "Oh, I don't know; he's been like this almost from the beginning! He's just a social butterfly, I guess." Shannon began to worry; why wasn't Will a social butterfly? Why, for example, did he seem to actually dislike being around other people, even his parents? Why did he still put everything in his mouth and not seem to want to play with "regular" toys? Why didn't he like being hugged by his own mother? Shannon took her concerns to the pediatrician at Will's 1-year check up. The doctor told her not to worry because some babies were "slow to warm up." At 18 months, Shannon told Matt that she believed something might be wrong with Will: he was walking later than the other children, still resisted engaging with others, and wasn't playing with the other kids. Most concerning, he hadn't yet started talking. Matt, though sympathetic, felt that Shannon was overreacting. After all, Will was a beautiful, healthy boy. What could possibly be wrong with him? Shannon's mother suggested that Will was simply an "intellectual" who preferred things to people, and reminded her that her cousin hadn't talked until age 3, but then in full sentences. "When he has something important to say, he will." At his 2-year doctor visit, Shannon again told the doctor of her concerns, this time explaining that Will had still not said his first words. Finally, the doctor took notice of Shannon's concerns. She asked Shannon a series of questions about Will's social skills, play behaviors, and communication (which at this time consisted primarily of grunts, whines, and tantrums). When she was finished, the doctor sat Shannon and Matt down and explained that Will might have autism. The couple was devastated. Matt, for one, did not believe it, and refused to entertain the possibility. For Shannon, though heartbreaking, the news came almost as a relief; she had *known* something wasn't right. Now it had a name: autism. Their beautiful, auburn haired, blue-eyed angel was not as perfect as they had first imagined. Suddenly, the Will they had wished for, dreamed of, and imagined they had was gone. In his place was the new Will, the one with autism. Although the answer had finally come, it brought with it many more questions and a rollercoaster ride of emotions and issues that would last for a lifetime.

Case of Sam

Walking onto the playground, you see mothers sitting and talking. You see their children playing together; running, jumping, laughing. A child asks her mother if she can swing. You watch the mother walk over, pick up the child, place her on the swing, and sit back down. Then without help from anyone, the child kicks her legs and swings. After several minutes, she yells "Hey, Mom, look at me!" She jumps off, lands on her feet and runs to the jungle gym. You are amazed. Staring at her, you think, "Four or five years old. She's at least that age." The mother looks at you. "How old is she?" you ask. "Three, going on 16!" she replies. Your stomach hurts. You have this awful feeling like you lost something. You muster up a smile and walk over to your son, your 5-year-old son, who is repeating the same word over and over. It doesn't matter what the word is; it's just the random word he's into today. He is sitting on another boy's bike. "Hey, that's my bike!" the boy yells from across the park. Everyone looks. "Get off my bike!" he yells. You try to get your kid off the bike without attracting too much attention. He doesn't listen. You raise your voice a bit. There's nothing. No response. The more you say to him, the less he seems to hear. You grab and pull him off the bike. It falls over. He's now screaming and trying to get back on the bike. With your child in one arm, kicking and screaming, you reach with the other and pick up the bike. The little boy runs over and takes his bike. You apologize to him like you killed his dog. The mothers are just staring. You can't think straight. Your boy continues to wail. He's repeating the word again, over and over. You try to calm him, but there's no way to get through. He's crying and yelling. All he wants is to sit on that bike. He doesn't understand. He never understands. He has a bike, but that doesn't matter. He wanted *that* bike and that's all that mattered. You drag him from the park. He's crying. You're crying. You finally get him strapped in his seat. You get in the car and put your head back. You suddenly feel a strange sense of accomplishment and you think to yourself, "Wow, that's the longest we've ever stayed at the park."

By Sam's Dad, Steven

Case of Carly

Rachel is a single mother of two daughters, one 18, the other 6. Six-year-old Carly has autism and mental retardation. She does not speak, does not respond when spoken to, does not feed herself, and wears diapers. She has beautiful, long curly brown hair and the face of an angel, although she rarely smiles. Carly spends her days in self-stimulation: flapping her hands in front of her face and walking on her tippy-toes back and forth, in about a 4-square-foot area. Carly's father and stepmother do not believe that anything is wrong with Carly. They think Rachel has overreacted, saying "She can't be 'retarded.' Look at her—she's beautiful." They think the reason Carly doesn't talk and will not comply with even the simplest directions is the result of Rachel's bad parenting; however, they will take her only one afternoon a month. Rachel's mother is elderly and unable to assist her with child care, and Carly's sister, Eden, is married with her own baby. Rachel has applied for respite care with a local agency, but is on a waiting list, and it may take another 6 months to a year before Rachel receives any help. Rachel can't afford a baby-sitter, and the teens in the neighborhood won't stay with Carly because of her tendency to "get loose" and run down the street. With the train tracks and the highway nearby, it's just not safe to have anyone other than Rachel stay home with Carly.

On her way home from picking up Carly at afterschool care one day, Rachel must make a stop at the grocery store. She avoids going out in public with Carly at all costs, but they are out of milk and Carly won't drink anything else. "I'll just run in and out; surely she can handle that," Rachel thinks to herself as she parks in the handicapped spot, thanks to the sticker her doctor reluctantly gave her so she didn't have to worry about Carly getting away and getting hit in by a car in the lot. Inside, Rachel quickly puts Carly into a cart and races to the back of the store to the dairy section. She grabs the milk and is almost to the checkout line when Carly spies something in one of the aisles. Rachel does not know what it is because Carly can't tell her and does not point. She knows only that Carly has seen something that she apparently wants and is now writhing back in the seat as if in pain, screaming as though she is receiving a shot. When she gets to the front of the line, Rachel picks up screaming Carly and tries to console her, knowing this will not work; it never does. Carly drops to the floor and begins scratching her mother's legs while simultaneously biting her own wrist. Rachel apologizes to the patron in front of her and tries to pick Carly up. Carly screams even louder and cannot be moved. After what seems like decades, a store manager and a police officer approach Rachel. In her fury, Carly has kicked the milk open and it has spilled on the floor; Carly's wrist is bleeding. The manager asks Rachel to come with him; the officer approaches to take Carly. They have called Child Protective Services, they say, and they want to question her. They believe Rachel is abusing Carly, and they want an investigation. Rachel begins to cry. This is not the first time the police have been called. She assumes it won't be the last. "She has autism!" Rachel screams; the policeman and the store manager look at her as if she's spoken a foreign language. "Ma'am, you'll have to lower your voice and come with us." Rachel, with the help of the officer, gets Carly up and goes to the manager's office. It will be another hour before she is allowed to leave the store, and the social workers will come over tomorrow to investigate the abuse allegations. Rachel is tired. Carly is tired. They are still out of milk. Rachel goes home and wishes for help. She wishes that Carly could just tell her what she wanted in that store.

INTRODUCTION

The case of Will is fictional. Shannon, Matt, and Will are all characters representing the lives of millions of families with children on the autism spectrum. Whereas there is no "typical" when it comes to Autism Spectrum Disorders, the story of Shannon and Matt provides a glimpse into some of the issues that are faced by families with a child on the spectrum: a nagging concern that something is "off" about the child or his/her development; continued attempts at reassurance from family and professionals that the child is fine; realization that there is something wrong; shock, disbelief, and even denial in the face of the diagnosis; and then moving forward with the loss of what was to the unknown of what is to come.

This chapter provides information on the issues and needs faced by families of children with Autism Spectrum Disorders (ASD) across the lifespan as well as how professionals in education can assist families in overcoming and meeting these needs. One purpose of this chapter is for the reader to recognize and respect what the families of children with ASD have been through, as well as the obstacles they continue to face. Through empathy and understanding, teachers can make a big difference in the lives of children with ASD and their families.

GETTING THE DIAGNOSIS

As Shannon and Matt's case illustrates, getting an early diagnosis can be a complicated process. Although the story you read above is fictional, the lag between parental suspicions regarding developmental delay and an actual diagnosis of autism is documented in the literature and is a source of frustration for parents (Smith, Chung, & Vostanis, 1994). Parents' first concern is often around language development, and these concerns happen even earlier for parents of children with more severe autism characteristics. In one study, parents of children with autism reported concern over development at 17½ months but did not seek assistance until about 22½ months (Coonrod & Stone, 2004). When parents bring language and behavior concerns to primary caregivers, such as a pediatrician, many are told to wait and see. A survey of parents with children with autism found that the median time from noticing a problem to the autism diagnosis was 9 months with a range of 0 months to 13 years (Harrington, Patrick, Edwards, & Brand, 2006). So although there may not be a consensus on the exact amount of time between noticing symptoms and receiving a diagnosis, there is undoubtedly a period that may be better used for intervention. It is no wonder that parents often have little confidence in a physician's ability to diagnose autism (Harrington, Patrick, Edwards, & Brand, 2006). The wait-and-see approach wastes valuable time and can have long-term financial implications. Early **cost-benefit analysis** estimates that early intensive behavioral intervention can save more than $2 million over the lifespan of the child (Jacobson, Mulik, & Green, 1998).

Once a diagnosis of autism has been established, many parents begin a grieving process. Koubler-Ross's (1969) famous **stages of grief** are as follows: denial, anger, bargaining, depression, and acceptance. These stages have been used to describe what a parent might experience when given a diagnosis. The loss parents feel is real and must be acknowledged. This grief over diagnosis has been written about by parents in works such as the essay "Welcome to Holland" by Emily Kingsley (1987). See Figure 4.1 and the essay "Holland Schmolland," by Laura Krueger-Crawford (2008), which is a response to "Welcome to Holland." In "Welcome to Holland," the mother comes to terms with her child's diagnosis by comparing autism to vacationing in Holland—a place she had not intended to go (her original destination was Italy), but a nice place nonetheless.

I am often asked to describe the experience of raising a child with a disability—to try to help people who have not shared that unique experience to understand it, to imagine how it would feel. It's like this . . .

When you're going to have a baby, it's like planning a fabulous vacation trip—to Italy. You buy a bunch of guidebooks and make wonderful plans. The Coliseum. The Michelangelo *David*. The gondolas in Venice. You may learn phrases in Italian. It's very exciting.

After months of eager anticipation, the day finally arrives. You pack your bags and off you go. Several hours later, the plane lands. The stewardess comes in and says, "Welcome to Holland."

"Holland?!?" you say. "What do you mean Holland? I signed up for Italy! I'm supposed to be in Italy. All my life I've dreamed of going to Italy."

But there's been a change in the flight plan. They've landed in Holland and there you must stay.

The important thing is they haven't taken you to a horrible, disgusting, filthy place full of pestilence, famine and disease. It's just a different place.

So you must go out and buy new guide books. And you must learn a whole new language. And you will meet a whole new group of people you never would have met.

It's just a different place. It's slower-paced than Italy, less flashy than Italy. But after you have been there for a while and you catch your breath, you look around . . . and you begin to notice Holland has windmills . . . Holland has tulips. Holland even has Rembrandts.

But everyone you know is busy coming and going from Italy . . . and they're bragging about what a wonderful time they had there. And for the rest of your life, you will say, "Yes, that's where I was supposed to go. That's what I had planned."

And the pain of that will never, ever, ever, ever go away . . . because the loss of that dream is a very, very significant loss.

But . . . if you spend your life mourning the fact that you didn't get to go to Italy, you may never be free to enjoy the very special, the very lovely things . . . about Holland.

FIGURE 4.1 Welcome to Holland

Source: From Kingsley, E. (1987), "Welcome to Holland." Retrieved April, 10, 2008, from http://www.upkidsoflawrencecounty.com/POEM.html

In "Holland Schmolland," the mother takes a different look. She writes of having read the "Welcome to Holland" piece:

> While I appreciated the intention of the story, I couldn't help but think, "Are they kidding? We are not in some peaceful countryside dotted with windmills. We are in a country under siege—dodging bombs, trying to board overloaded helicopters, bribing officials—all the while thinking, "What happened to our beautiful life?" . . . That was 5 years ago. My son is now 8 and though we have come to accept that he will always have autism, we no longer feel like citizens of a battle torn nation. . . . It's not a war zone, but it's still not Holland. Let's call it Schmolland. (pp. 2–3)

She goes on to describe Schmolland as a "nation" where its citizens "lick walls," line up toys, and bounce on the couch for hours (p. 3). In this analogy, it is not Schmolland that is difficult to deal with; rather, it is "people from other countries" and even those from Schmolland, who present the occasional challenge (p. 4):

> Where we live, it is not surprising when an 8-year-old boy reaches for the fleshy part of a woman's upper torso and says, "Do we touch boodoo?" We simply say, "No we don't touch boodoo" and go on about our business. It's a bit more startling in other countries, however, and can cause all sorts of cross-cultural misunderstandings. . . . Other families

who are affected by autism are familiar and comforting to us, yet are still separate entities. . . . [W]e share enough similarities in our language and customs to understand each other, but conversations inevitably highlight the diversity of our traditions. "My child eats paper. Yesterday he ate a whole video box." "My daughter only eats four foods, all of them white." "My son wants to blow on everyone." (pp. 4–5)

Together, "Welcome to Holland" and "Holland Schmolland" provide some insight into what it is like raising a child with autism. Specifically, "Holland Schmolland" provides some perspective on how it feels being an outsider, not just an outsider to those with typically developing children, but also an outsider to those with other children on the spectrum. The differences each family faces are highlighted in this passage, reminding professionals that just as no two children with autism are the same, no two families with a child with autism are the same. We must be willing to recognize and respect these differences, and also to appreciate that one parent's "Holland" may be another's "Schmolland."

Some parents feel a sense of relief upon hearing an autism diagnosis. Whereas few are glad to hear that their children have a disability, having a diagnosis means that there is a reason and a name for what is going on. As one parent states, upon hearing the diagnosis of autism, "I was so thankful. I finally had something that made sense. Other labels did not make sense" (Hutton & Caron, 2005).

PARENTAL PRIORITIES FOR THEIR CHILDREN WITH AUTISM

Like all parents or primary caregivers, parents of children with autism have hopes and dreams for their children. They also have worries and concerns. This section will provide information on those issues cited most frequently in the literature as important to parents of children with autism. It is important for teachers to be aware of these generalities but to also make efforts to learn the dreams and nightmares of the individual families with whom they work. Consider this example of a second-grade general education teacher who truly shared concerns over the education of one of her students, and how she worked with the parent to understand the student and his needs better. The teacher asked the mother, Liz, "If you could wave a magic wand, what would you wish for your son?" The mother's response appears in Figure 4.2. Liz was very impressed with the teacher for asking; no one had made such an attempt to get to know her son in the entirety of his education (since age 3). Liz's response was so moving that the building principal printed it in the school newsletter (under a pseudonym) for all parents and teachers to see what it would take to help a youngster with autism.

Liz's list of wishes reflects many of the priorities of parents of children with autism. Researchers (Ivey, 2004; Spann, Kohler, & Soenksen, 2003) have found the following priorities as most important to families for their children with autism:

- Play with classmates.
- Have friends.
- Receive an invitation to a birthday party.
- Improve language skills.
- Have adequate **vocational** and leisure skills.
- Be happy.
- Receive acceptance in the community.
- Live independently.

If I could wave a magic wand, here are my wishes . . .

By: Liz Bullington

- First and foremost, accept and *include* him as a part of your class—just like everyone else.
- Try to understand and respect his differences. He did not choose to have autism and learning to live with it is harder for him than it is for us.
- Be patient with his limited communication skills.
- Encourage him to try new things, but go slow. New experiences can be scary for him.
- Give *lots* of praise for his accomplishments, no matter how small.
- Understand that he learns differently, but *believe* that he can learn.
- Help him feel comfortable in the classroom. Give him the space he needs, but don't isolate him.
- Embrace the fact that he is a visual learner. Pictures and examples are better than just words.
- Encourage him to interact with his classmates when appropriate, but realize that social situations are difficult for him.
- Focus on the positive, and be careful not to reinforce the negative.

Finally—

- Have realistic expectations, but don't underestimate his potential. As the old saying goes—if you don't expect much, you won't get much. Even though some things are harder for my son, you'll be *amazed* at what he can achieve. His successes may not be the same as the rest of the class, but they are still something to be proud of.

FIGURE 4.2   A Mother's Wishes for Her Son with Autism

Sadly, when asked whether or not they perceived that the school was addressing these priorities, nearly half of the 45 families surveyed as part of the research by Spann and colleagues (2003) stated that they felt the school was doing little or nothing.

With regard to worries or concerns, Biernat discusses concerns about acceptance and prejudice toward both her son and herself by her community, friends, and family (2000). Another concern is fear that someone will take advantage of their child. In addition, parents are also highly concerned about ensuring their children's safety from physical harm (Ivey, 2004).

IMPACT OF AUTISM ON PARENTS

The impact of autism on the family has been the focus of some, although few, research studies in recent years. Chief among the issues facing parents are their concerns about raising their child with autism, as well as stressors and depression that occur as a result of raising such a child. As Biernat (2000) states:

> It is a hard adjustment to realize that we are the parents of a "special" child. It is learning the new language of therapy and adjusting our paradigm of what we expect for and of our children. It is difficult to have no medical cause to blame, no concrete diagnosis. It is hard not knowing what we can expect and not having answers to our questions. There are days when I feel nothing short of desperate. There are days when I am frustrated and angry and sad. There are other days when it is worse. There are times when I feel a profound sense of sadness and yet I realize how lucky we are, how much worse it could be. (p. 210)

STRESS   According to Boyd (2002), "Mothers of children with autism are one of the most stressed parental groups" (p. 214). Boyd further emphasizes that parent and child variables contribute to the level of stress felt by a parent or other caregiver of a child with autism. Specifically, children with lower-functioning autism "place a greater degree of stress on their mothers because of their potential for long-term dependency" (p. 213). Children with autism who exhibit the most challenging behaviors create increased stress not only because of the difficulty in raising these children, but also because of fear of public scrutiny, from both strangers as well as friends and families (Boyd, 2002). Further, behavioral challenges may limit a parent's ability to obtain social supports (known to relieve some of the stress), thereby exacerbating the stress (Boyd, 2002). Finally, stress for any parent often comes with perceived difficulty in parenting; for parents of children with autism, "consistent and pervasive stress makes it even more difficult to parent" (Boyd, 2002, p. 214). This stress over behaviors of a child with autism, combined with the lack of reinforcement in the parenting process, culminates in an even more stressful situation for the parent (Siklos & Kerns, 2007). A variety of factors may influence the stress level felt by parents of children with ASD. Cultural differences are discussed in Box 4.1, while in Box 4.2 a study is presented that suggests that parent involvement in treatment may be a factor in a parent's level of stress.

BOX 4.1   Diversity Notes

It must be noted that the family research in autism, particularly around diagnosis and family stressors, consists mostly of a Caucasian and middle-class subject pool (Dale, Jahoda, & Knott, 2006; Kuhn & Carter, 2006). Whereas there is an emerging base of literature that includes children and families from a variety of cultures, this is an area that requires further investigation.

Cuccaro et al. (1996) point out that the common symptoms of autism vary little across "culture, ethnic group, and socioeconomic status (SES)" (p. 462). In other words, autism is readily recognizable as such regardless of where you go in the world. This is supported by a recent test of validity of instruments such as the ASQ in British and Japanese cultures, which found no differences in the ability to detect autism or Asperger Disorder in both groups of children despite the fact that they come from vastly different cultures (Wakabayashi et al., 2007).

If autism "looks" the same regardless of culture, it is worth investigating whether culture may play a role in how a parent deals with the diagnosis and challenge of raising a child with autism. This chapter has already discussed the impact of autism on maternal stress; however, we did not make a distinction between cultures. Research from Blacher and McIntyre (2006) indicates that Latino mothers have levels of stress similar to those of their Caucasian counterparts. However, Latino mothers may have significantly higher levels of depression, while at the same time are better able to see the positive impact of the disability. The authors suggest that more research is needed on these and other differences within the Latino culture if professionals are going to better support these families.

Race may also play an important role in the age at which low-income children with autism first receive a diagnosis. A study of Medicaid-eligible children with autism found that while Caucasian children receive a diagnosis at an average age of 6.3 years, African American children were diagnosed at an age of 7.9 years (Mandell, Listerud, Levy, & Pinto-Martin, 2002). It is theorized that these differences may result from the fact that different racial groups have different styles of interaction with medical professionals; some may ask for help right away, whereas others may wait longer.

The studies discussed above all suggest that culture and race influence how families deal with autism. Much more research is needed in order to enable school professionals to properly address the needs of *all* families of children with autism. In the meantime, teachers must be sensitive to cultural practices when interacting with families.

BOX 4.2 Research Notes #1

In 2007 researchers examined the extent to which intensity of applied behavior analysis (ABA) therapy impacted family stress and the well-being of mothers in particular (Schwichtenberg & Poehlmann, 2007). Forty-one mothers of children with autism ages 3 to 14 (mean age of 6.9) completed a five-item assessment protocol consisting of questionnaires related to autism characteristics/behaviors, family needs, depression, personal strain, and the child's ABA program. The average number of hours per week of ABA therapy ranged from 6 to 50 with a mean of 22. The average number of hours per week that mothers spent involved with their child's ABA program ranged from 0 to 30 with a mean of 3.1. Two important findings were noted in this study. First, symptoms of depression were fewer for those mothers whose children were in more intensive ABA programs compared to those in less intensive programs. Second, mothers reported more "feelings of personal strain" (p. 603) when they spent more hours per week involved in their child's ABA program. The researchers report that their findings support intensive ABA programs but do not support using mothers as therapists or as therapy coordinators.

DEPRESSION Along with stress, depression is the most common associated negative impact of autism on families. Hastings et al. (2005) found greater depression for mothers than fathers, although mothers were also more positive toward their child with autism than were fathers in the study. Fathers' stress and perceptions (positive or negative) were based on maternal depression; mothers' stress was dependent on their partner's depression, suggesting a cycle of interdependency and influence of psychosocial well-being among married parents or partners of children with autism. In this same study, the authors point out that the greater the behavioral problems of their child, the greater the mothers' stress.

POSITIVE IMPACT A small fraction of the literature supports the idea that families, particularly parents and primary caregivers, experience positive effects of raising a child with autism. In a two-part special series on parenting children with autism, the journal *Focus on Autism and Other Developmental Disabilities* published several pieces written by parents of individuals with autism. In their own words, parents provide insights into the positive effects of raising a child with autism, relating the greater impact it has had on their lives beyond the well-published difficulties. "Daily life with our son is such a pleasure and truly makes us feel that we are the lucky ones who have been blessed with this handsome and bright child. . . . Even on those days when I am at the end of my rope, I sit back and am very thankful for Josh" (Welteroth, 2001, p. 9). Patricia Roth states that "the experience of having this rather unusual son has considerably expanded my mind" (2001, p. 19). "Stephen's total dependence on and trust in me teaches me an important human relationship. He silently tells me, 'I can live meaningfully and happily if you love me completely.'. . . Through Stephen, I have learned a truth of my life—to give my love when I am strong and to receive the love of others when I am weak. If I want to live meaningfully, peacefully, and happily, I have to love other people completely without any conditions attached" (Tsai, 2000, p. 205). Tsai (2000) goes on to state, "I have learned from Stephen that the beauty of caregiving is not just in giving but also in receiving. . . . Thus, my care for Stephen is not a burden but a privilege" (p. 205). The feeling that one's child with autism is a gift is a concept expressed by other parents as well, including Kathy Biernat, who wrote, "Each of our children is a precious gift, but the fact that God has entrusted us with Luke is both an awesome responsibility and a tremendous blessing" (2000, p. 210).

IMPACT OVER TIME   There is also **longitudinal research** that suggests that the impact of autism on a family changes over time. Grey (2002) conducted a 10-year follow-up of parents of children with autism and found that initial concerns of parents, including high levels of emotional stress like depression and anger, were still present in the sample 10 years later but at much lower level. Overall parents had developed some coping methods and it was mostly the parents of children with severe aggressive or obsessive behaviors that still experienced high levels of stress. All of this points to the idea that teachers must be sensitive to the changing needs of families of children with autism.

Family Needs

Families of children with autism face a number of obstacles related to caring for their child with autism. In addition to the emotional burdens they may face, treatments may be expensive or require a great deal of time, taking away from other duties and family members. Common needs associated with raising a child with autism include:

- Financial support
- Emotional support
- Respite care (child care)
- Resources to aid in understanding the child's disorder
- Resources for dealing with the child's disorder

Teachers may find themselves wondering what their role is in addressing these needs for the families of the children with whom they work. In truth, meeting these needs may not be feasible. Few of us have enough of our own resources (time or money) to donate to another person. However, teachers can play a crucial role in *empowering* families to meet their own needs. Teachers can provide information to families upon request about community and state resources that can help meet financial, emotional, informational, and respite care needs. For families that may be uncomfortable asking for help, teachers may choose to have a "Family Information Center" (e.g., a bulletin board) in or just outside their classroom containing contact information for a variety of resources. Or, teachers may send home a monthly newsletter highlighting a new community resource each month. Still other teachers may hold an "Information Night," inviting parents to come to the classroom and learn about community resources both from the teacher as well as from other parents. On such an occasion, the teacher may make his or her classroom computer (if connected to the Internet) available for families with limited Internet access to browse the options within their community. Teachers may wish to conduct a Family Needs Assessment (see Figure 4.3) to determine areas of need for the individual families with whom they work and prepare information sessions accordingly. Another way is to assist families with meeting their needs is to be empathetic to the fact that the families of students with autism have unique needs that may be very different from your own needs or those of other students with disabilities. The first step to helping a family in need is to be receptive to their issues and have an open mind.

Family Involvement

"Parent involvement is widely acknowledged to be a critical 'best practice' in the education of young children with ASD" (Benson, Karlof, & Siperstein, 2008, p. 47). For children with autism, family involvement is necessary for a number of reasons, including generalization of skills, parent support and training, collaboration across home and school, and ensuring that necessary skills are being addressed through the education plan. (See Box 4.3 for a study on the use of parent training to aid with generalization of skills.) It is often observed by teachers that parents of children with autism are

To help us better understand your family and your child's needs, please respond to the following questions. You are free to skip questions that either do not apply to your situation or that you would rather not answer. Use additional paper as needed. Thank you for your time.

1. What are your child's greatest strengths?
2. What are your goals for your child in the **next 6 months**?
3. What are your goals for your child in the **next 2–3 years**?
4. What are your goals for your child **when he/she is an adult**?
5. What one skill, if your child had it or was improved in it, would make your life or that of your family easier?
6. What does your family like to do together? Does your child with autism participate in these activities?
7. What activities does your child participate in with the family?
8. What activities would you like to see yourself or your family be able to do with your child with autism, and what is currently preventing you from doing them?
9. What are your child's favorite activities or areas of interest?
10. What does your child enjoy most with each member of the family?
11. What are your child's least favorite activities?
12. What are your child's favorite toys or objects?
13. What are his or her least favorite toys or objects?
14. Does your child engage in play or other activities independently? Please describe.
15. Describe your favorite moments with your child.
16. Describe your least favorite moments with your child and how you feel at those times (e.g., frustrated, sad, angry, helpless, etc.).
17. What are your greatest hopes and dreams for your child?
18. What are your greatest fears for your child?
19. What are your expectations for the services that we may provide for your family and your child?
20. What other things would you like us to know about you, your family, or your child that you think may assist us in our work?

FIGURE 4.3 Family Needs Assessment

some of the most well informed when it comes to their child's disability, their needs, and the family's rights. This should be seen as positive, rather than something to be defensive of. In this section, we discuss some of the ways that parents should be encouraged to be involved in their child's education, how teachers can encourage parents to do so, and how to bridge gaps and foster positive collaborative relationships with families.

BOX 4.3 Research Notes #2

Training parents to apply applied behavior analysis (ABA) strategies has often been a key component to a home-based program for children with autism, despite some evidence that suggests that it may not be personally satisfying for the parents to do so (see Schwichtenberg & Poehlmann, 2007). Of particular benefit is the generalization of skills to the natural environment when parents are trained in and can continue skill training beyond the therapy session (see Lovaas, Koegel, Simmons, & Long, 1973). Crockett and colleagues conducted a study in 2007 that investigated the effects of parent training on acquisition and generalization of specific teaching procedures (discrete trial teaching [DTT]). Participants were two parents (mothers) of 4-year-old children diagnosed with autism (one was also diagnosed with mental retardation). The parent training model used by the researchers was individualized for each parent and consisted of between 6 and 9 weeks of weekly trainings lasting 2 hours each. Training involved lecture, demonstration of both correct and incorrect DTT procedures, role play with feedback, practice with their own children with direct and immediate feedback, and videotaped practice with feedback. Results indicated that both parents were able to learn appropriate DTT procedures and to generalize them to skills beyond the training model. However, despite the gains in parental skill acquisition, child skill acquisition as a result of parent training was only minimal in the current study. The authors suggest that the duration of the study was insufficient to realize any meaningful gains in child skill acquisition, and that longer-term treatment is necessary for gains to be observed.

Legal Mandates

EARLY INTERVENTION   The Individuals with Disabilities Education Act (IDEA, 2004) includes a provision providing for the development of an **Individualized Family Service Plan (IFSP)** for every child served under age 3 receiving services for a disability, which must be completed by a team of individuals including parents. By law, parents must be a part of all decisions made relative to the education and treatment of their child with a disability. However, how much and what type of involvement are not clearly delineated within the law; in fact, it is up to **early intervention** (EI) personnel and parents themselves to determine the degree of participation parents will have beyond the minimum required by law.

The IFSP itself is perhaps a more family-friendly document than the Individualized Education Program (IEP), with which most teachers are familiar. The IFSP requires that the team consider not only the child's needs and services but also those of the family. If the parents require training or support, it can be written into the IFSP and becomes the responsibility of the EI agency to ensure that the services are provided. The authors of Part C of IDEA (which covers services for infants and toddlers) made a good observation: In order to best serve an infant or toddler with a disability, we must also serve the family. The family is the child's first teacher, the primary caretakers, and may themselves have needs, which, if not addressed, could prevent successful intervention for the child. Furthermore, because non–school-aged children are cared for primarily in the home or child care facility, significant training and support should go to the parents, grandparents, child care providers, and so on—hence, the IFSP.

Early interventionists typically do a satisfactory job of including the family and supporting their needs during the EI years (birth through age 3); this job is, after all, required by law. What is less clear is the nature of family involvement in the IEP process, as required by Part B of IDEA. We will examine this next.

SPECIAL EDUCATION   Many, though certainly not all, children with autism will transition from services outlined in **Part C of IDEA** to those in **Part B of IDEA** at age 3. Part B is commonly referred to as "traditional special education" and includes children between ages 3 to 21. It is important to note that families may be alarmed by the sudden lack of focus on their needs, having moved from an Individualized *Family* Service Plan to an Individualized *Education* Plan, which focuses solely on their child. Further, there may be some terminology, requirements, and paperwork that are new to the family that may contribute to the family's feeling "left out" or of less importance than the professionals. It is important for teachers working with young children, especially those transitioning from Part C, to make the family feel welcome, and to be cognizant of the fact that up until that time, the family was central to the services and the meetings to determine those services. A smooth transition, then, concerns itself not only with the child, but also with the family.

Even if a child has not received Part C services, when he comes into Part B, or special education, teachers need to be aware of the family's needs. At whatever age the child enters special education, the process will likely be new to the family, and there will be an understandable period of adjustment. Schools are required to provide a handbook of special education to the parents, but we suggest taking it a step further. For example, teachers should offer to sit down with parents before the first IEP meeting and discuss the handbook with them, explaining things that may be unclear and helping to familiarize them with the processes. In addition, because parents sometimes feel more comfortable speaking to other parents rather than to school personnel, we suggest that teachers ask parents of children already in the program if they would be willing to speak with families coming into the program for the first time to help put them at ease. Having available a handful of parents who will allow you to give their e-mail or phone numbers to new parents is suggested for all teachers who may receive newly diagnosed students into their programs. Finally, we want to remind professionals that the use of educational jargon can be confusing and off-putting to parents, particularly those new to the system. When families do not understand the lingo, some will ask for clarification, but others may not, which leaves them confused and feeling particularly inept and left out. It is the role of the special educator to bridge the gap between the family and the school during IEP meetings so that true collaboration can be achieved.

The IEP meeting itself may be overwhelming for families because of the differences between Part C (which focuses on the needs of families) and Part B, which, according to Stoner and colleagues (2005), "included new vocabulary, new staff, new agency cultures, and a new set of assumptions, which can cause confusion for families. All families in this study reported feelings of confusion during their initial IEP meeting, which was their first formal contact with the special education system" (p. 47). There are some tips that can help to put the family at ease and create a feeling of collaboration rather one of confrontation (see Figure 4.4).

Collaboration

As professionals in the field, the authors of this chapter have frequently heard teachers comment on the lack of cooperation from parents of students with autism, and as a consequence, a lack of collaboration between home and school. There are a number of reasons cited in the research that may foster a lack of collaboration between home and school. We examine this literature here.

STRUGGLE FOR DIAGNOSIS   Parents of children with autism may come into the educational system having already met with an array of difficulties with professionals, chief among them the difficulty in obtaining a diagnosis for their child as described above (Stoner et al., 2005). Among the difficulties experienced by parents in an attempt to get an accurate diagnosis for their child are "being rebuffed or dismissed by . . . professionals, and requesting referrals repeatedly" (Stoner et al., 2005, p. 47). As a result, according to the authors of this study, many parents of children with autism come to distrust professionals, which in turn negatively impacts their relationship with educational personnel (Stoner et al., 2005). The authors further submit that as a result of these early rejections, "parental trust in the recognized experts . . . was reduced while parents' trust in their own instincts was reinforced" (p. 47). As Stoner and Angell (2006) noted, parents' "repeated and often negative interactions with experts and professionals . . . left them skeptical and cautious" (p. 185).

FIGHTING FOR SERVICES   According to the Stoner et al. study (2005), because parents felt that they had to fight for services, their trust in the educational system charged with providing help for their children decreased. "Once reduction in trust occurred between the parents and the education professionals, parents became increasingly watchful and diligent in their efforts to ensure that their children received all services they deemed necessary to meet the needs of their child" (Stoner et al., p. 47).

- Start and end each communication (face-to-face, written, or via telephone) with a positive statement about the child.
- Send communication (make phone calls or send e-mails or notes) regularly, not just when something is wrong. Send "Bragging Notes" as well, because all parents love to hear someone else praise their child.
- Send home a draft agenda for each meeting (including the time allotted), requesting that the family add their needs or concerns to the agenda before the meeting.
- Come to meetings on time and avoid giving the impression that you are in a hurry to leave. Encourage others to follow this example.
- Remember that although it may be "just another meeting" for you, it is not just another meeting for the parents, as it concerns the well-being of their child. Show parents through your actions and words that meeting with them, whether annually or at other times, is important to you as well.
- Start each meeting by allowing the family to discuss how they feel about their child's education. Encourage them to ask questions or put items on the agenda.
- Continue to ask the family for their input throughout the meeting, not just at the beginning.
- Make sure that the family has understood each discussion item before moving on; avoid using jargon that the family may not understand.
- Position yourself at the meeting near the family, rather than having school representatives on one side of the table and the family on the other. Sitting next to the parents conveys your support for them and also gives you more opportunity to lean in and check for understanding periodically.
- Disagreements sometimes arise; we recommend these strategies for dealing with upset parents in a professional manner:
  1. Make every attempt to meet with the family immediately upon discovering there is an issue.
  2. If a parent approaches you with a problem unexpectedly, try to schedule a meeting at a later time so that you can have time to prepare for it; ask politely what the issue is and explain that you will look into the matter and get back to the parent.
  3. Keep written documentation of the meeting.
  4. If possible, have a third party present when you meet with the parent (e.g., an administrator) who can serve as a mediator if necessary (many school districts have parent/family liaisons who may be available to serve in this role).
  5. Listen to parents with an open mind, rather than thinking about how to respond; save thinking about how to respond until you have heard all of what they have to say.
  6. When the parents have finished speaking, convey that you heard what they said and rephrase it back to them to ensure that you heard them correctly (e.g., "I appreciate your taking time to share this with me. I hear you saying that you feel that Polly is not spending enough time in general education, is that correct?")
  7. Ask the parent to share what actions they feel will resolve the issue and give consideration to those that are within your school or district policies.
  8. Before leaving, make a list of actions for both you and the parent to take and come to agreement on what steps need to be taken, by whom, and in what time frame, to resolve the matter.
  9. End the meeting on a positive note by sharing something positive about the child with the parent.
  10. Follow-up with a phone call, e-mail, or note expressing again your appreciation for the opportunity to discuss the issue with the parent and reiterating the actions to be taken that you discussed.
  11. Keep a written log of the actions as they are accomplished and share that with the parent; follow-up after all actions listed have been completed to ensure that the parents' issue is resolved.

FIGURE 4.4 Tips for Working Collaboratively with Families

COMMUNICATION   Communication, often cited as critical to the family-educator relationship, takes on added importance when the student is unable to speak or otherwise communicate what happens on a daily basis. Unfortunately, some research suggests that families are dissatisfied with the communication between themselves and their child's teacher. "'Communication is a one-way street,' 'I have to do all of the initiating,' 'The only time the teacher sends me a note is when there is a problem'" (Spann, Kohler, & Soenksen, 2003, p. 235). Informal means of communicating with parents can be very important, especially for those families whose children lack sufficient functional communication skills to relay information about their school day. Informal options such as communication logs or notebooks sent to and from home daily, e-mail, or periodic conferences may be useful in establishing open lines of communication with families. Even if a child lacks functional communication, parents of nonverbal children are able to determine the success of a day based on their children's behavior (Stoner & Angell, 2006). Trust is a critical factor in communication between school personnel and parents; as parental trust of the school increased and perceived problems decreased, the need for communication by the parents increased (Stoner & Angell, 2006).

TRUSTING RELATIONSHIP   As illustrated in previous sections, trust is central to a collaborative partnership between home and school. In their research with parents, Stoner et al. (2005) identified teacher dispositions that either enhanced trust or reduced trust. Trust-enhancing characteristics in teachers included "having the heart to teach" (p. 48), being consistently positive, and being willing to do whatever was necessary to assist the parents' child. Trust-reducing characteristics included negativity, limited or insufficient communication, and personnel doing no more than they were forced to do. In addition, increased communication is associated with greater trust, and shared desires and priorities are associated with enhanced communication, also resulting in greater trust. Again, teachers are encouraged to get to know not only their students with autism, but their families as well.

Getting to Know the Child and Family

The author remembers when her daughter went to kindergarten. About a week before school even started the teacher sent home a questionnaire for her and her husband to fill out so that the teacher could get to their child to some degree. In first grade, about a week before school, a postcard arrived in the mail from the teacher just to say hello and to welcome the family and child to the class. Both teachers made the author, as a parent, feel more at ease and a part of the going-to-school process. This is important for all teachers to do, especially considering the close relationship that often forms between teachers of children with disabilities and their parents. Figure 4.3, the Family Needs Assessment presented earlier (p. 104), is an example of a questionnaire that can be filled out by parents to help teachers learn more about a student and his or her family. It can be adapted for any age level; its intent is to elicit from families information to help teachers teach their child better. Figure 4.5, a

---

Who Am I?

My name is _____

I like to be called _____

Some of my favorite things/activities are _____

Some things I do not like are _____

I am really good at _____

I am not so good at _____

One thing my family wishes you knew about me is _____

_____

FIGURE 4.5 Who Am I? Sheet

WHO AM I?

Georgia, Age 8

Wants to be the first
woman president

Loves cooking,
arts/crafts, and playing

Can run really fast, is a
good reader

Does not like mean
people

Sometimes gets
distracted

FIGURE 4.6 Completed "Who Am I?" Example
Courtesy of Susan Gaetz

"Who Am I?" Sheet, includes more open-ended questions that family members can answer to provide teachers with even more information about the children in their class. Figure 4.6 is a completed "Who Am I?" Sheet. To complete the "Who Am I?" Sheet, start with a picture or drawing of the child in the center of the page. Then add prompts written in the first person, such as "My favorite thing to do is _____ ." We recommend that you elicit information from a variety of family members (including the students themselves as appropriate) at least once per year, and especially when they are coming into the program for the first time. You might complete the sheet with the family in the form of an interview or simply send the sheet home. Either way, it is important to follow up with parents to determine if they have anything to add that was not addressed and to make sure you understand everything they are sharing. Taking the time to interact with parents and solicit their input can prevent or diffuse the trust issues mentioned above.

Keep in mind, however, that some parents may feel uncomfortable answering some of the questions or completing a "Who Am I?" Sheet. Don't pressure them; an informal conversation may be a better option for these parents, or you may need to wait until they are more comfortable with you and special education before you try again. Showing genuine interest and making efforts to get to know the child are the objectives.

SIBLINGS

Autism affects the entire family, not just the parents. There may be grandparents, aunts and uncles, or other family members who are equally as involved as the parents. Teachers may feel that their primary involvement with the family is with the parents. However, understanding the needs of the family unit and recognizing that the family unit impacts the overall development of everyone in the family (including the child with autism) is an important part of being a teacher of children with autism. In this section, we will examine the impact of autism on one familial group in particular: siblings.

Impact of Autism on Siblings

Siblings of children with autism have been the focus of research in recent years for a variety of reasons. Children with autism frequently require a great deal of their parents' attention, time, and energy. When there are other children in the family, parents may worry about the effects of autism on their other children (Biernat, 2000). Although some research has shown that having a sibling with autism has a positive impact on children (Hastings, 2003; Kaminsky & Dewey, 2001), the majority of studies have found that siblings of children with autism are negatively affected. Some negative impacts include less intimacy, fewer interactions, less nurturance, and negative relationships with parents (Hastings, 2003; Kaminsky & Dewey, 2001; Orsmond & Seltzer, 2007; Rivers & Stoneman, 2003). Rivers and Stoneman (2003) found that the greater the stress level of the parents, the more negative the sibling relationships, particularly when there were marital stressors. Most research, however, has focused on the psychosocial and emotional adjustment of children when they have a sibling with an ASD. Results of these studies have been inconsistent, as noted by Macks and Reeve (2007): "Some studies have reported poor adjustment, higher rates of depression, and poor social competence. . . . However, other studies have reported siblings . . . are typically well-adjusted, with positive self-concepts and good social competence. . . ." (p. 1061). Most recent research supports difficulties with adjustment for siblings of children with ASD, although Macks and Reeve report a paucity of ASD sibling research (2007).

ADJUSTMENT   Previous studies have identified a number of factors associated with increased risk for adjustment problems for siblings of children with autism, such as number of children in the family, socioeconomic status, gender, and birth order (Macks & Reeve, 2007). Specifically, "females and siblings from two-child families are at a greater risk for poor adjustment" (Macks & Reeve, 2007, p. 1061). The number of children in the family may affect adjustment. For example, when there are more children, they can share the responsibilities of helping to care for their sibling with an ASD among them. In addition, siblings in families with more than two children have someone they can talk to and relate to about living with someone with an ASD (Macks & Reeve, 2007). Age of siblings may also be a factor: "Older siblings appear to have greater difficulty with feelings, behaviors, and coping abilities . . .   [as well as] higher rates of internalizing and externalizing behavior problems" (Macks & Reeve, 2007, p. 1061). Despite inconsistent evidence regarding specific factors associated with poor adjustment, recent research supports that adjustment problems may be an issue for siblings of children with ASD.

Ross and Cuskelly (2006) assessed psychological adjustment of 25 siblings with ASD using maternal report as well as structured sibling interviews. Of interest in this study was the degree to which the sibling's understanding of ASD and/or the strategies they used to cope with the siblings impacted their adjustment. Consistent with other researchers (Gold, 1992, as cited in Ross & Cuskelly, 2006), the researchers found significantly higher levels of both internalizing (e.g., depression) and externalizing (e.g., aggression) behaviors than would be expected in the normal population. Whereas 84% of siblings in this study were found to engage in aggression toward their sibling with ASD, the authors note that this may reflect typical sibling interactions and may not be directly related to the ASD. Neither coping strategies nor understanding of ASD were found to be correlated with level of adjustment, suggesting that these areas do not impact the degree to which a sibling of a child with an ASD will have internalizing or externalizing behaviors greater than the norm.

In their study comparing 51 siblings of children with ASD to 35 siblings of children without disabilities, Macks and Reeve (2007) found that the siblings of children with ASD had a more positive self-concept than siblings of children without disabilities. "They were much more likely to have a positive view of their behavior, intelligence, scholastic performance, and anxiety than were siblings of non-disabled children. These children also had a more positive view of their overall personal characteristics" (p. 1065). The researchers posit that these positive responses may be attributable to the siblings of someone with ASD comparing themselves to that sibling. "It would only be natural to assume that these children would view themselves favorably in such a comparison" (p. 1065). Another explanation offered by Macks and Reeve is based on Gray's (1998) findings that siblings of children with autism are frequently more mature than those of children without disabilities. "Perhaps this maturity leads to improved behavior, better social skills, and improved academic performance, thereby increasing their overall self-concept" (p. 1065). Interestingly, parental reports in this study were more negative than the siblings' self-reports. The authors suggest this may be due to less opportunity to observe the behaviors of their children without autism, given the time and attention taken by the one with autism. One purpose of the study was to identify risk factors that would predict poor psychological adjustment among siblings of children with autism. These risk factors included gender (male), low SES, more than one sibling, and being younger than the child with autism. Though inconsistent with the findings of Macks and Reeves (2007, as noted previously), these findings are consistent with the work of Hastings (2003) who found that younger siblings of children with autism and those who were male had more behavioral problems. Interestingly, having a sibling with autism did not itself appear to be a risk factor, but instead was a positive factor. The authors conclude that "children with autism may even have a positive influence on the life of the non-disabled sibling. However, when multiple . . . risk factors are present, it becomes more difficult for the non-disabled sibling to deal with the child with autism. . . . Hence, the presence of a child with autism appears to have an increasingly negative effect on the non-disabled sibling as the number of . . . risk factors increase" (p. 1065).

In the previous sections we have identified how siblings of children with autism may be impacted as a result of their sibling's autism. Given the discrepancies, more research is needed to clarify these "risk factors" as well as to determine how teachers and parents can help these children overcome these issues. One additional area with regard to siblings cannot be overlooked—that of adulthood. For many of these siblings, once their parents are no longer alive or able to care for their adult child with autism, the burden falls to the sibling or siblings. Although research supports that finding a suitable living situation for their adult siblings with ASD (e.g., a group home) is a common experience of surviving children once their parents pass away, they may feel guilt about having to move their sibling from their parents' home, even though no one remains there to care for them (Benderix, Nordstrom, & Sivberg, 2006).

FAMILY ISSUES ACROSS THE LIFESPAN

In this section we examine the changing role of families as well as their changing needs across the lifespan of an individual with an ASD.

Infancy and Early Childhood

As discussed earlier in this chapter, upon initial diagnosis, parents and other family members may mourn the "loss" of the child they had hoped for. Although they may come to terms and "accept" the disorder as a part of their lives, it is important that professionals realize that depression, anger, and denial can recur at any time, especially in the early years after diagnosis. Further, this is the time when families may be having more children, thereby creating some of the sibling issues and concerns mentioned in a previous section. Parents may become concerned over the well-being of their other children or feel guilt over the time and attention they bestow on their child with autism. Finally, intensive early intervention may take time and resources that the family would otherwise share among their children, which may foster feelings of guilt in the parents or resentment in the siblings. In these early years, families are learning to navigate the educational system, researching treatments, and perhaps trying a variety of options to determine that which brings about the most success. Many parents mention a feeling of urgency as the child gets older, and this urgency may create a feeling of panic or that time is "running out" to find the best treatment approach. Further, with some parents and even professionals suggesting that autism can be cured with a particular treatment, or that children may "outgrow" their autism, the early years may be a time of both hope and disappointment as parents begin to face the reality that autism is a lifelong disorder. The move from early intervention to early childhood special education is the first of many **transitions** for a child with autism. IDEA 2004 allows for an EI professional to accompany a parent to an IEP meeting to help ease transition issues and to help the parent feel more comfortable with the process.

Elementary School Years

Issues at home are at the forefront even when children with autism head off to school. Whereas there may have been some help through the EI system to address problem behaviors that influence the activities of daily life, many parents still struggle with routines such as getting a child ready for school. Dependency on sameness can hamper spontaneous family activities and create difficulties in the daily transition from home-to-school environments (Larson, 2006).

Parents of children in elementary school may have decided on the treatments that they believe work best for their son or daughter, and may be more relaxed in their pursuit of knowledge about this disorder. During this time, however, physicians may prescribe a variety of medications and make adjustments to those medications for the child with an ASD. The school years may be the time when a child with Asperger Syndrome is first diagnosed. Families of these children will face the same issues as those with younger children when their child is first diagnosed (e.g., stages of grief). It is important to be sensitive to the reaction of diagnosis by families and to have available resources for families to help them better understand both the disorder and their options for treatment at home and school.

Also during the elementary years, families may become more aware of the differences between their child and others without autism. As children age, the gaps in their language and cognitive abilities become more pronounced. Families may have concerns over a lack of friends and social opportunities for their child with an ASD. Whereas some families may encourage inclusion in order to promote more interactions with typically developing peers, others may have concerns that being in a general education classroom will further exacerbate and draw attention to their child's differences and challenges. The siblings of children with autism also may have concerns during the elementary school years. For example, some siblings may have issues with going to the same school as their sibling with autism. Consider Mark, whose younger sibling Madeline has autism. When the school team decided to move Madeline from the early childhood special education program she was attending to kindergarten in her neighborhood school, Mark began to act out behaviorally in his third grade class. His teacher reported a short temper, noncompliance, irritability, and even cussing—behaviors she had never before seen in Mark. One of Madeline's team members realized Mark's behavior might be a result of concerns over having his sister with autism at "his" school. When the counselor talked with him about it, he discovered that Mark had told only a handful of friends about his sister's disability, believing that no one would ever find out. Now with her impending arrival on the home campus, Mark feared what his peers would think both about him and about his baby sister. During elementary school, professionals may need to be more considerate of the siblings and willing to provide support and information when needed.

Transition needs for the child and family at the end of the elementary school years include preparing students for differences in middle school and high school. Often this is the first time students are exposed to an interdisciplinary approach where students go to different classes every 50 minutes or so. Because children with autism often have difficulty with transition, professionals will need to work with the family to make sure proper supports are in place to make these daily transitions as smooth as possible.

Adolescence

The teen years, beginning in middle school, are often challenging even for families of typically developing children. Many parents of children without disabilities dread the onset of puberty. The same is true for parents of children with autism. However, for some parents, particularly of children who are lower functioning, puberty may take them by surprise. Having heard their child described as "functioning" at a lower level for most of his or her educational career, the onset of puberty may be a wake-up call for families that heretofore thought of their child as always a child. Families must deal with many issues when their child with autism enters puberty. For females, the onset of menstruation is of greatest concern. Hygiene skills become critical during menstruation, and because of the relative infrequency of opportunities to practice using feminine products, these skills may take a while to teach. For males, puberty brings a very different, but just as challenging, issue. While higher-functioning children can be taught that masturbatory behaviors in public are not appropriate, the concept of appropriateness may be more difficult for lower-functioning students. Further, until the lesson is learned, teachers must deal with the issue. A common recommendation is to remove the student from view of others so as not to draw attention to the issue and also to find ways to prevent the student from becoming aroused in the first place (e.g., wearing belted pants rather than elastic banded waists may prevent manual access). Professionals are cautioned to speak with families immediately when masturbation becomes an issue. Although some families will accept masturbation as a normal part of puberty, others may have religious or cultural beliefs that impact their reaction to this change in their son's behavior. Teachers should be considerate of any and all such cultural beliefs. It is also important for teachers to understand that females may also engage in masturbatory behaviors. Finally, with regard to puberty, lessons in sexuality may be necessary to educate and protect youth with ASD. Parents often cite concerns over sexual predators; still others have concerns over their child's sexual acting-out behaviors and the "message" they send to others.

In addition to puberty issues, adolescents with ASD are like all other teenagers: they want increased independence and autonomy. Consider Alan, who at age 17 realized that most of his peers were driving, prompting him to decide that he should be driving as well. Although verbal and mostly independent in many areas, Alan has autism, and his parents were concerned for his safety if he were to get behind the wheel of a car. However, they conceded that he could take a driver's education class, suspecting rightfully that he would quickly discover how difficult such a task would be for him. The instructor convinced Alan that he needed to wait a while before attempting to get his license. However, his father continued to teach him, and when he was 20 Alan got his first driver's license. When asked how he felt about this, Alan responded, "GREAT! Finally I don't have to have my parents with me everywhere I go!" Increasing opportunities for independence should be a priority for adolescents with ASD. In addition, teachers should work with families to identify age-typical activities that the child with an ASD can participate in actively and successfully.

At adolescence, transition becomes less about moving from class to class and more about deciding and planning for what children with autism will do once they leave the school environment at the age of 18–21. IDEA mandates that a formal transition plan be in place by the time a child is

16, but most professionals begin the process of transition as soon as the child enters high school. Any plan for a child's postsecondary outcomes must be made in consultation with the families. Some families want their child to have a job and live independently or in a group setting while others expect a child to live at home. Each of these options has very different implications for how a teacher will help prepare a student for life outside of school. Parents, therefore, must be at the center of this planning process.

Adulthood

Children with autism grow up and become adults with autism. Although teachers will work with a particular child only during their childhood and/or youth, families will be responsible for that child's well-being throughout his or her life. As discussed in the previous section, as adults with autism age, and their parents pass on, siblings begin to take on increased responsibility for their care—a task they may not be emotionally, psychologically, or financially ready to take on. As teachers, we need to be aware of potential difficulties in adulthood and to be willing to discuss these difficulties with the entire family before the child with autism graduates or ages out of public schools. Preparing the family for adulthood requires careful research on the part of professionals, who may be the first to broach the subject with families. Teachers should familiarize themselves with adult service agencies within their community that work specifically with individuals on the autism spectrum. If possible, visit these places to determine their appropriateness for the students with whom you work and compile a list of reputable and successful agencies and programs that families may contact as they near transition to adulthood for their student with autism.

Summary

Autism presents a variety of challenges to the family, from getting a diagnosis, evaluating treatment options, navigating the special education system, and minimizing the effect on siblings. Teachers must be aware of how the characteristics of families with children with autism may differ from those of families of children without disabilities. Further, educators must be aware that families' needs may change over time and differ by culture. By collaborating with families, developing a relationship, and recognizing that parents know their child best and have valuable information to share, teachers can help promote positive school experiences for all.

Chapter Review Questions

1. How does autism impact parents? How are siblings affected by autism? (Objectives 1 and 2)
2. What are a parent's options for supplemental services for a child with autism? (Objective 3)
3. What effects does autism have on the family during infancy? Once the child is ready for elementary school? As a teenager? (Objective 4)
4. What impact does transition from high school to adult life have on the family? What support services are available for family members? (Objective 5)

Key Terms

Internet Resources

National Dissemination Center for Children
   with Disabilities:*http: //www.nichcy.org/resources/
   autism.asp*
Families for Early Autism Treatment:*http: //www.feat.
   org/Default.aspx*

Autism Society of America:*http: //www.autism-society.
   org/site/PageServer*

References

Bendrix, Y., Nordstrom, B., & Sivberg, B. (2006). Parents' experience of having a child with autism and learning disabilities living in a group home: A case study. *Autism, 10*(6), 629–641.

Benson, P., Karlof, K. L., & Siperstein, G. N. (2008). Maternal involvement in the education of young children with autism spectrum disorders. *Autism, 12*(1), 47–63.

Biernat, K. A. (2000). To raise a son with autism. *Focus on Autism and Other Developmental Disabilities, 15*(4), 206–207.

Blatcher, J., & McIntyre, L. L. (2006). Syndrome specificity and behavioural disorders in young adults with intellectual disability: Cultural differences in family impact. *Journal of Intellectual Disability Research, 50*(3), 184–198.

Boyd, B. A. (2002). Examining the relationship between stress and lack of social support in mothers of children with autism. *Focus on Autism and Other Developmental Disabilities, 17*(4), 208–215.

Coonrod, E. E, & Stone, W. L. (2004). Early concerns of parents and children with autistic and nonautistic disorders. *Infants and Young Children, 17*(3), 258–268.

Crockett, J. L., Fleming, R. K., Doepke, K. J., & Stevens, J. S. (2007). Parent training: Acquisition and generalization of discrete trials teaching skills with parents of children with autism. *Research in Developmental Disabilities, 28*, 23–36.

Cuccaro, M. L., Wright, H. H., Rownd, C. V., Waller, J., & Fender, D. (1996). Brief report: Professional perceptions of children with developmental difficulties: The influence of race and socioeconomic status. *Journal of Autism and Developmental Disorders, 26*(4), 461–469.

Dale, E., Jahoda, A., & Knott, F. (2006). Mother's attributions following their child's diagnosis of Autism Spectrum Disorder: Exploring links with maternal levels of stress, depression and expectations of their child's future. *Autism 10*(5), 463–479.

Gray, D. E. (1998). *Autism and the family: Problems, prospects, and coping with the disorder.* Springfield, IL: Charles C. Thomas.

Grey, D. E. (2002). Ten years on: A longitudinal study of families and children with autism. *Journal of Intellectual and Developmental Disability, 27*(5), 215–222.

Harrington, J. W., Patrick, P. A., Edwards, K. S., & Brand, D. A. (2006). Parental beliefs about autism; Implications for the treating physician. *Autism, 10*(5), 452–462.

Hastings, R. P. (2003). Brief report: Behavioral adjustment of siblings of children with autism. *Journal of Autism and Developmental Disorders, 33*(1), 99–104.

Hastings, R. P., Kovshoff, H., Ward, N. J., degli Espinosa, F., Brown, T., & Remington, B. (2005). Systems analysis of stress and positive perceptions in mothers and fathers of pre-school children with autism. *Journal of Autism and Developmental Disorders, 35*(5), 635–644.

Hutton, A. M., & Caron, S. L. (2005). Experience of families with children with autism in rural New England. *Focus on Autism and Other Developmental Disabilities, 20*(3), 180–189.

Ivey, J. K. (2004). What do parents expect? A study of the likelihood and importance issues for children with autism spectrum disorders. *Focus on Autism and Other Developmental Disabilities, 19*(1), 27–33.

Jacobson, J. W, Mulick, J. A., & Green, G. (1998). Cost-benefit estimates for early intensive behavioral intervention for young children with autism. *Behavioral Interventions, 13,* 201–226.

Kaminsky, L., & Dewey, D. (2001). Sibling relationships of children with autism. *Journal of Autism and Developmental Disorders, 31*(4), 339–410.

Kingsley, E. (1987). Welcome to Holland. From http://www.upkidsoflawrencecounty.com/POEM.html, retrieved April 10, 2008.

Koubler–Ross, E. (1969). *On death and dying.* New York: MacMillan.

Krueger-Crawford, L. (2008) Holland Schmolland. From http://groups.msn.com/TheAutismHomePage/schmolland.msnw, retrieved April 10, 2008.

Kuhn, J. C, & Carter, A. S. (2006). Maternal self-efficacy and associated parenting cognitions among mothers of children with autism. *American Journal of Orthopsychiatry, 76*(4), 564–575.

Larson, E. (2006). Caregiving and autism: How does children's propensity for routinization influence participation in family activities? *OTJR: Occupation, Participation and Health, 26*(2), 69–76.

Lovaas, I, Koegel, R., Simmons, J. Q., & Long, J. S. (1973). Some generalization and follow-up measures on autistic children in behavior therapy. *Journal of Applied Behavior Analysis, 6,* 131–165.

Mack, R. J. & Reeve, R. E. (2007). The adjustment of non-disabled siblings of children with autism. *Journal of Autism and Development Disorders, 37*(6), 1060–1067.

Mandell, D. S., Listerud, J., Levy, S. E., & Pinto-Martin, J. (2002). Race differences in the age at diagnosis among Medicaid-eligible children with autism. *Journal of the American Academy of Child and Adolescent Psychiatry, 41*(12), 1447–1453.

Orsmond, G. I., & Seltzer, M. M. (2007b). Siblings of individuals with autism or Down Syndrome: Effects on adult lives. *Journal of Intellectual Disability Research, 51*(9), 682–696.

Rivers, J. W., & Stoneman, Z. (2003). Sibling relationships when a child has autism: Marital stress and support coping. *Journal of Autism and Developmental Disorders, 33*(4), 383–394.

Ross, P., & Cuskelly, M. (2006). Adjustment, sibling problems and coping strategies of brothers and sisters of children with Autistic Spectrum Disorder. *Journal of Intellectual and Developmental Disability, 31*(2), 77–86.

Roth, P. H. (2001). A mother's account. *Focus on Autism and Other Developmental Disabilities, 16*(1), 9–12.

Schwichtenberg, A., & Poehlmann, J. (2007). Applied behaviour analysis: Does intervention intensity relate to family stressors and maternal well-being? *Journal of Intellectual Disability Research, 51*(8), 598–605.

Siklos, S., & Kerns, K. A. (2007). Assessing the diagnosis of a small sample of parents of children with autism spectrum disorders. *Research in Developmental Disabilities, 28,* 9–22.

Smith, B., Chung, M. C., & Vostanis, P. (1994). The path to care in autism: Is it better now? *Journal of Autism and Developmental Disorders, 24,* 551–563.

Spann, S. J., Kohler, F. W., & Soenksen, D. (2003). Examining parents' involvement in and perceptions of special education services: An interview with families in a parent support group. *Focus on Autism and Other Developmental Disabilities, 18*(4), 228–237.

Stoner, J. B., & Angell, M. E. (2006). Parent perspectives on role engagement: An investigation of parents of children with ASD and their self-reported roles with education professionals. *Focus on Autism and Other Developmental Disabilities, 21*(3), 177–189.

Stoner, J. B., Bock, S. J., Thomson, J. R., Angell, M. E., Heyl, B. S., & Crowley, E. P. (2005). Welcome to our world: Parent perceptions of interactions between parents of young children with ASD and education professionals. *Focus on Autism and Other Developmental Disabilities, 20*(1), 39–51.

Tsai, L. Y. (2000). I learn about autism from my son and people like him. *Focus on Autism and Other Developmental Disabilities, 15*(4), 202–205.

Wakabayashi, A., Baron-Cohen, S., Uchiymam, T., Yoshido, Y., Tojo, Y., Kuroda, M., & Wheelwright, S. (2007). The Autism-Spectrum Quotient (AQ) children's version in Japan: A cross-cultural comparison. *Journal of Autism and Developmental Disorders, 37*, 491–500.

Welteroth, D. (2001). A parent perspective. *Focus on Autism and Other Developmental Disabilities, 16*(1), 9–12.

5

Environmental Planning

Brenda Smith Myles, Ph.D.
Autism Society of America

Kai-Chien Tien
Kun Shan University

Yu-Chi Chou, and Hyolung Lee
University of Kansas

CHAPTER OBJECTIVES

After reading this chapter, learners should be able to:

1. List the characteristics of individuals with Autism Spectrum Disorders (ASD) in terms of the ways they interact with the environment.

2. Identify environmental items that need to be modified based on the characteristics of individuals with ASD.

3. Identify visuals supports appropriate for individuals with ASD across settings.

4. List safety modifications that can be made in the home and community for individuals with ASD.

 CASE STUDY Examples

The following three examples illustrate common environmental needs that individuals with ASD encounter regularly, such as coping with noises, lights, and crowds. These slight disturbances may be easily ignored by people in the environment because they are more focused on the ongoing activities. However, these small details could be the main factors that prevent individuals with ASD from participating in the activities like other people do. Fortunately, several environmental supports could make huge differences in their participation of daily activities and enhance their quality of life.

Case of Aaron

Aaron is a third grader in Mrs. Taylor's class. Mrs. Taylor thinks that Aaron has a unique sense of humor and is a very polite student. Everyone in his class knows that Aaron's main interests are dinosaurs and rockets. Mrs. Taylor is amazed at his incredible knowledge of these subjects as well as his enthusiasm that keeps him talking continuously. Other than those areas of interest, Aaron is easily distracted by various stimuli such as posters on the wall, outside noises, or even very slight sounds that anyone else in the room can barely hear. Aaron has even commented on the tick-tock sound of Mrs. Taylor's watch.

Mrs. Taylor has tried to minimize visual or auditory distractions by seating Aaron toward the front of the class, facing away from the posters on the wall, the door, and the windows. In addition, she applies Aaron's interests in many ways, including using dinosaur pictures for the self-checklist to organize his supplies and making social narratives to explain the importance of finishing his independent work in the name of the National Aeronautics and Space Administration (NASA). Those strategies have been successful in getting his attention and in motivating him to participate in activities. In addition, Mrs. Taylor has conferred with a special education teacher to update and develop more repertoires of his interests. By doing so, Mrs. Taylor could tailor her instructions according to Aaron's special interests or encourage him in developing a variety of interests for maximizing class participation.

Case of Jacob

Jacob is a 4-year-old boy who was diagnosed with ASD at the age of 2. On weekdays, he attends a preschool located near his house in the morning and spends the rest of the day with his mom at home. Jacob is very active and always in motion. He likes to jump up and down, run around, and climb high. In fact, on several instances Jacob has run out of the house and gotten lost. Jacob's mom is stressed and in a state of constant worry when Jacob is home because she has to spend every second watching him to prevent danger or injury.

At a family gathering, Jacob's mom expressed her frustration to Jacob's aunt, who is a special education teacher. A couple of days later, Jacob's aunt visited their home and helped Jacob's mom create a safer and more supportive home environment for Jacob. For example, they placed the sofas against the wall and put away some rarely used armchairs to create a large open area in the living room where Jacob can play unobstructed. They also securely screwed all the freestanding shelves and cabinets to the wall to prevent them from flipping over when Jacob climbs up on them. They used colored tape on the floor as boundary markers to create a small area in the corner of the living room to allow Jacob his own space to do any activity he wants. All of Jacob's toys and books were organized in see-through plastic boxes with labels designating the contents and stored in the lower level of the shelves so that he can have easy access. Furthermore, by Jacob's aunt's suggestion, a sensory monitoring system was installed on all of the doors and windows around the house so that his parents will be alerted when Jacob opens a door or window. In addition, a big stop sign was hung on the front door as a visual sign to tell Jacob not to open the door and leave the house alone.

After the home environment has been modified, Jacob's mom is now able to enjoy her afternoon with Jacob without constant worry. She can leave him alone playing in the living room for short periods of time—for example, while she is cooking in the kitchen or doing other housework in another room.

Case of Abbey

Abbey is a 6-year-old girl who has autism. She is particularly fond of reading books. She regularly attends the Parent-Child Fun Reading Club on Saturday mornings with her parents and her younger sister. The activity is held inside or outside of the community building, depending on the weather. The reading club usually lasts an hour and half.

In the beginning, Abbey had a hard time concentrating on reading the materials or listening to storytelling. She usually screamed and tried to run away, which was different from her behavior when she read at home. When the reading club was held outdoors, she usually ran away and stayed inside of the building the whole time.

Her parents consulted Abbey's special education teacher, who recognized possible reasons for Abbey's behavior at the community activity, including unpredictable noises in the environment, constant movement of other children, and the sunlight when they were outside. Therefore, the teacher and Abbey's parents came up with several solutions to assist Abbey with participating in this community activity. First, Abbey carries a headset along with her books. When the noise gets unbearable, she puts on her headset and reads the books she has brought. Second, the family arrives 5 minutes earlier to choose a suitable seat for Abbey to avoid placing her in the center of the crowd. For instance, she likes to sit at the corner with her younger sister or sit in front of the storyteller with the crowd behind her. Third, when the reading club is held outside, Abbey brings her sunglasses or wears her favorite hat to protect her from the sunlight. With these environment supports, Abbey no longer screams or runs away from the activity. Instead, she now looks forward to the reading club every Saturday morning. Also, Abbey's family now is less worried about unexpected incidents during the reading club and is very happy to have quality time with Abbey during this family event. Observed by her parents, Abbey and her younger sister are much closer because they have common interests and a preferred activity.

INTRODUCTION

Autism Spectrum Disorders (ASD), as discussed in previous chapters, can be understood with regard to the domains of social interaction, repetitive and stereotyped patterns of behavior, impaired **verbal communication**, and/or **nonverbal communication**, and sensory processing difficulties. In order to better draw correlations between individual student need relative to characteristic and environmental supports, the following paragraphs review the characteristics of individuals with ASD and their relationship to environmental needs.

According to the *Diagnostic and Statistical Manual of Mental Disorders,Fourth Edition* (*DSM-IV*; American Psychiatric Association [APA], 1994), *DSM-IV,* Text Revision (*DSMV-IV-TR*; APA, 2000), and the *International Classification of Diseases* (*ICD-10*; World Health Organization, 1993), ASD are neurological disorders that present challenges in social interaction, repetitive and stereotyped patterns of behavior, and verbal and/or nonverbal communication. Another noticeable characteristic, although currently not included in the official diagnosis, is sensory processing differences (Dunn, Myles, & Orr, 2002; Myles et al., 2004; Ornitz & Ritvo, 1968; Scheuermann & Webber, 2002).

Social Interaction

One of the most manifest characteristics of ASD with regard to social interaction is difficulty with nonverbal behaviors, such as eye contact and facial expressions (Kanner, 1943; Ornitz & Ritvo,

1968; Wing & Gould, 1979). Nonverbal behavior also includes body posture. In this area, individuals with ASD may display inflexible and awkward physical movement, further affecting social interactions. Given these characteristics the arrangement of the physical environment clearly plays an important role.

Individuals with ASD also are lacking in emotional expression and age-appropriate social skills. For example, in classroom activities, students with ASD may seldom engage in eye-to-eye contact or reciprocal interactions with the teacher or with peers. It is also common for individuals with ASD to show little interest in working or playing with people or in groups. For example, they demonstrate few socially meaningful interactions, such as taking turns, asking questions, or exchanging ideas. Instead, they may prefer visual or tangible objects. For these reasons, students with ASD very often need a lot of prompting and visual supports to achieve successful social interaction.

Repetitive and Stereotyped Patterns of Behavior

In terms of repetitive and stereotyped patterns of behavior, another of the core characteristics of ASD (Kanner, 1943; Ornitz & Ritvo, 1968; Rutter, 1978; Wing & Gould, 1979), individuals with ASD demonstrate varying levels of intensity in focusing on particular objects or preoccupation with restricted patterns of behaviors or activities. For instance, a student with ASD may devote repetitive hours to a certain computer program to the exclusion of anything else. In the same way, individuals with ASD display many routine-driven characteristics that may involve little functional importance, such as always walking in a straight line or arranging things in a particular way. Due to the intensity of focus and preference for sameness and predictability, change in routine activities, food, physical arrangements, and so on, may be a great challenge to persons with ASD (Koegle, Rincover, & Egel, 1987), and may lead to behavioral outbursts or anxiety. Related to repetitive and stereotypical behavior, self-stimulation is widespread, such as spinning, rocking, and so on. As discussed below, self-stimulation may be related to sensory processing problems; that is, it is serves as a means of obtaining additional sensory input.

Impaired Verbal and/or Nonverbal Communication

One of the most noticeable behaviors of individuals with ASD is impairment in verbal and/or nonverbal communication (Kanner, 1943; Rutter, 1978; Wing & Gould, 1979). For example, challenges in initiating or maintaining conversation with a social meaning or functional intention are common. Further, **echolalia**, repeating words that have been said by others, is not uncommon, nor are language comprehension difficulties. An example of discrepancy between language use and comprehension is that a person may very well articulate in telling a story but does not understand the theme or underlying meaning of it. As suggested earlier, social communication also causes challenges for this population, such as joint attention and the ability to pay attention to a topic or object shared by people in the same social situation (Mundy, Sigman, & Kasari, 1994). That is, students with ASD may not be able to be attentive and participate in a particular goal with other peers on group projects that require shared attention and idea exchanging. For these reasons, many students with ASD work with speech-language pathologists on a regular basis, and need a lot of communicative supports across settings, such as prompts on the playground for conversational initiatives. In this way, the skill learned could be generalized to a variety of social situations.

Sensory Processing Difficulties

Atypical response to sensory stimuli (Field et al., 1997) is another challenging area across the spectrum. Even though they are not directly addressed in the official diagnostic criteria, sensory processing difficulties are commonly recognized by research studies (Baranek, 1999; Baranek, Foster, & Berkson, 1997a, 1997b; Dunn, Myles, & Orr, 2002; Myles et al., 2004; Ornitz & Ritvo, 1968). Indeed, it has been suggested that some stereotyped behaviors or unique social responses are the results of sensory processing difficulties, such as auditory hypersensitivity, tactile defensiveness, sensorimotor differences, and so on. It is important to note that individuals with ASD may be hyper- or hyposensitive to noise, light, touch, and/or smell and that the condition varies from individual to individual and sometimes from setting to setting. It is generally agreed that the use of visual stimuli is the most effective way to catch and maintain the attention of individuals with ASD.

To conclude, the characteristics of individuals with ASD primarily include (a) challenges in social interaction, (b) displays of stereotyped behavior and narrow interests, (c) difficulties with communication skills, and (d) differences in sensory processing. In planning and promoting more supportive learning and living environments, it is important to take these characteristics into consideration. This chapter addresses environmental planning in general, including management of physical structures and the use of visual supports, followed by environmental planning for school, home, and community. In addition, the discussion includes implementation and evaluation. See Figure 5.4 on page 130 for a list of questions for school team members for environmental considerations and Figure 5.7 on page 135 for a home and community environment checklist in order to carry out an environmental plan.

STRATEGIES FOR CREATING A SUPPORTIVE ENVIRONMENT

In this section, strategies are introduced to give educators, parents, and community members an idea of what modifications could be made to rearrange the physical environment so that individuals with ASD could actively participate in their daily activities. In addition to rearranging the physical environment, the use of visual supports is an effective way to prepare and guide individuals with ASD on how to interact in various environments.

Modifications of the Physical Environment

Interaction with their environment can be frustrating for individuals with ASD when the environment is not supportive of their individual needs. Understanding specific individual needs as well as general characteristics of ASD is critical for providing appropriate supports and making modifications in various settings. A well-organized and predictable environment is often considered the most desirable condition for individuals with ASD.

The following paragraphs provide an overview of general considerations when making modifications of the physical environment. They are categorized as sensory considerations, assisting individual needs, school environment, and home environment. General considerations for the school environment include seating, learning space, and space for relaxation. Examples of general considerations for the home environment are also discussed.

SENSORY CONSIDERATIONS Lighting, sounds, smells, and temperature are the major sensory considerations when making modifications to the physical environment. Individuals with ASD who have sensory issues such as atypical sensory seeking or avoiding often need environmental modifications. Using soft light, screening bright windows, using earphones or ear plugs, wearing minimal amounts of perfume, and keeping proper room temperature are examples of what teachers or parents can do to modify the environment (Bellini, 2006). The *Adolescent/Adult Sensory Profile* (AASP; Brown & Dunn, 2002) is an example of an assessment one could use to determine a child's sensory needs. See Chapter 11 for more information on sensory issues for students with ASD.

More specifically, many individuals with ASD are sensitive to light, sound, touch, or smell. Use of blinds and curtains may prevent exposure to too much sunlight. An environment free of bright colors or patterns can help to modulate sensory processing. In terms of touch, feel and texture of carpets or furniture should be chosen based on children's level of comfort. Further, rooms may be arranged in ways that are conducive to quieter environments. Finally, portable items, such as sunglasses, headsets, and sensory items may improve and modulate sensory processing and can easily be transported to community environments.

ASSESSING INDIVIDUAL NEEDS   When a school or family team develops a **supportive environment**, it is important to keep in mind that no one solution fits all children. Consequently, it is important to assess individual needs as part of planning the classroom and home layout. In addition, teachers should take into consideration individual family needs and cultural differences (see Box 5.1). Teachers and parents may consider the following factors when arranging their classroom and home environment:

1. What aspects of the child's behavior have affected his/her interaction in the environment and therefore need to be included in the environmental plan?
   a. Sensory needs (e.g., hyper- or hyposensitivity to light, sounds, or smells)
   b. Anxiety
   c. Restrictive and repetitive pattern of behavior
   d. Level of understanding of visual or written cues
   e. Level of communication (e.g., using alternative augmentative communication devices or systems)
2. What is the appropriate seating accommodation for the child, based on the following considerations?
   a. Level of modifications for seating device: Can the child support herself or himself when sitting on a chair? Is a cushion needed to reduce sensory overload?
   b. Light
   c. Fresh air
   d. Distractions
   e. Personal space
   f. Traffic pattern
3. Where can the student store books, materials, and equipment? Are they easily accessible?
4. Are materials placed sequentially?
5. Are learning and leisure spaces clearly defined?
   a. Independent work
   b. Group work
   c. Leisure/Break
   d. Transition
   e. **Relaxing space**
6. Will visual cues be provided appropriately?
   a. Use of pictures, icons, symbols, and so on
   b. Labeling
   c. Color coding
7. Are there dangerous items or equipment to be considered?
   a. Electric outlets/cables
   b. Sharp objects
   c. Arrangement of furniture

BOX 5.1   Diversity Notes

McMahon, Malesa, Yoder, and Stone (2007) addressed family stressors especially related to parental concerns about having a second child with disabilities. Their research showed that parents of children with autism experience extensive stress, often at clinical levels. However, the study pointed out that little research has explored parental perceptions of the development of infants in families that have an older child with an ASD.

Koegel and Brown (2007) noted that the lack of a system of supports is a societal problem. As part of providing a supportive environment for families with children with disabilities, a social support system, quality intervention programs, lifespan planning, and other psychological supports that can reduce their depression, anxiety, and distress are needed. The challenged and unsafe environment can affect the entire family, regardless of the ability and disability level of the children.

Dunlap (2007) pointed to the importance of empowering parents and families as central members of intervention teams. The diversity of families' characteristics and cultural uniqueness must play an essential role if an intervention is to be successful.

School Environment

SEATING   Special seating may be appropriate for students with ASD who feel overwhelmed because of their sensory needs. In general, seating students away from bright windows, posters on the wall, doors, or hallways may be considered ways to reduce sensory stimuli and distractions. Depending on the classroom setup, seating in the front row in a classroom can be helpful to allow more personal space.

Alternative seating is another way to support students' learning. Alternative seating such as therapy balls have been found to be effective for improving students' engagement in classroom activities and in-seat behavior (see Research Box 5.2, Schilling & Schwartz, 2004). Further, typical seating devices such as chairs, benches, or carpet squares can be modified by using a specially designed inner seat or covering chair legs with soft fabric or tennis balls. This could reduce the sensory load and help students to modulate their sensory process.

BOX 5.2   Research Notes #1

The purpose of Schilling and Schwartz's study was to (a) investigate the effectiveness of therapy balls in in-seat behavior and maintained engagement and (b) assess teachers' perceptions of the intervention. Participants were four preschool children (3 years 11 months to 4 years 2 months) with a diagnosis of Autism Spectrum Disorders. A single-subject withdrawal design was employed within the natural classroom setting for a minimum of two school weeks. Momentary real-time sampling and frequency counts were used for data collection. The results indicated substantial improvements in both classroom seating and engagement after implementing the therapy ball intervention. Moreover, the results suggested a decrease in oppositional behavior of refusal to follow a routine teacher request. Finally, teachers reported positive classroom behavior as a result of the use of therapy balls.

Source: Information from Schilling, D. L., & Schwartz, I. S. (2007). Alternative seating for young children with autism spectrum disorder: Effects on classroom behavior. *Journal of Autism and Developmental Disorders, 34,* 423–432.

LEARNING SPACE   **Classroom layout**, such as the placement of learning materials, plays an important role in encouraging and structuring students' learning. As mentioned, a predictable and visual learning environment is very beneficial for students with ASD. **Accessibility** of materials and resources for learning within the classroom is also important for motivating and keeping students' interests. Materials may be made accessible by arranging them into learning sections and by placing materials on a table or desk, thereby guiding students to the right place (McClannahan & Krantz, 1999). Color coding and labeling materials are also effective ways to organize materials as they appeal to students' visual learning style.

SPACE FOR RELAXATION   Individuals with ASD often have challenges regulating and controlling their emotions. A home base, a quiet and separate place in the school, and a defined area in the classroom are examples of locations where students can restore calm and relax when their emotions and anxiety start to escalate (Myles, 2005; Myles & Adron, 2001). This includes those occasions when they are overwhelmed by sensory overload and they need to get away from light, sounds, people, and so on.

CREATING A SAFE ENVIRONMENT

Safety is a significant concern in the home. Installing gates in stairwells and doorways, covering electrical outlets, and equipping cabinets with childproof locks are examples of ways to make the home environment safe. Examples of **environmental modifications** at home include the following:

- Arranging the furniture to make rooms easier to navigate to prevent children from getting hurt by bumping into things
- Storing unnecessary materials and keeping a center space clean to prevent children from stumbling when mobility is a concern
- Using safety locks or putting handles higher than a child's height to secure dangerous items, such as cleaning products and other chemicals, medications, and so on
- Safeguarding windows and stairs
- Covering electrical outlets and knobs on appliances
- Organizing everyday items, especially cleaning supplies or prescription drugs and keeping them out of children's reach
- Providing appropriate alternative seating devices, if necessary, such as inner seats to keep children from falling
- Using visual supports, including signs or symbols with or without written words, such as a stop sign at the entrance door
- Keeping bath items and toys away from the tub and unavailable until after bathing
- Planning proper fire and other evacuation procedures

The aforementioned modifications give parents and caregivers strategies to keep a safe home environment for children with ASD. Parents and caregivers are also encouraged to consult with their child's teacher regarding implementing the safety devices used in the school environment so that there is consistent guidance for the child to follow at home.

VISUAL SUPPORTS

Because individuals with ASD tend to be strong visual processors and learners, visual supports are highly effective with this population (Cardon, 2007; Savner & Myles, 2000.) **Visual supports** come in many different forms, such as objects, photographs, pictures, symbols, signs, and written words, and are used to increase comprehension of language and environmental expectations as well as to provide **structure** and predictability by allowing individuals with ASD to scan, select, and make sense of the relevant and important details in the environment, thus helping them to understand what is happening to and around them.

It is generally agreed that for learners with ASD, information presented visually is easier to process and comprehend than information that is presented verbally. In addition, because information presented visually is more concrete than verbal information, it allows for greater processing time. In short, visual supports not only help individuals with ASD to be better prepared for changes in setting and routines, but also assist them in learning concepts, clarifying information, organizing their thoughts, making transitions in the environment, and understanding unfamiliar situations and cues presented by others.

Examples of visual supports that may be used to accommodate and support the needs of individuals with ASD at home, in school, and in the community include visual schedules, choice boards, boundary markers, maps, and labeling.

VISUAL SCHEDULES   **Visual schedules** present abstract concepts such as time in a more concrete and manageable form. For instance, a visual schedule gives a child a clear sense of what activity is going on right now and what is next. By making clear when activities, tasks, or classes will occur, visual schedules allow individuals with ASD to anticipate upcoming events and activities. This in turn allows them to develop an understanding of time and facilitates the ability to predict change, thereby reducing anxiety about the unknown. Further, by showing when a preferred activity comes amidst activities or tasks that may be uncomfortable and unpleasant, visual schedules serve as motivators.

Visual schedules may be created to present a range of information. For example, visual schedules may come in the form of a daily schedule of activities that must be completed during each time period, or a schedule of activities that must be completed over a longer period of time. Decisions about what and how the information is presented on the visual schedule and where the schedule is displayed should be based on the individual's specific characteristics and preferences, including age and developmental needs. It is important to ensure that the individual understands the information on the visual schedule and knows how to access it. Therefore, careful consideration should also be given to the format of the visual schedule and how and where it will be used.

The information on a visual schedule may be presented through written words, objects, photographs, line drawings, symbols, or a combination thereof. Furthermore, depending on their function, visual schedules may be displayed in different settings and made in different formats. For instance, a daily or weekly visual schedule may take the form of a big poster placed on the board, and an activity schedule may be simply a small strip that is set on the student's desk. Figure 5.1 provides a sample of a visual schedule for a child with ASD.

CHOICE BOARDS   A choice board presents available choices in a visual rather than, or in addition to, a verbal format. The use of a visual display provides the individual with an ASD time to see and comprehend all the possible choices, to think about the potential choices, and to consider the available options as frequently as necessary prior to making a decision. Most important, choice boards allow users a sense of control over certain situations and consequently reduce situational behavior problems that are caused by uncertainty and anxiety.

In terms of creating a supportive environment for this population, it is beneficial to utilize choice boards across environments, such as the classroom, the dining room, the living room, and so on, for any activities that involve the individual with an ASD. For example, you may create a food choice board in the dining room as a visual support to tell a child with an ASD what options she has for a snack or a sensory activity choice board in the classroom to show a student what choice of

FIGURE 5.1   Sample Visual Schedule for My Morning Class

sensory input she has (for example, jumping on the trampoline or swinging). As for visual schedules, the choices on a choice board may be presented through pictures, words, or objects, or a combination thereof. Figure 5.2 is an example of what a choice board may look like.

BOUNDARY MARKERS   Boundary markers are **visual cues** that can be used to guide individuals with ASD through physical spaces within the environment by delimiting areas for study, play, and so on. Boundary markers may be made by arranging rugs, bookcases, and other furniture to serve as barriers, or by attaching colored tape to the floor to define areas for specific activities.

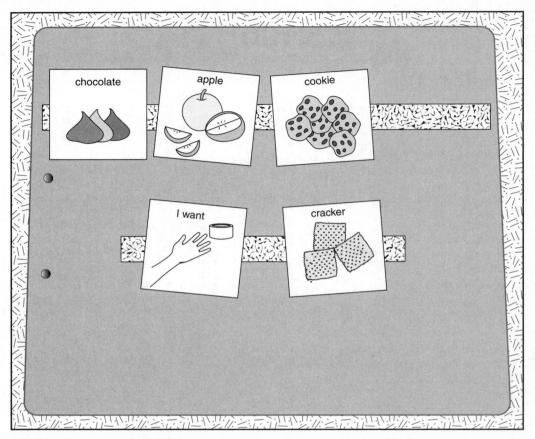

FIGURE 5.2 Sample Choice Board

MAPS Maps can help individuals with ASD to scan an environment and analyze and select relevant details while ignoring irrelevant details and to further elicit meaning and purpose. For example, simple maps of the layout of the classroom or the route to the gym help orient students with ASD to new settings and serve as a reference for locating materials or moving from one room or building to another. In addition, maps can further help reduce anxiety from distractions and overwhelming sensory stimulation while highlighting the critical important information in an environment. Figure 5.3 is an example of a map used in a classroom to tell a student with an ASD where the various activity areas in the classroom are.

LABELING Labeling is one of the simplest and easiest ways to provide visual supports. The main purpose of using labels is to provide cues to help individuals with ASD to function efficiently and independently. In school, home, and community environments, labeling may be used on shelves, drawers, and cupboard and closet doors to (a) show what and where to find and return items; (b) designate an individual's personal space and belongings and thereby help identify personal possessions; or (c) assist in accentuating the organization of the space by demarcating activity areas, such as the art table, the play rug, the work table, the leisure area, the break corner, and the book table.

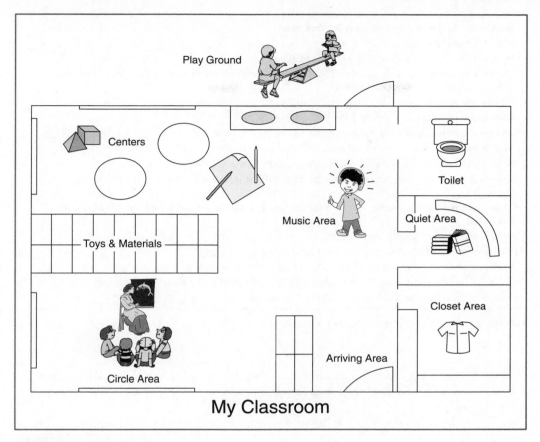

FIGURE 5.3 Sample Map

To conclude, this section provides educators, parents, and caregivers with a general overview of what could be modified in the physical environment in order to create a safer and more appropriate environment based on the sensory challenges and the unique patterns of behavior displayed by children with ASD. Environmental modification includes physical environment arrangement, seating/learning space/relaxation place, as well as visual supports such as visual schedules, choice boards, boundary markers, maps, and labeling.

MAKING IT WORK

The following paragraphs discuss how to plan and implement environmental supports at school as well as at home and community. Examples of how to arrange classroom settings and organize learning materials are illustrated. Also, strategies for creating a safer and more appropriate home environment to meet the needs of children with ASD are provided.

Environmental Planning in Schools

IMPORTANCE OF UNDERSTANDING STUDENTS WITH ASD   Getting a clear picture of the student's needs and characteristics based on observation, interviews, and other forms of data collection

---

Questions To Be Answered by a School Team

Who is the student?

What are the student's strengths and difficulties?

What is so unique about the student? (e.g., unique behaviors, communication skills, learning abilities, social skills, special interests)

What is the educational goal (long- and short-term) for the student?

What is the priority in supporting the student?

What is the most significant challenge to supporting the student?

What is the most desirable outcome for this student this school year?

What is the least desirable outcome for this student this school year?

What was the most successful outcome for this student last year? (including modifications or strategies)

What was the least successful outcome for this student last year? (including modifications or strategies)

What is the student's daily schedule?

In what settings will the student participate throughout the day?

What has been done to support the student academically and socially in these settings?

What can be done to better support the student academically and socially in these settings?

What is each team member's role in supporting the student?

FIGURE 5.4   A List of Questions for Team Members

is critical for preparing a successful environment (Koegel & Koegel, 2006; Myles, 2005). Figure 5.4 is a list of questions that school team members need to address to understand the student and his or her environment.

By developing a snapshot of the learner together, team members get the "big picture" of themselves as well as the student and his environment. One can gather information as to the child's present level of performance in a variety of skill domains (e.g., self help, communication, academic, etc.) through examination of the Individualized Education Program (IEP.) However, information specific to sensory issues (e.g., sensitivity to light or sound) may not be available as part of the IEP and thus may require additional observations or interviews with caregivers and former teachers.

Making the Classroom Work for All Students

A well-organized classroom is the cornerstone of providing meaningful opportunities to learn. Careful and thoughtful development of the classroom layout, taking into consideration all students' needs, should include everything from work space, to accessibility of materials, to areas for relaxation, and so on. Such data-based planning helps both teachers and students. Teachers are better prepared and don't need to spend valuable instructional time searching for materials, moving students around when problems occur, and so on. Students with ASD, in turn, benefit from an orderly environment as it helps them develop greater independence and reduce anxiety and subsequent problem behaviors often caused by unpredictable situations.

Organizing various areas in a classroom increases predictability for students. Instructional areas are often set up as "centers" or "stations," which designate either (a) the type of skill to be taught in that area (e.g., math) or the type of activity (e.g., free time) or (b) the type of instruction (e.g., one-to-one, independent, small group).

Stations or centers at the elementary level based on the type of skill may include:

- Math
- Reading/Writing
- Self-Help
- Pretend Play
- Sensory
- Building Vocabulary

At the secondary level, stations or centers based on the type of skill may include:

- Math
- Language Arts
- Vocational
- Independent Living
- Community Use
- Self-Help

Stations or centers based on general activities in a classroom may include:

- Snack or Group Activities
- Play or Leisure
- Transition
- Relaxing/Quiet Place

Stations or centers based on type of instruction may include:

- Independent Work
- One-to-one Instruction
- Small-group Instruction
- Whole-class Instruction

Clearly defined spaces can help students to know what they are supposed to do and what they can expect will happen in a given area, as well as to understand where to go and when to start and stop an activity. Figure 5.5 is an example of a well-organized classroom layout for all students. Note that in the example in Figure 5.5, shelves are used to separate different areas of the classroom; this provides the visual boundary needed for students with ASD as well as promotes easy access to materials needed in that area. Room dividers and tables can provide additional visual boundaries, as can color-coding areas (e.g., red chairs at the one-to-one work areas, blue chairs at the small group area, etc.).

Teachers can also ensure that their instruction is presented in an orderly and organized manner. For example, using simple directions and minimizing unnecessary words can enable students to focus and, therefore, to work more independently. Further, having materials and forms for data collection handy before beginning instruction cuts down on the time between arriving at the location and beginning instruction, thereby increasing the likelihood that the student will begin to associate a particular area of the room with specific activities or instructional strategies. Another way to ensure this shortened wait time is to make sure that all adults in the room know with whom they are to be working, on what activities, and where at all times throughout the day. Given that most self-contained classrooms will likely have a variety of children working on a number of different IEP objectives each day across different functioning levels, it is often difficult to create meaningful large-group activities for the class. Teachers must rely on small-group activities or one-to-one instruction for the majority

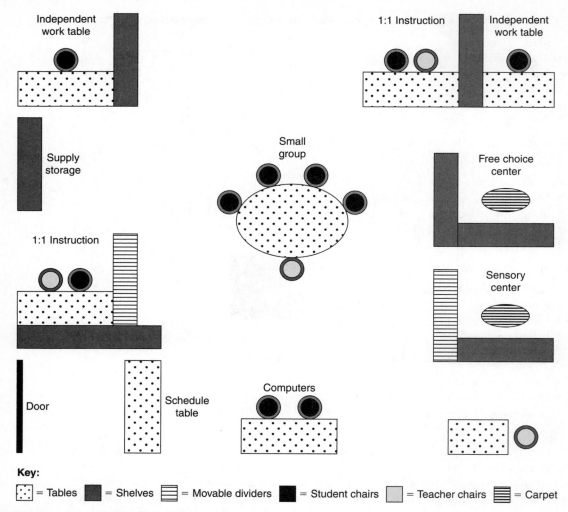

FIGURE 5.5 Sample Well-organized Classroom Layout

of their instruction each day. Figure 5.6 is an example of one teacher's schedule, which depicts what each of the paraprofessionals, the teacher, and the students are doing throughout the day. This prevents loss of instructional time and helps the day to flow more smoothly between activities. Teachers may post such a schedule somewhere in the room so that all adults can easily view it while they work, or provide a copy to each adult at the start of the day or week. Having a well-organized classroom, from materials, to furniture, to stations, to instruction, is key to creating the predictability that students with ASD need.

Creating a Successful Learning Environment

One of the ultimate goals of the school setting is to support students' learning. In general, beyond the physical layout, a supportive classroom environment for students with ASD offers structure and makes use of visual strategies such as pictures, icons, and symbols along with written or verbal directions. Moreover, the method of how to present and deliver learning materials determines the effectiveness of

Time	Teacher, Mrs. B	Paraprofessional Mrs. W.	Paraprofessional Mr. S	Independent/ Inclusion
7:15–7:45	Prep room Restroom Backpacks Schedules	Meet students at bus Restroom Backpacks Schedules	Meet students at bus Restroom Backpacks Schedules	TS: Kindergarten SZ: Third Grade
7:45–8:15	CM: Math, Writing	MT, JT: Calendar, Weather, Self-Help	TG: Receptive Identification; Sorting by Class	PP: Independent Work Station
8:15–8:45	MT, JT, PP: Social Play Group	TG: Self-Help	Pick up boys in Inclusion; Take to Restroom	CM: Independent Work Station
8:45–9:15	TG, PP: First Grade	TS, MT, JT: Classroom jobs; Reading	CM: Reading, Spelling, Typing	SZ: Independent Work Station
9:15–9:45	Return from First Grade @ 9:35; Restroom; Set up for snack	SZ: Math, Writing	MT: Fine motor, Vocabulary	CM: OT (Tue) or Computer TS & JT: Independent Work Stations
9:45–10:15	All-Class: Snack, Motor Lab	All-Class: Snack, Motor Lab	Take MT & JT to Inclusion @ 9:55	

Key:

■	One-to-One Work Station #1
▤	Inclusion
▦	Independent Work Stations
▥	Small Group Table
▧	One-to-One Work Station #2
	Other

FIGURE 5.6   Sample Classroom Organization Schedule

instruction. For instance, the best way for most children with ASD to process learning is through a combination of clear verbal instruction and explicit visual prompts. In addition to more traditional instructional tools, assistive technology must be considered as a means of supporting students' learning.

Types of instructional materials and tools include:

- Standard textbooks
- Projected visuals (e.g., using Microsoft PowerPoint slides, overhead projector, and tangible objects)
- Alternative textbooks (e.g., audiobooks, CD-ROMs, or Web-based textbooks)
- Tape recorders
- Computers and software
- Alternative writing tools (e.g., word processors, writing aids, note-taking assistant, and word prediction and speech recognition software)

In addition to visual supports and explicit presentation of learning materials, the interactive social environment plays an important role for successful learning. Therefore, an interactive classroom climate could be created when teaching children with ASD appropriate social skills to participate in instructional activities. Also, a productive learning environment could be created through cooperative teamwork and hands-on activities related to life experiences. Other examples such as encouraging words (praises) or facial expressions (smiles) could foster a positive environment and motivate learning.

SCHEDULES Types of schedules vary based upon students' needs. As mentioned earlier, visual schedules tend to be beneficial for students with ASD because they help them to predict what will happen and when. The way information on various kinds of schedules is presented depends on students' functioning level. For students who have high reading skills, written schedules with directions can be supportive, whereas picture cues, icons, symbols, and other visual formats are more effective for students who are nonreaders. Visual cues may be paired with words or phrases to enhance students' understanding of the schedule.

Unexpected changes in schedules or routines are typically difficult for students with ASD. Social Stories™ (Gray, 2000) and other social narrative strategies, including social scripts and the Power Card Strategy (Gagnon, 2001) can help students with ASD not only to understand social situations but also that their schedules can change under certain situations. Warnings about how to handle changes and unexpected situations need to be embedded in schedules for students with ASD. For example, one such warning might be "Stay calm and talk to the teacher when there is a change in the schedule." Further, scheduling priming (Zanolli, Daggett, & Adams, 1996) closer to a given activity is a good way to provide scheduling information and prepare students so that they are aware of what activity will happen next. (See below for an explanation of *priming*.)

SCHEDULE PLANNING

- *Visual Supports* Using visual cues and material organizers to make important directions or activities clearer than when using words alone; unifying symbols or color to define the same materials or activities; using the same pictures when representing the same activity in different contexts
- *Priming* Providing information in advance of an activity to help prepare students for what is to come; time for priming should be embedded in the schedule
- *Social Narratives* Writing stories about how to cope with activities that happen unexpectedly or accidentally; discussing what the student can do or what kinds of options he or she might have in these situations
- *Checklists* Using self-checklists to enable students to monitor their own progress and predict next steps

ENVIRONMENTAL PLANNING IN THE HOME/COMMUNITY

The major purposes of modifying and planning environmental supports are to promote safety as well as to increase quality of life (McLean, Wolery, & Bailey, 2004). With this idea in mind, this section focuses on building supports in home/community environments to meet the behavioral and sensory needs of children with ASD.

Several environmental and safety modifications can be made in the **home/community environment** and strategies can be developed to prevent unsafe or undesired behaviors, such as climbing on a shelf or running out of the door. Although it is unrealistic to consider modifying every aspect of a particular environment, awareness of potential dangers is important, based on the individual needs of a given child or person with an ASD.

The following paragraphs contain information that teachers can share with families to help with planning or modifying a safe and supportive living environment for individuals with ASD. The checklist in Figure 5.7 helps evaluate the home environment and further identify potential safety risks and precautions that need to be taken to prevent injury.

Go around the house and pay careful attention to the following elements. As you do so, please check the items in the checklist as appropriate.

1. Furniture Arrangement

1.1 There is enough indoor space for children and adults to move around freely.

1.2 There is more than one space available for privacy and relaxation.

1.3 Furnishings do not crowd the room.

1.4 Furnishings are placed to provide open space for play.

1.5 Big pieces of furniture (e.g., bookcases) are secured with wall brackets so that they can't be tipped over.

1.6 Floors, walls, and other built-in furnishings are in good condition, with no peeling or cracking paint.

1.7 Rugs are secured to floors or fitted with anti-slip pads underneath.

1.8 There is protective padding on any corners of furniture.

1.9 Stairways are clear of tripping hazards.

2. Doors and Windows

2.1 Safety locks or latches are placed on doors and windows appropriately.

2.2 Doorknob covers or keyless locks are used.

2.3 All glass doors contain decorative markers so that they won't be mistaken for opened doors.

2.4 Safety bars or window guards are installed on upper-story windows.

2.5 Window blind cords are tied with clothespins or specially designed cord clips.

2.6 Doors and windows have sensory monitors connected to the alarm system or other alternative system.

2.7 The glass panes are replaced with strengthened safety glass or Plexiglas™ or are covered with plastic.

3. Fire and Electricity Safety

3.1 Unused electrical outlets are covered with safety plugs, or the power access to the electrical appliances are covered or removed.

3.2 All wiring for appliances and electronics are concealed in a way that they cannot be played with.

3.3 All major electrical appliances are grounded.

3.4 Cord holders are used to keep extended cords fastened against walls.

3.5 There are no potential electrical fire hazards, such as overloaded electrical sockets and electrical wires running under carpets.

3.6 All radiators and baseboard heaters are covered with childproof screens if necessary.

3.7 Safety covers are placed over gas stoves and oven knobs.

3.8 Gas fireplaces have been secured with a valve cover or key.

3.9 All working fireplaces have a screen.

4. Storage of Dangerous Items

4.1 Household chemicals (e.g., detergents, cleaning products, pesticides, bleach) are stored in locked cabinets or out of reach.

4.2 All prescription and nonprescription medications are stored in a locked cabinet.

4.3 All bottles of mouthwash, perfumes, hair products, nail products, and so forth are stored in a locked cabinet or out of reach.

(continued)

FIGURE 5.7 Home and Community Environment Checklist

> 4.4 All tools and supplies used for gardening, automotive, and lawn care are stored in a locked container.
>
> 4.5 Lighters, matches, sharp objects/utensils (scissors, knives, razor blades), and so forth are out of reach.
>
> **5. Organization**
>
> 5.1 The organization of the room is predictable (e.g., items of the same category are grouped together; items are labeled).
>
> 5.2 Functional items are organized in see-through plastic bins/boxes with visual labels.
>
> 5.3 Things (e.g., books or toys) are placed on shelves or in places that are visible with easy access.
>
> 5.4 Visual supports (e.g., boundary markers, labels, and signs) are used as needed.
>
> **6. Sensory Considerations**
>
> 6.1 Natural light can be controlled, such as adjustable blinds or curtains.
>
> 6.2 Dimming switches for the lights are used to control the brightness of the room.
>
> 6.3 Soft lighting or deep-colored lightbulbs are used.
>
> 6.4 There are no extreme-smelling cleaners and chemicals.
>
> 6.5 There are no high-frequency sounds (e.g., CRT monitors and television sets) or irritating noise (e.g., grinders, electric saws).
>
> 6.6 Temperature and humidity of the room are comfortable.
>
> 6.7 Comfortable texture materials are used for bedding, sofa, rug, and so on.

FIGURE 5.7 (*continued*)

Importance of Understanding Children with ASD

Understanding a child's patterns of behavior and observing his or her interaction with home/community environments are initial steps for an environmental plan. For instance, if the child is a runner and not aware of potential danger outside the house, safety locks on interior doors may be necessary. Other children with ASD may be very sensitive to noises, and screaming or kicking could result from the frustration of sensory overload. Therefore, appropriate arrangement is needed to meet behavioral and sensory needs. Figure 5.7 on pages 135–136 shows a checklist regarding the safety arrangement that parents or caregivers need to consider before making an environmental plan.

Arrangement of Furniture and Other Furnishings

Just as in the classroom, furniture and other furnishings should be arranged so as to provide individuals with ASD a secure environment in which to carry out their daily activities. The following considerations should be incorporated when arranging furniture. First, rooms should not be crowded with furniture or decorative items but should instead allow spacious, open areas for moving around, playing, or carrying out everyday activities. Second, the furniture should be arranged in a way that limits the need for excessive movement and transitions, such as keeping the traffic smooth when transitioning from one place to another. Third, to prevent children from getting hurt, the furniture should be arranged so that they cannot climb up onto high shelves or cabinets. Fourth, large pieces of furniture should be secured to the floor or wall so they cannot easily be tipped over. Furthermore, it is important for parents and caregivers to keep furniture surfaces clean and clear and make sure that the furniture is in good condition with no peeling or cracking paint, and so on.

DOORS AND WINDOWS   Some individuals with ASD have little or no awareness of danger and may run away or leave the house at any given opportunity without supervision. Thus, it is important to place locks on exterior doors to prevent them from running away. Also, safety locks on interior doors may be necessary to secure places to which the individual should have no access. It is strongly recommended that parents and caregivers install an alarm system that goes off when doors and windows are opened. Furthermore, some individuals with ASD like to pound on windows. To prevent injury in such cases, parents and caregivers may consider replacing ordinary glass with strengthened safety glass, Plexiglas™, or a plastic seal.

FIRE/ELECTRICAL SAFETY   Individuals with ASD, especially children, should not have easy access to electrical outlets and wiring unless they fully understand their use and purpose as well as potential dangers. For outlets, plastic covers are recommended. Further, some electrical appliances such as stoves, ovens, washers, and dryers should be out of children's reach or should be labeled with warning signs, such as a bold red "X" mark. It is also recommended that parents and caregivers frequently communicate with children about the potential danger of lighters, matches, fire, or heat around the house. Safe behavior in the event of a fire should also be taught and practiced on a regular basis. When participating in community activities, parents and caregivers should remind the children of safe environments and behaviors and frequently supervise children. For instance, remind the child of the danger of fire before camping.

STORING DANGEROUS ITEMS   Parents and caregivers should safeguard dangerous items around the house, such as detergents, chemicals, medicines, cleaning materials, and so on. These items should be kept out of children's reach when possible, and visual signs should be used to remind children of potential danger. If possible, parents and caregivers should teach children to differentiate items that are safe to use from items that they are to stay away from. This habit of being aware of dangerous items should be generalized to community environments, such as being aware of warning signs in public buildings.

Organization

Predictability is strongly needed by individuals with ASD to effectively function and participate in their daily lives. In addition, a sense of order and structure are critical for their well-being. The need for organization goes beyond the desire to have a neat and clean house. A well-organized, structured, and ordered environment reduces the frustration level of an individual with an ASD and, consequently, diminishes and/or eliminates undesirable behavior, such as screaming or tantrums.

There are several ways that parents and caregivers can create a well-structured home environment. For example, items belonging to the same category (e.g., clothing, books, and toys) can be stored together in see-through plastic bins or boxes with visual labels so that the child can see the contents, gain access, and use them. Things such as toys or books may be placed on shelves or in places that allow the child to see and access them independently. Further, visual supports, such as labeling or simple maps can enhance the child's understanding of how things are organized and where to find desired items.

Summary

ASD is a neurological disorder that presents challenges in the areas of social interaction, **repetitive and stereotyped behavior**, verbal and/or nonverbal communication (APA, 2000), and in atypical sensory processing patterns—although the latter is not included in current definitions of ASD (Dunn et al., 2002; Field, 1997; Myles et al., 2004). As a result of those challenges, individuals with ASD interact with the environment differently than the rest of the population. Interactions between an individual with an ASD and his environment can be frustrating when the environment does not accommodate his needs. An understanding of the general characteristics of ASD as well as specific individual needs is critical for providing appropriate supports across settings, including planning and creating supportive learning and living environments.

Most individuals with ASD function best and are most comfortable in environments that are well organized and predictable. Lighting, sounds, smells, temperature, seating, as well as special spaces for both learning and relaxation are factors that need to be taken into consideration when planning and modifying physical environments for individuals with ASD. In addition, vi-sual supports, such as visual schedules, choice boards, boundary markers, maps, and labels, are valuable tools for assisting individuals with ASD in navigating their environment. Further, several environmental and safety modifications can be made in school and home/community environments and strategies can be implemented to prevent unsafe or undesired behaviors, such as running away or screaming. Despite commonalities, it is important to remember that no two individuals with ASD are the same and that, consequently, their needs vary. Thus, in environmental planning, as in any other intervention or treatment, each person's characteristics and needs must be considered individually.

Chapter Review Questions

1. What are the commonly observed characteristics of individuals with Autism Spectrum Disorders (ASD) and how do those characteristics affect this population in terms of the ways they interact with the environment? (Objective 1)

2. A well-organized and predictable environment is considered the most desired and beneficial setting for individuals with ASD. Identify what modifications you can make in your classroom to create a supportive learning environment for a student with an ASD. (Objective 2)

3. What are visual supports and what are examples of such supports that may be applied in planning a supportive environment to accommodate the needs of individuals with ASD? Give examples across various settings (e.g., school, home, workplace). (Objective 3)

4. What environmental and safety modifications may be made in a home/community environment? (Objective 4)

Key Terms

Accessibility   *125*
Classroom layout   *125*
Echolalia   *121*
Environmental modifications   *125*
Home/Community environment   *134*
Nonverbal communication   *120*

Predictability   *137*
Priming   *134*
Relaxing space   *123*
Repetitive and stereotyped behavior   *137*
Social narratives   *134*
Social Stories™   *134*

Structure   *126*
Verbal communication   *120*
Visual cues   *127*
Visual supports   *125*
Visual schedules   *126*
Supportive environment   *123*

Internet Resources

Do2learn is specifically designed for individuals on the autism spectrum. The site has a collection of graphics, picture schedules, and task analyses that parents have created for home and school use. Do2learn (*http://www.do2learn.com*)

The Autism Society of America (ASA) is the oldest and largest grassroots organization within the autism community. It is dedicated to increasing public awareness about autism and the day-to-day issues facing families affected with autism. The website

provides good sources of information, research, and references on autism, such as "Safety in the Home" and "Resources to Help."
http://www.autism-society.org

The Access Center is a national technical assistance (TA) center funded by the U.S. Department of Education's Office of Special Education Programs to improve outcomes for elementary and middle school students with disabilities. The website includes various teaching strategies as well as technology applications designed to enhance accessibility, both environmentally and instructionally.
http://www.k8accesscenter.org/index.php

The National Autistic Society provides the most comprehensive services and events for people with Autism Spectrum Disorders in the United Kingdom. The website includes information about autism-friendly environments, including a booklet titled "Creating an Autism-Friendly Environment."
http://www.nas.org.uk

TEACCH (Treatment and Education of Autistic and Related Communication Handicapped Children) is an evidence-based service, training, and research program for individuals of all ages and skill levels with Autism Spectrum Disorders. The website provides information about structured teaching and physical organization as ways of teaching students with Autism Spectrum Disorders effectively.
http://www.teacch.com

References

American Psychiatric Association. (1994). *Diagnostic and statistical manual of mental disorders* (4th ed.). Washington, DC: Author.

American Psychiatric Association. (2000). *Diagnostic and statistical manual of mental disorders* (4th ed., text revision). Washington, DC: Author.

Baranek, G. T. (1999). Autism during infancy: A retrospective video analysis of sensory-motor and social behaviors at 9–12 months of age. *Journal of Autism and Developmental Disorders, 29*, 213–224.

Baranek, G. T., Foster, L. G., & Berkson, G. (1997a). Sensory defensiveness in persons with developmental disabilities. *Occupational Therapy Journal of Research, 17,* 173–185.

Baranek, G. T., Foster, L. G., & Berkson, G. (1997b). Tactile defensiveness and stereotyped behaviors. *American Journal of Occupational Therapy, 51,* 91–95.

Bellini, S. (2006). *Building social relationships: A systematic approach to teaching social interaction skills to children and adolescents with autism spectrum disorders and other social difficulties.* Shawnee Mission, KS: Autism Asperger Publishing Company.

Brown, C., & Dunn, W. (2002). *Adolescent/Adult sensory profile: User's manual.* San Antonio, TX: The Psychological Corporation.

Cardon, T. A. (2007). *Initiations and interactions: Early intervention techniques for parents of children with autism spectrum disorder.* Shawnee Mission, KS: Autism Asperger Publishing Company.

Dunlap, G. (2007). Some thoughts on the evolving arena of autism services. *Research and Practice for Persons with Severe Disabilities, 2,* 161–163.

Dunn, W., Myles, B. S., & Orr, S. (2002). Sensory processing issues associated with Asperger Syndrome: A preliminary investigation. *American Journal of Occupational Therapy, 56,* 97–102.

Field, T., Lasko, D., Mundy, P., Henteleff, T., Kabat, S., Talpins, S., et al. (1997). Brief report: Autistic children's attentiveness and responsivity improve after touch therapy. *Journal of Autism and Developmental Disorders, 27*(3), 333–338.

Gagnon, E. (2001*). Power cards: Using special interests to motivate children and youth with Asperger Syndrome and autism.* Shawnee Mission, KS: Autism Asperger Publishing Company.

Gray, C. A. (2000). *The new social story book.* Arlington, TX: Future Horizons, Inc.

Kanner, L. (1943). Autistic disturbances of affective contact. *Nervous Child, 2*(3), 217–250.

Koegel, L. K., & Brown, F. (2007). autism spectrum disorders: Trends, treatments, and diversity. *Research and Practice for Persons with Severe Disabilities, 2*, 87–88.

Koegel, R. L., & Koegel, L. K. (2006). *Pivotal response treatments for autism.* Baltimore: Paul H. Brookes.

Koegel, R. L., Rincover, A., & Egel, A. L. (Eds.) (1987). *Educating and understanding autistic children.* San Diego: College Hill Press.

McClannahan, L. E., & Krantz, P. J. (1999). *Activity schedules for children with autism: Teaching independent behavior.* Bethesda, MD: Woodbine House, Inc.

McLean, M., Wolery, M., & Bailey, D. B. (2004). *Assessing infants and preschoolers with special needs* (3rd ed.). Upper Saddle River, NJ: Pearson Education.

McMahon, C., Malesa, E. E., Yoder, P., & Stone, W. L. (2007). Parents of children with autism spectrum disorders have merited concerns about their later-born infants. *Research and Practice for Persons with Severe Disabilities, 2*, 154–160.

Mundy, P., Sigman, M., & Kasari, C. (1994). Joint attention, developmental level, and symptom presentation in autism. *Development and Psychopathology, 6*, 389–401.

Myles, B. S. (2005). *Children and youth with Asperger Syndrome: Strategies for success in inclusive settings.* Thousand Oaks, CA: Corwin Press.

Myles, B. S., & Adreon, D. (2001). *Asperger syndrome and adolescents: Practical solutions for making sense of the world.* Shawnee Mission, KS: Autism Asperger Publishing Company.

Myles, B. S., Hagiwara, T., Dunn, W., Rinner, L., Reese, M., Huggins, A., et al. (2004). Sensory issues in children with Asperger Syndrome and autism. *Education and Training in Developmental Disabilities, 39*, 283–290.

Ornitz, E. M., & Ritvo, E. R. (1968). Perceptual inconstancy in early infantile autism: The syndrome of early infant autism and its variants including certain cases of childhood schizophrenia. *Archives of General Psychiatry, 18*(1), 76–98.

Savner, J., & Myles, S. B. (2000). *Making visual supports work in the home and community: Strategies for individuals with autism and Asperger Syndrome.* Shawnee Mission, KS: Autism Asperger Publishing Company.

Scheuermann, B., & Webber, J. (2002). *Autism: Teaching does make a difference.* Belmont, CA: Wadsworth/Thomson.

Schilling, D. L., & Schwartz, I. S. (2004). Alternative seating for young children with autism spectrum disorder: Effects on classroom behavior. *Journal of Autism and Developmental Disorders, 34*, 423–432.

Wing, L., & Gould, J. (1979). Severe impairments of social interaction and associated abnormalities in children: Epidemiology and classification. *Journal of Autism and Developmental Disorders, 9*, 11–29.

World Health Organization. (1993). *International statistical classification of diseases and related health problems.* Geneva, Switzerland: Author.

Zanolli, K., Daggett, J., & Adams, T. (1996). Teaching preschool age autistic children to make spontaneous initiation to peers using priming. *Journal of Autism and Developmental Disorders, 46*, 547–551.

6

Teaching Students with Autism Using the Principles of Applied Behavior Analysis

Melissa Olive, Ph.D. BCBA
Center for Autism and Related Disorders

E. Amanda Boutot, Ph.D. BCBA-D
Texas State University

Jonathan Tarbox, Ph.D. BCBA-D
Center for Autism and Related Disorders

CHAPTER OBJECTIVES

After reading this chapter, learners should be able to:

1. Describe and use the discrete trial training techniques.

2. Describe and use errorless teaching strategies.

3. Describe and use error correction procedures.

4. Describe generalization and maintenance strategies.

5. Describe and use incidental teaching strategies.

6. Describe and use basic data collection.

CASE STUDY   Examples

Case of Enrique

Enrique is a 3-year-old male who was referred to his school district from the local early childhood intervention team. Enrique has a delay in expressive and receptive language as well as delays in social skills. Enrique engages in high rates of stereotypical behaviors such as hand-flapping, vocalizations, and eye gazing. Enrique also slaps himself in the head and he has recently begun slapping his parents. Enrique's parents speak Spanish and they are learning English. They have expressed a desire for Enrique to learn English and they report that they speak to Enrique in English. Enrique participates in the school district's early childhood special education program for half days 5 days per week.

Case of Jashonne

Jashonne is an 8-year-old who was diagnosed with Asperger Syndrome at age 4. Her language vocabulary is equivalent to that of an 11-year-old. However, Jashonne has delays in her social skills. She often stands too close to her peers and teachers. She also insists that all conversations, games, and activities include princesses. Jashonne becomes very upset if she is not allowed to talk about princesses. She often asks to include princesses appropriately on the first attempt. If she is told no she begins to ask louder. If she is told again, she begins crying and stating that she wants to have a princess at which point she leaves and cries in a corner.

Case of Aidan

Aidan is a 16-year-old male with autism. He cannot read or write and his verbal expression is limited to simple phrases such as eat, drink, bathroom, and video. He engages in challenging behavior almost daily. His behaviors include elopement, aggression, and self-injury. Aidan can complete some self-care skills independently but he needs close supervision to ensure that he is thorough. He is learning some job skills but he does not remain on task for very long.

INTRODUCTION TO APPLIED BEHAVIOR ANALYSIS

Applied behavior analysis (ABA) is the utilization of the basic principles of learning and motivation to address socially important problems. The principles of learning and motivation, also known as the **principles of behavior**, upon which ABA is based, are found in Figure 6.1. First, all behavior is learned. Individuals learn through two mechanisms: classical conditioning and operant conditioning. In classical conditioning, individuals learn to associate an unknown stimulus with a known stimulus. The best example of this was Pavlov's experiment with his dog (Pavlov, 1927). Pavlov rang a bell each time he presented his dog with food. His dog began to associate the bell with the food. In the future, when the bell rang, the dog began to salivate in anticipation of food presentation. Operant conditioning involves the modification of stimuli following behaviors in order to change the occurrence and/or form of the behavior (Skinner, 1953). When an infant learns to make a raspberry sound, his parents often cheer or giggle. The raspberry sound is the behavior of interest and the cheering and giggling are the stimuli following the behavior. If the baby enjoys hearing cheering and giggling, he will learn to engage in more raspberry behaviors in order to obtain more cheering and giggling.

The second principle of applied behavior analysis is that all behavior serves a purpose. Each person has her own reasons for engaging in behaviors and the reasons may change based on age, contextual situations, and prior experiences. Behaviors may be exhibited in order to obtain a social outcome, or behaviors may be exhibited in order to experience an internal feeling. Social outcomes

All Behavior is Learned	All Behavior Serves a Purpose	All Behavior is Contextual
• Through association learning (classical conditioning) • Through operant conditioning	• Functions vary from person to person • Some functions may include escape or avoidance of task, attention, to obtain something tangible or a preferred activity, or for self-soothing/self-stimulation	• Behavior is influenced by the environment in which it occurs; sometimes referred to as the trigger for behavior • Antecedent events in the immediate environment or setting events that have happened previously

FIGURE 6.1 Principles of Behavior

may include access to or avoidance from social interaction or tangible outcomes. These may include getting a preferred chair color during instruction or avoiding difficult activities such as math instruction. Students may engage in behaviors for nonsocial outcomes as well. The nonsocial outcomes, or what behavior analysts refer to as *automatic reinforcers*, may include access to feelings of euphoria and pride. Nonsocial outcomes may also include avoiding things such as headaches, loud noises, and embarrassment.

The third and final principle of behavior analysis is that all behaviors are contextual. Behaviors are influenced by contextual factors within the student's learning environment. The contextual factors may be stimuli associated with environments, or behaviors may be related to states of deprivation (e.g., lack of access to stimuli) or satiation (e.g., exposure to too much stimuli). The contextual factors that influence behaviors may also be related to the culture of the environment. For example, kicking is a widely accepted behavior in school activities such as cheerleading, football, dancing, karate, and kickball. Conversely, kicking is not generally accepted in environments such as basketball, reading instruction, lunchtime, baseball, or hallway transitions.

ABA has been used to address a large variety of issues, including anxiety, depression, weight management, substance abuse, job performance, and behavior disorders (Greene, Winett, Van Houten, Geller, & Iwata, 1987). Autism is just one of the many areas addressed by ABA. Procedures and areas of specialization within ABA go by various names, including discrete trial training (Smith, 2001), incidental teaching (Hart & Risley, 1975), pivotal response teaching (Koegel, Camarata, Valdez-Menchaca, & Koegel, 1998), verbal behavior (Wallace, Iwata, & Hanley, 2006), and positive behavioral supports (Sugai & Horner, 2002). All of these approaches are part of the field of ABA, all are based on the same principles of learning and motivation, and all require advanced training in the science of ABA. Comprehensive ABA programs for children with autism often include some elements of each of these approaches.

Research has demonstrated that for a significant proportion of children with autism, intensive early intervention will result in increases in appropriate behaviors and decreases in inappropriate behaviors (e.g., Lovaas, 1987; Sallows & Graupner, 2005). For some children, the outcome has been so great that the children with autism become indistinguishable from their typically developing peers (e.g., Lovaas, 1987).

The first controlled study to evaluate long-term, intensive, early ABA intervention for children with autism was conducted by Lovaas (1987). This study compared a group of children who received intensive (40 hours per week) ABA intervention to two control groups; one who received 10 hours per week of ABA intervention and one who received 10 hours per week of non-ABA intervention. All children received interventions for 2 or more years. Assignment to groups was not random but based on availability of staff that could provide therapy. However, the groups did not vary significantly on any measures at intake. At follow-up, 47% of the children in the intensive ABA group achieved both normal IQ and successful first grade placement in general education classrooms. Children in the control groups, however, made much smaller gains, with only 2% of children across both control groups achieving normal intellectual functioning and placement within general education settings. In 1993, McEachin, Smith, and Lovaas published a follow-up study, wherein participants in the intensive ABA group were reevaluated at a mean age of 11.5 years. Eight of the nine participants demonstrated intellectual and adaptive functioning within the normal range.

Subsequent studies on intensive ABA have produced similar results. Sallows and Graupner (2005) found that 48% of children who had received 4 years of intensive early ABA scored in the normal range on measures of intelligence and adaptive behavior. The children were able to transition to general education with no support. Cohen, Amerine-Dickens, and Smith (2006) studied the effects of 3 years of intensive ABA for young children with autism and found that children receiving intensive ABA outperformed controls on measures of intelligence and adaptive behavior. Moreover, 28% of participants were successfully transitioned to general education placements, whereas only 4% of controls were placed in general education.

Eikeseth, Smith, Jahr, & Eldevick (2007) extended previous research by evaluating intensive ABA intervention for slightly older students with autism. They found that students who began intensive ABA at ages 4 through 7 attained statistically significant increases in intellectual and adaptive functioning when compared to a control group who received the same amount of services consisting of "eclectic" special education services.

A number of reviews of the research on ABA for children with autism have been completed. The most recent review (Eikeseth, 2009) noted that four studies demonstrated that children who received ABA made significantly more gains than control group children in a variety of measures. These four studies also met the highest criteria for scientific merit. Similarly, in their review of autism treatment research, Rogers and Vismara (2008) concluded that early intensive ABA is the only "well-established" treatment. Reichow and Wolery (2009) recently completed a meta-analysis of early intensive behavior intervention for children with autism. They reported that on average, ABA is an effective treatment for these children. In summary, research has demonstrated that intensive ABA can produce substantial gains in children with autism.

The robust research base supporting ABA treatment for children with autism has led to widespread endorsement by independent entities, including the U.S. Surgeon General (U.S. Department of Health and Human Services, 1999), the New York State Department of Health (New York State Department of Health, Early Intervention Program, 1999), the National Academy of Sciences (National Academy of Sciences, 2001), and the American Academy of Pediatrics (Myers & Johnson, 2007). Major public policy changes have also begun to occur, including state funding being allocated to ABA for autism treatment and state-level legislative decisions mandating insurance coverage for ABA treatment (e.g., "Steven's Law," Arizona House Bill 2487).

USING ABA TO TEACH STUDENTS WITH AUTISM

A comprehensive approach to teaching new skills to students involves a variety of ABA procedures. Everything that a student with autism needs to learn is viewed as a skill that can be taught, including daily living skills, language, social skills, academic skills, motor skills, perspective taking, and advanced or meta-cognition. Each skill area is broken down into small, teachable units and then taught systematically. Each student's unique strengths are built upon in the gradual process of teaching all skills the student needs to know in order to catch up to his or her typically developing peers. The two major ways that ABA is used to teach students with autism will be described further: (a) using ABA to teach new skills and (b) using ABA to address challenging behaviors.

USING ABA TO TEACH SKILL ACQUISITION (NEW LEARNING)

Discrete Trial Training

Discrete trial training (DTT) is a particular ABA teaching strategy that enables the student to acquire complex skills and behaviors through multiple practice opportunities. Discrete trial training is comprised of multiple and repeated discrete trials. A discrete trial includes what is known as the three-term contingency, which includes an antecedent, a behavior, and a consequence. The first step is the Antecedent or **discriminative stimulus** (S^D). For example, when teaching a child to say "car," the adult models "Say 'car,'" which is the Antecedent for the desired behavior. The student says "car" which is the targeted behavior. Then the student is given access to the toy car. This is the Consequence or reinforcer for saying "car." Figure 6.2 shows an example of a three-term contingency learning opportunity for this example.

The key element to this single discrete trial is that the student must be interested in the car when the instruction begins. If the student is not interested in the car, then other reinforcers may be needed to reinforce the child when she says car. If the student is not capable of saying "car," she is allowed to use an easier version of the skill such as touching a picture of a car, signing the word car, or touching an assistive technology device that says the word "car" for her. As the student masters easier versions of the skill, the adult scaffolds the student's learning by increasing the behavioral expectations (e.g., moving from "car" to "I want car").

The DTT procedure used for any particular student is customized to match the difficulty of the task and to the current skill level of the student. For example, when first introducing a new skill, a "mass trialing" procedure may be used wherein the same task is presented repeatedly several times in a row. Mass trialing has been shown to result in faster skill acquisition (Losardo & Bricker, 1994). An everyday analogy for mass trialing is teaching a student to shoot basketball free throws, or teaching a student to play scales on a piano. The student is required to repeat the same skill over and over until the skill is mastered. Once the student is able to perform the basic skill, then that skill is mixed with other skills in "random rotation" wherein the student must switch back and forth between varieties of learned skills in order to ensure that all skills are truly mastered.

Discrete trial training requires training and practice for teachers in order to become fluent in instructional delivery. (See Box 6.1 for review of a research study on teaching DTT to paraprofessionals.) There are a number of variables that can negatively influence the learning opportunities,

Antecedant	Behavior	Consequence
"Say car"	"Car"	Child is given car

If the car serves as a reinforcer, the next time someone says, "Say car" there is a high probability the learner will do so.

FIGURE 6.2 Three-Term Contingency

BOX 6.1 Research Notes

The provision of appropriate programming for students with autism in public schools is frequently a collaborative effort among multiple professionals, including teachers, therapy providers, and paraprofessionals. In a study by Bolton and Mayer (2008), the effectiveness of a training package for paraprofessionals was examined. Because of the increase in the number of paraprofessionals providing services to students with autism, adequate training is of highest concern. In this study, discrete trial teaching (DTT) was taught to three paraprofessionals working in a state agency serving children with autism. The study implemented a training package using "didactic instruction, modeling, rehearsal, and performance feedback" (p. 104). A delayed multiple baseline across subjects design was used to determine the efficacy of the treatment package as well as the generalization of skills beyond the training setting. Each of the participants took part in a 30-minute training session using a PowerPoint presentation on ABA and DTT. Following the presentation, baseline data for each participant was taken to determine the level of accuracy in implementation of seven steps in the DTT process (see below). Immediately following baseline measurement, participants were provided with an additional 45 minutes of specific instruction, which involved lecture and demonstration of the seven steps. Following the more specific instruction, general case instruction, in which "multiple teaching examples are chosen systematically to ensure that they sample the span of stimulus and response variations that occur within the environment where the behavior is desired" (p. 104) was provided. Ten different programs were used in this training sample, including such skills as "responding to name, pointing, gross motor imitation, identifying body parts, object discrimination, matching, color identification, object identification, verbal imitation, and toy play" (p. 106). Paraprofessionals spent the remainder of the training session practicing DTT for each of the programs and received performance feedback on each trial from the trainer. Treatment data were collected for each paraprofessional participant during the practice trials. For generalization, each paraprofessional was observed providing DTT to an assigned child with autism in the natural setting—in this case either the home or a community-based setting. Data was collected on the performance of each paraprofessional during generalization and compared to both baseline and treatment performance.

The training package examined in this study incorporated several aspects of training shown previously in the literature to be effective in teaching professionals to perform DTT, including general case instruction, performance feedback, and the use of common stimuli (e.g., toys and other materials during the training that were most likely to be used in actual child instruction). The study demonstrated that this rapid training program was successful in teaching three paraprofessionals, each of whom had little to no prior training in DTT, how to implement the steps of DTT. In treatment, each participant was able to achieve 98% to100% accuracy while in generalization each was able to achieve 90% to 100% accuracy on the seven steps of DTT with a child with autism. Both treatment and generalization accuracy levels were higher than baseline, which were between 50% and 63%. This study supports that training for paraprofessionals is effective in achieving high levels of accuracy of teaching strategies and that such training may be effective in a relatively short amount of time, given appropriate procedures. In this case the general case instruction, performance feedback, and programming common stimuli were cited as components of the training package leading to the gains of these participants.

Seven Steps of DTT:

1. Have materials ready?
2. Gain child's attention
3. Present discriminative stimulus
4. Prompt
5. Reinforce
6. Use correction procedure as necessary
7. Collect data

Source: Information from Bolton, J. & Mayer, M. D. (2008). Promoting the generalization of paraprofessional discrete trial teaching skills. *Focus on Autism and Other Developmental Disabilities, 23*(2), 103–111.

Some things to keep in mind during DTT
- Ensure motivation to learn
- Establish Instructional Control
- Use natural cues when possible
- Clear the field between trials
- Keep the A-B-C separate; no overlapping
- Reinforce immediately
- Use errorless learning for new skill acquisition

FIGURE 6.3   Discrete Trial Training

which make learning for the student difficult. Teachers can prevent or reduce the negative factors by adhering to several key "rules" for DTT instruction (See Figure 6.3). First, it is important that the student is motivated to participate in the learning opportunity. A preference assessment may be necessary at the start of each training session to determine what the student wants to work for. For example, the teacher may have a box of several of the student's favorite items. The teacher can place the box in front of the student and record what he seems most interested in. For students who are verbal, teachers may ask students what they would like to work for. A second preference assessment strategy is to hold two known reinforcers in front of the student to see which he chooses. If a student is not motivated to learn, learning is not likely (Iwata et al., 1997). When instruction moves to natural environments, reinforcers will become more natural. For example, if the child is playing in the housekeeping center, his motivation may be to obtain the pretend sandwich for his pretend picnic.

The second variable to consider in a discrete trial is the student's level of focus, or readiness to learn. Securing the student's attention and focus prior to delivery of the S^D is known as instructional control. **Instructional control** includes having the student sit up straight, hands in lap, looking toward the teacher. Securing instructional control between each trial will aid in successful student responses and it will help students learn to notice the appropriate stimuli on which to focus.

Third, teachers should try to use the most natural cue or antecedent for each skill. This is also known as the S^D. In the initial phases of instruction, it is important for teachers and their teaching assistants to keep the S^D the same. This helps the student learn more quickly. Once the student has demonstrated an understanding of the instructional task, the S^D should be varied gradually to ensure that the student learns to use the skill in a variety of situations. For example, when teaching students to respond to greetings, the teacher initially says, "Hi Enrique!" After Enrique learns that he should say "hi," the teacher moves to "Hey Enrique!" or "Hello Enrique" or even "What's Up?" It is unlikely that Enrique will be able to generalize his skill to the playground or neighborhood park if the S^D does not match the different ways that students greet each other.

A fourth suggestion to improve DTT efficiency is to remove teaching materials from the student's view between trials (for multiple trial sessions). This is known as "clearing the field." Clearing the field ensures that each new trial is presented "cleanly" which prevents confusing the student during learning opportunities. For example, if a teacher is teaching Enrique to learn colors, the teacher will use a simple color card. At the beginning of each trial, the teacher brings out the red card and says "touch red." When Enrique touches red he is given brief access to his reinforcers while his teacher removes the red card from his line of sight and records his response on the data sheet. Then the teacher begins the instructional trial again by presenting the red card and simultaneously delivering the S^D.

As with S^D delivery, it is important that instructional materials remain consistent until the student demonstrates an understanding of the learning opportunity. When the instruction moves to more natural contexts, it is important to have many materials present to ensure that the student learns to focus his attention on the appropriate learning materials.

Fifth, teachers must ensure that the components of the discrete trial do not overlap. For example, the S^D must precede response prompts, so that the response prompt does not become accidentally "chained" to or associated with the S^D. For example, when Enrique's teacher prompts him to "touch red," she waits to prompt him until after the red card is presented and after she has said, "touch red."

A sixth consideration is that the reinforcement must be delivered immediately following the correct behavioral response, regardless of the level of prompting. Initially during instruction, the student will receive a reinforcer immediately following each correct response that has been emitted following the S^D. When the student demonstrates an understanding of the learning trial, then the reinforcement is "thinned." Thinning reinforcement consists of requiring more behaviors before reinforcement is delivered. Initially, Enrique receives a reinforcer following each instance that he touches red when asked to touch red. Over time, he will need to have two correct responses before the reinforcer is delivered. This is adjusted to three and so on until he can work for an extended time before earning reinforcement. Further, reinforcement should be as natural as possible. Initially, reinforcers may be contrived (e.g., candy or tokens). Figure 6.4 shows a hierarchy of reinforcement from least to most natural. Over time, the student learns to work for social praise with the ultimate goal being that the student works for internal motivation. Although some students will require more extrinsic reinforcement than others, it is important that teachers plan for and fade reinforcement as quickly as the student's learning will allow. Moving students to more natural reinforcers will also ensure that **maintenance** (i.e., ability to perform the skill over time) and **generalization** (i.e., ability to perform the skill with novel teachers, teaching aids, instructional materials, and settings) will occur (Stokes & Baer, 1977). Paying careful attention to the way one is using DTT can help teachers ensure student success.

Errorless Learning

Effective prompting is also an important part of any ABA program. A prompt is additional help that is provided to a student to make sure each learning attempt is successful. For example, when teaching a student to name objects, one might hold up a picture of an apple and say, "What is it?" Rather than simply taking a trial-and-error approach and potentially allowing the student to make frustrating errors, the student is given a response prompt that assists him in answering correctly on the first few trials. For example, initially the instructor may say, "What is it? Apple." This process of instruction is referred to as "most-to-least" prompting or "errorless learning." Errorless learning has been

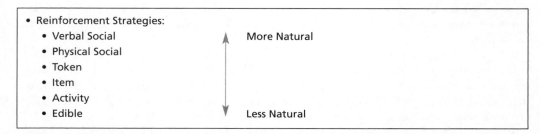

- Reinforcement Strategies:
  - Verbal Social
  - Physical Social
  - Token
  - Item
  - Activity
  - Edible

More Natural

Less Natural

FIGURE 6.4 Hierarchy of Reinforcement from Most to Least Natural

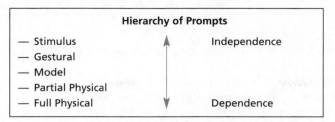

FIGURE 6.5 Hierarchy of Prompting Strategies from Most to Least Independent

shown to be effective in teaching new skills to students, particularly in that the student has less frustration (Touchette & Howard, 1984).

Once a student demonstrates mastery of a skill, maintenance is addressed by adjusting the prompts accordingly. The instructor moves to a "least-to-most" prompting strategy and provides a prompt only if the student does not engage in the correct response. This approach helps ensure that students do not become dependent on prompts but rather learn to use new skills independently. Figure 6.5 and Figure 6.6 present a hierarchy of prompting procedures that may be used during instruction and an overview of prompt-fading procedures.

Error Correction Procedures

During instruction, prompts should be faded systematically. However, it is possible that a student will make an error at some point during instruction. When this occurs, teachers must use appropriate **error correction** procedures, sometimes called correction trials, in order to prevent such errors from happening in the future. When the student makes a mistake, the teacher should clear the field for the next trial, ensure instructional control is regained, and re-present the S^D as in the previous trial. This time, however, the teacher should immediately provide assistance in the form of a prompt to ensure the student does not make the error a second time.

The level of prompt used in the error correction procedure is selected based on data collection from previous lessons (see data collection strategies later in this chapter). Data from previous trials will indicate the last known prompt level required for that particular skill. In other words, if the student has previously been able to perform the skill with a gesture prompt, the teacher would use a gesture prompt rather than a full physical prompt. If a physical prompt was used when only a gesture

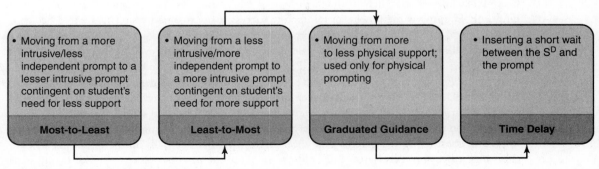

FIGURE 6.6 Overview of Prompting Systems

> **Error Correction**
> - Trial 1: mistake
> - Clear field, present Trial 2 with prompt (at last required level prior to mistake)
> - Reinforce prompted trial
> - Clear field, present Trial 3 at level to Trial 1
> - Repeat until child can perform skill at the desired level
> - Variation: insert easy trials between prompted trial and repeated mistake trial

FIGURE 6.7 Error Correction Procedure

prompt was needed, the student may develop prompt dependency. In such a case, the teacher would either deliver a gesture prompt or a prompt one level up from that (e.g., a model prompt) to support the student's success. If that prompt level does not lead to the correct response, then a most-to-least prompting procedure should be reinstated until the student regains the skill.

After the student performs the correct behavior with the prompt, the student receives the reinforcement. The teacher may at this point either (a) re-present the same trial without the prompt to probe the student's ability to perform the skill independently, or (b) move on to another skill for two or three trials and then come back to the corrected trial without the prompt. In either case, the least intrusive prompt should be used and the correction trial repeated until the student can reliably perform the skill on her own. Figure 6.7 provides an overview of error correction procedures.

Discrimination Training

Another critical component within an ABA program is discrimination training. Many types of discrimination training exist, but receptive language training is among the most important. When students learn receptive language discrimination, a basis is formed for later instruction. In receptive language discrimination training, an instructor makes two or more items available to the student and asks the student to respond to one of them. For example, a red car and a green car might be placed on a table. The instructor says "Where's red?" and then prompts the student to touch red. After the student learns to discriminate red, another color is taught. In this manner, the basic building blocks of language comprehension are taught. As the student progresses, the complexity of the instructor's language expands (e.g., "Where's the red car?" versus "Where's the red truck?").

Shaping

Complex behaviors are taught through the use of ABA strategies such as shaping, chaining, and modeling. **Shaping** is the process of reinforcing successive approximations of the desired behavior (Skinner, 1953). Over time, closer approximations of the behavior are required before reinforcement is provided. Interestingly, this instructional strategy is used by parents every day. One example is a parents' desire to teach their child to walk. Parents do not expect their child to walk before it is developmentally appropriate to do so. However, parents use shaping to encourage a child to get closer and closer to walking. Specifically, parents teach their child to pull up to a table. The child is reinforced when she learns to do this because her parents clap and cheer. The child soon learns that fun things are located on top of tables so this becomes a natural reinforcer for pulling up. Once the child learns to pull up consistently, her parents stop cheering for her when she pulls up. Now, her parents will cheer only when she takes steps while holding on. Soon, the parents stop cheering for taking steps and now they cheer only when she no longer holds on to the table. Before long, the child is walking and the parents cheer madly. Within weeks, the child walks in the absence of cheering.

One example of using shaping in behavior analysis is when a student is taught to say a word. Initially, the instructor will reinforce a sound such as "m." Then the instructor refrains from reinforcing the "m" sound and reinforces only sound blends such as "mu." When that skill is acquired, the instructor stops reinforcing "mu" and reinforces only when the student says a word approximation such as "muk." Finally, the instructor provides reinforcement only when the student says "milk."

Chaining

Chaining is another instructional strategy that is used to teach a series of behaviors. Behavior chaining occurs when a series of behaviors occurs in the presence of a specific stimulus. The instructional aspect is that students are taught to put multiple behaviors together in succession (Skinner, 1953). Putting on a coat, brushing teeth, and hand washing are all examples of behavior chains. When teaching a student to chain behaviors together, instructors may use forward chaining (McWilliams, Nietupski, & Hamre-Nietupski, 1990). In forward chaining, the student is taught to engage in the first and second behaviors together. When the two behaviors are exhibited together, then the student is taught to do the first three skills together and so on.

Backwards chaining is another way to teach a series of behaviors (cf., Hagopian, Farrell, & Amari, 1996). In this approach, the instructor teaches the student to chain together the last two behaviors in the sequence. When those two behaviors are learned, then the preceding behavior is taught. This continues until the student successfully engages in the chain of behaviors from the beginning.

Finally, the instructor may use total task presentation wherein the entire chain is taught simultaneously (cf., Werts, Caldwell, & Wolery, 1996). For example, when a student is learning to wash hands, he learns to turn on the water, get soap, rub hands together, rinse, turn water off, and dry hands. Each of those steps is an individual behavior that is not really meaningful unless performed in the chain.

Chaining could be used to teach Aidan how to complete work tasks. For example, teaching Aidan how to shred paper includes many steps: (a) retrieve paper from bin, (b) insert paper into shredder, (c) hold paper until shredder begins, (d) empty shredder when full, and (e) adjust shredder should it become jammed. Initially, Aidan will be taught how to shred one single sheet of paper. When he learns this skill and receives reinforcement for engaging in the skill, then he will be taught to shred single sheets of paper successively. Once he is able to shred single sheets successfully, then he is taught to retrieve paper from each person's office before he begins his shredding job. Once he is able to do this set of skills, he is taught how to make adjustments to the shredder if it becomes too full. Over time, Aidan is taught to shred more paper before receiving reinforcement (e.g., 10 sheets, 20 sheets, 30 sheets, etc).

Modeling

Modeling as an instructional strategy is the process of demonstrating a behavior for a student to imitate; modeling may also be referred to as "imitation learning." There are several types of models for students to imitate. A live model is most often used. However, written, picture, and audio models are also effective forms of instruction. Recently, many studies have shown the effectiveness of video modeling in teaching students with autism (e.g., LeBlanc et al., 2003). Before modeling can be used, however, the student must have prerequisite skills. These necessary skills include the ability to:

- Attend to the model
- Remember the behavior to be performed
- Reproduce the behavior

Finally, the student must be motivated to attend to and reproduce the behavior. Jashonne would benefit from video modeling as part of her social skills instruction. Specifically, a social skills interaction could be shown to her on a video. Following the video, the teacher could ask Jashonne what behaviors the models used. The teacher could also use pausing during the video. Specifically, when the video is paused, the teacher could ask Jashonne to look at facial expressions of the models and interpret their thoughts. The teacher could also have Jashonne predict what might happen in the conversation based on what the models have said.

Progress Monitoring

An essential element to any comprehensive ABA program is the use of progress monitoring. The most widely used progress monitoring is observational recording or what teachers may refer to as "data collection." Data are collected on each and every trial that a child experiences during DTT. Trial-by-trial data collection involves recording the child's response to virtually every learning opportunity occurring during daily therapy sessions. Each child's response is recorded as one of the following: independently correct, correct but prompted, incorrect, or no response. All child responses are summarized at the end of each therapy session (e.g., 2- to 3-hour blocks of therapy). For each individual skill, data are summed and graphed as a rate or percent correct. All instructional data are graphed and visually analyzed daily. Instructors modify their instruction based on the accomplishments achieved in the previous instructional session. As the child moves to more naturalistic intervention, data collection opportunities are then modified to ensure that representative samples of data are collected during an intervention session.

This chapter does not allow the space necessary to fully describe different progress monitoring techniques. Readers are referred to *Applied Behavior Analysis for Teachers* by Alberto and Troutman (2008) for additional information on ABA and progress monitoring.

VARIATIONS OF INSTRUCTIONAL FOCUS AND DELIVERY

Early phases of ABA instruction are often referred to as drill and practice because instructors present multiple discrete trials in close succession, hence the term discrete trial training (DTT). In DTT, the instructor may teach in blocks of 10 trials allowing the student short work breaks between blocks. However, as students acquire simple behaviors, instructors alter their procedures to reflect a more flexible instructional sequence. This is done through the presentation of varied discriminative stimuli as well as through the use of naturalistic behavioral teaching procedures such as natural environment training (NET), incidental teaching, and pivotal response teaching (PRT).

Verbal Behavior

In the past two decades, comprehensive ABA programs for students with autism have incorporated a consideration of "verbal behavior." **Verbal behavior** is the term B. F. Skinner (1957) coined for a behavioral approach to language. The primary contribution of incorporating Skinner's analysis of verbal behavior into instructional plans is that it reminds us to consider all possible functions of language during instruction. For example, asking for a car when you want a car is not necessarily the same thing as mentioning that you see a car when you are walking past one. Similarly, being able to imitate the word "car" is not the same thing as being able to have a conversation about cars. For typically developing children and adults, learning word meaning often results in being able to use that word in whatever manner is desired. However, research has shown that if individuals with developmental disabilities are taught to use a word in one manner (e.g., to label something), they may not necessarily be able to generalize the use of that same word for other purposes (e.g., to request something)

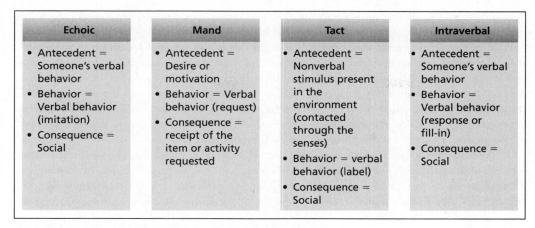

Echoic	Mand	Tact	Intraverbal
• Antecedent = Someone's verbal behavior • Behavior = Verbal behavior (imitation) • Consequence = Social	• Antecedent = Desire or motivation • Behavior = Verbal behavior (request) • Consequence = receipt of the item or activity requested	• Antecedent = Nonverbal stimulus present in the environment (contacted through the senses) • Behavior = verbal behavior (label) • Consequence = Social	• Antecedent = Someone's verbal behavior • Behavior = Verbal behavior (response or fill-in) • Consequence = Social

FIGURE 6.8 Overview of Skinner's Analysis of Verbal Behavior

(Sigafoos, Doss, & Reichle, 1989). Therefore, assessing and teaching each individual function of a word is often necessary when working with individuals with autism who are beginning to learn language.

Although language is commonly divided into expressive or receptive skills, Skinner provides us with expanded components of language that go beyond these more simplistic types and include the function of the language, rather than just its form (Barbera, 2007). Figure 6.8 and Figure 6.9 provide an overview of Skinner's verbal behavior components with examples of each and an example of an adult conversation with the components of verbal behavior highlighted.

Echoics are typically one of the first verbal operants taught in behavioral intervention programs for children with autism. **Echoic** instruction teaches students to imitate spoken words. This is also the same as a verbal model prompt. Specifically, the teacher says, "Say 'ball'" and the student echoes or imitates this by saying "ball." Learning to engage in echoics is the foundation of all remaining verbal

---

Two mothers at the neighborhood playground.

Alice: "This is a great park." (tact)

Jamie: "I know; I love it. My name is Jamie, are you new here?" (intraverbal; mand for information)

Alice: "I'm Alice, and we just moved in yesterday." (intraverbal)

Jamie: "Welcome. How old are your kids? Do you have only the one?" (mand for information)

Alice: "Thank you. No, we have one older one in school; she's 5. This one is 20 months. How old are yours?" (intraverbal; mand for information)

Jamie: "I have five actually; my older two are in school also—second and fifth grade. These guys are 4, 2, and almost a year."

Alice: "Wow, you're busy." (intraverbal)

Jamie: "Busy." (echoic)

Jamie (looking at watch): "It's almost 2:00. I need to go. Will I see you here tomorrow?" (tact; mand for information)

Alice: "I think so. I'll have to see how unpacking goes. Nice to meet you." (intraverbal)

Jamie: "You, too." (intraverbal)

FIGURE 6.9 Example of Adult Conversation Analyzed Using Skinner's Verbal Behavior

behavior because it teaches the student the ability to imitate vocal model prompts during future instruction.

Concurrent with echoic instruction, most verbal behavior programs focus on teaching basic mands, or requests (Barbera, 2007). The primary advantage of beginning with mand instruction is that it builds upon the student's natural motivation (Barbera, 2007). For example, a teacher may hold an item the student wants, such as a cookie, just out of reach and prompt her to sign "cookie"; the consequence is receipt of the cookie. **Mand** training helps the student build simple associations between desired items and the words that represent them, which in turn increases the likelihood that she will make that sign or say that word to get the item in the future.

Tact instruction is often used to increase a student's vocabulary. Tacting consists of basic naming, labeling, and commenting on stimuli in the environment. Tacting in typical development is often observed when toddlers "show off" newly learned names of objects by pointing out those objects every time they see them. Tact instruction should focus on establishing independent or spontaneous tact abilities by preventing prompt dependence as much as possible. Tact instruction is also used to increase a student's vocabulary for a variety of words including common nouns, verbs, adjectives, adverbs, prepositions, and so forth.

Receptive language instruction may precede tact instruction or they may occur simultaneously through what is known as a "transfer trial." A transfer trial transfers the behavior from one language form to another in two back-to-back discrete trials. For example, the teacher places two color cards on the table in front of the student and delivers the S^D, "Show me red." When the student points to red, the teacher praises the student, then immediately picks up the card and delivers the S^D, "What color is it?" Having just heard the teacher name the color as red, the student is more likely to say red in response to the S^D than if the tact trial had been presented in isolation, thus eliminating the need for a prompt. One must be careful in transfer trials that the student does not become dependent upon the receptive trial to get the expressive or tact trial correct. Probing tact trials in isolation will determine whether or not the student is able to truly tact the item.

An **intraverbal** is a verbal behavior that occurs in response to another verbal behavior (Skinner, 1957). Examples of intraverbal instruction include teaching higher-level verbal skills such as categorization (Petursdottir, Carr, Lechago, & Almason, 2008) and antonyms (Perez-Gonzalez, Garcia-Asenjo, Williams, & Carnerero, 2007). Intraverbal instruction may also include "fill-ins." In a fill-in, the student essentially finishes a sentence delivered as the S^D. For example, the teacher may say, "You sleep in a . . ." and the student is expected to finish or fill in the sentence with the intraverbal, "bed." Intraverbal instruction can include answering questions, asking for more information, and carrying out conversations. A critical element of intraverbal instruction is to teach multiple examples and vary instructions frequently in order to avoid rote learning. For example, when teaching a child to respond to the instruction "Name some animals," one should take care to teach as many different animals as possible answers and to not always list the same ones in the same order.

In the very early days of ABA programs for students with autism, some programs focused on teaching receptive and expressive labels only. This resulted in the failure to address spontaneous requesting, spontaneous commenting, and conversational skills. Therefore, a comprehensive approach to ABA for students with autism should include a consideration of verbal behavior skills and a range of communicative functions when developing instructional plans for skill acquisition.

Maintenance and Generalization

Quality instructional programs must be developed with a plan for maintenance and generalization. Years of research in behavior analysis have shown that instruction using multiple exemplar training, intermittent schedules of reinforcement, and natural reinforcement are likely to promote both maintenance and generalization (Stokes & Baer, 1977). Additionally, procedures such as sequential modification, mediation, and general case instruction can be used to promote generalization.

One way of using multiple exemplar training is to transition from strict presentations of the discriminative stimuli (S^D) and uniform phrases (e.g., "Hi Johnny!") to more generalized or loose S^D presentations (e.g., "Hi," "Hello," "How's it going?"). This is often referred to as "training loosely" and is used in programs designed to facilitate generalization (e.g., Horner, Eberhard, & Sheehan, 1986).

Contingency management is another strategy that has been shown through research to promote generalization and maintenance of skills (e.g., Baer, 1999; Craft, Alber, & Heward, 1998; Hoch, McComas, Thompson, & Paone, 2002). Contingency management is accomplished by changing the type and schedule of reinforcement. Specifically, reinforcement is moved from primary and contrived reinforcers (e.g., candy or "good job") to natural and secondary reinforcers (e.g., access to requested item or high five). Contingency management may also include teaching students to ask for reinforcement in the generalization setting. Meanwhile, the reinforcement schedule is faded from a fixed predictable schedule to a more variable and natural schedule. For example, during the early stages of learning, students gain access to the reinforcer on every trial. However, when skills are acquired, the schedule of reinforcement must change to meet a more natural schedule of reinforcement. For example, when a student is first learning body parts, he may be praised each time he touches his nose. Once the skill is acquired, the reinforcement is faded to an unpredictable and more natural schedule.

A comprehensive ABA program should consider various strategies for instruction based on the skills to be taught as well as the individual student. While ABA is proven via decades of research to be effective, the specific programs vary from student to student and include the myriad of approaches discussed here.

Incidental and Milieu Teaching

As discussed in Chapter 3, incidental and **milieu teaching** strategies are used within the context of the natural environment and often during daily routines. Some environmental arrangement strategies may be used to elicit language or to increase the likelihood of manding (Hemmeter & Kaiser, 1994). Environmental arrangement strategies include sabotage, blocking, missing pieces, and small portions. Sabotage involves setting up a learning opportunity in advance so that the desired behavior is most likely to occur. For example, a teacher places a preferred magazine on a high shelf and waits for Aidan to show interest in obtaining it. When Aidan shows an interest in the magazine, the teacher prompts Aidan to request the item if Aidan is in skill acquisition. If Aidan is in maintenance and generalization, the teacher uses a time delay prompt to see if Aidan will request independently. Another example would be handing the student a closed container that he cannot open and prompting him to ask for help. Blocking is used incidentally when the student attempts to gain access to a desired item or activity and the teacher blocks access contingent on a specific requesting behavior. Missing pieces may be used in a number of situations. For example, the teacher may present Jashonne with a puzzle that she is motivated to complete, but the teacher withholds one or more pieces. When Jashonne notices the missing pieces, the teacher uses the situation to capitalize on social skills instruction. Another example would be to give Enrique something to eat but not give him a fork. The teacher would use an appropriate prompt (e.g., most to least or least to most) depending on Enrique's learning phase. Enrique would obtain the fork, but only after the desired behavior of requesting the fork.

In each of these examples, the behavioral response is communicative. Other examples of **incidental teaching** include teaching self-help skills during naturally occurring opportunities. For example, when it is time to go outside, the teacher may take that opportunity to teach Aidan the steps of putting on his jacket. Discrete trials may also be used during incidental or learning opportunities. For example, at recess on the playground the teacher may deliver the S^D "slide" and then prompt Enrique to slide down the slide. Enrique receives a high five for sliding when asked to slide. It is a common myth that DTT must be done "at a table" or only in multiple trials. Boutot, Guenther, and Crozier (2005) successfully taught a 4- year-old with autism to engage in typical play activities through the use of DTT in the natural environment.

USING ABA TO ADDRESS CHALLENGING BEHAVIORS

Increased prevalence of challenging behaviors, such as stereotypy, tantrums, aggression, self-injury, and property destruction are common in students with ASD. As such, a foundational component of an instructional package is a positive, functional approach to addressing challenging behaviors.

Before any intervention plan is developed for challenging behaviors, a functional behavioral assessment should be completed in order to determine the antecedents and consequences that are evoking and/or reinforcing the challenging behavior. Intervention plans are then developed based on the function of the behavior. Chapter 5 provides a comprehensive description of functional behavioral assessment and the development of behavioral interventions for students with ASD.

Family Involvement

As discussed in Chapter 4, family involvement is not only required by law (e.g., IDEIA, 2004), but is also critical to student success. A key component to ABA programming is stakeholder participation in decision making. Specifically, skills that are to be taught within an ABA program must be "socially important" (Schwartz & Baer, 1991). Thus, in order to determine the social importance of a particular skill, family members should be consulted. Further, cultural differences and priorities of the family should also be considered. (See Box 6.2, Diversity Notes, for more suggestions.) Identifying and teaching skills that have social importance and are agreed upon by the family increases the likelihood that we are teaching skills that (a) the student needs to learn for his everyday life and (b) will be supported in the natural environment of the home and community.

BOX 6.2   Diversity Notes

In one of the few studies available examining the impact of culture on application of the principles of applied behavior analysis for students with autism, Wang and colleagues examined the role of cross-cultural competence in using positive behavior supports (PBS) to change the challenging behavior of a 14-year-old Chinese-American girl with autism (2007). The authors define "cross-cultural competence" as "'the ability to think, feel, and act in ways that acknowledge, respect, and build upon ethnic, socio-cultural, and linguistic diversity'" (Lynch & Hanson, 1993, p. 50, as cited in Want, McCart, & Turnbull, 2007, p. 38). The researchers provide tips for professionals working with culturally diverse families when implementing PBS to change a challenging behavior at each of three stages in the process. In the first stage, the planning stage, the researchers suggest that professionals should reflect on their own cultural values and beliefs and learn the families' expectations, their perceptions on the disability, their discipline practices, and their nonverbal communication style. In the second stage, during the conducting of a functional behavioral assessment and development of the behavior intervention plan, they suggest taking time to build trust and rapport with the family using a mediator (for example, a family friend) to help build this trust, identify natural supports within the family and/or community, communicate honestly, clear up misunderstandings and disagreements, and recognize that families can take time to make decisions. Finally, in the third stage, during implementation of the intervention, the researchers suggest that professionals listen to the opinions of the family regarding the efficacy of the intervention strategies, respond to the family's questions and concerns, help the family establish goals, and recognize that "development of cultural reciprocity requires time and persistence" (p. 48). Results of their study in which cross-cultural competence was utilized found that the young lady's behavior improved and was maintained over time.

Source: Information from Wang, M., McCart, A., & Turnbull, A.P. (2007). Implementing positive behavior support with Chinese American families: Enhancing cultural competence. *Journal of Positive Behavior Interventions, 9*(1), 38–51.

Another component of family involvement that should be considered within a comprehensive ABA program is family training. Although family members may not wish to be their child's "therapist," research supports that the more families understand and are able to carry out the various ABA strategies within the context of their daily routines, the more opportunities their children have for learning specific skills (Lovaas, Koegel, Simmons, & Long, 1973). Early childhood professionals have long suggested that parents are their children's first teachers (Sandall, Hemmeter, Smith, & McLean, 2005). For typically developing children, this teaching includes incidental strategies that are often not even considered true "teaching." However, because children with ASD may require more direct and systematic instruction and may not learn skills just through exposure to them, teaching families to use specific, proven ABA strategies is a way of ensuring that when learning opportunities present themselves the child has the opportunity to be successful in that learning.

Determining Intensity of Individual Instructional Time

WEEKLY INTENSITY OF INTERVENTION   The recommended intensity of intervention is an often debated topic. However, the research on intervention intensity should be used to determine the amount of intervention that is recommended for students.

The initial Lovaas (1987) study included a group of children who received low-intensity and high-intensity ABA. Low-intensity intervention was defined as approximately 10 hours per week while high-intensity intervention was defined as 40 hours per week. Results showed that children in the high-intensity group had significantly better outcomes in intellectual and adaptive functioning.

Eldevick, Jahr, Eikeseth, and Smith (2006) compared low-intensity ABA to a control group. There was no high-intensity group in this study. The authors conducted a study wherein children with autism received low-intensity ABA therapy (approximately 12 hours per week) for 2 years. These participants achieved statistically significant gains when compared to a control group but the gains were considerably lower than those found in studies of high-intensity ABA. Reed, Osborne, and Corness (2006) descriptively compared 9-month outcomes of a group of children who received a mean of 30 hours per week of ABA therapy to a group of children who received a mean of 12 hours of ABA therapy per week and found that the high-intensity group achieved significantly greater gains. Smith, Groen, and Wynn (2000) evaluated the effects of 25 hours per week of ABA therapy for 2 years. Results indicated that the ABA group achieved gains that were statistically significant when compared to a control group but that were considerably lower than those produced by studies of higher-intensity ABA (e.g., 30 to 40 hours per week). Taken together, the four studies summarized above appear to indicate that 1:1 intervention at less than 25 hours per week is not likely to result in as many developmental gains. On the other hand, optimal outcomes are associated with ABA instruction that is provided at higher weekly intensities.

It is often difficult for classroom teachers to provide instruction at such intensive levels. Rarely do classrooms have a 1:1 ratio of staff to students to support high-intensity levels. Therefore, teachers must develop creative ways to deliver instruction as intensively as possible. Teachers can improve the intensity of services through classroom structure, student grouping procedures, and incidental teaching procedures.

When setting up classrooms, teachers should structure the daily schedule so that each student has the opportunity for one-to-one instruction as much as possible each day. The instructional day should include little or no down time. Students with autism are more likely to engage in stereotypical behaviors (e.g., non learning behaviors) during down time. Teachers should arrange classroom schedules with minimal transitions. Transitions are often difficult for students with autism. Moreover, tantrums are most often associated with transition activities. As such, decreasing the number of transitions will result in fewer challenging behaviors and increased time for student learning. Finally, teachers should develop lesson plans that result in as many learning trials as possible each day. Learning trials should be comprised of a variety of types of learning including 1:1, small group, large-group choral responding, and natural environment training.

Teachers can utilize effective grouping to increase 1:1 instructional opportunities. One-to-one instruction with a student can take place while the other students are being taught in small groups or working on independent activities. Students with similar Individualized Education Program (IEP) objectives can be grouped together in groups of two or three at the same table using the same or similar materials. In this situation the teacher delivers DTT to one student while the others are working on an independent task or engaged with a reinforcing activity. At the end of the trial, the teacher then moves to the next student until each student has received 1:1 instructional trials.

Finally, teachers may use incidental teaching strategies, as discussed previously, to provide increased opportunities for 1:1 instruction. Incidental teaching trials can be delivered in the lunch line, in the restroom, on the playground, during hallway transitions, and during centers or free-play activities. Incidental teaching trials should be delivered in different ways as opposed to identical instructional delivery. Students may predict the instructional situation rather than learn how to exhibit the behavior under different contexts.

DURATION OF INTERVENTION   The total duration of intervention (i.e., in years, months, etc.) required to produce optimal gains for students with autism is also commonly debated. However, several research studies suggest that intensive intervention for 2 or more years is likely needed to produce optimal results. Howard, Sparkman, Cohen, Green, & Stanislaw (2005) compared 14 months of intensive ABA therapy to eclectic therapy of the same duration for young children with autism. Results showed that the ABA group made statistically significant gains when compared to the control group. However, the gains were less than those in studies that evaluated intensive ABA for 2 or more years (e.g., Cohen, et al., 2006; Lovaas, 1987; Sallows & Graupner, 2005). Similarly, Eikeseth, Smith, Jahr, and Eldevick (2002) evaluated the effects of intensive ABA therapy for 1 year and found significant results, but still lower than those in studies evaluating longer-term ABA therapy. Reed, Osborne, and Corness (2006) found that 9 months of intensive ABA produced significant gains but lesser gains than studies evaluating long-term ABA. Finally, Scheinkopf and Siegel (1998) evaluated ABA therapy that was both lower in intensity (approximately 20 hours per week) and shorter in duration (approximately 15 months) and found that children again achieved statistically significant gains in IQ when compared to controls but that the gains were smaller than those found in studies that implemented ABA for 2 or more years. These four studies, particularly when contrasted with existing studies on longer-term ABA therapy, provide evidence that ABA therapy for children with autism should be provided for 2 or more years, if optimal outcomes are desired. Given that most students with autism enter school settings at ages 3 through 5 and remain there until at least age 18, teachers should be able to provide long-term intervention for their students on the autism spectrum.

Given the significant volume of research on the outcome of intensive ABA intervention for students with autism, it seems clear that ABA is the methodology of choice for teaching students from this population. Additionally, all research cited above was published in peer-reviewed scientific journals, thus meeting the requirement under IDEA of 2004. Furthermore, it should be noted that there is not a single controlled study published in a peer-reviewed journal that demonstrates robust intervention effects in students with autism without the use of ABA therapy. Finally, studies that have evaluated ABA therapy of short duration and/or of low intensity indicate that optimal outcomes are not produced. In order for students with autism to achieve maximal intervention effects, multiple studies have demonstrated that ABA should be provided for more than 25 hours per week and for a minimum duration of 2 years.

Summary

Many peer-reviewed research studies have concluded that an intervention approach using the principles of ABA yield significant results for students with autism. In fact, Simpson (2005) as discussed in Chapter 3, finds that ABA is the only practice currently available that meets the requirements of being evidence-based. Given the fact that both the No Child Left Behind Act (NCLB, 2001) and the Individuals with Disabilities Education Improvement Act (IDEIA, 2004) require that teachers use research-based practices, the use of ABA strategies in teaching students with autism is an essential component of any comprehensive program for these students. Teachers are encouraged to seek advanced training in the use of ABA strategies and to remain current on the research in the field in order to best serve their students on the autism spectrum.

Chapter Review Questions

1. Describe and give an example of discrete trial training for a student with autism. (Objective 1)
2. Describe and give an example of errorless teaching for a student with autism. (Objective 2)
3. Describe and give an example of error correction with a student with autism. (Objective 3)
4. Describe and give an example of both generalization and maintenance for a student with autism. (Objective 4)
5. Describe and give an example of incidental teaching for a student with autism. (Objective 5)

Key Terms

Applied behavior analysis (ABA) *142*
Chaining *151*
Discrete trial training (DTT) *145*
Discriminative stimulus *145*
Echoic *153*
Error correction *149*

Generalization *148*
Incidental teaching *155*
Instructional control *147*
Intraverbal *154*
Maintenance *148*
Mand *154*

Milieu teaching *155*
Modeling *151*
Principles of Behavior *142*
Shaping *150*
Tact *154*
Verbal Behavior *152*

References

Alberto, P. A., & Troutman, A. C. (2008). *Applied behavior analysis for teachers.* Upper Saddle River, NJ: Pearson Education.

Baer, D. M. (1999). *How to plan for generalization* (2nd ed.). Austin, TX: Pro-Ed.

Barbera, M. (2007). *The verbal behavior approach: How to teach children with autism and related disorders.* London: Jessica Kingsley Publishers.

Bolton, J., & Mayer, M. D. (2008). Promoting the generalization of paraprofessional discrete trial teaching skills. *Focus on autism and other developmental disabilities, 23*(2), 103–111.

Boutot, E. A., Guenther, T., & Crozier, S. (2005). Lets play! Teaching play skills to young children with autism. *Education and Training in Developmental Disabilities, 40*(3), 285–292.

Cohen, H., Amerine-Dickens, M., & Smith, T. (2006). Early intensive behavioral intervention: Replication of the UCLA model in a community setting. *Developmental and Behavioral Pediatrics, 2,* S145–S157.

Craft, M. A., Alber, S. R., & Heward, W. L. (1998). Teaching elementary students with developmental disabilities to recruit teacher attention in a general education classroom: Effects on teacher praise and academic productivity. *Journal of Applied Behavior Analysis, 31*, 399–415.

Eikeseth, S. (2009). Outcome of comprehensive psycho-educational interventions for young children with autism. *Research in Developmental Disabilities, 30*, 158–178.

Eikeseth, S., Smith, T., Jahr, E., & Eldevik, S. (2002). Intensive behavioral intervention at school for 4- to 7-year-old children with autism. *Behavior Modification, 26*, 49–68.

Eikeseth, S., Smith, T., Jahr, E., & Eldevik, S. (2007). Outcome for children with autism who began intensive behavioral intervention between ages 4 and 7: A comparison controlled study. *Behavior Modification, 31*, 264–278.

Eldevik, S., Eikeseth, S., Jahr, E., & Smith, T. (2006). Effects of low-intensity behavioral intervention for children with autism and mental retardation. *Journal of Autism and Developmental Disorders, 36*, 211–224.

Greene, B. F., Winett, R. A., Van Houten, R. V., Geller, E. S., & Iwata, B. A. (1987). *Behavior analysis in the community: 1968–1986* (Reprint Series, Volume 2). Lawrence, KS: Society for the Experimental Analysis of Behavior.

Hagopian, L. P., Farrell, D. A., & Amari, A. (1996). Treating total liquid refusal with backward chaining and fading. *Journal of Applied Behavior Analysis, 29*, 573–575.

Hart, B. M., & Risley, T. R. (1975). Incidental teaching of language in the preschool. *Journal of Applied Behavior Analysis, 8*, 411–420.

Hemmeter, M. L., & Kaiser, A. P. (1994). Enhanced milieu teaching: Effects of parent-implemented language intervention. *Journal of Early Intervention, 18*, 269–289.

Hoch, H., McComas, J. J., Thompson, A. L., & Paone, D. (2002). Concurrent reinforcement schedules: Behavior change and maintenance without extinction. *Journal of Applied Behavior Analysis, 35*, 155–169.

Horner, R. H., Eberhard, J. M., & Sheehan, M. R. (1986). Teaching generalized table bussing: The importance of negative teaching examples. *Behavior Modification, 10*, 457–471.

Howard, J. S., Sparkman, C. R., Cohen, H. G., Green, G., & Stanislaw, H. (2005). A comparison of behavior analytic and eclectic interventions for children with autism. *Research in Developmental Disabilities, 26*, 359–383.

Iwata, B. A., Bailey, J. S., Neef, N. A., Wacker, D. P., Repp, A. C., & Shook, G. L. (1997). *Behavior analysis in developmental disabilities* (3rd ed.). Lawrence, KS: Society for the Experimental Analysis of Behavior.

Koegel, L. K., Camarata, S., Valdez-Menchaca M., & Koegel, R. L. (1998). Generalization of question asking in children with autism. *American Journal on Mental Retardation, 102*, 346–357.

LeBlanc, L. A., Coates, A. M., Daneshvar, S., Charlop-Christy, M. H., Morris, C., & Lancaster, B. M. (2003). Using video modeling and reinforcement to teach perspective taking skills to children with autism. *Journal of Applied Behavior Analysis, 36*, 253–257.

Losardo, A., & Bricker, D. (1994). A comparison study: Activity-based intervention and direct instruction. *American Journal on Mental Retardation, 98,* 744–765.

Lovaas, I. O. (1987). Behavioral intervention and normal educational and intellectual functioning in young autistic children. *Journal of Consulting and Clinical Psychology, 55,* 3–9.

Lovaas, I. O., Koegel, R., Simmons, J. O., & Long, J. S. (1973). Some generalization and follow-up measures on autistic children in behavior therapy. *Journal of Applied Behavior Analysis, 6,* 131–166.

McEachin, J. J., Smith T., & Lovaas, I. O. (1993). Long-term outcome for children with autism who received early intensive behavioral intervention. *American Journal on Mental Retardation, 55,* 359–372.

McWilliams, R., Nietupski, J., & Hamre-Nietupski, S. (1990). Teaching complex activities to students with moderate handicaps through the forward chaining of shorter total cycle response sequences. *Education and Training in Mental Retardation, 25,* 292–298.

Myers, S. M., & Johnson, C. P. (2007). Management of children with autism spectrum disorders. *Pediatrics, 120,* 1162–1182.

National Academy of Sciences (2001). *Educating children with autism.* Commission on Behavioral and Social Sciences and Education. Washington, DC: Author.

New York State Department of Health, Early Intervention Program (1999). *Clinical practice guideline: Report of the recommendations: Autism / Pervasive developmental disorders: Assessment and intervention for young children (age 0–3 years).* New York: Author.

Pavlov, I. P. (1927). *Conditioned reflexes: An investigation of the physiological activity of the cerebral cortex* (G. V. Anrep, Trans.). London: Oxford University Press.

Pérez-González, L. A., García-Asenjo, L., Williams, G., & Carnerero, J. J. (2007) Emergence of intraverbal antonyms in children with pervasive developmental disorder. *Journal of Applied Behavior Analysis, 40,* 697–701.

Petursdottir, A. I., Carr, J. E., Lechago, S. A., & Almason, S. M. (2008). An evaluation of intraverbal training and listener training for teaching categorization skills. *Journal of Applied Behavior Analysis, 41,* 53–68.

Reed, P., Osborne, L. A., & Corness, M. (2006). Brief report: Relative effectiveness of different home-based behavioral approaches to early teaching intervention. *Journal of Autism and Developmental Disorders.* Manuscript published electronically, ahead of print.

Reichow, B., & Wolery, M. (2009). Comprehensive synthesis of early intensive behavioral interventions for young children with autism based on the UCLA young autism project model. *Journal of Autism and Developmental Disorders, 39,* 23–41.

Rogers, S. J., & Vismara, L. A. (2008). Evidence-based comprehensive treatments for early autism. *Journal of Clinical Child & Adolescent Psychology, 37,* 8–38.

Sallows, G. O., & Graupner, T. D. (2005). Intensive behavioral intervention for children with autism: Four-year outcome and predictors. *American Journal on Mental Retardation, 110,* 417–438.

Sandall, S., Hemmeter, M. L., Smith, B. J., & McLean, M. E. (2005). *DEC recommended practices: A comprehensive guide.* St. Paul, MN: Red Leaf Press.

Schwartz, I. S., & Baer, D. M. (1991). Social validity assessments: Is current practice state of the art? *Journal of Applied Behavior Analysis, 24,* 189–204.

Sheinkopf, S. J., & Siegel, B. (1998). Home-based behavioral intervention of young children with autism. *Journal of Autism and Developmental Disorders, 28,* 15–23.

Sigafoos, J., Doss, S., & Reichle, J. (1989). Developing mand and tact repertoires in persons with severe developmental disabilities using graphic symbols. *Research in developmental disabilities, 10,* 183–200.

Simpson, R. L. (2005). *autism spectrum disorders: Interventions and treatments for children and youth.* Thousand Oaks, CA: Corwin Press.

Skinner, B. F. (1953). *Science and human behavior.* New York: Macmillan.

Skinner, B. F. (1957). *Verbal behavior.* New York: Appleton-Century-Crofts.

Smith, T. (2001). Discrete trial training in the treatment of autism. *Focus on Autism and Developmental Disabilities, 16,* 86–92.

Smith, T., Groen, A. D., & Wynn, J. W. (2000). Randomized trial of intensive early intervention for children with pervasive developmental disorder. *American Journal on Mental Retardation, 105,* 269–285.

Stokes, T. F., & Baer, D. M. (1977). An implicit technology of generalization. *Journal of Applied Behavior Analysis, 10,* 349–367.

Sugai, G., & Horner, R. H. (2002). The evolution of discipline practices: School-wide positive behavior supports. *Child and Family Behavior Therapy, 24,* 23–50.

Touchette, P. E., & Howard, J. S. (1984). Errorless learning: Reinforcement contingencies and stimulus control transfer in delayed prompting. *Journal of Applied Behavior Analysis, 17,* 175–188.

U.S. Department of Health and Human Services (1999). *Mental health: A report of the surgeon general.* Rockville, MD: U.S. Department of Health and Human Services, Substance Abuse and Mental Health Services Administration, Center for Mental Health Services, National Institutes of Health, National Institute of Mental Health.

Wallace, M. D., Iwata, B. A., & Hanley, G. P. (2006). Establishment of mands following tact training as a function of reinforcer strength. *Journal of Applied Behavior Analysis, 39,* 17–24.

Wang, M., McCart, A., & Turnbull, A.P. (2007). Implementing positive behavior support with Chinese American families: Enhancing cultural competence. *Journal of Positive Behavior Interventions, 9*(1), 38–51.

Werts, M. G., Caldwell, N. K., & Wolery, M. (1996). Peer modeling of response chains: Observational learning by students with disabilities. *Journal of Applied Behavior Analysis, 29,* 53–66.

7

Comprehensive Behavior Interventions for Individuals with Autism Spectrum Disorders

Barry G. Grossman, Ph.D. and Ruth Aspy, Ph.D.
The Ziggurat Group

CHAPTER OBJECTIVES

After reading this chapter, learners should be able to:

1. Describe the purpose of functional behavior assessment (FBA) and the elements of an FBA.

2. Explain the importance of considering the underlying characteristics of ASD when addressing behavioral concerns.

3. Describe the five levels of behavior intervention and identify them as antecedent, behavior, or consequences strategies.

4. Outline the elements of a comprehensive behavior intervention plan.

5. Explain how the demands of typical daily activities may differ for people with ASD and discuss suggested strategies for increasing support and decreasing demands for these individuals.

INTRODUCTION

Individuals with Autism Spectrum Disorders (ASD) often experience behavioral difficulties that have widespread impact on their lives (Horner, Carr, Strain, Todd, & Reed, 2002; Myles & Southwick, 2005) and can negatively affect those who care for them (Lecavalier, Leone, & Wiltz, 2006; Sakai, 2005). Without appropriate treatment and support, behavior difficulties may be present across the lifespan. Children and adolescents with ASD often display a number of emotional and behavior problems that are stable over time and result in increased stress for the family (Herring et al., 2006; Lecavalier et al., 2006) and educators (Lecavalier et al., 2006). Long-term outcomes for individuals on the autism spectrum are improving; however, most require ongoing support (Howlin, 2000; Howlin, Goode, Hutton, & Rutter, 2004). "Optimal development depends on the successful identification and treatment of [behavior] problems, achieved through the strategies of functional assessment (Horner & Carr, 1997) and **comprehensive intervention**" (cited in Bregman, Zager, & Gerdtz, 1997, p. 897). Whereas functional assessment is widely accepted as the status quo, comprehensive approaches to intervention are considered to be revolutionary. This chapter provides a brief review of the role of functional assessment in behavior intervention. Discussion of the need for comprehensive intervention follows. Last, this chapter introduces a framework, known as the **Ziggurat Model**, for the development of comprehensive behavior interventions.

FUNCTIONAL BEHAVIORAL ASSESSMENT

According to behavior theory, events that precede (**antecedents**) and follow (**consequences**) a behavior affect that behavior. Careful analysis of antecedents, behavior, and consequences (the ABCs) provides insight into the purpose or function of a behavior. This analysis is called a **functional behavior assessment (FBA)**. Studies have demonstrated that functional behavior assessments increase the effectiveness of interventions (Carr et al., 1999; Ellingson, Miltenberger, Stricker, Galensky, & Garlinghouse, 2000). The first step in a functional behavior assessment is careful definition of the behavior in observable and measurable terms—an operational definition. Once the behavior is carefully defined, information is gathered through observation, interviews, and other methods. Based on analysis of the ABC data, a function is determined. Figure 7.1 contains a list of common antecedents to behavioral difficulties. Common functions of behavior include: escape/avoidance, attainment of attention, attainment of a tangible item, access to a preferred activity, and sensory stimulation.

Case Illustration

Dianne is a 4-year-old girl diagnosed with autism. She has little verbal communication and tends to "be in her own world." Dianne attends a preschool program for students with special needs. She has had difficulty adjusting to the school program and experiences frequent "meltdowns," especially when there are unexpected changes in the environment or school routine. Her teacher is concerned

---

- Time of day
- Presence of specific peers
- Specific classroom subject
- Transition from more preferred to less preferred activity (e.g., playing video game to homework)
- Change in routine
- Settings with decreased/increased structure (e.g., hallways, classroom, grocery store)
- Request to stop a behavior
- Punishment
- Medication changes
- Family circumstances (e.g., new baby, parental divorce, parent's new job, financial stress)
- Environmental changes (e.g., new paint at home, different classroom desk arrangement, weather)

FIGURE 7.1 Common Antecedents

Antecedent	Behavior (Off task)	Consequence
• Morning circle time • Request to join the circle • Unexpected changes	• Leaves the circle • Screams • Plays in rice tray	• Adult redirects Dianne to return to circle • Adult eventually withdraws request (to return to circle) • Play in rice tray

FIGURE 7.2 Functional Behavior Assessment for Diane

because Dianne frequently wanders away during morning group activities. Additionally, although her peers enjoy imaginary play with blocks, Dianne simply lines them up in rows. Many of her preferred activities center around sensory exploration. For example, she repetitively scoops up rice and closely examines the grains as she pours them back into the bin.

Dianne's teacher is concerned that she wanders off during morning group activities. Each time she is asked to join the morning circle, Dianne screams, leaves the circle, and plays in the rice tray. She is guided to return to the circle two or three times. Dianne eventually leaves again. She is then allowed to play with the rice until the circle time is over. During other class activities, such as one-on-one instruction and center time, Dianne remains on task. She does not go to the rice table that is still at her access. As depicted in Figure 7.2, the antecedents are circle time requests to join the morning activity, and unexpected changes in the school routine or in the environment. The behaviors include leaving the circle time activity, screaming, and playing in the rice tray. The consequences include adult redirection, withdrawal of request to return to the circle, and access to the rice tray (see Figure 7.2). The school team concluded from this FBA that avoidance of circle time is the function of Dianne's behavior. The possibility that access to the rice tray was an additional function was considered. Because Dianne participated in other daily activities without leaving the area for rice play, they determined that the avoidance of the circle time was more strongly maintaining the behavior than was access to the rice tray.

Note that change in routine was identified as an antecedent to behavioral difficulties for Dianne. The information in Box 7.1 provides current research on the types of changes that are often challenging for individuals with ASD.

BOX 7.1   Diversity Box

Many behavioral difficulties experienced by individuals with ASD are triggered by the need for sameness and the resulting lack of behavioral flexibility. Researchers conducted a survey of parents of three different groups of individuals—those with autism, Asperger Syndrome, and Down's Syndrome—to identify the situations in which these individuals insist on sameness. Situations identified included losing a game, objects breaking, and activities interrupted. Those with Asperger Syndrome were rated as having the least behavioral flexibility followed by those diagnosed with autism. Those with the diagnosis of Down's Syndrome had the least challenges in this area. No gender or age differences were found.

Source: Information from Green, V. A., Sigafoos, J., Pituch, K. A., Itchon, J., O'Reilly, M., & Lancioni, G. E. (2006). Assessing behavioral flexibility in individuals with developmental disabilities. *Focus on Autism and Other Developmental Disabilities, 21*(4), 230–236.

Antecedent	Behavior	Consequence
Cover the rice tray	Teach Dianne to sit on the carpet square	Reinforce Dianne for sitting correctly on the carpet square

FIGURE 7.3   Interventions Based on Dianne's FBA

INTERVENTION BASED ON AN FBA   As discussed above, behavior interventions are strengthened by an understanding of the pattern of behavior (antecedent-behavior-consequence). Each of these points provides an opportunity for intervention. Antecedent interventions are those that precede and prevent behavior problems from occurring. Interventions that occur at the point of behavior involve teaching a new skill, often called **replacement behaviors**. Consequence interventions alter the response to a behavior and often take the form of **reinforcement**. Figure 7.3 illustrates interventions at each of these three points for Dianne. The discussion that follows demonstrates that addressing the strengths and characteristics of individuals with ASD results in more effective and comprehensive behavior interventions.

BEYOND FUNCTIONAL ASSESSMENT: ADDRESSING UNDERLYING NEEDS

Those who do not understand the characteristics of autism are more likely to perceive those with the disorder as being poorly behaved or as "needing more discipline." It is critical for those in helping roles with individuals with ASD to be able to recognize characteristics of autism that underlie challenging behaviors. Not all behavioral difficulties are related to the underlying disorder. Indeed, individuals with ASD may willfully choose to engage in inappropriate behaviors; however, *misinterpreting behaviors as willful when they are not carries great risks*. A history of being punished for behavior that is related to an underlying disorder may result in low self-esteem, hopelessness, depression, and a lack of opportunity to learn alternative behaviors. *When in doubt, it is best to respond to a behavioral difficulty as if it is related to the underlying autism*. For this reason, those who wish to design effective behavior interventions must know the characteristics of the disorder.

Schopler (1994) used an **iceberg** as a metaphor to illustrate the concept that visible behaviors (the portion of the iceberg above the surface of the water) are manifestations of underlying or "hidden" characteristics of autism (the portion of the iceberg beneath the surface of the water). According to Schopler, effective behavior interventions must address underlying needs and not simply visible or "surface" behaviors. Recognizing when problem behaviors are a manifestation of ASD may be a challenging task that requires more than "common sense." Further, there must be a willingness and conscious determination to consider the possible role of the ASD in the behavior of concern.

Targeting underlying needs will lead to interventions that are more proactive and fundamental. In comparison, interventions that are designed solely to address surface behavior without consideration of the underlying ASD are potentially less effective and less likely to result in sustained behavior change. "Consideration of patterns of behavior in addition to underlying characteristics will lead to a better understanding of specific behavioral concerns and their unseen causes" (Aspy & Grossman, 2007, p. 47).

According to Horner et al. (2002), an effective behavior plan "should be developed based on a thorough analysis of biological, antecedent, and consequence events that control them" (p. 435). Further, intervention plans must be comprehensive. Horner et al. state that comprehensive interventions involve multiple strategies applied across all or most of the individual's day.

The strategies are informed by functional assessment and address multiple behavior challenges. The current trend toward use of positive behavioral supports (PBS) incorporate these critical features as well (see Box 7.2 for more information on PBS). The current authors assert that a comprehensive intervention plan also must be responsive to the characteristics of the individual with autism—both strengths and needs. Finally, comprehensive plans should address each of the three points of intervention—antecedent, behavior, and consequence.

BOX 7.2   Trends and Issues Notes

A recent trend is the emergence of **positive behavior supports (PBS)**. "PBS is a set of research-based strategies used to increase *quality of life* and decrease problem behavior by teaching new skills and making changes in a person's environment (Association for Positive Behavior Support, n.d.)." PBS's influence is perhaps most apparent in the public school setting. The Individuals with Disabilities Education Improvement Act (IDEIA), emphasizes preventative early intervention services and the use of positive behavior intervention approaches (2004).

Critical Features (from Carr, Dunlap, Horner, Koegel, Turnbull, Sailor et al., 2002, pp. 6–11) of PBS are described below.

Critical Features	Description
Comprehensive lifestyle change and quality of life	The goal is to comprehensively improve the quality of life for individuals and improve the systems in which they live.
Life span perspective	Intervention is viewed as a continuous process. Support must continue as the person matures and is required to interface in new settings.
Ecological validity	The intervention must be applicable in real life—not just in a laboratory setting.
Stakeholder participation	All stakeholders (e.g., parents and professionals) play an active role and collaborate in order to develop and implement an intervention plan.
Social validity	In order to be socially valid, interventions must be seen by the stakeholders as practical, effective, and so forth.
Systems change and multi-component intervention	The focus of intervention should be on changing the systems or contexts in which problem behaviors occur. Interventions will not be effective unless there is systemic change. This necessitates the use of multiple interventions.
Emphasis on prevention	"Intervention takes place in the absence of problem behavior so that such behavior can be prevented from occurring again" (p. 9).
Flexibility with respect to scientific practices	Appreciation and use of alternative practices.
Multiple theoretical perspectives	Appreciation of other perspectives that contribute to change.

Sources: Association of Positive Behavior Support (n.d.). *What is positive behavior support?* From http://www.apbs.org/PBSTopics.htm#OACA, retrieved October 13, 2007.

Carr, E., Dunlap, G., Horner, R. H., Koegel, R. L., Turnbull, A. P., Sailor, W. et al. (2002). Positive behavior support: Evolution of an applied science. *Journal of Positive Behavior Interventions, 4*(1), 4–16.

Individuals with Disabilities Education Act. (2004). *The Individuals with Disabilities Education Act Amendments of 2004.*

- Has difficulty imitating actions or words of others
- Chooses or prefers solitary activities
- Appears to be in "own world"
- Seems to be unmotivated by customary rewards
- Has little or no speech
- Has problems handling transition and change
- Has difficulty following instructions
- Seeks activities that provide touch, pressure, or movement (e.g., swinging, hugging, pacing, etc.)
- Appears to be unresponsive to others (e.g., unaware of presence of others; ignores greetings, questions, requests, and own name, etc.)
- Displays atypical activity level (e.g., overactive/hyperactive, underactive/hypoactive)

FIGURE 7.4 Characteristics of Autism that May Be Related to Dianne's Off-task Behavior

Recall the case example of Dianne. Her staff considered aspects of autism that were believed to underlie her off-task behavior (see Figure 7.4). Because Dianne does not have the social and communication skills required to be successful in interacting with others during circle time, she leaves the group and protests returning to this activity. For a behavior intervention to be effective, staff need to target these skills. Targeting underlying characteristics (i.e., autism) as opposed to looking solely at the behavior was a paradigm shift for Dianne's staff. Before staff considered the underlying autism, Dianne's behavior plan included covering the rice tray and teaching and rewarding her for sitting in her place. Because the context of autism was incorporated into the new intervention plan, staff included strategies to expand Dianne's communication skills and social interactions with peers. They understood that as Dianne's awareness of others increased, participation in circle time would become more meaningful to her. Communication and social skills were addressed by the speech therapist during individual and group sessions. The speech therapist also helped the staff to work on these skills throughout the course of a typical day. For example, her teacher observed that Dianne enjoyed movement. Staff encouraged play on the seesaw because the activity required cooperation with a peer. In time, staff would teach Dianne the communication skills associated with this activity (e.g., requesting). Other activities were designed to increase social interaction. Staff were aware of the importance of reinforcement in helping Dianne to learn and maintain these skills. With their new understanding of the impact of underlying characteristics, staff also decided to include interventions to address sensory needs.

In summary, when designing a comprehensive plan to address behavior difficulties, one must move beyond functional behavior assessment. It is critical to understand (a) characteristics of ASD and (b) what causes and maintains behavior. In order to be comprehensive, the plan must be (a) multi faceted, (b) implemented across all or most of an individual's day, and (c) responsive to unique needs and strengths that individuals with ASD present. Behavior interventions based on these principles require innovative thought. The Ziggurat Model provides a framework for designing comprehensive interventions (Aspy & Grossman, 2007). The model is consistent with the principles discussed above. The following is a discussion of behavior strategies outlined by the Ziggurat Model grouped into five areas that address the underlying autism at each point of intervention—antecedent, behavior, and consequence. Figure 7.5 depicts the five levels of the Intervention Ziggurat.

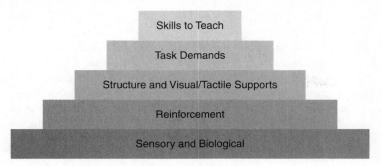

FIGURE 7.5 The Five Levels of the Intervention Ziggurat

ANTECEDENT INTERVENTIONS

Antecedent interventions are those that prevent behaviors from occurring by changing the environmental factors that precede them. It is generally preferable to be proactive rather than to be reactive. Research supports the power of these interventions (Reeve & Carr, 2000) to prevent severe behaviors. Based on the Ziggurat Model (Aspy & Grossman, 2007), antecedent interventions that are responsive to the needs of individuals with ASD are grouped into three broad areas: sensory differences and biological needs; **task demands**; and structure, **visual supports** and **tactile supports**.

SENSORY AND BIOLOGICAL INTERVENTIONS   There is an increasing awareness of sensory and biological differences among those with ASD. Unmet sensory and biological needs will necessarily result in changes in behavior. Differences in sensory processing are related to increases in behavioral difficulties such as self-stimulatory behaviors, crying, running away, withdrawing/failing to participate, becoming easily distracted, noise making, and tantrumming. Sensory differences are also related to increased levels of anxiety in adults and children. Hunger, fatigue, sleep disorders, fine and gross motor deficits, and illness also may be antecedents to behavioral difficulties. Designing the environment to minimize aversive sensory experiences and to be responsive to other biological needs will result in decreased behavioral challenges.

Sensory and biological strategies may be used as antecedent interventions, preventing behavioral difficulties rather than addressing them after they occur. For this reason, the development of comprehensive behavior intervention programs requires the consideration of biological and sensory factors and inclusion of interventions to address these needs.

Because sensory needs vary across individuals and across time, a current assessment of sensory functioning is a critical step in the development of a behavior intervention plan for those with ASD. Changes can then be made to adjust for identified areas of oversensitivity or undersensitivity. For example, interventions such as decreasing the number of wall decorations, adjusting the lighting, or decreasing the requirement to copy from a board may result in fewer behavior difficulties for individuals with visual **hypersensitivity**. Likewise, provision of headphones, simplification of verbal instructions, and provision of a warning before a fire drill may serve as behavior interventions for individuals with auditory hypersensitivity. Sensory interventions are available for each sensory area. Occupational therapists have expertise in identifying sensory needs and in developing sensory interventions; therefore, their participation may be key in the prevention of behavior difficulties.

TASK DEMANDS   Imagine the difficulties that individuals with ASD experience on a daily basis. Every activity or task may present unique challenges for them. Consider just a few of the skills required to be successful during recess. Children must have the social and communication skills necessary to start and join conversations and play. They must be able to tolerate the sounds and temperature encountered outdoors and to understand the unwritten playground rules (e.g., how to take turns on a swing). When tasks such as these are too demanding, they often become antecedents to challenging behaviors. When these behaviors occur, who is to blame—the person with ASD or the adult who placed the demands on them? All too often, individuals with ASD are seen as "the problem." They are labeled *defiant* or *oppositional* when given tasks that exceed their skills. Statements such as "He can do it if he wants to" or "He's 18 years old, he should know not to say that in public" are common. This perspective is harmful for the individual with an ASD and often is associated with a reluctance to employ one of the most effective strategies—an antecedent intervention.

Mr. Blackwell is the father of two children with ASD. He eloquently states, "We don't fix things that aren't broken, we remove obstacles for kids with infinite potential. I am in the obstacle removal business" (Blackwell et al., 2007). Mr. Blackwell understands the importance of addressing antecedents or "obstacles." In short, when behavior difficulties are observed, parents and professionals need to analyze the demands they are placing on an individual with an ASD and determine whether they exceed the abilities of the person on whom they are placed.

Figure 7.6 depicts a continuum of task demands. Demands may be considered to be easy, challenging, or too demanding. When skills required to be successful are all mastered, the task places few

Task Demands	
Level of Demand	**Applications**
Easy (independent skills–with or without modification and structural supports)	• Independent functioning • Review • Provide opportunity for success • Increase self-esteem
Challenging/Emerging (possible with assistance) Zone of Proximal Development	• Expand knowledge through scaffolding—learning new skills that build on those previously mastered • Generalization of skills to new situations/settings
	• Assessment to find the upper-limit of current skill development
Too Demanding	

FIGURE 7.6 Continuum of Task Demands
Source: Aspy, R., & Grossman, B. (2007). From *The Ziggurat Model: Designing Comprehensive Interventions for Individuals with High-Functioning Autism and Asperger Syndrome* (p. 77). Shawnee Mission, KS: Autism Asperger Publishing Company. Copyright 2007 by AAPC. Reprinted with permission.

demands on the individual. Such "easy" tasks are optimal when there is a desire for the individual to work independently. Some tasks may present a challenge when the required skills are emerging, but not yet mastered. This area is depicted in the center of the continuum—Vygotsky's zone of proximal development (ZPD) that is described below (1978, as cited in Miller, 1993, pp. 380–381).

The **zone of proximal development** defines those functions that have not yet been mastered but are in the process of maturation—functions that will mature tomorrow but are currently in an embryonic state. The functions could be termed the "buds" or "flowers" of development rather than the "fruits" of development.

Presenting tasks that are challenging is appropriate when there is a desire to expand skills. It is risky to present tasks that exceed an individual's skills; therefore, when tasks are challenging, it is necessary to provide support in order to facilitate success. The last area depicted on the continuum represents the point at which demands exceed ability. Behavior problems can be expected when tasks are too demanding. Failure to provide adequate support to accomplish easy and challenging tasks will result in demands that exceed ability. In summary, when developing a comprehensive plan to address behavior, it is essential to consider the demands being placed on an individual and to prevent problems through antecedent interventions. Obstacles must be removed and supports offered in order to facilitate success.

STRUCTURE AND VISUAL/TACTILE SUPPORTS   Addressing behavioral challenges through providing structure and visual/tactile supports is responsive to core characteristics of ASD including deficits in verbal communication and a need for routine and order. Failure to follow spoken instructions is often interpreted as noncompliance or defiance. Such behavior may actually be a reflection of difficulty with processing information delivered verbally. Providing instructions or rules through the use of visual (or tactile) supports allows those with ASD to understand expectations and decreases behavioral challenges.

While typically developing individuals are able to respond readily to spoken information, spoken instructions are often "lost" for individuals with ASD. Visual and tactile supports are less fleeting than auditory input. These supports hold information "still" to allow more time for processing.

Visual reminders or lessons, called visual supports, are often provided to address these concerns. Tactile supports are an additional alternative to verbal communication and should be considered, especially for students with a vision impairment. Interventions that increase structure and visual/tactile supports often overlap. Visual supports such as pictures, written schedules, and task strips may be used as tools to clarify the structure of an activity. Visual schedules have been shown to be effective for improving the speed of transitions (cf., Dettmer, Simpson, Myles, & Ganz, 2000), decreasing behavior problems during transition (cf., Dooley, Wilczenski, & Torem, 2001), increasing on-task behavior (cf., Bryan & Gast, 2000), and enhancing independence (cf., Pierce & Schreibman, 1994).

There is substantial research support for the effectiveness of other visual strategies, such as Social Stories™ (Odom et al., 2003; cf., Sansosti, Powell-Smith, & Kincaid, 2004) and video modeling (cf., Nikopoulos & Keenan, 2004) in reducing behavioral difficulties. **Video modeling** may involve the use of actors to demonstrate a skill. Alternatively, the observer may watch himself or herself performing a skill on video (video self-modeling). Video modeling has been effective in reducing tantrums and pushing (Buggey, 2005). Coyle and Cole (2004) found video self-modeling combined with self-monitoring to be effective in decreasing off-task behaviors in the classroom. The behavior improvement occurred rapidly and skills were maintained after the treatment ended. Video that is taped from the child's perspective has been found to be helpful in decreasing behavioral difficulties during transitions (Schriebman, Whalen, & Stahmer, 2000). Box 7.3 reviews a meta-analysis on current research on the use of video modeling with students with ASD.

BOX 7.3   Research Notes

The use of video in addressing behavior concerns seems a natural match for those with ASD. Video-based strategies capitalize on the visual processing strengths often present in those with ASD. Is the use of video-based behavior intervention strategies supported in the research? Bellini and Akullian (2007) address this question in their meta-analysis of video modeling and video self-modeling (VSM) interventions for children with Autism Spectrum Disorders.

In video modeling, an individual watches a behavior demonstrated on video and then imitates that behavior. In video-self modeling the positive behavior is demonstrated by the individual with the ASD and then reviewed in order to encourage imitation of that behavior. In the meta-analysis, Bellini and Akullian examine the maintenance effects—change in behavior over time—and generalization effects—transfer of skills across settings and persons—of these two strategies for individuals with ASD.

The results of the meta-analysis indicate that video modeling and VSM are effective strategies for addressing behavior concerns in those with ASD. One study found VSM to be effective in decreasing tantrums and pushing behaviors and in increasing prosocial language and social initiations. Effects were immediate and maintained over time. Studies examining the impact of VSM on off-task behaviors found less consistent results. The median duration of the videos used across all of the studies in the analysis was 3 minutes. The videos used in the studies were watched nine and a half times (median).

Bellini and Akullian observe that one advantage of VSM and video modeling is time effectiveness. They also note elements of these strategies that make them particularly helpful for those with ASD. For example, there is a tendency among some individuals with ASD to focus on irrelevant aspects of the environment. Video strategies allow removal of irrelevant details. Furthermore, by removing the social interactions often involved in instruction, video strategies allow the delivery of information without the related social stressors. Finally, because watching a video is often a preferred activity, video strategies provide a built-in source of reinforcement.

Source: Information from Bellini, S., & Akullian, J. (2007). A meta-analysis of video modeling and video self-modeling interventions for children and adolescents with autism spectrum disorders. *Exceptional Children, 73,* 364–287.

The predictability and information that structure and visual/tactile supports make available to those on the spectrum are critical aspects of any comprehensive behavior intervention plan.

In summary, antecedent interventions help to prevent behaviors from occurring by changing the environmental factors that precede them. The **Intervention Ziggurat** contains three levels that consist primarily of antecedent strategies. Dianne's antecedent interventions addressing the three levels of the Intervention Ziggurat are presented in Figure 7.7.

Behavior

Whereas it is possible to prevent many problem behaviors using antecedent interventions, another approach to addressing intervention is to teach new skills. Interventions that occur at this point focus on teaching new skills or alternative behaviors.

SKILLS TO TEACH   Behavior is communicative. Noncompliance and aggression speak volumes if one is willing to listen. Behavior problems often communicate that there are hidden skill deficits. As discussed earlier, it is important to look at behavior patterns in order to effectively intervene. Although it is possible to resolve some behavioral concerns through antecedent and consequence interventions, only teaching skills (i.e., replacement behaviors) increases the ability to function independently and

Antecedent	• Provide visual supports using pictures and symbols to structure the school day and to assist Dianne to communicate her wants and needs.
	• Shorten the length of circle time for Dianne and increase her interest by permitting her to hold her favorite stuffed animal only while seated with the group. Dianne's teacher says that she can currently sit for approximately 5 minutes. Staff will give her an alternate activity to complete and then require her to be in circle time for the last 5 minutes. Staff will gradually increase group time.
	• Build activities that provide movement into the school day.
	• Use a first-then visual chart. Before circle time, have Dianne select a reinforcer from a menu and place the symbol on the chart.
	• Assign Dianne an optimal location on the floor at the edge of the group so she is less crowded.

FIGURE 7.7 Dianne's Antecedent Interventions Based on Three Levels of the Intervention Ziggurat

decreases the need for support. It is for this reason that the ultimate goal of all comprehensive behavior interventions is skill acquisition.

As discussed earlier, when behavior problems emerge, there is a tendency to view the person with ASD as "the problem." This belief leads to punitive approaches to intervention. Recall that behavior difficulties are a strong indicator of skill deficits. Therefore, when behaviors persist, it is important to ask, "What skills are missing?" Scheuermann and Webber (2002, p. 73) offer the following rule of thumb: "If you seldom see the [person] exhibit the desired behavior under similar circumstances, assume the [person] does not know how to do the behavior (i.e., assume a skill deficit)."

Individuals with ASD often require direct instruction in skills that others seem to learn naturally. Seeing the missing skills can be difficult—especially when working with individuals who have average or above average skills in other areas of functioning. For example, a 12-year-old with Asperger Syndrome may be capable of producing college-level work; however, she may lack an understanding of simple social graces. Effective behavior intervention depends on the ability to recognize this "hidden curriculum." The **hidden curriculum** refers to standards and rules that are assumed to be known by everyone (Myles, Trautman, & Schelvan, 2004) and that most learn through observation.

Returning to Dianne, staff observed some hidden deficits and sought to help her by teaching new skills. Figure 7.8 summarizes the interventions at the point of behavior.

Behavior	• Provide speech language therapy to address language acquisition and social skills.
	• Under the guidance of a speech therapist, teach Dianne alternative ways to communicate in order to facilitate language development.
	• Teach Dianne to recognize her new location on the floor by using a colored mat and placing her preferred stuffed animal on her spot.
	• Select activities that are enjoyable to Dianne that require interaction/cooperation. For example, Dianne enjoys movement. Staff can have her play with a peer on a seesaw. Gradually teach her the communication skills associated with these activities.
	• Teach Dianne to use a first-then visual symbol chart.
	• Teach Dianne to use a visual timer so that she learns to recognize how much time she has remaining.
	• Use natural classroom routines to promote guided interaction with peers. For example, when cleaning up after centers, prompt Dianne to hand her toy to a peer. Reinforce.

FIGURE 7.8 Dianne's Behavior Interventions Based on the Intervention Ziggurat

Consequence

By definition, a reinforcer increases the likelihood that a behavior will recur; therefore, when a new behavior or skill is needed, reinforcement is essential.

REINFORCEMENT *Reinforcement* is defined as "a situation or event that follows a particular behavior, resulting in an increased likelihood that a behavior will recur in the future" (Bregman & Gerdtz, 1997, p. 611). Therefore, if a behavior occurs frequently, it is assumed that the event that follows it maintains or reinforces it. A behavior may be reinforced by something desired that is delivered following a behavior (positive reinforcement) or by something aversive that is removed following a behavior (negative reinforcement).

The importance of reinforcement cannot be overstated. In order to decrease a problem behavior, an alternative or replacement behavior must be taught. Reinforcement is key to increasing the frequency of more appropriate behaviors.

Some characteristics of ASD (e.g., narrow and unusual interests, less responsive to social motivators such as praise) may impact the nature of reinforcers for this population. It may be necessary to think creatively about reinforcement for individuals with ASD. Whereas social opportunities are often reinforcing for typically developing students, the same is sometimes not the case for those with ASD for whom socialization presents a significant challenge. Furthermore, in seeking to identify effective reinforcers, it is often helpful to consider the individual's preoccupations (Sakai, 2005). Indeed, research has found that activities or objects related to obsessions are often more effective reinforcers than food (cf., Charlop-Christy, Kurtz, & Casey, 1990) for individuals on the autism spectrum.

In the case of Dianne, reinforcement was critical to the comprehensive plan. Figure 7.9 summarizes the reinforcement interventions.

Case Illustration

Regardless of age or level of functioning, the process for designing a comprehensive behavior intervention is the same. The case presented here, Glenn, illustrates the application of this process to an individual with needs very different from Dianne. Glenn is a 14-year-old who is diagnosed with Asperger Syndrome. He has no real friends at school and tends to associate better with his 10-year-old brother and adults. Glenn is preoccupied with World War II history and tends to talk excessively on this topic. Glenn carries books on this subject with him at all times. While other students talk and enjoy each others' company in the hallway, Glenn reads as he transitions from one class to the next. During lunch, he eats quickly so he will have time to leave the cafeteria to sit on a bench and read. He appears to be anxious when around groups of peers and complains that the cafeteria is too loud. Although he learns quickly and is able to do grade level assignments, he often does not complete class work. Instead, he reads a book hidden inside his binder. Any time he is not in very close proximity to an adult, Glenn reads his World War II books. His comprehensive

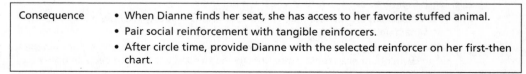

Consequence	• When Dianne finds her seat, she has access to her favorite stuffed animal. • Pair social reinforcement with tangible reinforcers. • After circle time, provide Dianne with the selected reinforcer on her first-then chart.

FIGURE 7.9 Dianne's Consequence Interventions Based on the Intervention Ziggurat

	Levels of Intervention	Interventions
Antecedent	Sensory and Biological	• Assign to lunch period with fewer students in cafeteria to reduce the noise level.
		• Reduce the amount of time spent at lunch to increase calming and decrease exposure to loud noise level.
		• Teach calming strategies.
	Structure and Visual/ Tactile Supports	• Provide Glenn a script for initiating conversations.
		• Hold up hand to indicate that it is time to change topics.
		• Use video to teach Glenn to recognize the nonverbal expressions of emotions.
		• Use video with pause button to help Glenn to recognize peers' responses to his behaviors.
	Task Demands	• Reduce the amount of time that Glenn is required to be in the cafeteria.
		• Assign Glenn to a lunch period with fewer students.
		• Assign a peer buddy who is trained to invite Glenn to join his table.
		• Train peer buddy to cue Glenn to change the subject when dwelling on one topic.
		• Provide Glenn a script to help him to initiate conversation with peers.
Behavior	Skills to Teach	• Use video to teach Glenn to recognize nonverbal expressions of emotions.
		• Teach Glenn to read the subtle signs that communicate a loss of interest in a conversation and fade the use of hand signal (discussed on the Structure and Visual/Tactile Support level).
Consequence	Reinforcement	• Include one or two peers with similar interests in his group of peer buddies.
		• Incorporate interests into class assignments.
		• Provide time to read WWII books after turning in class work.
		• Provide unique WWII materials that he can access only after completing assignments.

FIGURE 7.10 Glenn's Interventions Based on the Intervention Ziggurat

intervention is detailed in Figure 7.10. Note how interventions address each of the five levels and each point of intervention (ABC), and are responsive to Glenn's strengths and to manifestations of his ASD. For example, consider the Task Demand interventions for Glenn detailed in Figure 7.10. Glenn becomes anxious in large groups and dislikes the noise. This results in additional social isolation for him. Task demands in the cafeteria include the crowds and the noise, length of the lunch period, and socialization (e.g., initiating and sustaining conversation, requesting, joining a group, and reading social cues). Task Demand interventions for Glenn may include removing obstacles by reducing the time he is required to remain in the cafeteria or assigning him to a lunch period with fewer students. Additionally, Task Demand interventions may involve increasing the level of support. Staff could assign a peer buddy who is trained to invite Glenn to join his table. His buddy could also be trained to cue Glenn to change the subject when dwelling on one topic. Glenn could also be given a script to help him to initiate conversation with peers. As illustrated with Glenn, by acknowledging and carefully adjusting task demands to match ability, one can often prevent problems. Moreover, consideration of task demands helps to set the stage for essential skill development.

Interventions do not always neatly fall onto one level or point (antecedent, behavior, consequence). Some of the strongest interventions draw their strength from the fact that they address multiple levels and points. For example, notice in Figure 7.10 that decreasing the number of students in the cafeteria addresses two levels (Sensory and Biological and Task Demands). Using video to help Glenn to understand nonverbal signs of emotion addresses two levels (Structure and Visual/Tactile Supports and Skills to Teach) at two points (antecedent and behavior).

Summary

A thoughtful and comprehensive approach is required for designing behavior interventions for individuals with ASD. One must address both the behaviors and their unseen causes. This requires knowledge of behavior principles in addition to an understanding and appreciation of this unique group of individuals. A comprehensive intervention plan must be responsive to the characteristics of the individual with autism—including both strengths and challenges. This chapter introduces a framework, known as the Ziggurat Model, for the development of comprehensive interventions. The model emphasizes five levels of intervention that are responsive to the unique needs of individuals with ASD. The levels address needs at three points (antecedent, behavior, and consequence). When well implemented, a comprehensive plan is a powerful tool for changing the lives of individuals as well as the settings in which they function.

Effective interventions are *designed.* They cannot be developed without assessment and understanding of those with ASD. Designing a quality intervention requires a thoughtful process that takes time and a willingness to effect change.

Chapter Review Questions

1. What is the purpose of an FBA? Describe the required elements. (Objective 1)
2. What is the importance of considering the underlying characteristics of ASD when addressing behavioral concerns? (Objective 2)
3. Select a routine activity and describe three ways that the demands of that activity might be expected to differ for an individual with ASD (in comparison with the demands for a typically developing individual). Suggest strategies for removing the obstacles so that the individual with ASD might be more successful when participating in the activity. (Objective 3)
4. Using the definition of a comprehensive intervention plan provided in the chapter, outline a comprehensive plan to address a specific behavior concern. (Objective 4)
5. For each level of the Intervention Ziggurat, describe a behavior intervention strategy to decrease off-task behaviors. (Objective 5)

Key Terms

Internet Resources

Website	Description
http:/www.pbis.org	This is the Web site for the U.S. Office of Special Education Programs (OSEP) National Technical Assistance Center on Positive Behavior Interventions and Supports (PBIS). This site contains a description of PBS and its use in the public schools. Research articles and training modules on this topic are available on the Web site.
http:/www.researchautism.org/index.asp	The Organization for Autism Research (OAR) Web site focuses on the application of research to the challenges of autism—practical research. The Web site provides practical resources for parents, teachers, service providers, and individuals with ASD.
http:/www.ocali.org	The Ohio Center for Autism and Low Incidence (OCALI) Web site has a wealth of information on autism. Resources such as a parent guide, services database, Internet training modules, and service guidelines are available to the public.

References

Aspy, R., & Grossman, B.G. (2007). *The Ziggurat Model: A framework for designing comprehensive interventions for individuals with high-functioning autism and Asperger Syndrome.* Shawnee Mission, KS: Autism Asperger Publishing Company.

Blackwell, J., Blackwell, E., Blackwell, C., Blackwell, D., Blackwell, J., & Blackwell, J. (September 2007). *Socks don't matter: Perspective of a family living with the spectrum.* Presentation at the Network of Autism Training and Technical Assistance Programs.

Bregman, J. D., Zager, D., & Gerdtz, J. (1997). *Behavioral interventions.* In D. J. Cohen & F. R. Volkmar (Eds.), *Handbook of autism and pervasive developmental disorders* (2nd ed., pp. 606–630). New York: John Wiley and Sons.

Bryan, L. C., & Gast, D. L. (2000). Teaching on-task and on-schedule behaviors to high-functioning children with autism via picture activity schedules. *Journal of Autism and Developmental Disorders, 30,* 553–567.

Buggey, T. (2005). Video self-modeling applications with children with Autism Spectrum Disorder in a small private school. *Focus on Autism and Other Developmental Disabilities, 20*(1), 52–63.

Carr, E. G., Horner, R. H., Turnbull, A. P., Marquis, J. G., Magito-McLaughlin, D., McAtee, M. L., et al. (1999). *Positive behavior support for people with developmental disabilities: A research synthesis.* Washington, DC: American Association on Mental Retardation.

Charlop-Christy, M. H., Kurtz, P. F., & Casey, F. (1990). Using aberrant behaviors as reinforcers for autistic children. *Journal of Applied Behavior Analysis, 23,* 163–181.

Coyle, C., & Cole, P. (2004) A videotaped self-modeling and self-monitoring treatment program to decrease off-task behaviour in children with autism. *Journal of Intellectual & Developmental Disabilities, 29*(1), 3–15.

Dettmer, S., Simpson, R. L., Myles, B. S., & Ganz, J. B. (2000). The use of visual supports to facilitate transitions of students with autism. *Focus on Autism and Other Developmental Disabilities, 15*, 163–169.

Dooley, P., Wilczenski, F. L., & Torem, C. (2001). Using an activity schedule to smooth school transitions. *Journal of Positive Behavior Interventions, 3*, 57–61.

Ellingson, S. A., Miltenberger, R. G., Stricker, J., Galensky, T. L., & Garlinghouse, M. (2000). Functional assessment and intervention for challenging behaviors in the classroom by general classroom teachers. *Journal of Positive Behavior Interventions, 2*, 85–97.

Herring, S., Gray, K., Taffe, J., Tonge, B., Sweeney, D., & Einfeld, S. (2006). Behaviour and emotional problems in toddlers with pervasive developmental disorders and developmental delay: Associations with parental mental health and family functioning. *Journal of Intellectual Disability Research, 50*(12), 874–882.

Horner, R. H., & Carr, E. G. (1997). Behavioral support for students with severe disabilities: Functional assessment and comprehensive intervention. *Journal of Special Education, 31*, 84–104.

Horner, R. H., Carr, E. G., Strain, P. S., Todd, A. W., & Reed, H. K. (2002). Problem behavior interventions for young children with autism: A research synthesis. *Journal of Autism and Developmental Disorders, 32*(5), 423–446.

Howlin, P. (2000). Outcome in adult life for more able individuals with autism or Asperger Syndrome. *Autism, 4*, 63–83.

Howlin, P., Goode, S., Hutton, J., & Rutter, M. (2004). Adult outcome for children with autism. *Journal of Child Psychology and Psychiatry, 45*(2), 212–229.

Lecavalier, L., Leone, S., & Wiltz, J. (2006). The impact of behavior problems on caregiver stress in young people with autism spectrum disorders. *Journal of Intellectual Disability Research, 50*(3), 172–183.

Miller, P. (1993). *Theories of developmental psychology* (3rd ed.). New York: W.H. Freeman and Company.

Myles, B. S., & Southwick, J. (2005). *Asperger Syndrome and difficult moments: Practical solutions for tantrums, rage, and meltdowns* (Rev. ed.). Shawnee Mission, KS: Autism Asperger Publishing Company.

Myles, B. S., Trautman, M. L., & Schelvan, R. L. (2004). *The hidden curriculum: Practical solutions for understanding unstated rules in social situations.* Shawnee Mission, KS: Autism Asperger Publishing Company.

Nikopoulos, C. K., & Keenan, M. (2004). Effects of video modeling on social initiations by children with autism. *Journal of Applied Behavior Analysis, 37*, 93–96.

Odom, S. L., Brown, W. H., Frey, T., Karasu, N., Smith-Canter, L, & Strain, P. S. (2003). Evidence-based practices for young children with autism: Contributions for single-subject design research. *Focus on Autism and Other Developmental Disabilities, 18*(3), 166–155.

Pierce, K. L., & Schreibman, L. (1994). Teaching daily living skills to children with autism in unsupervised settings through pictorial self-management. *Journal of Applied Behavior Analysis, 27*, 471–481.

Reeve, C. E., & Carr, E. G. (2000). Prevention of severe behavior problems in children with developmental disorders. *Journal of Positive Behavior Interventions, 2*(3), 144–160.

Sakai, K. (2005). *Finding our way: Practical solutions for creating a supportive home and community for the Asperger Syndrome family.* Shawnee Mission, KS: Autism Asperger Publishing Company.

Sansosti, F. J., Powell-Smith, K. A., & Kincaid, D. (2004). A research synthesis of social story interventions for children with autism spectrum disorders. *Focus on Autism and Other Developmental Disabilities, 19*(4), 194–204.

Scheuermann, B., & Webber, J. (2002). Autism: *Teaching does make a difference.* Belmont, CA: Wadsworth/Thomson Learning.

Schopler, E. (1994). Behavioral priorities for autism and related developmental disorders. In E. Schopler & G. B. Mesibov (Eds.), *Behavioral issues in autism* (pp. 55–75). New York: Plenum Press.

Schreibman, L., Whalen, C., & Stahmer, A. C. (2000). The use of video priming to reduce disruptive transition behavior in children with autism. *Journal of Positive Behavior Interventions, 3*, 2–11.

8

Teaching Students with Autism to Communicate

Christina Carnahan, Ph.D.
University of Cincinnati

CHAPTER OBJECTIVES

After reading this chapter, learners should be able to:

1. Describe typical social communication development.
2. Discuss the variance in development of social communication seen in children with autism.
3. Describe the acquisition and importance of joint attention, communication intent, and symbol use in social communication for children with autism.
4. Discuss the strategies employed for assessment of social communication skills in children with autism.
5. Discuss the importance of incorporating assessment into decisions for interventions addressing social communication skills.
6. List and describe available interventions to increase communication skills for students with autism.

 ## CASE STUDY Examples

Case of Audrey

Audrey is a 4-year-old with autism. She does not use verbal language to have her needs met. Audrey utilizes a picture exchange communication system to request a preferred item or activity. She will not walk across a room to request an item, instead relying on climbing, reaching, or opening compartments to get what she desires. Audrey spends most of her day actively avoiding social communication interactions. She prefers to engage in individual activities like jumping, spinning, swinging, and looking at books. Audrey's assessment of social communication skills indicates that she rarely engages in joint attention experiences, uses little eye contact, and primarily uses communication to have wants or needs met. Audrey engages in few parallel play interactions with her peers. She is beginning to follow one-step directions and indicates an understanding of the back-and-forth nature of communication during structured activities.

Case of Tyler

Tyler is a 35-year-old man with autism. He works at the local library as part of a work program with his independent living community. Tyler rides the bus to work and home. His job is to repair damaged items, place scanning stickers on new books and to shelve returned items. Tyler often stops patrons and tells them about the book he is shelving, such as the author's last name and genre (mystery, etc). He has difficulty changing the topic within a conversation and interactions are often ended abruptly by the other party. The most recent assessment of Tyler's social communication skills indicates that he needs instruction in several areas of communication. Although Tyler uses verbal communication, he often uses the wrong tense and/or incorrect word order in sentences. He clearly demonstrates an understanding of the back-and-forth of communication, but does not appear to be aware of or read the body language of others. Tyler is a very literal thinker.

Case of Graham

Graham is a 9-year-old boy with autism. As a third grader, he spends most of his day in the general education classroom. With adult support, he uses an augmentative device to engage in classroom interactions. Graham uses his "talker" to answer questions in class, ask questions of his teacher and peers, and to comment on class activities. He usually plays by himself at recess and occasionally plays games with other peers during small group time. Graham sometimes comments inappropriately within the classroom, saying things like "big nose" to a girl at his table. Graham's assessment of social communication skills indicates that he understands the reciprocal nature of communication and is beginning to engage in interactive play activities. Graham does not use spoken language. He often uses incorrect word order and word endings when using his augmentative device. Graham does not follow the eye gaze of peers in communication exchanges and does not appear to utilize context cues to assist in topic maintenance.

INTRODUCTION

Autism Spectrum Disorders (ASD) are neurological disorders characterized by differences in social communication. Verbal and nonverbal social **communication** patterns represent key features of autism (Attwood, 1998; Chiang, Soong, Lin, & Rogers, 2008; Noens & van Berckelaer-Onnes, 2005; Tager-Flusberg, 1999). At the base of the variations in nonverbal and verbal social communication are differences in communicative intent and joint attention (Baranek, 1999; Baron-Cohen, et al., 1996; Leekam & Moore, 2001; Lord, 1995; McArthur & Adamson, 1996; Mundy & Burnette, 2005; Mundy, Sigman, & Kasari, 1990; Noens & van Berckelaer-Onnes, 2004; Quill, 2000;

Robins, Fein, Barton, & Green, 2001; Sigman & Ruskin, 1999; Stone, Ousley, Yodar, Hogan, & Hepburn, 1997; Werner & Dawson, 2005; Wetherby, Watt, Morgan, & Shunway, 2007). From a very early age, students with autism exhibit differences in their interactions with others (Charman, 2004; Dawson et al., 2004; DiLavore & Lord, 2005; Leekam & Ramsden, 2006; Leekam, Lopez, & Moore, 2000; Naber et al., 2008; Osterling, Dawson, & Munson, 2002; Rutherford & Rogers, 2003; Sullivan et al., 2007; Toth, Munson, Meltzoff, & Dawson, 2006). These differences influence the development of important communicative behaviors needed at home, school, and in the community. For a comprehensive discussion of communication development in typically developing children, visit the American Speech and Hearing Association (ASHA) at http://www.asha.org/public/speech/development/chart.htm.

WHAT IS SOCIAL COMMUNICATION AND WHY IS IT IMPORTANT?

The essence of communication is the ability to use symbols (i.e., spoken words, nonverbal gestures, etc.) and to convey to or receive a feeling or idea from another person (Paul, 2005). Messages are conveyed in countless ways such as speech, sign language, written words, facial expressions, gestures, Braille, signs or symbols, body movement, and so forth. Hulit & Howard (2006) note that "communication is so much a part of the human experience that we are constantly sending and receiving messages" (p. 3). Prizant & Wetherby (2005) describe social communication as the use of "conventional and socially appropriate verbal and nonverbal means to communicate for a variety of purposes across social settings and partners" (p. 925). Social communication requires some level of understanding of social settings and events and the ability to continually monitor and engage in exchanges with others. Communication consists of several components, making it a complex skill to learn. These components include joint attention, symbol use and communicative intent, and **language** (See Figure 8.1).

Below are a few important points related to social communication and autism:

1. Social-communication impairments often lead to a variety of challenging behaviors. Addressing the social-communication needs of students with ASD is an important component of promoting positive behavior (Lord et al., 2005).
2. Even if an individual with ASD has verbal language, he or she will continue to need instruction in the pragmatic aspects of communication.

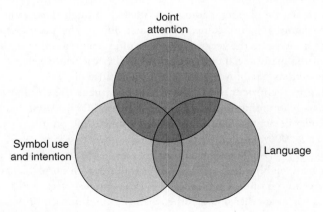

FIGURE 8.1 Components of Communication

BOX 8.1   Diversity Notes

Communication norms differ across cultures. We must attend to differences between cultures and of the cultures in which the students in our classroom are involved. Communication norms vary in several ways: direct versus indirect language, formal versus informal communication, expressive versus neutral, low context versus high context, and contact versus no contact. For more information or specific examples on variances across cultures see *Communicating with Diverse Cultures*, a workshop sponsored by the Diversity Committee of the Michigan College Personnel Association.

Students with high-functioning autism are known to have social-communication issues and issues with generalization. These students must receive explicit instruction in appropriate interactions including how to interact in accordance to cultural norms. For example, if a child with Asperger Syndrome was placed in a classroom with a teacher from outside the student's cultural experience, both the student and the teacher would need explicit instruction in how to interact. The student will likely be unable to differentiate the cultural difference between himself and the teacher, therefore resulting in an increased need for specific and explicit instruction in the differing rules of communicative exchange. The modification of an already taught system of appropriate communication with the dominant culture is required in order for the student to respond to the norms of differing cultures.

3. Social-communication skills are imperative for community participation, increased independence, relationship development, and so on. Thus, intensive instruction related to social-communication skills is crucial for students with autism. The sections below highlight key differences in the language development of children with ASD. These differences provide a foundation for ongoing assessment and instruction.

Joint Attention

Joint attention is an important component of communication. The term *joint attention* refers to not only the ability to engage in an experience with someone else, but also the knowledge of and active participation in the experience. Quill (2000) defines joint attention as the "coordination of attention among oneself, social partners, and an object" (p. 8). Joint attention implies active, shared experience.

Babies develop joint attention in the first year of life. Caregivers help babies move from self-centered attention to engage in interactions with others. Through these interactions that occur during the first few months, babies come to recognize objects and people separate from themselves; they begin to understand the very social nature of interacting. Joint attention development is the foundation of the many social communication skills that will develop through childhood. Joint attention interactions not only teach children specific skills (i.e., communication involves two people engaging in **reciprocal interactions**) but also make the child available for learning other important social-communication concepts (Charman, 2004; Dawson et al., 2004; Happe, 1998; McDuffie, Yoder & Stone, 2005; Sigman & Ruskin, 1999; Smith, Mirenda, & Zaidman-Zait, 2007; Toth et al., 2006).

Owens (2005, pp. 173–174) describes four phases in the development of joint attention. These phases occur between birth and 12 months for children with normal language development. In phase one (4 weeks to 6 months), babies learn to look toward objects and recognize when their attention is being called to another object (other than the child himself or herself). During phase two, around 7 to 8 months, children begin to make efforts to communicate independently. These initial communicative bids involve the child reaching with an open hand to indicate an object of interest. Over time, the reaching becomes a point and eventually the child begins moving toward and reaching for the objects. Between 8 and 12 months, children enter phase three of joint attention development. They now use all available resources to obtain objects of interest or the attention of a parent by combining gestures and vocalizations. By the time a child is around 1 year, he begins to pair single words with eye gaze and/or a gesture to draw attention to objects or to obtain an object or action of interest.

Hulit & Howard (2006) suggest the construction of conversation as one additional type of joint attention. Through the give and take of conversation, children learn the back-and-forth routines and dialogues that exist in everyday communication. They begin to understand nuances of conversation such as the type of communication dialogue appropriate for different settings. Similar to the first three phases of joint attention, this advanced skill clearly influences the child's involvement and skill development in other areas during early social communication exchanges.

Adamson, Bakeman, Deckner, & Romski (2008) made an important distinction between two different joint attention (or joint engagement) experiences. They categorized joint attention into supported and coordinated joint attention. The distinction between the two is the ability of the child to not only attend to the shared topic (supported joint attention) but to also attend to the partner (coordinated joint attention). In their study of joint attention, they found that "children with autism rarely coordinated attention to a shared object and a partner, a deficit that was no less marked in children who had acquired relatively large vocabularies" (p. 91).

To illustrate the development of joint attention, let us consider Philip, a child with typical language development. As a young child, his parents buy him a new stuffed giraffe. As they play with him, Phillip's parents hold the giraffe where he can see it, saying, "Look, giraffe" while looking at him and back to the giraffe. By the time he is 6 months old, Philip recognizes that the change in pitch of his parents' voice indicates a shift in attention; his parents are drawing his attention to an object. Philip responds to the change in pitch by looking at the giraffe and smiling back at his mother or father. As he gets a little older, Philip reaches toward his giraffe and looks toward his mother or father in the hope of playing. He eventually adds a vocalization to his point and eye gaze. "Uh-uh-ooh," he says. As his first birthday approaches, Philip begins using word approximation to indicate his interest in an object other than himself. He no longer says Uh-uh-ooh" as he reaches for the giraffe. Instead, as he points to the stuffed giraffe, he says "Raffe" while glancing repeatedly between his mother and the toy. When his mother picks up the toy while teasing Philip, he falls to the floor in a heap of giggles.

Two types of joint attention support the development of verbal and **nonverbal communication skills**. The first, **response to joint attention (RJA)**, involves an individual's ability to respond to initiations from others. Philip demonstrated RJA as he responded with a smile and a glance to the giraffe and his mom as she engaged him with the toy giraffe. The second, **initiating joint attention (IJA)** interactions, involves initiating joint attention interactions with a communication partner (Bruinsma, Koegel, & Koegel, 2004; Jones & Carr, 2004). In our example above, Philip demonstrates IJA as he points to the giraffe, comments "Raffe," and looks between his mother and the toy. Children use protodeclarative initiations to share or engage in social interactions. Protoimperative initiations allow children to direct the behavior (i.e., to obtain an object) of others.

Active engagement in joint attention experiences contributes to and is crucial for social cognitive development (Mundy & Newell, 2007). The importance of the progression is multifaceted. Joint attention is crucial for language development. It signals a child's understanding of the social nature of communication. Through joint attention, the child is beginning to understand communication as a back-and-forth process between two individuals. As a child engages in joint attention interactions, he learns his role in directing the attention of others. Over time, he comes to understand that he cannot only direct the attention of others but also that others direct his attention. Thus, the child begins to understand communicative intent in others (Bruinsma et al., 2004).

Symbol Use and Communicative Intent

Through experience, a child comes to understand that the intent of others is different from his own. The term **communicative intent** refers to the notion that a speaker has an intended outcome in sharing a message with others (Adams, 2002). Symbols are the means by which we convey our communicative messages. Symbols include spoken words, pictures, and nonverbal gestures such as pointing, and so forth. The power of a symbol is not in the symbol itself, but rather, in the ability of the speaker to use the symbol to convey a message to another person. Augmentative communication tools make it possible for children with limited functional communication to convey their message and engage in social interactions with others. An important point is that augmentative communication devices are not only for students who do not use verbal communication. These systems support any individual who does not yet have a functional means by which to communicate with others. For more information on this topic, see Chapter 12 on Assistive Technology.

In the previous sections, we discussed the stages and importance of joint attention in communication development. Around the first year, young children begin to use important symbols to demonstrate communicative intent. These symbols include pointing, eye gaze, and verbal approximations. **Symbol use** and communicative intent are intertwined in that the emergence of symbol use for social purposes indicates a developing understanding of communicative intent.

Bates, Camaioni, and Volterra (1975), building on the work of Austin (1962) and Searle (1969), discussed the stages of communication intention in children. Communicative intent is described as a three-stage process. The development of communicative intent takes a child from using reflexive cries to complex communication to get his wants and needs met and engaging in a social exchange regarding a topic of interest. As we saw in an earlier illustration, the development of joint attention interplays with the development of communicative intent between birth and 12 months. As a child's experiences grow and social awareness develops, he learns that communication occurs for a multitude of purposes. Through joint attention, a child engages with others who model the many different purposes of communication.

Bates et al. (1983) described the first stage of intention development, the **perlocutionary stage**, as a time in which a child moves from the use of reflexive cries to an increased understanding of the function of common objects. Without an understanding of the function of common objects, it is difficult to request those objects (Bates, Bretherton, Shore, & McNew, 1983). In the second stage of intention development, the **illucionary stage**, a child begins to use gestures to signal intentionality. Children begin using gestures to both engage other individuals in an activity of interest (protodeclarative intent) and to use gestures to have needs and wants met (protoimperative intent). The final stage, the **locutionary stage**, takes a child from the point of gesture use to the initial use of single words to communicate intent.

It is generally accepted that communicative function is seen in children before the use of verbal words (Bruner, 1981; Hallliday, 1975). The number of functions identified by each researcher and every language development book differs, although common among most are the abilities to control the behavior of others, expression of emotions, satisfaction of needs or wants, sharing knowledge, and gaining attention.

Let us once again consider Philip. Development of communicative intent starts with Philip's use of reflexive cries when he is hungry. Eventually, Philip understands that the function of the bottle is to give him milk. As Philip continues to develop, he reaches out to indicate hunger and request the bottle. Eventually, Phillip's reach becomes a point paired with a single word or approximation, such as "ba-ba," indicating his desire for the bottle. Similar to requesting, Philip develops the ability to demonstrate refusal. As a very young infant, he may cry when in distress or when presented with something he does not enjoy. Eventually, Philip turns his face and pushes the item away with his hands. By the third stage of development, Philip says "no" while vigorously shaking his head from left to right to indicate refusal.

Although it will be addressed in detail later in the chapter, at this point it is important to note the dissonance in the development of joint attention and communicative intent in children with ASD. Children with ASD demonstrate a difference in the function of their interactions with others. Specifically, research suggests that individuals with ASD are more likely to engage in protoimperative than protodeclarative interactions. These differences correlate with the differences in development in joint attention. Disordered joint attention impedes the understanding of the social nature of communication (Adamson et al., 2008). If a child does not understand the social function of communication (i.e., communication to share an interest), his communicative interactions will continue to focus on personal needs/desires.

Language

Communication is often confused or used synonymously with language. Language, one component of communication, is a rule-governed system of abstract symbols. The components of language include **syntax**, **semantics**, and **pragmatics**.

Syntax refers to the structure of language. Children begin to develop syntax when they combine two or more words together in utterances. When one-word utterances are used, there are structural rules to follow. It is when words are combined that rules apply. For example, in the English language, the subject precedes the action (e.g., "I run."). The knowledge of semantics requires the use of the parts of language and words that influence meaning. While vocabulary is the basis of meaning, in order to move beyond the use of one-word utterances, a child must start to understand the additional components of words and language. Bound morphemes occur at the beginning and end of words to influence meaning. For example, the addition of an "s" to the end of a word changes the meaning from singular to plural (e.g., "cat" and "cats"). Complex language skills require an understanding of syntactical rules such as the influence of bound morphemes. The semantics of language include the ways in which words change to incorporate quantity (plural vs. singular), temporal information (verb tense) and state (prefixes such as "un," "non," etc.) as well as other properties.

COMMUNICATION IN INDIVIDUALS WITH AUTISM SPECTRUM DISORDERS

Although children with ASD demonstrate relatively intact understanding of the grammatical rules of language, there are differences in some areas. Two examples include the acquisition of certain vocabulary forms and the use of morphemes to indicate temporal relationships. First, students with ASD often demonstrate a greater capacity for learning nouns (e.g., "runner") over verbs (e.g., "running"). Additionally, individuals with ASD appear to have difficulty using bound morphemes (e.g., "play" vs. "played," "work" vs. "worked," etc.) to mark past tense.

In addition to knowledge of syntax and semantics, pragmatics plays a critical role in expressive and **receptive language**. Pragmatics is the ability to integrate meaningful information from a context or setting to inform language comprehension and use. Components of pragmatics include communicative intent, responsiveness and initiation, repairs and turn taking, cohesion, topic, and coherence (Adams, 2002).

For young children, understanding an object's real-world function influences comprehension. However, as children develop, they utilize context clues to inform comprehension rather than relying on knowledge of object use (Loukusa et al., 2007; Tager-Flusberg, Paul, & Lord, 2005; Volden, Coolican, Garon, White, & Bryson, 2009). For example, if a child hears the statement, "The baby gives Daddy a bottle," an understanding of how these objects work in the real world would influence his interpretation. He may presume that the speaker intended to say, "Daddy gives the baby a bottle." However, as the child matures, he is more inclined to integrate contextually relevant information to inform his interpretation.

Whereas children with typically developing language learn the syntax, semantics, and pragmatics of a language by overhearing and engaging in communication exchanges, the development of the different aspects of language is often impaired in individuals with ASD. Although syntax and semantics may be relative strengths in the face of pragmatics for some individuals with ASD, these are still areas of concern that need attention (Bara, Bosco & Bucciarelli, 1999; Eigsti, Bennetto, & Dadlani, 2007; Geurts & Embrechts, 2008; Kjelgaard & Tager-Flusberg, 2001; Lord & Paul, 1997; Rapin & Dunn, 2003).

Children with global language delays experience differences in all three areas of language. Pragmatics often becomes the focus of intervention since it is often more clearly identified and appears to have the largest social impact on a child's interaction. It is important to understand that impaired semantic and/or syntactic understanding can also cause social isolation for individuals with ASD, especially those on the higher functioning end of the spectrum. Incorrect use of syntax or semantics can make communication less fluent and distracting to the communication partner and significantly impair the ability to gain information. If a child does not understand the use of some morphemes, his ability to gain or understand information presented by a communication partner will be impaired, resulting in a communication breakdown. Volden et al. (2009) note that both structural language and pragmatics play a role in everyday communicative functioning but do not indicate how well a child will navigate social interactions. It is important then to consider the addition of targets in all areas of language for children with ASD rather than focus on only the pragmatic aspects of language development.

Further Discussion of Social-Communication Skills in Children with ASD

Approximately 33% to 50% of children with autism do not develop functional speech (Noens & van Berckelaer-Onnes, 2005). Although the others do develop speech, both groups demonstrate impairments with the pragmatic aspects of language (Mundy & Markus, 1997; Rapin & Dunn, 2003). Research suggests that these differences correlate with the cognitive processing style and joint attention deficits described earlier (Hale & Tager-Flusberg, 2005; Mundy, 2003; Quill, 2000). For example, people with autism may attend to specific words or phrases without regard for the situation or context that influences meaning (Noens & van Berckelaer-Onnes, 2004). As a result, their verbal skills often overshadow their comprehension abilities. A person with autism may have a large vocabulary, but not understand simple comments or directions from others (Lord & Rhea, 1997). Similarly, he or she may also have strong word decoding skills but struggle with reading comprehension (Attwood, 1998). Other challenges include a propensity toward literal/factual thinking (Noens & van Berckelaer-Onnes, 2004). For example, a student with an ASD, when told to put his eyes on the speaker, may actually walk to the teacher, leaning in an attempt to place his eye on the other person. The following paragraphs provide an overview of common social communication features in ASD.

As previously discussed, engagement and experience are the basis for learning and development (Twachtman-Cullen, 2008). Young children with autism demonstrate qualitative differences in engagement and interactions with both the individuals in their environment and the environment itself. For these children, there is somewhat of a vicious cycle in that the behavioral manifestations (i.e., lacking motivation to engage in joint attention interactions) of the disorder decrease availability for engagement. Differences in quantity and quality of interactions lead to decreases in social experiences thereby influencing social-cognitive development (Mundy & Burnette, 2005). That is, it is not that individuals with ASD never engage in joint attention interactions (Franco & Wishart, 1995; Kasari, Freeman, Mundy, & Sigman, 1995; Legerstee & Weintraub, 1997; Sigman & Ruskin, 1999), but that the form (i.e., style) and function (i.e., purpose) of the interactions are different (Adamson et al., 2008).

Children with ASD tend to experience the most difficulty initiating joint attention (Jones & Carr, 2004). When children with ASD do initiate joint attention interactions, they are more likely to engage in protoimperative initiations (i.e., make a request) than protodeclarative initiations (Murray et al., 2008; Chawarska & Volkmar, 2005). They may not point to objects or use eye gaze to engage others for social purposes. Instead, individuals with ASD may use interactions such as hand pulling to indicate a desire. The form (i.e., symbol used to convey the message) of the interaction differs in that the child is using a hand pull rather than a point. The function (i.e., message) is different in that the child uses the interaction to make a request or indicate a desire rather than to share a social experience (Calloway, Smith-Myles, & Earles, 1999; Carter, Davis, Klin, & Volkmar, 2005; Toth et al., 2006).

Joint attention interactions provide children with opportunities to develop a variety of language and social skills (Toth et al., 2006). Examples of such skills include vocabulary building, receptive language development, pragmatic skills, emotional regulation, and pretend play (Jones & Carr, 2004; Morales, Mundy, Crowson, Neal, & Delgado, 2005; Markus, Mundy, Morales, Delgado, & Yale, 2000). Given the importance of joint attention for typically developing young children, the differences exhibited by children with ASD most certainly influence the development of social-communication behaviors including communicative intent and pragmatic language use (Bruinsma et al., 2004; Charman, 2004; Dawson et al., 2004; Happe, 1998; McDuffie et al., 2005; Murray et al., 2008; Sigman & Ruskin, 1999; Smith et al., 2007; Toth et al., 2006).

It is difficult to separate the effects of differences in joint attention, symbol use, and communicative intent on the communicative behavior of young children. These characteristics manifest in the number and type of interactions exhibited by children on the spectrum. Namely, differences in eye gaze or eye contact, types of symbols used, and the purpose (i.e., social vs. directive) of communicative interactions are defining features of symbol use and communicative intent in individuals with ASD (Bruinsma et al., 2004).

COMMUNICATION ASSESSMENT AND INTERVENTION

Our primary role as interventionists is to support the development of social communication for meaningful, functional purposes in the children we serve (Adams, 2002; Ogletree, Oren, & Fischer, 2007; Prizant & Wetherby, 2005). Although it is important to understand the characteristics or defining features of ASD, understanding the unique interests, strengths, and behavioral manifestations of our students is also important. Boxes 8.1 (p. 182) and 8.2 (p. 188) provide an overview of areas for social-communication assessment in ASD. These differences warrant assessment and, based on data analysis, intervention for individuals on the spectrum. In the following sections, we discuss some foundational principles to guide the assessment process and then provide a brief overview of possible interventions.

BOX 8.2 Research Notes

Current research findings suggest two forms of **video modeling** as effective intervention strategies for increasing the social-communication skills in students with ASD (Ayers & Langone, 2005; Bellini & Akullian, 2007). These interventions include video modeling (VM) and video self-monitoring (VSM). VM and VSM refer to the use of a videotaped demonstration to teach children specific, targeted behaviors.

Through video modeling, students receive repeated exposure to skills they need to learn. After watching the videotaped demonstration, students have opportunities to imitate or practice in real world situations. The distinction between VM and VSM is the subject (i.e., actor) of the demonstration model. If the student is videotaped, it is considered a VSM.

Between the years of 1980–2005, 29 studies were published on VM and VSM (Bellini & Akullian, 2007). Bellini & Akullian found 9 studies utilizing VM/VSM specifically targeting social-communication skills and play behaviors. Three other studies specifically addressed conversation skills. Targeted behaviors varied across studies with most or all students involved demonstrating improvement. Below is a list of communications skills addressed through VM and VSM:

- spontaneous verbal requests (Wert & Neisworth, 2003)
- play-related verbal responses (Buggey, Toombs, Gardener & Cervetti, 1999; D'Ateno, Mangiapanello, & Taylor, 2003)
- social initiations and reciprocal play behaviors (Nikopoulos & Keenan, 2003, 2004)
- engagement in extended pretend play sequences (MacDonald, Clark, Garrigan, & Vangala, 2005)
- increasing play-related statements (Taylor, Levin, & Jasper, 1999)
- compliment-giving responses and initiations (Apple, Billingsley, & Schwartz, 2005)
- social skills (Simpson, Langone, & Ayers, 2004)
- conversation skills (Charlop & Milstein, 1989; Charlop-Christy, Le, & Freeman, 2000; Sherer et al., 2001)

The effectiveness of video modeling may be due to the matching of learner preference to intervention modality in that a student's desire to watch themselves or others on video may increase interest (Bellini & Akullian, 2007; Sherer et al., 2001; Wert & Neisworth, 2003). This relates directly to the argument presented in this chapter for assessing and addressing the joint attention deficits in children with ASD. Without adequate joint attention, a child is unable to attend to the model being presented.

Communication Assessment

The purpose of this section is to provide interventionists with resources to conduct meaningful assessment in authentic settings. It is beyond the scope of this chapter to detail all of the formal **communication assessments** available. Rather, we offer an overview of areas for consideration and specific suggestions to support the assessment process. As a guide, we focus on the skills suggested by the National Research Council (NRC, 2001) as important for social-communication development. These include:

Social skills to enhance participation in family, school, and community

Expressive verbal language, receptive language, and nonverbal communication skills

Increased engagement and flexibility in developmentally appropriate tasks and play

Cognitive skills, including symbolic play, and basic concepts

Replacement of problem behaviors with more conventional and appropriate behaviors

Paul (2005) suggests that the role of assessment is to develop a communication profile detailing the "functions an individual is currently expressing and the means by which he or she attempts to do so" (p. 802). Based on the assessment, practitioners develop intervention plans for increasing the function for which an individual communicates and the conventional forms through which those functions are communicated. It is important to recognize that different assessments approach the process in many different ways (i.e., different formats, data collection strategies, etc.). Quill (2000), for example, uses an extended checklist to assess four broad areas of social-communication skills. These include social-communication behaviors, core skills, social skills, and communication skills.

Figure 8.2 offers three general considerations related to social-communication assessment. The considerations include communication frequency, or how often the child interacts; form, or the mode the child uses to engage in social-communication interactions; and function, or the purpose of the child's interaction.

In addition to the general **frequency, form, and function of social-communication interactions**, attention to specific communication behaviors is important. The child's strengths, needs, and interests must guide the intervention process. For children with advanced verbal language skills, additional considerations are necessary (see Figure 8.3). Twachtman-Cullen (2008) suggests that assessment and interventions for these individuals focuses on "pragmatics comprehension," or the influence of context and social information on language (p. 104).

Figure 8.4 offers additional resources for building a social-communication assessment. These resources include references that practitioners may find helpful.

As previously mentioned, the focus of assessment should be the development of a communication profile that leads to interventions that support functional social-communication skills. Thus, assessment strategies that occur in natural settings and provide a true picture of the child's skills are important (Twachtman-Cullen, 2008). Below is a list of strategies that support such assessment based on the work of Mesibov, Shea, and Schopler (2005), Paul and Sutherland (2005), and Twachtman-Cullen (2008).

Consider the Frequency, Form, and Function of Communicative Interactions

1. How often does the child initiate and respond to social-communication interactions with others?
   a. Track and compare the number of incidences in which the child responds to and initiates interactions with others.
2. How does he or she initiate these interactions?
   a. Examples include pointing versus reaching with an open hand toward items, grabbing someone's hand, etc.
3. What are the functions of the social-communication interactions (for what purposes)?
   a. Request (object, action, or interaction)
   b. Protest
   c. Social engagement (i.e., share experience)

FIGURE 8.2 General Points Related to Social-Communication Assessment

*The following questions and considerations serve only as a guide. For extensive assessment guidelines, see the resources in Figure 8.4.

Interests and Strengths

1. What activities, topics, or themes does the child enjoy or find interesting?
   a. Consider activities that hold the child's interests and attention.
   b. When does the child demonstrate independent, active engagement?
2. Describe the child's strengths.
3. What is the child's preferred learning style?

Joint Attention

1. Does the child engage in joint attention experiences? Specifically, does the child use eye gaze to actively engage in a shared triad experience (i.e., the child, another individual, and an object)?

Symbol Use and Intention

1. Consider the nonverbal symbols the child uses. What are these symbols (i.e. eye gaze, gestures, facial expression)?
2. Consider how the child responds to the nonverbal symbols others use. Does he or she follow an eye gaze? Does the child recognize and respond to the facial expressions of others?
3. Consider the child's play.
   a. Does the child engage in parallel play or initiate play interactions with others?
   b. How does the child respond to bids from adults and peers?
   c. Does the child demonstrate pretend play?

Language

1. Describe the child's verbal communication skills. Consider word use.
2. Does the child use morphemes to mark temporal relationships?
3. Consider the child's pragmatic language skills.
   a. Consider the conversational skills of the child. Does the child use context to inform his understanding?
   b. Does the child understand the basic rules of conversation (i.e., turn taking, topic maintenance, maintaining a reciprocal conversation)?
   c. How does the child's cognitive style influence his social-communication skills? Is the child a literal thinker?
   d. Does the child recognize the thoughts, feelings, or emotions of others?

FIGURE 8.3 Additional Assessment Considerations

Preschool Language Scale (PLS-4). Zimmerman, Steinek, & Pond, 2002.
Clinical Evaluation of Language Fundamentals–Preschool (CELF-P). Semel, Wiig, & Secord, 2003.
Clinical Evaluation of Language Fundamentals (CELF-4) (4th ed.). Semel, Wiig, & Secord, 1992.
Peabody Picture Vocabulary Test (PPVT). Dunn, Dunn, Robertson, & Eisenberg, 1981.
Comprehensive Assessment of Spoken Language (CASL). Carrow-Woolfolk, 1999.
Oral and Written Language Scales (OWLS). Carrow-Woolfolk, 1995.
Goldman Fristoe Test of Articulation. Goldman, & Fristoe, 2000.
Social Communication Questionnaire. Rutter, Bailey, & Lord, 2003.
Do, Watch, Listen, Say: Social and communication intervention for children with autism. Quill, 2000.

FIGURE 8.4 Assessment References

Note: The references in this figure include a sample of assessment references. These resources serve as guides as educational teams work to understand each student's specific strengths, interests, and needs.

1. Whenever possible, work with the individual in his or her natural environment and give consideration to home, school, and other community settings. Pay special attention to settings where parents or other professionals report challenges.
2. Provide structure and visual supports as needed to ensure that the child understands the task expectations. For example, use a schedule (i.e., picture or written) to indicate the number of activities the child must complete before a break.
3. Use high rates of reinforcement. Reinforcers include edible items and other tangible items such as stickers, social activities, games, computer activities, and so on.
4. Create enticing situations or scenarios. Examples of strategies for enticement include hiding objects, using physical play interactions, showing the child an unopened bag of his favorite snack, playing a repetitive game and suddenly stopping the interaction, using dolls or puppets and dressing them in unlikely outfits, and placing items of interest out of reach, but in the child's sight.
5. Embed assessment in shared reading or other literacy experiences.
6. Use engaging learning materials—specifically, topics, items, or themes of interest. Ask the child, parent, siblings, past teachers or other therapists, and so forth, for items or activities that the child finds interesting.
7. Use prompts or repeat/revisit a task or skill to increase understanding. For example, if assessing receptive vocabulary comprehension, use a prompt to demonstrate how you want the child to identify the item or object. This ensures that the assessment truly targets the child's vocabulary rather than his understanding of the direction.

Intervention

The work of designing and implementing interventions for individuals with ASD is crucial to future success and must be considered as such by all team members. The most important skills are those that promote an individual's ability to independently engage in meaningful social-communication interaction in a variety of settings (NRC, 2001; Ogletree et al., 2007; Prizant & Wetherby, 2005). To achieve these social communication skills, the NRC makes several recommendations. We have summarized a few of these recommendations below:

> Interventions should target functional, spontaneous communication.

> Interventions should provide social skills instruction across settings, namely in the setting in which the child will most likely apply the skill.

> Active engagement in intensive intervention with many learning opportunities is critical.

At this point, it is important to note the critical nature of ongoing assessment and data-based decision making. The NRC (2001) suggests 3 months as the mark for evaluating the effectiveness of an intervention and making any necessary adjustments. Given this time line, continuous assessment and data collection are critical.

There are a variety of intervention techniques available to support the social-communication development of individuals with ASD. These interventions exist along a continuum from behavioral to pragmatic development (Ogletree et al., 2007; Paul & Sutherland, 2005). As with assessment, it is beyond the scope of this chapter to provide a full review of all available interventions. However, we will highlight a few common interventions and offer suggestions for designing comprehensive programming.

The work of Ivar Lovaas conducted in the 1970s and 1980s serves as the basis for much of the literature about behavioral interventions for individuals with ASD (1987, 1989). Examples of behavioral interventions include discrete trial instruction and verbal behavior. Traditional **discrete trial instruction** often occurs in a one-on-one setting involving the presentation of multiple, systematic learning opportunities (Smith, 2001). Each learning trial begins with a cue or teacher directive designed to elicit a specific student response. If the student has not learned to demonstrate the correct response, the instructor pairs the cue with a prompt (e.g., gesture, physical prompt, etc.). The student then responds. If the student responds correctly, the instructor provides reinforcement. If the response is incorrect, the instructor implements specific error correction procedures.

Another teacher-directed, behaviorally based approach is verbal behavior. The **verbal behavior (VB)** program is based on Skinner's analysis of verbal behavior (Sundberg & Michael, 2001). There are five broad classes of verbal behavior including echoes, mands, tacts, reception by feature, function, class, and intraverbals. Verbal behavior uses teaching principles similar to those in other behavioral programs to systematically move students through language acquisition. Once children learn to echo or repeat specific words, they learn to use words for a variety of purposes or functions (i.e., label, request, and respond to verbal communication of others).

In the middle of the continuum are naturalistic intervention strategies including the **picture exchange communication system (PECS)** and **pivotal response training (PRT)**. These interventions apply behavioral principles in more naturalistic settings across the child's day (Ogletreen et al., 2007). PECS is a system used to teach individuals with ASD "a rapidly acquired, self-initiated functional communication system" (Bondy & Frost, 2001, p. 727). The system follows initial language development in that it begins by targeting initiation, a pivotal skill acquired by very young children. Individuals learn to initiate interactions by exchanging pictures for highly desired items. Initially, individuals exchange one picture for one object. However, over time the individual acquires other skills (e.g., phrase development, commenting, answering questions, and verbal communication). PECS involves five different phases of instruction that incorporate behavioral teaching principles such as systematic prompting and reinforcement. For more information on PECS, visit http://www.pecs.com/.

PRT is an intervention strategy that applies behavioral principles in naturalistic settings (Koegel, Carter, & Koegel, 2003; Koegel, Koegel, & McNerney, 2001). PRT is designed to target a small set of keystone or pivotal behaviors that will lead to the development of skills in other important areas (e.g., social-communication skills). Pivotal behaviors for individuals with autism include increased motivation, the ability to respond to multiple cues, the ability to self-regulate, and increased incidence of self-initiation. PRT addresses concerns of traditional behavioral interventions related to the generalization and utility of skills learned in one-on-one teaching settings to new environments, and the maintenance of these skills over time (Koegel, Koegel, & Carter, 1999). For example, students with autism may learn to follow the direction "sit down" while working with one adult but cannot follow the direction in the presence of several other children or in environments that are more chaotic. Another concern relates to teacher efficiency, especially in classroom settings (Taubman et al., 2001). For example, in a classroom with six students, it is difficult for a teacher to provide one-on-one instruction for each student throughout the school day. This is not to say that discrete trial teaching strategies no longer apply. Rather, the principles of discrete trial instruction are effective in contexts that are more natural. For more information on PRT, visit http://education.ucsb.edu/autism/.

Finally, on the other end of the continuum are social pragmatic interventions including programs such as **Social Communication Emotional Regulation Transactional Supports (SCERTS)** (Prizant, Wetherby, Rubin, & Laurent, 2003). Prizant and colleagues describe the SCERTS model as "a comprehensive, multidisciplinary approach to enhancing communication and socioemotional abilities of children from early intervention to the early school years" (p. 289). The model is embedded throughout the individual's day and emphasizes three different priorities. The priorities include social communication (joint attention and symbol use), emotional regulation to promote self-control and active engagement, and transactional supports to promote generalization across all aspects of the child's life. The SCERTS model does not prescribe specific strategies, but instead offers a framework for designing an intervention plan. For additional information on SCERTS, visit http://www.scerts.com/.

The interventions above represent a small sampling of the interventions available for supporting the social-communication development of individuals with ASD. Presenting the interventions along a continuum provides a visual for understanding the many different options. However, such a visual also sets up a dissonance between the various interventions. Although others may suggest differently, these interventions are not diabolically opposed and using one intervention does not preclude using another. All of the interventions are somewhat flexible and can be employed as an individual's needs necessitate (Ogletree, 2007; Ogletree et al., 2007). To guide the intervention planning process we offer a few big ideas and several supporting strategies. The big ideas include:

1. Use assessment data to guide intervention planning. Rather than focusing on buying or selling one specific intervention, comprehensive, person-centered planning aligns the needs of the individual with specific intervention strategies.
2. Comprehensive interventions promote functional, authentic outcomes. Functional, authentic outcomes are determined by the ecological factors such as the individual's interests and goals, support system, and culturally responsive practices (Ogletree, 2007).
3. Comprehensive interventions occur within meaningful contexts (i.e., a setting that as closely as possible mimics the environment in which the skill will be used).
4. Comprehensive interventions include plans for generalizing learned skills across environments.
5. Most importantly, comprehensive interventions include collaboration between families, school professionals, community professionals, and other community agencies. Ongoing problem solving promotes an environment with high standards and tenacity toward goals. The teamwork approach allows for increased social validity and shared strategies across settings. Concurrently, collaboration supports generalization of new skills across environments.

The following are several suggestions to support the big ideas:

1. Increase active engagement by allowing the child to initiate or lead the interaction and by using motivating learning materials (e.g., special interests, strengths, tangible reinforcers).
2. Structure the learning setting to promote understanding. Structures include physical boundaries (i.e., furniture arrangements), visual supports, and clear task organization (Mesibov et al., 2005). Students demonstrate increased engagement when the environment is well structured.
3. Recognize symbolic sequences. If a child does not yet use words, try pictures (i.e., photographs, colored line drawings, black and white line drawings, writing) or even objects (real objects and miniature objects) (Paul, 2005).
4. Plan for data collection. Develop a systematic strategy for tracking and analyzing student progress over time.
5. Communicate, communicate, communicate. Share your intervention data with all team members. Ask for anecdotal reports of the individual's success in other settings. Engage all team members in problem solving.

Summary

Social communication is at the center of the human experience. Children with autism differ in their development of social communication skills. Throughout this chapter, we discussed typical **social-communication development** and how social communication differs for children with Autism Spectrum Disorders. Joint attention, communication intent, and symbol use are critical components of development. Data-based decision making and interventions guided by thorough assessments are crucial to increasing a student's social-communication repertoire. A collection of strategies to assist with this assessment and intervention planning was presented.

Chapter review Questions

1. Describe the typical stages of joint attention and communicative intent development. (Objective 1)
2. Describe common deficits in social-communication skills seen in children with ASD. (Objective 2)
3. Describe the importance of addressing joint attention, symbol use, and communicative intent in children with ASD. (Objective 3)
4. Describe the process of assessing social-communication skills in students with ASD. (Objective 4)
5. Compare and contrast the different methods of intervention approach for students with ASD. (Objective 5)
6. Discuss considerations when selecting an appropriate social communication intervention for students with ASD. (Objective 6)

Key Terms

Communication   *180*
Communication assessments   *188*
Communicative intent   *184*
Discrete trial instruction   *192*
Expressive verbal language   *188*
Frequency, form, and function of social-communication interactions   *189*
Illucionary stage   *184*
Initiating joint attention (IJA)   *183*
Joint attention   *182*
Language   *181*

Locutionary stage   *184*
Nonverbal communication skills   *183*
Perlocutionary stage   *184*
Picture exchange communication system (PECS)   *192*
Pivotal response training (PRT)   *192*
Pragmatics   *185*
Receptive language   *186*
Reciprocal interactions   *182*

Response to joint attention (RJA)   *183*
Semantics   *185*
Social-communication development   *185*
Social Communication Emotional Regulation Transactional Supports (SCERTS)   *192*
Syntax   *185*
Verbal behavior (VB)   *192*
Video modeling   *188*

Internet Resources

The American Speech and Hearing Association (ASHA) has several resources, position papers, and so on related to students with ASD.
http://www.asha.org/about/publications/leader-online/archives/2005/050301/f050301c3.htm.).

Online modules detailing a variety of interventions
http://www.autisminternetmodules.org/mod_list.php
UCSB Koegel Autism Center (PRT)
http://education.ucsb.edu/autism/

The SCERTS Model
http://www.scerts.com/
Picture exchange communication system (PECS)
http://www.pecs.com/
Center for Autism and Related Disabilities (CARD) (incidental teaching, etc.)
http://www.coe.fau.edu/card/Free%20Resource%20Materials.htm
Treatment and Education of Autistic and Related Communication Handicapped Children
http://www.teacch.com/communication.html

Hanen Early Language Center
http://www.hanen.org/web/Home/tabid/36/Default.aspx
Augmentative and Alternate Communication Connecting Young Kids
http://aac.unl.edu/yaack/index.html
Route 66: Literacy for Adolescent and Adults Beginning Readers
http://www.route66literacy.org/?gclid=CMe4wt_wxpgCFQu-GgodkzDC1w

References

Adams, C. (2002). Practitioner review: The assessment of language pragmatics. *Journal of Child Psychology and Psychiatry, 43,* 973–987.

Adamson, L. B., Bakeman, R., Deckner, D. F., & Romski, M. A. (2008). Joint engagement and the emergence of language in children with autism and Down Syndrome. *Journal of Autism and Developmental Disorders, 39,* 84–96.

Apple, A. L., Billingsley, F., & Schwartz, I. S. (2005). Effects of video modeling alone and with self-management on compliment-giving behaviors of children with high-functioning ASD. *Journal of Positive Behavior Interventions, 7*(1), 33–46.

Attwood, T. (1998). *Asperger's Syndrome: A guide for parents and professionals.* London: Jessica Kingsley Publishers.

Austin, J. L. (1962). *How to do things with words.* Oxford, England: Oxford University Press.

Ayers, K. M., & Langone, J. (2005). Intervention and instruction with video for students with autism: A review of the literature. *Education and Training in Developmental Disabilities, 40*(2), 183–196.

Bara, B. G., Bosco, F. M., & Bucciarelli, M. (1999). Developmental pragmatics in normal and abnormal children. *Brain and Language, 68*(3), 507–528.

Baranek, G. T. (1999). Autism during infancy: A retrospective video analysis of sensory-motor and social behaviors at 9–12 months of age. *Journal of Autism and Developmental Disorders, 29,* 213–224.

Baron-Cohen, S., Cox, A., Baird, G., Swettenham, J., Nightengale, N., Morgan, K., et al. (1996). Psychological markers in the detection of autism in infancy in a large population. *The British Journal of Psychiatry, 168,* 158–163.

Bates, E., Bretherton L., Shore, C., & McNew, S. (1983). Names, gestures, and objects: The role of context in the emergence of symbols. In K. Nelson (Ed.), *Children's language* (Vol. 4, pp. 59–123). Hillsdale, NJ: Erlbaum.

Bates, E., Camaioni, L., & Volterra, V. (1975). The acquisition of performatives prior to speech. *Merrill Palmer Quarterly, 21*(3), 205–226.

Bellini, S., & Akullian, J. (2007). A meta-analysis of video modeling and video self-monitoring interventions for children and adolescents with autism spectrum disorders. *Exceptional Children, 73*(3), 264–287.

Bondy, A., & Frost, L. (2001). The picture exchange communication system. *Behavioral Modification, 25*(5), 725–744.

Bruinsma, Y., Koegel, R., & Koegel, L. (2004). Joint attention and children with autism: A review of the literature. *Mental Retardation and Developmental Disabilities, 10,* 169–175.

Bruner, J. (1981). The social context of language acquisition. *Language and Communication, 1,* 155–178.

Buggy, T., Toombs, K., Gardener, P., & Cervetti, M. (1999). Training responding behaviors in students with autism: Using videotaped self-modeling. *Journal of Positive Behavior and Intervention, 1*(4), 205–214.

Calloway, C., Smith-Myles, B., & Earles, T. (1999). The development of communicative functions and means in students with autism. *Focus on*

Autism and Other Developmental Disabilities, 14 (3), 140–149.

Carrow-Woolfolk, E. (1999). *Comprehensive Assessment of Spoken Language.* Circle Pines, MN: American Guidance Services.

Carrow-Woolfolk, E. (1995). *Oral and Written Language Scales.* Circle Pines, MN: American Guidance Services.

Carter, A., Davis, N., Klin, A., & Volkmar, F. (2005). Social development in autism. In F. Volkmar, R. Paul, A. Klin, & D. Cohen (Eds.), *Handbook of autism and pervasive developmental disorders* (3rd ed., pp. 312–344). New York: Wiley.

Chalop, M. H., & Milstein, J. P. (1989). Teaching autistic children conversational speech using video modeling. *Journal of Applied Behavior Analysis, 22*(3), 275–285.

Chalop-Christy, M. H., Le, L., & Freeman, K. A. (2000). A comparison of video modeling with in vivo modeling for teaching children with autism. *Journal of Autism and Developmental Disorders, 30*(6), 537–552.

Charman, T. (2004). Why is joint attention a pivotal skill in autism? In U. Frith & E. L. Hill (Eds.), *Autism: Mind and brain* (pp. 68–87). Oxford, England: Oxford University Press.

Chawarska, K. & Volkmar, F. (2005). Autism in infancy and early childhood. In F. Volkmar, R. Paul, A. Klin, & D. Cohen (Eds.), *Handbook of autism and pervasive developmental disorders* (3rd ed., pp. 223–246). New York: Wiley.

Chiang, C. H., Soong, W. T., Lin, T. L., & Rogers, S. J. (2008). Nonverbal communication skills in young children with autism. *Journal of Autism and Developmental Disorders, 38*, 1898–1906.

D'Ateno, P., Mangiapanello, K., & Taylor, B. (2003). Using video modeling to teach complex play sequences to a preschooler with autism. *Journal of Positive Behavior Interventions, 5*(1), 5–11.

Dawson, G., Toth, K., Abbott, R., Osterling, J., Munson, J., Estes, A. et al. (2004). Early social attention impairments in autism: Social orienting, joint attention, and attention to distress. *Developmental Psychology, 40*, 271–283.

DiLavore, P., & Lord, C. (1995, March). *Do you see what I see? Requesting and joint attention in young autistic children.* Paper presented at the Biennial

Conference of the Society for Research in Child Development, Indianapolis, IN.

Dunn, L., Dunn, L., Robertson, G., & Eisenberg, J. (1981). *Peabody Picture Vocabulary Test* (Rev. ed). Circle Pines, MN: American Guidance Services.

Eigsti, I., Bennetto, L., & Dadlani, M. (2007). Beyond pragmatics: Morphosyntactic development in autism. *Journal of Autism and Developmental Disorders, 37*, 1007–1023.

Franco, F., & Wishart, J. G. (1995). Use of pointing and other gestures by young children with Down Syndrome. *American Journal of Mental Retardation, 100*, 160–182.

Geurts, H. M., & Embrechts, M. (2008). Language profiles in ASD, SLI, and ADHD. *Journal of Autism and Developmental Disorders, 38*, 1931–1943.

Goldman, R., & Fristoe, M. (2000). *Goldman-Fristoe Test of Articulation–2.* Circle Pines, MN: American Guidance Service.

Hale, C. M., & Tager-Flusberg, H. (2005). Brief report: The relationship between discourse deficits and autism symptomatology. *Journal of Autism and Developmental Disorders, 35*(4), 519–524.

Halliday, M. (1975). *Learning how to mean: Explorations in the development of language.* New York: Arnold.

Happe, F. (1998). Language and communication disorders in autism and Asperger's Syndrome. In B. Stemmer & H. A. Whitaker (Eds.), *Handbook of neurolinguistics* (pp. 525–534). San Diego: Academic Press.

Hulit, L., & Howard, M. (2006). *Born to talk: An introduction to speech and language development* (4th ed.). Boston: Allyn & Bacon.

Jones, E., & Carr, E. (2004). Joint attention in children with autism: Theory and intervention. *Focus on Autism and Other Developmental Disabilities, 19* (1), 13–26.

Kasari, C., Freeman, S. F., Mundy, P., & Sigman, M. D. (1995). Attention regulation by children with Down Syndrome: Coordinated joint attention and social referencing looks. *American Journal of Mental Retardation, 100*, 128–136.

Kjelgaard, M. M., & Tager Flusberg, H. (2001). An investigation of language impairment in autism: Implications for genetic subgroups. *Language and Cognitive Processes, 16*(2–3), 287–308.

Koegel, L., Carter, C., & Koegel, R. (2003). Teaching children with autism self-initiations as a pivotal response. *Topics in Language Disorders, 23*(2), 134–145.

Koegel, R., Koegel, L., & Carter, C. (1999). Pivotal teaching interactions for children with autism. *School Psychology Review, 8*(4), 576–594.

Koegel, R., Koegel, L., & McNerney, E. (2001). Pivotal areas in intervention for autism. *Journal of Clinical Child Psychology, 30*(1), 19–32.

Leekam, S. R., Lopez, B., & Moore, C. (2000). Attention and joint attention in preschool children with autism. *Developmental Psychology, 36*, 261–273.

Leekam, S., & Moore, C. (2001). The development of attention and joint attention in children with autism. In J. A. Burack, T. Charman, N. Yirmiya, & P. R. Zelazo (Eds.), *The development of autism: Perspective from theory and research* (pp. 105–129). Mahwah, NJ: Erlbaum.

Leekam, S. R., & Ramsden, A. H. (2006). Dyadic orienting and joint attention in preschool children with autism. *Journal of Autism and Developmental Disorders, 36*, 185–197.

Legerstee, M., & Weintraub, J. (1997). The integration of person and object attention in infants with and without Down Syndrome. *Infant Behavior and Development, 20*, 71–82.

Lord, C. (1995). Follow-up of two-year-olds referred for possible autism. *Journal of Child Psychology and Psychiatry, 36*, 1365–1382.

Lord, C., & Paul, R. (1997). Language and communication in autism. In D. J. Cohen & F. R. Volkmar (Eds.), *Handbook of autism and pervasive developmental disorders* (pp. 195–225). New York: John Wiley & Sons.

Lord, C., & Rhea, P. (1997). Language and communication in autism. In D. V. Cohen, (Ed.), *Handbook of autism and pervasive developmental disorders* (2nd ed., pp. 195–225). New York: John Wiley & Sons.

Lord, C., Wagner, A., Rogers, S., Szatmari, P., Aman, M., Charman, T., et al. (2005). Challenges in evaluating psychosocial interventions for Autistic Spectrum Disorders. *Journal of Autism and Developmental Disorders, 35*(6), 695–708.

Loukusa, S., Leinonen, E., Jussila, K., Mattila, M.L., Ryder, N., Ebeling, H., et al. (2007). Answering contextually demanding questions: Pragmatic errors produced by children with Asperger Syndrome or high-functioning autism. *Journal of Communication Disorders, 40*, 357–381.

Lovaas, O. I. (1987). Behavioral treatment and normal educational and intellectual functioning in young autistic children. *Journal of Consulting and Clinical Psychology, 55* (1), 3–9.

Lovaas, O. I., & Smith, T. (1989). A comprehensive behavioral theory of autistic children: Paradigm for research and treatment. *Journal of Behavioral Therapy & Experimental Psychology, 20* (1), 17–29.

MacDonald, R., Anderson, J., Dube, W., Geckeler, A., Green, G., Holcomb, W., et al. (2006). Behavioral assessment of joint attention: A methodological report. *Research in Developmental Disabilities, 27*, 138–150.

MacDonald, R., Clark, M., Garrigan, E., & Vangala, M. (2005). Using video modeling to teach pretend play to children with autism. *Behavioral Interventions, 20*(4), 225–238.

Markus, J., Mundy, P., Morales, M., Delgado, C., & Yale, M. (2000). Individual differences in infant skills as predictors of child-caregiver joint attention and language. *Social Development, 9* (3), 302–315.

McArthur, D., & Adamson, L. B. (1996). Joint attention in pre-verbal children: Autism and developmental language disorder. *Journal of Autism and Developmental Disorders, 26*, 481–496.

McDuffie, A., Yoder, P., & Stone, W. (2005). Prelinguistic predictors of vocabulary in young children with autism spectrum disorders. *Journal of Speech, Language, and Hearing Research: JSLHR, 48*, 1080–1097.

Mesibov, G., Shea, V., & Schopler, E. (2005). *The TEACCH approach to autism spectrum disorders.* New York: Kluwer Academic/Plenum Publishers.

Morales, M., Mundy, P., Crowson, M., Neal, A. R., & Delgado, C. (2005). Individual differences in infant attention skills, joint attention, and emotional regulation behavior. *International Journal of Behavioral Development, 29* (3), 259–263.

Mundy, P. (2003). Annotation: The neural basis of social impairment in autism: The role of the dorsal medial-frontal cortex and anterior cingulated system. *Journal of Child Psychology and Psychiatry, 44*, 793–809.

Mundy, P., & Burnette, C. (2005). Joint attention and neural developmental models of autism. In F. Volkmar, R. Paul, A. Klin, & D. Cohen (Eds.), *Handbook of autism and pervasive developmental disorders* (3rd ed., pp. 650–681). New York: Wiley.

Mundy, P., & Markus, J. (1997). On the nature of communication and language impairment in autism. *Mental Retardation and Developmental Disabilities, 3,* 343–349.

Mundy, P., & Newell, L. (2007). Attention, joint attention, and social cognition. *Current Directions in Psychological Science, 16*(5), 269–274.

Mundy, P., Sigman, M., & Kasari, C. (1990). A longitudinal study of joint attention and language development in autistic children. *Journal of Autism and Developmental Disorders, 20,* 115–128.

Murray, D., Creaghead, N., Manning-Courtney, P., Shear, P., Bean, J., & Prendeville, J. A. (2008). The relationship between joint attention and language in children with autism spectrum disorders. *Focus on Autism and Other Developmental Disabilities, 23*(1), 5–14.

Naber, F. B. A., Bakermans-Kranenburg, M. J., van IJzendoorn, M. H., Dietz, C., van Daalen, E., Swinkels, S. H. M., et al. (2008). Joint attention development in toddlers with autism. *European Journal of Child and Adolescent Psychiatry, 17,* 143–152.

National Research Council. (2001). *Educating children with autism,* Washington, DC: National Academy Press.

Nikopoulos, C. K., & Keenan, M. (2003). Promoting social initiation in children with autism using video modeling. *Behavioral Interventions, 18*(2), 87–108.

Nikopoulos, C. K., & Keenan, M. (2004). Effects of video modeling on social initiations by children with autism. *Journal of Applied Behavior Analysis, 37,* 93–96.

Noens, I., & van Berckelaer-Onnes, I. (2004). Making sense in a fragmentary world: Communication in people with autism and learning disabilities. *Autism, 8*(2), 197–218.

Noens, I., & van Berckelaer-Onnes, I. (2005). Captured by details: Sense-making, language and communication in autism. *Journal of Communication Disorders, 38,* 123–141.

Ogletree, B. (2007). What makes communication intervention successful with children with autism spectrum disorders? *Focus on Autism and Other Developmental Delays, 22*(3), 190–192.

Ogletree, B., Oren, T., & Fischer, M. (2007). Examining effective intervention practices for communication impairment in Autism Spectrum Disorder. *Exceptionality, 15*(4), 233–247.

Osterling, J., Dawson, G., & Munson, J. (2002). Early recognition of 1-year-old infants with Autism Spectrum Disorder versus mental retardation. *Development and Psychopathology, 14,* 239–251.

Owens, R. (2005). *Language development: An introduction* (6th ed.). Boston: Allyn & Bacon.

Paul, R. (2005). Assessing communication in autism spectrum disorders. In F. Volkmar, R. Paul, A. Klin, & D. Cohen (Eds.), *Handbook of autism and pervasive developmental disorders* (3rd ed., pp. 799–816). New York: Wiley.

Paul, R., & Sutherland, D. (2005). Enhancing early language in children with autism spectrum disorders. In F. Volkmar, R. Paul, A. Klin, & D. Cohen (Eds.), *Handbook of autism and pervasive developmental disorders* (3rd ed., pp. 946–976). New York: Wiley.

Prizant, B., & Wetherby, A. (2005). Critical issues in enhancing communication abilities in persons with autism spectrum disorders. In F. Volkmar, R. Paul, A. Klin, & D. Cohen (Eds.), *Handbook of autism and pervasive developmental disorders* (3rd ed., pp. 925–945). New York: Wiley.

Prizant, B., Wetherby, A., Rubin, E., & Laurent, A., (2003). The SCERTS model: A transactional, family-centered approach to enhancing communication and socioemotional abilities of children with Autism Spectrum Disorder. *Infants and Young Children, 16*(4), 296–316.

Quill, K. A. (2000). *Do-watch-listen-say: Social and communication intervention for children with autism.* Baltimore, MD: Paul H. Brookes.

Rapin, I., & Dunn, M. (2003). Update on the language disorders of individuals with autistic spectrum. *Brain & Development, 25,* 166–172.

Robins, D., Fein, D., Barton, M., & Green, J. (2001). The Modified Checklist for Autism in Toddlers: An initial study investigating the early detection of autism and pervasive developmental disorders.

Journal of Autism and Developmental Disorders, 31,131–144.

Rutherford, M. D., & Rogers, S. J. (2003). Cognitive underpinning of pretend play in autism. *Journal of Autism and Developmental Disorders, 33*, 289–302.

Rutter, M., Bailey, A., & Lord, C. (2003). *The Social Communication Questionnaire: Manual.* Los Angeles: Western Psychological Services.

Searle, J. R. (1969). Linguistics today: Substance and structure of language/speech acts. *Quarterly Journal of Speech, 55*(3), 329–330.

Semel, E., Wiig, E., & Secord, W. (1992). *Clinical evaluation of language fundamentals preschool.* San Antonio: Psychological Corporation, Harcourt Assessment, Inc.

Semel, E., Wiig, E., & Secord, W. (2003). *Clinical evaluation of language fundamentals–4.* San Antonio, TX: Psychological Corporation, Harcourt Assessment, Inc.

Sherer, M., Pierce, K. L., Paredes, S., Kisacky, K. L., Ingersoll, B., & Schreibmen, L. (2001). Enhancing conversation skills in children with autism via video technology: Which is better, "self" or "other" as a model? *Behavioral Modifications, 25*(1), 140–158.

Sigman, M., & Ruskin, E. (1999). Continuity and change in the social competence of children with autism, Down Syndrome, and developmental delays. *Monographs of the Society for Research in Child Development, 64.*

Simpson, A., Langone, J., & Ayers, K. M. (2004). Embedded video and computer based instruction to improve social skills for students with autism. *Education and Training in Developmental Disabilities, 39*(3), 24–252.

Smith, T. (2001). Discrete trial training in the treatment of autism. *Focus on Autism and Other Developmental Disabilities, 16* (2), 86–92.

Smith, V., Mirenda, P., & Zaidman-Zait, A. (2007). Predictors of expressive vocabulary growth in children with autism. *Journal of Speech Language and Hearing Research: JSLHR, 50,* 149–160.

Stone, W. L., Ousley, O. Y., Yodar, P. J., Hogan, K. L., & Hepburn, S. L. (1997). Nonverbal communication in two- and three-year old children with autism. *Journal of Autism and Developmental Disorders, 27,* 677–696.

Sullivan, M., Finelli, J., Marvin, A., Garrett-Mayer, E., Bauman, M., & Landa, R. (2007). Response to joint attention in toddlers at risk for autism spectrum disorders: A prospective study. *Journal of Autism and Developmental Disorders, 37,* 37–48.

Sundberg, M., & Michael, J. (2001). The benefits of Skinner's analysis of verbal behavior for children with autism. *Behavior Modification 25*(5), 698–724.

Tager-Flusberg, H. (1999). A psychological approach to understanding the social and language impairments in autism. *International Review of Psychiatry, 11,* 325–334.

Tager-Fluseberg, H., Paul, R., & Lord, C. (2005). Language and communication in autism. In F. Volkmar, R. Paul, A. Klin, & D. Cohen (Eds.), *Handbook of autism and pervasive developmental disorders* (3rd ed., pp. 335–364). New York: Wiley.

Taubman, M., Brierley, S., Wishner, J., Baker, D., McEachin, J., & Leaf, R. (2001). The effectiveness of a group discrete trial instructional approach for preschoolers with developmental disabilities. *Research in Developmental Disabilities, 22,* 205–219.

Taylor, B. A., Levin, L., & Jasper, S. (1999). Increasing play-related statements in children with autism toward their siblings: Effects of video modeling. *Journal of Developmental and Physical Disabilities, 11,* 253–264.

Toth, K., Munson, J., Meltzoff, A., & Dawson, G. (2006). Early predictors of communication development in young children with Autism Spectrum Disorder: Joint attention, imitation, and toy play. *Journal of Autism and Developmental Disorders, 36* (8), 993–1005.

Twachtman-Cullen, D. (2008). Symbolic communication: Common pathways and points of departure. In K. Dunn Buron & P. Wolfberg (Eds.), *Learners on the autism spectrum: Preparing highly qualified educators* (pp. 89–113). Shawnee Mission, KS: Asperger Publishing Company.

Volden, J., Coolican, J., Garon, N., White, J., & Bryson, S. (2009). Brief report: Pragmatic language in Autism Spectrum Disorder: Relationships to measures of ability and disability. *Journal of Autism and Developmental Disorders, 39,* 388–393.

Werner, E., & Dawson, G. (2005). Validation of the phenomenon of autistic regression using home videotapes. *Archives of General Psychiatry, 62,* 889–895

Wert, B. Y., & Neisworth, J. T. (2003) Effects of video self-modeling on spontaneous requesting in children with autism. *Journal of Positive Behavior Interventions, 5*(1), 30–34.

Wetherby, A. M., Watt, N., Morgan, L., & Shunway, S. (2007). Social communication profiles of children with autism spectrum disorders late in the second year of life. *Journal of Autism and Developmental Disorders, 37,* 960–975.

Zimmerman, L., Steinek, V. & Pond, M. A. (2002). *Preschool Language Scale* (4th ed.). New York: The Psychological Corporation.

9

Social Challenges of Children and Youth with Autism Spectrum Disorders

Scott Bellini, Ph.D.
University of Indiana

CHAPTER OBJECTIVES

After reading this chapter, learners should be able to:

1. Increase knowledge of common social skills deficits.
2. Increase awareness of the relationship between social skills deficits and deleterious outcomes.
3. Increase awareness of skill acquisition versus performance deficits.
4. Increase knowledge of meta-analytical research regarding social skills training.
5. Increase knowledge of social skills assessment techniques.
6. Increase awareness of available social skills training strategies.

 ## CASE STUDY   Examples

Case of Kelly

Kelly is a kindergartener with autism and significant expressive communication deficits. She is primarily echolalic, and seldom uses her language spontaneously with classmates and teachers. Kelly is extremely fearful of social situations and often avoids social interactions. Consequently, Kelly spends the vast majority of her playground time by herself, with little peer interaction. A social skills assessment concluded that she had significant skill deficits in initiating interactions and maintaining interactions with peers. A peer-mediated intervention (PMI) was implemented that taught Kelly's peers how to initiate and respond to her initiations.

Case of Khalil

Khalil is a 28-year-old man with autism. Khalil said that he had a best friend once, but that the two of them had stopped spending time together. He currently has no friend and spends the majority of his time alone. He stated that he did have a girlfriend for a brief time but the relationship ended, according to Khalil, because he grew tired of spending time with her. He stated that he becomes anxious in crowded environments and often avoids social settings. Khalil received an associate's of science degree in information technology from a local community college. Khalil has worked in primarily menial labor jobs (e.g., custodial work); however he is currently unemployed. Khalil stated that his difficulties with social interactions and hypersensitivity to crowded environments may be impacting his ability to find and keep a job. Vocational rehabilitation services were implemented that targeted social skills essential for finding and keeping a job. Khalil was also taught coping strategies to help him regulate his response to sensory stimuli.

Case of Carlos

Carlos is a 9-year-old boy with autism who engages in a number of problem behaviors, such as touching and pushing other children. Carlos also makes inappropriate comments in class, such as calling the teacher "ugly" and telling his classmates that they are "stupid." A functional behavior assessment was conducted to assist with the development of an intervention plan. During the playground observation, Carlos ran into the girls' bathroom. As he ran in, about a dozen girls ran out screaming and giggling, followed by Carlos who was doing the same. Carlos was immediately taken to the principal's office. At the conclusion of the observation and teacher interview, it was determined that the function of the problem behavior was peer attention. That is, Carlos was engaging in inappropriate social behaviors to gain peer attention. As a result, an intervention was developed that focused on providing Carlos with ample opportunities to gain peer attention during the course of the day through the use of structured play groups. Each day, Carlos had the opportunity to invite two friends to play games with him for 10 to 15 minutes. The thought was that if Carlos had ample opportunity to satisfy his craving for peer attention, he would not have any need to engage in inappropriate behaviors to gain their attention. The intervention also focused on providing frequent reinforcement for appropriate behavior. Unfortunately, the intervention failed miserably. In the structured play group, Carlos engaged in all the inappropriate behaviors (e.g., touching, name calling) that he had engaged in prior to the intervention. The primary reason for the failure was that the intervention did not teach replacement behaviors. That is, Carlos still did not have the skills necessary to effectively and appropriately gain peer attention.

INTRODUCTION

Social skills have been defined as "socially acceptable learned behaviors that enable a person to interact with others in ways that elicit positive responses and assist in avoiding negative responses" (Gresham & Elliot, 1990). Effective social skills allow children to elicit positive reactions and evaluations from peers as they perform socially approved behaviors (Ladd & Mize, 1983). Social skills are distinguished from **social competence** in that social skills represent behaviors that must be learned and performed, and social competence represents judgments of those behaviors by others (Gresham, 2002).

Although some individuals with Autism Spectrum Disorders (ASD) experience excellent outcomes, a majority of individuals will have persistent social impairment (Szatmari, Bartolucci, Bremner, Bond, & Rich, 1989). This could be attributed to the fact that few children receive adequate social skills programming (Hume, Bellini, & Pratt, 2005). This dearth of services is an unfortunate reality, especially considering that social skills deficits have been linked to other deleterious outcomes, such as poor academic performance, peer rejection, isolation, **social anxiety**, depression, and other forms of psychopathology (Bellini, 2006a; Tantam, 2000; Welsh, Park, Widaman, & O'Neil, 2001). Furthermore, based on a recent meta-analytical study (Bellini, Peters, Benner, & Hopf, in press), those few children who are receiving social skills programming may not be receiving *effective* social skills programming. Social skills training should be an integral part of a child's overall programming and an emphasis should be placed on implementing effective, empirically tested interventions.

The chapter will provide an overview of common social skills deficits in individuals with ASD and discuss methods for assessing social skills and social competence. The chapter will also provide a summary of the results and recommendations produced by meta-analytical research studies on social skills programming. The chapter will conclude with a description of social skills strategies that have been empirically examined via research. The chapter is separated into three broad sections: (a) common social skills deficits, (b) social skills assessment, and (c) social skills training.

COMMON SOCIAL SKILLS DEFICITS

Impairment in social functioning is a fundamental characteristic of ASD and is well documented in the literature (Attwood, 1998; Baron-Cohen, 1989; Brown & Whiten, 2000; Dawson & Fernald, 1987; Rogers, 2000). According to the *Diagnostic and Statistical Manual of Mental Disorders,* Fourth Edition, Text Revision (*DSMV-IV-TR*; American Psychiatric Association [APA], 2000), essential diagnostic criteria in the social domain include: "(a) marked impairment in the use of multiple nonverbal behaviors such as eye-to-eye gaze, facial expression, body postures, and gestures to regulate social interaction; (b) failure to develop peer relationships appropriate to developmental level; (c) a lack of spontaneous seeking to share enjoyment, interests, or achievements with other people; and (d) lack of social and emotional reciprocity" (p. 75). In addition, social avoidance and withdrawal is a hallmark feature of many individual with ASD. This was noted more than a half-century ago by Leo Kanner (1943), who described autism as a disorder with two primary clinical features: extreme aloneness and insistence on preserving sameness.

Some professionals have interpreted social withdrawal as an indication that individuals with ASD lack motivation and interest in interacting with others and in establishing relationships. This assumption has been challenged by others (Attwood, 1998; Bellini 2006b) who emphasize that many individuals with ASD do have an interest and desire to establish and maintain meaningful relationships. However, significant social skills deficits, history of peer failure and rejection, and intense social anxiety make it very difficult for these individuals to achieve or even attempt social success. The result is sometimes a life absorbed in solitary hobbies and interests. For others it leads to a pattern of inappropriate behavior that is intended to gain peer attention and affiliation, but instead it often leads to peer failure and rejection.

It is also important to discern between behaviors that are effective with peers and behaviors that are effective with adults. One need only consider the behaviors of popular children to realize that effective social behavior does not always represent "appropriate" social behavior. Sometimes the behaviors that are targeted for reduction by adults are the behaviors that are quite effective when interacting with peers (talking loudly, vulgar language, etc.). As such, it is imperative to view social skills from a developmental perspective.

The following is a description of common social skills deficits in individuals with ASD. Social skills deficits are separated into four broad categories of social functioning: (a) nonverbal communication, (b) social initiation, (c) social reciprocity, and (d) social cognition.

Nonverbal Communication

Successful social skills require the ability to read and understand the nonverbal cues of others and to clearly express thoughts, feelings, and intentions through facial expressions, gestures, and body language. In many ways, our nonverbal communication is more meaningful than our verbal communication. Difficulty in reading body language or nonverbal cues of others is a common problem for individuals with ASD. Some fail to look for nonverbal cues and are virtually oblivious to the nonverbal communication of others. Others may look for nonverbal cues, but interpret them incorrectly or fail to understand their message. Understanding nonverbal communication requires that we recognize the body language of others and infer the meaning of the nonverbal communication. This occurs by integrating all the available nonverbal and contextual cues in the environment. For instance, imagine yourself arriving home from school and finding your mother standing in the doorway, arms folded, and with a scowl on her face … and holding your report card! You would probably be able to (a) recognize your mother is upset, and (b) infer based on the contextual cues (i.e., holding the report card and scowling) that her consternation has something to do with the report card in her hand.

Social Initiation

Difficulties with initiating interactions are common among individuals with ASD (Hauck, Fein, Waterhouse, & Feinstein, 1995). Many children fall into one of two initiation categories: those who rarely initiate interactions with others, and those who initiate frequently, but inappropriately. Children in the first category often demonstrate fear, anxiety, or apathy regarding social interactions. It was once believed that the vast majority of children on the autism spectrum fit into this category. In fact, many social skills interventions have been designed with the express goal of increasing social initiations. However, in recent years an increasing number of children fit within the latter category. These children initiate interactions frequently, but their initiations are often ill timed and ill conceived. For example, they may interrupt or talk over someone. They may ask repetitive questions or questions that pertain only to their own interests. They may talk with others in settings that require silence, such as a library or church. For these children, the goal of social skills training is not to get them to initiate more frequently, but to get them to initiate more appropriately.

Social Reciprocity

Social **reciprocity** refers to the give-and-take of social interactions. Successful social interactions involve a mutual, back-and-forth exchange between two or more individuals. If you have ever been on a date where your date would not stop talking about himself, or perhaps you had to do all the talking because your date had little to say, you will understand how problems with social reciprocity can hinder social interactions. Many individuals with ASD engage in one-sided interactions in which they are either doing all the talking or fail to respond to the social initiations of others and to build on conversations with others. Individuals with ASD may continually derail conversations by changing the subject to fit their own self-interests. Joint attention is also a key component of social reciprocity. Joint attention refers to the ability to attend in unison to an object with another person. Travis, Sigman, and Ruskin (2001) demonstrated that initiating joint attention was significantly related to social competence in individuals with ASD.

Social Cognition

Several social skills difficulties exhibited by children and adolescents with ASD may be attributed to the manner in which they process social information, or **social cognition** (Baron-Cohen, 1989). Social cognition directly impacts the success of social functioning. Social cognition involves understanding the thoughts, intentions, motives, and behaviors of ourselves and others (Flavell, Miller, & Miller, 1993). Knowing and understanding social norms, customs, and values is essential to healthy social interactions and is influenced by our social cognition (Resnick, Levine, & Teasley, 1991). Within the social-cognitive domain, three processes are particularly important in social functioning: knowledge (know-how), perspective taking, and self-awareness. Individuals with ASD often experience difficulties in all three of these areas.

Knowledge is an essential component of successful social interactions. Cognitive theorists describe two types of knowledge: declarative and procedural (Pressley & McCormick, 1995). Declarative knowledge is responsible for understanding the often unwritten social rules and customs of society. Declarative knowledge also helps us interpret "figures of speech" or idioms, most of which make no literal sense. It tells us that "raining cats and dogs" means "raining hard." Children with ASD also have difficulties understanding idioms and the unwritten rules of social relationships. For example, the individual with ASD might tell a stranger that he is overweight, or that his breath stinks. Or, she might try to find the location of her thinking cap when her teacher says "It is time to put your thinking cap on."

The ability to understand the internal psychological processes of others and to take another person's point of view is critical to social cognition, and to successful social interaction (Frith, 1991). In children and adults who have an inadequate theory, or knowledge of mind, such as those with ASD, social functioning is significantly impaired (Baron-Cohen, 1989). Specifically, Baron-Cohen has found that individuals with autism demonstrate significant deficits in the ability to attribute mental states to others and correctly predict the beliefs of others. The results of such "mindblindness" (Attwood, 1998) are usually social interactions that lack social and emotional reciprocity.

Successful social interaction requires that we continually monitor and regulate our behaviors, thoughts, and feelings during social interactions. Self-awareness encompasses the ability to monitor, regulate, and evaluate our thoughts and actions. By doing this, we are able to modify our actions to ensure that our interactions will be enjoyable and successful. Self-awareness is also inextricably linked to the ability to read nonverbal cues and perspective-taking. Self-awareness allows us to monitor how our actions or behaviors impact others. Without proper self-awareness we would engage in one-sided interactions, and perhaps seemingly inappropriate or embarrassing behaviors.

Types of Skill Deficits: Performance Deficits versus Skill Acquisition Deficits

Social skills deficits are often conceptualized from a skill acquisition/performance deficit dichotomy. A **skill acquisition deficit** refers to the absence of a particular skill or behavior. For example, a young child with ASD may not know how to effectively join in activities with peers; therefore, she will often fail to participate. If we want this child to join in activities with peers, we need to teach her the necessary skills to do so. A **performance deficit** refers to a skill or behavior that is present, but not demonstrated or performed. To use the same example, a child may have the skill (or ability) to join in an activity, but for some reason, fails to do so. In this case, if we want the child to participate we would not need to teach the child to do so (since she already has the skill). Instead, we would need to address the factor that is impeding performance of the skill, such as lack of motivation, anxiety, or sensory sensitivities.

The benefit of using a skill acquisition/performance deficit model is that it guides the selection of intervention strategies. Most intervention strategies are better suited for either skill acquisition or performance deficits. The selected intervention should match the type of deficit present (Gresham, Sugai, & Horner, 2001). That is, you would not want to deliver a performance enhancement strategy if the child was mainly experiencing a skill acquisition deficit. Examples of skill acquisition strategies include: Social Stories™, video modeling, pivotal response training, social scripting, and social problem-solving strategies. (See Box 9.1 for more information on the use of video modeling). Performance enhancement strategies include: reinforcement strategies, environmental modifications, prompting strategies, peer-mediated interventions (PMIs), and social priming. It is important to note that these two categories are not mutually exclusive. Some strategies are capable of both teaching a new skill and enhancing the performance of existing skills (e.g., video modeling, Social Stories™, prompting, and self-monitoring). In addition, performance enhancement strategies are often used to supplement skill acquisition strategies. That is, when a skill is being taught via a skill acquisition strategy, it is necessary to implement performance enhancement strategies to facilitate the performance of the newly learned skill.

BOX 9.1   Trends and Issues Notes

The Use of Technology in Instruction

In recent years, the use of technology has played a prominent role in the implementation of social skills programming. Technological tools have been integrated with existing treatment modalities, such as Social Stories™ and modeling to create promising new practices. Storymovie (see The Gray Center, information) is a video application of Social Stories™ that allows the child watch videos of children demonstrating the behavior or situation portrayed in the story. Video modeling (see "Video Modeling and Video Self-Modeling" in this chapter for more information) is a technique that incorporates video technology to teach children new skills. In addition, several computer programs have also been developed to address both emotions and perspective-taking abilities in individuals with ASD. Perhaps the most popular of these computer programs is *Mind Reading: An Interactive Guide to Emotions* developed by Simon Baron-Cohen (2004). The program contains three areas to teach children how to recognize the thoughts and emotions of others: "emotions library," "learning center," and "game zone." The emotions library contains an extensive collection of video clips depicting actors (children and adults) displaying a variety of emotions organized into a helpful collection of "emotion groups." The learning center teaches the child about the various emotion groups by providing a pictorial and video example depicting an actor displaying the emotion in a social setting. This area also provides lessons and quizzes that can be tailored to match the child's individual needs and skill level. The third part of the program, "game zone," provides a collection of five emotions-related games.

SOCIAL SKILLS ASSESSMENT

The first step in social skills training programs should consist of conducting a thorough evaluation of the child's current level of social functioning (Bellini, 2006a). The purpose of the social skills assessment is to identify skills that will be the direct target of the intervention, and to monitor the outcomes of the social skills program. The evaluation details both the strengths and weaknesses of the individual related to social functioning. The identification of personal strengths is an important element of a social skills program because it allows the interventionist to leverage the individual's strengths in a manner that facilitates social relationships. For instance, if the adolescent with ASD has an encyclopedic knowledge of baseball statistics, or is a math whiz, then the interventionist can connect the child with other children with similar interests. The identification of weaknesses allows the interventionist to identify skills that will be the direct target of the intervention.

The assessment often involves a combination of observation (both naturalistic and structured), interview (e.g., parents, teachers, playground supervisors), and social skills rating forms (parent, teacher, and self-reports). Social skills assessment involves the direct assessment of social skills (via systematic observation), and the evaluation of social competence (via interview and rating scales).

Evaluation of Social Competence

Evaluations of social competence are typically conducted through the use of interviews or rating scales. Interviews are a valuable method for obtaining information regarding social functioning in a relatively short time by allowing us to collect and synthesize information from a variety of respondents representing a wide range of settings. That is, they allow the evaluator to make decisions regarding the direction and focus of the program. The interviews also allow the evaluator (who may be a professional unfamiliar with the child) to learn about the child's strengths and weaknesses related to social functioning. Interviews can be broad and encompassing or a more focused problem identification and analysis interview that breaks social skills into component parts.

Rating scales are indirect assessment tools that provide a wealth of information on the child across a variety of functioning areas. These measures range from informal checklists to standardized rating scales and may be administered to parents, teachers, and the child. Rating scales can measure social functioning, anxiety, self-concept and self-esteem, and behavioral functioning. A major advantage of behavior rating scales is their ability to quickly and efficiently obtain large quantities of information regarding social behavior from a variety of sources and across a variety of settings (Elliott, Malecki, & Demaray, 2001). The use of rating scales can also increase the social validity of the social skills program when information gleaned from the assessment is linked directly to the development of treatment goals and objectives (Gresham et al., 2001).

Evaluation of Social Skills

Observation of social behaviors should follow the interviews and administration of rating scales. Two traditional methods of observation may be used to assess the social functioning of children with ASD, naturalistic and structured. The purpose of both methods is to observe the child's social performance across settings, persons, and social contexts. Naturalistic observation involves observing and recording the child's behavior in real-life social settings, such as the school playground and cafeteria, or in various social settings at or near the child's home. Naturalistic observation is the ideal method of observing social behavior because it involves behavior that is authentic and spontaneous, allowing us to record behavior in settings that the child typically encounters in the course of his daily life. It also allows us to observe behavior across settings and across persons. This is particularly important in cases where the child might be interacting well in structured settings (i.e., the classroom) but not in unstructured settings (i.e., the playground) or interacting well with certain peers, or with adults, but not with other children or unfamiliar adults. Structured observations involve observing the child in an environment that has been artificially established to facilitate social interactions between the target child and pre-selected peers. Structured observations involve observing social behavior in a structured play group, or structured social group. The child with ASD is grouped with one or two non-disabled peers in a setting that is rich in social opportunities (games, toys, and other age-appropriate play objects). Non-disabled peers may also be coached prior to the observation to make sure that they include the child with ASD in their activities.

Social Validity

Social validity refers to the social significance of the treatment objectives, the social significance of the intervention strategies, and the social importance of the intervention results (Gresham & Lambros, 1998). It involves ensuring that the consumers believe that the selected treatment objectives are indeed important for the child to achieve. If consumers do not believe that the objectives are important, they will be less likely to exert the effort necessary to achieve those objectives. This aspect of social validity is established during the initial social skills assessment, specifically during the interview process.

Gresham (2002) provides a classification system that separates social skills assessment methods into three categories that represent different levels of social validity. Type I measures include rating scales and interviews designed to measure social competence. Type I measures are the most socially valid assessment measures because they directly measure the impressions of key stakeholders. That is, the results of Type I measures represent the judgments of parents and teachers. As such, treatment objectives developed from these measures are likely to be accepted and viewed as socially acceptable by these key stakeholders. A major advantage of Type I measures is their ability to efficiently obtain information regarding social behavior from a variety of sources and across a variety of settings. A major disadvantage of Type I measures is the fact that they are often not sensitive to short-term changes in behavior. For instance, the child might be demonstrating an increase in the target behaviors without key stakeholders noticing these changes. Type II measures involve the direct assessment of the child's social skills. As such, these measures are valuable to progress monitoring and are used extensively in applied research studies involving single-subject methodology. Type II measures are sensitive to small changes in behavior because they are linked directly to the treatment objects. For instance, if the interventionist identifies "joining in activities with peers" as a treatment objective, the intervention would then observe the child to measure whether "joining-in" behavior has increased over the course of the intervention. Type III measures are the least socially valid assessment measures. Type III measures involve conducting role-play scenarios or asking questions of the individual related to social cognition (e.g., social problem solving or perspective-taking scenarios). Although these are important areas to address via intervention, research has demonstrated that these measures are not related to measures of social competence (Type I measures) or measures of social skills (Type II measures).

The **social acceptability** of intervention strategies is also critical to the success of the social skills training. If consumers do not think that an intervention strategy will be effective, or if they think it may be harmful to the child, they will be less likely to implement it. The social importance of intervention results represents the consumer's perceptions of the intervention results. If the consumer does not believe that the intervention resulted in positive and meaningful change for the child, then the consumer is likely to disengage, or discontinue, the social skills program.

Functional Behavior Assessment (FBA) and Social Skills

Functional behavior assessment (FBA) refers to a process of determining what is maintaining the problem behavior (See Chapter 7 for more information on FBA). FBA integrates a variety of data, including interviews, observations, and rating forms. An FBA might determine that a child engages in inappropriate touching behavior to gain peer attention. The function of this behavior would be peer attention. Another purpose of the FBA is to determine what antecedent stimulus (also referred to as a discriminative stimulus) might be triggering, or occasioning, the problem behavior. For instance, the FBA might reveal that the child engages in aggressive behaviors towards individuals with loud voices. In this case, the loud voices would be serving as a trigger for the aggressive behavior. Yet another purpose of the FBA is to identify potential **establishing operations (EOs)** for the problem behavior. An EO is a condition that increases (or decreases) the probability that a problem behavior will occur. In this way, social skills deficits, isolation, and social anxiety serve as EOs for many problem behaviors. For instance, a child with social skills deficits who is socially isolated, may be more likely to engage in inappropriate behavior to gain peer attention than a child with effective social skills who receives copious amount of peer attention throughout the day. Or, a child with severe social anxiety may be more likely to engage in appropriate behavior to avoid or escape interactions, and thereby reduce her anxiety level, than would a child without anxiety.

A fundamental purpose of the FBA is to develop a behavior intervention plan. The intervention is linked directly to the data gathered via the FBA process and addresses the function, the antecedent stimulus, and/or the EO. A key feature of the intervention plan is to teach replacement behaviors. A replacement behavior is an appropriate behavior that serves the same function as the problem behavior. As such, social skills are considered replacement behaviors, and social skills training often takes on a level of importance in the development of intervention plans. For instance, the child who engages in inappropriate touching to gain peer attention can be taught replacement behaviors (i.e., social skills) to effectively initiate interactions with peers. Performance of these newly learned skills will allow her to gain the peer attention she desires, and thus diminish the need to engage in inappropriate touching.

SOCIAL SKILLS TRAINING

Social skills training refers to instruction or support designed to improve or facilitate the acquisition and/or performance of social skills. Social skills training programs address three primary objectives: promote skill acquisition, enhance the performance of existing skills, and facilitate the **generalization** of skills across settings and persons. For most children, social skills are acquired through learning that involves observation, modeling, coaching, social problem solving, behavior rehearsal, feedback, and reinforcement-based strategies (Gresham & Elliot, 1990). Two underlying assumptions of all social skills training programs are that individuals can be taught to behave differently, and they will elicit more positive reactions and evaluations from peers as they acquire and perform more socially approved behaviors (Ladd & Mize, 1983). Elliot and Gresham (1991) discuss five factors that contribute to social skills deficits: (a) lack of knowledge, (a) lack of practice or feedback, (c) lack of cues or opportunities, (d) lack of reinforcement, and (e) the presence of interfering problem behaviors. Social skills training programs should identify which factors are contributing to the social skills deficits of the target child and attempt to ameliorate these deficits through programming. The following section provides a summary of meta-analytic research and literature reviews that have been conducted on social skills training for children with and without ASD. These research studies provide a valuable synthesis on the existing knowledge base regarding social skills training, and also provide helpful recommendations for effective programming. The section concludes with a description of specific social skills training strategies commonly used with individuals with ASD.

Results of Meta-Analytical Research: Ingredients of Effective Social Skills

PROGRAMS A number of qualitative reviews have examined the effectiveness of social skills interventions for children with ASD and have provided suggestions for increasing the effectiveness of social skills programming (Hwang & Hughes, 2000; McConnell, 2002; Rogers, 2000). Hwang and Hughes (2000) reviewed 16 studies involving social skills programming for children with ASD between the ages of 2 and 12. The researchers concluded that social skills programming shows "considerable promise for increasing social and communicative skills" of children with ASD (p. 340), pointing to "positive" changes in social behaviors across the studies in the literature review. Rogers (2000) provided a comprehensive narrative of social skills strategies for children with ASD. Rogers concluded that children with ASD are "responsive" to a wide variety of social skills intervention strategies to facilitate both adult-child and child-child interactions. These strategies include pivotal response training, adult prompting, environmental modifications, social skills groups, Social Stories™, video modeling, and peer-mediated instruction.

McConnell (2002) conducted a literature review of 55 studies examining social skills interventions for young children with ASD. McConnell divided social skills interventions into five categories: (a) environmental modifications, (b) child-specific interventions, (c) collateral skills interventions, (d) PMIs, and (e) comprehensive interventions. According to McConnell, *environmental modifications* involve modifications to the physical and social environment that promote social interactions between children with ASD and their peers. **Child-specific interventions** involve the direct instruction of social behaviors, such as initiating and responding. **Collateral skill interventions** involve strategies that promote social interactions by delivering training in related skills, such as play behaviors and language, rather than training specific social behaviors. PMIs involve training non disabled peers to direct and respond to the social behaviors of children with ASD. Finally, comprehensive interventions involve social skills interventions that combine two or more of the aforementioned intervention categories. McConnell concluded that young children with ASD can benefit from arranged environments that include structured, preferred activities and opportunities for positive interactions with more socially competent peers coupled with targeted, direct intervention to enhance his or her own individual skills.

A number of quantitative meta-analyses have been performed on social skills intervention studies involving children and adolescents with and without ASD. Although these studies have failed to support the effectiveness of social skills training in general, they do provide helpful guidance in determining the ingredients of effective social skills interventions. In general, studies have demonstrated that traditional social skills training programs are only minimally effective in teaching social skills to children and adolescents (Bellini., et al., in press; Gresham, et al., 2001; Quinn, Kavale, Mathur, Rutherford, & Forness, 1999). Quinn et al. (1999) found small effect sizes in their **meta-analysis** of 35 studies examining social skills interventions in children and adolescents with emotional and behavioral disorders. In addition, no significant differences in outcomes were observed for the duration of the intervention, quality of the research design, age of the participant, and the specific construct used to measure social skills. The researchers concluded that social skills programs must be designed to fit the individual needs of the child as opposed to forcing the child to "fit" into the chosen social skills strategy or strategies. Finally, the researchers concluded that the type of skill deficit (i.e., performance deficit versus skill acquisition deficit) must also be considered when developing a social skills intervention plan. Results were consistent with the low treatment effects observed in the meta-analysis performed by Mathur, Kavale, Quinn, Forness, and Rutherford (1998).

After reviewing numerous studies, Gresham et al. (2001) concluded that meta-analytic reviews of social skills training have yielded a wide variety of results, ranging from ineffectual to highly effective interventions. The authors provided a number of recommendations for promoting effective social skills interventions. First, the researchers recommended that social skills training should be implemented more frequently and more intensely than what is typically implemented. They concluded that "thirty hours of instruction, spread over 10–12 weeks is not enough" (p. 341). Second, they concluded that a major weakness of social skills interventions is due to the fact that social skills training often takes place in "contrived, restricted, and decontextualized" (p. 340) settings, such as resource rooms or other "pull-out" settings. Third, the researchers posited that the ineffectiveness of many social skills programs is a result of the interventionists' failure to match the social skills strategy to the type of skill deficit presented. For instance, if the child is experiencing skill acquisition deficits, then intervention strategies designed to teach new skills should be selected. Finally, Gresham et al. concluded that the traditionally weak treatment effects of many social skills programs may be the result of outcome measures that do not match the skills that are being taught.

Bellini et al. (in press) conducted a meta-analysis of school-based social skills interventions for children and adolescents with ASD. Results of this meta-analysis suggest that school-based social skills interventions are only minimally effective for children with ASD. A major finding of the study was that students receiving social skills programming in their typical classroom setting had substantially more favorable treatment outcomes than did students who received services in a pull-out setting. Environmental modifications, child-specific interventions, collateral skills interventions, PMIs, and comprehensive interventions produced similar treatment results, and there were no differences observed between individual and group intervention formats. The results support the recommendations offered by Gresham et al. (2001), which include (a) increasing the dosage of social skills interventions, (b) providing instruction within the child's natural setting, (c) matching the intervention strategy with the type of skill deficit, and (d) ensuring intervention fidelity.

Specific Social Skills Training Strategies

Social skills training can be delivered across a variety of settings (e.g., home, community, classroom, resource room, playground, and therapeutic clinic) and with multiple persons (e.g., family members, teachers, counselors, speech and language pathologists, social workers, occupational and physical therapists, psychologists, physicians, and case managers). In addition, social skills can be taught in an individual, group, or classwide format. Successful social skills training programs promote cooperation between both parents (and other family members and caregivers) and professionals and should take into consideration the child's and family's culture (see Box 9.2). There are a number of important questions to consider when selecting social skills strategies. For instance, does the strategy target the skill deficits identified in the social assessment? Does the strategy enhance performance? Does the

BOX 9.2   Diversity Notes

In social skills training, it is critical to understand the role of culture in the interaction and communication patterns of our students or clients. What may be viewed as a social skills "deficit" by the dominant culture may in fact be an extremely functional and effective social behavior when viewed within the context of the person's culture. For instance, some persons from Latino cultures may view direct eye contact as disrespectful, especially when communicating with an elder (LaFrance & Mayo, 1976). It would be insensitive to instruct this child to maintain eye contact during interactions, and even worse, it would undermine the values instilled in him by his family. In addition to eye contact, culture may influence a number of social behaviors such as personal space, conversational turn taking, voice volume, and emotional expression. It is also extremely important to recognize that there is great variation within cultures regarding interaction patterns. That is, we can not accurately predict a person's interaction or communication style simply by knowing her cultural affiliation. Social behavior should be evaluated on a person-by-person basis and always viewed within the context of the person's culture.

strategy promote skills acquisition? Does the strategy facilitate generalization? If not, what is the plan to facilitate generalization? Is there research to support its use? If not, what is your plan to evaluate its effectiveness with the child? Is it developmentally appropriate for the child? (See Figure 9.1 for more on a developmental perspective of social skills training.) The following section summarizes a number of social skills strategies that have been systematically tested via research. This section is separated into three categories: promoting skill acquisition, enhancing performance, and facilitating generalization. It is important to note that these strategies do not represent an all-inclusive list of available social skills training strategies. The field of autism is dynamic with new strategies being developed

---

An examination of social skills requires a developmental perspective. That is, social skills change during the course of the child's development, and as such the focus of social skills training should also change. The following captures the typical development of social skills across three developmental levels: early childhood, middle childhood, and adolescence (adapted from Bierman & Montimy, 1993). These developmental issues are important to consider in both teaching social skills to the individual with ASD, and in the implementation of PMIs.

Early Childhood
- Engage in shared-play activities
- Require interactive play skills
- Interactions are brief in duration
- Engage in frequent squabbles with peers
- Concrete social perceptions
- View themselves and others in physicalistic terms (skin color, hair length, size, etc.)
- Sociometric status (popularity among peers) more variable
- Grudges and preferences for peers tend to be modified continually

Middle Childhood
- Peer-approved social behavior becomes more complex and demanding
- Play becomes more organized and rule–bound
- Acquire skills related to sustained interpersonal relationships
- Acquire self-regulation skills
- Compare abilities and characteristics of self and others across time and context
- Focus more on relationship aspects of friendship
- Become more norm-based in their evaluations of self and peers
- Underestimate the competencies of disliked peers (intelligence, physical stature, athletic abilities, etc.)

Adolescence
- Social activities become more diverse
- Expectations of friendship develop to include intimacy, self-disclosure, and loyalty
- Social withdrawal and isolation increases, especially following peer rejection
- Able to anticipate social encounters and consider multiple perspective or viewpoints
- Social reasoning develops beyond rigid, rule-based expectations
- Perceptions of peers become more rigid and difficult to change
- Extremely susceptible to peer influences
- More likely to view peer rejection as an indication of personal unworthiness
- More vulnerable to social anxiety

FIGURE 9.1 Social Skills from a Developmental Perspective

and evaluated on a frequent basis. The strategies selected for this chapter represent a sampling of strategies with documented effectiveness with individuals with ASD.

Skill Acquisition Strategies

SOCIAL STORIES   Social Stories™ (Gray, 2000) is a frequently used strategy to teach social skills to children with ASD. Sansosti, Powell-Smith, and Kincaid (2004) conducted a research synthesis of eight Social Stories™ intervention studies. The researchers concluded that Social Stories™ is an effective intervention strategy in addressing the social, communication, and behavioral functioning of children and adolescents with ASD. Social Stories™ present social concepts and rules to children in the form of a brief story, and may be used to teach a number of social and behavioral concepts, such as initiating interactions, making transitions, playing a game, and going on a field trip. Gray emphasizes that the story should be written in response to the child's personal need and that the story should be something the child wants to read on her own (depending upon ability level). She also stresses that the story should be commensurate with the child's ability and comprehension level. Perhaps most important, Gray recommends that the story should use less directive terms such as "can" or "could," instead of "will" or "must."

VIDEO MODELING AND VIDEO SELF-MODELING (VSM)   **Video modeling** is a technique that involves demonstration of desired behaviors through active video representation of the behavior. A video modeling intervention typically involves an individual watching a video demonstration and then imitating the behavior of the model. Video self-modeling (VSM) is a specific application of video modeling wherein the individual learns by watching her own behavior. Results of a recent meta-analysis suggest that video modeling and VSM are highly effective intervention strategies for addressing social-communication skills, behavioral functioning, and functional skills in children and adolescents with ASD (Bellini & Akullian, in press). Results demonstrate that video modeling and VSM effectively promote skill acquisition and that skills acquired via video modeling and VSM are maintained over time and transferred across persons and settings.

The effectiveness of video modeling and VSM for individuals with ASD can be attributed in part to the fact that video modeling and VSM integrate an effective learning modality for children with ASD (visually cued instruction) with a well-studied intervention technique (modeling). In addition to capitalizing on the effectiveness of visual instruction, there are a number of other factors that make video modeling and VSM effective interventions for children with ASD. As Bandura (1977) theorized, attention is a necessary component of modeling. That is, a person cannot imitate the behavior of a model if the person does not attend to the model's behavior. Some individuals with ASD exhibit overselective attention or attend to irrelevant details of the environment. The use of video modeling allows interventionists to remove irrelevant elements of the modeled skill or behavior through video editing. The removal of irrelevant stimuli allows the individual with ASD to better focus on essential aspects of the targeted skill or behavior. In addition, video modeling and VSM can be implemented with minimal human interaction, thereby reducing much of the distress and anxiety related to social interactions. (See Box 9.3 for more on anxiety issues in individuals with ASD.) Motivation could be another factor contributing to the success of video modeling and VSM interventions. Watching videos is a highly desired activity for many children with and without ASD, leading to increased motivation and attention to the modeled task. In VSM, motivation to watch oneself on the video may be enhanced by the portrayal of predominantly positive and successful behaviors, which may also increase attention and enhance self-efficacy.

BOX 9.3 Research Notes

The Relationship Between Socials Skill Functioning and Social Anxiety

Recent research suggests that individuals with Autism Spectrum Disorders may exhibit significantly higher levels of anxiety than the general population (Bellini, 2004; Gillott, Furniss, & Walter, 2001; Green, Gilchrist, Burton, & Cox, 2000; Kim, Szatmari, Bryson, Streiner, & Wilson, 2000). These studies suggest that individuals with ASD exhibit a broad range of anxious symptoms, including physiological arousal, panic, separation anxiety, and social anxiety. Anxiety can be a debilitating disorder, often associated with excessive worry and fear, and isolation. Social anxiety is particularly salient to a discussion of social skills, given the impact that it has on social functioning. The essential feature of social anxiety is an intense fear of social situations or performances. Bellini (2006) presents a developmental pathway that describes both the development of social skills deficits and social anxiety in adolescents with ASD. The research indicates that the path to social skills deficits and social anxiety for individuals with ASD begins with an early temperament that is marked by a high degree of physiological arousal. This physiological arousal makes it more likely that the young child with ASD will become overwhelmed by interactions with others and avoid subsequent social interactions. Social withdrawal then limits the opportunity for the child to develop effective social skills by limiting her ability to interact with peers. Impairment in social skills functioning significantly increases the chances for negative peer interactions and social failure. To complete the pathway, the presence of physiological hyper-arousal makes it more likely that the individual will be conditioned by these negative social experiences, leading to increased social anxiety. The model provides valuable treatment implications for practitioners working with individuals with ASD and co-morbid social anxiety. As a result of this research, Bellini offers the following recommendations for practitioners addressing the social-emotional functioning in children with ASD:

1. It is imperative that we assess anxiety in children with ASD to examine how it may be influencing their social performance.
2. Social skills programs should include teaching the child how to regulate her physiological responses to stressful events.
3. Early intervention to decrease social withdrawal is critical to the development of social skills.
4. Social skills training should be an integral component of a child's individual education program (IEP) throughout her education career.
5. Peer intervention strategies should be used to facilitate an atmosphere of acceptance and caring to minimize the possibility of negative peer interactions.

SOCIAL PROBLEM SOLVING Many children with ASD have difficulties interpreting and analyzing social situations. This is due to a number of factors, including lack of self-awareness, failure to read nonverbal and contextual cues, difficulties with perspective taking, and failure to understand social rules. It is also due to the fact that they lack the necessary skills and strategies to analyze social situations. Research has demonstrated that **social problem solving (SPS)** can be taught to children with ASD. A meta-analysis conducted by Beelman, Pfingsten, and Losel (1994) found that SPS strategies were effective in increasing performance on social problem tasks. However, a major limitation noted by the researchers was that these increases in social problem-solving ability had no carryover effect to other areas of social functioning, such as specific social behaviors or skills. That is, SPS strategies may increase social problem solving, but their impact on social skills and social competence is questionable.

Many different methods and techniques have been used to facilitate the development of social reasoning in children with and without ASD (Elias, Butler, Bruno, Papke, & Shapiro, 2005). SPS strategies can be used in individual and group social skills programs, or they can be incorporated into a classroom curriculum. The following represents an example of a SPS strategy that incorporates many of the basic elements of social problem solving. The first step of the SPS process may be to describe the social scenario, setting, behavior, or problem (what's happening or what has happened?). The next step may be to predict the consequences (What do you think will happen next? What will be the consequences of this behavior?), and then select an alternative behavior (What could he/she/you have done differently?). Finally the child may be asked to predict a consequence for the alternative behaviors.

PIVOTAL RESPONSE TRAINING   **Pivotal response training (PRT)** (Koegel & Koegel, 2006) is an intervention program based on the principles of applied behavioral analysis that is utilized in natural environments and capitalizes on the availability of naturally occurring reinforcers. PRT targets so-called *pivotal behaviors* (behaviors that lead to widespread changes in other behaviors), which facilitates transfer of skills to multiple settings and collateral improvements in non-targeted behaviors. PRT directly targets behaviors related to initiation and responding to environmental cues. PRT targets four pivotal areas: **responsivity to multiple cues, initiation, motivation,** and **self-management**. PRT teaches children to attend and respond to multiple cues in the environment. Intervention in this area teaches the child to select cues that are relevant in a given context or situation. Intervention in the initiation area teaches the child to effectively initiate interactions with others. Intervention in the motivation area addresses the child's lack of motivation related to social situations. Intervention includes giving the child a choice in activity, using natural reinforcers, and reinforcing reasonable attempts at interacting. Interventions in self-management teach the child to be more independent and less reliant on prompts from others in their environment. Humphries (2003) conducted a research synthesis of 13 studies that investigated the effectiveness of PRT. Humphries concluded that PRT is an effective strategy for addressing the behavior, communication, and social functioning of children with ASD.

SOCIAL SCRIPTING AND SCRIPT FADING   **Scripting** involves the presentation of a structured "script" to the child that provides an explicit description regarding what the child will say or do during a social interaction (Mayo & Waldo, 1994). The script may provide a narrative of what to say during a conversation or what to do during an activity. The script may contain the entire sequence of the interaction or only the initiation. For instance, the child might be taught a script for initiating an interaction with a peer who is also taught to respond in a scripted fashion. The benefits of scripting for individuals with ASD have been demonstrated in research involving both conversational scripts (Loveland & Tunali, 1991) and play scripts (MacDonald, Clark, & Garrigan, 2005). A major limitation of scripting is that the child may become reliant on the script and be unable to engage in spontaneous, unscripted interactions. Script fading is a research-based practice designed to address this limitation (Krantz & McClannahan, 1998). Script-fading involves the introduction of script to facilitate an increase in social interactions and then a systematic fading of the script over time to promote maintenance, generalization, and elaboration of the interaction.

Additional Strategies to Promote Skill Acquisition

There are a number of additional strategies that have been used extensively to teach social skills in other populations. This section will summarize two of those skill acquisition strategies: behavioral rehearsal and coaching. Behavioral rehearsal, or role-playing, is used primarily to teach basic social interaction skills. It is an effective approach to teaching social skills that allows for the positive practice of skills (Gresham, 2002). Behavioral rehearsal involves acting out situations or activities in a structured environment to practice newly acquired skills and strategies or previously learned skills that the child is having difficulties performing. Coaching utilizes verbal and visual instruction to facilitate the development and performance of social skills. Coaching is a flexible teaching strategy that may take many shapes and forms, but typically contains the following three basic steps: (a) introduce the social rule to the child, (b) provide opportunities to practice or rehearse the skill with a coach, and (c) provide immediate feedback to the child regarding her performance.

Strategies to Enhance Performance of Existing Skills

PRIMING **Priming** refers to the "incidental activation of knowledge structures" (Bargh, Chen, & Burrows, 1996), which facilitates memory recall or behavioral performance. The positive effects of priming to facilitate social behavior is supported by other researchers, who used priming to increase the social initiations of preschool children with ASD (Zanolli, Daggett, & Adams, 1996) and to decrease problem behaviors in the classroom (Koegel, Koegel, Frea, & Green-Hopkins, 2003). Video priming has been used to reduce problem behaviors during transitions for children with ASD (Schreibman, Whalen, & Stahmer, 2000). The researchers selected transitions in settings deemed most problematic by the children's parents. The researchers then videotaped the settings to show the environment just as the child would see it (moving through the store, getting ready in the morning, etc.). The children were not depicted in the video.

The usefulness of priming procedures to activate knowledge structures and to facilitate social cognition and social behaviors makes it a valuable intervention component in social skills programming. Social cognitions and social behaviors can be primed by presenting cognitive or behavioral "primes" just prior to performance of the skill or behavior in the natural environment.

Cognitive priming strategies can be either visual (e.g., pictures, videos, modeling, or visual prompts) or verbal instruction (e.g., verbal description of the behavior, discussion of the behavior, or verbal prompts). *Behavioral priming strategies* involve behavioral rehearsal or practicing the skill or behavior just prior to performing it in the natural environment. Priming does not teach new skills or behaviors; however, it is a powerful strategy for activating skills and behaviors already in our behavioral repertoire.

PROMPTING **Prompts** are highly effective in facilitating child-adult and child-child interactions in children with ASD (McConnell, 2002; Rogers, 2000). Prompts are supports and assistance provided to the child to help her acquire skills and successfully perform behaviors. Prompts can be used to teach new social skills (in the case of physical and modeling prompts) and to enhance performance of previously acquired skills. In addition, they may be used with novice or advanced performers, in individual sessions or in group sessions, with verbal children or with nonverbal children, and with preschoolers or with adults. Prompts may be delivered by adults or by other children. A limitation of prompting strategies is that the child with ASD may limit social interactions to only instances in which prompting is provided. As such, a prompt-fading plan is implemented to systematically fade prompts from most to least supportive.

There are five primary types of prompts that may be used to facilitate social behavior. They are discussed from "most" to "least" supportive. The most supportive prompts require the greatest amount of adult support and the least amount of independence on the part of the child, whereas least supportive prompts require more independence on the part of the child and less adult assistance. The goal is to use the prompt that provides "just enough" support—or the least supportive prompt necessary for the child to successfully complete a task. *Physical prompts* consist of physically guiding a child's performance of a target skill or behavior and are the most supportive type. Physical prompts range from hand-over-hand guidance (most supportive), to a simple physical touch to facilitate a specific movement (least restrictive). *Modeling prompts* consist of demonstrating or performing all (most supportive) or part (least supportive) of the desired skill or behavior to the child, who imitates the skill or behavior immediately. Verbal prompts include specific verbal directives (most supportive) or instructions or single words and phrases designed to trigger, or jog, a child's memory of how to perform a task (least supportive). This type of prompt can be used to teach new skills or behaviors and also to enhance performance of existing skills or behaviors. *Gestural prompts* involve providing a nonverbal gesture that visually directs or reminds an individual to perform a task. Gestural prompts typically include various hand signals but may also include visual cues and supports (pictures, cards, etc.). They range from elaborate (pointing to a location and pantomiming an activity) to simple (pointing to another student to facilitate a social initiation). Natural prompts are the least supportive type of prompt. These are stimuli that naturally occur in the child's environment that direct a behavior to occur. This may include a bell ringing or kids lining up to go outside. There are many natural prompts for social interactions. A common natural (and direct) prompt occurs when a person initiates an interaction with us (i.e., asks us a question). This prompt naturally directs our behavior to respond to the person.

SELF-MONITORING   **Self-monitoring** strategies have demonstrated considerable effectiveness for teaching children with and without disabilities to both monitor and regulate their own behavior (Carter, 1993). Self-monitoring can be considered a skill acquisition strategy because it teaches the child to monitor her own behavior, but it may also be considered a performance-enhancing technique because through self-monitoring, the child is able to enhance the performance of an existing skill. The self-recording of behavior can be used during the behavioral performance or after the performance (or both). Strategies can target a number of externalizing behaviors, such as time on task, work completion, and disruptive behaviors, as well as internal processes, such as thoughts (self-talk) and feelings (both positive and negative). Self-monitoring strategies may involve having the child record occurrences, duration, and frequencies of behaviors (whether the behavior was performed, for how long, how frequently it was performed) and the quality of the behavioral performance (how well the behavior was performed). Self-monitoring strategies have also been used effectively to address the social and behavioral functioning of children with ASD (Coyle & Cole, 2004; Shearer, Kohler, Buchan, & McCullough, 1996). Shearer et al. used self-monitoring to increase the social interactions of preschool children with ASD. Coyle and Cole used self-monitoring in combination with video self-modeling (positive self-review) to decrease off-task behavior in school-aged children with ASD. Finally, self-monitoring strategies support generalization of skills because they teach children to independently monitor their own behavior.

PEER-MEDIATED INTERVENTION   **Peer-mediated intervention (PMI)** is an effective strategy for facilitating social interactions between young children with ASD (and other disabilities) and their non-disabled peers (Laushey, & Heflin, *2000;* Odom, McConnell, & McEvoy, 1992; Sasso, Mundschenk, Melloy, & Casey, 1998; Strain & Odom, 1986). In PMI programs, non disabled children in the class are selected and trained to be "peer buddies" for a child with ASD. As such, the non-disabled peers participate in the intervention by making social initiations or responding promptly and appropriately to the initiations of children with ASD during the course of their school day. PMI allows children with ASD to perform social behaviors through direct social contact and by modeling the social behaviors of peers.

PMI allows us to structure the physical and social environment so as to promote successful social interactions. PMI can be used in naturalistic settings (classroom and playground), and also in structured settings (structured play groups). For maximum effectiveness, it is recommended that PMI programs are used in both settings. The use of peer mentors allows the teacher and other adults to act as facilitators rather than participate as active playmates. The use of trained peer mentors also facilitates generalization of skills by ensuring that newly acquired skills are performed and practiced with peers in the natural environment.

POSITIVE REINFORCEMENT   Social interactions can be stressful and excruciatingly difficult for children with ASD, at least until they acquire sufficient skills and confidence. Therefore, reinforcement is often integrated into most social skills programs. Positive reinforcement is a powerful motivator of human behavior. Individuals are driven to perform behaviors to obtain a positive reinforcer. A child who receives a reinforcer for initiating an interaction with another child is likely to initiate interactions again in the future. The opposite is also true: a child who does not receive a reinforcer for initiating an interaction (e.g., the other child rejects his initiation attempt) will be less likely to initiate interactions in the future. Specific types of reinforcers include attention (from peers or adults), social praise, sensory items, tangible items (toys, stickers, food, etc.), and preferred activities (playing a video game or extra recess time).

In addition to increasing wanted behavior, the delivery of positive reinforcement communicates to the child that adults are monitoring his behavior. This is a very important concept for reducing problematic behaviors. Reinforcement also provides feedback to the child about his behavioral performance. And since it is the delivery of positive reinforcement, it will involve feedback regarding positive behaviors rather than the negative ones.

Facilitating Generalization

A critical aspect of all social skills programs is to develop a plan for generalization, or transfer of skills across settings, persons, situations, and time. The ultimate goal of social skills training is to teach the child to interact successfully with multiple persons and in multiple natural environments. From a behavioral perspective, the inability to generalize a skill or behavior is a result of too much stimulus control. That is, the child performs the skill or behavior only in the presence of a specific stimulus (person, prompt, directives, etc.). For instance, the child may respond to the social initiations of other children, but only if his mother is there to prompt him. If Mom is not there, he does not respond. Generalization is particularly important for children with ASD who often have pronounced difficulties transferring skills across persons and settings. A number of strategies may be used to facilitate generalization of social skills across settings, persons, situations, and time, including: (a) reinforce the performance of social skills in the natural environment, (b) train with multiple persons and in multiple settings, (c) ensure the presence and delivery of natural reinforcers for the performance of social skills, (d) practice the skill in the natural environment, (e) fade prompts as quickly as feasible, (f) provide multiple exemplars for social rules and concepts, (g) train skills loosely (i.e., vary the instruction, directives, strategies, and prompts used during skill instruction), (h) teach self-monitoring strategies, and (i) provide "booster" sessions (i.e., provide follow-up training after initial instruction has been discontinued).

Summary

Impairment in social functioning is a central feature of ASD. Individuals with ASD experience difficulties related to social initiation, social reciprocity, nonverbal communication, and social cognition. These skill deficits can be separated into either skill acquisition or performance deficits. A skill acquisition deficit refers to the absence of a particular skill or behavior. A performance deficit refers to a skill or behavior that is present, but not demonstrated or performed. It is critical to select strategies that match the type of skill deficit. Skill acquisition strategies involve techniques to teach new skills. They involve the introduction and demonstration of behaviors that are not presently in the child's behavioral repertoire. Performance enhancement strategies are designed to facilitate, or enhance the performance of, existing, or newly learned skills. These strategies enhance performance by either addressing the factor diminishing performance (e.g., lack of motivation, sensory sensitivities), or by providing opportunities to perform newly learned skills. An essential first step of social skills training is to identify the skills that will be targeted during intervention. This is done through social skills assessment. The assessment often involves a combination of observation (both naturalistic and structured), interview (e.g., parents, teachers, playground supervisors), and social skills rating forms (parent, teacher, and self-reports). The types of social skills training strategies that should be selected are supported by research and match the type of skill deficit, and social skills training programs should be intensive and implemented in natural settings.

Chapter Review Questions

1. Describe common social skills deficits in individuals with ASD. (Objective 1)
2. Why is it important to teach social skills to individuals with ASD? (Objective 2)
3. How are social skills and social competence evaluated? (Objective 3)
4. Distinguish between a skill acquisition deficit and performance deficits. How is this dichotomy important to intervention? (Objective 4)
5. What does meta-analytical research tells us about the effectiveness of social skills training for individuals with ASD? (Objective 5)
6. What social skills training strategies are available to teach social skills to individuals with ASD? (Objective 6)

Key Terms

Child-specific interventions *210*
Cognitive priming strategies *216*
Collateral skill interventions *210*
Establishing operations
   (EOs) *209*
Functional behavior assessment
   (FBA) *208*
Generalization *209*
Initiation *215*
Meta-analysis *210*
Motivation *215*

Peer-mediated intervention
   (PMI) *217*
Performance deficit *205*
Pivotal response training
   (PRT) *215*
Priming *216*
Prompts *216*
Reciprocity *204*
Responsivity to multiple cues *215*
Scripting *215*
Self-management *215*

Self-monitoring *217*
Skill acquisition deficit *205*
Social acceptability *208*
Social anxiety *203*
Social cognition *205*
Social competence *202*
Social skills *202*
Social problem solving (SPS) *214*
Social Stories™ *213*
Social validity *208*
Video modeling *213*

References

American Psychiatric Association. (2000). *Diagnostic and statistical manual of mental disorders* (4th ed., text revision). Washington, DC: Author.

Attwood, T. (1998). *Asperger's Syndrome: A guide for parents and professionals.* Philadelphia: Kingsley.

Bandura, A. (1977). *Social learning theory.* Upper Saddle River, NJ: Prentice Hall.

Bargh, J. A., Chen, M., & Burrows, L. (1996). The automaticity of social behaviour: Direct effects of trait concept and stereotype activation on action. *Journal of Personality and Social Psychology, 71*, 230–244.

Baron-Cohen, S. (1989). The autistic child's theory of mind: A case of specific developmental delay. *Journal of Child Psychology and Psychiatry, 30*, 285–297.

Baron-Cohen, S. (2004). *Mind reading: An interactive guide to emotions.* London: Jessica Kingsley Publishing.

Beelman, A., Pfingsten, U., & Losel, F. (1994). Effects of training social competence in children: A meta-analysis of recent evaluation studies. *Journal of Clinical Child Psychology, 213*, 260–271.

Bellini, S. (2004). Social skill deficits and anxiety in high functioning adolescents with autism spectrum disorders. *Focus on Autism and Other Developmental Disabilities, 19*, 78–86.

Bellini, S. (2006a). The development of social anxiety in high functioning adolescents with autism spectrum disorders. *Focus on Autism and Other Developmental Disabilities, 21*, 138–145.

Bellini, S. (2006b). *Building social relationships: A systematic approach to teaching social interaction skills to children and adolescents with autism spectrum disorders and other social difficulties.* Shawnee Mission, KS: Autism Asperger Publishing.

Bellini, S., & Akullian, J. (in press). A meta-analysis of video modeling and video self-modeling interventions for children and adolescents with autism spectrum disorders. *Exceptional Children.*

Bellini, S., Peters, J., Benner, L., & Hopf, A. (in press). A meta-analysis of school-based social skill interventions for children with autism spectrum disorders. *Remedial and Special Education.*

Bierman, K., & Montminy, K. (1993). Developmental issues in social skills assessment and intervention with children and adolescents. *Behavioral Modification, 17*(5), 229–254.

Brown, J., & Whiten, A. (2000). Imitation, theory of mind and related activities in autism: An observational study of spontaneous behaviour in everyday contexts. *Autism: The International Journal of Research and Practice, 4*, 185–205.

Carter, J. F. (1993). Self-management: Education's ultimate goal. *Teaching Exceptional Children, 18*(4), 272–276.

Coyle, C., & Cole, P. (2004). A videotaped self-modeling and self-monitoring treatment program to decrease off-task behaviour in children with autism. *Journal of Intellectual & Developmental Disabilities, 29*(1), 3–15.

Dawson, G., & Fernald, M. (1987). Perspective taking ability and its relationship to the social behavior of autistic children. *Journal of Autism and Developmental Disorders, 17*, 487–489.

Elias, M. J., Butler, L. B., Bruno, E. M., Papke, M. R., & Shapiro, T. F. (2005). *Social decision making/social problem solving: A curriculum for academic, social, and emotional learning.* Champaign, IL: Research Press.

Elliot, S., & Gresham, F. (1991). *Social skills intervention guide.* Circle Pines, MN: American Guidance.

Elliott, S. N., Malecki, C. K., & Demaray, M. K. (2001). New directions in social skills assessment and intervention for elementary and middle school students. *Exceptionality, 9*, 19–32.

Flavell, J. H., Miller, P. H., & Miller, S. A. (1993). Cognitive development (3rd ed.). Upper Saddle River, NJ: Prentice Hall.

Frith, U. (Ed.). (1991). *Autism and Asperger Syndrome.* Cambridge: Cambridge University Press.

Gillott, A., Furniss, F., & Walter, A. (2001). Anxiety in high-functioning children with autism. *Autism, 5*, 277–286.

Gray. C. (2000). *The new social story book: Illustrated edition.* Arlington, TX: Future Horizons.

Green, J., Gilchrist, A., Burton, D., & Cox, A. (2000). Social and psychiatric functioning in adolescents with Asperger Syndrome compared with conduct disorder. *Journal of Autism and Developmental Disorders, 30*, 279–293.

Gresham, F. M. (2002). Best practices in social skills training. In A. Thomas & J. Grimes (Eds.), *Best practices in school psychology* (4th ed., pp. 1029–1040). Bethesda, MD: NASP.

Gresham, F. M., & Elliot, S. N. (1990). *Social skills rating system manual.* Circle Pines, MN: American Guidance Service.

Gresham. F. M., & Lambros, K. M. (1998). Behavioral and functional assessment. In T. S. Watson &

F. M. Gresham (Eds.), *Handbook of child behavior therapy* (pp. 3–22). New York: Plenum Press.

Gresham, F. M., Sugai, G., & Horner, R. H. (2001). Interpreting outcomes of social skills training for students with high-incidence disabilities. *Teaching Exceptional Children, 67*, 331–344.

Hauck, M., Fein, D., Waterhouse, L., & Feinstein, C. (1995). Social initiations by autistic children to adults and other children. *Journal of Autism and Developmental Disorders, 25*, 579–595.

Hume, K., Bellini, S., & Pratt, C. (2005). The usage and perceived outcomes of early intervention and early childhood programs for young children with Autism Spectrum Disorder. *Topics in Early Childhood Special Education, 25*, 195–207.

Humphries, A. (2003). Effectiveness of PRT as a behavioral intervention for young children with ASD. *Bridges Practice-based Research Syntheses, 2*(4), 1–10.

Hwang, B., & Hughes, C. (2000). The effects of social interactive training on early social communicative skills of children with autism. *Journal of Autism and Developmental Disorders, 30*, 331–343.

Kanner, L. (1943). Autistic disturbances of affective contact. *Nervous Child, 2*, 217–230.

Kim, J. A., Szatmari, P., Bryson, S. E., Streiner, D. L., & Wilson, F. J. (2000). The prevalence of anxiety and mood problems among children with autism and Asperger Syndrome. *Autism, 4*, 117–132.

Koegel, R. L., & Koegel, L. K. (2006). *Pivotal response treatment for autism: Communication, social, and academic development.* Baltimore: Paul Brookes.

Koegel, L. K., Koegel, R. L., Frea, W., & Green-Hopkins, I. (2003). Priming as a method of coordinating educational services for students with autism. *Language, Speech, and Hearing Services in Schools, 34*, 228–235.

Krantz, P. J., & McClannahan, L. E. (1998). Social interaction skills for children with autism: A script-fading procedure for beginning readers. *Journal of Applied Behavior Analysis, 31*, 191–202.

Ladd, G. W., & Mize, J. (1983). A cognitive-social learning model of social skill training. *Psychological Review, 90*, 127–157.

LaFrance, M., & Mayo, C. (1976). Racial differences in gaze behavior during conversation: Two systematic observation studies. *Journal of Personality and Social Psychology, 33*, 547–552.

Laushey, K. M., & Heflin, L. J. (2000). Enhancing social skills of kindergarten children with autism through the training of multiple peers as tutors. *Journal of Autism and Developmental Disorders, 30*, 183–193.

Loveland, K. A., & Tunali, B. (1991) Social scripts for conversational interactions in autism and Down Syndrome. *Journal of Autism and Developmental Disorders, 21*, 177–186.

MacDonald, R., Clark, M., & Garrigan, E. (2005). Using video modeling to teach pretend play to children with autism. *Behavioral Interventions, 20*, 225–238.

Mathur, S. R., Kavale, K. A., Quinn, M. M., Forness, S. R., & Rutherford, R. B. (1998). Social skills interventions with students with emotional and behavioral problems: A quantitative synthesis of single subject research. *Behavioral Disorders, 23*, 193–201.

Mayo, P., & Waldo, P. (1994). *Scripting: Social communication for adolescents.* Eau Claire, WI: Thinking Publications.

McConnell, S. R. (2002). Interventions to facilitate social interaction for young children with autism: Review of available research and recommendations for educational intervention and future research. *Journal of Autism and Developmental Disorders, 32*, 351–372.

Odom, S. L., McConnell, S. R., & McEvoy, M. A. (1992). *Social competence of young children with disabilities: Issues and strategies for intervention.* Baltimore: Paul H. Brookes.

Pressley, M., & McCormick, C. (1995). *Cognition, teaching and assessment.* New York: Harper Collins College Publishers.

Quinn, M. M., Kavale, K. A., Mathur, S. R., Rutherford Jr., R. B., & Forness, S. R. (1999). A meta-analysis of social skills interventions for students with emotional and behavioral disorders. *Journal of Emotional and Behavioral Disorders, 7*, 54–64.

Resnick, L. B., Levine, J. M., & Teasley, S. D. (1991). *Perspectives on socially shared cognition.* Washington, DC: American Psychological Association.

Rogers, S. (2000). Interventions that facilitate socialization in children with autism. *Journal of Autism and Developmental Disorders, 30*, 399–409.

Sansosti, F. J., Powell-Smith, K. A., and Kincaid, D. (2004). A research synthesis of social story interventions for children with autism spectrum disorders. *Focus on Autism and Other Developmental Disabilities, 19,* 194–204.

Sasso, G. M., Mundschenk, N. A., Melloy, K. J., & Casey, S. D. (1998). A comparison of the effects of organismic and setting variables on the social interaction behavior of children with developmental disabilities and autism. *Focus on Autism and Other Developmental Disabilities, 13*(1), 2–16.

Schreibman, L., Whalen, C., & Stahmer, A. (2000). The use of video priming to reduce disruptive transition behavior in children with autism. *Journal of Positive Behavior Intervention, 2,* 3–12.

Shearer, D. D., Kohler, F. W., Buchan, K. A., & McCullough, K. M. (1996). Promoting independent interactions between preschoolers with autism and their nondisabled peers: An analysis of self-monitoring. *Early Education & Development, 7,* 205–220.

Strain, P. S., & Odom, S. L. (1986). Peer social initiations: An effective intervention for social skill deficits of preschool handicapped children. *Exceptional Children, 52,* 543–552.

Szatmari, P., Bartolucci, G., Bremner, R., Bond, S., & Rich, S. (1989). A follow-up study of high-functioning autistic children. *Journal of Autism and Developmental Disorders, 19,* 213–225.

Tantam, D. (2000). Psychological disorder in adolescents and adults with Asperger Syndrome. *Autism, 4,* 47–62.

Travis, L., Sigman, M., & Ruskin, E. (2001). Links between social understanding and social behavior in verbally able children with autism. *Journal of Autism and Developmental Disorders, 31,* 119–130.

Welsh, M., Park, R. D., Widaman, K., & O'Neil, R. (2001). Linkages between children's social and academic competence: A longitudinal analysis. *Journal of School Psychology, 39,* 463–481.

Zanolli, K., Daggett, J., & Adams, T. (1996). Teaching preschool age autistic children to make spontaneous initiations to peers using priming. *Journal of autism and developmental disorders, 26*(4), 407–422.

10

Teaching Academic and Functional Skills

Gena Barnhill, Ph.D. BCBA
Lynchburg College

CHAPTER OBJECTIVES

After reading this chapter, learners should be able to:

1. Describe the importance of educators understanding the unique characteristics of students with ASD.

2. Identify current trends in education, including universal design for learning (UDL), **Individuals with Disabilities Education Improvement Act** (IDEIA) 2004, and No Child Left Behind (NCLB).

3. List the six agreed-upon critical components of preschool educational programs and the six interventions that should have precedence in teaching young children with ASD, as defined by the National Research Council.

4. Discuss the debate on inclusion of students with ASD.

5. Explain the current research on effective teaching for students with ASD in the areas of reading, writing, mathematics, and functional skills.

6. Describe executive dysfunction in individuals with ASD and explain how to teach executive skills.

 CASE STUDY Examples

Case of Marissa

Marissa is a 7-year-old girl who was diagnosed with autism at the age of 3 years. Concerned friends suggested that the family have her evaluated when she was almost 3 years old because she typically did not respond when her name was called, she seemed to "be in her own world," and she was not talking. Her parents suspected that she might have a hearing problem. After Marissa received the diagnosis of autism, she attended an early intervention program that used applied behavior analysis (ABA) techniques. During the morning she worked one-on-one with an adult focusing on learning readiness skills and communication skills. In the afternoons she attended a class that focused on social skills and learning preschool routines with typically developing peers and with peers who also had been diagnosed with autism. Marissa began talking in sentences and reading prior to kindergarten. Her school team decided to place her in a general education class for kindergarten and to have a paraprofessional work with the entire class and be available if Marissa needed any extra help. Her parents are extremely pleased with her current academic progress, but are concerned about how she will function when she gets older because friends in their support group have told them that the academic material becomes more abstract and is often harder for children with Autism Spectrum Disorders (ASD) to handle without some individualized special education supports.

Case of Justin

Justin is a 15-year-old high school student who was recently diagnosed by his psychologist as having Asperger Syndrome (AS). Justin speaks in a college professorial manner and gives the impression to others that he is very bright and articulate. However, he has been described by many as an enigma. There are times when he appears to be very insightful and other times when he seems to not have a clue as to what is going on around him. His responses at these times suggest that he is functioning socially and emotionally more like a 10-year-old boy. When he is speaking about his favorite interest, observatories, he bores same-age peers, but is able to speak to his father and grandfather who seem to have interest in this topic, too. In fact, whenever the family goes on vacation, Justin's father always makes sure they find an observatory to visit and photograph. Justin's mother was concerned that something might be wrong when he was younger, but the rest of the family assured her that he was fine and they told her that boys typically develop slower than girls. Furthermore, they reminded her that he was just like his father and grandfather, who were excellent engineers and successful in their careers. His mother did take him to the family doctor, who diagnosed him with Attention-Deficit/Hyperactivity Disorder (ADHD) at age 7. However, he later began having significant social problems and was intimidated by other students to sell his Ritalin during eighth grade. This led to a school suspension and failing grades in all subjects, except math, because he was not allowed to make up the schoolwork when he was suspended. His mother suspected that he was depressed and took him to a psychologist, who conducted a thorough developmental history. This psychologist diagnosed him with AS at age 15. Following this diagnosis, the school made several modifications in his academic program. He began attaining excellent grades, except in English. He does not like reading fiction and has difficulty following character plots and understanding idioms and expressions. He still has difficulty getting along with peers, but he has found a niche in the chess club.

Case of Michael

Michael was diagnosed with Pervasive Developmental Disorder (PDD) at the age of 4 after his preschool teacher suggested that his family might want to have him evaluated. Michael taught himself how to read and was fascinated with numbers at the age of 2. His parents were very proud of their son's abilities. They were also relieved when he began talking as a toddler and appeared to be so bright because they had twin nephews who were diagnosed with autism, did not speak, and exhibited some serious self-injurious behaviors. They believed that surely their son could not have autism because he was affectionate with them and he was so smart. They did not know any other 2-year-old children who could read and do basic math problems like Michael could. They assumed he was a genius. Michael began having problems getting along with his peers when he went to preschool. His mother felt that the children were jealous of his academic abilities. When he corrected the teacher's grammar and told her how to teach the class, Michael's parents were asked to conference with his teacher. It was at this time that the teacher discussed Michael's academic strengths and also her concerns that perhaps he needed a different curriculum or environment to meet his advanced academic needs. Michael's parents agreed to have him evaluated at that time.

INTRODUCTION

Several considerations must first be addressed when designing effective academic and functional skills instructional programs for individuals with Autism Spectrum Disorders (ASD). There is no one program, one recipe, or "one-size-fits-all" treatment (Schreibman, 2005, p. 267; Zager & Shamow, 2005). As has been discussed in previous chapters, students with ASD are a heterogeneous group of individuals who have a wide range of abilities and present with different strengths and areas of weaknesses. They have different learning styles, behavioral issues, and sensory issues that impact their ability to acquire information in the classroom. The students in the above case studies all fall on the autism spectrum, but their academic and functional skills programs will all look very different and will be based on their individual needs and strengths. "No one program or service (e.g., self-contained class for autism) is likely to meet the needs of the population as a whole" (Iovannone, Dunlap, Huber, & Kincaid, 2003, p. 153). Furthermore, "No one has all the answers!" (Gill, 2005, p. 209). That is why it is critical to collaborate as a team with other professionals and the students' parents when designing academic and functional skills programs for students with ASD.

The fundamental goal of education is to prepare individuals to lead constructive and gratifying lives. When developing Individualized Education Programs (IEPs) for students, educators need to consider lifelong goals for their students with ASD (Zager & Shamow, 2005). Furthermore, teachers need to understand the characteristics of these students and how these characteristics specifically affect their students in order to effectively teach. Teachers also need to know what to teach and how to teach these students. The likelihood of general education teachers having a student with high-functioning autism (HFA) or Asperger Syndrome (AS) in their classroom is relatively high (Gill, 2005), which makes it critical not only for special education teachers to understand ASD, but for general education teachers to understand this spectrum as well.

IMPORTANCE OF DEVELOPING AN UNDERSTANDING OF ASD

Researchers and practitioners have described individuals with ASD as enigmas (Gill, 2005; Herbert, Sharp, & Gaudiano, 2002). Oftentimes, these students confuse their teachers because of their uneven skill development, unique learning styles, roller-coaster rides of intense emotions, fragile self-esteem, and paradoxical behavior (Barrett, 2006; Gill, 2005). An example of paradoxical behavior is that they may appear to demonstrate great insights in one setting, but not in another.

This can lead teachers to misinterpret their behaviors or make false assumptions about the cause of their behavior (Barrett, 2006). Educators need to take time to look beneath the surface behaviors to understand the impact autism has on the lives of their students (Gill, 2005). Unlike other physical or mental disabilities that affect specific areas of functioning while leaving others intact, the effects of ASD are all-encompassing and affect most areas of functioning (Herbert et al., 2002). Listening to the parents of these children, attending workshops given by professionals experienced in this field, and reading books written by individuals on the autism spectrum can provide valuable insight about the challenges these students face on a daily basis. Anxiety is often part of their daily life and they typically do not learn from previous mistakes (Zager & Shamow, 2005). Being told by a teacher that a student with ASD seems to "need to be bouncing off the walls today," could frighten the student who easily misinterprets idioms and expressions into thinking that the teacher wants him to hurt himself and smash into the walls. Students with HFA or AS frequently experience fear of failure, which may be demonstrated by noncompliance or avoidance behaviors (Gill, 2005). Teachers need to look beneath the student's outward appearance or facade to understand that he or she is not purposely being disobedient or manipulative, but instead is reacting to the fear and anxiety that he or she cannot express verbally. Oftentimes realizing that the student is acting in an inappropriate manner to hide fear of failure is overlooked because these students can be extremely verbal and articulate. Furthermore, it is easy to fall into the trap of taking their misbehavior personally. Gill (2005) suggested that we need to continually remind ourselves that all the student's interactions are affected by ASD and their misbehavior is typically not an attack against the teacher. These students typically are not able to express their fears, frustrations, and feelings, despite the fact that they may have good verbal skills.

This author's adult son, who has AS, described his mind as a computer (Barnhill, 2002). When correct data is entered, he can produce great results. However, if too much information is given to him at one time, he cannot process the information and he shuts down and crashes. He also indicated that if unexpected or unwanted changes occur, alarms go off in his head similar to the error messages displayed on a computer. To prevent this from happening, he takes precautionary measures by working in short spurts and taking breaks to reduce stress. This analogy to a computer provides insight into the possible cognitive style of individuals with AS as well as to some of the triggers and stressors that we need to consider when designing their academic programs. Gill (2005) suggested that teachers consider the following list of potential challenges and stress triggers when designing educational plans for students with AS: (a) providing too much choice, (b) giving vague assignments and open-ended tasks, (c) assigning tasks that require sequencing and organization, (d) using idioms and multiple-meaning words, (e) needing the student to shift to other solutions, (f) expecting the student to imagine something he or she has never experienced, (g) requiring the student to understand the gist of something, and (h) having the student integrate and organize information.

Designing academic and functional programs for students with ASD can be very challenging given that the characteristics associated with these conditions affect social functioning, communication, interests, play, sensory responses, motor coordination, adaptive behavior, organizational skills, and abstract thinking (American Psychiatric Association [APA], 2000; World Health Organization, 1993). These characteristics are often in conflict with the physical, social, and instructional components of general education classrooms, which further impair the student's ability to learn (Kunce, 2005). Kunce proposed a model of effective educational intervention for students with HFA or AS. Kunce's three foundational elements for developing an effective educational plan are (a) accepting and knowledgeable people, (b) parent and teacher collaboration, and

BOX 10.1   Diversity Notes

Traditional intervention techniques have focused on the acquisition of academic learning, adaptive skills, communication, and the reduction of problem behaviors for students with autism to develop independence and self-responsibility (Wilder, Dyches, Obiakor, & Algozzine, 2004). However, multicultural students with autism have "triple layered problems—they are culturally different, they may be linguistically different, and they have an exceptionality that is loaded with behavioral repertoires" (Wilder et al., 2004, p. 105). Evidence seems to support the idea that multicultural students have more challenges with the academic and behavioral customs of the school culture than do students from the dominant culture. Given the relative paucity of research specific to the challenges multicultural students with autism face, it is not clear if the traditional focus of interventions will be effective for multicultural students with autism and their families. Research in this area is in its infancy (Wilder et al., 2004). Therefore, educators are strongly encouraged to learn about their students' cultures and infuse the curriculum with materials that reflect their students' cultures. Furthermore, given the research support for parents' involvement in the educational planning of their children with ASD, it is important for educators to understand the multicultural family's customs and the importance they place on teaching academic skills. Not all cultures view independence and community-based competence—which are components of middle- to upper-class European American cultural values in the United States—as valuable (Wilder et al., 2004). This is important information to consider when developing IEP goals for multicultural students with autism.

(c) comprehensive assessment to determine the strengths and areas of concern for each individual. Again, this reiterates the importance of having people who are knowledgeable about autism and who are also tuned in to how autism affects the individual they are teaching, including the individual's cultural differences (see Box 10.1). This has been a key element in the success of this author's son, and it still is a critical element in his success in the adult world of work. Oftentimes, his employers did not understand his behavior and interpreted it as a purposeful act of willful disobedience of the rules, when, in fact, he incorrectly interpreted the rules literally. He might not have been fired from several of his jobs if the employers and co-workers better understood AS and how it impacted him. Also, the importance of collaborating with parents is supported in the research literature (e.g., Dawson & Osterling, 1997; National Research Council [NRC], 2001; Zager & Shamow, 2005) and mandated by law (**Individuals with Disabilities Education Improvement Act [IDEIA]**, 2004).

A meaningful education plan can begin to be designed after the three foundational elements discussed above are in place. However, deciding how to implement the structural elements or infrastructure for the educational program is the next consideration. In Kunce's (2005) model, the structural elements include the provision of environmental supports to compensate for learning and behavioral differences that typically distinguish students with HFA or AS. These structural elements include (a) cognitive-organizational supports, (b) social supports, and (c) behavioral-emotional supports. The curriculum or content elements are the third major set of elements in Kunce's model. These include (a) traditional academics, (b) adaptive behavior, (c) vocational skills, (d) metacognition, (e) social communication, (f) self-management, and (g) sensory and motor needs. It is this author's experience that academics and functional skills are not taught in isolation and that all of these factors must be considered in planning the educational program of students with ASD. Other chapters in this textbook describe several of these areas in depth, and they will not be discussed in this chapter. Traditional academics, functional skills, and cognitive-organizational supports will be addressed, as well as the concepts of **inclusion** and **universal design for learning (UDL)**. See Box 10.2.

> ## BOX 10.2 Trends and Issues
>
> Recent legislation (e.g., No Child Left Behind [NCLB]; IDEIA 2004) and current philosophies and trends (e.g., universal design for learning) have stressed the need to provide effective educational practices for *all* children. NCLB is considered to be the most significant expansion of the federal government into education in our country's history. It holds states accountable for improving student achievement in reading and math and requires that educators use scientifically based strategies and interventions (Yell, Drasgow, & Lowrey, 2005). The Individuals with Disabilities Education Improvement Act (IDEIA, 2004), which is the reauthorization of the Individuals with Disabilities Education Act (IDEA, 1990), was designed to align with NCLB (Hyatt, 2007). The teacher who incorporates universal design for learning (UDL) recognizes that each student has his or her own route toward learning. The Council for Exceptional Children (CEC, 2005) described this teacher as one who makes use of all available resources in the classroom, school, and community; designs diverse and inclusive environments to the extent possible that use assistive technology; knows how to implement proven teaching methods; and provides students access to the general curriculum while supporting their progress toward the same standards of learning as their non-disabled classmates. In other words, the teacher makes every effort to uphold the spirit and intent of IDEIA and NCLB. "The central, underlying premise behind the concept of UDL is that flexibility is intrinsic in teaching, learning, and assessment to accommodate all learners" (CEC, 2005, p. 52). The two essential features of UDL are (a) built-in tools that promote access to the range of learners, and (b) a flexible delivery of the general education curriculum that can meet the individual needs of students. UDL is inclusive by design because rather than establishing an alternate curriculum, teaching methods and assistive technologies are built in or readily available and do not have to be added on as afterthoughts by the teacher (CEC, 2005). The Center for Universal Design in North Carolina (2002) described the intent of UDL as to simplify life for everyone by making products, communications, and the environment more usable by as many individuals as possible at little or no extra expense.

CORE ELEMENTS OF EFFECTIVE INSTRUCTIONAL PROGRAMS

Scientifically Based Research

One of the significant restructuring efforts in education has involved initiatives that require teachers to use practices that are supported by research. Simpson (2005) pointed out that **No Child Left Behind (NCLB)** mentioned the use of **scientifically based research** more than 100 times. Scientifically based research is defined as "research that involves the application of rigorous, systematic, and objective procedures to obtain reliable and valid knowledge relevant to education activities and programs" (NCLB, 2002). Furthermore, Simpson (2005, p. 142) reported that NCLB considers the "gold standard" of scientifically based practices to include resources and materials that were validated by means of research designs that used random samples and control and experimental groups. However, for several sound and ethical reasons, randomized control group designs are not often used in research with individuals with ASD. Simpson (2005) concluded that the scientifically based research requirement of NCLB seems to be restricting and impeding the identification of effective practices involving students with ASD. He also pointed out that the **National Research Council** (**NRC**, 2001) recognized that there were times when randomization was not feasible. It is critical for educators and families to be informed about the research literature regarding effective treatments for autism so that harm is not done in promoting unproven treatments and time and money is not wasted when another more effective method could have been implemented (Herbert et al. 2002). Simpson recommended three basic questions be used when selecting a program or method of instruction for students with ASD based on previous work of Heflin and Simpson (1998). They are:

- What are the efficacy and expected outcomes with this practice, and are the expected outcomes in agreement with the student's needs?
- What are the possible risks with this practice?
- What are the most effective ways of evaluating this method or approach?

Recognizing the need to provide some guidelines for educators on what to teach, how to teach, and how to design appropriate academic and functional skill programs for students with ASD, the NRC (2001) was requested to investigate the scientific evidence of the effects of early educational intervention on young children with ASD by the U.S. Department of Education's Office of Special Education Programs. The Committee on Educational Interventions for Children with Autism was formed by the NRC "to integrate the scientific, theoretical, and policy literature and create a framework for evaluating the scientific evidence concerning the effects and features of educational interventions for young children with autism" (NRC, 2001, p. 2). Their primary concentration was early intervention programs and school programs for children from birth to age 8. They made the following recommendations: (a) Any child who receives a diagnosis of any ASD should be eligible for special education programming under the category label of autism and (b) The educational goals of children with ASD should be the same as those for other children: personal independence and social responsibility.

In addition, the Committee on Educational Interventions for Children with Autism (NRC, 2001) provided the following agreed-upon critical components of preschool programs:

- Educational services need to begin as soon as the diagnosis of ASD is *seriously considered.*
- Services should include a minimum of 25 hours per week of active student participation in intensive instruction, with full-year programming varied according to the student's chronological age and developmental level.
- Repeated, planned teaching opportunities need to be provided around short periods of time such as 15–20 minutes for young children, including adult attention in one-on-one and small-group instruction to meet individual student goals.
- Families need to be included and parent training provided.
- Low student/teacher ratios (no more than two young students with ASD per adult) are needed.
- Methods for formative program evaluation and assessment of the individual student's progress are essential so that adjustments can be made as needed.

Furthermore, the committee (NRC, 2001) reported that the following interventions should have precedence:

- The primary focus of early education needs to be functional, spontaneous communication.
- Social instruction needs to be taught throughout the day.

- Play skills should focus on play with peers.
- Other teaching aimed at goals for cognitive development should be taught in the context in which the skills will be carried out, with generalization and maintenance in natural settings as important as the acquisition of new skills.
- Proactive approaches to behavioral problems that include functional behavior assessment, reinforcement of alternative behaviors and functional communication training need to be used.
- Functional academic skills need to be taught when appropriate to the skills of the student.

To date, there is still a dearth of empirically sound research on effective interventions for students with HFA and AS (Kunce, 2005) and older students with ASD since most of the research focus has been on effective practices for children ranging from 0–8 years (Iovannone et al., 2003). However, Iovannone and colleagues reviewed research from four respected scholars and groups within the field of autism, including the NRC, and indicated that the areas identified were "consistent with effective practices for children of any age with ASD" (Iovannone et al., 2003, p. 152). Their synthesized list of six core components or essential themes to be included in effective programming for students with ASD were similar to the NRC's (2001) and included (a) individualized supports and services for families and children, (b) systematic instruction, (c) structured and/or understandable environments, (d) specialized curriculum subject matter, (e) a functional approach to behavior challenges, and (f) family participation.

CORE ACADEMIC AND FUNCTIONAL SKILLS

Reading

According to O'Connor and Klein (2004), there has been relatively little attention given to reading instruction in the research literature on autism. They hypothesized that this might be because the behavioral and social needs of individuals with classic autism were thought to need more urgent attention. However, there is research focusing on individuals with high-functioning autism and AS that demonstrates that the decoding and reading comprehension skills of this group demonstrate a continuum of performance levels, with reading comprehension typically falling below both decoding skills and age-level norms (O'Connor & Klein, 2004). Church, Alisanski, and Amanullah (2000) published the first study that investigated the reading skills of children and youth with AS. Their examination of chart reviews revealed that many children with AS entered elementary school with reading skills and many were reading above grade level. However, comprehension challenges were noted, especially when the material was not factual. Myles et al. (2002) found a significant difference between literal/factual and inferential comprehension skills of the children and youth with AS in the Asperger Syndrome Project (see Box 10.3). These students incorrectly answered almost two thirds of the inferential questions they were asked about the stories read. The students were able to comprehend almost one third more material that was rote based. Poorer reading comprehension was observed during silent reading versus reading aloud. Griswold, Barnhill, Myles, Hagiwara, and Simpson (2002) found that children and youth with AS demonstrated relative strengths in oral expression and word-calling or decoding skills and relative weaknesses in listening comprehension and difficulties related to problem solving and language-based critical thinking.

Based on the areas of weaknesses demonstrated in reading assessments conducted by the Asperger Syndrome Project, Barnhill (2001) suggested the following interventions: (a) provide

BOX 10.3   Research Notes #1

O'Connor and Klein (2004) were the first researchers to conduct an experimental study to examine the effects of facilitating strategies on reading comprehension. Twenty adolescent high-functioning students with ASD read passages under the following four conditions: (a) responding to prereading questions, (b) finishing cloze sentences embedded in text, (c) receiving cues to relate pronouns to antecedent nouns (anaphora), and (d) reading only (control condition). Prereading was selected as an intervention to address the possibility that students with ASD do not regularly access prior knowledge while reading; cloze procedures were used to help the students use the information in the reading passages to make predictions while reading; and "anaphoric cueing" (p. 118) was used to prompt students to stop and monitor whether or not they were understanding the passage and also to look back in the passages to repair their comprehension. The only condition that demonstrated statistical significance was the anaphoric cuing. The researchers reported that for some students, prereading questions actually activated prior knowledge that was irrelevant or inaccurate, and the students perseverated on this information, which negatively affected their comprehension.

Based on the results of their study, O'Connor and Klein (2004) tentatively recommended that teachers, parents, and paraprofessionals suggest to students with ASD that they need to check the antecedents of pronouns as they read. This could be facilitated by using computer software, which highlights pronouns and other forms of anaphora on the computer screen. The student would need to click on the highlighted area before continuing to read. Another independent intervention could be to teach the students to check the referents of pronouns.

Source: Information from O'Connor, I. M., & Klein, P. D. (2004). Exploration of strategies for facilitating reading comprehension of high-functioning students with autism spectrum disorders. *Journal of Autism and Developmental Disorders, 34,* 115–127.

opportunities for auditory and visual cues during reading; (b) teach using direct instruction on idioms, figures of speech, and interpreting abstract concepts; (c) furnish opportunities for students to demonstrate their strong decoding skills in the classroom; and (d) raise the awareness level of educators, paraprofessionals, and parents that the student will be able to read more than he or she can comprehend, so that they can take this into consideration when teaching.

Written Language

Hans Asperger reported on the school functioning of the boys that he studied in his writings in 1944. He indicated that they had writing deficiencies and stated, "The very same children who can astonish their teachers with their advanced and clever answers fail miserably at their lessons" (Asperger, 1991, p. 75). Church et al.'s (2000) review of records of students with AS concluded that overall handwriting was an extremely difficult task for most students and many of the students had paraprofessionals to assist them with scribing. Some teachers reported that their elementary-aged students erased their work so many times in an effort to make it perfect that they left holes in their papers. More than half of the students had occupational therapy to assist with fine motor skills such as pencil grasp and handwriting. Handwriting problems continued through high school, at which time their handwriting was almost illegible (see Box 10.4).

BOX 10.4   Research Notes #2

Griswold et al. (2002) and Myles et al. (2003) did not find significant differences in the written language skills as measured by norm-referenced tests administered to children and youth with AS in their studies. However, analysis of aggregate data can lead to incorrectly assuming that these students did not need assistance in written language skills. Furthermore, in the study by Griswold and colleagues, one participant refused to take the written language test, and several did not complete the test because of fatigue and ending of the testing session and an inability to reschedule more testing time. Interestingly, visual analysis of the data in the Myles et al. (2003) study found that the individuals with AS exhibited more variability in their performance than the neurotypical peers and they produced considerably less legible letters and words than the neurotypical group. There were significant differences observed in letter alignment, formation, size, and spacing of the two groups, with the neurotypical participants making fewer errors in three out of the four areas. Informal analysis appeared to reveal a more informative picture of the students' writing skills. Although the students with AS could produce sentences similar in number to their neurotypical peers, the sentences produced were brief and not as complex as shown by the number of morphemes, t-units, and words. However, the participants with AS did seem to understand the rules of sentence construction as demonstrated by run-ons and sentence fragments that were similar to their neurotypical peers. Future research that focuses on analyzing differences within the group of students with AS was recommended, as well as analyzing differences within individual students' test profiles. Myles et al. (2003) also suggested using a scribe in future research to determine if the lower written language scores were due to lack of elaborated thoughts or a motoric problem in putting the thoughts on paper.

Myles et al. (2003) suggested that educational programs for students with AS may need to focus on teaching embellishment of written thoughts rather than writing conventions such as spelling and punctuation. They also recommended that programming suggestions not be taken from norm-referenced assessments. This is not the purpose of norm-referenced tests; they were designed to compare student performance to a norm group. Other implications for practice included: (a) allowing the student to tape-record his or her verbal answers if the process of writing was so taxing that it limited the student's ability to create written products commensurate with his or her ability; then the student could copy the tape-recorded answers onto paper to increase elaboration and the number of words used; (b) teaching how to write drafts and proof read so that students can learn to write content first and concentrate on the mechanics of writing second; (c) motivating students by allowing them to write about their special interest; (d) permitting the use of a computer if repeated instruction in penmanship that focuses on letter formation, size, and alignment has not lead to increased legibility; and (e) using pre-constructed paragraphs so that students could practice identifying construction errors.

Source: Information from Myles, B. S., Huggins, A., Rome-Lake, M., Hagiwara, T., Barnhill, G. P., & Griswold, D. E. (2003). Written language profile of children and youth with Asperger Syndrome: From research to practice. *Education and Training in Developmental Disabilities, 38,* 362–369.

Other factors to consider in developing interventions are the writing device, position of the paper, and whether or not the student should use cursive writing instead of printing (Heflin & Alaimo, 2007). Teachers could allow the students to use fat pencils, felt-tip pens, pencil grips, or natural cedar pencils if they are preferred. Using a marker on a white board may be easier for some students than writing with crayons. Other students who have challenges writing legibly because of the position of the paper could use slant boards. Older students can purchase a slant board that looks like a clip board. Cursive writing may be easier than printing for some students with ASD because they do not need to lift their pencil or pen between each letter. Each letter is connected in a discrete unit in cursive writing, which may help prevent difficulties in learning how to properly space between words (Heflin & Alaimo, 2007).

Delano (2007) used a multicomponent intervention that included the Self-Regulated Strategy Development (SRSD) Model delivered via video self-modeling for three students with AS. The SRSD Model was developed about 20 years ago for students with academic problems and has been used to teach writing interventions and self-regulation to students with and without disabilities (Graham, Harris, & Troia, 2000, as cited in Olson, Platt, & Dieker, 2008). SRSD entails interactive learning between the teacher and student and is organized so that students gradually learn to select and use specific writing strategies independently. Delano (2007) reported that SRSD instruction has been empirically supported for students with learning disabilities, but, to date, SRSD had not been evaluated with individuals with AS. During the intervention sessions in Delano's study, each participant watched a video of himself using the strategies for increasing the number of words written and the number of functional essay elements. The students then wrote a persuasive essay. Results revealed that each student showed gains in the number of words written and number of functional essay elements. However, a longer intervention may need to be implemented in future studies since the students did not maintain gains after 3 months. Neither the video self-modeling nor the SRSD was assessed in isolation. Therefore, the positive results obtained cannot be attributed to any one component of the intervention.

Mathematics

There is very limited research on instructional strategies to effectively teach mathematics skills to children with ASD (NRC, 2001) and limited research on the mathematical abilities of students with HFA and AS using standardized achievement tests (Chiang & Lin, 2007). Church et al. (2000) mentioned that several of the students' records that they reviewed indicated outstanding performance in math. However, Jordan (2005) and Griswold et al. (2002) did not find this to always be the case. Jordan (2005) indicated that there has not yet been a systematic review of the existence of dyscalculia in individuals with HFA and AS; however, anecdotal notes from teachers imply that it is not uncommon. Furthermore, Jordan (2005) indicated that most problems with math involved generalizing procedures to other settings, such as real-life ones, and understanding processes such as estimation because there are no precisely correct answers. Griswold et al. (2002) conducted the first empirical study that focused on the academic achievement of students with AS. They found that the aggregate math scores of the individuals studied fell within the average range when compared to peers. However, the lowest scores, still within the average range, were in the areas that assessed the student's ability to write dictated numbers, answer mathematical problems, and solve equations using addition, subtraction, multiplication, and division. Aggregate scores measuring math reasoning were higher, but not statistically significantly different. It is important to note that visual cues were provided for some questions and the text was read to the individual and printed on his or her booklet on the math reasoning assessment. Griswold and colleagues concluded that these visual cues may have helped the students and that teachers may find hands-on instructional activities or visual representations helpful in assisting students to understand numerical operations and concepts.

TOUCHMATH™ TouchMath™ (http://www.touchmath.com) is a "concrete psychomotor designed math curriculum program" (Berry, 2004, p. 1) that "is a pencil paper approach to basic computation" (Berry, 2004, p. 4). Students work directly with numbers. Dots are used on the numbers to show the quantity each number represents. Children typically see, say, hear, and touch the numbers in order to solve calculation problems. Auditory reinforcement, flashcards and timed tests are used to teach students math facts. Students are instructed to count forward for addition problems and backward for subtraction problems. Berry (2004) found that 10 students with autism increased their math fluency by using a modified version of TouchMath™ in a 2-year study (see Box 10.5).

BOX 10.5   Research Notes #3

Berry (2004) conducted a 2-year study with 10 children identified with autism to determine if TouchMath™ was an effective instructional strategy for this population. His results revealed that TouchMath™ led to an increase in math fluency, with the participants averaging a 3-year gain in addition and subtraction skills over 2 years. These results were statistically significant. Berry indicated that his findings may demonstrate that children with autism may learn in a "whole-part-whole sequence" (p. 1). Furthermore, the touchpoints allowed the participants to focus on the number and math items without looking away from their worksheet. This allowed them to look at the whole concept at a glance. "They could stare at the numbers and without lifting their gaze or attention, input in one chunk of information both the number (abstract) and the number amount (concrete)" (p. 7). Some modifications were made in this study to accommodate three students who could not write or verbally state their answers. Teachers laminated individual numbers 1 through 10 and placed Velcro on the back of them. The students could then use these pieces to correctly solve calculation problems. This also provided a clear understanding of whether or not the student knew the answer because there was no interpretation of messy written numbers or challenging speech patterns. Another modification was the deletion of all participatory oral instructional techniques due to the fact that the instruction was done individually and language is one of the primary deficit areas in autism.

Source: Information from Berry, D. (2004). *The effectiveness of TouchMath™ curriculum to teach addition and subtraction to elementary aged students identified with autism.* From http://www.touchmath.com/research, retrieved December 24, 2007.

Chiang and Lin (2007) examined a total of 18 studies that included either mathematical ability demonstrated on one subtest of an individual IQ test or mathematical achievement demonstrated on a standardized academic assessment of individuals with HFA and AS ($n = 8$) who ranged in age from 3 to 51 years. They concluded that most students with AS/HFA exhibit average mathematical ability when compared to same-age peers in the normed population. Their mathematical ability was somewhat lower than their IQ, but the clinical significance of the difference was small. Moreover, some of the individuals with AS/HFA demonstrated mathematical giftedness.

Functional Skills

Educators need to evaluate the functionality of the skills targeted within the student's curriculum. In 1991, Dunlap and Robbins (as cited in Iovannone et al., 2003) reported that these skills should be those that (a) are most likely to have utility in the individual's life so that he or she can control the environment, (b) will increase the individual's independence and quality of life, and (c) increase the individual's capable performance. A good test of the functionality of a skill is to ask whether the result of not learning a specific skill will necessitate another person to carry out the task. One critical goal for all individuals with ASD is to learn to communicate, even if the form of communication is not traditional. Otherwise, someone else will always need to be present to assist the individual in making his or her communication needs known (Iovannone et al.).

No matter where on the autism spectrum the individual falls, he or she will need to be taught how to be ready to learn. This includes skills such as learning how to attend to specific tasks; how to attend in a group; how to work independently and complete tasks; how to follow rules, timetables, and work schedules; and how to avoid irrelevant stimuli and attend to relevant stimuli when possible (Jordan, 2005). One model that may be considered for instruction is the Treatment and Education of Autistic and related Communication-handicapped Children (**TEACCH**) program based out of the University of North Carolina. TEACCH is as an evidenced-based service, training, and research model that was developed as a result of a 5-year research project funded by the National Institutes of Mental Health in 1964. Children are taught how to learn through structured teaching and the use of visual supports (http://www.teacch.com).

The following skills are considered by Powers (1992), as cited in Dawson and Osterling (1997, p. 319), as a beginning list of survival skills that are taught in preschool programs to children to help them to function independently in a general education classroom:

- Complying with adult requests
- Taking turns
- Listening to directions from afar or near
- Sitting quietly during activities
- Volunteering
- Raising one's hand to solicit attention
- Walking in line
- Using toilets in classroom versus in the hallway
- Picking toys up after use
- Communicating about basic needs.

Preparing individuals with ASD to live in their communities is a critical teaching area. These individuals need to be taught self-preservation skills or safety skills to increase their ability to respond to dangerous and possibly life-threatening situations at home, school, and in their community. These skills need to be prioritized and instructed with long-range planning in mind. Some examples of these skills include: keeping the seatbelt fastened in cars or buses, looking both ways before crossing the street, following the rules of a fire drill, dialing 911 when there is an emergency, and identifying safety signals and important community signs. Identifying the daily living skills that the individual needs to learn and teaching them are also essential. These skills include eating, toileting, dressing, grooming, and maintaining a clean and safe home environment (Zager & Shamow, 2005).

COGNITIVE ORGANIZATIONAL SUPPORTS   Research on the cognitive profiles of individuals with ASD of varying ages and ability levels in more than 20 separate studies indicated that individuals with ASD demonstrated an unusually uneven profile (Barnhill, Hagiwara, Myles, & Simpson, 2000). A review of 22 studies revealed a relatively consistent pattern of strong performance on the cognitive subtest that measures nonverbal concept formation and relatively weak performance on the subtest that was designed to assess an individual's understanding of social values and rules and interpersonal situations. Only 4 of the 22 studies specifically included individuals with AS. Barnhill et al.'s (2000) study examined the cognitive profiles of 37 individuals diagnosed with AS, and their results concurred with the majority of the previous studies. The participants attained lower, but not statistically significant scores, on the Arithmetic subtest, which requires mental math. Barnhill et al. suggested that mental math might have been more difficult because there were no visual supports to help with problem solving. One theory that has been proposed to explain the uneven cognitive performance of individuals with ASD is executive dysfunction.

EXECUTIVE DYSFUNCTION   Executive functions are defined as "the ability to regulate one's behavior through working memory, inner speech, control of emotions and arousal levels, and analysis of problems and communication of problem situations to others" (Hallahan & Kauffman, 2006, p. 534). Ozonoff and Schetter (2007) reviewed the literature on executive dysfunction in autism and found that it is clear that individuals with ASD experience executive impairments at a high rate. Most of the research has been conducted with individuals with IQs above the mentally retarded range. Executive dysfunction impairments cause a multitude of difficulties in the classroom that may not be recognized or may be misinterpreted. Frequently maladaptive behaviors exhibited in the classroom are directly related to executive dysfunction and are not intentional, malicious, or manipulative. However, because many of these students are verbal and function intellectually above the range of mental retardation, their deficits are unrecognized until about third grade when the curriculum and expectations of students make an important shift. It is at this time that more conceptual knowledge is required, prediction and abstraction are necessary, and the student is expected to be able to initiate self-organization and learning.

Singular focus on specific topics, difficulty transitioning between favorite activities or giving up favored objects, resistance to change, repetitive motor behavior and language, and perseveration on ways to do things are all signs of executive dysfunction. Ozonoff and Schetter (2007) cited several researchers (e.g., Brian, Tipper, Weaver, & Bryson, 2003; Kleinhans, Akshoomoff, & Delis, 2005; Ozonoff, Cook, Coon, Dawson, Joseph, & Klein et al., 2004) as concurring that the current research involving school-age children, adolescents, and adults with ASD indicates that ASD involves significant challenges in both planning and flexibility, which includes shifting of attention and conceptual set. However, difficulties are not apparent in inhibitory functions such as stopping motor reactions, inhibiting the processing of unrelated material or distractors or suppressing prepotent but incorrect responses.

Persons with ASD and executive dysfunction have not successfully learned effective habits to perform tasks or the skills essential for creating effective action plans and coping strategies. They need interventions that are geared toward their learning strengths and learning styles in order to learn different ways of performing tasks. Typically, visual-spatial processing and memory are areas of strength. The two components of intervention recommended are (a) using accommodations, modifications, and compensatory strategies to work around weaknesses; and (b) directly training missing or weak skills (Ozonoff & Schetter, 2007).

ACCOMMODATIONS, COMPENSATORY SKILLS, AND MODIFICATIONS

Accommodations are physical or environmental changes that help the student with a disability access the general education curriculum and participate in a course or a test. The purpose of the accommodation is to give the student access to the general education curriculum in the least restrictive environment, without having to modify or lower the curriculum standards. In a classroom based on UDL principles, these supports would already be in place. **Modifications**, on the other hand, provide structural, cognitive changes in the level of the curriculum. Compensatory skills are skills that a student needs to independently access and effectively use the accommodations provided. Writing accommodations into the student's IEP does not necessarily mean that he or she will be able to make use of them without some direct instruction. For example, even if the student is permitted to work independently on assignments rather than in a group, he or she still needs to learn how to identify the needed information, make a list of the priorities and order of activities to complete, collect needed materials, and complete the work on time (Ozonoff & Schetter, 2007).

There are several programs specifically for children with ASD that focus on accommodations and compensatory skills and help with executive impairments. For example, the TEACCH program teaches students to follow visual schedules, provides very structured and predictable routines, organizes environment and task requirements using visual cues to increase independent work, and uses work systems to explain task expectations and work demands. When the student is able to independently use the accommodations and compensatory skills, the focus needs to shift to self-advocacy, with the student requesting the needed accommodations for himself or herself (Ozonoff & Schetter, 2007). Several examples of accommodations used for students with ASD suggested by Ozonoff and Schetter (2007) are (a) pacing by extending or adjusting time or providing breaks; (b) varying the presentation of material by emphasizing visual, tactile or multimodal approaches; taping instruction; preteaching material; using organizers; providing visual cues; allowing small-group or individual instruction; (c) utilizing materials and equipment such as assistive technology, books on tape, calculators, computers, or color overlays; (d) adjusting assignments by giving directions in small, discrete increments; giving prompts; reducing paper/pencil tasks; allowing recorded or dictated answers; adjusting the length of the assignment; (e) using **reinforcement** and follow-through including positive reinforcement, peer tutoring, study guides, and checklists; providing behavioral contracts; requesting parent reinforcement; and (f) testing adaptations such as reading the exam to the student, shortening the length of the exam, changing the format, allowing oral answers, scribing answers for the student, and allowing open book or open notes testing.

Several modifications suggested by Ozonoff and Schetter (2007) are (a) using specialized curriculum written at a lower cognitive level; (b) adapting or simplifying books for a lower level of understanding; (c) modifying content areas by simplifying vocabulary, concepts, and rules; (d) modifying the weight of tests when grading; and (e) lowering the reading level of the exam.

Teaching Executive Skills

In order for the student to learn independent completion of any complex task, the student must be explicitly taught the process of task analysis, which involves breaking down the tasks, prioritizing and ordering the incremental steps, and planning for task completion (Ozonoff & Schetter, 2007). This skill is critical to teach because gathering materials for task completion is often a trigger for off-task behavior and poor use of time. Ozonoff and Schetter (2007) contend that few programs specifically teach these underlying cognitive skills. In fact, there are no published efficacy studies of cognitive remediation programs for students with ASD. It is a challenge to write goals about a process, especially one that occurs internally and is only inferred after observation of a successful result. Many strategies focus on teaching students with ASD how to finish tasks through rote compliance and rule following—for example, "If _____ happens, then do _____," (Ozonoff & Schetter, 2007, p. 145). This can be effective because many students with ASD have strong memorization skills and can follow explicitly stated rules. However, there are problems generalizing to new situations if the if-then rules have not been explicitly taught. Moreover, students with ASD can become rigid with rules they have been taught because they do not understand why an action plan was selected or needed and they lack the flexibility to modify the rule. Therefore, any program designed to remediate executive dysfunction in ASD needs to use students' visual-spatial strengths and teach how to generalize skills by teaching across settings with different people and within functional, real-life routines.

Schetter (2004) developed a cognitive remediation program specifically for children with ASD called "Learning the R.O.P.E.S. for Improved Executive Functioning" (cited in Ozonoff & Schetter, 2007). The program uses graphic organizers, "which are visual representations of knowledge that

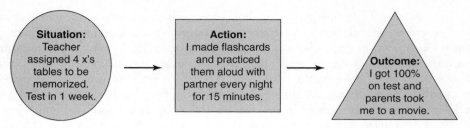

FIGURE 10.1 Graphic Organizer
Source: Graphic organizer information adapted from model in Ozonoff, S. & Schetter, P. L. (2007). Executive dysfunction in autism spectrum disorders: From research to practice. In L. Meltzer (Ed.), *Executive function in education: From theory to practice* (pp. 133–160). New York: Guilford Press.

organize information for later functional use" (Ozonoff & Schetter, 2007, p. 147). (See Figure 10.1 for an example of a graphic organizer.) The graphic organizer describes a *situation,* which is placed in a circle. A line is drawn from the right side of the circle to a square, which describes possible *actions.* A line is drawn from the right side of the square to a triangle, which contains possible *outcomes.* This assists students in thinking sequentially and visualizing the relationships among situations, actions, and outcomes. The teacher **prompts** through directed questions to help the student complete the graphic organizer. Independent completion of the graphic organizer is shaped through differential reinforcement of closer approximations to independent completion. Graphic organizers are used to teach task analysis, how to evaluate a novel situation, how to identify needed materials for a task, and how to prioritize based on due dates and deadlines and possible penalty and bonus outcomes.

When the student learns how to independently complete the executive skills discussed above, the focus of intervention then becomes teaching self-management and maintenance of the skills (Ozonoff & Schetter, 2007). Cooper, Heron, and Heward (2007) define *self-management* as "the personal application of behavior change tactics that produce a desired change in behavior" (p. 578). The four uses of self-management are to (a) live a more successful and efficient lifestyle, (b) break bad habits and learn good ones, (c) complete difficult tasks, and (d) attain personal goals (Cooper et al., 2007). There are several components to a self-management program. Self-monitoring, which is also called self-recording, self-observation, or self-assessment, involves the student observing and recording the occurrence or nonoccurrence of the target behavior (Ozonoff & Schetter, 2007). Self-monitoring is frequently combined with goal setting and self-evaluation (Cooper et al., 2007). Self-reinforcement involves having the student identify and self-administer his or her own reinforcers (Ozonoff & Schetter, 2007).

INCLUSION

One of the most controversial concerns about integrating students with disabilities in schools is inclusion, especially the concept of full inclusion (Hallahan & Kauffman, 2006). Schreibman (2005) contended that the controversy is actually one main issue, which is the question as to whether it is best to educate children with ASD in general education classes with typically developing students or to educate them in special education classes with children with ASD and other disabilities. This is a difficult decision because the best possible choice of classroom needs to balance the student's basic civil rights to be fully included in the community and the student's individual need for instruction. There are strong advocates and arguments on both sides of this issue. Schreibman (2005) described mainstreaming and reverse mainstreaming as other options to full inclusion.

Mainstreaming is a term that is used when a child with a disability attends a non-special-education classroom for at least some part of the day. Reverse mainstreaming is described as having typically developing students spend part of the day in the special education class with the students with disabilities. Although there are different ideas as to what full inclusion should entail, most definitions contain the following key elements: (a) there are no separate education classes because all students, regardless of their disability, attend only general education classes; (b) all students attend their neighborhood schools; and (c) general education is primarily responsible for the students with disabilities, not special education (Hallahan & Kauffman, 2006). Some practitioners believe that inclusive education in the general education curriculum is an appropriate consideration for students with ASD (Ozonoff & Schetter, 2007; Schreibman, 2005; Schwartz & Davis, 2006/2007). Jordan (2005) reminds us that inclusion "is not about a location but about how a child is educated and the attitudes and understanding, and experiences involved" (p. 216). Furthermore, Jordan stated that the long-term goal of inclusion is social inclusion in society. Schreibman (2005) reported that the compelling arguments for full inclusion are (a) the civil rights issue that no one should be denied access to the mainstream community because of his or her disability, (b) the belief that integration with typically developing students will increase the social development of children with autism, and (c) the academic achievement of children with ASD will be improved in inclusion environments. Other issues to consider are that the normally developing students are likely to learn tolerance and acceptance of individual differences in a full inclusion setting.

Schreibman (2005) further reported that we know that children with ASD can be included if the situation is "right" (p. 264). The "right" situation includes: (a) teachers who are trained in a wide variety of teaching methods appropriate to a wide range of students, (b) good support and consultation opportunities for teachers, (c) adequate academic and social supports for the student with ASD, and (d) the curriculum for the student with ASD is integrated into the general education classroom activities. Unfortunately, inclusive environments have been sabotaged when school districts did not realize that support and training were essential for inclusion to work.

Others have reported that although the societal level of inclusion is best attained through inclusive schooling, this may not always be best in every situation (Jordan, 2005). For example, a student who is very sensitive to all forms of stimulation may find the physical conditions in a mainstream school unbearable to tolerate. Supports such as headphones and physical adaptations to the school (e.g., screening fluorescent lighting) may help to relieve some of the distress; however, there are practical limitations to these accommodations and also times when other children's needs are in conflict (Jordan, 2005). Reiter and Vitani (2007) reported that it was their experience that students in first grade demonstrated willingness and enthusiasm in including peers with autism in their classes, but they became less willing during second and third grade by exhibiting detachment and negative thoughts about the students with ASD. In their intervention program, which focused on improving the quality of inclusion of students with ASD in a regular fourth-grade class, they found that the regular education students who had previously demonstrated signs of burnout stemming from the inclusion demonstrated less burnout at the end of their intervention program. Also, the attitudes of the regular education students to the included students with ASD changed and became more positive.

Opponents to full inclusion note that many of the studies on the effects of integration on social development have been derived from studies in laboratories or other highly controlled settings. In addition, many of the participants with disabilities in these studies did not have ASD. Given that social relationships are a hallmark feature of ASD and that these students are less likely to imitate their peers, opponents to full inclusion contend that students with ASD are at a disadvantage in these settings without specialized support. Bryna Siegel (1996) argued that placing students with

ASD in inclusive environments denied them the special attention they needed to be successful when she stated the following:

> Mainstreaming and full inclusion are positive words. They sound much better than saying that the school district can save money by partly or fully depriving a child of the special help he or she needs to best overcome a learning disability. (*as cited in Schreibman, 2005, p. 253*)

Harrower and Dunlap (2001) reviewed data-based interventions used for facilitating the educational inclusion of children with ASD and found that antecedent procedures (priming, prompt delivery, and picture schedules), self-management strategies, delayed and unpredictable contingencies, peer-mediated interventions, and multi-component interventions demonstrated empirical support. Antecedent procedures were discussed in an earlier section and self-management strategies were discussed under the section Teaching Executive Skills. Delayed and unpredictable contingencies were effective in establishing entirely independent task completion by a young man with ASD who had profound intellectual challenges after a gradual process of thinning reinforcement schedules and delaying the corrective feedback (Dunlap, Plienis, & Williams, 1987, as cited in Harrower & Dunlap, 2001). Peer-mediated interventions included providing peer tutoring, recruiting typically developing peers to act as supports for students with ASD, and utilizing cooperative learning. A successful multi-component intervention used for students with ASD that increased their interactions with peers involved the development and use of conversation books, rotating peer buddies, weekly class conferences, media-related activities, and staff prompting (Hunt, Farron-Davis, Wrenn, Hirose-Hatae, & Goetz, 1997, as cited in Harrower & Dunlap, 2001).

Summary

Individuals with ASD are a varied group with different talents, strengths, and interests, as well as different areas of weakness. It is important for educators to understand the unique characteristics of students with ASD so that they do not misinterpret their misbehavior as intentional or manipulative, when in fact it may be due to anxiety or challenges with pragmatic language skills (e.g., taking language literally, misinterpreting idioms). No one academic program can meet the needs of this diverse population. It is important for educators and parents to work together collaboratively to design effective education programs using scientifically based research to select interventions based on the individual student's needs. Some students with ASD will make progress in the general education curriculum with trained teachers and the use of accommodations and compensatory skills in inclusive classrooms. Others may need more specialized instructional programs to learn the skills their peers have already mastered. Generally, students with ASD tend to perform better on reading decoding than they do on reading comprehension tasks, especially inferential questions. Writing tends to be an area of difficulty for many students; however, accommodations and the use of assistive technology can be used to help students. There is little research in the area of math; however, TouchMath™ has shown some promise as a technique to teach math addition and subtraction skills. Teaching students to use organizational supports such as graphic organizers to learn the process of task analysis, prioritizing, and planning for completion of tasks is important in addressing executive skills dysfunction.

Chapter Review Questions

1. Why is it important for teachers to understand the unique characteristics of individuals with ASD? (Objective 1)

2. Describe universal design for learning (UDL) and indicate how this philosophy can be used to design classrooms and classroom instruction for students

with ASD. How have IDEIA 2004 and NCLB impacted the educational practices for students with ASD? (Objective 2)

3. The National Research Council (NRC, 2001) provided guidelines for the critical components and essential interventions of preschool programs for children with ASD. Name these components and interventions and explain why they are important in the education of young children with ASD. Take a critical look at preschool programs you are familiar with and determine if they meet these guidelines. (Objective 3)

4. Discuss the pros and cons of inclusion for students with ASD. When would you recommend inclusion for students with ASD? Are there situations or conditions that would cause you not to recommend inclusion? If so, describe them. (Objective 4)

5. Outline the current research findings on effective teaching for students with ASD in the areas of reading, writing, mathematics, and functional skills. (Objective 5).

6. Describe executive dysfunction in individuals with ASD and explain how you would teach executive skills to students with ASD. (Objective 6)

Key Terms

Accommodations   *236*
Inclusion   *228*
Individuals with Disabilities
    Education Improvement Act
    [IDEIA]   *227*

Modifications   *236*
National Research Council
    (NRC)   *229*
No Child Left Behind (NCLB)   *228*
Prompts   *238*

Reinforcement   *237*
Scientifically based research   *228*
TEAACH   *235*
Universal Design for Learning
    (UDL)   *228*

References

American Psychiatric Association. (2000). *Diagnostic and statistical manual of mental disorders* (4th ed., text revision). Washington DC: Author.

Asperger, H. (1991). "Autistic psychopathy" in children. In U. Frith (Ed. & Trans.), *Autism and Asperger Syndrome* (pp. 37–92). New York: Cambridge University Press. (Original work published 1944).

Barnhill, G. P. (2001). What's new in AS research: A synthesis of research conducted by the Asperger Syndrome Project. *Intervention in School and Clinic, 36,* 300–305.

Barnhill, G. P. (2002). *Right address . . . wrong planet: Children with Asperger Syndrome becoming adults.* Shawnee Mission, KS: Autism Asperger Publishing.

Barnhill, G. P., Hagiwara, T., Myles, B. S., & Simpson, R. L. (2000). Asperger Syndrome: A study of the cognitive profiles of 37 children and adolescents. *Focus on Autism and Other Developmental Disabilities, 15,* 146–153.

Barrett, M. (2006). "Like dynamite going off in my ears": Using autobiographical accounts of autism with teaching professionals. *Educational Psychology in Practice, 22,* 95–110.

Berry, D. (2004). *The effectiveness of TouchMath curriculum to teach addition and subtraction to elementary aged students identified with autism.* From http://www.touchmath.com/research, retrieved December 24, 2007.

Brian, J. A., Tipper, S. P., Weaver, B., & Bryson, S. E. (2003). Inhibitory mechanisms in autism spectrum disorders: Typical selective inhibition of location versus facilitated perceptual processing. *Journal of Child Psychology and Psychiatry, 44,* 552–660.

Center for Universal Design, North Carolina State University. (2002). From http://www.design.ncsu.edu/cud/, retrieved December 21, 2007.

Chiang, H., & Lin, Y. (2007). Mathematical ability of students with Asperger Syndrome and high-functioning autism: A review of the literature. *Autism, 11,* 547–556.

Church, C., Alisanski, S., & Amanullah, S. (2000). The social, behavioral, and academic experiences of children with Asperger Syndrome. *Focus on Autism and Other Developmental Disabilities, 15*, 12–20.

Cooper, J. O., Heron, T. E., & Heward, W. L. (2007). *Applied behavior analysis* (2nd ed.). Upper Saddle River, NJ: Pearson Education.

Council for Exceptional Children. (2005). *Universal design for learning: A guide for teachers and educational professionals.* Arlington, VA: Merrill Education/Author.

Dawson, G., & Osterling, J. (1997). Early intervention in autism. In M. Guralnick (Ed.), *The effectiveness of early intervention* (pp. 307–326). Baltimore: Brookes.

Delano, M. E. (2007). Improving written language performance of adolescents with Asperger Syndrome. *Journal of Applied Behavior Analysis, 40*, 345–351.

Dunlap, G., Plienis, A. J., & Williams, L. (1987). Acquisition and generalization of unsupervised responding: A descriptive analysis. *Journal of the Association for Persons with Severe Handicaps, 12*, 274–279.

Dunlap, G., & Robbins, F. R. (1991). Current perspectives in service delivery for young children with autism. *Comprehensive Mental Health Care, 1*, 177–194.

Gill, V. (2005). Challenges faced by teachers working with students with Asperger Syndrome. In M. Prior (Ed.), *Learning and behavior problems in Asperger Syndrome* (pp. 194–211). New York: Guilford Press.

Graham, S., Harris, K. R., & Troia, G. A. (2000). Self-regulated strategy development revisited: Teaching writing strategies to struggling writers. *Topics in Language Disorders, 29*(4), 1–14.

Griswold, D.E., Barnhill, G. P., Myles, B. S., Hagiwara, T., & Simpson, R. L. (2002). Asperger Syndrome and academic achievement. *Focus on Autism and Other Developmental Disabilities, 17*, 94–102.

Hallahan, D. P., & Kauffman, J. M. (2006). *Exceptional learners: An introduction to special education* (10th ed.). Upper Saddle River, NJ: Pearson Education.

Harrower, J. K., & Dunlap, G. (2001). Including children with autism in general education classrooms: A review of effective strategies. *Behavior Modification, 25*, 762–784.

Heflin, L. J., & Alaimo, D. F. (2007). *Students with autism spectrum disorders: Effective instructional practices.* Upper Saddle River, NJ: Merril/Pearson Education.

Heflin, L. J., & Simpson, R. L. (1998). Interventions for children and youth with autism: Prudent choices in a world of exaggerated claims and empty promises. Part II: Legal/policy analysis and recommendations for selecting interventions and treatments. *Focus on Autism and Other Developmental Disabilities, 13*, 212–220.

Herbert, J. D., Sharp, I. R., & Gaudiano, B. A. (2002). Separating fact from fiction in the etiology and treatment of autism: A scientific review of the evidence. *The Scientific Review of Mental Health Practice, 1*, 23–43.

Hunt, P., Farron-Davis, F., Wrenn, M., Hirose-Hatae, A., & Goetz, L. (1997). Promoting interactive partnerships in inclusive educational settings. *Journal of the Association for Persons with Severe Handicaps, 22*, 127–137.

Hyatt, K. J. (2007). The new IDEIA: Changes, concerns and questions. *Intervention in School and Clinic, 42*, 131–136.

Individuals with Disabilities Education Improvement Act of 2004, 20 U.S.C. § 1400 *et seq.* (2004) (reauthorization of the Individuals with Disabilities Education Act of 1990).

Iovannone, R., Dunlap, G., Huber, H., & Kincaid, D. (2003). Effective educational practices for students with autism spectrum disorders. *Focus on Autism and Other Developmental Disabilities, 18*, 150–165.

Jordan, R. (2005). School-based intervention for children with specific learning difficulties. In M. Prior (Ed.), *Learning and behavior problems in Asperger Syndrome* (pp. 212–243). New York: Guilford Press.

Kleinhans, N., Akshoomoff, N., & Delis, D. C. (2005). Executive functions in autism and Asperger's Disorder: Flexibility, fluency, and inhibition. *Developmental and Neuropsychology, 27*, 379–401.

Kunce, L. (2005). The ideal classroom. In M. Prior (Ed.), *Learning and behavior problems in Asperger Syndrome* (pp. 244–268). New York: Guilford Press.

Myles, B. S., Hilgenfeld, T. D., Barnhill, G. P., Griswold, D. E., Hagiwara, T., & Simpson, R. L. (2002). Analysis of reading skills in individuals with Asperger Syndrome. *Focus on Autism and Other Developmental Disabilities, 17*, 44–47.

Myles, B. S., Huggins, A., Rome-Lake, M., Hagiwara, T., Barnhill, G. P., & Griswold, D. E. (2003).

Written language profile of children and youth with Asperger Syndrome: From research to practice. *Education and Training in Developmental Disabilities, 38*, 362–369.

National Research Council (2001). *Educating children with autism.* Washington, DC: National Academy Press.

No Child Left Behind Act of 2001, 20 U.S.C. 70 § 6301 *et seq.* (2002).

O'Connor, I. M., & Klein, P. D. (2004). Exploration of strategies for facilitating the reading comprehension of high-functioning students with autism spectrum disorders. *Journal of Autism and Developmental Disorders, 34*, 115–127.

Olson, J. L., Platt, J. C., & Dieker, L. A. (2008). *Teaching children and adolescents with special needs* (5th ed.). Upper Saddle River, NJ: Merrill/Pearson Education.

Ozonoff, S., Cook, I., Coon, H., Dawson, G., Joseph, R., Klin, A., et al. (2004). Performance on subtests sensitive to frontal lobe function in people with autistic disorder: Evidence from the CPEA network. *Journal of Autism and Developmental Disorders, 34*, 139–150.

Ozonoff, S., & Schetter, P. L. (2007). Executive dysfunction in autism spectrum disorders: From research to practice. In L. Meltzer (Ed.), *Executive function in education: From theory to practice* (pp. 133–160). New York: Guilford Press.

Powers, M. (1992). Early intervention for children with autism. In D. Berkell (Ed.), *Autism: Identification, education, and treatment* (pp. 223–251). Hillsdale, NJ: Lawrence Erlbaum Associates.

Reiter, S., & Vitani, T. (2007). Inclusion of pupils with autism: The effect of an intervention program on the regular pupils' burnout, attitudes and quality of mediation. *Autism, 11*, 321–333.

Schetter, P. (2004). *Learning the R.O.P.E.S. for improved executive functioning: A cognitive-behavioral approach for children with high-functioning autism and other behavioral disorders.* Woodland, CA: Autism and Behavior Training Associates.

Schreibman, L. (2005). *The science and fiction of autism.* Cambridge, MA: Harvard University Press.

Schwartz, I. S., & Davis, C. A. (2006/2007, Fall/Winter). Early intervention for children with ASD. *Impact, 19*(3), 14–15.

Siegel, B. (1996). *The world of the autistic child.* New York: Oxford University Press.

Simpson, R. L. (2005). Evidence-based practices and students with autism spectrum disorders. *Focus on Autism and Other Developmental Disabilities, 20*, 140–149.

TEACCH. From http://www.teacch.com, retrieved December 24, 2007.

Wilder, L. K., Dyches, T. T., Obiakor, F. E., & Algozzine, B. (2004). Multicultural perspectives on teaching students with autism. *Focus on Autism and Other Developmental Disabilities, 19*, 105–113.

World Health Organization (1993). *International classification of diseases and related health problems: Tenth revision.* Geneva: Author.

Yell, M. L., Drasgow, E., & Lowrey, K. A. (2005). No Child Left Behind and students with autism spectrum disorders. *Focus on Autism and Other Developmental Disabilities, 20*, 130–139.

Zager, D., & Shamow, N. (Ed.). (2005). Teaching students with autism spectrum disorders. In D. Zager (Ed.), *autism spectrum disorders: Identification, education, and treatment* (3rd ed.) (pp. 295–326). Mahwah, NJ: Lawrence Erlbaum Associates.

11

Autism Spectrum Disorders and Sensory Integration

Jenny Clark Brack, OTR/L BCP

CHAPTER OBJECTIVES

After reading this chapter, learners should be able to:

1. Define *sensory processing/integration*.
2. Explain how Sensory Processing Disorder affects children with ASD.
3. Outline sensory strategies that can be implemented at home and school.
4. Discuss how collaboration between school staff, families, and community members is essential for the success of a child with ASD.
5. Summarize current sensory processing evidence for best practice with children on the autism spectrum.

 CASE STUDY Examples

Case of Troy

Troy is a 13-year-old adolescent who has autism, Attention-Deficit/Hyperactivity Disorder (ADHD), Obsessive Compulsive Disorder (OCD), epilepsy, and Tourette's Syndrome. Troy's adoptive mother was concerned about how Troy's difficulty with sensory processing might be affecting his motor coordination, boundary awareness, emotional control, and social skills with peers, especially when he engages in extracurricular sports—his motivator. Troy's initial occupational therapy (OT) evaluation results indicated that he had decreased motor coordination and strength for his age, as well as sensory overresponsivity and sensory underresponsivitiy, which equates to a modulation disorder. Troy often would become angry and aggressive if a peer accidentally touched him (tactile defensive) or yelled too loudly (auditory defensive), and sometimes Troy would physically get "too close" due to poor spatial boundary awareness. Because of Troy's apparent sensory processing dysfunction, the OT recommended that Troy begin attending occupational therapy. Through OT Troy learned how to identify his state of alertness by labeling his "engine speed" (fast, slow, just right). Troy also learned to change his state of alertness by choosing sensory tools to attain "Just Right" through a program called the "Alert Program: How Does Your Engine Run?" The strategies from the Alert Program allow Troy to understand what his body is experiencing physiologically when he is upset and also help him in making sensory choices to calm down. Such choices may include asking for a "break" or jumping on a mini trampoline. As a result of these OT interventions, the Alert Program, sensory strategies used at school and a sensory "diet" for home, Troy now participates in his favorite sport—basketball. He is also more successful with teamwork and peer social interactions and he demonstrates improved motor coordination. Raising a child truly does take a whole village. Everyone involved in Troy's life collaborated to help him in all environments to experience success.

Case of Joey

Joey is a 7-year-old boy with Asperger Syndrome and Fetal Alcohol Syndrome. Joey has increased anxiety, a short attention span, poor motor coordination, difficulty tying his shoes and managing snaps and buttons, and sensory-seeking needs. Joey plays roughly because he has difficulty with grading touch pressure due to poor proprioceptive feedback. He often seeks out deep pressure touch such as pushing his feet into a pillow at night and likes to be wrapped tightly in a blanket. In addition, he has a need to move and has difficulty sitting still, is "on the go," likes to swing, and enjoys twirling himself (vestibular). Joey tends to get into other children's "space" because he wants to interact with his peers but has difficulty judging appropriate social distance. At school, the staff does not understand sensory processing and misinterprets Joey's "behaviors." As a result, Joey is often in "time-out" and misses out on much schoolwork. After the occupational therapist educated the staff about sensory processing and gave suggestions for a sensory diet and strategies, Joey is better able to attend to task and has decreased frequency, duration, and intensity of the "problem behaviors." Joey wears a weighted vest intermittently throughout the day and the OT monitors appropriate wearing schedule and weight. In addition, Joey pushes his feet against a resistive therapy band that is tied around his desk chair legs. He sits on a chair ball to help him get movement input while seated, and he squeezes a stress ball for deep pressure to his hands. Joey also engages in heavy work "jobs" at school, such as carrying library books, carrying the crate of milk cartons for snack, and helping to put chairs on the desks at the end of the day. The understanding of sensory processing helps Joey's parents and the school staff to create innovative solutions to aid Joey at home and school.

INTRODUCTION*

Sensory Processing Disorder (SPD) is a neurological condition that interferes with the daily lives of approximately 1 in 20 children (Ahn, Miller, Milberger, & McIntosh, 2004). SPD occurs when the brain inaccurately perceives sensation from touch, sight, sound, smell, and movement. Many

*Source: The material on pp. 245-250 originally appeared in Chapter 1 of *Learn to Move, Moving Up! Sensorimotor Elementary-School Activity Themes* (2009). Author Jenny Clark Brack, OTR/L, BCP. Used with permission of Autism Asperger Publishing Company.

people experience occasional difficulties processing sensation, such as not being able to tolerate loud sounds when having a headache or being bothered by tags in their clothing.

Children with SPD, however, experience significant and chronic symptoms that can disrupt daily living activities and negatively affect their participation in everyday life. For example, a child with SPD not only cannot tolerate tags in his clothing, but he may also have emotional meltdowns from the texture of sock seams, certain types of clothing materials, toothbrush bristles, food textures, art media, and having his fingernails cut. These symptoms are a daily occurrence and impact food choices, hygiene, participation in school activities, and social interactions.

Sensory Integration

The concept of Sensory Processing Disorder has its roots in **sensory integration theory**, developed in the 1970s by Jean Ayres. Dr. Ayres earned B.S. and M.A. degrees in occupational therapy and a Ph.D. in educational psychology from the University of Southern California. She completed a postdoctoral traineeship at the UCLA Brain Research Institute under Dr. Arther Parmelee. In addition to her occupational therapy credentials, Dr. Ayres was also a licensed psychologist in California.

Ayres defined sensory integration as "the neurological process that organizes sensation from one's own body and from the environment and makes it possible to use the body effectively within the environment" (Ayres, 1979, p. 11). In other words, sensory integration allows us to participate in daily activities and experience sensations such as the taste of a hotdog, the feel of clothing textures, the sounds of birds while playing in the park, and the movement from riding a bicycle.

Children who have difficulty with sensory processing experience sensory input as confusing, upsetting, or not meaningful. For example, at school during a fire drill when the fire alarm sounds, a child reacts by covering her ears, becomes upset and cries, and has difficulty re-engaging in the task at hand. At home, a child avoids brushing his teeth because the toothbrush texture does not feel good in his mouth. In the community, a child steers clear of playground equipment because he is afraid of heights.

Certain types of sensation, especially in new environments, can be so overwhelming for a child that her emotional reactions present as willful behavior to others. Such rigid and controlling behavior impacts social interactions with others and interferes with engaging in everyday activities.

A child attending a typical birthday party experiences a wealth of sensory input: the sounds of all the children talking, singing, and blowing horns; the sights of balloons, gifts, and candles; the sensation of other children accidentally bumping into him; the texture of the elastic string under his chin from the birthday hat; and the taste, texture, and temperature of the cake and ice cream.

A typical child is able to take in all the sensations—usually without even being aware of them—and have an enjoyable time. A child with SPD, on the other hand, may experience the sounds as too loud and the sights as overwhelming. The tactile sensation of children accidentally bumping into him may disrupt his personal boundary space, leading him to misinterpret the sensation as purposefully hurtful. Finally, he may not like the texture of the chocolate cake or the coldness of the ice cream.

In an effort to cope with these uncomfortable and sometimes painful sensations, the child may shut down or lash out. Not surprisingly, such behavior can negatively impact social interaction with the people around him. This example illustrates only one type of sensory processing pattern; there is a broad spectrum of processing patterns, from sensory sensitive to sensory underresponsive, with various symptoms across developmental age groups of children.

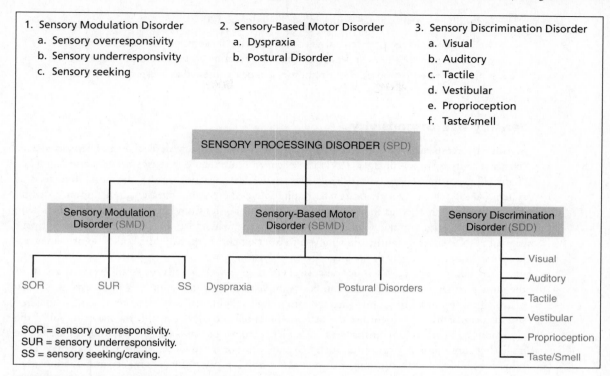

1. Sensory Modulation Disorder
   a. Sensory overresponsivity
   b. Sensory underresponsivity
   c. Sensory seeking

2. Sensory-Based Motor Disorder
   a. Dyspraxia
   b. Postural Disorder

3. Sensory Discrimination Disorder
   a. Visual
   b. Auditory
   c. Tactile
   d. Vestibular
   e. Proprioception
   f. Taste/smell

SOR = sensory overresponsivity.
SUR = sensory underresponsivity.
SS = sensory seeking/craving.

FIGURE 11.1 Sensory Processing Disorder
Source: From Miller, L. J., Anzalone M. E., Lane, S. J., Cermak, S. A., & Osten, E. T. (2007). Concept evolution in sensory integration: A proposed nosology for diagnosis. *American Journal of Occupational Therapy, 61*(2), p. 137.

It is important to accurately categorize a child's sensory processing patterns in order to develop treatment plans that target the child's needs. Miller, Anzalone, Lane, Cermak, and Osten (2007) have suggested that SPD be divided into three patterns, each with subtypes (Figure 11.1).

SENSORY PROCESSING CONCEPTS

In the following section, we will take a closer look at SPD using Miller et al.'s (2007) classification.

Sensory Modulation Disorder

SENSORY MODULATION   Sensory Modulation Disorder (SMD) "is a problem with turning sensory messages into controlled behaviors that match the nature and intensity of the sensory information" (Miller & Fuller, 2006, p. 12). **Sensory modulation** occurs every moment of our day, allowing us to focus on important input while ignoring irrelevant input. Modulation takes place at an unconscious level such that most of us are unaware of the small adjustments our nervous system makes to help us participate smoothly in daily life activities.

When input is not properly modulated, it can affect the ability to attend to task. For example, if a teacher is giving instructions for a math assignment, the child who has poor modulation may have difficulty tuning out extraneous background sounds, such as children's voices in the hallway or the noise from the heater, be distracted by them, and consequently miss the point of the instructions.

According to Henry, Kane-Wineland, & Swindeman (2007):

> We all have sensory preferences, yet students with sensory modulation disorder have very strong sensory likes and dislikes and their reaction to sensory input departs from typical expected responses. Their responses can be manifested as overresponsivity and/or sensory seeking behaviors (p. 4).

Sensory Overresponsivity

Sensory overresponsivity is also commonly referred to as **sensory defensiveness**. Sensory defensiveness (Wilbarger & Wilbarger, 1991) can occur in more than one sensory system and involves a "fight, flight, or freeze" reaction. When a sensory defensive reaction occurs, the autonomic nervous system (ANS), which regulates heart rate, respiration, and digestion, releases adrenaline and cortisol. This is intended to assist us in preparing to protect our bodies from harm, and is useful when there is a real threat. For example, if you are driving down the road and a deer jumps out in front of your car, your ANS works instantly, allowing you to react quickly by putting the brakes on or maneuvering your car out of the way to be safe.

In children who have sensory defensiveness, their ANS responds to typical everyday events in the same manner, even if not called for. For example, a child who is auditorily defensive—has a low neurological threshold to sound—may go into a "fight, flight, or freeze" reaction when a school bell sounds because his ANS identifies the bell as a potential threat. As a result, she may run out of the classroom or hit the child sitting next to her. If teachers, parents, and others are unaware of the child's sensory sensitivity to sound, such behavior will not make sense. As a result, they may discipline the child rather than problem-solve and develop sensory strategies and accommodations that possibly will prevent future occurrences.

Sensory Underresponsivity

Another subtype of SMD is **sensory underresponsivity**. Children with sensory underresponsivity require intense sensory input to notice sensations and lack initial awareness of stimuli. These children tend to have decreased **sensory registration**, defined as "the initial awareness of a sensation" (Williamson & Anzalone, 2001, p. 13). Thus, in order to notice a new sensation in her environment, such as a change in temperature, sound, or lighting, the child has to become aware of the new stimulus before she can attend to it. Children with underresponsivity appear to be sedentary, lethargic, and apathetic, and they tend to lack an inner drive, be withdrawn, and may take longer to respond. Such children are often mislabeled as "lazy" or "unmotivated" (Miller et al., 2007).

Children with Autism Spectrum Disorder (ASD), a major focus of this book, fall into both categories of over- and underresponsivity in multiple sensory systems (Tomchek & Dunn, 2007). For example, a child may demonstrate poor tolerance for tactile sensation such as getting paint on her fingers in art or having her hair or nails cut (overresponsivity), but may need to feel the heavy sensation of a weighted blanket to calm for sleeping (underresponsivity).

Sensory Seeking

A third subtype of SMD is **sensory seeking**. Children who are sensory seeking prefer intense and extreme sensory input. These children may be viewed as "daredevils," who prefer to climb rocks or go fast on the merry-go-round. They may not easily feel pain, they may make sounds with their mouth as a way to stimulate their auditory system, and they often play roughly with toys and other children.

The consequence of such behavior is poor impulse control, leading to physical contact that can harm another individual or the child himself.

Sensory-Based Motor Disorder

Sensory-based Motor Disorders (SBMD) are divided into two subtypes: dyspraxia and Postural Disorder (PD).

DYSPRAXIA   The term **dyspraxia** (sometimes called Developmental Coordination Disorder [DCD]) comes from the word *praxis*, which refers to paying conscious attention to a task while relying on stored sensory information from each of the sensory systems. For example, adults skiing for the first time rely on the sense of vision to navigate around obstacles, hearing to listen to instructions, tactile sensations to feel the ski boots and ski poles, and movement sensations to learn the new skill of snow skiing. While relying on sensations of which they are not consciously aware, they learn the motor patterns by consciously focusing on manipulating the skis and the poles to perform the motions with smooth movements.

Dyspraxia, in contrast, refers to difficulty in executing unfamiliar motor actions, which affects oral, fine-motor, and gross-motor coordination. Children with dyspraxia have poor awareness of their body in space, thus displaying symptoms such as bumping into other people or objects, poor articulation, illegible handwriting, and awkward motor skills in physical education class as well as sports. Children with dyspraxia need excessive repetition to learn new motor skills and have to cognitively "think" about how to move their bodies.

POSTURAL DISORDER   **Postural Disorder** is described as "difficulty stabilizing the body during movement or at rest to meet the demands of the environment or of a given motor task" (Miller et al., 2007, p. 138). Thus, it is characterized by poor motor control, poor stability, or poor balance due to an imbalance in muscle tone (hypertonic—high muscle tone, or hypotonic—low muscle tone). Children with poor postural control have difficulty with movement against gravity and may slump at their desk or fall out of their chair.

Sensory Discrimination Disorder

Sensory Discrimination Disorder involves difficulty perceiving the details of sensation to identify differences or similarities (see Figure 11.2). Poor discrimination can occur in one or more sensory systems. Ultimately, a child's learning, self-esteem, and behavior are impacted by a Sensory Discrimination Disorder, as extra time is required to process information. For example, a child with poor visual

---

- Poor auditory discrimination
  - Trouble discerning speech sounds
  - Delays with processing verbal directions
- Poor tactile discrimination
  - Difficulty manipulating fasteners unless looking at them
  - May not notice food on face after eating
- Poor discrimination with movement (vestibular)
  - Difficulty with balance tasks such as navigating stairs

- Poor discrimination with muscles (proprioception)
  - May misjudge the amount of pressure to use when coloring, consequently breaking crayons
  - Trouble judging body space; bumping into objects
- Decreased taste/smell discrimination
  - May be particular about food choices

FIGURE 11.2   Examples of Discrimination Disorder

discrimination may have difficulty discerning "b" from "d" and therefore, struggles with reading. He may be very much aware that his peers are reading more fluently than he is, which affects his self-confidence and his sense of "fitting in." This, in turn, may cause him to display inappropriate behaviors in the classroom and act out as the "class clown" to hide his difficulties and try to be accepted by his peers.

As illustrated, children with SPD struggle with participating in daily activities and routines at school, at home, and in the community. These children need emotional support and physical accommodations to experience success in all environments.*

THE SEVEN SENSORY SYSTEMS

There are seven sensory systems that play a role in sensory processing. Each sensory system affects a child's occupation in daily life activities. Five of these sensory systems are well known and two are considered the "hidden senses" and not as commonly recognized. Disturbances in any of the sensory systems may occur for a variety of reasons (see Box 11.1) and are common among individuals with ASD.

Tactile System

The **tactile system** is made of cells in our skin (mechanoreceptors) that send information to our central nervous system (brain) for light touch, pain, vibration, and temperature (thermoreceptors). Tactile receptors on the chest and back have low receptor density in large receptor fields, whereas tactile receptors in the hands and mouth have high receptor density in small receptor fields. Since tactile receptors in the hands have high receptor density in small receptor fields, children who have tactile defensiveness do not like to have their hands touch messy media, such as finger paint or glue. The tactile system serves two purposes: as protection by alerting to danger (such as touching something hot and quickly moving away from harm) and as discrimination by orienting to the touch sensation by answering questions (What touched me? Where did it touch me?). Children with underresponsivity to tactile input seek out touch sensation and display behaviors of fidgeting with items such as pencils, erasers, and fingernails, as well as touching other kids or dragging their hand along the wall in the hallways. A child with an overresponsivity to touch sensation (tactile defensiveness) responds to non-noxious stimuli in a "fight, flight or freeze" response. Forty percent of children with ASD are both overresponsive (sensory defensive) and underresponsive to touch (Rimland, 1990).

Auditory System

The **auditory system** allows us to hear sound, process what we are hearing (auditory processing), discriminate between sounds (phonics), and focus on foreground sound while tuning out background sound (auditory figure-ground). The auditory system has neurological connections to the vestibular system (see below) due to the anatomical proximity. A child with an underresponsive auditory system may display poor sensory registration and demonstrate delayed processing and response to an auditory stimulus. A child with an overresponsive auditory system responds in a defensive manner to typical environmental sounds. For example, children with ASD may cover their ears with their hands during music class or in the gymnasium during physical education. In addition, they may go into "fight, flight, freeze" reaction during community activities that have decibels greater than 85 such as at a movie theatre, a birthday party, or a restaurant.

*End of material appearing in *Learn to Move, Moving Up!*

Visual System

The **visual system** has several functions. One function is that it allows us to see clearly for acuity (focusing mechanism). Secondly, our visual system assists in functional vision as eye muscles team together for ocular tracking and convergence/divergence. Functional vision helps a child to read across a page without losing his place, copy text from the chalkboard, navigate stairs, and catch a ball. A third function of the visual system is visual motor integration, which is the ability to coordinate vision with motor control. Visual motor integration skill is the foundation necessary for legible handwriting. Lastly, visual perception provides a child with the skills to interpret visual information, such as visual memory or discrimination, and is the foundation for reading and mathematics. Visual perception tends to be a well-developed skill for many children with ASD, as observed by their amazing ability to assemble puzzles.

Gustatory System

The **gustatory system** is comprised of chemical receptors located on the tongue that allow us to taste sweet, sour, salty, and bitter and perceive textures such as soft, hard, crunchy, gummy, sticky, and chewy. One in four people are "super-tasters" who are born with an excess taste buds (papiliae). For these children, vegetables tend to taste bitter, textures are noxious, and sweet tastes are increased. About a quarter of the population are "non-tasters," and everyone else is in between. Children with an underresponsive gustatory system prefer food with extreme bitter, sweet, sour, and other strong tastes. Children with an overresponsive gustatory system prefer bland foods such as breads, meats, and potatoes. Many children on the autism spectrum have difficulty tolerating a variety of tastes, but especially textures in foods, and prefer to eat foods that are either bland or very spicy and textures that are smooth and familiar. Keep in mind that typical children have to be exposed to a food 20 different times before determining whether they like it or not.

Olfactory System

The **olfactory system** is made of chemical receptors located in the nasal structure that allow us to smell and discriminate between smells. In October 2004, two scientists won a Nobel Prize for discovering that humans have 1,000 olfactory odor receptor cells that register 10,000 different smells. The sense of smell is often underestimated for its important role in emotion. The olfactory system has direct neuronal connections to the limbic system, which is responsible for emotional memory. Therefore smells can evoke an emotional response. For example, if you notice the smell of bread baking, it might evoke an emotional memory of your grandmother who used to bake homemade bread when you were a child. However, it brings up powerful memories whether they are pleasant or not. A child with an overresponsive olfactory system may respond to scents in the environment such as cafeteria food, perfumes, or locker room odors in a "fight, flight, freeze" reaction. A child with an underresponsive sense of smell displays inappropriate behaviors and seeks out olfactory sensation by sniffing items such as markers, crayons, clothes, or magazines.

Vestibular System

The **vestibular system** is comprised of hair cells in two structures in the inner ear. Otolith organs respond to linear movement and gravity, and semicircular canals respond to angular movement. The vestibular system detects movement and changes in head position so that we can orient in space, sense the speed at which we are moving, and determine in which direction we are moving. Linear movement tends to be more organizing to the nervous system while angular or rotary movement tends to be alerting to the nervous system. Vestibular input is cumulative and can last in the nervous system for hours depending on the intensity, duration, and frequency of the movement input.

Children with an overresponsive vestibular system avoid moving and may steer clear of playground equipment, get car sick, or may become distressed when their head is tipped for hair washing. Children with an underresponsive vestibular system crave movement and have difficulty sitting still, rock while seated, and enjoy being upside down. The use of a chair ball (therapy ball) is sometimes used to help children get the needed extra movement input that their underresponsive vestibular systems are craving. Research has shown that children with ASD benefit from sitting on a therapy ball to improve in-seat behavior and engagement in the task at hand (Shilling & Schwartz, 2004).

Proprioceptive System

The **proprioceptive system** involves receptors in the joints, muscles, and tendons that perceive contraction, stretching, and compression. It provides us with awareness of joint position and movement. This helps us to have appropriate fine and gross motor coordination. Children with poor proprioceptive feedback may appear clumsy during physical education class, fall out of their chair frequently at school, or have poor articulation. The proprioceptive system also allows us to grade touch pressure so that we know exactly how much pressure to apply when picking up a light paper cup versus a heavy glass. Children with poor proprioceptive feedback may have difficulty grading touch pressure and color with heavy crayon pressure, break their pencil lead when writing, or pet a cat with so much force that they are hitting it. Children with ASD show signs of overresponsivity to tactile sensation (Tomcheck & Dunn 2007) and thus seek out proprioceptive input as a way to modulate the nervous system. In addition, studies suggest that children with ASD rely on visual input to maintain balance, suggesting a possibility of poor vestibular and proprioceptive processing (Minshew et al., 2004; Molloy et al., 2003). Signs and symptoms of poor proprioceptive processing may appear as playing roughly and breaking toys, deliberately falling, chewing hard on food or non-food items, or preferring tight clothing. Children with ASD may seek out strong, deep pressure touch input as a way to self-regulate. If the input is intense enough to meet their neurological thresholds, then the child will feel an overall calming response. This proprioceptive input can last in the nervous system for one and a half to two hours. Endorphins from the brain are released when the deep pressure touch input occurs. These endorphins then metabolize in the nervous system in about 90 minutes. This may be why children with ASD appear to have a strong need for deep pressure touch. A common practice that provides this input is the use of a weighted vest. Research supports the efficacy and benefits for children with ASD wearing a weighted vest (see Box 11.1). Findings suggest that the use of a weighted vest helps to increase attention to task and decrease self-stimulatory behaviors (Fertel-Daly, Bedell, & Hinojosa 2001).

BOX 11.1   Research/Trends and Issues Notes

Weighted vests are a common sensory strategy among practicing occupational therapists. However, until recently, evidence to support the efficacy was limited. One study examined five preschool children with a diagnosis of Pervasive Developmental Disorder and the effectiveness of wearing a weighted vest for increasing attention during fine motor tasks and decreasing self-stimulatory behaviors over a 6-week time period. Results indicated that all participants demonstrated a decrease in the number of distractions and an increase in attention during the intervention phase. In addition, all but one participant demonstrated a decrease in duration of self-stimulatory behaviors; however, for that child, the self-stimulatory behavior altered and was less violent.

The most common questions that arise from using the weighted vest as a sensory strategy include:

1. What is the wearing schedule?
2. How much weight is used in the vest?

In response to the first question, because the nervous system responds to change in sensory input, wearing the weighted vest ON for a period of time then OFF for a period of time is most effective. Wearing the weighted vest all day is not effective because the nervous system accommodates to the input. Also, stimulation to the proprioceptive system wears off after one and a half to two hours, thus, needing to have more input after this length of time. It is common practice with therapists to have a child wear the weighted vest for 20 minutes at a time; however, there is no evidence to support this intervention time decision. This study had the children wearing the weighted vests ON for 2 hours and OFF for 2 hours, and results were favorable.

In response to the second question, Honaker and Rossi (2005) designed a protocol entitled "CAT (Critically Appraised Topics) Brief" analyzing evidence from previously published literature in determining the amount of weight used for effectiveness. This system allowed for a very structured and organized manner in which to analyze all of the available evidence for best practice decisions. Results determined that the amount of weight, which the evidence showed most effective, was 5% of the child's body weight.

Source: Information from Fertel-Daly, D., Bedell, G., & Hinojosa, J. (2001). Effects of a weighed vest on attention to task and self-stimulatory behaviors in preschoolers with Pervasive Developmental Disorders. *American Journal of Occupational Therapy, 55,* 629–640.

ACCOMODATIONS/SIMPLE SOLUTIONS

There are many innovative accommodations that can allow children with ASD who have sensory processing difficulties to function at their best during school and at home for attention, behavior, and work productivity. The list below includes only a sampling of suggestions. It is the hope of this author that readers will have a better understanding of sensory processing and will begin to create their own unique solutions that are specific for each child's sensory needs in every moment of the child's daily life. The term *Sensory Diet* was coined by Patricia Wilbarger, Ph.D., OTR, occupational therapist. A **sensory diet** is best described as sensory strategies and accommodations that children engage in and utilize throughout their daily routines as "food" for their nervous system. Just like we eat breakfast, lunch, and dinner as well as snacks between meals to maintain our blood sugar levels, our nervous system needs specific sensory and motor input to maintain our regulatory system for alertness. We digest food after we eat, and our nervous system "digests" sensory input after we are exposed to it. When sensory strategies and accommodations are carefully chosen, utilized intermittently throughout the day, and meet a child's sensory processing needs, the child is able to maintain a "just right" alertness for focusing and emotional well-being.

Before strategies and accommodations are recommended, the student is observed by an occupational therapist in a variety of environments such as the classroom, lunchroom, recess, music class, physical education, and so forth. In addition, one or more teachers may complete a checklist for specific concerns they observe in the school environment. The observation checklist in Figure 11.3 is one example that might be used (Brack, 2004).

In addition, an occupational therapist may perform formal assessment to glean more detailed and standardized data about how the student is processing sensory input. A variety of assessments may be used for formal assessment and listed here are just two examples: *The Sensory Profile School*

Signs and Symptoms of Sensory Integration/Processing Dysfunction

Tactile
- ❏ Dislikes standing in line
- ❏ Bothered by tags on shirts
- ❏ Dislikes playing with messy things
- ❏ Reacts aversively to textured foods
- ❏ Likes only highly textured foods
- ❏ Does not react to falls, scrapes or bumps
- ❏ Touches everything, walks touching the wall
- ❏ Constantly puts things in mouth

Proprioceptive
- ❏ Stamps feet or bangs with hands
- ❏ Writes or holds pencil too hard (or too soft)
- ❏ Plays too roughly
- ❏ Seems unaware of body in space – clumsy
- ❏ Handles toys roughly – lots of banging and breaking
- ❏ Deliberately falls or tumbles a lot
- ❏ Chews hard on things
- ❏ Demonstrates poor motor planning in gross-/fine-motor skills

Vestibular
- ❏ Wiggles around during seated activities
- ❏ Craves spinning or swinging
- ❏ Rocks while seated or standing
- ❏ Likes being upside down
- ❏ Is constantly in motion
- ❏ Is afraid of movement
- ❏ Experiences car sickness
- ❏ Avoids playground equipment
- ❏ Fears having head titled backward (e.g., hair washing)
- ❏ Is afraid to sit on a toilet

Auditory
- ❏ Covers ears or screams with sudden loud noises (e.g., vacuum cleaner, toilet flushing)
- ❏ Has difficulty locating sound
- ❏ Enjoys constantly making sounds (e.g., humming)
- ❏ Is constantly distracted by background sounds (e.g., fluorescent lights humming)
- ❏ Prefers very loud music

Vision
- ❏ Demonstrates poor eye contact
- ❏ Turns head to the side when looking at things
- ❏ Holds head very close to work
- ❏ Loses place on page when reading
- ❏ Has difficulty copying from the board
- ❏ Uses hand as a "visor" in bright sunlight or fluorescent lighting
- ❏ Has difficulty tracking a ball to catch

Arousal and Attending
- ❏ Is hyperactive and difficult to calm
- ❏ Has difficulty modulating emotional response
- ❏ Startles easily
- ❏ Is difficult to arouse and does not react to loud sounds, bright lights, etc.
- ❏ Has difficulty completing tasks
- ❏ Has difficulty transitioning from one task to another

Social Consciousness
- ❏ Reacts with laughter when someone expresses anger, sadness, fear
- ❏ Becomes fearful in social situations
- ❏ Does not spontaneously interact in a group
- ❏ Appears to be unaware of others' feelings
- ❏ Unable to identify happy/sad/angry faces

Olfactory/Gustatory
- ❏ Complains of things "smelling bad"
- ❏ Notices how people smell
- ❏ Reacts violently to smells
- ❏ Smells objects constantly
- ❏ Prefers foods that are highly spiced or totally bland
- ❏ Chooses very limited repertoire of foods (e.g., prefers smooth vs. texture)

FIGURE 11.3 Observation Checklist
Source: Brack, J. C. (2004). *Learn to Move, Move to Learn Sensorimotor Early Childhood Activity Themes* (p. 4.) Shawnee Mission, KS: Autism Asperger Publishing Company. Reprinted with permission.

Companion (Dunn, 2006) and *Sensory Processing Measure* (Kuhaneck, Henry, & Glennon, 2007). Once the sensory processing difficulties are identified through formal assessment, observation, and interview, the simple solutions listed below may be suggested, adjusted, and in come cases monitored by an occupational therapist. Some of these strategies are used for calming the nervous system and some are used for alerting the nervous system. Moreover, specific strategies are used for calming and alerting specific sensory systems. Consulting an OT is necessary to determine how best to tailor sensory strategies to specific sensory needs of a child.

Vestibular Simple Solutions for School

- Have the child use a chair ball or air-filled cushion for additional movement while seated.
- Let the child have movement breaks throughout the day, such as running an office errand.
- Allow the child to assume non-sitting positions such as standing or lying down while reading.
- Do not take away recess privileges to finish work. Movement helps with attention and behavior.
- Schedule movement prior to seatwork, not as a reward.
- Incorporate movement into teaching activities.

Vestibular Simple Solutions for Home

- Extracurricular sports such as soccer, basketball, baseball.
- Swinging.
- Bike riding.
- Have the child avoid movement activity prior to bedtime, as this will make it difficult for him to fall asleep.

Proprioception Simple Solutions for School

- Have the child wear a weighted vest with an occupational therapist's guidance.
- Have the child wear a neoprene pressure vest for deep pressure. Some children prefer this to a weighted vest.
- Let the child use a weighted lap bag.
- Provide a beanbag chair in the classroom.
- Incorporate naturally occurring heavy work into the child's day, such as carrying library books or a crate with milk cartons for snack.
- Provide the child with a weighted wristband for distal proprioceptive feedback to help with functional fine motor control.
- Let the child use a mechanical pencil if he pushes so hard that his pencil lead breaks. This will give immediate feedback when writing to use less pressure.

Proprioception Simple Solutions for Home

- Give hugs.
- Have the child engage in extracurricular sports such as swimming, karate, and yoga.
- Let the child help with chores such as wiping off the table, carrying groceries, and digging in the garden.
- Have the child climb on playground equipment.
- Buy lycra clothing for the child to wear such as Under Armour, Starter Brand, or a swimsuit.

Tactile Simple Solutions for School

- Offer hand fidgets.
- Let child trace tactile letters with sandpaper or Wikki Stix®.

- Mark personal space with a large carpet square so that child does not get bumped accidentally.
- Place the child in front or back of the line.

Tactile Simple Solutions for Home

- Use firm touch, not light touch or tickling.
- When cutting hair, massage the scalp, use a weighted vest or have the child engage in a heavy work activity prior to cutting hair.
- At the dentist's office, ask for the child to wear the X-Ray vest for heavy pressure calming.
- Buy clothes without tags or cut tags out of clothing.
- When cutting nails, first soak the nails, then compress each nail bed prior to cutting.

Visual Simple Solutions for School

- Let the child wear a visor in the classroom if lighting is too bright.
- Provide a table easel or slant board to prop book or paper.
- Cut out a window guide for ease in tracking during reading without losing place on page.
- Consult an occupational therapist regarding adapted handwriting paper.
- Provide a small piece of a sticky note for the child to use for spacing between words when writing.
- Use visual pictures for the daily schedule.
- Incorporate Social Stories™ for new situations.

Visual Simple Solutions for Home

- Use a fish tank for visual relaxation.
- Place a blue-colored light bulb in the bedroom lamp.
- Give the child sunglasses to wear for visual sensitivity.

Auditory Simple Solutions for School

- Allow the use of headphones or earplugs for sound sensitivity.
- Incorporate classical music for background sound.
- Simplify language, give directions one at a time, and allow longer response time.
- Pair directions with physical and visual prompts.

Auditory Simple Solutions for Home

- Use soft music for calming and focusing at mealtime, bedtime, and homework time.
- Respect your child's sensitivity to sound and give him a verbal warning prior to a noxious sound, such as the vacuum cleaner, garbage disposal, or toilet flushing.
- Be the first one to arrive at a birthday party to allow your child to accommodate to the increasing sounds as other children arrive.

Olfactory Simple Solutions for School and Home

- Use vanilla scents for calming and peppermint or citrus scents for alerting.
- Adults should avoid wearing perfume or cologne as this can cause the overresponsive child to go into "fight, flight, or freeze" reaction to smell.
- Use scent-free fabric softeners and laundry detergents to wash clothes.
- For negative reactions to scents, have the child smell cinnamon, cloves, or coffee beans.

Gustatory Simple Solutions for School and Home

- Allow the child to chew gum. This can help with sensory organization and has even been shown to improve memory.

- Offer oral motor fidgets such as chew tubes or straws.
- Provide a straw for the child to drink from. The stronger the suck (thick liquids or looped straws) the more organizing it is to the nervous system.
- Use a vibrating toothbrush for extra proprioceptive input in the mouth.

INTERVENTIONS

More specific and intensive interventions may be necessary to meet the sensory needs of the child with ASD. These interventions need to be carried out by trained professionals.

The Alert Program

The Alert Program (Williams & Shellenberger, 1994) teaches children sensory self-regulation. Self-regulation is when an individual is able to make sensory choices that help them to attain and maintain a "just right" state of alertness. The Alert Program begins with teaching children that their body is like a car engine: sometimes it runs too fast, sometimes too slow, and sometimes it runs just right. Adults begin to label their own "engine" speed and then the child's "engine speed" throughout the day. Labeling the engine speed allows children to build associations and understanding of events that may trigger "fight, flight, or freeze" reactions and tune into their own body signals such as heartbeat, temperature, and breathing rate. Children are then introduced to different "tools" that can change their engine speed. Sensory tools may include tools for the body, hands, mouth, ears, and eyes. After children learn which tools help change their "engine speed" to "just right," they then have a repertoire of activities and items that they can use as needed in any environment and during any event for sensory self-regulation.

Animal-Assisted Therapy

Recent research supports the use of animals to assist children with ASD with developing important life skills. Sams, Fortney, and Willenbring (2006) compared language and social interactions between children with ASD receiving standard OT techniques and children with ASD incorporating animals into therapy sessions. Results indicated that the children receiving therapy sessions with animals had significantly greater use of language and social interactions. In a single case study over a 15-week period, Jennifer Barol (2007), a graduate student in New Mexico Highland University School of Social Work, observed a 5-year-old child on the autism spectrum engaging in therapy sessions with a specially trained dog named Henry. The purpose of the study was to find out if animal-assisted therapy increased social skills in children with autism. The boy was nonverbal prior to the study. Halfway through the research study, he spoke his first sentence. In addition, the boy began to make social interactions with the therapists working with him and became more aware of others' needs.

Sensory Integration Therapy

Sensory integration therapy is "a program of intervention involving meaningful therapeutic activities characterized by enhanced sensation especially tactile, vestibular, and proprioceptive, active participation, and adaptive interaction." (Bundy et. al., 2002, p. 479). There is controversy over sensory integration (SI) treatment and its effectiveness on the functional performance in children. (For the purposes of this chapter, only children with ASD will be mentioned.) However, some research has shed light on interventions that do indeed have an affect on children with SPD. One study examined the effectiveness of OT and SI with children on the autism spectrum. Results found improvement in play skills, social interaction, adult interaction, and approach to motor tasks. In addition, sensory sensitivities decreased. No changes were noted in interactions with peers (Baranek, 2002).

BOX 11.2 Diversity Notes

Lin, Cermak, Coster, and Miller (2005) studied the relationship between the length of institutionalization and sensory integration in children adopted from Eastern Europe. Participants consisted of 60 school-age children between 4 years and 8 years 11 months who had been adopted from Eastern European countries into the United States. Half of the participants had longer lengths of institutionalization histories, which on average was 34 months, whereas the other 30 participants had been in orphanages for an average of only 3 months. The Sensory Integration and Praxis Tests (SIPT) were used to measure visual, tactile, and kinesthetic perception and motor performance in each participant. In addition, the Developmental and Sensory Processing Questionnaire was completed by the adoptive parents, which asked questions for both sensory processing and behaviors. Results found that the children adopted from Eastern Europe orphanages with longer lengths of institutionalization histories had more atypical sensory discrimination, praxis (motor planning), and sensory modulation scores. In addition, tactile, vestibular, proprioceptive, visual, and auditory processing were more affected by deprived environmental conditions in early childhood.

COLLABORATION

Collaboration is communication between one or more people in order to achieve an end result. Because children with ASD have needs in multiple areas, it is imperative that all team members work together for a common goal resulting in best practice and functional outcomes. Team members may consist of a speech-language pathologist, special education teacher, regular education teacher(s), occupational therapist, physical therapist, peers, family members, and others in the child's community. Using a transdisciplinary approach is most effective. This allows an integrative team to share treatment ideas, roles, and functions across disciplinary lines so that everyone works with the whole child, rather than focusing on each discipline's perspective. This approach is used routinely in the *Learn to Move, Move to Learn* (Brack, 2004) program in early childhood classrooms. Children with ASD benefit as they participate in all the activities through integration alongside their peers, building social skills while developing important motor, language, and cognitive skills. Collaboration allows all involved with the child to think "outside the box" when problem solving, and can help children with ASD flourish in school, at home, and in their community.

Summary

It is well documented that many children on the autism spectrum have sensory processing difficulties, especially in the areas of sensory defensiveness and underresponsivity to sensory input, which results in a modulation disorder. These sensory difficulties affect motor coordination for functional activities such as handwriting, shoe tying, bike riding, and extracurricular sports. In addition, behavior, attention, self-esteem, and social skills are greatly impacted by poor sensory processing. Collaboration between professionals, community, and families is essential for creating practical and innovative solutions to meet the sensory processing needs of each child. Intervention helps children with ASD improve self-regulation, functional engagement, and participation in everyday life. Through sensory interventions, sensory diets, and environmental strategies and accommodations, each child has a greater opportunity to be successful with acquisition of social skills, pre-vocational skills, play skills, and academic skills for an enriched and meaningful life.

Chapter Review Questions

1. Describe sensory defensiveness and explain how this can impact a child with ASD in the school setting. (Objectives 1 and 2)
2. Create three sensory strategies to be used in an educational setting for a child who has an underresponsive nervous system. (Objective 3)
3. Explain the importance of collaboration and how this can best meet the needs of a child with ASD. (Objective 4)
4. Discuss how the Alert Program can assist a child with ASD in the process of sensory self-regulation. (Objective 5)

Key Terms

Auditory system   *250*
Collaboration   *258*
Dyspraxia   *249*
Gustatory system   *251*
Olfactory system   *251*
Postural Disorder   *249*
Proprioceptive system   *252*
Sensory defensiveness   *248*

Sensory diet   *253*
Sensory Discrimination
   Disorder (SDD)   *249*
Sensory integration theory   *246*
Sensory modulation   *247*
Sensory overresponsivity   *248*
Sensory Processing Disorder
   (SPD)   *245*

Sensory registration   *248*
Sensory seeking   *248*
Sensory underresponsivity   *248*
Sensory-based Motor Disorders
   (SBMD)   *249*
Tactile system   *250*
Vestibular system   *251*
Visual system   *251*

Internet Resources

This site contains valuable resource information for parents and professionals. The Sensory Processing Disorder (SDP) network is a project of the KID Foundation, a nonprofit organization based in Littleton, Colorado. The SDP network has a treatment directory for locating a therapist in your community, scientific research information, access to other links about sensory processing and conferences and workshops listed.
http://www.spdnetwork.org/
This site has an educator, parent, and health-care professional guide with many activity ideas, free downloads with checklists and lesson plans, articles and links to sensory resources and products, and sensory quick fixes for home and school.
http://www.spdconnection.com/links. htm#parentresources
This site includes a Sensory Processing Disorder newsletter, symptom checklist, equipment and product suggestions, resources for parents and teachers, ideas for setting up a sensory room, and loads of sensory activities.
http://www.sensory-processing-disorder.com/

References

Ahn, R. R., Miller, L. J., Milberger, S., & McIntosh, D. N. (2004). Prevalence of parents' perceptions of Sensory Processing Disorders among kindergarten children. *American Journal of Occupational Therapy, 58*, 287–293.

Ayres, A. J. (1979). *Sensory integration and the child.* Los Angeles: Western Psychological Services.

Baranek, G. (2002). Efficacy of sensory and motor interventions for children with autism. *Journal of Autism and Developmental Disorders, 32*(5), 397–442.

Barol, J. (2007). *The effects of animal-assisted therapy on a child with autism.* Albuquerque: New Mexico Highland University School of Social Work.

Brack, J. C. (2004). *Learn to move, move to learn sensorimotor early childhood activity themes.* Shawnee Mission, KS: Autism Asperger Publishing Company.

Bundy, A., Lane, S., & Murray, E. (2002). *Sensory integration theory and practice* (2nd ed.). Philadelphia: F. A. Davis Company.

Dunn, W. (2006). *Sensory profile school companion.* San Antonio, TX: The Psychological Corporation.

Fertel-Daly, D., Bedell, G., & Hinojosa, J. (2001). Effects of a weighted vest on attention to task and self-stimulatory behaviors in preschoolers with Pervasive Developmental Disorders. *American Journal of Occupational Therapy, 55*, 629–640.

Henry, D., Kane-Wineland, M., & Swindeman, S. (2007). *Tools for Tots: Sensory strategies for toddlers and preschoolers.* Glendale, AZ: Henry Occupational Therapy Services, Inc.

Honaker, D., & Rossi, L. M. (2005). Proprioception and participation at school: Are weighted vests effective? Appraising the evidence Parts 1 and 2. *Sensory Integration Special Interest Section Quarterly, 3, 4.*

Lin, S. H., Cermak, S., Coster, W. J., & Miller, L. (2005). The relation between length of institutionalization and sensory integration in children adopted from Eastern Europe. *The American Journal of Occupational Therapy, 59*(2), 148–152.

Kuhaneck, H. M., Henry, D. A., & Glennon, T. J. (2007). *Sensory processing measure.* Los Angeles: Western Psychological Services.

Miller, L. J., & Fuller, D.A. (2006). *Sensational kids: Hope and help for children with Sensory Processing Disorder.* New York: G. P. Putnam's Sons.

Miller, L. J., Anzalone M. E., Lane, S. J., Cermak, S. A., & Osten, E. T. (2007). Concept evolution in sensory integration: A proposed nosology for diagnosis. *American Journal of Occupational Therapy, 61*, 135–140.

Minshew, N. J., Sung, K., Jones, B. L., & Furman, J. M. (2004). Underdevelopment of the postural control system in autism. *Neurology, 63*, 2056–2061.

Molloy, C. A., Dietrich, K. N., & Bhattacharya, A. (2003). Postural stability in children with Autism Spectrum Disorder. *Journal of Autism and Developmental Disorders, 33*, 643–652.

Rimland, B. (1990). Sound sensitivity in autism. *Autism Research Review International, 4* (1), 6.

Sams, M. J., Fortney, E. V., & Willenbring, S. (2006). Occupational therapy incorporating animals for children with autism: A pilot investigation. *American Journal of Occupational Therapy, 60*, 268–274.

Schilling, D., & Schwartz, I. (2004). Alternative seating for young children with Autism Spectrum Disorder: Effects on classroom behavior. *Journal of Autism and Developmental Disorders, 34*, 423–432.

Tomchek, S., & Dunn, W. (2007). Sensory processing in children with and without autism: A comparative study using the Short Sensory Profile. *American Journal of Occupational Therapy, 61*, 190–200.

Wilbarger, P., & Wilbarger, J. L. (1991). *Sensory defensiveness in children aged 2–12. An intervention guide for parents and other caretakers.* Denver, CO: Avanti Educational Programs.

Williams, M. S. & Shellenberger, S. (1994). *How does your engine run? A leader's guide to the Alert Program for self-regulation.* Albuquerque, NM: Therapy Works, Inc.

Williamson, G., & Anzalone, M. (2001). *Sensory integration and self-regulation in infants and toddlers: Helping very young children interact with their environments.* Washington, DC: Zero to Three.

12

Assistive Technology for Students with Autism

Elizabeth West, Ph.D.
University of Washington

CHAPTER OBJECTIVES

After reading this chapter, learners should be able to:

1. List the benefits of assistive technology for students with Autism Spectrum Disorders.

2. Identify the categories of assistive technology.

3. Discuss the framework and rationale for considering the student, the environment, and the task when selecting an assistive technology device.

4. List the steps in the service delivery of assistive technology.

5. Discuss the components of collaboration when working with assistive technology.

 CASE STUDY **Examples**

Case of Gabriel

Gabriel is a student who has autism and is learning to read. When Gabriel was in preschool, he used a computer with preschool computer software to learn cause-and-effect skills. He accessed programs on the computer by using a modified mouse and a touch screen. Gabriel is getting older and needs access to literacy and communication skills, both written and expressive. Gabriel now uses a standard mouse and he benefits from hearing information on the computer with voice-output software. Gabriel is highly motivated by certain cartoon characters. Consequently, these characters were used as the foundation for many of the activities created for him. Gabriel's teacher took digital photographs of the cartoon characters and loaded them into computer programs to personalize the activities and increase Gabriel's motivation to learn literacy skills and improve communication. The programs allowed for individualization, visual cues, voice output, and options for scaffolding emergent skill development. Gabriel is provided with custom files that contain motivating graphics and are relevant to his understanding of language, provide for repetition and practice, and allow him to integrate new concepts in a way that supports his learning style.

Case of Grace

Grace is a teenager who benefits from the use of activity schedules to assist her with transitions across her school day. Grace was diagnosed with autism at an early age and is primarily nonverbal. Grace had difficulty with transitions and it was determined that Grace required more information to assist her with transitions. Grace learned how to use activity schedules at school that contained photographs of the various tasks and activities that she does throughout her school day. The photographs were sequenced in a portable, age-appropriate photo album. Initially, Grace was provided with prompts to access the schedule and initiate transitions. Gradually, the prompts were systematically faded and now Grace independently opens her book, turns to the appropriate page, and does the activity. Use of activity schedules has progressed from providing Grace with more information about her daily schedule to providing her with visual information about specific steps of activities. Use of this mid-tech solution—activity schedules—has assisted Grace in becoming more independent across her school day.

INTRODUCTION

Technology plays a pivotal role in the education of children with autism. Technology can take many forms and serve many functions. Integral to many programs developed for children with autism is the use of technology to assist in the attainment of critical skills necessary to lead a productive life.

Assistive technology (AT) is a generic term that includes assistive, adaptive, and rehabilitative devices and the process used in selecting, locating, and using them. AT promotes greater independence for students with disabilities and can be an equalizing force as these students gain access to inclusive environments. AT provides enhancements to or changed methods of interacting with the technology needed to accomplish tasks that promote positive educational outcomes. A formal, legal definition of AT was first published in the Technology-Related Assistance for Individuals with Disabilities Act of 1988 (The Tech Act). This act was amended in 1994 and in 1998 it was replaced with the Assistive Technology Act of 1998 ("AT Act"). Throughout this history, the original definition of assistive technology has remained consistent. The Tech Act of 1998 defines assistive or adaptive technology as "equipment or devices that are used to improve functioning of people with disabilities. The definition refers to products that are commercial as well as those that are customized for an individual."

The consideration of AT devices and services is required during the development of every individualized educational program (IEP) and every individual family service plan (IFSP) for children birth to school age. The Individuals with Disabilities Education Act (IDEA) of 1997 requires that each IEP/IFSP team considers and documents any AT devices and/or services that a child may need, with input from the family (see Box 12.1). Important to the IDEA mandate, upheld in the recent reauthorization, is the focus on both "**device**" and "**service**." It is not sufficient to merely provide access to a device with no "service." Services extend to students with disabilities or their caregivers to help

BOX 12.1   Diversity Notes #1

Generally thought to be helpful to any student whose needs seem to require them, assistive devices or services are useful only if the student's family wants them. In establishing assistive technology (AT) goals, IEP teams need to consider certain factors relating to the family's perception of their child's disability and also their ability to understand and implement the devices. Some families, for instance, prefer that their children remain dependent on family and community resources rather than have them gain independence by means of the AT device or service. Some families may want their children to be included with their peers, but others may be afraid that the device will mark their child as out of the ordinary, and still others may feel doubly stigmatized by the AT, already having to cope with the stigma of their minority status. The key to successful implementation of AT in the IEP is to consider the appropriateness of the device or service for a particular child, within the context of the family. Parette and McMahan (2002) formulated a detailed list of family goals and expectations regarding assistive technology, potential positive and negative outcomes, and possibly IEP responses in light of those outcomes. These researchers also provide a helpful set of questions that team members can pose to families regarding acceptance of the device within the family and community, expectations of results to be gained from its use, and the resources available.

---

them select, acquire, or use adaptive devices. Such services can include functional evaluations, training on devices, product demonstration, and equipment purchasing or leasing.

Students with autism can benefit from technology in many arenas of their lives: education, recreation, employment, and social. AT can assist students with autism by increasing their independence, developing communication and literacy skills, and building social competence. Influences in these areas serve to improve students' overall quality of life and equalize educational opportunities by promoting access to the general education setting.

Use of technology, specifically technology that relies heavily on visual input, may be of particular benefit for learners with ASD. One of the general trends that has been noted in children with autism is that they are visual learners and thinkers (Dettmer, Simpson, Myles, & Ganz, 2000; Edelson, 1998; Grandin, 1995a; Mesibov, 1998; Prizant & Rubin, 1999; Quill, 1997; Wheeler & Carter, 1998). Use of visual supports and strategies are of benefit for many individuals with autism which aligns well with the visual nature of technology (see Box 12.2).

BOX 12.2   Research Notes # 1

Sturmey (2003) authored an article highlighting the use of video technology across several studies. The use of video is an expanding technology and has potential to promote positive social, language, and academic outcomes for children with a variety of disabilities. Videos have been used in many ways, particularly to present peer, self, or adult models of appropriate behavior, to promote stimulus control of appropriate child behavior through nonsocial stimuli, and as one element in a comprehensive positive behavioral support package. New behaviors are addressed in this special section where research focused on perspective taking; independent, cooperative, and imaginative play; spontaneous requesting, and academic skills. Use of video technology across these novel areas demonstrated its power as a tool to support students with autism.

Source: Information from Sturmey, P. (2003). Video technology and persons with autism and other developmental disabilities: An emerging technology for PBS. *Journal of Positive Behavior Interventions, 5*(1), 3–4.

Recommended competencies in the area of AT have been identified by the Council for Exceptional Children. A subcommittee appointed by the National Association of State Directors of Special Education (NASDSE), called "Partnership of States," developed a statement of competencies for school district staff members working in the area of AT. See Figure 12.1 for a complete listing of the competencies. These competencies serve as a useful guide in the arena of technology, which advances at such a rapid pace that it may be difficult for the practitioner to keep up with current trends and recommendations in the field. This chapter serves to provide an overview of technology and its potential for applied use in the everyday lives of those students who are diagnosed with ASD.

I. Basic Knowledge of Assistive Technology (AT) Services and Devices
- Understand AT, including legal requirements, its purpose, and functional application for the student's educational program.
- Demonstrate awareness of a variety of AT devices and services and the ability to integrate technology into educational programs.
- Demonstrate knowledge in their specialty area of AT (e.g., access, alternative/augmentative communication, computer-based instruction, mobility, positioning, assistive listening and signaling devices, recreation/leisure/play, vision technology, environmental control, and activities of daily living).
- Demonstrate the ability to apply discipline specific knowledge regarding AT.
- Demonstrate the ability to use appropriate AT in a variety of educational settings.
- Demonstrate the recognition of the need for ongoing individual professional development and maintaining knowledge of emerging technologies.

II. Collaboration and Communication
- Understand the transdisciplinary nature of AT application and contribution of a variety of disciplines to the service delivery process.
- Understand skills required to serve as a member of a transdiciplinary team providing services for AT.
- Include parents as team members.
- Listen and respond to input from other team members.
- Demonstrate effective group process skills.
- Know when and where to refer to other resources for AT.
- Utilize resources to meet technology needs for students with disabilities.
- Demonstrate the ability to network with others in the community, including parents and general educators, for technical information and problem solving.

III. Assessment, Planning, and Implementation Process
Assessment:
- Identify appropriate, qualified team members necessary to determine AT needs and strengths.
- Determine, in collaboration with other members of the assessment team, AT needs as part of a comprehensive transdisciplinary evaluation that addresses all areas related to the disability and is based on student's strengths, tasks, and expectations.
- Use appropriate data-gathering procedures and strategies to conduct an AT evaluation utilizing a team approach to assess the student in customary environments.
- Integrate and discuss, in collaboration with the transdisciplinary team, all evaluation information including formulating recommendations and preparing a report.

FIGURE 12.1 Assistive Technology Competencies

Planning:
- Develop a plan utilizing appropriate, qualified team members.
- Identify and design appropriate AT devices, services, and strategies in the plan.

Implementation:
- Implement the plan using a collaborative approach.
- Evaluate, measure, and report on the effectiveness of the plan to meet the student's needs.
- Modify the plan as required to meet the student's needs.
- Identify areas that require further assessment or reevaluation on an ongoing basis.

IV. Resources
- Identify, in collaboration with team members, AT resources at the classroom, building, district, region, community, state, and national level; funding resources; product resources (e.g., augmentative communication, computer access); print and electronic resources (e.g., books, Web sites, journals, list serves); human resources (e.g., individuals who can provide assessment, training, and customization); and problem solving (e.g., maintenance and repair).
- Recognize own scope of knowledge and skills, and utilize identified resources to augment knowledge and skills represented within the team.
- Serve as a resource for others.
- Identify staff development needs and opportunities that meet needs.
- Participate in staff development opportunities that address identified needs.

FIGURE 12.1 (*continued*)

AREAS OF HUMAN FUNCTION

Categories

When decisions are being made about the provision of AT services for individuals with ASD, it is important to base them on factors related to human function rather than on diagnosis. The real issue is the difficulties the student has in functioning within his or her environment and how to provide adequate supports.

The term *function* can be defined as an action that a person takes in response to a demand to meet some need. Human functions can be grouped into several categories. The National Assistive Technology Research Institute (NATRI; see Internet Resources) staff have categorized AT according to seven **areas of human function**. This conceptualization is adapted from Melichar's (1978) work to categorize and locate assistive and adaptive devices according to their functional applications. These seven categories are highlighted below.

EXISTENCE   The first and most basic category, existence, refers to those functions that are needed to sustain life. These functions include feeding, elimination, bathing, dressing, grooming, and sleeping. Services for students with ASD may focus on teaching them how to perform such functions. Numerous devices exist to assist students in performing these functions.

COMMUNICATION   Numerous communicative functions exist; specifically, oral and written expression, visual and auditory reception, internal processing of information, and social interaction. Use of technology, specifically use of **augmentative and alternative communication (AAC)**, is of great benefit given that communication difficulties are a core deficit for children with ASD. An AAC system is an "integrated group of components, including the symbols, aids, strategies, and techniques used by individuals to enhance communication" (American Speech-Language-Hearing Association,

1991, p. 10). Qualities of visual systems for communication appear to match the cognitive strengths of students with autism (Quill, 1995). Given the communicative needs of students with ASD, practitioners have relied upon AAC to assist students in becoming functional communicators both in the present and with a vision toward the future (Beukelman & Mirenda, 1998).

AAC systems can range from relatively **low-tech** systems (i.e., simple adaptations with no batteries or electronics, such as communication boards and conversation books) to **high-tech** devices (i.e., complex electronic or computer driven technologies). AAC systems may be roughly classified into one of two categories: unaided communication systems and aided communication systems (Beukelman & Mirenda, 1998; Romski & Sevcik, 1988). **Unaided AAC systems** do not require any sort of external communication device for production of expressive communications and may include sign language, facial expressions, gestures, and nonsymbolic vocalizations. **Aided AAC systems** require an external communication device for production and include the use of picture communication boards and voice output devices (Beukelman & Mirenda, 1998; Miller & Allaire, 1987).

The primary emphasis of communication intervention has shifted to the acquisition of functional communication skills within natural environments. Although structured approaches are still utilized, best practices today emphasize functional language skills within natural daily routines and natural environments (Beukelman & Mirenda, 1998; Calculator & Jorgensen, 1991). **Functional communication** is "the actual use of language to achieve predetermined purposes. In order to be functional, language must influence others' behaviors and bring about effects that are appropriate and natural in a given social context" (Calculator & Jorgensen, 1991, p. 204). Functional communication may promote literacy learning given the visual nature of reading and writing and the strong visual-spatial strengths of children with ASD.

One example of a contemporary and frequently used approach to functional communication is the **Picture Exchange Communication System (PECS)** (Bondy & Frost, 1994). Practitioners utilizing the PECS program emphasize communicative exchanges as students are taught to request and comment by giving picture cards to a communication partner. The effectiveness of PECS with individuals having autism has been established (Charlop-Christy, Carpenter, Le, LeBlanc, & Kellet, 2002; Kravits, Kamps, Kemmerer, & Potucek, 2002; Liddle, 2001).

Numerous AAC devices exist, focusing on output and input methods. **Voice output communication aids (VOCA)** are portable AAC devices that produce synthesized or digitized speech. In addition to using output methods for communication, AAC interventions have also been used to communicate input from others. Several case studies demonstrate the effectiveness of using visual symbols to augment communication (Hodgdon, 1995; Quill, 1997; Peterson et al., 1995). Several "input" methods exist—specifically the use of visual schedules, where children with ASD access a visual representation to assist with comprehension of activity sequences. Visual schedules have been used in many ways to facilitate the attainment of numerous skills. See Box 12.3 for examples of innovative uses of **multimedia supports** with **activity schedules**.

BOX 12.3   Research Notes #2

Stromer et al. (2006) reviewed selected literature that focused on integrating multimedia computer supports with activity schedules. It is suggested that this is an effective way to teach students to manage their work, play, and skill-building activities independently. Originally, activity schedules were used to promote independent performance by using pictures and words to cue a student's performance through a sequence of activities. Activity schedules have become more technologically advanced, resulting in an expansion of existing repertoires. Activity schedules have progressed to a computer format that engages the learner with videos, sounds, dialogue, images, and words as instructional stimuli. The authors of this article suggest that this new avenue has implications for both researchers and teachers. The researcher is provided with a framework to study play, socialization, and communication using a blend of computer and notebook activity schedules. For the teacher, use of activity schedules in varied formats may facilitate the attainment of generative and functional skills.

Source: Information from Stromer, R., Kimball, J. W., Kinney, E. M., & Taylor, B. A. (2006). Activity schedules, computer technology, and teaching children with autism spectrum disorders. *Focus on Autism and Other Developmental Disabilities, 21*(1), 14–24.

Closely aligned with the category of communication is the need for behavioral support. Strong empirical support exists for the use of functional communication training to replace challenging behaviors. Individuals with ASD are able to learn to use AAC to replace challenging behavior (Mirenda, 1997). The AAC form must serve as a functional equivalent to the challenging behavior (Horner et al., 1990) and a systematic approach has been designed to assist practitioners in this endeavor.

BODY SUPPORT, PROTECTION, AND POSITIONING   Some students need assistance to maintain a stable position or support portions of their body. Students with ASD who have fine- and/or gross-motor difficulties as well as sensory difficulties may require the support of devices in this functional category. An array of materials may be used to meet the student's need for support and input. Examples include the use of weighted vests, stability balls, tactile toys, vibrating pens, and platform swings.

TRAVEL AND MOBILITY   Functions in this category include crawling, walking, using stairs, lateral and vertical transfers, and navigation of the environment. Wheelchairs, special lifts, canes, walkers, specially adapted tricycles, and crutches can be used to support these functions.

ENVIRONMENTAL INTERACTION   The environment can be adapted or the student can adapt to the environment. Environmental interaction includes functions associated with these adaptations as seen in the performance of many of the activities of daily living, both indoors and outdoors. Examples include food preparation, operation of appliances, accessing facilities, and alteration of the living space. It may be necessary to make a number of modifications to school facilities to accommodate functions in this category.

EDUCATION AND TRANSITION   Functions in this category include those associated with school activities and various types of therapies. Numerous technologies may be used within the context of schools and can include **computer-assisted instruction (CAI)**, audio instructional tapes, print magnifiers, book holders, and other materials and equipment that can facilitate education. CAI includes the use of computer-delivered prompts, systematic learning programs, technology-based curricular adaptations, writing programs with word predication, and virtual reality. Computer software, such as Boardmaker, allows for the creation of environmentally specific visual language tools for language boards or VOCA displays. Other software programs, such as Picture-It, Pix-Writer, and Writing with Symbols 2000, provide iconic representations for phrases and sentences and can be used to create Social Stories™ and adapted curricular materials. Children with autism may also benefit from CAI in reading. Chen and Bernard-Optiz (1993) compared delivery of academic tasks by an instructor through a computer monitor and found higher performance and more interest from children in the CAI than the adult-delivered intervention. Heimann et al. (1995) used a CAI program and a traditional instructional approach to present lessons to students. Children with autism made significant gains in the CAI program compared with traditional instruction. Collaborative virtual environments have also been used to facilitate the attainment of specific skills (see Box 12.4).

BOX 12.4 Trends and Issues Notes #2

A *virtual environment* (VE) can be defined as a computer-generated three-dimensional simulation of a real or imaginary environment (Cobb, Kerr, & Glover, 2001). One emerging area for children with autism is the use of collaborative virtual environments (CVE; Moore, D., Cheng, Y., McGrath, P., & Powell, N. J., 2005). CVEs have begun to be used as an assistive technology, as an educational technology, and as a means of helping address potential theory-of-mind impairments. Central to the use of CVEs is the notion of an on-screen avatar. The user can interact within this environment using a self-selected avatar, defined as a representation of the user's identity within the computer environment (Gerhard, 2003). In a CVE, there can be more than one user, and the users can communicate with each other using their self-selected avatars. Moore, Cheng, McGrath, and Powell (2005) define a *CVE* as a "distributed computer-based virtual space... in which people can meet and interact with others via their avatars" (p. 232). Avatars can potentially provide presence and social facilitation for those involved in a CVE. Given the impairments that individuals with autism exhibit, use of a CVE may have potential benefit. CVEs may promote communication amongst users and facilitate social skills as a range of scenarios to practice are provided. Use of this technology is in its infancy, however, and as technology advances, research will be needed to demonstrate its efficacy.

Source: Information from Moore, D., Cheng, Y., McGrath, P., & Powell, N. J. (2005). Collaborative virtual environment technology for people with autism. *Focus on Autism and Other Developmental Disabilities, 20*(4), 231–243.

SPORTS, FITNESS, AND RECREATION Functions associated with group and individual play, sports, games, hobbies, and leisure time are included in this functional category. There is a wide array of equipment and devices that can facilitate functions in this category to promote active participation.

Technology can take many forms to serve the above functions—from the low-tech picture drawing to the high-tech voice output system. Blackhurst (1997) provides a continuum of technology-based solutions ranging from no-tech, low-tech, **medium-tech**, and high-tech tools (see Table 12.1). As illustrated in the table, AT can be used for different objectives with different children with disabilities.

Handleman and Harris (2000) describe several areas that are important in comprehensive early education programs for children with ASD. These areas are: social and cognitive development, verbal and nonverbal communication, adaptive skills, increased competence in motor activities, and

TABLE 12.1 Examples of Technology Solutions

	Technology to Increase Access	Technology as Instructional Tool
No-Tech	Physical, speech, or occupational therapy	Systematic teaching procedures
Low-Tech	Pencil with rubber grip Velcro fastener Raised desk to accommodate wheelchairs	Flash cards Overhead projector Chalkboard
Medium-Tech	Wheelchair Hearing aid	Calculators Instructional videotape
High-Tech	Adaptive keyboards Speech synthesizer Virtual reality devices	Instructional computer software Interactive multimedia systems Computer text with hypermedia links

Source: Information adapted from Blackhurst, E. (1997, May/June). Perspectives on technology in special education. *Volume number required*, 41–48.

amelioration of behavioral difficulties. These areas are not specific to early education programs as each domain is critical to the lives of individuals with autism at every age. As noted, AT can take many forms and serve many functions as it is used in interventions to assist students to meet specific goals in comprehensive educational programs.

ASSISTIVE TECHNOLOGY SERVICE DELIVERY SYSTEMS

The Process

A typical AT delivery system consists of assessment, acquisition, application, and an evaluation (refer to the Wisconsin Assistive Technology Initiative [WATI] Internet resource for detail on delivery systems). Service delivery should include a detailed, systematic process for examining a student's abilities and difficulties and the demands of the environments and tasks. When considering AT, the environment and the tasks must be considered before tools are selected. To support this belief, the **SETT Framework** has been developed to aid in gathering and organizing data that can be used to make appropriate AT decisions. The SETT Framework considers first, the Student, the Environment(s), and the Tasks required for active participation in the activities of the environment; and, finally, the Tools needed for the student to address the tasks. Information about the Student, the Environments, and the Tasks, must be gathered and thoughtfully considered before an appropriate system of Tools can be proposed and acted upon. The outline of questions to consider in each area of the SETT Framework was developed as a guideline and a place to start. Teams gathering and acting upon this data may wish to seek answers to numerous additional questions. In virtually every case, however, any questions that arise will relate to one of the areas of the SETT Framework. Refer to Figure 12.2 for specific questions related to the framework.

The Student

1. What does the Student need to do?
2. What are the Student's special needs and current abilities?

The Environments

1. What are the instructional and physical arrangements? Are there special concerns?
2. What materials and equipments are currently available in the environments?
3. What supports are available to the student and the people working with the student on a daily basis?
4. How are the attitudes and expectations of the people in the environment likely to affect the student's performance?

The Tasks (be as specific as possible)

1. What activities occur in the student's natural environments that enable progress toward mastery of identified goals?
2. What is everyone else doing?
3. What are the critical elements of the activities?
4. How might the activities be modified to accommodate the student's special needs?

The Tools

1. What no-tech, low-tech, and high-tech options should be considered for inclusion in an assistive technology system for a student with these needs and abilities doing these tasks in these environments?
2. What strategies might be used to invite increased student performance?
3.. How might students try out the proposed system of tools in the customary environments in which they will be used?

FIGURE 12.2 SETT Questions

ASSESSMENT   The first step in the process involves assessing the technology-related needs of students with disabilities to determine if any equipment may be needed. Consideration of AT should occur during the very earliest stages of evaluating a student's eligibility for special education services. The successful use of any educational tool or strategy begins with an effective assessment of a student's individual needs. In order for AT to be effective, its selection and use must be grounded in a solid understanding of (a) a child's needs, strengths, and suitability for different assistive technologies; and (b) the technology's features, characteristics, demands, and suitability for the child (Office of Special Education Programs [OSEP], 2000).

During the assessment process, professionals must understand family needs for information, recognize the impact on and changes in family routines the AT will cause, and consider the extent to which family members desire themselves or their children to be accepted in community settings (Hourcade, Parette, & Huer, 1997). A clear understanding of these issues will provide the practitioner with culturally relevant information to assist in establishing a process that is culturally responsive (see Box 12.5).

BOX 12.5   Trends and Issues Notes #1

Access to the general education curriculum is emphasized by IDEA and includes the ability to obtain materials as well as the ability to understand and use them. Internet communications, multimedia, and universal design are providing new learning tools. Internet communications can transport students beyond their physical environments, allowing them to interact with people faraway and engage in interactive learning experiences. Students can also access electronic multimedia encyclopedias, library references, and online publications. Multimedia tools are another way in which information can be made accessible to students. Multimedia use of text, speech, graphics, pictures, audio, and video in reference-based software is especially effective. Although a picture can be worth a thousand words to one student, audio- or text-based descriptive video or graphic supports may help another student focus on the most important features of the materials. Used in conjunction with assistive technology, e-books can use the power of multimedia to motivate students to read. They include high-interest stories: the computer reads each page of the story aloud, highlighting the words as they are read. Fonts and colors can be changed to reduce distraction. Additional clicks of the mouse result in pronunciation of syllables and a definition of the word. When the student clicks on a picture, a label appears. A verbal pronunciation of the label is offered when the student clicks the mouse again. Word definitions can be added by electronic dictionaries and thesauruses. These books are available in multiple languages, including English and Spanish, so students can read in their native language while being exposed to a second language. The Center for Applied Special Technology (CAST) promotes the concept of universal design (Rose & Meyer, 2002), which asserts that alternatives integrated in the general curriculum can provide access to all students, including a range of backgrounds, learning styles, or abilities. Providing material in digital form, which can easily be translated, modified, or presented in different ways, can often attain the goal of universal design.

Source: Information from Behrmann, M., & Kinas, M. (2002). *Assistive technology for students with mild disabilities:Update.* Arlington VA: ERIC Clearinghouse on Disabilities and Gifted Education. (ERIC Document Reproduction Service No. ED463595).

Many barriers exist related to assessment, including lack of current and thorough information, lack of understanding of a child's environment, supplementary supports, changing needs of children, and costs of assessments (OSEP, 2000). **Education Tech Points** is a system that was developed to assist in consideration of AT (Bowser & Reed, 1995, 1998). Each Education Tech Point identifies the specific times within the planning and provision of specially designed instruction that the need for AT (both

- Education Tech Point #1—Initial Referral Questions
  When a child has an identified educational difficulty, assistive technology questions at the referral stage center around the specific problem that the student is experiencing and whether simple, readily available assistive technology utilized in the classroom might provide enough support that referral to special education would not be necessary.
- Education Tech Point #2—Evaluation Questions
  Questions for the evaluation team include whether the student can be evaluated accurately without assistive technology and what types of assistive technology might enhance the student's performance. The implications for school districts here are that evaluation center staff must have the same awareness-level training recommended for student service teams; in addition they need specific training on the requirements of IDEA and Section 504 for accommodations and modifications. They also need access to an array of assistive technology devices to use for evaluation purposes and to colleagues with expertise about assistive technology for various difficulties, including positioning, hand use, augmentative communication, computer access, and print access.
- Education Tech Point #3—Extended Assessment Questions
  Extended assessment is generally understood to mean a trial period. The questions to be addressed at the point of extended assessment of assistive technology needs are related to what specific tasks the student needs to be able to do and what, if any, assistive technology could possibly help.
- Education Tech Point #4—Plan Development Questions
  After the evaluation and assessment data have been assembled, an appropriate educational program must be developed. The school district must determine if assistive technology is needed for the child to receive a free, appropriate public education (FAPE). Implications for the school district include ensuring that staff members are trained in writing assistive technology into the IEP and that they include appropriate periodic review to identify and deal with unanticipated problems.
- Education Tech Point #5—Implementation Questions
  Implementation questions focus on responsibility for day-to-day operation. This area includes questions such as who will make sure the equipment is up and running, what will happen when it needs repair, and what the district will provide in the interim if they are going to seek outside funding to purchase a device.
- Education Tech Point #6—Periodic Review Questions
  IDEA requires the periodic review of each student's IEP. This review should include evaluation of the effectiveness of the assistive technology solutions in the child's plan. Questions at the point of periodic review center around whether the assistive technology devices and services that were planned and provided have actually had the intended effect.

FIGURE 12.3 Overview of Education Tech Points

devices and services) should be considered. Education Tech Points offer a way to integrate AT into the thinking of the IEP/IFSP team and the management system that each school district uses to ensure provision of appropriate services to children with disabilities. Key points to assist in making decisions regarding utilization of AT services and resources are identified and incorporated into the regular educational planning system. Initial Education Tech Point questions guide the IEP/IFSP team through the necessary steps to determine if a child may need an AT device or service. For a brief overview of each Education Tech Point, refer to Figure 12.3.

ACQUISITION Once a determination is made, the AT team sets out to acquire the device. A large barrier to acquisition is funding of services and supports.

APPLICATION Once a device has been acquired, the next step is to actually use the device with the student. During implementation, the Education Tech Point questions at points 5 and 6 can assist the education staff in monitoring the program in order to ensure that needed changes are addressed in a timely and efficient manner. Training of consumers is critical during the service delivery process. Determining exactly what to teach and how to teach it must be highly individualized not only to meet the needs of the child, but to fit into the beliefs and lifestyle of the family as well as teachers, therapists, and other persons who are involved. Whatever the family is counted upon to do must fit into their lifestyle and routines, and not be burdensome. To ensure that this occurs, everyone involved, and the family in particular, must have fundamentally agreed with both the choice of technology and its accompanying teaching program (see Box 12.6).

BOX 12.6   Diversity Notes #2

Professionals need to take into account and understand how a family's cultural, ethnic and/or socioeconomic background may impact decisions about the use of assistive technology with young children. A number of studies have found differences in family reactions to assistive technology across cultures. For example, many Asian and Native American families value and expect a certain degree of dependence on the family (Hourcade, Parette & Huer, 1997). In these cultures, the use of assistive technology for increased independence by very young children may not be considered important. On the other hand, a strong value of many African American families is to fit into their communities, rather than appear different (Parette, VanBiervliet & Hourcade, 2000). AT devices that draw considerable attention to a child's disability in public places may not be acceptable to these families. Additionally, families from low socioeconomic backgrounds often have pressing concerns about basic needs such as health care, food, work, and transportation that make it difficult for them to participate in AT evaluation and training sessions (Kemp and Parette, 2000). The priorities of these families may be very different from those of the professionals working with their child. These kinds of considerations obviously have important implications for the AT decision-making process.

During the application stage, it is critical for the trainer to identify and use those "teachable moments." Ideally, formal instruction should occur frequently and for short periods of time. This is easier to do when teaching is integrated into daily activities and routines, including playtime (i.e., naturalist teaching methods are useful). Children should be taught in natural settings, places in which the child is familiar and feels at ease. The essential philosophy of service provision has evolved from a focus on isolated skills taught during pullout therapy to an inclusive model in which functional skills are taught within natural environments.

EVALUATION   The success of the AT solution must be periodically evaluated and necessary adaptations must be made to the devices. A nationwide group of AT practitioners, known as the **Quality Indicators for Assistive Technology (QIAT)**, has developed a list of indicators of AT quality that can be used to guide the delivery and evaluation of AT services. The current version provides intent statements and identifies errors that are often committed when attempting to implement various AT services. The QIAT has focused its efforts on defining a set of descriptors that could serve as overarching guidelines for quality AT services (for more information visit the QIAT Web site at http://www.qiat.org). Descriptors developed by the Consortium can assist practitioners to develop and provide quality AT services.

COLLABORATION

Essential to the service delivery process is effective collaboration amongst a variety of individuals. In addition to the family and student, several people should be involved in the service delivery process, namely, a person knowledgeable about the student, a person knowledgeable in the area of curriculum, a person knowledgeable in the area of language, a person knowledgeable in the area of motor, and a person who can commit the district's resources. During an AT assessment, team members work together to find the most promising solutions for a student. This collaborative process that occurs within teams leads to the most appropriate solutions. The collaborative process should not stop after assessment is complete but be present to ensure sustainability of programs. Assessment and intervention should form a continuous and dynamic process that is directly influenced by collaboration.

Summary

Assistive technology (AT) can serve as a powerful equalizer in the lives of students with ASD and can facilitate access to a range of meaningful opportunities. Culturally relevant and responsive AT services and supports must be provided during each step of the decision-making, implementation, and evaluation process. AT can either be a blessing or a barrier. A collaborative process must be established where partnerships are forged to adequately reflect needs and desires. One of the greatest potentials for the use of technology is in the education of children with disabilities. Technology has the potential for dramatically improving the quality of education and the quality of life for children with ASD. Effective use of technology can foster independence, promote the development of communication and literacy skills, and build social competence.

Chapter Review Questions

1. Interview either a student who uses AT, a family member of a student who uses AT, or school personnel who support a student who uses AT and identify the reported benefits of AT. (Objective 1)
2. Create a diagram or visual representation of the categories of assistive technology and seven areas of human function. (Objective 2)
3. You have been asked to lead an IEP meeting where team members are considering the use of AT for a particular student. Identify and discuss the framework and rationale for considering the student, the environment, and the tasks required for active participation first before selecting the tools needed to address the tasks. (Objective 3)
4. Create a Venn diagram or another type of visual aid that outlines the service delivery system and depicts each step in the process. (Objective 4)
5. You have just received a new student who you feel needs AT supports and services. Identify the core components of collaboration and who you think should be involved in the process. (Objective 5)

Key Terms

Activity schedules *266*
Aided AAC systems *266*
Areas of human function *265*
Assistive technology (AT) *262*
Augmentative and alternative communication (AAC) *265*
Computer-assisted instruction *267*
Device *262*

Education Tech Points *270*
Functional communication *266*
High-tech *266*
Low-tech *266*
Medium-tech *268*
Multimedia supports *266*
Picture Exchange Communication System (PECS) *266*

Quality Indicators for Assistive Technology (QIAT) *272*
Service *262*
SETT Framework *269*
Unaided AAC systems *266*
Voice output communication aids (VOCA) *266*

Internet Resources

The TAM (Technology and Media) Division of the Council for Exceptional Children offers a variety of information about assistive technology and special education instructional technology.
http://www.tamcec.org

Florida Assistive Technology Education Network (ATEN) Homepage has tutorials that can be downloaded on a variety of assistive technology devices.
http://www.aten.scps.k12.fl.us/

Trace Research and Design Center includes software tool kits and many disability-related articles and papers.
http://trace.wisc.edu/world/computer_access/multi/sharewar.htm

The Family Village is a Web site designed to provide information for families with children with disabilities. This site offers extensive resources on AT.
http://www.familyvillage.wisc.edu/

Closing the Gap offers a variety of articles, resources, and interactive activities related to assistive technology.
http://www.closingthegap.com/index.lasso

Augmentative and alternative communication resource guide for young children.
http://aac.unl.edu/yaack/toc.html

Contains information on creating literacy-based communication boards and an excellent resource list on AAC.
http://www.aacintervention.com

The Wisconsin Assistive Technology Initiative (WATI) is recognized as a leader in the provision of statewide support for assistive technology services. Their site offers a wealth of practitioner-friendly resources.
http://www.wati.org/index.html

The National Assistive Technology Research Institute (NATRI) conducts assistive technology (AT) research, translates theory and research into AT practice, and provides resources for improving the delivery of AT services.
http://natri.uky.edu

The Quality Indicators for Assistive Technology (QIAT) Web site includes the work done to date to develop a comprehensive set of quality indicators for effective assistive technology services. Managed by Joy Zabala.
http://www.qiat.org/

CAST researches and develops ways to support all learners according to their individual strengths and needs through Universal Design for Learning (UDL).
http://www.cast.org/

This project provides information and consultation to AT programs. Locate the AT program in your state and read articles relating to legislation and AT.
http://www.resna.org/

This is a general site with information and resources for a range of assistive technology.
http://www.abilityhub.com/

ABLEDATA provides objective information about assistive technology products and rehabilitation equipment available from domestic and international sources.
http://www.abledata.com/

Matrices are provided to serve as resources that match technology tools with supporting literature on promising practices for the instruction of K–8 mathematics and reading for students with disabilities.
http://www.techmatrix.org/

Selected links on ASD including articles and sites with practical strategies.
http://www.lburkhart.com/index.html

This site contains information and resources as well as free printable picture symbols and charts to use for visual schedules and steps within tasks.
http://www.dotolearn.com/

This is a weekly newspaper for AAC users as well as emergent readers. Communication symbols are used along with the text.
http://news-2-you.com/

References

American Speech-Language-Hearing Association. (1991). Report: Augmentative and alternative communication. *ASHA, 33* (Suppl. 5), 9–12.

Assistive Technology Act of 1998. P.L. 105-394.

Behrmann, M., & Kinas, M. (2002). *Assistive technology for students with mild disabilities: Update 2002.* Arlington VA: ERIC Clearinghouse on Disabilities and Gifted Education. (ERIC Document Reproduction Service No. ED463595).

Beukelman, D. R., & Mirenda, P. (1998). *Augmentative and alternative communication: Management of severe communication disorders in children and adults* (2nd ed.). Baltimore: Brookes.

Blackhurst, E. (1997, May/June). Perspectives on technology in special education. *Teaching Exceptional Children, May/June, 29,* 41–48.

Bondy, A., & Frost, L. (1994). The picture-exchange communication system. *Focus on Autistic Behavior, 9,* 1–19.

Bowser, G., & Reed, P. (1995). Education TECH points for assistive technology planning. *Journal of Special Education Technology, 12*(4), 325–338.

Calculator, S., & Jorgensen, C. M. (1991). Integrating AAC instruction into regular education settings: Expounding on best practices. *Augmentative and Alternative Communication, 7,* 204–212.

Charlop-Christy, M., Carpenter, M., Le, L., LeBlanc, L., & Kellet, K. (2002). Using the picture exchange communication system (PECS) with children with autism: Assessment of PECS acquisition, speech, social-communicative behavior, and problem behavior. *Journal of Applied Behavioral Analysis, 35,* 213–231.

Chen, S. H. A., & Bernard-Optiz, V. (1993). Comparison of personal and computer-assisted instruction for children with autism. *Mental Retardation, 31,* 368–376.

Cobb, S., Kerr, S., & Glover, T. (2001). The AS interactive project: Developing virtual environments for social skills training in users with Asperger Syndrome. In K. Dautenhahn (Ed.), *Robotic and virtual interactive systems in autism therapy.* Hatfield, UK: University of Hertfordshire.

Dettmer, S., Simpson, R. L., Myles, B. S., & Ganz, J. B. (2000). The use of visual supports to facilitate transitions of students with autism. *Focus on Autism and Other Developmental Disabilities, 15,* 163–169.

Edelson, S. M. (1998). *Learning styles and autism.* From http://www.autism.org, retrieved January 16, 1998.

Gerhard, M. (2003). *A hybrid avatar/agent model for educational collaborative virtual environments.* Unpublished doctoral dissertation, Leeds Metropolitan University—UK.

Grandin, T. (1995). How people with autism think. In E. Schopler & G. Mesibov (Eds.), *Learning and cognition in autism: Current issues in autism* (pp. 137–156). New York: Plenum Press.

Handleman, J. S., & Harris, S. L. (2000). *Preschool education programs for children with autism.* Austin, TX: Pro-Ed.

Heimann, M., Nelson, K. E., Tjus, T., & Gilberg, C. (1995). Increasing reading and communications skills in children with autism through an interactive multimedia computer program. *Journal of Autism and Developmental Disorders, 25,* 459–480.

Hodgdon, L. (1995). *Visual strategies for improving communication.* Troy: MI: QuirkRoberts.

Horner, R. H., Dunlap, G., Koegel, R. L., Carr, E. G., Sailor, W., Anderson, J., et al. (1990). Toward a technology of nonaversive behavior support. *Journal of the Association for Persons with Severe Handicaps, 10*(3), 172–175.

Hourcade, J. J., Parette, H. P., & Huer, M. B. (1997). Family and cultural alert! Considerations in assistive technology assessment. *Teaching Exceptional Children, 30*(1), 40–44.

Kemp, C. E., & Parette, H. P. (2000). Barriers to minority family involvement in assistive technology decision-making processes. *Education and Training in Mental Retardation and Developmental Disabilities, 35*(4), 384–392.

Kravits, T., Kamps, D., Kemmerer, K., & Potucek, J. (2002). Brief report: Increasing communication skills for an elementary-aged student with autism using the picture exchange communication system.

Journal of Autism and Developmental Disorders, 32, 225–230.

Liddle, K. (2001). Implementing the picture exchange communication system (PECS). *International Journal of Language & Communication Disorders, 36*(Suppl.), 391–395.

Melichar, J. F. (1978). ISAARE: A description. *AAESPH Review, 3*, 259–268.

Mesibov, G. B. (1998). *Learning styles of students with autism.* From http://www.autism-soceity.org/packages/edkids_learning-styles.html, retrieved January 16, 1998.

Miller, J. F., & Allaire, J. (1987). Augmentative communication. In M. A. Snell (Ed.), *Systematic instruction of persons with severe handicaps* (3rd ed., pp. 273–296). Upper Saddle River, NJ: Merrill/Pearson Education.

Mirenda, P. (1997). Functional communication training and augmentative communication: A research review. *Augmentative and Alternative Communication, 13*, 207–225.

Moore, D., Cheng, Y., McGrath, P., & Powell, N. J. (2005). Collaborative virtual environment technology for people with autism. *Focus on Autism and Other Developmental Disabilities, 20*(4), 231–243.

Office of Special Education Programs (2000). *Synthesis on the selection and use of assistive technology.* Washington, DC: U.S. Department of Education.

Parette, H. P., VanBiervliet, A., & Houcade, J. J. (2000). Family-centered decision making in assistive technology. *Journal of Special Education Technology, 15*, 45–55.

Peterson, S., Bondy, A., Vincent, Y., & Finnegan, C. (1995). Effects of altering communicative input for students with autism and no speech: Two case studies. *Augmentative and Alternative Communication, 11*, 93–100.

Prizant, B. M., & Rubin, E. (1999). Contemporary issues in interventions for autism spectrum disorders: A commentary. *Journal of the Association for Persons with Severe Handicaps, 24*, 199–208.

Quill, K. A. (1995). Visually cued instruction for children with autism and Pervasive Developmental Disorders. *Focus on Autistic Behavior, 10*, 10–20.

Quill, K. A. (1997). Instructional considerations for young children with autism: The rationale for visually cued instruction. *Journal of Autism and Developmental Disorders, 27*, 697–714.

Romski, M. A., & Sevcik, R. A. (1988). Augmentative and alternative communication systems: Considerations for individuals with severe intellectual disabilities. *Augmentative and Alternative Communication, 2*, 83–93.

Rose, D. H., & Meyer, A. (2002). *Teaching every student in the digital age: Universal design for learning.* Alexandria, VA: ASCD.

Stromer, R., Kimball, J. W., Kinney, E. M., & Taylor, B. A. (2006). Activity schedules, computer technology, and teaching children with autism spectrum disorders. *Focus on Autism and Other Developmental Disabilities, 21*, 14–24.

Sturmey, P. (2003). Video technology and persons with autism and other developmental disabilities: An emerging technology for PBS. *Journal of Positive Behavior Interventions, 5*(1), 3–4.

Technology-Related Assistance for Individuals with Disabilities Act of 1988. P.L. 100-407.

Wheeler, J. J., & Carter, S. L. (1998). Using visual cues in the classroom for learners with autism as a method for promoting positive behavior. *B.C. Journal of Special Education, 21*, 64–73.

13

Transition and Adulthood

Charles Dukes, Ph.D. BCBA
Florida Atlantic University

CHAPTER OBJECTIVES

After reading this chapter, learners should be able to:

1. Describe the different dimensions of adulthood and how each may or may not apply to individuals with Autism Spectrum Disorders (ASD).

2. Discuss the advantages and disadvantages of using a distinct point in time as an indicator of adulthood, from the perspectives of families, professionals, and individuals with ASD.

3. Define *transition* according to the Individuals with Disabilities Education Improvement Act (IDEIA) of 2004 noting important changes from 1997 (ASD).

4. Relate each of the guiding principles of transition to a specific outcome appropriate for an individual with ASD.

5. Summarize the roles of families, professionals, and the personal responsibility of individuals with ASD in the transition process.

 ### CASE STUDY   Examples

Case of Sam

Sam is an 11th grader with autism. He has done well academically in school attending some classes with his typically developing peers, while also attending classes exclusively for students with disabilities. Parents and educators at Sam's high school have been discussing the move toward inclusive education for a number of years and recently the goal has been to create a continuum of services that include academic courses where both students with and without disabilities attend the same classes. Under the old system Sam would not have had any classes with general education students. This transition to inclusive education has been challenging for students and educators. Sam is still in need of additional time to complete some assignments and his Individualized Education Program (IEP) requires that he receive direct instruction in social skills. As a result, the IEP team struggled with where exactly to embed social skills instruction into an already loaded curriculum sequence. The process has taken planning and active participation from all members of the IEP team, including Sam's parents and Sam himself. Sam's involvement is encouraged as both his teachers and parents are concerned that he be able to articulate his needs and recruit help when needed once he leaves high school. Sam is doing well and the inclusion in general education classrooms has been advantageous on a number of fronts.

Case of Jonathan

Jonathan is a young adult with autism in his second year of postsecondary education at a 4-year institution. The transition from high school to the university has been quite difficult. Both the academic and social challenges have been more than he expected. Many of his professors report that he seems distracted and unable to engage in content-related discussions during class. Jonathan has trouble following the often quickly paced verbal-only lectures the professors seem to use exclusively. The differences between high school and the university are vast and have had an impact on Jonathan's academic performance. Individual help is available in the Office for Students with Disabilities (OSD), but this requires a formal process that Jonathan was not familiar with until late in the second semester. In addition, assistance from OSD requires individual students to approach professors and negotiate appropriate accommodations. Jonathan has found this most challenging as some professors are more open than others and some seem to be completely unresponsive to his requests for assistance with some assignments. There are some advantages to the university experience, as some restaurants surrounding the university and even some restaurants on campus allow students to hang out late at night. This experience has been fun for Jonathan as he learns to interact with some other students in these social settings.

Case of Donald

Donald is married with two children. He was not diagnosed with Asperger Syndrome until the age of 50; he is now 57. He can recall a long history of never quite understanding his social environment. In spite of his talent for working with almost all things electrical (e.g., stereos), he seemed to find a reason to lose a number of jobs throughout his life. That is how his friends described his knack for losing jobs; somehow it was always his fault. Of course, Donald did not see it that way and he has spent the later part of his life trying to gain some clarity about his strengths and weaknesses in social situations. Donald has slowly gained a better understanding of his own limitations, but at the same time he has learned that he was not the only one with limitations and that many adults did not have all the answers to the most pertinent questions in life either. Donald has been able to leave the frequent misunderstandings and awkward social situations behind by asking questions when he does not understand something and asking people to allow him time to make a point if necessary. While these strategies certainly do not eliminate all problems, it does create a better overall social experience. He now enjoys living with his wife and children and making connections with others to form friendships on terms he can accept and understand.

INTRODUCTION: BECOMING AN ADULT: WHAT DOES IT MEAN FOR INDIVIDUALS WITH ASD?

On the surface, this is a very simple question. For an individual with an ASD, becoming an adult represents the same developmental stage that all humans reach at a point in their lives. In other words, eventually we all grow up and become an adult. The meaning of **adulthood** can be elusive when more closely examined; it is inevitable that humans will age, but there are other factors related to adulthood that also require development. It almost goes without saying that many individuals without disabilities have moments, perhaps more than others, when a parent says or does something that somehow transforms the situation from a completely legitimate conversation to one reminiscent of childhood. The dimensions of adulthood are vast and may never be fully mastered. The legal age of adulthood in many Western countries is 18, but using age as an indicator of adulthood seems extremely inadequate even for individuals without disabilities. For individuals with ASD, it is even more problematic, as many of these individuals are still receiving services in secondary schools (i.e., high schools) where there are oftentimes only limited opportunities to live and be treated as an adult. (For more information on adult outcomes of individuals with ASD, see Box 13.1.)

BOX 13.1   Research Notes

There is little known about the long-term outcomes of individuals with ASD. A number of issues impact our current state of knowledge. The diagnostic methods used at different points in history and the variability among treatment are only two reasons why understanding the long-term prognosis for individuals with ASD is so difficult. In this study, 120 individuals were followed up after a period of between 17 and 40 years. All individuals were diagnosed in the 1970s or 1980s and were rated on their outcomes at the time of the follow-up. Sets of criteria were used to create a scale ranging from good to very poor outcomes. The criteria included employment status, having friends, social progress, and others. A majority of the 108 individuals who were included in the follow-up study reported outcomes that were rated as poor or very poor. This result may be due in part to the presence of a disability, but in addition, low IQ has been cited as an important factor in predicting outcomes as well. The implication is that although the symptoms of autism do contribute to outcomes, it is also possible that IQ also plays a role.

Source: Information from Billstedt, E., Gillberg, C., & Gillberg, C. (2005). Autism after adolescence: Population-based 13- to 22-year follow-up study of 120 individuals with autism diagnosed in childhood. *Journal of Autism and Developmental Disorders, 35*(3), 351–360.

The meaning of adulthood is not completely straightforward, but for many, there are a number of dimensions that can be used to indicate adulthood. Age is one of the most prominent indicators. There are a number of privileges (e.g., operating a motor vehicle) and responsibilities (e.g., voting in local and national elections) that coincide with becoming an 18-year-old. But in the case of individuals with ASD, this age threshold does not make sense. For some, turning 18 may lead to a new level of **independence** (see Sam in the opening case example), but there is still a need for a greater level of support in comparison to typically developing peers. It is important to note that many individuals regardless of disability status will need support from parents and others after turning 18 and graduating from high school, but the point here is that many of the specialized supports that benefit individuals with ASD in high school will need to be re-conceptualized to fit the new environment even after leaving high school. Thus, age does not seem to constitute an adequate indicator of adulthood for individuals with ASD.

Employment is one of the most popular indictors of adulthood. Many individuals begin working shortly after becoming 16 years old, and the movement to prepare individuals with disabilities for the world of work has a storied history (see Stull & Sanders, 2003, for a review). The notion of people working directly after leaving high school is not a new concept and movement along a career path is a clear indicator of adulthood. In spite of the low rates of employment for individuals with disabilities in general (National Organization on Disability, 2004) and individuals with ASD specifically (Holmes, 2007), employment is also an inadequate indicator of adulthood. Job placement and employment experiences in contrast to **competitive employment** often make up the limited options for individuals with ASD. These contrived employment options are necessary and should be continued, but it should be noted that these contrived experiences do not match typical experiences and should not be used as an indication that an individual has or has not achieved adulthood.

Yet another possible indicator of adulthood is independence from one's parents (e.g., financial, residential, etc.). The ability to engage in self-care is perhaps one of the most highly anticipated yet feared events during the course of raising children. The daily tasks of adulthood are broad, including routine personal hygiene, care for the home, and seeking assistance when medical care is needed or even preparing for a natural disaster. Living independently is highly valued in many Western societies but requires a great deal of skill and access to a number of resources. The scope of independence is so broad and dependent on a number of factors that using it as a single indictor of adulthood is also inadequate for individuals with ASD.

Cultural diversity is a well-documented reality in the greater society as well as in schools specifically (Shakespear, Beardsley, & Newton, 2003). The previously mentioned indicators of adulthood were largely based on Western traditions of child rearing that lead to generally accepted outcomes associated with adulthood (see Turnbull & Turnbull, 2001 for a comparison of cultural perspectives). These indicators are not based on empirical investigations but rather on cultural conceptions of adulthood. In this sense, culture refers to the broad exchange of traditions in Western countries. There are of course other exchanges of traditions based on experiences of people from other countries as well. These cultural traditions may have an impact on the conception of adulthood and even be in contrast to some of the previously mentioned indicators above. As children age and needs change, many families may make decisions based on their cultural identity and not based on the disability status (see Harry, Kalanpur, & Day, 1999, for a number of examples). This may have implications for indicators of adulthood as some families may be concerned with their children making certain contributions to the family or carrying on particular family traditions. These concepts of adulthood may be just as important as the previously mentioned indicators (e.g., employment). Similar to the other indicators of adulthood already discussed, culture is also an insufficient single indicator of adulthood, but rather one in addition to several other dimensions (see Box 13.2).

At this point the picture may seem bleak and muddled with a number of variables and considerations that do not necessarily lead in one clear direction. This is only partially true. The indicators of adulthood are multidimensional and will be at least somewhat different for different individuals on the spectrum. A critical consideration for the **transition** to adulthood for individuals with ASD is that the dimensions of adulthood cannot be viewed in terms of presence or absence, but rather as a matter of degree. In other words, it may be that for some individuals, living independently simply means having a corner of the family home. Or perhaps another individual works in a restaurant for part of the day and uses public transportation to get to and from her family home. In each of these

BOX 13.2   Diversity Notes # 1

Families and professionals work diligently to ensure that individuals with ASD receive the most effective treatment available. As individuals with ASD age, needs change and therefore services and supports must change as well. Currently, there is little known about how culture may affect families' choices for interventions early or later in life. In a review of studies conducted by Mandell and Novak (2005), several studies were reviewed in an effort to answer this question. While the literature base is small, there are several findings of note. Families from different cultural backgrounds may interpret symptoms slightly differently, leading to different choices for treatment. In addition, families from different cultural backgrounds may also hold different beliefs about the causes of autism, also leading to different choices in treatment. Finally, diverse families differentially interact with professionals from the health care system. Some groups, most notably African Americans, may not have regular contact with health care professionals, leading to later diagnosis and different interpretations about recommendations for treatment. In spite of the paucity of literature, it is important to note culture may very well account for some of the variance in decision making for intervention both early and later in life.

examples, the adult may be viewed as not meeting the generally accepted status for independent living or employment, but each individual is living and employed to a particular degree. This is critical for individuals with ASD, as adulthood can be achieved if families and professionals can conceptualize adulthood as a fluid concept that is defined differently for different individuals (autobiographies by individuals with ASD also shed light on individual differences; see Box 13.3).

BOX 13.3   Trends and Issues Notes # 1

In recent years there has been a great interest in autism. Part of this interest may be traced back to the popular film, *Rain Man*, starring Dustin Hoffman and the many amazing feats he seemed to be able to perform with his memory. This combined with the fact that some individuals with ASD have verbalized their experiences and shared with the rest of the world the so called "mysteries of autism." Several individuals have written autobiographical accounts of their experiences in books that seemingly recount for others the trials, tribulations, and success of living with autism. This body of work may provide families and professionals with a personal perspective that is unlike any other. These books may serve as a starting point for understanding the realities of adulthood for individuals with ASD. This body of work provides families and professionals with stories about "real people" encountering "real life situations." By reading these personal accounts, it may be possible to identify similarities and even gain greater insight into the life of an individual with an ASD. Clearly, families and professionals will need to do more than read research studies or personal accounts, but having access to sound information about outcomes for adults with ASD can have a positive impact on perspectives for the future.

For further reading, refer to the partial list of works below:

Grandin, T., & Scariano, M. (1986). *Emergence labeled autistic.* Tunbridge Wells, Kent.
Costello. Novato: Arena Press.
Grandin, T. (1995). *Thinking in pictures: and other reports from my life with autism.* New York: DoubleDay.
Williams, D. (1992). *Nobody nowhere.* London: Corgi Books.
Williams, D. (1994). *Somebody somewhere.* London: Corgi Books.

In the absence of a clear comprehensive list that can serve as a starting point for the transition to adulthood, it is necessary to choose a point in time to think about an individual as an adult. This point in time does not imply that the transition process should not start earlier in life. In fact, the Individuals with Disabilities Education Improvement Act (IDEIA, 2004) requires that transition be a part of the Individualized Education Program (IEP) process beginning at the age of 16. The point here is that transition services should start early, but adulthood and all the related dimensions start at a different point. Individuals with ASD are served well by a clear point of departure from childhood to adulthood to help guide families, professionals, and most importantly the individuals themselves to re-conceptualize services and supports in the adult context. A logical starting point from which to begin the transition process to adulthood is the point in time when individuals are no longer the responsibility of the public schools (Chadsey-Rusch & Gonzalez, 1988). This view allows both families and professionals to anticipate a clear point in time from which all stakeholders should work collaboratively to interact with the individual with an ASD to the greatest extent possible as an adult. There are a number of advantages to framing the context of adulthood as a distinct period in one's life. First, in spite of deficits or lack of skill, all individuals will leave school and thus reach adulthood and can be treated as such. Second, this perspective eliminates the need for individuals to obtain employment, live independently, or engage in any of the other often-used adult indicators. This is important for many individuals, as many of these adult dimensions will not necessarily resemble typically developing peers, yet still may be obtainable to some degree. In this view, transition to adulthood is defined as a period in time when services and supports simply change and growth is not viewed as the end to a particular process, but rather a process whereby individuals can eventually live as happy adults. A final advantage of framing the context of adulthood as a distinct period in one's life is that families and professionals can begin to think about services and supports in a different context outside school. Professionals associated with the school system provide many of the services and supports individuals with ASD require. This is simply a reality of the current service delivery models, but life after the school system can be difficult for families, as the organization of the adult service system is not the same and in fact may require more time, resources, and perhaps a high level of assertiveness from the families.

The requirements of adulthood are many and do not follow a distinct developmental trajectory for individuals with or without disabilities. In an effort to better understand adulthood and its impact on individuals with ASD, a collection of unifying themes for consideration will be put forth. These themes are not exhaustive, but rather provide a broad basis by which to lay a foundation for the transition process to adulthood. These themes should be thought of as pertaining to all aspects of the process. There are three unifying themes that provide continuity to the transition process. First, the unique needs of individuals with ASD must be understood. Families, professionals, and individuals with ASD (to the extent possible) must be able to articulate their needs to individuals unfamiliar with ASD. Particularly, as individuals with ASD age, they will need to develop skills in self-advocacy and learn how to articulate their needs to a range of different people (see Test, Fowler, Wood, Brewer, & Eddy, 2005 for a description of a self-advocacy model). According to Morgan (1996), individuals with ASD must make sense of their world, discover services meaningful to them, and then based on this exploration, to the greatest extent possible, take an active role in designing their own services and supports. The idea that individuals with ASD must act as their own advocate is not insignificant by any means. Although three different themes are included in this section, it is also possible to see each of these themes as an outgrowth of some aspect of **self-determination**. For the sake of clarity, self-determination will be described last, but it is important to note that transition to adulthood cannot be discussed without a clear understanding and promotion of all aspects of self-determination. In addition, when discussing self-determination, there are a number of related issues that also must be discussed (see below for details). A second theme providing continuity to the transition process is the concept of

person-centered planning (PCP). There are a number of planning processes using PCP (see Holburn & Vietze, 2002) as a central theme, but here the meaning is general in nature. It is necessary to place the individuals with ASD at the center of the planning process by ensuring that unique needs are recognized. In addition, the transition process must take into account that individuals with ASD are members of a family network and cultural/linguistic group. These additional considerations are also necessary to fully understand transition as a comprehensive planning process that involves not only the tasks of adulthood (e.g., employment), but also the responsibilities of adulthood (e.g., making decisions about activities). The third theme unifying the transition process is self-determination. The extant literature discussing self-determination is vast and the discussion here will be limited to those aspects pertaining to transition and adulthood, but it should be noted that self-determination is not confined to older adolescents or adults and should be a consideration for younger children as well (see Wehmeyer & Palmer, 2000; Palmer & Wehmeyer, 2003). Self-determination is a central focus for individuals with disabilities and is considered a "best practice" that should be included in the transition process (Wehmeyer, Garner, Yeager, Lawerence, & Davis, 2006). Self-determination is actually a collection of skills and behaviors most readily indicated by one's ability to self-regulate, problem-solve, and make informed choices. There have been four components of self-determination identified in the literature: (a) the ability to act autonomously, (b) the capacity to self-regulate behaviors, (c) the ability to act in an empowered way, and (d) being able to act in a self-realizing manner (Smith, Polloway, Smith, & Patton, 2007). As self-determination is a collection of several different skills and behaviors, it is not easily taught or practiced. The importance of self-determination is well documented in the literature and is seen as an important aspect of the curriculum for students with and without disabilities (Agran, Blanchard, & Wehmeyer, 2000; Carter, Lane, Pierson, & Stang, 2008). Although it is possible to view self-determination as a global construct and there is indication that students who exhibit many of the aforementioned components seem to experience success in everyday tasks after leaving high school (Wehmeyer & Pamler, 2003), it is also possible to consider particular components of self-determination to enhance various aspects of the transition process. For example, choice making and problem solving stand out as essential to the development of the global concept of self-determination (Wehmeyer, Palmer, Soukop, Garner, & Lawrence, 2007). Thus, if there is an expectation that someone is to be self-determined in her actions, then it is necessary to promote several different skills and behaviors. The point here is that self-determination should be an integral part of the transition process. Moreover, self-determination should be seen as a collection of skills and behaviors that can be incorporated into a host of experiences beginning well before leaving the school system.

In review, three themes underlie the transition process: uniqueness of autism, placing the person at the center of the planning process, and self-determination. These themes should be considered in tandem with each of the factors discussed below. In this chapter, the authors briefly discuss the general dimensions of transition to adulthood for individuals with ASD. This discussion is limited to the specific components of transition to include the creation of a formal transition plan. Then, the discussion will shift to include specific factors to consider when developing services and supports for individuals with ASD necessary for the transition to adulthood. Finally, the authors pose a number of critical questions for families, professionals, and individuals to consider when thinking about the transition to adulthood.

A PRIMER ON TRANSITION FOR INDIVIDUALS WITH ASD

The topic of transition is not confined to adulthood, and many have argued that the transition process should begin well before the age of 14 or 16 (deFur & Patton, 1999; Sitlington & Clark, 2006). Transition is a broad concept but generally accepted to refer to the movement from one stage in life to another. This movement from one stage to the next requires close monitoring and deliberate actions to assist those in need of the skills necessary to function in the next stage of life. In the early years of life, transition is largely school-based and centered on the acquisition of skills necessary to function in school environments. Transition to adulthood stands out in the transition process as a fundamentally different stage in which the outcome is not another school-based environment, but rather the adult world. There are many more components to transition than space allows here, but it is possible to focus on some of the fundamental aspects of the transition process and directly relate this information to adults with ASD. First, much of special education is driven by legislation and transition is no different. The IDEIA of 2004 will be discussed, highlighting differences from its immediate predecessor, Individuals with Disabilities Education Act (IDEA, 1997). It is necessary to understand the impact of legislation on the way supports and services are conceptualized. Second, there are several general principles that can help guide the transition process. A list will be presented based on several sources from the vast literature sources available. Finally, one of the keystones of transition is the **Individualized Education Problem/Individualized Transition Plan** (**IEP/ITP**). This document can serve as the foundation for structuring the planning process for individuals with ASD moving into adulthood and help all stakeholders understand the services and supports that will facilitate the transition process.

One of the basic tenants of special education is federal legislation. IDEA has been in existence in one form or another since 1975. There have been a number of changes that impact transition services dating back to 1997. To better understand the impact on services and supports today, it is necessary to briefly discuss some of the content contained in both the 1997 and 2004 versions of IDEA. Transition services were actually defined in the 1990 version of IDEA, but remained the same in the 1997 version. Transition services were described as a "coordinated set of activities for a student, designed within an outcome-oriented process promoting movement from school to post-school activities" (Department of Education, 1992, p. 44804). The post-school activities were to include an array of options for students, including vocational training, **supported employment**, competitive employment, postsecondary education, living options, and others. The coordination of services is important to bring together a number of different services, agencies, and personnel to ensure that an individual with a disability can live as an adult.

In 1997, the definition of transition services remained the same, but some additions were made. One of the significant additions included the age at which transition services should begin. As part of the IEP process, it was required that at the age of 14 a transition statement should be added to the IEP. Then each year after, this statement should be reviewed and related to the goals and objectives included in the IEP. In other words, educational goals, course selection, academic, and social skills should all be related to transition to the next educational environment and beyond. This requirement influenced both families and professionals to begin thinking about transition earlier and to use transition as an underlying theme for decisions made earlier in life that clearly impact options later in life. Another point of note from the 1997 legislation is the "transfer of rights at the age of majority." This provision requires that 1 year before reaching the **age of majority** (18 in most states), the IEP must include a statement that students have been informed of his or her rights. This aspect of transition is reflective of the need for early planning as reaching the age of majority has implications for legal standing and perhaps particular responsibilities that must be addressed (e.g., ownership of property).

In 2004, IDEA was reauthorized once again with some changes affecting transition services. One change indirectly affecting transition was the emphasis placed on access to the general curriculum for students with more significant disabilities. The trend toward students with mild disabilities (e.g., learning disabilities) spending a majority of the day (i.e., 79%) in general education classrooms has been and seemingly continues to be on an upward trend. This is not the case for individuals with more significant disabilities, including students with ASD. The mandate for access to the general curriculum will impact the way in which services are delivered, as there should be a greater push to include students with more significant disabilities in general education classrooms. As a result, it may be possible to also allow greater access to content-oriented information and more opportunity for social skills development. Currently, it is not exactly known how the movement toward greater access to the general curriculum will impact students, but there is evidence that some educational practices have changed (Browder & Spooner, 2006).

The definition of transition services changed in 2004. The definition has been expanded and includes the following. Transition is:

❏ designed to be within a results-oriented process, that is focused on improving the academic and functional achievement of the child with a disability to facilitate the child's movement from school to post-school activities, including postsecondary education; vocational education; integrated employment (including supported employment); continuing and adult education; adult services; independent living or community participation. [602(34)(A)]
❏ based on the individual child's needs, taking into account the child's strengths, preferences and interests. [602(34)(B)]
❏ instruction, related services, community experiences, the development of employment and other post-school adult living objectives, and, when appropriate, acquisition of daily living skills and functional vocational evaluation. [602(34)(C)]

In addition to changes in transition services, there have also been some changes to the IEP. Beginning not later than the first IEP to be in effect when the child turns 16 and then updated annually thereafter, the IEP must include:

❏ appropriate measurable postsecondary goals based upon age-appropriate transition assessments related to training, education, employment and independent living skills, where appropriate
❏ transition services needed to assist the child in reaching those goals, including courses of study; and
❏ beginning not later than one year before the child reaches the age of majority under state law, a statement that the child has been informed of the child's rights under this title, if any, that will transfer to the child on reaching the age of majority under Section 615(m). [614(d)(1)(A)VIII] (H.R. 1350 -PL 108-446 (A)).

The significance of the changes made in 2004 continues to encourage educators to consider the importance of transition services. There is a greater emphasis on outcome and the process by which to get there based on systematic efforts that should begin well before reaching the age of majority (18 in most states) and before leaving public school (age 22 according to federal legislation).

It is possible to extrapolate guiding principles from the extant literature on transition to form a list that serves as a basis for conceptualizing transition services and the practices that result from the conceptualization. These principles are not exhaustive and it is possible to slightly alter these principles in an effort to better fit the individual in question. There are a number of sources that can provide some background on these and other potential principles (Patton & Dunn, 1998;

Pierangelo & Giuliani, 2004; Wehman, McLaughlin, & Wehman, 2005; Steere, Rose, & Cavaiuolo, 2007). What follows is a partial list of principles:

- ❏ Transition should be a part of the educational process from the very beginning.
- ❏ Transition planning should be comprehensive, taking into account the vast dimensions of adulthood.
- ❏ All possibilities should be explored, taking into account the availability of services and supports.
- ❏ Families must be involved in aspects of the transition process.
- ❏ Cultural diversity will impact some decisions made in the transition process and must be respected as such.
- ❏ Transition requires the collaborative efforts of families, professionals, and work with agencies outside of schools.
- ❏ Transition requires the development of skills in a number of different areas and must be coordinated so that individuals can work toward outcomes in a number of areas.
- ❏ Self-determination and transition are inextricably linked. Thus, all four components of self-determination (i.e., the ability to act autonomously, the capacity to self-regulate behaviors, the ability to act in an empowered way, and the ability to act in a self-realizing manner) must be promoted as part of a number of different experiences.

As stated previously, these principles are not exhaustive but serve as a starting point for guiding the transition process. These principles can be used when developing the IEP/ITP. What follows is a brief description of this document and how areas of interest for individuals with ASD can contribute to the transition process.

An IEP is the document that is used to detail the services and supports for students with disabilities required to successfully gain access to the general education curriculum. The IEP is not intended to supplant the general curriculum, but to serve as a plan for helping students with disabilities access the already existing curriculum. The ITP is a component of the IEP, and beginning at the age of 16 (see previous section) transition is a required part of the IEP process. Essentially, the transition to adulthood requires planning over a long period. Beginning at the age of 16 (ideally earlier), families, professionals, and individuals should begin using the guiding principles mentioned above as well as considering the dimensions of adulthood described in the next section to develop a plan for making the transition to adulthood. Unlike academic skill development, the goals for adulthood are not discrete; there is no clear beginning and end. Instead the dimensions of adulthood are continuous variables that require differential attention. In other words, living in a home may require a great deal of attention at some points, while not requiring more than paying rent or mortgage at another time. Thus, the ITP does not have to address all dimensions of adulthood at one time; it is necessary to always keep ultimate outcomes in mind. If independent living and competitive employment are important, then the skills necessary to obtain such goals should not wait until reaching age 18 or later. Some even suggest using a 5-year time horizon for making decisions about skill development. The implication here is that any skill development should begin well before the time period when the skill is needed. The coordination of skills must begin earlier in life so that individuals can make the transition to adulthood without the limitations of a narrow exposure to age-inappropriate skills and experiences.

The ITP must be comprehensive. This means that questions that drive its development must be expanded to include a consideration of areas germane to all aspects of transition (e.g., self-determination). For example, transition to adulthood should be driven by four basic questions: (a) "Where do you want to work and with whom do you want to work?", (b) "Where do you want to live and with whom do you want to live?", (c) "What do you want to do for fun and with whom do you want to have fun with?", and finally (d) "Do you want to sustain a friendship with someone and what kind of friendship do you want it to be?" These questions go well beyond the basic IEP process, and rather than focusing on discrete social skills, these questions broaden the discussion to include consideration of life beyond school. A comprehensive ITP requires considerations of the dimensions of adulthood to better understand the vast universe of possibilities that should be contemplated. What follows is a discussion of the dimensions of adulthood further describing the process that should shape the ITP.

SUPPORTING THE TRANSITION TO ADULTHOOD

There are a number of factors to consider when developing a comprehensive transition plan. Beyond the transition plan itself, it is necessary for families, professionals, and individuals to think about life after secondary school as fundamentally different from life in secondary school. Quite simply, life after secondary school is different and expectations for life after school require the collaborative efforts of all stakeholders to progressively move toward creating a satisfying life. In the following sections a select collection of considerations for stakeholders to use as a foundation for shaping discussions is put forth. The areas of (a) independence, (b) employment, (c) social relationships, and (d) postsecondary education will be discussed. These areas are selected in an effort to help stakeholders understand the range of possibilities related to the transition to adulthood.

Independence

Independence is a broad area that is not necessarily easy to define. As with many issues pertaining to transition, many concepts are interpreted depending on a number of factors (e.g., skill level). According to Jordon (2001) independence is having the ability to mobilize all forms of help (including other people) as needed and not just depending on what is readily available. Recognizing self-needs and then seeking assistance from another individual who can potentially provide this assistance is critical for individuals with ASD. It is quite often the case in secondary education settings that students must adhere to a highly structured schedule surrounded by professionals who anticipate almost every need, disallowing students to engage in problem solving that resembles postsecondary life. Independent movement and decision making will be limited for some individuals, but it is possible to create opportunities that foster some level of independence. For example, choice making has been a topic well discussed in the special education literature (Brown, Belz, Corsi, & Wenig, 1993). It is important to note that even when only two alternatives are presented, a meaningful choice can be made (i.e., choices that relate to lifestyle enhancement) (Storey, 2005). Because choice making is an essential part of self-determination and also quite literally a part of almost every aspect of life, some effort should be made to expand thinking related to transition and the possibilities for life after secondary education to include a continuum of options. Although the concept of independence is broad, the focus here will be on living arrangements and use of community resources.

Living options are an important consideration within the transition process. It is worth noting that there is no clear standard for determining the best living option for an individual. In general, typically developing adults do live outside of their parents' home after completing education or specialized training; it is not a necessary condition for the transition process. There are both advantages and disadvantages to living outside of the family home for individuals with ASD. Both parents and individuals must make adjustments to the new living arrangements, and living outside of the family home may actually require more involvement from families in comparison to staying in the family home. For example, parents may feel less pressure to provide daily care to an adult child with ASD, but there also may be a need to handle the day-to-day responsibilities associated with maintenance of the property, depending on the living situation. In addition, some parents enjoy the companionship of their adult child staying in the family home and may miss her presence if she were to live elsewhere (Krauss, Seltzer, & Jacbson, 2005).

The lack of skill is not the single factor determining living options for individuals with ASD. According to Smith and Philippen (1999), the presence of a disability simply dictates the amount of support services necessary to achieve community adjustment. There are a number of living arrangements possible, and each of these options should be carefully considered when deciding on living options. Living arrangement options include: (a) living with family, (b) living with a foster family, (c) partially **supported living**, (d) fully supported living, and (e) independent living. There are many responsibilities associated with maintaining a home or apartment; therefore any decision made regarding living arrangements should be individualized. For some, living at home may be necessary even after leaving school, but this living arrangement need not be permanent. It is possible for some to take on more responsibility and live independently, while still remaining within the confines of the family home. Living options can be modified to meet the needs of families and individuals with ASD.

Remaining with family is one of the most popular living options, as this may be the only option available for many families. Living with family should not be excluded as an option simply because of preconceived notions about the indicators of adulthood. Instead, families and professionals should consider the prospects of living in the family home with appropriate supports, and if possible, some modifications can be made to the living situation to foster independence to the greatest extent possible.

Living with a foster family can be an option for some individuals when the biological family will not or cannot provide living arrangements. A foster family must be able to provide not only the physical structure (e.g., enough space to sleep), but the social structure (e.g., opportunities to interact with others) as well. This living arrangement does require the individual to leave home, causing families to carefully consider the prospects of a family member living with an entirely new family. In addition, the needs and desires of the individual must be carefully weighed against the options available to ensure that the living arrangement reflects the choice of the individual.

Partially supported, fully supported, or independent living arrangements offer other possibilities. These living arrangements can be conceptualized from different viewpoints. For example, it is possible to live with partial support in the family home. The individual can be responsible for preparing her own meals or arranging her transportation to and from work. This arrangement may later translate into independent living. The importance of considering the individual's needs, desires, and successful supports from the past are essential when deciding on the most appropriate living arrangement. Similar to other areas of adulthood discussed in this chapter, the transition process does not stop with certain milestones. Even adults without disabilities encounter problems associated with daily living and many do not always make the most effective decisions in each case. It is possible that one living arrangement will work for a while, and then an alternative arrangement will have to be made. In many cases, this does not indicate failure, but rather growth.

The identification and use of community resources is another important aspect of adult life for individuals with ASD. Support available via community agencies and the resources available in the community can serve as an important link to the greater community and people outside of the family. In this sense, community should be understood not only as those people and places in close proximity to the family home, but also agencies that may operate on the national and local level (e.g., Autism Society of America). Families and professionals will need to understand the individual's community functioning level. This assessment should not only reflect the deficits associated with recruiting supports, but just as importantly, this assessment should also identify strengths and desires of the individuals to ensure that services are driven by basic needs as well as desires (see Clark, Patton, & Moulton, 2006; Clark & Patton, 2000, for transition assessment tools).

Making connections with other families and individuals is also a necessary step when attempting to assess available resources. Exchanging information by word of mouth about past experiences and/or the names of people who have been helpful at a particular agency can make some experiences a little easier. In addition to other families and professionals, helpful resources in the community may not be specifically designed for individuals with disabilities, but still may serve a role for them. For example, community colleges provide a plethora of services for their students and the public at large. It is possible to obtain transportation listings, job listings, or even access some recreation activities. Although some of the activities are restricted to students only, the convenience of having many different kinds of information together in one place should not be discounted. The caution of course is that using community agencies that are not specifically intended for individuals with disabilities means that individuals with ASD will need to be prepared to articulate needs and desires to those who may not understand the nature and needs of autism.

The key for families is to understand the options available and to understand the level of involvement necessary to help their adult children choose a living arrangement that makes sense for them. Families and school-based professionals will have to make decisions about services and supports that are qualitatively different from those provided during the school years. In fact, it may be necessary to ask fundamentally different kinds of questions about needs, as individuals with ASD will be entering a world where they will encounter many who may not understand the nature and needs of individuals with autism. Once a decision has been reached about a particular living option, it is then necessary to decide on the resources necessary to make the living arrangement a reality. It is possible that a supported living arrangement (e.g., group home) provides a great deal of support, while other options may require the direct intervention of family members and others (e.g., single family home). There is not a definitive list of skills associated with a particular living option; families and professionals will have to work collaboratively with service providers connected with the living option and create a plan that includes the necessary services and supports with a special emphasis on the context where the services and supports are to be delivered. The transition plan should specifically address this area, as living options should be a point of discussion for all individuals with ASD regardless of ability. Even for those individuals with highly limited skills, it is necessary to discuss possible living options in the event the family is no longer able to provide direct care.

Employment

There are a number of options available for employment. Many families and professionals may actually limit the employment experience by focusing on a limited number of options in light of an individual's skill deficits. There are a number of reasons why individuals with ASD cannot or do not obtain employment, but the responsibility for obtaining employment does not solely reside with the individual (Holmes, 2007). Much of the transition process requires an open mind and a willingness to approach issues by imagining how things can be in comparison to their current state. In addition, the purpose of employment must also be questioned. A common purpose for employment is to earn money to sustain necessities in life (i.e., food and shelter). But it is possible that employment can offer an opportunity to make social connections, continue skill development, and of course provide financial rewards.

The employment rate for individuals with disabilities is severely low (National Organization on Disability, 2004). This is a problem with a long history and has been addressed from a number of different perspectives (Wehman, 2006). It is possible for adults with ASD to work in a number of different contexts performing many different kinds of work. The continuum of employment options may include supported employment, non-sheltered workshops with specialized support on the job, and competitive employment with the assistance of a job coach (Trainor, Patton, & Clark, 2005;

Wehman, Sale, & Parent, 1992). There is no scarcity of models proposed to assist adults with ASD to obtain employment. In fact employment is generally one of the areas that is discussed while individuals still attend secondary schools. In most cases, this ensures that families and professionals have held conversations about possible employment options well before the individual leaves school.

According to Smith and Philippen (1999), there are a number of models for facilitating employment for individuals with ASD. These models have been proposed as an alternative to those models predicated on providing direct individual support. Many job coach models can be limiting for individuals with ASD, as the direct service may actually stunt growth in the development of skills for the job itself as well as inhibit natural interactions with co-workers. These limitations can be detrimental to individuals with ASD, as success on a job is linked to the ability to perform the job as well as making social connections with co-workers. The three models include mentor, job sharing, and training consultant. The **mentor model** calls for the job coach to do the initial training, and then a co-worker assumes the role of mentor for the individual with an ASD. This eliminates the dependence on an outside person for providing support to ensure completion of the tasks. In the **job-sharing model**, the worker shares a job with a nondisabled peer who assumes some of the responsibility for providing support. By working with another individual, there is at least the opportunity for social relationships to form. One of the key aspects of employment is gaining confidence in the completion of the task as well as the ability to work with others. In the third alternative, the training consultant option, a consultant from a human services agency provides training to co-workers on-site who in turn supports the individual with an ASD. The advantage of each of these models is that the primary responsibility for providing support is identified and facilitated within the context of the employment environment. This is important for individuals with ASD, as the prospects for gradually fading support is more plausible if co-workers provide support in the context of the employment setting and have a clear understanding of the employment tasks. Each of these models offers alternatives to the use of a job coach as the sole method of support on the job. It is essential for adults to receive assistance in seeking, obtaining, and maintaining employment.

As stated previously, employment is included in transition plans developed as part of the IEP. The inclusion of transition plans is a required part of the IEP process and should be included no later than age 16. In spite of this requirement, the transition plan may not tap into the real employment desires of individuals with ASD. There is evidence that individuals with ASD choose jobs for some of the same reasons as others: financial security, challenges, and value of the job itself (Stephens, Collins, & Dobber, 2005). The idea here is that a discussion confined to the IEP meeting may be insufficient to ensure that the needs and desires of individuals are truly captured within the pages of the IEP. Employment will require that families and professionals assess skills as well as the mechanisms for obtaining employment. In other words, the end result of actually obtaining a job is not the only important point to consider. Instead, it is necessary to consider where to look for employment, supports available within the employment context, and requirements of employment, as well as to identify who can assist in obtaining employment. These tasks will require the coordination of services and the consideration of transporting some services and supports to the employment context if necessary. The transition plan should be supplemented with a discussion highlighting the goals for obtaining employment and the personnel barriers that may impede performance on the job (e.g., the pace work is completed) as well as any barriers associated with the job itself (e.g., transportation to and from work). These tasks are not insurmountable and will simply require a well-coordinated effort that includes consideration of how services and supports complement and relate to potential employment.

Social Relationships

A great deal of emphasis is placed on understanding the mechanisms by which children with autism can form social connections with others. Indeed, one of the hallmarks of ASD is the inability to understand the social world. Making and sustaining social connections does not lose relevance in adulthood and may actually hold more significance, as many aspects of adulthood require at least a limited ability to understand the intentions and desires of others. Whether it involves interacting with a co-worker or simply attempting to initiate an interaction while attending a social event, creating social relationships remains an essential part of life for individuals with ASD. The cadres of social skills necessary to successfully navigate the social world are often learned in informal situations outside of the supervision of an educator or related service provider. A host of efforts have been directed at creating social situations through inclusive education or related efforts, but after leaving secondary school, opportunities for contrived social interactions may be limited or virtually impossible. The informal social networks of adults with ASD may be limited. The interactions that take place while using public transportation, eating lunch, taking a break at work, or exchanging communication via e-mail all have an impact on social relationships. For many with ASD, these interactions simply do not occur. An underlying philosophy of inclusive education is that individuals with and without disabilities should have the opportunity to learn and develop in an integrated environment (Heward, 2006). This philosophy is not intended to create a one-way interaction, whereby students without disabilities impart their store of academic and social knowledge on students with disabilities. Instead, the goal is for both sets of students to gain from each other and make exchanges of skills and experiences that allow both to benefit (see Ryndak & Fisher, 2003 for a description of inclusive education for students with more significant needs). These efforts are essential for individuals with ASD and should be continued. In regard to transition to adulthood, less is known about how these experiences contribute to life after secondary school. The social contacts made through particular classes or social clubs in secondary schools do not always translate into post-school friendships. This limited generalization of social relationships may be due in part to the tentativeness of relationships formed in schools (some last while others do not), as well as the lack of social skills. School experiences are by design to be educational in a highly structured environment where individuals with ASD can learn academic and functional skills. These school experiences are limited, in that a number of the requirements of adulthood simply do not have a direct correlate in the school environment, and thus there is no real opportunity to practice these skills in a context similar to the future environment.

Developing social relationships is a critical aspect of the transition to adulthood. There are more expectations placed on adults, and for those with non-obvious disabilities, it is quite possible that there will be no assumption of need in regard to making initial social contacts with others. Thus, it is possible that in spite of the need for support to clearly communicate needs and desires, when making an initial social contact, the typically developing adult in the interaction may not communicate effectively or make the extra effort to understand. It has been noted that social demands increase with age, but so do the maturity and understanding of others as well (Ozonoff et al., 2002). After leaving secondary school, many adults with ASD have a highly limited social world. In fact the immediate family may be the extent of their social world. This can make social connections difficult, as there is no interaction outside of the family home. A social relationship can actually serve as a conduit to the adult world. Making and maintaining a social relationship is certainly not the cure for all ills, but it may serve as a mechanism for exposure to fundamentally different kinds of experiences that may not take place if the social world is limited to the immediate family. When individuals with ASD attempt to make the transition to adulthood and seek employment or social experiences outside of the family home, having a non-paid individual outside of the immediate family can be critical to understanding these experiences and gaining appreciation for making choices that are grounded in an attempt to enjoy a high quality of life. In other words, spending time with another individual or with a group of people can be fulfilling. These connections may be possible through employment, living arrangements, or recreation opportunities. Entering each of these situations may be more easily facilitated with a social relationship outside of the family home. It is possible that social relationships formed outside of the family may contribute to one's ability to become independent. A relatively challenging aspect of independence is assessing the costs and benefits of particular situations, and then making a final decision based on the information available. This line of decision-making sequence applies to social relationships as well.

Social relationships are one of the most difficult aspects of transition, as there is not a clear outcome that is understood the same way by all stakeholders. Some may question the meaning of a social relationship and how can it be determined that someone has a social relationship or simply an acquaintance. These are valid questions and will need to be answered for the purpose of the transition plan. There are some more concrete markers of social relationships that can be used to assist all stakeholders in making definite decisions. First, social relationships will have to be categorized in terms of support. What kinds of assistance will an individual need to make this connection on a regular basis? Is special transportation required or are the contacts confined to a particular meeting time or place? Questions about how to facilitate the contact must be understood and answered. Second, all stakeholders will have to decide how social relationships fit into the overall context of an individual's life. Part of this decision is related to the first point about support, but context is also important in terms of making initial social contacts and sustaining them. Friendships are quite often centered around common interests and most importantly in environments where these common interests can be enjoyed (e.g., chess club). Thus, it is necessary for adults with ASD to be able to have access to these contexts on a regular basis in order to see and actually enjoy the social connections. All aspects of a transition plan are interrelated and must be viewed as such. Social relationships are critically important to be considered in relation to each of the other areas addressed in the plan, as it is possible to take an opportunity to make a social connection in each of the other areas of transition. For example, when choosing a living arrangement, there may be an opportunity to facilitate a social connection within the same apartment complex or perhaps even seek a living arrangement for two individuals with ASD with the support of other families. Goals related to social relationships should be embedded in the other areas addressed in the transition plan.

Postsecondary Education

It is well known that individuals with disabilities can attend secondary school until the age of 22 and even longer in some states (Millar, 2003). The idea that students with disabilities may require additional years of education is warranted as the variability in learning rates, regression of skills, and the need for multiple exposures to content are only some of the reasons why an extended stay in secondary school may make sense for certain students. The philosophy of normalization served as part of the philosophy of inclusive education leading families and professionals to work toward allowing greater access to general education environments for individuals with disabilities. As part of the normalization philosophy, it stands to reason that typical experiences should not be confined to schools, and in fact for individuals 18 years old or older, secondary school is not the typical experience. Thus, in recent years some have questioned the logic of keeping individuals with disabilities in a secondary school setting (i.e., high school) after reaching the age of 18. In short, postsecondary education has become a viable option for individuals with disabilities (Adreon & Stella-Duricher, 2007; Alpren & Zager, 2007; Neubert, Moon, & Grigal, 2004; VanBergeijk, Klin, & Volkmar, 2008).

On the surface, the idea of individuals with ASD attending a postsecondary institution of education may seem far-fetched. This is not an impossible idea by any means. Postsecondary education is not an appropriate option for all, but this is true of typically developing adults as well. Thus, the following note of caution is warranted. Attending a post secondary institution should be approached with the same caution and care as all other options available to individual with ASD. Specific options should be made to fit the individual in comparison to finding a program and hoping the individual will fit. In an effort to understand the make-up of postsecondary education and some of the possible elements of programs, some differences between secondary and postsecondary education will be discussed, followed by some of the possible components of the programs currently available.

The services and supports provided to individuals with ASD are driven by IDEA 2004. This powerful piece of legislation is generally well understood by educators, and programs are designed with the rules and regulations associated with IDEA 2004. The consequences for not following the stated rules and regulations are severe, and it is uncommon for entire schools or districts to avoid following the legislation at least in part. No such contingency exists at the postsecondary level; therefore there are a number of differences between services in K–12 schools and postsecondary institutions. First, the extent of services is different at postsecondary institutions (Eckes & Ochoa, 2005). There is no mandate for identifying students who may be in need of services. Thus, it is necessary for students to self-identify and actually advocate for themselves and recruit assistance from the instructors. Most postsecondary institutions have OSDs, where it is possible to register and receive accommodations for academic tasks. But, as it is necessary to self-identify, it is possible for an individual to attend an institution and never receive any services or supports. Second, the documentation required for receiving services is different for post secondary institutions. Provisions in IDEA 2004 have lifted the requirement to perform annual evaluations. According to Madaus and Shaw (2006), this will impact individuals with disabilities as it is possible to leave the secondary school without having the appropriate documentation demonstrating the presence of a disability and a detailed explanation of appropriate services. There is a provision in IDEA 2004 for the development of a Summary of Performance (SOP), "a document intended to summarize the child's academic achievement and functional performance" (Madus & Shaw, 2006, p. 16). But the description included in the legislation is vague and may not provide enough guidance for the creation of a comprehensive document with the required detail. A third difference between postsecondary institutions and secondary schools is that students with disabilities will interact with professors who may have little to no knowledge of the nature of needs of students with disabilities in general or autism specifically. The implications of this may translate into the need for educating the professor about accommodations that allow access to content while maintaining the integrity of the task (Sitlington, 2003).

BOX 13.4   Trends and Issues Notes # 2

Postsecondary education has been considered an option for individuals with mild disabilities for a long time. It is only in more recent years that individuals with more significant disabilities have been included in postsecondary education settings. Part of this trend is due in part to the large-scale efforts at the elementary and secondary level to include children with more significant disabilities in general education settings. This trend is also due in part to the realization that if students with more significant disabilities stay in secondary schools until the age of 22, then they are essentially not interacting with their age-appropriate peers. As a result, there have been some descriptions in the literature of programs that serve individuals with more significant disabilities attending postsecondary institutions. These programs are generally partnerships between a public school district and a postsecondary institution. This trend is in line with the inclusive philosophy of assisting individuals with disabilities to access general education environments and provide the necessary services and supports in the inclusive environment, instead of creating two parallel systems of education or service delivery.

For further reading, refer to the partial list of works below:

Moon, M. S., & Inge, K. V. (2000). Vocational preparation and transition. In M. Snell & F. Brown (Eds.), *Instruction of students with severe disabilities* (5th ed., pp. 591–628). Upper Saddle River, NJ: Merrill/Pearson Education.

Neubert, D. A., Moon, M. S., & Grigal, M. (2002). Post-secondary education and transition services for students ages 18–21 with significant disabilities. *Focus on Exceptional Children, 34*, 1–11.

Neubert, D. A., Moon, M. S., & Grigal, M. (2004). Activities of students with significant disabilities receiving services in post-secondary settings. *Education and Training in Developmental Disabilities, 39*(1), 16–25.

The differences between secondary education and postsecondary education must be understood in context. If one is to attend a postsecondary institution as a student only, then many of the differences may apply, but it is also possible to attend a postsecondary institution as a non-traditional student, as many programs are now in operation (see Box 13.4). Most programs operate in conjunction with a school district and actually deliver some of the same services on the campus of a postsecondary institution that would have been delivered on the campus of a secondary school. In essence, a school-based professional works on the postsecondary campus and provides assistance to the students who attend the institution. In this sense, attendance means something different for these students. It is possible to attend some classes for additional training in a particular area or as a result of a particular interest. However, it is also possible to engage in a host of other activities that are not simply possible at a typical secondary school. For example, it is possible to obtain employment in environments where age-appropriate peers are present on a regular basis. It is also possible to gain access to age-appropriate recreation on a regular basis, again with age-appropriate peers. The academic and social opportunities are vast and virtually unmatched at the typical secondary school. Postsecondary programs are still in development and much of the current state of knowledge is still in its infancy. More work is needed to understand the possible benefits of receiving services on a postsecondary campus and how these kinds of programs can be sustained over the long term (Benz, Lindstrom, Unruh, & Waintrup, 2004) (see Box 13.5).

BOX 13.5   Diversity Notes # 2

Postsecondary education has become a popular alternative to seeking employment following high school. Attending a postsecondary institution is not an option for everyone, but there are many individuals who can benefit from such an arrangement and some have investigated their experiences. In a study conducted by Dowrick, Anderson, Heyer, and Acosta (2005), they formed a series of focus groups consisting of somewhere between 3 and 19 individuals. The groups were convened across 10 states and represented a cross-section of racial and ethnic groups (e.g., African American, Asian, and Latino) with a variety of disabilities, including developmental disabilities. These investigators designed a series of questions intended to capture the participants' experiences in relation to obtaining supports within the postsecondary institution, one of the most interesting issues related to natural supports. The participants were asked to discuss the significance of their families and peers in their postsecondary institution. Whereas all participants identified receiving support from family and peers, the minority participants reported identifying more closely with their racial/ethnic identity group rather than with their disability group in regard to some supports (e.g., social outlets). This finding may indicate the need to recognize not only disability, but also cultural identity when designing supports for individuals with ASD.

The transition to postsecondary education requires some basic decisions to be made before actually considering a specific program. First, it is necessary to decide on the purpose of attending a postsecondary school. Is it to receive training in a particular area, access recreation or peers, or locate employment in an environment with age-appropriate peers? Whatever the reason, this decision must be made in order to fully appreciate the preparation necessary to guide the next steps. As stated previously, an annual reevaluation is not necessary, but an SOP is necessary and should be developed to detail student strengths and weaknesses (see Cosden, Koegel, Koegel, Greenwell, & Klein, 2006, for an explanation of strength-based assessment). A comprehensive transition plan will include this information, and if the decision is made to attend a postsecondary institution, then a supplemental SOP can be developed to ensure that this documentation can be used when gaining entrance to the school. One advantage of postsecondary institutions is that these institutions are there to serve the public, and even if it is not appropriate for an individual with an ASD to attend the institution, it is possible to access the school for recreation activities or social activities with age-appropriate peers.

Summary

Transition to adulthood can pose a challenge for families, professionals, and, of course, the individuals making the transition. Adulthood is an elusive concept that is often interpreted differently leading to different notions about what should and should not be considered when making the transition. When age or particular milestones are used as clear indicators of adulthood, then it may be difficult for families and professionals to treat an individual with ASD as an adult. Instead, by designating a particular point in time or the specific "transition point" (Kochhar-Bryant & Izzo, 2006) of leaving secondary school as entrance into adulthood, both families and professionals have a starting point for treating an individual as an adult. Limited notions about particular milestones may actually inhibit many individuals from ever being seen or treated as adult. In addition to some of the well-accepted dimensions of adulthood, such as employment or living arrangements, additional options have been considered for individuals with more significant disabilities. Postsecondary education to include 2- or 4-year institutions has become a viable option for individuals with ASD and can provide both training and social opportunities. Including education as an option for adults with ASD more closely matches the experiences of typically developing adults as a number of 18- to 21-year-old adults do not directly enter employment. This expansion of options may also be accompanied by considerations for an expanded view of the available options that do result in an isolated existence confined to the family home. The literature base on transition to adulthood and adult outcomes for individuals with ASD is steadily growing; this is very much a work in progress. Since the emergence of the extensive early intervention literature, there are now thousands of children with autism who were diagnosed earlier, with more accuracy, and receiving qualitatively better services much earlier in life. What will this mean in 10, 15, or 20 years? There may be an entire population of adults with ASD with extensive skills with the need for minimal supports. In spite of these bright prospects for the future, families and professionals will need to be cognizant of the entire transition process and prepare to tailor services and supports to meet individual needs. At the core of the transition process are people who want a satisfying quality of life.

Chapter Review Questions

1. What are the dimensions of adulthood and how do they apply to individuals with ASD? (Objective 1)
2. What are the advantages and disadvantages of using a distinct point in time as an indicator of adulthood, from the perspectives of families, professionals, and individuals with ASD? (Objective 2)
3. What is the definition of transition according to IDEA 2004 and how does this definition differ from IDEA 1997? (Objective 3)
4. What specific outcomes appropriate for an individual with ASD can be achieved through each of the guiding principles of transition? (Objective 4)
5. What are the roles of the family, professionals, and individuals with ASD in the transition process? (Objective 5)

Key Terms

Adulthood *279*
Age of majority *284*
Competitive employment *280*
IEP/ITP *284*
Independence *279*

Individualized Education Plan *284*
Individualized Transition Plan *284*
Job-sharing model *290*
Mentor model *290*

Person-centered planning (PCP) *283*
Self-determination *282*
Supported employment *284*
Supported living *288*
Transition *280*

Internet Resources

Council for Exceptional Children, Division on Career Development and Transition
http://www.cms4schools.com/dcdt/
National Association of Special Education Teachers, Transition Information page
http://www.naset.org/transervices4.0.html

National Center on Secondary Education and Transition
http://www.ncset.org/
National Secondary Transition Technical Assistance Center
http://www.nsttac.org/
National Transition Network
http://ici2.umn.edu/ntn/

References

Adreon, D., & Stella-Durocher, J. (2007). Evaluating the college transition needs of individuals with high-functioning autism spectrum disorders. *Intervention in School and Clinic, 42*(5), 271–279.

Agran, M., Blanchard, C., & Wehmeyer, M. L. (2000). Promoting transition goals and self-determination through student self-directed learning: The self-determined learning model of instruction. *Education and Training in Mental Retardation and Developmental Disabilities, 35*(4), 351–364.

Alpren, C. S., & Zager, D. (2007). Addressing communication needs of young adults with autism in a college-based inclusion program. *Education and Training in Mental Retardation and Developmental Disabilities, 42*(4), 428–436.

Benz, M. R., Lindstrom, L., Unruh, D., & Waintrup, M (2004). Sustaining secondary transition programs in local schools. *Remedial and Special Education, 25*(1), 39–50.

Billstedt, E., Gillberg, C., & Gillberg, C. (2005). Autism after adolescence: Population-based 13-to 22-year follow-up study of 120 individuals with autism diagnosed in childhood. *Journal of Autism and Developmental Disorders, 35*(3), 351–360.

Browder, D. M., & Spooner, F. (2006). *Teaching language arts, math, and science to students with significant cognitive disabilities.* Baltimore: Paul H. Brookes.

Brown, F., Belz, P., Corsi, L., & Wenig, B. (1993). Choice and diversity for people with severe disabilities. *Education and Training in Mental Retardation, 28,* 318–326.

Carter, E. W., Lane, K. L., Pierson, M. R., & Stang, K. K. (2008). Promoting self-determination for transition-age youth: Views of high school general and special educators. *Exceptional Children, 75*(1), 55–70.

Chadsey-Rusch, J., & Gonzalez, P. (1988). Adults with developmental disabilities. In J. L. Matson & A. Marchetti, (Eds.), *Developmental disabilities: A life-span perspective* (pp. 228–255). Philadelphia: Grune & Stratton.

Clark, G. M., & Patton, J. R. (2000). *Informal assessments for transition planning.* Austin, TX: Pro-Ed.

Clark, G. M., Patton, J. R., & Moulton, L. R. (2006). *Transition planning inventory* (Rev. ed.). Austin, TX: Pro-Ed.

Cosden, M., Koegel, L. K., Koegel, R. L., Greenwell, A., & Klein, E. (2006). Strength-based assessment for children with autism spectrum disorders. *Research and Practice for Persons with Severe Disabilities, 31*(2), 134–143.

DeFur, S., & Patton, J. R. (1999). *Transition and school-based services: Interdisciplinary perspectives for enhancing the transition process.* Austin, TX: Pro-Ed.

Dowrick, P. W., Anderson, J., Heyer, K., & Acosta, J. (2005). Postsecondary education across the USA: Experiences of adults with disabilities. *Journal of Vocational Rehabilitation, 22,* 41–47.

Eckes, S. E., & Ochoa, T. A. (2005). Students with disabilities: Transitioning from high school to higher education. *American Secondary Education, 33*(3), 6–20.

Grandin, T., & Scariano, M. (1986). *Emergence labeled autistic.* Tunbridge Wells, Kent. Costello. Novato: Arena Press.

Grandin, T. (1995). *Thinking in pictures: and other reports from my life with autism.* New York: Doubleday.

Heward, W. L. (2006). *Exceptional children: An introduction to special education* (8th ed.). Upper Saddle River, NJ: Merrill/Pearson Education.

Holmes, D. L. (2007). When the school bus stops coming: The employment dilemma for adults with autism. *Autism Advocate, 46*(1), 16–21.

Houlburn, S., & Vietze, P. M. (Eds.). (2002). *Person-centered planning: Research, practice, and future directions.* Baltimore: Paul H. Brookes.

Jordon, R. (2001). *Autism with severe learning difficulties.* London: Souvenir Press.

Kochhar-Bryant, C. A., & Izzo, M. V. (2006). Access to post-high school services: Transition assessment and the summary of performance. *Career Development for Exceptional Individuals, 29*(2), 70–89.

Krauss, M. W., Seltzer, M. M., & Jacobson, H. T. (2005). Adults with autism living at home or in non-family settings: Positive and negative aspects of residential status. *Journal of Intellectual Disability Research, 49*(2), 111–124.

Madaus, J. W., & Shaw, S. F. (2006). Disability services in post-secondary education: Impact of IDEA 2004. *Journal of Developmental Education, 30*(1), 12-14, 16, 18, 20–21.

Mandell, D. S., & Novak, M. (2005). The role of culture in families' treatment decisions for children with autism spectrum disorders. *Mental Retardation and Developmental Disabilities Research Reviews, 11,* 110–115.

Millar, D. S. (2003). Age of majority, transfer of rights and guardianship: Considerations for families and educators. *Education and Training in Developmental Disabilities, 38*(4), 378–397.

Moon, M. S., & Inge, K. V. (2000). Vocational preparation and transition. In M. Snell & F. Brown (Eds.), *Instruction of students with severe disabilities* (5th ed., pp. 591–628). Upper Saddle River, NJ: Merrill/Pearson Education.

Morgan, H. (1996). Underpinning philosophy in the provision of services for adults with autism: A critique of global values related to specific practice. In H. Morgan (Ed.), *Adults with autism: A guide to theory and practice* (pp. 31–52). Cambridge, United Kingdom: Cambridge University Press.

National Organization on Disability. (2004). *N.O.D./ Harris survey of Americans with disabilities: Landmark survey finds pervasive disadvantages.* Washington, DC: Author. Available at http://www.nod.org.nod.org/content.cfm?id=1537.

Neubert, D. A., Moon, M. S., & Grigal, M. (2002). Post-secondary education and transition services for students ages 18–21 with significant disabilities. *Focus on Exceptional Children, 34,* 1–11.

Neubert, D. A., Moon, S., & Grigal, M. (2004). Activities of students with significant disabilities receiving services in postsecondary settings. *Education and Training in Developmental Disabilities, 39*(1), 16–25.

Ozonoff, S., Dawson, G., & McPartland, J. (2002). *A parent's guide to Asperger Syndrome and high-functioning autism: How to meet the challenges and help your child thrive.* New York: The Guilford Press.

Palmer, S., & Wehmeyer, M. L. (2003). Promoting self-determination in early elementary school. *Remedial and Special Education, 24*(2), 115–126.

Patton, J., & Dunn, C. (1998). *Transition from school to young adulthood: Basic concepts and recommended practices.* Austin, TX: Pro-Ed.

Pierangelo, R., & Giullani, G. A. (2004). *Transition services in special education: A practical approach.* Upper Saddle River, NJ: Merrill/Pearson Education.

Ryndak, D. L., & Fisher, D. (Eds.) (2003). *The foundation of inclusive education* (2nd ed.). Baltimore: TASH.

Shakespear, E., Beardsley, L., & Newton, A. (2003, September). *Preparing urban teachers: Uncovering communities. A community curriculum for interns and new teachers.* Evaluation report from Jobs for the Future. Boston: Jobs for the Future.

Sitlington, P. L. (2003). Postsecondary education: The other transition. *Exceptionality, 11*(2), 103–113.

Sitlington, P. L., & Clark, G. M. (2007). The transition assessment process and IDEIA 2004. *Assessment for Effective Intervention, 32*(3), 133–142.

Smith, M. D., & Philippen, L. R. (1999). Community integration and supported employment. In D. B. Zager, (Ed.), *Autism: Identification, education, and treatment* (pp. 301–321). Mahwah, NJ: Lawrence Erlbaum.

Smith, T. L., Polloway, E. A., Smith, D. J., & Patton, J. R. (2007). Self-determination for persons with developmental disabilities: Ethical considerations for teachers. *Education and Training in Developmental Disabilities, 42*(2), 144–151.

Steere, D. E., Rose, E., & Cavaiuolo, D. (2007). *Growing up: Transition to adult life for students with disabilities.* Boston: Allyn & Bacon.

Stephens, D. L., Collins, M. D., & Dodder, R. A. (2005). A longitudinal study of employment and skill acquisition among individuals with developmental disabilities. *Research in Developmental Disabilities, 26,* 469–486.

Storey, K. (2005). Informed choice: The catch-22 of self-determination. *Research and Practice for Persons with Severe Disabilities, 30*(4), 232–234.

Stull, W. J., & Sanders, N. M. (Eds.). (2003). *The school-to-work movement: Origins and destinations.* Westport, CT: Praeger.

Test, D. W., Fowler, C. H., Wood, W. M., Brewer, D. M., & Eddy, S. (2005). A conceptual framework of self-advocacy for students with disabilities. *Remedial and Special Education, 26*(1), 43–54.

Trainor, A. A., Patton, J. R., & Clark, G. M. (2005). *Case studies in assessment for transition planning.* Austin, TX: Pro-Ed.

Turnbull, A., & Turnbull, R. (2001). Self-determination for individuals with significant cognitive disabilities and their families. *The Journal for the Association for Persons with Severe Handicaps, 26* (1), 56–62.

VanBergeijk, E., Klin, A., & Volkmar, F. (2008). Supporting more able students on the autism spectrum: College and beyond. *Journal of Autism and Developmental Disorders, 38,* 1359–1370.

Wehman, P. (2006). *Life beyond the classroom: Transition strategies for young people with disabilities* (4th ed). Baltimore: Paul H. Brookes.

Wehman, P., McLaughlin, P. J., & Wehman, T. (Eds.). (2005). *Intellectual and developmental disabilities: Toward full community inclusion* (3rd ed.). Austin, TX: Pro-Ed.

Wehman, P., Sale, P., & Parent, W. (1992). *Supported employment: Strategies for integration of workers with disabilities.* Boston: Andover Medical Publishers.

Wehmeyer, M. L., Garner, N., Yeager, D., Lawrence, M. & Davis, A. K. (2006). Infusing self-determination into 18–21 services for students with intellectual or developmental disabilities: A multi-stage, multiple component model. *Education and Training in Developmental Disabilities, 41*(1), 3–13.

Wehmeyer, M. L., & Palmer, S. B. (2000). Promoting the acquisition and development of self-determination in young children with disabilities. *Early Education and Development, 11*(4), 466–481.

Wehmeyer, M. L., & Palmer, S. B. (2003). Adult outcomes for students with cognitive disabilities three years after high school: The impact of self-determination. *Education and Training in Developmental Disabilities, 38*(2), 131–144.

Wehmeyer, M. L., Palmer, S. B., Soukup, J. H., Garner, N. W., & Lawrence, M. (2007). Self-determination and student transition planning knowledge and skills: Predicting involvement. *Exceptionality, 15*(1), 31–44.

Williams, D. (1992). *Nobody nowhere*. London: Corgi Books.

Williams, D. (1994). *Somebody somewhere*. London: Corgi Books.

INDEX

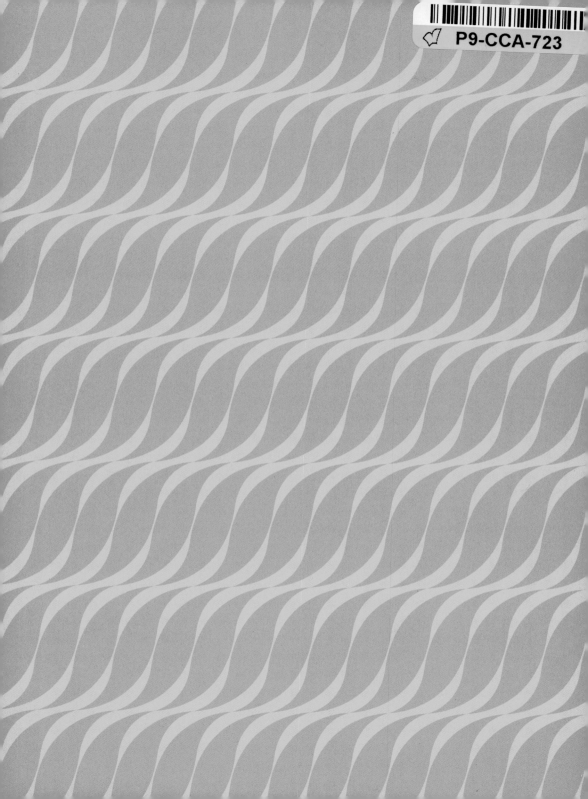

All about
VOLCANOES
Amazing explosions, earthquakes and eruptions

Robin Kerrod

<small>CONSULTANT</small> John Farndon

southwater

This edition is published by Southwater

Southwater is an imprint of
Anness Publishing Limited
Hermes House
88–89 Blackfriars Road
London SE1 8HA
tel. 020 7401 2077
fax 020 7633 9499

Distributed in the UK by
The Manning Partnership
251–253 London Road East
Batheaston
Bath BA1 7RL
tel. 01225 852 727
fax 01225 852 852

Distributed in the USA by
Anness Publishing Inc.
27 West 20th Street
Suite 504
New York
NY 10011
tel. 212 807 6739
fax 212 807 6813

Distributed in Australia by
Sandstone Publishing
Unit 1
360 Norton Street
Leichhardt
New South Wales 2040
tel. 02 9560 7888
fax 02 9560 7488

Publisher: Joanna Lorenz
Managing Editor, Children's Books: Gilly Cameron Cooper
Editor: Peter Harrison
Photographer: John Freeman
Stylist: Melanie Williams
Designer: Caroline Grimshaw
Picture Researcher: Kay Rowley
Illustrator: Peter Bull Art Studio
Production Controller: Don Campaniello

10 9 8 7 6 5 4 3 2 1

The publishers would like to thank the following children, and their parents, for modeling in this
book—Anum Butt, Dima Degtyarov, Roxanne Game, Fawwaz Ghany, Angelica Hambrier, Larrissa
Henderson, Lori Hey, Louis Loucaides, Malak Mroue, Tom Swaine-Jameson, Sophie Viner.

PICTURE CREDITS
b=bottom, t=top, c= centre, l= left, r= right
Bryan & Cherry Alexander: page 48bl. Ardea/R. Gibbons: page 19tl;/F Gohier page 17b;/A Warren
page 37cl. BBC Natural History Unit/B Davidson: page 35br;/C Buxton page 34bl. Biofotos:
page 27tr;/B Rogers page 34br;/S Summerhays pages 8tr, 56br. Bridgeman Art Library: page 41tr.
CEPHAS/M Rock page 35bl. Bruce Coleman: page 7br;/C Atlantide page 22br;/F Bruemmer
page 35c;/G Cubitt page 15cr;/M Freeman page 60t. FLPA/M Withers: page 27bl;/S Ardito(Panda Photo)
page 53tr;/S Jonasson page 11cr;/S McCutcheon pages 33bl, 49cl. Gamma/Frank Spooner: pages 23cl, 47br,
49t, 60br, 60bl, 61d, 61br, 61bl. Genesis Space Photo Library: page 53tl. GSF Picture Library: page 26tl.
Robert Harding Picture Library: page 5cl;/R Frerck(Odyssey,/Chicago) page 49bl. Michael Holford: pages
16tl, 54t. Hulton-Getty: page 4tr. Image Select: page 22bl;/Caltech: page 52b. JS Library: page 56bl;/G
Tonsich page 25cr. Landform Slides: page 29cr. Mountain Camera/C Monteath: page 53br;/J Cleare page
48t;/T. Kajiyama pages 45br, 50t, 51cr. Oxford Scientific Films/J Frazier: page 33tl, 63tl;/V Pared page
5bl;/W Faioley page 53c. Planet Earth/Bourseiller&Durieux: pages 32br, 57t;/C Weston pages 17tr,
28b;/I & V Krafft pages 2, 5tr&br, 23bl, 45cl;/J Corripio page 23cr;/J Waters page 7cl;/K Lucas pages 33tr,
33br;/R Chesher page 10tr;/R Hessler page 11tl;/R Jureit page 36br;/WM Smithey page 34tl. Rex
Features: pages 1, 22tl, 45bl, 46t, 61tr. Science Photo Library: pages 5tl, 6tr, 11cl, 11bl, 11br, 14tl, 17tl, 17cl,
18c, 19cl, 40br, 63br;/A Pasieka page 30tl;/D Hardy pages 3tl, 29l, 40tl;/D Parker pages 3tl, 44t, 56t;/D
Weintraub page 26c, endpapers;/G Garradd page 41c;/G Olson page 49br;/GECO(UK) page 58t;/J Hinsch
page 32b;/JL Charmet page 44b;/L Cook page 49cr;/NASA pages 41b, 42t;/P Menzel page 45t;/R de
Guglielmo page 32tr;/S Fraser pages 3tl, 28t, 36t, 36bl, 37cr, 38tr;/S Stammers pages 33c, 42bl;/US
Geological Survey pages 3br, 43tl, 43t, 45cr. Spacecharts: pages 3cl, 15cl, 23br, 26bl, 26br, 42br, 43c, 43b,
57bl. Still Pictures;/A Maslennikov: page 37t;/C Caldicott page 29br;/G&M Moss page 17cr. Telegraph
Colour Library: pages 3cr, 20tl. Topham Picture Point: pages 27br, 53bl, 61cr. Tony Waltham: pages 3t, 3bl,
6b, 7bl, 15t, 15br, 18b, 19bl, 23t, 27tl, 35t, 37b, 41tl, 57br. Woodmansterne: page 29tr.

Previously published as *Investigations: Volcanoes and Earthquakes*

All about
VOLCANOES

Amazing explosions, earthquakes and eruptions

CONTENTS

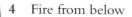

FIRE FROM BELOW

At this moment in various parts of the world volcanoes are erupting. Fountains of red-hot rock are hurtling high into the air, and rivers of lava are cascading down the volcanoes' sides. Volcanoes are places where molten (liquid) rock pushes up from below through splits in the earth's crust. They may be beautiful, but they can also be very destructive. Earthquakes are another destructive part of nature. Every year violent earthquakes destroy towns and kill hundreds, sometimes thousands, of people. The constant movements that take place in and beneath the rocky crust that covers the earth cause volcanoes and earthquakes. The word volcano comes from the name that the people of ancient Rome gave to their god of fire. He was called Vulcan. Volcanology is the term given to the study of volcanoes, and the scientists who study them are known as volcanologists.

The greatest
An artist's impression of the massive eruption of the volcano Krakatoa, near Java in southeast Asia, in 1883.

From the depths
When a volcano erupts, magma (red-hot molten rock) forces its way to the earth's surface. It shoots into the air along with clouds of ash and gas, and runs out over the sides of the volcano. In time layers of ash and lava build up to form a huge cone shape.

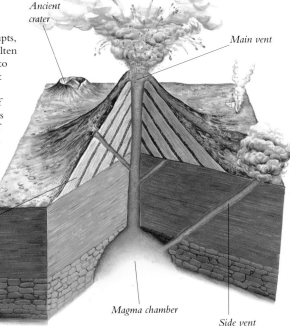

Ancient crater

Main vent

Layers of lava and ash

Magma chamber

Side vent

FACT BOX

• The explosion of Krakatoa in Indonesia, in 1883, caused a massive tidal wave that killed 36,000 people.

• A powerful earthquake killed 5,500 people in the city of Kobe, Japan, in January 1995. Kobe was one of the largest ports in Japan, and thousands of homes were destroyed. It was estimated it would take several years to rebuild the city completely.

Piping hot
Hot water often bubbles to the surface in volcanic regions. This creates geothermal (heated in the earth) springs. The hot spring pictured is in Yellowstone National Park.

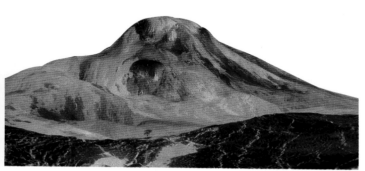

Suited up
Heatproof suits and helmets like this make it possible for volcanologists to walk near red-hot lava. This volcanologist is taking samples of lava on the volcano Mauna Loa, on Hawaii.

Out of this world
There are huge volcanoes like this on the planet Venus. Volcanoes have helped shape many bodies in the solar system, including Mars and the moon.

Shaking earth
A badly-damaged village in India after a severe earthquake in 1993. Two plates (sections) of the earth's crust meet in India. The plates push against each other and cause earthquakes.

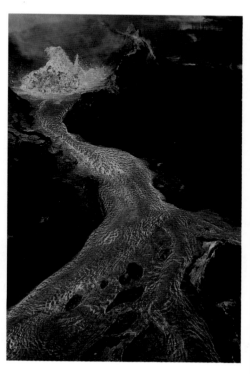

Red-hot river
A river of molten rock races down the sides of the Hawaiian volcano Kilauea in a 1994 eruption. Kilauea is one of the most active volcanoes known on earth.

THE ACTIVE EARTH

The causes of volcanoes and earthquakes begin many miles beneath the surface of the earth. Our planet is covered with a thin layer of hard rock called the crust. Soil, in which trees and plants grow, has built up on top of the rock. Underneath the hard rock of the crust, however, there is a much hotter layer of the earth called the mantle. The center of the earth, deep inside the mantle, is intensely hot. That heat moves out from the center and heats everything in the mantle. In the mantle the rocks become semi-liquid and move and flow like molasses. Because of the intense heat from the center of the earth, the rocks move in currents. Very hot liquid rocks (magma) are lighter than cooler rocks and float up toward the top of the mantle. Where there are gaps in the crust, the magma bubbles up through them and shoots out in volcanoes.

Volcanoes have been erupting on earth for billions of years. During all that time they have pushed out enormous amounts of lava (magma pushed out of a volcano), ash and rocks. These hardened and built up in layers to form part of the landscapes around us. Volcanoes also produced water vapor that eventually condensed (turned to liquid) to form the earth's seas and oceans.

The newborn earth
Thousands of millions of years ago the earth probably looked similar to the picture above. Molten rock was erupting from volcanoes everywhere on the earth's surface, creating huge lava flows. These hardened into rocks.

Fit for giants
Looking like a spectacular, jumbled-up stairway, this rock formation is on the coast of County Antrim in Northern Ireland. It is known as the Giant's Causeway, because people in the past believed that giants built it. However, it is a natural formation made up of six-sided columns of basalt, one of the commonest volcanic rocks. Basalt often forms columns like these when it cools, and this is called columnar basalt. There are similar structures on Staffa, an island in the Inner Hebrides group off northwestern Scotland. Among the many caves along Staffa's coastline is Fingal's Cave, about which the composer Mendelssohn wrote a famous overture.

Inside the earth

The earth is made up of a number of different layers. The top layer is the hard crust. It is thinnest under the oceans, where it is only some 3–6 miles thick. Underneath the crust there is a thick layer of semi-liquid rock known as the mantle. Beneath the mantle is a layer of liquid metal, mainly iron and nickel, that makes up the earth's outer core. The inner core at the center is solid, made up of iron and other metals.

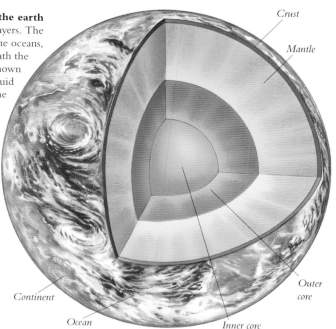

Crust

Mantle

Continent

Ocean

Outer core

Inner core

Fire and ice

This bleak landscape in Iceland was created by the country's many volcanoes. Iceland is one of the most volcanically active places in the world, and hardened lava covers most of the country.

Iron from space

Iron is also found in meteorites that fall to our planet from space. This 60-ton iron meteorite is the world's largest. It was found in 1920 at Hoba, Namibia, in southwest Africa. Scientists estimate that it fell to earth about 80,000 years ago.

A rocky layer cake

There are other rocks on earth besides those made by volcanoes. Sedimentary rocks were formed out of sediment, or material produced when older surface rocks were worn away by wind and rain. These kinds of rocks build up in layers. This picture of the Grand Canyon in Arizona shows an enormous area of sedimentary rocks. You can see how they are built up in layers of different colors.

ERUPTION

People usually think of volcanoes as mountains of fire that shoot fountains of red-hot rock high into the air and pour out rivers of lava. But much more comes out of volcanoes besides molten rock. Water that has been heated and turned into a gas in the volcano comes out as water vapor and steam. Once it is outside the volcano the vapor cools down and condenses (turns back into water). The hot rock inside volcanoes produces many other kinds of gas, such as carbon dioxide. Some of these gases go into the air outside the volcano, and some are mixed with the lava that flows from it. The second project shows you how to make a volcano that releases lava mixed with carbon dioxide. As you will see, the red floury lava from your volcano comes out frothing, full of bubbles of this gas. In a real volcano, it is the gas that is mixed with the lava that makes the volcano suddenly explode. The gas bubbles and swells inside the volcano and pushes out the mixture of lava and gas violently.

Hawaiian fire
The gigantic Hawaiian volcano Mauna Loa erupted in 1984, sending rivers of red-hot lava cascading down its slopes. The lava came dangerously close to the coastal town of Hilo. If the lava had reached Hilo, the town would have been set on fire.

WATER VAPOR

You will need: heat-proof pitcher, saucepan, oven mitt, plate.

1 Fill up the pitcher with water from the hot tap. Pour the water into the saucepan. Switch on one of the hotplates or light a stove burner and place the saucepan on it.

2 Heat the water in the saucepan until it is boiling hard and steam is coming from it. Pick up the plate with the oven mitt and hold it upside-down above the saucepan.

3 After a few minutes, turn off the burner and remove the plate using the oven mitt. You will see that the plate is covered with drops of water. This water is water vapor (steam) that has cooled and turned back to liquid.

1 Make sure the pitcher is dry, or the mixture will stick to the sides. Empty the baking soda into the pitcher and add the flour. Thoroughly mix the two using the stirrer.

ERUPTION

You will need: pitcher, baking soda, flour, stirring rod, funnel, plastic bottle, sand, seed tray (without holes), large plastic container lid, vinegar, red food coloring.

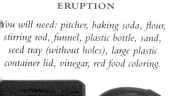

5 Pour the vinegar into the pitcher. Then add enough food coloring to make the vinegar a rich red color.

2 Place the funnel in the neck of the plastic bottle. Again, make sure that the funnel is perfectly dry first. Now pour in the mixture of soda and flour from the pitcher.

6 Place the funnel in the mouth of the plastic bottle and quickly pour into it the red-colored vinegar in the pitcher. Now remove the funnel from the bottle.

3 Empty sand into the tray until it is half-full. Fill the pitcher with water and pour it into the tray to make the sand sticky but not too wet. Combine with the stirring rod.

4 Stand the bottle containing the flour and soda mixture in the center of the plastic lid. Then start packing the wet sand around it. Make the sand into a cone shape.

7 The sandy volcano you have made will begin to erupt. The vinegar and soda mix to give off carbon dioxide. This makes the flour turn frothy and forces it out of the bottle as red lava.

SPREADING SEAS

The earth's crust is not all in one piece. but is made up of many sections, called plates. They are solid and float on currents circulating in the deep layer of semi-liquid rock beneath them in the mantle. All the plates of the crust move in different directions. Some plates are moving apart and others are moving toward one another. The plates that move apart are usually under the oceans. Magma pushes up from below the sea-floor and squeezes through gaps between the edges of the ocean plates. The magma squeezing up pushes the plates in opposite directions. As the plates move apart they make the ocean floor wider and push continents apart. This is known as sea-floor spreading. Sea-floor spreading builds up plates because when the magma cools it adds new rock at the edges of the plates. This kind of boundary between two plates is called a constructive boundary. The magma pushes up the seabed to form a long mountain range called a ridge or rise. Ridges are very noticeable features on the floors of both the Atlantic and the Pacific Oceans.

Underwater explorer
The deep-diving research submersible (midget submarine) *Alvin*. The submersible can carry a pilot and two scientific observers to a depth of 13,000 feet. *Alvin* can dive so deeply that scientists were able to study the Mid-Atlantic Ridge. The submersible also helped scientists to discover mineral deposits on the ocean floor.

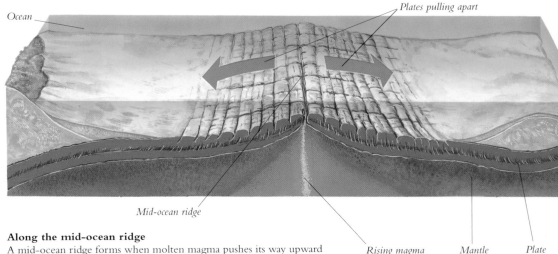

Ocean

Plates pulling apart

Mid-ocean ridge

Rising magma   Mantle   Plate

Along the mid-ocean ridge
A mid-ocean ridge forms when molten magma pushes its way upward from the mantle, the semi-molten layer under the crust. The magma bubbles up through cracks in the crust as they are pulled apart. When the magma meets the sea water, it hardens to form ridges.

Strange life

Hot water full of minerals streams out of the vents (openings) along the mid-ocean ridges. Strange creatures live around them. They include the giant tube worms pictured here around vents in the Galapagos Islands in the eastern Pacific Ocean. Other creatures that thrive on the ridges include species of blind crabs and shrimps.

New island

The island of Surtsey, off Iceland, did not exist before November 1963. In that month the top of an erupting volcano broke through the sea's surface close to Iceland. The volcano continued erupting for more than three years. There were times when the ash and steam rising from the new volcano reached more than 3 miles into the sky.

Volcanoes underwater

A computer-colored picture of three underwater volcanoes in the South Pacific Ocean. They were found close to the East Pacific Rise, the main mid-ocean ridge in the Pacific Ocean.

Black smoker

Water as hot as 662°F, hotter than a domestic oven, pours out of vents along the ocean ridges. The water often contains particles of black sulphur minerals that make it look like smoke. This is why these vents are called black smokers.

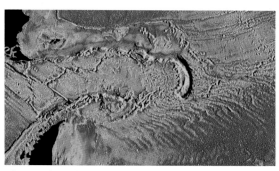

Plate and sandwich

A satellite view showing a small ocean plate on the floor of the South Atlantic Ocean between the tip of South America (top left) and Antarctica (bottom left). The curved shape in the center is the South Sandwich Trench.

MOVING MAGMA

The temperature of the rocks in the earth's mantle can be as high as 2,700°F. At this temperature the rocks would normally melt. They are under so much pressure from the rocks above them that they cannot melt completely. They are, however, able to flow slowly. This is like a solid piece of modeling clay that flows slightly when you put enough pressure on it. This kind of flow is called plastic flow. In places, the rocks in the upper part of the mantle do melt completely. This melted rock, called magma, collects in huge pockets called magma chambers. The magma rises because it is hotter and lighter than the semi-liquid rocks. Volcanoes form above magma chambers when the hot magma can rise to the surface. The second project demonstrates this principle using hot and cold water. The hot water rises through the cold because it is lighter.

1 Make sure that the table is protected by a sheet. Knead the lump of clay in your hands until it is quite flexible. Now shape it into a ball. Place it on the table.

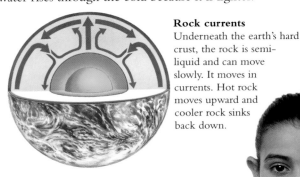

Rock currents
Underneath the earth's hard crust, the rock is semi-liquid and can move slowly. It moves in currents. Hot rock moves upward and cooler rock sinks back down.

3 Roll the clay into a ball again and press it with the board. But this time push the board forward at the same time. The clay will again flow and let the board move forward. The board is moving in the same way as the plates in the earth's crust move.

2 Place the wooden board on top of the ball of clay and press down. The clay flattens and squeezes out at the sides. It is just like semi-liquid rock flowing under pressure.

1 Pour some of the food coloring into the small jar. You may need to add more later to give your solution a deep color. This will make the last stage easier to see.

2 Fill the small pitcher with water from the hot tap. Pour it into the small jar. Fill it right to the brim, but not so it's overflowing. Wipe off any that spills down the sides.

3 Cut a circular patch from the plastic wrap an inch or so bigger than the top of the small jar. Place it over the top and secure it with the rubber band.

BLACK SMOKERS

You will need: dark food coloring, small jar (such as baby food jar), small pitcher, transparent plastic wrap, strong rubber band, sharpened pencil, large jar, oven mitts, large pitcher.

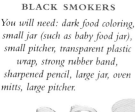

4 With the sharp end of the pencil, carefully make two small holes in the plastic covering the top of the jar. If any colored water splashes out, wipe it off.

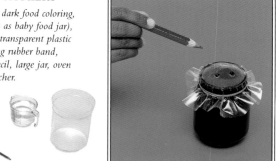

6 Watch what happens. The colored hot water begins rising from the holes. This happens because the hot water is lighter, or less dense, than the cold water around it.

5 Now place the small jar inside the larger one. Use oven mitts because it is hot. Fill the large pitcher with cold water and pour it into the large jar, not into the small one.

WHEN PLATES MEET

The plates on the sea floor that spread out from the mid-ocean ridges meet edge-to-edge with the plates carrying the continents. The edges of the plates then push against each other. Because continental rock is lighter than ocean-floor rock, the edge of the continental plate rides up over the edge of the ocean plate. The ocean plate is then forced back into the mantle inside the earth. As the ocean plate goes down into the mantle, it melts and is gradually destroyed. This kind of boundary between colliding plates is called a destructive boundary because the edge of the ocean plate is destroyed. Where the ocean plate starts to descend, a deep trench forms in the sea-bed. The continental plate is also affected by the ocean plate pushing against it. It wrinkles up and ranges of fold mountains are formed. The great mountain chains of North and South America—the Rockies and the Andes—were formed in this way. Earthquakes also occur at destructive boundaries. So do volcanoes, as parts of the destroyed ocean plate force their way through the weakened continental crust.

Around the Pacific
Most of the Pacific Ocean sits on one huge plate moving northwest. This rubs against other plates and creates a huge arc of volcanoes (shown in red) along the plate edges.

Continental crust wrinkles up

Ocean trench

Ocean

Ocean plate

Continental plate   Ocean plate descends

FACT BOX

• The Andes Mountains of South America were formed by the collision between the South American plate and the Nazca plate. With a length of nearly 5,600 miles, they form the longest mountain range in the world.

• The deepest part of the world's oceans is Challenger Deep, which lies in the Marianas Trench in the North Pacific Ocean. The depth there is almost 7 miles.

Along ocean trenches
In many places around the world, a plate moving away from an ocean ridge meets a plate carrying a continent. When this happens, the ocean plate (which is made up of heavier material) is forced down underneath the continental plate. This causes a deep trench to form where the plates meet.

14

Youngest and tallest

The Himalayas in southern Asia form the highest mountain range in the world. They include Mount Everest which, at 29,141 feet, is the earth's highest single peak. The range began rising only about 50 million years ago. The plate carrying India collided with the Asia plate at that time. The Himalayas is one of the youngest mountain ranges on earth. In the long history of the earth, 50 million years is not a particularly long time.

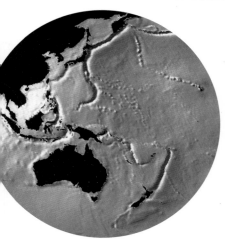

The ocean trenches

This satellite photograph of the earth shows Australia at lower center with the huge land mass of Asia at the top of the globe. The North and South Pacific Oceans are to the right, while the Indian Ocean is on the left. Variations in the height of the sea surface are clearly visible. The surface dips in places where there are deep trenches on the ocean bed many miles below. The deep trenches to the right of Australia in this view are the Kermadek and Tonga Trenches. The Marianas Trench is in the upper center.

Volcanoes on the edge

The volcano on White Island, off the North Island of New Zealand, lies close to an ocean trench, where the Pacific plate is descending. As the plate descends, it heats up and changes back to magma. This forces its way to the surface as a volcano. White Island volcano is one of hundreds that ring the Pacific Ocean. Together they form a ring of volcanoes which is called the Ring of Fire.

Above the clouds

The tops of volcanoes rise above the clouds on the Indonesian island of Java. Most of the country's islands lie near the edge of a descending plate and have active volcanoes.

HOT SPOTS

Most of the world's volcanoes lie at the edges of plates. A few volcanoes, however, such as those in Hawaii, are a long way from the plate edges. They lie over hot spots beneath the earth's crust. A hot spot is an area on a plate where hot rock from the mantle bubbles up underneath. While the plate above moves, the hot spot stays in the same place in the mantle. The hot spot keeps burning through the plate to make a volcano in a new place. A string of dead volcanoes is left behind as the plate moves over the hot spot. Some form islands above the ocean surface. Others, called sea mounts, remain submerged. The best known active volcanoes far from plate boundaries are Kilauea and Mauna Loa on the main island of Hawaii. The Hawaiian archipelago lies in the middle of the Pacific plate, thousands of miles from plate boundaries. Its volcanoes erupt because it lies directly above a hot spot. The other Hawaiian islands formed over the same hot spot but were carried away by plate movement. In time, the main island will be carried away also. Volcanoes erupting from the hot spot will create a new island to take its place. The island of Réunion in the Indian Ocean is another example of a hot-spot location.

Powerful Pele
This is the name of the fire goddess of Hawaii. According to legend, Pele lives in a crater at the summit of the volcano Kilauea. When she wants to, she melts the rocks and pours out flows of lava that destroy everything in their path. When Pele stamps her feet, the earth trembles.

FACT BOX

• The Hawaiian hot-spot volcano of Mauna Kea is 29,500 feet high from the ocean floor. That is taller than Mount Everest. Half of Mauna Kea is below sea level.

• When sea mount volcanoes die, they cool and shrink. It is possible that the legendary lost city of Atlantis could have been built on top of a flat sea mount. Then the sea mount shrank and Atlantis sank beneath the waves.

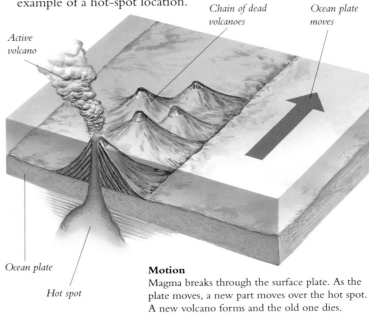

Chain of dead volcanoes

Ocean plate moves

Active volcano

Ocean plate

Hot spot

Motion
Magma breaks through the surface plate. As the plate moves, a new part moves over the hot spot. A new volcano forms and the old one dies.

Islands in line

Astronauts took this picture of the Hawaiian island chain in the North Pacific from the space shuttle *Discovery* in 1998. This island group is formed over a hot spot on the Pacific plate. The largest island is Hawaii which appears at the top of this picture.

Lanzarote's lunar landscape

Huge volcanic eruptions took place on Lanzarote, another Canary Island, in the 1800s and 1900s. They covered most of the island with lava and ash. The landscape is similar to the landscape on the Moon. Very few plants can grow in a landscape of this kind. Lanzarote has more than 300 volcanic craters. Many are to be seen in the area of the most recent lava flows, in the spectacular "Mountains of Fire."

Canary hot spot

Snow-capped Mount Teide, the highest peak on Tenerife, in the Canary Islands. It rises to 12,200 feet and was formed 10 million years ago by volcanic activity over the Canary Islands' hot spot. Teide last erupted in 1909.

Pacific atoll

There are many ring-shaped coral islands, or atolls, in the Pacific Ocean. These began as coral grew around the mouth of a volcano that rose above the ocean's surface. The volcano then sank, but the coral went on growing.

Pele is angry!

The volcano Kilauea, on Hawaii, is shown erupting here. At such times Hawaiians say that their fire goddess Pele is angry. She is supposed to live in Kilauea's crater. Kilauea, on the main island of Hawaii, is located over a hot spot on the Pacific plate. It formed only about 700,000 years ago.

CONES AND SHIELDS

Sticky rock
A volcano erupts with explosive force on Bali. It is one of a string of islands that make up Indonesia. There are more than 130 active volcanoes on the islands. They all pour out the sticky type of lava Hawaiians call aa.

Around the world there are more than 1,000 active volcanoes. They are all very different. Some erupt fairly quietly and send out rivers of molten lava that can travel for many miles. Others erupt with explosive violence, blowing out huge clouds of ash. The kind of magma inside a volcano makes the difference between it being quiet or explosive. Quiet volcanoes, such as those that form on the ocean ridges and over hot spots have magma with very little gas in it. The Hawaiian volcanoes formed over a hot spot. Their lava flows far, and they grow very broad. They are called shield volcanoes. Explosive volcanoes have magma inside them that is full of gas. Gas pressure can build up inside a volcano until it explodes. This is the kind of volcano found in the Ring of Fire around the Pacific plate. Because of their shape these volcanoes are called cone volcanoes. The blast and ash clouds these volcanoes give off can and do kill hundreds of people. The ash clouds can even cause changes in the weather. Large clouds of dust in the earth's atmosphere from volcanoes block out the sun's heat, making the weather on earth colder.

Red river
A river of molten lava flows down the slopes of the volcano Kilauea on the main island of Hawaii. Like the other volcanoes on the island, Kilauea is a shield volcano. It pours out very runny lava that flows for long distances, usually at speeds up to about 300 feet an hour. The fastest lava flows are called by their Hawaiian name of pahoehoe.

Long mountain
The volcano Mauna Loa on the main island of Hawaii is over 13,000 feet high. It is a shield-type volcano, meaning it is broad, with gently sloping sides. The main dome measures 75 miles across and its lava flows stretch for more than 13,000 square miles. In the Hawaiian language, the name means Long Mountain. This is a good name for it because it is very long and is the biggest mountain mass in the world.

Building layers

Explosive volcanoes blast rock and ash into the air. These eventually fall to the ground and lie there. Geologists call the rock and ash on the ground tephra. Here on Mount Teide, in Tenerife, layers of tephra have built up on top of each other after repeated eruptions.

Sacred mountain

Snow-covered Mount Fuji on the island of Honshu, Japan. Also called Fujiyama, it is one of the most beautiful volcanoes in the world and is considered sacred by the Japanese. It has an almost perfect cone shape. Five lakes ring the base of the volcano.

At the top

The caldera (crater) at the summit of the volcano Kilauea, on the island of Hawaii. There are vents (holes) in the caldera from which lava flows. The most active vent in the caldera is named Halemaumau. This is the legendary home of the fire goddess Pele.

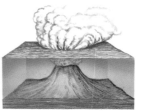

Submarine (undersea) volcanoes may grow in size until they rise above the surface of the sea. Scientists believe that this is how atolls are formed.

Hawaiian volcanoes have runny lava and gentle slopes.

Strombolian volcanoes spit out lava bombs in small explosions.

Plinian volcanoes produce thick, gassy lava and shoot columns of ash high into the air.

Fissure volcanoes are giant cracks in the ground from which lava flows.

Vulcanian volcanoes produce thick, sticky lava and erupt with violent explosions.

Pelean volcanoes produce clouds of very hot ash and gases. These clouds are dense and roar or gush quickly downhill.

Volcano types

Although all volcanoes behave in different ways, we can group them into a number of different kinds. In fissure volcanoes, magma forces its way up through long cracks in the earth's crust. Then it flows out on either side and cools to form broad plateaus. Other volcanoes grow in various shapes caused by how runny or thick their lava is. Some of these volcanoes are famous for their violent eruptions of thick clouds of ash and gas.

FLOWING LAVA

LAVA VISCOSITY

You will need: two paper plates, jar of honey, pen, stopwatch, container of liquid soap.

In some parts of the world, there are ancient lava flows that are hundreds of miles long. Long flows like these have come from fissures (cracks) in the crust, which have poured out runny lava. Runny lava is much thinner than the lava produced by explosive volcanoes, which is sometimes called pasty lava. The correct name for the thickness of a liquid is viscosity. Thin liquids have a low viscosity, thick liquids a high viscosity. The first project below investigates the different viscosities of two liquids and how differently they flow. The second project looks at at the effect on substances of temperature. Heating solids to a sufficiently high temperature makes them first turn soft, then melt and then flow. Rock is no exception to this rule. If you make rock hot enough it softens, becomes liquid, and then flows. Deep inside a volcano, hot rock becomes liquid and flows up and out onto the surface as lava. When the lava comes out, its temperature can be as high as 2,200°F. This is the temperature of most of the runny lavas of the Hawaiian shield volcanoes. There are two kinds of lava flows from these volcanoes. One is called pahoehoe and the other aa by the Hawaiians. Volcanologists use these names for similar flows the world over. Pahoehoe and aa flows have different kinds of surfaces. Pahoehoe has quite a smooth skin and wrinkles up like coils of rope. Aa flows have a very much rougher surface that is full of rubble.

1 Mark a large circle on the plates by drawing around the edge of a saucer. Pour a tablespoon of honey from the jar into the middle of the circle. Start the stopwatch.

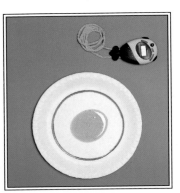

2 After 30 seconds, mark with the pen how far the honey has run. After another 30 seconds mark again. Stop the watch when the honey has reached the circle.

3 Pour some liquid soap into the center of another plate. Use the same amount as the honey you poured. Start the stopwatch.

4 After 30 seconds, note how far the liquid has run. You will probably find that it has reached the circle. It flows faster because it has a much lower viscosity than honey.

MAGMA TEMPERATURE

You will need: stick of margarine, jam jar, pitcher, large mixing bowl, stopwatch.

1 Scoop out some margarine and drop it onto the bottom of the jar. For the best results, use hard margarine, not a soft margarine spread.

2 Pick up the jar and tilt it slightly. See what happens to the margarine. The answer is, not a lot. It sticks to the bottom of the jar and does not slide down.

3 Fill the pitcher with hot water and pour some into the bowl. Shake it around to heat the bowl, then pour it away. Now pour the rest of the hot water into the bowl.

4 Pick up the jar and tilt it again. The margarine still will not move. Now place the jar on the bottom of the bowl. Keep your fingers clear of the hot water.

6 Continue checking the jar for another three or four minutes. After even a minute, the margarine will start to slide along the bottom as it warms and starts to melt. After several minutes, it is quite fluid.

5 Start the stopwatch and after one minute, take out the jar. Tilt it, and see if the margarine moves. Return it to the bowl and after another minute, look at it again.

VICIOUS VOLCANOES

Erupting volcanoes can be among the most impressive sights in nature. They are almost always destructive, however, and can be deadly. Quiet volcanoes are the least dangerous to life, but their lava flows will destroy anything in their path. Explosive volcanoes are the most destructive. Their lava does not flow far because it is so thick. However, the clouds of ash, shattered rock and gas they blast out can be deadly. It was an exceptionally heavy ash fall that killed people by the thousands in ancient Pompeii. When the volcanoes explode first, they often give off a glowing cloud of white-hot ash, gas, and rocky debris. This is called a *nuée ardente* (glowing avalanche) and can travel at speeds of up to 60 mph. Such a cloud killed tens of thousands of people in St. Pierre in the Caribbean in 1902. The gases that all volcanoes give out can also be deadly. They include sulphur dioxide and hydrogen sulphide. Both gases are highly poisonous. Vast amounts of carbon dioxide are also given off. This is not poisonous in itself, but it can kill by suffocation (inability to breathe). The carbon dioxide blocks out oxygen. When there is no oxygen, people cannot breathe. In 1986, more than 1,500 people and many animals died in this way at Lake Nyos in Cameroon.

Menace on Montserrat
Ash clouds billow high into the sky from this volcano in the Soufrière Hills on the Caribbean island of Montserrat early in 1997. Many people had to flee from the island.

Long ago in Herculaneum
The excavated remains of one of the houses in the Roman town of Herculaneum, near Naples in Italy. It was destroyed at the same time as nearby Pompeii in August A.D. 79. It was blasted by hot gas and buried by repeated avalanches of hot ash and rock from Vesuvius.

Plaster casts of bodies

The Garden of Fugitives
In this part of the excavated city of Pompeii plaster casts of victims of the A.D. 79 eruption of Vesuvius are displayed. Their lifelike casts show how they huddled together in fear.

The death of Pompeii

In A.D. 79, Mount Vesuvius, near Naples in Italy, erupted with explosive violence. A huge, choking cloud of gas, hot ash, and cinders blew down and covered the Roman town of Pompeii. At least 2,000 people are thought to have been killed either in their homes, or trying to flee from the deadly cloud. In a short time most of the city was buried. Over the past century more than half of the city has been uncovered. The ash and cinders have been dug away from many different buried buildings.

Silent killer
Carbon dioxide killed these cattle in fields near Lake Nyos, in Cameroon. The gas was released during a volcanic explosion under the lake in August 1986.

Lava rain
Volcanic bombs on the slopes of Mount Teide, on Tenerife, in the Canary Islands. They were thrown out during an eruption of the volcano as lumps of partly molten lava.

Gas sampling
A volcanologist takes a sample of gases from a volcanic vent. He wears a gas mask to avoid being suffocated.

Indian burial
The cinder field around Sunset Crater in Arizona. The volcano that created the crater erupted in about A.D. 1064. Thick lava flows, fumaroles (gas vents) and ice caves have been found in the surrounding area. It has been a national park since 1930.

FACT BOX

• In April 1815 on the island of Sumbawa, in Indonesia, the volcano Tambora exploded. An estimated 90,000 people died directly from the eruption or from famine caused by ruined crops.

• In May 1902, a glowing cloud of gas from the Mount Pelée volcano on the Caribbean island of Martinique destroyed the city of St. Pierre and killed its 30,000 inhabitants.

DANGEROUS GASES

The two projects here look at two effects the gases given out by volcanoes can have. In the first project you will see how the build up of gas pressure can blow up a balloon. If you have put enough gas–making mixture in the bottle, the balloon may explode. Be careful. When the gas pressure builds up inside a volcano, an enormous explosion takes place, often releasing a deadly hot gas cloud like the one that killed thousands of people in Pompeii. The second project shows the effect of carbon dioxide, a gas often released by volcanoes. The project uses the gas to prevent oxygen from reaching a candle. The candle cannot burn without oxygen. This explains how carbon dioxide kills people by suffocation: it stops oxygen from getting into their lungs. The project also shows that carbon dioxide is heavier than air. Being heavy makes it dangerous because clouds of the gas can push away the air from around people and animals.

GAS PRESSURE

You will need: funnel, soda bottle, baking soda, vinegar, pitcher, balloon.

Plaster casts
Gas killed many of those who died at Pompeii. Archaeologists (people who study the past) can recreate the shapes of their bodies. First they fill hollows left by the bodies with wet plaster of Paris and let it harden. Then they remove the cast from the rock in which the bodies fell.

1 Make sure the funnel is dry first. Place it in the top of the bottle and pour in some baking soda. Now pour the vinegar into the funnel from the pitcher and into the bottle.

2 Remove the funnel. Quickly fit the neck of the balloon over the top of the bottle. Notice that the vinegar and soda are fizzing and giving off bubbles of gas.

3 The balloon starts to blow up because of the pressure, or force, of the gas in the bottle. The more gas released, the more the balloon fills. Don't burst the balloon!

SUFFOCATING GAS

You will need: funnel, bottle, baking soda, vinegar, pitcher, modeling clay, pencil, long straw, tall and short candles, large jar, matches.

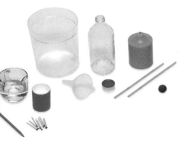

1 Place the funnel in the bottle and add the baking soda. Pour in the vinegar from the pitcher. This bottle is your gas generator. The gas produced is carbon dioxide.

2 Knead a piece of modeling clay until it is soft, then push it into the mouth of the bottle. Make sure it fits tightly. This will ensure that no gas will escape past it.

Deadly fumes
Clouds of poisonous sulphur fumes billow out from holes on the slopes of Mount Etna, on the Italian island of Sicily. It is one of the most active volcanoes in the world.

3 Make a hole in the clay stopper with the pencil. Carefully push the straw through the hole. Press the clay around the straw.

5 Direct the straw of your gas generator into the bottom of the jar. Keep your arms well away from the candle flames. Soon you will find that the short candle goes out. The carbon dioxide gas has covered it and blocked out the oxygen that would let it burn.

4 Stand both candles in the bottom of the large jar. Ask an adult to light them. Light the short one first to avoid the danger of being burned if the tall candle were lit first.

MOUNT ST. HELENS

Picture perfect
Mount St. Helens before the May 1980 eruption.

Mount St. Helens in Washington lies in the Cascade range of mountains. This mountain range includes many volcanoes. Before 1980, Mount St. Helens had not erupted for 130 years. The mountain began to shake in March of 1980. Scientists knew there was about to be an eruption. Many scientists and tourists traveled to photograph what would happen. The progress of the eruption was recorded by hosts of people on the ground, in the air and also by satellite. Nothing prepared the geologists who had gathered there for the spectacular explosion on the morning of May 18, 1980, however. The blast, the ash clouds, the rain of debris from the volcano, the mud slides and the poisonous fumes killed 60 people that morning. When the clouds cleared, the mountain had lost about 1,300 feet in height and acquired a crater about 2 miles across. Mount St. Helens was no longer a beautiful piece of tourist scenery.

Blast off
An enormous cloud of thick ash billows from the huge new crater formed when the top of Mount St. Helens blew off on May 18, 1980. The cloud rose to a height of more than 12 miles. It dropped ash over the surrounding region and on towns far away as it blew toward them. In some towns the ash blocked out the sun. The city of Yakima was particularly badly hit. Over 500,000 tons of ash later had to be removed from the area surrounding Mount St. Helens.

Before and after
These satellite photographs of the Mount St. Helens region were taken before and after the eruption. They show how much land was devastated and covered by ash. The picture on the left was taken a few months before the eruption occurred. The mountain's snow cap is beginning to grow as autumn sets in. The picture on the right was taken about a year after the eruption. Ash covers thousands of acres of what was once forest land.

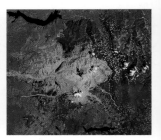

Like ninepins

This photograph shows what remained of a forest on the slopes of Mount St. Helens after it erupted. Thousands of trees were knocked over by the powerful blast. In places the fallen trees were swept away by an avalanche of rocks, dust and mud, which caused even greater destruction.

Ominous dome

Since the 1980 eruption, Mount St. Helens has been quiet. Domes like this near the summit show that magma is still pushing up to the top of the volcano, however. This shows that it is still active.

FACT BOX

• Native Americans of the Pacific Northwest called Mount St. Helens *Tah-one-lat-clah* (fire mountain).

• Mount St. Helens was previously active between 1832 and 1857.

• The first indication of a forthcoming eruption occurred on March 20, 1980, when an earthquake measuring over 4 on the Richter scale was recorded in the Mount St. Helens area.

• On March 27 an explosion rocked the area, caused by an eruption of steam.

• Mount St. Helens blew up at precisely 8:32 on the morning of May 18, 1980.

• The crater formed by the eruption measured 2 miles long and 1 mile wide.

Blooming again

Only a year after the eruption in 1980, plants are making a comeback on Mount St. Helens. Flowers are blooming again on slopes washed clean by rain, and shrubs are pushing their way through the ash.

Dark as night

Seven hours after Mount St. Helens blew, street lighting was needed about 85 miles away in the town of Yakima because the air was filled with black, choking dust.

VOLCANIC ROCKS

The lava that flows out of volcanoes eventually cools, hardens and becomes solid rock. Volcanoes can give off several different kinds of lava that form different kinds of rocks. All these rocks are known as igneous, or fire-formed rocks, because they were born in the fiery heart of volcanoes. They contrast with sedimentary rock, the other main kind of rock found in the earth's crust. This was formed from layers of silt that built up in ancient rivers and seas. Two of the main kinds of igneous rocks formed by volcanoes are basalt and andesite. Basalt is the rock most often formed from runny lava. This kind of lava pours out of the volcanoes on the ocean ridges and over hot spots. It is dark and dense. Andesite is the rock most often formed from the pasty lava that comes out of the explosive volcanoes on destructive plate boundaries. Because the crystals in both rocks are very small, they are called fine-grained rocks.

Road block
Lava flowing from the Kilauea volcano on Hawaii has cut off one of the island's roads. When the flow stopped, the molten lava had solidified into black volcanic rock with a smooth surface.

Intrusions
Here in Lanzarote, in the Canary Islands, molten rock has intruded, or forced its way through, other rock layers and then hardened. When this happens, geologists call it an intrusion. Volcanic intrusions like this most often occur underground when molten rock forces its way toward the surface. Sheet-like intrusions are known as dikes if they are vertical. If intrusions are horizontal and form between the rock layers, or strata, geologists call them sills.

Obsidian

This volcanic rock is formed when lava cools very quickly. It looks like black glass and is often called volcanic glass.

Basalt

Dark, heavy basalt is one of the most common volcanic rocks. This sample is known as vesicular basalt because it is riddled with holes.

Andesite

Andesite is a lighter-colored rock than basalt. It is so-called because it is the typical rock found in the Andes Mountains.

Rhyolite

This is another fine-grained rock like basalt and andesite. It is much lighter in color and weight than the other two, however.

Pumice

Pumice is a very light rock that is full of holes. It forms when lava containing a lot of gas pours out of underwater volcanoes.

Tuff

Tuff is rock formed from the ash ejected in volcanic eruptions. It is fine-grained and quite soft and porous.

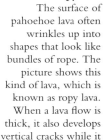

The wrinkly skin

The runny type of lava called pahoehoe quickly forms a skin on its surface. This cools first. The lava underneath is still moving and causes the skin to fold and wrinkle. In large flows the surface may cool to form a solid crust, while lava still runs underneath.

Ropy lava

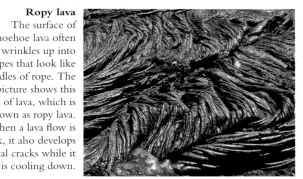

The surface of pahoehoe lava often wrinkles up into shapes that look like bundles of rope. The picture shows this kind of lava, which is known as ropy lava. When a lava flow is thick, it also develops vertical cracks while it is cooling down.

Sandy shores

In most parts of the world, the beaches are covered with pale yellow sand. But in volcanic regions, such as here in Costa Rica, the beaches have black sand. The sand has been formed by the action of the sea beating against dark volcanic rocks and grinding them into tiny particles.

BUBBLES AND INTRUSIONS

In the first project on this page we see how keeping a liquid under pressure stops gas from escaping. The liquid magma in volcanoes usually has a lot of gas dissolved in it. As it rises through the volcano, the pressure drops and the gases start to leak. They help push the magma up and out if the vent is clear. But if the vent is blocked, the gas pressure builds up and eventually causes the volcano to explode. The lava that comes from volcanoes with gassy magma forms rock riddled with vesicles (holes). The pasty lava from some explosive volcanoes sometimes contains so much gas that it forms a light, frothy rock that floats on water. We know this rock as pumice. When rising magma becomes trapped underground, it forces its way into gaps in the rocks and between the rock layers. This process is known as intrusion. The rocks that form when the magma cools and solidifies are called intrusive rocks. Granite is the most common intrusive rock. Often the heat of the intruding magma changes the surrounding rocks. They turn into what are called metamorphic (changed form) rocks, and are the third main rock type, after igneous and sedimentary.

Rock slice
A highly magnified picture of a thin slice of the intrusive rock called andesite. When looked at through a microscope, it is possible to see the tiny crystals in this slice of rock.

DISSOLVED GAS

You will need: small jar with tight-fitting lid, bowl, pitcher, antacid tablets.

3 Now quickly unscrew the lid from the jar, and see what happens. The whole jar starts fizzing. Removing the lid releases the pressure, and the gas in the liquid bubbles out.

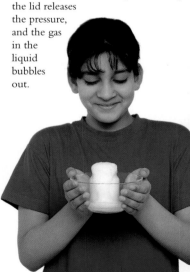

1 Stand the jar in the bowl. Pour cold water into the jar from the pitcher until it is nearly full to the top. Break up two antacid tablets and drop them into the jar.

2 Quickly screw the lid on the jar. Little bubbles will start to rise from the tablets but will soon stop. Pressure has built up in the jar and prevents any more gas from escaping.

IGNEOUS INTRUSION

You will need: plastic jar, awl (hole punch), pieces of broken tiles, modeling clay, tube of colored toothpaste.

1 Make a hole in the bottom of the plastic jar with an awl, enough to fit the neck of the toothpaste tube in. Keep your steadying hand away from the sharp end of the awl.

2 Place the pieces of broken tiles on the bottom of the jar. Keep them as flat as possible. They are meant to represent the layers of rocks we find in the earth's crust.

5 Squeeze the toothpaste tube. You will see the toothpaste pushing, or intruding, into the tile layers and making the disk on top rise. Molten magma often behaves in the same way. It intrudes into rock layers and makes the earth's surface bulge.

3 Flatten out the modeling clay into a disk as wide as the inside of the jar. Put the disk of modeling clay inside the jar. Push it down firmly on top of the tiles.

4 Unscrew the top of the toothpaste tube. and force the neck into the hole you have made in the bottom of the bottle. You may have to widen it a little to get the neck in, but don't make it too wide.

FIERY MINERALS

Some of the rocks that volcanoes produce are very useful to people because they contain valuable minerals. These minerals are a source of metals, such as copper, silver and gold. Minerals are compounds (combinations) of chemical elements that are in the earth. They form in the intense heat of volcanoes. Rock from volcanoes, such as basalt, looks as though it is a solid black lump. If you look at it under a microscope, however, you can see millions of little specks. These specks are crystals of minerals. The mineral crystals need time to grow. Lava cools so quickly that this does not happen. In volcanic rocks that cool more slowly, crystals have time to grow big enough to see without a microscope. Granite is a rock that forms when magma cools slowly underground. It contains three main kinds of mineral crystals: milky white quartz, pink feldspar and black mica. Some of the most valuable mineral materials occur in streaks, or veins, in the rocks. They include ores (minerals from which metals such as the lead ore galena can be extracted) and precious metals such as gold.

Quartz crystals
Pure quartz is colorless and is known as rock crystal. It forms hexagonal (six-sided) crystals that end in pyramid shapes. Colored crystals, such as amethyst, are used as precious stones.

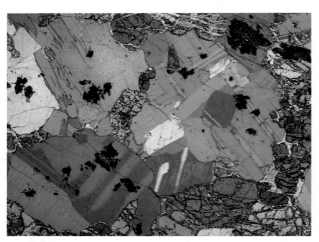

A slice of olivine
The tiny crystals in olivine can be seen here in many colors. Olivine is a mineral often found in volcanic rocks. A special kind of light called polarized light has been shone through a very thin slice of the olivine. Then the slice has been viewed through a special microscope. Transparent, pale green crystals of olivine, known as peridot, are used as gems in the making of jewelry.

Friend or foe?
Most volcanoes give off sulphur when they erupt, and this can collect into huge deposits after a time. Here a worker is cutting sulphur from deposits found around a volcano in Indonesia. Sulphur is very useful in modern industry, but it can damage the lungs of those who mine it.

Bomb filling

Volcanic bombs such as these are often blasted out by erupting volcanoes. They are made of cooled lava and may contain other pieces of rock. Inside this bomb a chunk of peridotite was found. Peridotite is a volcanic rock tinged green by olivine crystals.

As nature intended

A diamond pictured in the rock in which it was found. When dug from the earth, diamonds look rather like dirty glass. Only when they are expertly cut and polished do they display their outstanding beauty and sparkle.

For industry

This collection of diamonds has been cut and polished. They will not be turned into expensive jewelry, however. Their color is not pure enough and they contain flaws. They are industrial diamonds, which will be used, for example, in drill bits for cutting into rock. Diamond is the hardest of all the minerals on the earth.

In the vein

The silvery-gray crystals in this rock sample are of the mineral galena, which forms cubic crystals. It is one of the main ores of lead and often contains the metal silver. It is often found with zinc and silver minerals.

Beautiful beryl

Crystals of emerald, one of the finest gems, can be seen buried in a mass of quartz from Colombia, in Central America. Emerald is the green variety of a mineral called beryl. Other colored varieties of beryl are gemstones too, including aquamarine, a bluish-green mineral.

VOLCANIC LANDSCAPES

Blooms in a cinder desert
Hot cinders once blanketed the ground here. Since then wind-blown seeds have settled, germinated, grown into plants, and flowered. Their roots will help break down the cinders into better soil.

The landscapes in active or recently active volcanic regions are bare and often drably colored. They do not look as if they could ever be covered with vegetation. However, they are not without beauty, and in time, plants will grow there. The constant action of wind, rain, heat and frost eventually breaks down the newly-formed rocks. The rocks turn into soil, in which wind-blown seeds soon germinate. Providing the climate is suitable, flowers, shrubs, and finally trees will eventually grow again. Sprinklings of ash from further eruptions may, in time, add to and increase the fertility of the soil. But there is always the danger that when a volcano erupts it will destroy all the plants that have grown since the last eruption. This can happen in hours. After the enormous eruption of Mount St. Helens in 1980, the blast, hot ash cloud and mud avalanches killed everything within 15 miles. Less than a month afterward, however, wildflowers began to grow, and soon insects and small animals began returning.

Dead landscape
A typical volcanic landscape in Iceland looks bleak before regeneration. Volcanic peaks tower in the distance, while in the foreground are bare, black volcanic rocks. Winter is coming, and temperatures are struggling to rise above freezing point. Conditions do not seem favorable for plant life.

Suitable soil
Here, in another part of Iceland, the ground is carpeted with low-growing plants. They are growing in the thin soil that now covers a former lava field. The action of the weather and primitive plants such as mosses and lichens have broken down the lava into soil deep enough to support larger plants.

Etna's attractions

Giant cinder cones known as the Silvestri craters are on the southern side of Mount Etna in Sicily. The 11,100 feet-high mountain erupts frequently. It is one of a string of volcanoes in the Mediterranean region. The others include Stromboli, Vulcano and, most famously, Vesuvius. Geologists estimate that Mount Etna has probably been active for more than 2.5 million years. More than 110 eruptions of the volcano have been recorded since 1500 B.C. A particularly long eruption in 1992 destroyed much farmland and threatened several villages. The city of Catania, on the lower slopes of the mountain, is often showered with ash.

Rich paddies

Terraces of paddy fields are built on the slopes of hillsides in Bali in Indonesia, southeast Asia. The soil is very fertile because of the ash blasted out by the many volcanoes on the island. Terracing helps increase the amount of farming land and conserves water. In the hot, humid conditions, farmers can grow several crops of rice every year.

Fruit of the vine

Grape vines grow in vineyards on fertile land on the Italian island of Sicily. The land has been fertilized for centuries by the ash from regular eruptions of the island's famous volcano Mount Etna, which looms menacingly on the skyline. Etna is Europe's most active volcano.

Unstoppable

Nothing can stop this thick ribbon of lava from an erupting volcano named Kimanura, from smashing its way through tropical forest in Zaire. There are a number of active volcanoes along Zaire's eastern border. The border is in the Great Rift Valley, where plates meet, causing volcanic activity.

LETTING OFF STEAM

Hothouses
Here in Iceland, the greenhouses are heated by hot water piped in from the many hot springs in the rocks. The people of Iceland rely more on geothermal heating than any other nation.

The molten rock, or magma, in the earth's mantle does not always break out to create volcanoes. Sometimes it stays beneath the earth's crust. There it causes other volcanic features. They are called geothermal features because they are almost always caused by the earth (geo) creating heat (thermal) in underground magma that then affects underground water. The most spectacular geothermal feature is the geyser. This is a fountain of steam and water that erupts from holes in the ground. Vents (holes) called fumaroles, where steam escapes gently, are more common. They may also give out carbon dioxide and sulphurous fumes. Also common are hot springs, where water becomes heated in underground rocks to a temperature above body heat (about 98.7°F). Some hot springs can be twice this hot. Many are rich in minerals. For centuries people have believed that bathing in these mineral-rich springs is good for health.

Iceland *geysir*
A column of steam and water spurts out of the ground and high into the air as Iceland's Strokkur geyser erupts. It is just one of hundreds of geysers found in Iceland. The word geyser comes from the Icelandic word *geysir* (upward force). Geysers may erupt every few days or hours. Some erupt at such exactly regular intervals that people can set their watches by them.

Boiling tar
In a volcanically active region in New Zealand, geothermal heating is causing this tarpit to boil and bubble. New Zealand was one of the first countries to tap geothermal energy for power production.

Hot dip

Icelanders enjoy the pleasures of a hot spring. There are hundreds of hot springs dotted around the island. The water from some of them is piped into towns to provide a cheap form of central heating for public buildings and homes. Geothermal heating has many advantages over conventional systems. It does not cause any pollution and will be available until the earth cools billions of years from now.

Yellowstone springs

A hot spring makes a colorful sight in Yellowstone National Park Wyoming. The intense blue of the clear water contrasts with the yellow and orange minerals that have been deposited by evaporation around the edges. Yellowstone is the foremost geothermal region in the United States.

Steam power

A geothermal power station in Iceland makes use of natural geyser activity. Steam is piped up from underground and fed to turbogenerators to produce electricity.

Gleaming terraces

Looking like a frozen waterfall, white terraces of travertine are found in many hot-spring regions, as here in Yellowstone National Park. Travertine is made up of the mineral calcite.

FACT BOX

• One of the most famous geysers in the world is Old Faithful, in Yellowstone National Park. This geyser erupts regularly about once every 45 minutes.

• Yellowstone National Park also boasts the tallest geyser in the world. Known as Steamboat, its spouting column has been known to reach a height of more than 375 feet.

GEYSERS AND MUDLARKS

All the different kinds of thermal (heat) activity that go on in volcanic regions have the same basic cause. Water on the earth's surface trickles down through holes and cracks into underground rocks that have been heated by hot magma far below. The water becomes superheated to temperatures far above the boiling point (355°F). It does not boil, however, because it is under huge pressure. Eventually, this very hot water may turn to steam and escape from a fumarole (vent where steam escapes). The hot water can also mix with cooler water to create a hot spring, or with mud to form a bubbling mud hole. Sometimes it turns into steam at the bottom of a column of water, creating a steam explosion that blasts water out of the ground as a geyser. The first project shows you how to make a geyser using air pressure to force out water. Blowing into the top of the bottle increases the air pressure there. This forces the colored water out of the bottle through the long straw.

Waterspout
Superheated steam and water spout high into the air from the Lady Knox geyser at Waiotapu, in New Zealand. A cone of minerals has built up around the mouth of the geyser, which usually erupts for about an hour.

GEYSER ERUPTION

You will need: modeling clay, long straws, pitcher, food coloring, large plastic bottle, large jar.

3 Place the jar under the other end of the lengthened straw and blow into the other straw. Water spurts out into the jar. If the long straw was upright, the water would spout upward like a geyser.

1 Make two holes in a little ball of clay and push two straws through it, as shown in the picture. Push another straw through the end of one of the first two straws.

2 Pour water into the pitcher and add the coloring. Then pour it into the bottle. Push the clay stopper into the neck so that the lengthened straw dips into the colored water.

MUDBATHS

You will need: cornstarch, cocoa powder, measuring pitcher, mixing bowl, wooden spoon, milk, saucepan, oven mitt.

1 Combine two tablespoons of cornstarch and two of cocoa powder in the bowl, using the spoon. Stir the mixture thoroughly until it is an even color.

2 Pour about 1¼ cups of milk into the saucepan, and heat it slowly on the stove. Keep the heat low to make sure the milk does not boil. Do not leave unattended.

4 Pour the creamy mixture into the hot milk in the saucepan, still keeping heat low. Holding the handle of the saucepan with the oven mitt, stir constantly to prevent the thick liquid from sticking to the bottom of the saucepan.

3 Add some cold milk, little by little, to the mixture of cornstarch and cocoa in the bowl. Stir vigorously until the mixture has become a thick smooth cream.

6 Soon your hot liquid mud will start sending up thick bubbles, which will burst with gentle plopping sounds. This is exactly what happens in hot mud pools in volcanic areas.

5 If you have prepared your flour and chocolate mixture well, you will now have a smooth hot liquid that looks something like liquid mud.

CHANGING CLIMATES

Volcanoes can have a noticeable effect on the weather locally (nearby) when they erupt. Over weeks or months, they can affect climates around the world. Locally, volcanoes can set off lightning flashes. These break out when static electricity builds up in the volcano's billowing ash clouds and then discharges like a gigantic electric spark. The ash clouds from volcanoes may be so thick that they block out the sunlight and turn day into night. This happened for hours in the region around Mount St. Helens after the eruption in 1980. It also happened for days during the eruption of Mount Pinatubo in the Philippines in 1991. The Mount Pinatubo eruption also had longer-term effects. The gas and dust it gave out stayed in the atmosphere (air) for months, producing spectacular sunsets. So much escaped into the high atmosphere that it cut down the sunlight reaching the ground. This cooled down the earth's climate enough to affect weather patterns for a number of years. The Mexican volcano El Chichon, which erupted in 1982, had the same effect. Its ash had a particularly high sulphur content. Chemicals containing sulphur are believed to block sunlight most.

Mighty blast
In August 1883, the volcano Krakatoa blasted itself apart. The ash clouds from the volcano rose high into the atmosphere, spreading out and traveling in a band around the world.

A dying breed
The fossil skeleton of a pterosaur, a flying dinosaur that became extinct (died out) about 65 million years ago. It might have perished as a result of the earth being plunged into darkness after planetwide volcanic eruptions.

Blowing its top
The crater at the top of the Mexican volcano El Chichon. Until April 1982 it had a jungle-covered conical summit. But on April 4, this was blasted away in an explosion that drove ash high into the atmosphere.

Fissure eruptions
This series of volcanic cones follows a long fault in Iceland called the Skaftar fissure. Massive ash eruptions occurred along the fissure in 1783 and caused cold winters in Europe.

Chilly winters
The ash and gases from volcanoes can stay in the atmosphere for years. If enough volcanoes erupted at the same time, winters could be much colder than usual. In very cold winters in the 1800s, people held markets called frost fairs on deep-frozen rivers.

Red night delights
Spectacular sunsets often occur when eruptions throw dust and ash into the air. In 1991, Australians saw sunsets like this following the eruption of Mount Pinatubo in the Philippines. Mud slides that followed the eruption killed more than 400 people.

Astronauts' eye view
Space shuttle astronauts took this picture of the ash cloud rising from the eruption of the volcano at Rabaul, New Guinea in 1994. It was estimated that the cloud rose between 12 and 18 miles into the sky. On the ground ash fell 30 inches deep and destroyed two-thirds of the town of Rabaul.

FACT BOX

• The Indonesian volcano Tambora, which erupted in 1815, produced so much ash that world temperatures fell sharply in the following year. New England had severe frosts in August.

• Mount Pinatubo, which erupted in the Philippines in June 1991, released nearly 4 cubic miles of ash. This totals eight times as much ash as at the eruption of Mount St. Helens.

OUT OF THIS WORLD

Earth is not the only place in the universe that has volcanic activity. Many other planets and moons in our solar system have had volcanoes erupting on their surface at some time in their history. Two of the planets nearest to us, Venus and Mars, were affected by volcanoes. Venus and Mars are both terrestrial (earth-like) planets, with a similar rocky structure to earth. The whole landscape of Venus, revealed by the Magellan radar probe between 1990 and 1994, is volcanic. There are volcanoes everywhere. Most of the surface consists of vast lava plains stretching for thousands of miles. Mars has fewer volcanoes, but they are gigantic. The record-breaker is Olympus Mons, which is more than five times the height of earth's highest mountain, Mount Everest. Nearer home, volcanoes have been a major force in shaping our moon. The dark patches we see on the moon at night are flat plains that flooded with lava when massive volcanic eruptions took place long ago. But some of the most interesting volcanoes lie much farther away, on one of Jupiter's moons, Io. Its volcanoes pour out liquid sulphur.

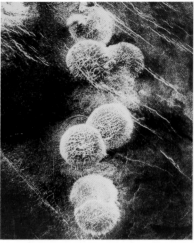

Volcanic pancakes
A series of volcanic features on Venus are called pancake domes. Scientists think they form when molten rock pours out of flat ground, spreads out and hardens.

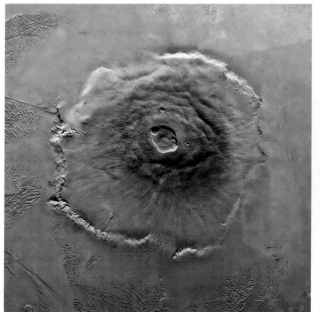

The greatest
This is the biggest volcano on Mars, and one of the biggest we know in the whole solar system. It is named Olympus Mons, or Mount Olympus. The volcano is 370 miles across at the base, and it rises to a height of some 17 miles.

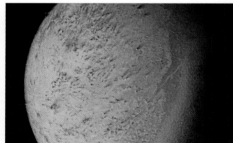

Triton's eruptions
Volcanic eruptions take place on Triton, the largest moon of Neptune. Because the moon is very cold (about −455°F), its volcanoes give off liquid nitrogen. Dark material comes out as well, causing the dark streaks visible in the picture.

Out on a limb

A volcano erupts on the edge, or limb, of Jupiter's moon Io. It shoots gas and dust hundreds of miles into space as well as pouring molten material over Io's surface. The material that comes out of the volcano is not molten rock, however. It is a liquid form of the chemical sulphur. Sulphur is a yellow-orange color, which explains why Io is such a colorful moon. Io's volcanoes were among the many astonishing discoveries made by the Voyager space probes. They visited the outer planets between 1979 and 1989.

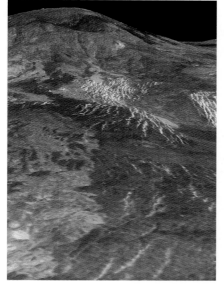

Volcano on Venus

One of Venus's many volcanoes recorded by the Magellan space probe. It has the typical broad dome shape of the shield volcanoes on earth. Most volcanoes on Venus are of this type and, like all shield-type volcanoes, they pour out runny lava. Repeated eruptions over millions of years have sent rivers of lava streaming for hundreds of miles around. Most of the landscape of Venus consists of rolling plains made up of such lava flows. Venus's biggest volcanoes are up to 300 miles across and several miles high, but most are much smaller. Venus has many other volcanic features, including strange, spidery structures called arachnoids.

The lunar seas

The seas on the moon are flat plains. They were created billions of years ago when lava flooded into huge craters made by meteorites. The picture shows part of the moon's largest sea, which is called the Ocean of Storms. This sea covers more than 5 million miles, and is more than half as big again as the Mediterranean Sea on earth. The large crater in the picture is called Kepler by astronomers. It is about 20 miles from one side to the other.

THE QUAKING EARTH

Famous fault
The most famous earthquake-producing fault in the world is the San Andreas in California. It runs for hundreds of miles, passing close to the cities of Los Angeles and San Francisco.

Many people consider the city of San Francisco, in California, to be one of the most beautiful in the world. It has a stunning setting and enjoys a pleasant climate. But living in the city has one major disadvantage. San Francisco sits nearly on top of a line of weakness in the earth's crust known as the San Andreas fault. The fault marks the boundary between two of the plates in the earth's crust, the eastern Pacific and the North American plates. These plates are trying to slide past each other. They do this jerkily and when they do, the ground shakes violently. Earthquakes occur around the boundaries of all the plates on the earth's surface, especially where the plates are colliding. This is why they often occur in the same places as volcanoes, which also occur at plate boundaries. Tens of thousands of earthquakes take place every year throughout the world, but only about 1,000 of them are powerful enough to cause damage. Such earthquakes are incredibly destructive. Most only last for a few seconds, but in that short time they can reduce whole cities to rubble and kill thousands of people. The main earthquake is always followed by smaller ones. These are called aftershocks and happen when the rocks along the edge of the fault settle into their new positions. These aftershocks can also cause a lot of damage.

Not so grand
This old print shows the chaos and destruction that earthquakes can bring. This earthquake was in 1843, in the port of Pointe-à-Pitre on the island of Grande Terre. It is one of the Guadeloupe group of islands in the Caribbean.

Housing slump
An earthquake in San Francisco in October 1989 caused whole rows of houses to collapse or damaged them beyond repair. In only a few seconds, more than 60 people were killed.

Anchorage in ruins
In March 1964, a powerful earthquake hit Anchorage, in Alaska. It was one of the longest ever recorded. The town and surrounding regions shook for four long minutes. Roads disappeared into the ground.

One-way street
An earthquake demolished one side of the Kalapana road in Hawaii in 1984. The ground was set shaking when the volcano Kilauea rumbled into life. Earthquakes occur frequently in volcanic regions.

No highway
In a 1994 earthquake that rocked Los Angeles, an elevated section of highway was shaken off its supporting piers (legs). Elevated roads are difficult to make earthquake-proof. The piers they stand on shake easily in earthquakes.

Kobe's killer waves
Some of the destruction caused by the powerful earthquake that struck the city of Kobe, Japan, in 1995. Multistorey apartment blocks collapsed like packs of cards. It was the country's most destructive earthquake since 1923.

SLIPS AND FAULTS

Every earthquake, from the slightest tremor you can hardly feel, to the violent shaking that destroys buildings, has the same basic cause. Two blocks of rock grind past each other along a fault line where the earth has fractured (the crust has split). There are several kinds of fault. At the San Andreas fault in California, the blocks are sliding past each other horizontally. This is called a transform fault, or strike-slip fault. In a normal fault, the rocks are pulling apart and one block slides down the other. In a thrust fault, the blocks are pressing together, causing one to ride up above the other. Because the edges of the blocks in contact at a fault are very uneven, friction (resistance to movement) locks them together. As they try to move, the rocks become strained and stretched. In the end, the strain in the rocks grows so great that it overcomes the friction. The two blocks suddenly move apart. The energy in the rocks is released as earthquake waves that cause great destruction.

All shook up
Traffic lights fell over in Los Angeles after an earthquake in January 1994 that killed 60 people.

FAULT MOVEMENTS

You will need: two wooden blocks, jar of baby oil, thumb tacks, sheets of sandpaper.

3 Tack sheets of sandpaper on the sides of the blocks, and try to make them slide now. You will find it much more difficult. The sandpaper is rough and increases friction between the blocks.

1 Hold a block in each hand so that the sides of the blocks are touching. Pushing gently, try to make the blocks slide past each other. You will find this quite easy.

2 Wet the sides of the blocks with the oil, and try to slide them again. You should find that it is easier. The oil has lessened the friction between the blocks.

QUAKES

You will need: scissors, strong rubber band, ruler, plastic tray (without holes), piece of cardboard, salt.

1 With the scissors, cut the rubber band at one end to make a long strip. This represents a layer of rock inside the earth before it is affected by an earthquake.

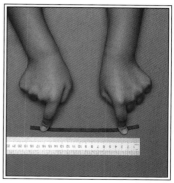

2 Measure the strip of rubber band with a ruler. This represents the original length of the rock in the ground. Make a note of how long the rubber band is at this stage.

3 Stretch the rubber band and hold it over the tray. Rocks get stretched by pulling forces inside the earth during an earthquake.

4 Ask a friend to hold the card-board on top of the rubber band and sprinkle some salt on it. The salt layer now on the card-board represents the surface of the ground above the stretched rock layer.

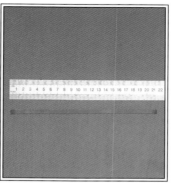

No highway
Part of the elevated highway in Kobe that collapsed during the 1995 earthquake. The supporting columns were shaken into pieces by the force of the tremors.

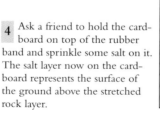

5 Now let go of the ends of the rubber band. Notice how the salt grains on the cardboard are thrown about. This was caused by the energy released when the rubber band shrunk.

6 Finally, measure the strip of rubber band again. You will find that it is slightly longer than it was at the start. Rocks are often permanently stretched a little after an earthquake.

TREMENDOUS TREMORS

The movement of rocks that causes earthquakes usually occurs deep inside the earth's crust. The exact point where the rocks start to break, or fracture, is known as the focus. This can lie as deep as hundreds of miles or as close as a few tens of miles. At the surface, the most violent disturbance occurs at a point directly above the focus, called the epicenter. The closer the focus, the more destructive is the earthquake. The earthquake that struck Kobe, Japan, in 1995 was so destructive because its focus was only about 9 miles deep. The focus of the great Alaskan earthquake of 1964 was not much deeper and caused massive destruction. The epicenter of that earthquake was on the coast of the Gulf of Alaska, and also caused the seabed to rise. This created a surge of water up to 70 feet high— it was a tidal wave, or tsunami. The tsunami devastated coastal towns and islands for hundreds of miles around.

Earthquake-proof
The Transamerica building in San Francisco is very distinctive. It has been built with flexible foundations. These should allow it to withstand the shaking that earthquakes bring.

Struts hold pipeline above ground

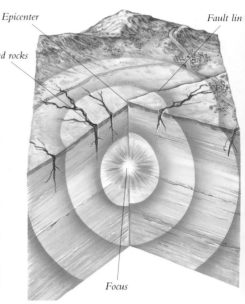

Epicenter

Fault lin

Cracked rocks

Focus

Flexible pipe
The Transalaska Pipeline snakes through the wilderness of Alaska, carrying oil south from the oilfields of the North Slope. It is built above ground. There are zigzags in places to let it move if and when earthquakes occur. The pipeline stretches for almost 800 miles.

Earthquakes in focus
Most earthquakes originate in rock layers many miles below the surface, at the focus. The most intense vibrations on the surface are felt immediately above the focus, at the epicenter.

Fire alarm

Fire breaks out in a gas main following a minor earthquake in Los Angeles. Underground pipelines carrying gas, oil or water are damaged easily when the ground vibrates. They can cause additional hazards to victims of the earthquake and their rescuers. The pipes break and their contents leak. Gas and oil catch fire easily. Water pipes can cause large floods.

Wall of water

This old print shows the tsunami (tidal wave) that followed the explosion of the volcano Krakatoa in 1883. Most of the people who died as a result of the eruption were drowned when this wall of water swept across the neighboring low-lying islands.

Shipwrecked

One of the many fishing boats that were wrecked by the tidal wave that followed the powerful earthquake in Alaska in 1964. The wave devastated all the coastal communities around the Gulf of Alaska.

Displaced persons

Tents provide temporary shelter for the inhabitants of a town in northern Turkey, following the earthquake in 1999. It is not yet safe to return home, even to houses that suffered little damage. A main earthquake is always followed by a number of aftershocks. If these are strong enough, they may bring down even more buildings.

The safest?

The designer of this odd-shaped building in Berkeley, California, boasts that it is the world's safest building. He claims that it can withstand the most powerful earthquakes. Berkeley is not far from the notorious San Andreas fault. It may not be long before we find out whether he is right or wrong about how safe his house is.

MAKING WAVES

The enormous energy released by an earthquake travels through the ground in the form of waves. Some waves are rather like water waves. They can literally make the ground ripple up and down. Others make the ground shake from side to side, which makes them very destructive. Waves also travel deep underground from an earthquake. The primary (P) waves travel fastest. They travel through rocks in the same way that sound travels through the air, as a series of pressure surges (pushing motions). The secondary (S) waves are slower than the P waves. They travel up and down and from side to side. They are a lot like the wave you can see in a rope when you shake it up and down.

Ripples in the street
The waves that travel through the surface rocks make the ground ripple. Afterwards, the ripples can often be seen. This road has been affected by waves in the ground. Now the surface of the road is like a wave.

NEWTON'S CRADLE

You will need: large beads, lengths of yarn, tape, cane, four wooden blocks.

1 Tie or tape the beads to the ends of the pieces of yarn. Tape the other ends to the cane. Make sure the threads are all the same lengths, and that the beads just touch when they hang down.

2 Prop up the cane at both ends on a pair of blocks supported by more blocks underneath. The blocks should be high enough to stop the beads from touching the table. Secure the ends with tape. Lift up the bead at one end of the row and let go. Look what happens to the other beads.

3 The beads in the middle do not move, but the one at the other end flies up. The energy of the falling bead at one end travels as a pressure wave through the middle ones. Then it reaches the bead at the other end and pushes it away.

TREMORS

You will need: set of dominoes, cardboard.

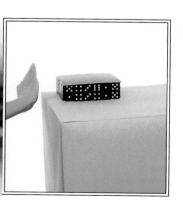

1 This project investigates how the energy in waves varies with distance. Near the end of a table, build a simple house out of dominoes. Stand them up on their ends.

2 Place the cardboard on the dominoes to make the roof of your house. Many people in earthquake zones live in the simplest of houses, built not too differently from this one.

3 Go to the opposite end of the table and hit it with your hand, but not too hard. What happens to your domino house? Probably it shakes, but still stays standing.

Leaning tower blocks
After a major earthquake, buildings lean at all angles as the shock waves destroy their foundations. The 1995 Kobe earthquake in Japan damaged nearly 200,000 buildings.

4 Now go back to the other end where your house is, and hit the table again with the same amount of force. What happens to your domino house this time?

5 Your house comes tumbling down. The waves you create when you hit the table are strong enough to knock down the house when it is nearby. When you hit the table from the opposite end, which is further away from the dominoes, the waves weaken as they travel. They are too weak to knock down the house by the time they reach it.

SEISMIC SCIENCE

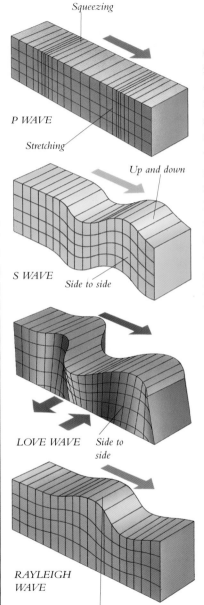

Squeezing

P WAVE

Stretching

Up and down

S WAVE

Side to side

LOVE WAVE *Side to side*

RAYLEIGH WAVE

Rippling up and down

Geologists who specialize in the study of earthquakes are called seismologists. These scientists call the waves that earthquakes create in the rocks seismic waves. The main instrument they use to detect and measure earthquakes is called a seismograph. Modern seismograms record the tremors (waves) an earthquake creates as a readout on a screen. The trace is known as a seismogram. It shows clearly the different waves earthquakes produce. The primary (P) waves, arrive first because they usually travel at speeds of more than 12,400 mph. The secondary (S) waves arrive next. They usually travel at only about half the speed of the P waves. Finally come the surface waves. Among other things, seismologists can tell from a seismograph how strong an earthquake is. The strength, or magnitude, of an earthquake is usually measured on the Richter scale, invented by Charles Richter. Other scales are also used, however, particularly one named after the Italian volcanologist Giuseppe Mercalli.

Making waves
This illustration shows four different ways in which earthquake waves travel through the ground. The primary (P) wave is a compression (squeezing) wave. It compresses, then stretches, rocks it passes through. The secondary (S) wave produces a side-to-side, shaking action. Love waves travel on the surface, making the ground move from side to side. Rayleigh waves are surface waves that move up and down. These two waves are named after the scientists who were the first to study them closely.

Charles Richter (1900–1985)
Charles F. Richter was an American seismologist. In 1931 he worked out a scale for measuring the relative strengths, or magnitudes, of earthquakes, based on the examination of seismographs.

On Vesuvius
An Italian seismologist looks at an old seismograph at the observatory on Mount Vesuvius, near Naples. The building dates from 1845.

Bad vibrations
This is a seismogram of a moderate earthquake in California, in 1989. The widest vibrations show the strongest earth tremors.

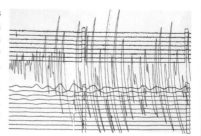

Looking for moonquakes
Apollo 11 astronaut Edwin Aldrin sets up instruments on the moon in 1969. One was a seismometer, designed to measure moonquakes, or ground tremors on the moon. Seismometers were set up at the other *Apollo* landing sites. They helped scientists work out the structure of the moon.

Vibrating needle
A close-up picture shows the needle and drum of a seismograph. These machines are being replaced by electronic ones. They will be linked to computers that are able to record waves from earthquakes digitally.

FACT BOX

• The work in the early 1900s of an Eastern European meteorologist (weather scientist) named Andrija Mohorovicic led to the discovery of the layered structure of the earth.

• The United States National Earthquake Information Service is one of the key seismic centers in the world. It records around 60,000 seismic readings every month.

Round and round
A seismologist changes the paper roll on a seismogram at an Antarctic research station. There are many scientific observation stations in the Antarctic. People stay in them for months studying the earth and weather.

BUILDING SEISMOGRAPHS

There are thousands of seismic centers scattered around the world. Within minutes of a quake, seismologists in different countries are analyzing the seismograms from their seismographs. Then they will compare notes with scientists in other countries and will be able to pinpoint the epicenter and focus of the quake, its strength and how long it lasted. The Italian scientist Luigi Palmieri built the first seismograph in 1856. All seismographs work on the same principle. They use a heavy weight supported by a spring inside a frame. When an earthquake occurs, it shakes the instrument. The heavy weight tends to stay where it is because of its inertia (resistance to change). A pen attached to the weight records the shaking movement as a wavy line drawn on paper wrapped round a rotating drum. The same principle of the inertia of a heavy weight is used to detect tremors in the do-it-yourself seismograph shown in the project here.

Out of a dragon's mouth
This is a model of a seismoscope built by a Chinese scientist of the past called Zhang Heng. The movement of an earthquake shakes a ball out of a dragon's mouth and into a toad's mouth below.

BUILDING A SEISMOGRAPH
You will need: cardboard box, awl (hole punch), tape, modeling clay, pencil, felt-tip pen, string, piece of cardboard.

1 The cardboard box will become the frame of your seismograph. It needs to be made of quite stiff cardboard. The open part of the box will be the front of your instrument.

2 Make a hole in what will be the top of the frame with the awl (hole punch). If the box feels flimsy, strengthen it by taping around the corners as shown in the picture.

3 Roll a piece of clay into a ball and make a hole in it with the pencil. Now push the felt-tip pen through the clay so that it extends a little bit beyond the hole.

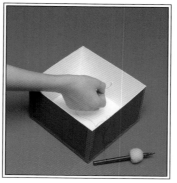

4 The pen and clay will be the pointer of your seismograph and make a record of earthquake vibrations. Tie one end of the piece of string to the top of the pen.

5 Thread the other end of the string through the hole in the top of the box. Now stand the box upright and pull the string through until the pen hangs free.

6 Tie the top end of the string to the pencil and roll the pencil to take up the slack. When the pen is at the right height (just touching the bottom) tape the pencil into position.

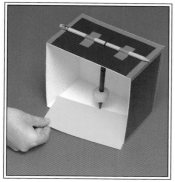

9 You do not have to wait for an earthquake to test your seismograph. Just shake or tilt the frame. The suspended pen does not move but it marks the piece of cardboard, giving you your very own seismogram.

7 Place the cardboard in the bottom of the box under the pen. If you have adjusted it properly the tip of the pen should just touch and mark the cardboard.

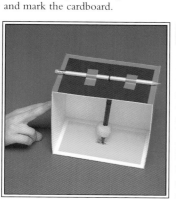

8 Your seismograph is now complete and ready for use. It uses the same principle as a proper seismograph. The heavy pendulum, will be less affected by shaking motions than the frame.

FIELDWORK

The scientists who study volcanoes and earthquakes spend a great deal of time in the field (on the spot) around active volcanoes and in earthquake zones (places where earthquakes commonly take place). Volcanologists keep an eye on many active volcanoes all the time, looking for any changes that may signal a new eruption. Permanent observatories have been built on volcanoes near centers of population, such as Mount Vesuvius and Mount Etna in Italy. Hopefully the volcanologists can give advance warnings to people who could be at risk. When eruptions do take place, they chart the direction of lava flows and take temperatures and samples of lava and gases. The thermometers they use are not the mercury-in-glass kind. Those would melt at 1,800°F and at the greater temperatures found around volcano sites. Volcanologists use thermocouples to measure temperatures. These are made of metals. Seismologists spend their time in earthquake regions setting up and checking instruments that can record ground movements. This is part of their study to try and predict earthquakes.

Studying creep
A scientist measures movements along a fault using a creepmeter. The two parts of the creepmeter are on either side of the fault line.

Watching Etna
Mount Etna, in Italy, is the highest volcano in Europe. It has been erupting for more than 2.5 million years. Shown above is one of the three observatories set up on its slopes in the mid 1800s. The town of Catania lies on the slopes of Mount Etna. The volcano is watched constantly because if it erupts it could destroy Catania and other villages nearby. Fortunately, eruptions on Etna happen quite slowly.

Hard hat job
A geologist checks a lava flow from Hawaii's highly active volcano Kilauea. The sides have already cooled and solidified, which helps shield him from the heat given out by the river of molten rock beneath. He wears a hard hat to protect himself from falling debris.

Space age suits

These volcanologists look quite similar to astronauts in their protective suits. They are carrying out research in Ethiopia about the lava lake at Erta Ale volcano. The suits they wear have a shiny silvery coating. This reflects the heat from the hot lava away from their bodies and so helps to keep them cool. The researchers also wear protective helmets to shield their faces, particularly their eyes, from the heat. Erta Ale has been erupting since 1967.

Laser checking

Seismologists sometimes use a space satellite called Lageos to check for ground movements. Two identical lasers are set up, one on each side of a fault. Movement in the ground affects the time it takes for the laser beams to go to and from the satellite. These time differences tell the scientists the ground is moving.

On the ice

Geologists carry out seismic surveys in Antarctica to study the rock layers under the ice. In places the ice is more than 13,000 feet thick. Mount Erebus is the only volcano on the continent.

Lageos satellite

Thumping good idea

In the past, seismologists set off explosives to send shock waves they could measure through the rocks. Nowadays they mostly use special vibrator trucks, which thump the ground to create waves.

MEASURING MOVEMENTS

The seismograph is the most important instrument for seismologists once an earthquake has happened. But these scientists use many other instruments, in particular to detect how the ground moves in areas where earthquakes might occur. The San Andreas fault in California is criss-crossed with seismic ground stations, some using laser beams and other electronic devices and others with relatively simple instruments. An extensometer measures stretching movements in the rocks. A magnetometer detects minute changes in the earth's magnetism that often occurs when rocks move. A creepmeter measures movements along faults. Our two projects show how to make simple versions of instruments called the gravimeter and the tiltmeter. The gravimeter measures slight changes in gravity. When changes occur, the pull on a heavy mass changes, which will make a mass and a pointer attached to it move over a scale. The tiltmeter detects whether rock layers are tilting by comparing the water levels in two connected containers.

Seismic survey
Seismic researchers carry out an accurate survey of the ground in an earthquake region. By comparing their readings with past records, they can tell if any ground movements have taken place.

GRAVIMETER

You will need: strip of contact paper, pen, large jar, modeling clay, rubber band, toothpick, pencil.

1 Draw a scale on a strip of contact paper using a ruler and pen. Stick the scale on the jar. In a real instrument this would measure slight changes in gravity.

2 Bury one end of a rubber band in a ball of clay. Stick in a toothpick at right angles to the band to act as a pointer. Pass the pencil through the loop of the band.

3 Lower the ball into the jar, dangling from the pencil, so that the tip of the pointer is close to the scale. Rest the pencil on the top of the jar and use bits of clay to stop it from moving. If you move the jar up or down, the pointer moves down and up the scale.

TILTMETER

You will need: awl (hole punch), two transparent plastic cups, transparent plastic tubing, modeling clay, pen, contact paper, wooden board, adhesive, food coloring, pitcher.

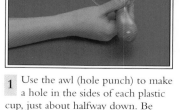

1 Use the awl (hole punch) to make a hole in the sides of each plastic cup, just about halfway down. Be careful not to prick your fingers. Ask an adult to help you if you prefer.

2 Push one end of the tubing into the hole in one of the cups. Seal it tight with modeling clay. Put the other end in the hole in the other cup and seal it also.

3 Using the pen, draw identical scales on two strips of the contact paper. Use a ruler and mark regular spaces. Stick the scales at the same height on the side of the cups.

4 Stick the cups to the wooden baseboard with adhesive. Position them so that the tube between is pulled straight, but make sure it doesn't pull out.

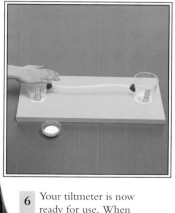

Tilt makes water flow out of upper cup

6 Your tiltmeter is now ready for use. When it is level, the water levels in the cups are the same. When it tilts, the water levels change as water runs through the tube from one cup to the other.

Tilt makes water flow down into lower cup

5 Add coloring to water in the pitcher, and pour into each of the cups. Make sure to fill them so that the water level reaches over the openings to the tubes.

TO THE RESCUE

Body heat
This is a picture taken by a thermal imaging camera. It records heat, not light. Rescuers use these cameras when searching in dark places for earthquake survivors.

When volcanoes erupt and earthquakes strike, they can unleash destructive power equal to hundreds of atomic bombs. The most destructive volcanoes explode and cause ash and mud slides that sweep away everything in their path. Most people caught by these stand no chance and are dead by the time any rescuers can arrive. Earthquakes are even more deadly than volcanoes. They often kill thousands of people when their houses crumble about them in a few seconds. Many people survive the earthquake itself but are buried alive and often badly injured. It is then a fight against time to rescue them before they die of suffocation or their injuries. Many cities in earthquake zones have well-trained rescue teams. But when disaster strikes in remote villages it can be days before any teams can reach them. Often the roads to the villages have become impassable. All earthquake rescue work is hazardous. Aftershocks can bring down damaged buildings on the rescuers. Fire may break out from fractured gas pipes, and there may not be enough water for firefighting because of burst water mains. There can also be great danger of disease from the decaying bodies of possibly thousands of people and animals.

With bare hands
A survivor of the 1995 Kobe earthquake in Japan uses his bare hands to remove debris. He is searching for other members of his family who might be buried in the ruins.

Ash and mud
An aerial view of Plymouth, the capital of the Caribbean island of Montserrat, after the volcanic eruption of 1997. Thick ash and torrents of mud have covered the city.

Still alive
Rescuers have heard faint cries from the rubble of a collapsed block of houses. Carefully, they remove the broken concrete and steel girders and find a survivor.

Stretcher bearers
Four members of the skilled rescue team that battled with the devastation caused by the Kobe earthquake in Japan, achieve another success as they carry a survivor to safety.

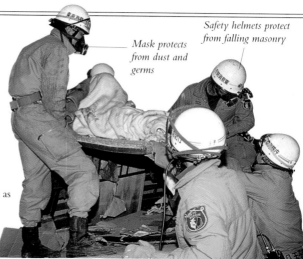

Mask protects from dust and germs

Safety helmets protect from falling masonry

Clearing up
Powerful excavators work round the clock to clear shattered concrete and twisted metal supports from the collapsed Hanshin expressway after the Kobe earthquake in Japan. It took nearly a week to get the road back to normal.

Rescue man's best friend
Earthquake rescue teams not only rely on the latest scientific equipment to find survivors but also use sniffer dogs. Sniffer dogs are specially trained to use their sensitive noses to pick up the scent of people buried in collapsed buildings after an earthquake.

Heavy lifting
A crane is lowered to help lift the heavy steel and concrete beams of a collapsed building in Erzican, Turkey. These rescue workers are trying to free people buried during an earthquake there.

GLOSSARY

active volcano
A volcano that is erupting or might erupt at any time in the near future.

archipelago
A large group of islands.

atmosphere
The layer of air surrounding the earth.

atoll
A small island made up of an almost circular strip of coral surrounding a lagoon of sea water.

creepmeter
An instrument that measures movements of the earth's crust along faults in the crust.

climate
The typical weather pattern of a place during the year.

constructive boundary
The edge of one of the earth's plates, where new plate material is forming.

continental drift
The gradual movement of the continents across the face of the earth.

core
The region at the center of the earth.

crust
The rocky surface layer of the earth.

destructive boundary
A region of the earth's crust where one of the plates of the crust is colliding with another and being destroyed.

dormant volcano
A volcano that is not active at present but might erupt one day in the future. The word dormant means sleeping.

earthquake
An often violent shaking of the earth's crust, caused when plates in the crust try to slide past or over each other.

epicenter
The region on the earth's surface that lies directly above the focus of an earthquake.

erosion
The gradual wearing away of the earth's surface by the action of wind, rain, heat, cold, and the movement of rivers.

extensometer
An instrument that measures whether stretching movements are occurring in the rocks in the earth's crust.

extinct volcano
A volcano that has not erupted for many years and is believed unlikely ever to erupt again.

fault
A crack in the earth's crust.

focus
The exact point underground where the rocks in the earth's crust move and cause an earthquake.

fossil
The remains in the earth's rocks of living things that have died and been preserved.

fumarole
An opening in the ground in volcanic regions, where steam and gases escape.

geologist
A scientist who carries out the study of the earth's surface and rocks.

geology
The scientific study of the earth and the changes that take place on its surface and in the rocks below.

geothermal energy
The energy created in areas of volcanic activity by the heating of rocks below the earth's surface.

geyser
A fountain of steam and water that spurts out of vents in the ground in volcanic regions.

gravimeter
An instrument that measures slight changes in gravity in the rocks in the earth's crust.

hot spot
A place in the earth's crust away from plate boundaries where hot rock forces its way to the surface to cause volcanoes.

hot springs
Places in volcanic regions where water that has been heated underground by rocks bubbles to the surface.

igneous rock
A rock that forms when magma (hot molten rock) cools and becomes solid. This can happen both on the earth's surface or underground.

intrusive rock
A rock that forms underground when hot molten rock forces its way into existing rock layers and then cools.

lava
The molten rock that pours out of volcanoes onto the surface of the ground and then cools. Lava can be very thin and runny or thick and pasty.

magma
The name given to hot molten rock while it is still inside the earth's crust.

mantle
The very deep layer of rock that lies underneath the earth's crust.

metamorphic rock
Rock that forms when existing rocks are changed because of great heat and pressure inside the earth's crust.

mineral
A chemical compound found inside the earth.

nuée ardente
A glowing cloud of very hot air and ash given out by some volcanoes. It spreads quickly over the area surrounding the volcano, causing death and destruction on a large scale.

planet
One of the nine large bodies in the solar system that circle around the sun. The earth is one of the nine planets.

plate
A section of the earth's crust that moves in a recognized direction across the earth's surface.

P waves
The primary waves produced by an earthquake that travel fastest and are detected first.

Richter scale
A scale for measuring the strength of earthquakes, devised by the American scientist Charles Richter.

S waves
The secondary waves produced by an earthquake, detected later than P waves.

sedimentary rock
Rock formed from layers of sediments, or materials such as eroded rock and chemical compounds that settled in layers millions of years ago at the bottom of seas and rivers.

seismogram
The wavy trace on paper that a seismograph makes.

seismograph
An instrument used by scientists to record earthquake waves.

seismologist
A geologist who carries out the study of earthquake waves.

seismology
The study of the waves that earthquakes send out.

Solar system
The family of planets, moons and other bodies that orbit around the sun.

thermocouple
A thermometer scientists use to measure very high temperatures.

thermometer
An instrument that is used for measuring temperature.

tidal wave
A huge ocean wave caused when an earthquake takes place on the seabed. It has nothing to do with tides.

tiltmeter
An instrument used to detect the tilting of the ground.

tremor
A shaking of the ground.

trench
A valley in the seabed, marking the region where one plate of the earth's crust meets another and is forced down into the crust.

tsunami
A huge ocean wave set up when an earthquake takes place on the seabed. It is popularly called a tidal wave.

vent
An opening in the ground.

viscosity
A measure of how thick or thin a liquid is. A liquid with low viscosity flows faster than one with a high viscosity.

volcanic bomb
A lump of molten material flung into the air from a volcano.

volcano
An opening in the earth's crust from which molten rock escapes.

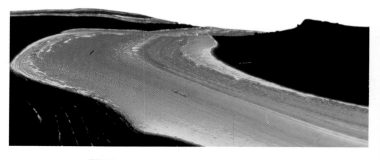

Index